The Final-over-Final Conditio

Linguistic Inquiry Monographs
Samuel Jay Keyser, general editor

A complete list of books published in the Linguistic Inquiry Monographs series appears at the back of this book.

The Final-over-Final Condition
A Syntactic Universal

Michelle Sheehan, Theresa Biberauer, Ian Roberts, and Anders Holmberg

The MIT Press
Cambridge, Massachusetts
London, England

This book was set in 10 on 13 pt Times Roman by Toppan Best-set Premedia Limited. Printed and bound in the United States of America.

Library of Congress Cataloging-in-Publication Data

Names: Sheehan, Michelle, author. | Biberauer, Theresa, author. | Roberts, Ian G., author. | Holmberg, Anders, author.
Title: The final-over-final condition : a syntactic universal / Michelle Sheehan, Theresa Biberauer, Ian Roberts, and Anders Holmberg ; foreword by David Pesetsky.
Description: Cambridge, MA : The MIT Press, [2017] | Series: Linguistic inquiry monographs. 76th | Includes bibliographical references and index.
Identifiers: LCCN 2016056889| ISBN 9780262036696 (hardcover : alk. paper) | ISBN 9780262534161 (pbk. : alk. paper)
Subjects: LCSH: Grammar, Comparative and general--Syntax. | Grammar, Comparative and general--Word order. | Head-driven phrase structure grammar.
Classification: LCC P295 .F56 2017 | DDC 415--dc23 LC record available at https://lccn.loc.gov/2016056889

10 9 8 7 6 5 4 3 2 1

Contents

Series Foreword by Samuel Jay Keyser   vii
Foreword by David Pesetsky   ix
Acknowledgments   xiii

1   Introduction   1
Anders Holmberg

2   Empirical Evidence for the Final-over-Final Condition   11
Theresa Biberauer, Anders Holmberg, Ian Roberts,
and Michelle Sheehan

3   Harmony, Symmetry, and Dominance in Word Order Universals   27
Ian Roberts

4   The Final-over-Final Condition and Linearization in
Generative Grammar   43
Anders Holmberg

5   The Final-over-Final Condition and Processing   79
Michelle Sheehan

6   The Final-over-Final Condition and Adverbs   97
Michelle Sheehan

7   The Final-over-Final Condition and the Head-Final Filter   121
Michelle Sheehan

8   The Final-over-Final Condition in DP: Universal 20 and the Nature
of Demonstratives   151
Ian Roberts

9   The Final-over-Final Condition and Particles   187
Theresa Biberauer

10   The Final-over-Final Condition in a Mixed-Word-Order Language   297
Anders Holmberg

11   The Final-over-Final Condition in Morphology   323
Ian Roberts

Notes   347
References   385
Index   437

Series Foreword

We are pleased to present the seventy-sixth volume in the series *Linguistic Inquiry Monographs*. These monographs present new and original research beyond the scope of the article. We hope they will benefit our field by bringing to it perspectives that will stimulate further research and insight.

Originally published in limited edition, the *Linguistic Inquiry Monographs* are now more widely available. This change is due to the great interest engendered by the series and by the needs of a growing readership. The editors thank the readers for their support and welcome suggestions about future directions for the series.

Samuel Jay Keyser
for the Editorial Board

Foreword

I have always been enamored of a bon mot attributed to Isaac Asimov:[1]

The most exciting phrase to hear in science, the one that heralds new discoveries, is not "Eureka!" (I found it!) but "That's funny ..."

This must describe how Anders Holmberg felt when, upon investigating word order alternations in the Finnish verb phrase near the end of the last century, he discovered that although the Finnish clause has fairly free word order, there is a sharp restriction. If the main verb precedes its complement, the auxiliary verb must precede VP (its own complement)—but if the main verb follows its complement, the position of the auxiliary verb is free.

"That's funny," Holmberg must have said to himself (in one of his several languages). "I wonder why that should be? Is there a broader generalization?" And after tinkering a bit (I like to imagine), he discovered that a very similar generalization holds within the Finnish nominal. Casting a quick glance at a wider range of languages, he conjectured that there might indeed be a broader generalization:

If a phrase α is head-initial, then the phrase β immediately dominating α is head-initial. If α is head-final, β can be head-final or head-initial.

This generalization, first reported in Holmberg 2000, was the essence of what came to be called the Final-over-Final Condition (FOFC), the topic of the present volume—and the rest is history.

Or more accurately, the rest will surely *become* history, when the story of our field is written—if this finding is as significant as I think it is. I vividly recall the day Anders told me during a conference break that he had made this discovery and had joined forces with Theresa Biberauer, Ian Roberts, and Michelle Sheehan to investigate its implications. Most casual conversations are immediately forgotten, but this one was different. This was real news: the unexpected discovery of a brand-new,[2] nontrivial universal property of human language.

The discovery is marvelous in another way as well: its fundamental simplicity, which makes it a wonderful educational tool for our field. To grasp the essence of FOFC, all one needs as background is the core concept of hierarchical phrase structure and the notion "head." Neither of these concepts is well-known among the general public, but both are easy to teach—with FOFC as a spectacular follow-up. As a consequence, FOFC has been the pièce de résistance of the syntax section of my undergraduate linguistics class for nearly a decade, and it forms a standard part of almost every lecture that I give about linguistics for nonspecialist audiences. I recommend this idea to all readers of this book who undertake similar tasks. Intellectually engaged audiences get the point easily and find it deeply exciting: the diversity of possible languages, the diversity of *impossible* languages, the discovery of general laws that distinguish the two groups, and the significance of such discoveries.

At the same time, every worthwhile discovery of course raises new questions and puzzles. The more exciting the discovery, the more urgent the questions and the more significant the puzzles. That is what prompts the present volume. To begin with, for all its simplicity, FOFC is also perplexingly quirky—and there are details missing from the simplest version of FOFC that run the risk of further quirkiness when they are filled in. Some of the most obvious questions and puzzles are these:

- **Precision:** What is the structural domain within which FOFC holds sway? The generalization makes clear and seemingly correct predictions for verbs, auxiliaries, and complementizers within a clause—but languages like German, for example, permit a head-initial DP embedded within a head-final VP. Consequently, it looks like FOFC constrains the linearization of particular syntactic domains as they are built, but also comes with a "reset button" at the edge of these domains. What are these domains, where are their reset buttons, and why does the system work this way?

- **Apparent counterexamples:** As discussed in Biberauer's solo contribution to this volume (chapter 9), uninflected particles that stand in for auxiliary verbs in certain languages can be found phrase-finally in apparent defiance of FOFC, and many languages show clause-final clause-typing particles that should not be there if they are instances of C. Do these phenomena spell doom for the FOFC generalization, or (less catastrophically) added complexity in its statement? Or are the particles themselves not the phrasal heads that they seem to be at first glance, so they might not pose a problem for FOFC in the first place?

- **The *why* question:** If FOFC is true, what deeper laws of language might explain why it should hold? Is it an artifact of processing in real time, as some have suggested, or a consequence of how the grammar regulates linearization in general (a brilliant proposal of this sort by Sheehan is discussed at several points in the volume)—or something else entirely?

- **Extensions (closely connected to the *why* question):** Are there other phenomena that have the "spirit of FOFC" but fail to follow directly from FOFC as initially stated? Can these phenomena be brought under the FOFC umbrella, and does the result reshape our understanding of the phenomena or of FOFC itself? Chapter 6 by Sheehan, for example, addresses this question in the domain of adverb placement, as does chapter 8 by Roberts in the context of Greenberg's famous Universal 20 (concerning the order of elements in noun phrases)—and almost every chapter addresses some questions with a similar logic.

It should be immediately obvious that these questions are interdependent. Answering any one of them has implications for the answers to the others. For this reason, studying FOFC (like studying any problem with conceptual and empirical depth) must be a team effort. The issues are too complex and too tightly interwoven for any one individual to sort them out alone. Nothing makes that clearer than the successful teamwork evident in this volume, which is largely devoted to the most pressing questions in all four of the categories listed above. Not only that: some chapters, reflecting the authors' expertise, go beyond the obvious categories of those questions to show how FOFC itself can shed light on language change and language development. In this way, the team effort reflected in this volume provides a model for us all, whatever questions we might be studying, since almost all these questions interact with others across the entire span of theoretical linguistics.

This volume is a model for us all in two other crucial respects as well:

- **Embedding within a tradition of research results:** Part of the thrill of FOFC is the fact the generalization leaps out at you, its excitement clear as day the minute you learn about it—but only in the context of modern hierarchical theories of syntactic structure. Without hierarchical structure of the sort characterized by the recursive application of the rule Merge (or its predecessors in earlier work) and without the notion "head," as motivated in decades of earlier research, there is no FOFC generalization to discuss. Because of its cross-categorial nature, it is not a theory about particular parts of speech, nor even about traditional grammatical relations such as subject and object. Instead, it is an abstract generalization about syntactic structures whose existence has been motivated independently by years of research into a wide variety of seemingly unrelated phenomena: displacement patterns, other word order generalizations, possible and impossible anaphora, semantic scope, and more. FOFC was detectable in the first place only because of a research tradition that seeks to understand linguistic knowledge as a *system* whose parts interact in a consistent manner, predicted by general laws.

- **Enlightened persistence in the face of apparent counterevidence:** One of the most noteworthy aspects of this volume is the authors' demonstration that a good idea should be abandoned only with the greatest reluctance (and, of course, that FOFC belongs in the category of "good ideas"). While good ideas may turn out to be false, every good idea, as noted above, is likely to be faced with numerous challenges. This is especially true in linguistics, where virtually every day researchers uncover new phenomena in the world's languages, none of which wear their explanations on their sleeves. For this reason, observations that appear to undermine a generalization such as FOFC must be explored, of course (not swept under the rug), but often turn out to be false alarms. Furthermore, these false alarms are often useful and informative, teaching us more about the phenomenon in question, or about the generalization they at first threatened to undermine. This attitude toward apparent counterevidence can be called *enlightened persistence*, and the present volume is as beautiful a demonstration of its value as I could imagine.

These points are worth making, because there are prominent traditions and trends in current research on linguistic diversity that differ from the present volume on both points (to varying degrees, of course). In my opinion, the present book implicitly presents the best possible argument against these traditions and trends. The evidence and arguments assembled in its various chapters make clear the value (indeed, the necessity) of examining linguistic phenomena through the lens of previous discovery, and of never taking apparent counterevidence at face value—not, at least, without first working hard to determine what that evidence is *really* teaching us.

One of the glories of this book is the degree to which it demonstrates the value of building on previous discovery and enlightened persistence, but an equal glory is the fact that its work is not done. Many questions remain open: this is no *Summa FOFCologica*. Like all excellent research, this volume is but a fragment of a larger scientific conversation that did not begin with its first page and does not end with its last page. So intriguing are the findings reported here by Sheehan, Biberauer, Roberts, and Holmberg that we can be certain that the FOFC conversation is not over—perhaps the volume's most enduring achievement.

David Pesetsky
Head, Department of Linguistics and Philosophy; Ferrari P. Ward Professor of Modern Languages and Linguistics, and Margaret MacVicar Faculty Fellow
Massachusetts Institute of Technology

Acknowledgments

First and foremost, we would like to thank the UK Arts and Humanities Research Council (AHRC) for funding the research on the Final-over-Final Condition in 2007–2011 (Grant No. AH/E009239/1, project: "Structure and Linearization in Disharmonic Word Orders"). Since 2011, our work on this book has been funded by the European Research Council Advanced Grant No. 269752, "Rethinking Comparative Syntax" (ReCoS).

Next, thanks to the participants at the various conferences and workshops we organized in conjunction with the above project: the GLOW workshop Principles of Linearization (Newcastle, 2008), the Particles workshop (Cambridge, 2008), the workshop on Universal 20 (Cambridge, 2008), the conference Theoretical Approaches to Disharmonic Word Order (Newcastle, 2009), the Cambridge Institute of Language Research workshop on the Final-over-Final Constraint (Cambridge, 2010), and the LAGB workshop Disharmony in Nominals (Leeds, 2010). Thanks to the students who took Theresa's Eastern Generative Grammar (EGG) course "Theoretical Approaches to Word Order" (Brno, 2007), those who took Michelle's EGG course "Word Order: From Typology to Theory" (Wroclaw, 2012), and the many University of Cambridge students who attended and enthusiastically contributed to different FOFC-themed seminars during the course of the project. Thanks also to the other members of the ReCoS project: Jenneke van der Wal, András Bárány, Tim Bazalgette, Alison Biggs, Jamie Douglas, Georg Höhn, Kari Kinn, Marieke Meelen, and Sam Wolfe.

Although many people have contributed to the ideas presented in this book either directly or indirectly at the many venues at which parts of it have been presented, we would particularly like to thank Glenda Newton, who was initially a member of the project, as well as (alphabetically, by first name) Ad Neeleman, Adam Ledgeway, Alastair Appleton, Ángel Gallego, Bob Freidin, Carlo Cecchetto, David Pesetsky, Edith Aldridge, Edwin Williams, Elena Anagnostopoulou, George Walkden, Giuliana Giusti, Guglielmo Cinque,

Hedde Zeijlstra, Henk van Riemsdijk, Iain Mobbs, Jack Hawkins, Jan-Wouter Zwart, Joe Emonds, Joy Philip, Klaus Abels, Laura Bailey, Maria Vilkuna, Neil Myler, Norma Schifano, Norvin Richards, Olaf Koeneman, Pino Longobardi, Richie Kayne, Sten Vikner, Waltraud Paul, and Wim van der Wurff. There are many other people who could be mentioned. Thanks also to all the informants who provided data (mentioned in the individual chapters). Thanks to everyone who has provided feedback or criticism or who has engaged with us in any way in the course of our work on this book. And thanks, finally, to the editors of MIT Press, especially Marc Lowenthal, who have shown great patience with us, and to our phenomenal copy editor, Anne Mark.

1 Introduction

Anders Holmberg

This book is about a phenomenon we call the *Final-over-Final Condition*, abbreviated *FOFC*, pronounced /fofk/ (in mild violation of English phonotactics). (1a) is a preliminary formulation of this condition, to be refined in various ways in the course of the book; (1b) is a slightly more concise formulation:

(1) a. *The Final-over-Final Condition (FOFC)*
     A head-final phrase αP cannot immediately dominate a head-initial phrase βP, if α and β are members of the same extended projection.
  b. *[$_\alpha$P [$_\beta$P β γ] α], where β and γ are sisters and α and β are members of the same extended projection.

To take just one example, a phrase consisting of a VP and an auxiliary verb, in that order, cannot immediately dominate a VP consisting of a verb and a complement, in that order:

(2) *[$_{AuxP}$ [$_{VP}$ V XP] Aux]

If AuxP is head-final, then the immediately dominated VP must be head-final, too—hence the name *Final-over-Final Condition*. This can be seen most clearly in languages that allow VO as well as OV order and Aux-VP as well as VP-Aux order. Finnish happens to be one such language. As shown in (3), the one combination of VP and Aux that is not allowed is (3d)—namely, the combination in (2). The sentences are synonymous, all meaning roughly 'He has indeed bought a car':

(3) a. Kylä se on ostanut auton.   [Aux [V O]]   [Finnish]
      indeed he has bought car
  b. Kylä se on auton ostanut.   [Aux [O V]]
  c. Kylä se auton ostanut on.   [[O V] Aux]
  d. *Kylä se ostanut auton on.   [[V O] Aux]

As will be discussed in chapter 2, this pattern is found in language after language where enough word order variation is allowed to put cooccurrence restrictions like this to the test.

In previous work, we have called this syntactic condition a constraint, the Final-over-Final Constraint (Biberauer, Holmberg, and Roberts 2007, 2008a,b, 2014, Biberauer, Newton, and Sheehan 2009a,b, Biberauer and Sheehan 2012b, 2013, Sheehan 2013a,b, Biberauer 2016a,b). We have occasionally been criticized for this nomenclature. Since syntactic constraints are typically named after a construction where some operation or relation is not permitted—for example, *Complex NP Constraint* names a construction where extraction is not permitted—*Final-over-Final Constraint* can mistakenly be taken to name a hierarchic relation that is not permitted, when in fact the opposite is the case. Maintaining the acronym *FOFC*, we therefore now call it a condition, a more neutral designation.

The precise extension of FOFC is one of the critical issues to be discussed in various places throughout this book. The preliminary formulation in (1) includes the condition "if α and β are members of the same extended projection." This is in order to include a case like (2) under FOFC, where Aux and V are members of the same extended projection in Grimshaw's (2001) sense, but not include, for example, a case like (3):

(3) a. Er hat [das Buch gekauft].   [German]
       he has the book bought
    b. [$_{VP}$ [$_{DP}$ D NP] V]

Although (3) has a head-initial DP (*das Buch* 'the book') dominated by a head-final VP, it is not ruled out by FOFC as formulated in (1) because D and V are not members of the same extended projection. Is "extended projection" the relevant notion, though? And do the categorial identity and function of γ in (1b) make any difference? We will take up both of these issues in chapters to follow.

FOFC is either a very strong tendency among the languages of the world or actually a language universal. In either case, it is a theoretically interesting phenomenon, radically limiting the variety of structures and word orders found in human languages. In this book, we will explore the consequences of the idea that it is a syntactic universal, an automatic consequence of how some of the most fundamental operations in syntax and morphology/phonology interact. But we do not take this idea for granted. Instead, we acknowledge that it is a strong hypothesis, which we put to the test by investigating to what extent it can shed light on a wide range of syntactic and morphosyntactic phenomena. We also discuss other, nonuniversalist approaches to FOFC, including the idea that it is ultimately due to constraints on processing.

We will examine in detail a number of syntactic constructions and construction types in a variety of languages where effects of FOFC are visible. We will not propose a single, unified explanation of FOFC. (For a review of theories proposed in order to explain FOFC, and for discussion of the idea that FOFC is a parsing-based constraint, see chapters 4 and 5, respectively.) Instead, we will explore the implications and consequences of certain grammatical models when applied to FOFC. An overarching idea, however, is that FOFC is a consequence of the fundamental asymmetry of syntax. Even though selected portions of syntactic structure appear to show symmetry, as the verb phrase can have the order VO or OV, the clause can have the order C-IP or IP-C, the noun phrase can have the order Dem-Num-N or N-Num-Dem, and so on, depending on the language, when the relation between structure and order is scrutinized in more detail, it turns out that the symmetry is mostly apparent: the system is fundamentally asymmetric, as argued in particular by Kayne (1994). FOFC is an expression and/or consequence of this asymmetry.

The chapters are almost self-contained. Chapters 2–4 provide background, demonstrating the empirical evidence for the constraint and locating FOFC and theories of FOFC in the wider context of linguistic theory. Chapters 5–11 deal with syntactic phenomena that in one way or other involve FOFC.

Chapter 2, by Theresa Biberauer, Anders Holmberg, Ian Roberts, and Michelle Sheehan, presents some of the empirical evidence that FOFC is a pervasive phenomenon in human language. The evidence comes from cooccurrence restrictions in the grammar of various languages, at various hierarchical levels (VP, TP, and CP), in nominal as well as in verbal constructions. FOFC makes predictions about (i) language change, since it rules out any stages in the evolution of the syntax of a language where it is violated (these predictions can be verified); (ii) effects of language contact, again since any effects must conform to it; and (iii) first and second language acquisition, since if it is truly a universal, there can be no interlanguage that violates it.

Chapter 3, by Ian Roberts, addresses the nature of cross-categorial word order harmony, first discussed by Greenberg (1963) and formally expressed in terms of a subset of his so-called universals, and further discussed and developed by Hawkins (1983) and Dryer (1992). The chapter explores the implications that FOFC has for this notion, and for word order typology more generally. It also takes up two related issues: (i), how FOFC relates to, and challenges, both typologically and formally defined notions of symmetry and harmony; and (ii), the fact that FOFC, as (2) indicates, concerns strong generative capacity. That is, it is a generalization, not about strings of formatives in the manner of Greenberg's word order universals, but about hierarchical structure. It does not rule out strings of a certain type; rather, it rules out strings under a given structural description.

FOFC provides another argument that there is a fundamental asymmetry in the grammar of human languages such that head-final order is (marginally) more marked than head-initial order. This is also a consequence of some of Greenberg's universals, discussed by Greenberg in terms of dominance, and related to the asymmetries that provide the basis for Kayne's (1994) Linear Correspondence Axiom (LCA). It is proposed that the crosslinguistic distribution of word orders is not a consequence of Universal Grammar, but instead derives from the inherent conservativity of the learner; that is, it is a third-factor effect, in Chomsky's (2005) terms.

Chapter 4, by Anders Holmberg, examines how the relation between structure and linear order has been viewed within generative linguistics; discusses the implications of FOFC for the theory of the relation between structure and linear order; and reviews some theoretical explanations of FOFC proposed in recent years, with particular focus on the theories outlined by Biberauer, Holmberg, and Roberts (2014) and (Sheehan 2011, 2013a,b), and one based on Roberts's (2010b) theory of incorporation. These are the theories that are assumed, discussed, and compared throughout the book.

In early versions of generative grammar, phrase structure rules encoded both structure and word order. In the 1980s and early 1990s, structure and linear order were in principle separated, structure being universal (earlier X-bar theory, nowadays bare phrase structure theory) and linear order being determined by a set of parameters. The LCA was an important step in the evolution of the theory of the relation between structure and order. According to this principle, asymmetric c-command determines linear order, thus explaining a wide range of asymmetries in the crosslinguistic distribution of grammatical properties. As FOFC is an expression of asymmetry in grammar, it seems a priori plausible that the explanation of FOFC involves the LCA. This idea is implemented in some of the theories discussed in this chapter, including those of Biberauer, Holmberg, and Roberts (2014) and Sheehan (2011, 2013a,b), but in quite different ways.

Chapter 5, by Michelle Sheehan, discusses the possibility that FOFC is a consequence of constraints on speech processing, an initially not implausible idea, especially if it is found that FOFC is not a universal but only a strong tendency. Two processing-based theories are addressed. The first is based on Hawkins's (1994) theory of parsing, including the principle of efficient parsing called Early Immediate Constituents (EIC). From a parsing point of view, the ideal situation—explained by EIC—is that two heads in a structurally local relation are also linearly adjacent. According to Hawkins (1994, 2004), this explains why harmonic (i.e., consistently head-final or head-initial) structures are the most common ones. The structure ruled out by FOFC is disharmonic, as a complement intervenes between the two heads (see (4a)), complicating parsing. The problem is that the disharmonic structure in (4b), although not nearly as common as harmonically head-initial or head-final structures, is still widely attested in various categories across languages:

(4) a. *$[_{\beta P} [_{\alpha P} \alpha XP] \beta]$ (higher head final, lower head initial)

    b. $[_{\beta P} \beta [_{\alpha P} XP \alpha]]$ (higher head initial, lower head final)

A challenge for explaining FOFC in terms of parsing is to explain why the "direction of disharmony" makes a difference. The other parsing-based theory reviewed in chapter 5, that of Cecchetto (2013), attempts to do just that. It is based on the idea that FOFC is a consequence of a constraint on the parsing of backward dependencies. In (4b), selection of α by β goes "forward" and is less sensitive to locality than the "backward" selection in (4a).

As chapter 5 shows, EIC can also explain the difference between (4a) and (4b). However, it turns out that Hawkins's and Cecchetto's theories both face considerable empirical and analytical problems and ultimately fail to explain FOFC. The chapter considers whether FOFC is merely a "statistical universal"—that is, a more or less strong tendency. It proposes that the LCA, the principle on which the explanation of FOFC discussed in chapter 3 is based, is itself ultimately based on a processing condition: the preference for forward dependencies. In this sense, FOFC would after all be an effect of the interplay of principles of phrase structure and constraints on speech processing.

Chapter 6, by Michelle Sheehan, deals with the issue of γ in (1b). Like the order *$[[_{VP} V O] Aux]$, the order *$[[_{VP} V Adv] Aux]$ appears to be banned in a number of natural languages, and plausibly universally. Linear strings with the surface order V-Adv-Aux are argued to have one of two underlying hierarchical structures: either $[[_{XP} [V] X] Aux]$, where the apparent adverb is actually a projecting head, or $[[_{VP} O V] [_{XP} X [Aux t_{VP}]]]$, where a head-final VP has raised over two inflectional heads. The apparent impossibility of *$[[_{VP} V Adv] Aux]$ then suggests that adverbs also count as "interveners" for FOFC, suggesting that FOFC could be an effect of processing after all. It is proposed, though, that the ban on *$[[_{VP} V Adv] Aux]$ actually follows from existing accounts of FOFC in conjunction with the independent ban on *$[[O V] Adv]$ noted by Ernst (2003, 2004). The chapter also takes up the derivation of V-O-Adv order, as it appears prima facie to be derived by a FOFC violation. Evidence suggests, however, that in instances of V-O-Adv the verb and the object move past the adverb separately rather than as a phrase, meaning that this order falls outside the condition. This kind of derivation is unavailable with V-O-Aux because of the Head Movement Constraint (Travis 1984), which blocks head movement of V past Aux.

Chapter 7, by Michelle Sheehan, examines Williams's (1982) Head-Final Filter (HFF), a restriction on the distribution of adjectives that is highly reminiscent of FOFC but does not obviously fall within its remit, at least as FOFC is formulated in (1) above. The HFF (which traces its lineage back to Emonds's (1976) Surface Recursion Restriction and Greenberg's (1963) Universal 21) bans anything from intervening between a prenominal modifier and the phrase it modifies. A typical example is (5), a noun phrase with a prenominal adjectival phrase containing a complement:

(5) *a [proud of his son] man

This is not a standard FOFC violation like (2), for example, because the adjective is not a head selected by the noun. In other words, the adjective and the noun are not members of the same extended projection (by standard assumptions). As others have noted (see, e.g., Cinque 2010), the HFF effect, though pervasive, is apparently not universal; some languages appear to allow right-branching prenominal adjectival phrases to varying degrees. Nonetheless, the chapter argues that the HFF should fall within the remit of FOFC, as apparent violations plausibly involve considerable hidden structure, which is sometimes visible, as in the case of Bulgarian and Macedonian. It also shows that Sheehan's (2011, 2013a,b) account of FOFC can accommodate the HFF as long as certain independently motivated assumptions are made about adjectival modification.

Chapter 8, by Ian Roberts, is about the structure of DP. It takes as its starting point Greenberg's (1963) Universal 20, concerning the order of demonstratives, numerals, adjectives, and nouns in the noun phrase, as discussed and modified by Cinque (2005a). After reviewing the various orders of these constituents found among the world's languages, Cinque formulates several generalizations and proposes that all the existing orders are derived from a common base structure by a series of movements, within a theory assuming the LCA plus certain additional constraints on movement. FOFC is implicated in the generation of the order Num-N-Dem. According to Cinque, it would be derived from the base structure [$_{DemP}$ Dem [$_{NumP}$ Num NP]] by movement of NumP to Spec,DemP. This should lead to a FOFC violation; compare (6) with (1) and (2):

(6) [$_{DemP}$ [$_{NumP}$ Num NP] Dem]

Though quite rare, the order Num-N-Dem in fact occurs. As FOFC predicts that this order/structure should not occur at all, (6) cannot be the right analysis of phrases exhibiting it. This prompts an analysis of DPs exhibiting the order Num-N-Dem in a range of languages, showing that these noun phrases indeed respect FOFC; the final demonstrative is not the head of a DP dominating the NumP, but a "low demonstrative." This finding leads to the hypothesis that demonstratives function as the external argument of DP, closely corresponding to the subject in clauses. The chapter ends by discussing this hypothesis and its consequences for the syntax and typology of DPs.

Chapter 9, by Theresa Biberauer, deals with a class of apparent counterexamples to FOFC. Many languages with head-initial syntax have certain phrase-final or clause-final particles. For instance, clause-final question particles and clause-final negation are common in both VO languages and OV languages in many parts of the world, while VP-final auxiliaries are common in VO languages in some parts of the world. This has led some researchers (see, e.g., Whitman 2013, Paul 2014) to conclude that FOFC is a tendency rather than an absolute universal. The chapter scrutinizes many of these apparent counterexamples in detail. It turns out that, while the particle-final structures are underlyingly quite varied, they do share one property: on closer investigation, none of them unambiguously violate FOFC. The chapter demonstrates that pursuing the idea that FOFC is a syntactic universal—a hierarchical universal, in Whitman's (2008) terms—that bans a particular configuration from narrow syntax is a useful heuristic for developing insight both into the nature of particles and into the syntax of a variety of, for the most part, understudied constructions.

This chapter also puts FOFC and the particular head-final and head-initial order that it entails into the context of other pairs of syntactic values that exhibit a strikingly similar pattern, such as verbal and nominal, masculine and feminine, singular and plural, A-movement and -movement. The common factor is this: when there is a switch from one value to the other in the bottom-up construction of a syntactic structure, the switch can only go one way and it is irreversible. In the case of word order, head-final order at the bottom of the syntactic tree can change to head-initial at certain points in the construction of the tree, but the opposite switch never happens; this is FOFC. The chapter conjectures that this particular constraint on structural harmony may be a special case of a much more general phenomenon in the syntax of natural language.

Chapter 10, by Anders Holmberg, is a case study of a language with very free order among clausal constituents. To put it simply, clauses can conform to the SVO pattern (the unmarked case) or the SOV pattern (as a marked case). Interestingly, when they conform to the SOV pattern, they observe FOFC, as exemplified in (2). When a sentence has more constituents—for example, when it is based on a ditransitive verb—the word order options multiply, but FOFC-violating orders are always ruled out. The question posed in this chapter is how to formally characterize this freedom of constituent order—which touches in turn on a fundamental question in syntactic theory and typology: How is crosslinguistic word order variation to be explained? Is it a matter of more freedom of movement, or of the relevant heads (V, Aux, etc.) having dual ordering specifications? The chapter shows that movement of the object in Finnish, in contexts that exclude OV order, conforms to Holmberg's Generalization: the object can move, but only if the verb moves as well. This indicates that Holmberg's Generalization may indeed be universal, and that variation in constituent order does not relate to freedom of movement—rather, it relates to ordering specifications on heads, in that some languages have heads with dual specifications. This finding is then formally couched in a theory based Sheehan's (2011, 2013a,b) theory, in which linear order is only in part determined by movement.

Chapter 11, by Ian Roberts, is about effects of FOFC on word structure. Assuming that (i) suffixes head the words they form together with a root (or stem), as is standard since Aronoff 1976 and Williams 1981b, and (ii) syntax (phrase structure) and morphology (word structure) are part of the same generative system, sometimes called the Single Engine Hypothesis, words with suffixes are an instance of head-final order, so FOFC should apply. This chapter argues that FOFC does apply inside words. To begin with, the crosslinguistic preference for suffixing over prefixing in inflectional morphology, and particularly in head-final languages, is shown to be explained by the LCA in conjunction with FOFC. Following Kayne (1994), Holmberg (2000a), and Julien (2002), suffixation of a head F to a head G is taken to be the result of either head movement or phrasal movement, as in (7a,b), respectively (see also section 4.8):

(7) a. $[_{FP} [_F G F] [_{GP} ...\langle G \rangle ...]]$
    b. $[^{FP} [^{GP} ...G] F \langle GP \rangle]$
    c. $[^{FP} F [^{GP} G...]]$

It follows from the LCA that head movement can only be adjunction to the left, resulting in suffixation. It follows from FOFC that phrasal movement as in (7b) is only possible when GP is head-final. This restricts the class of configurations where prefixation is possible to (7c). Data from the literature, including the *World Atlas of Language Stuctures*, show that this theory makes the right predictions regarding the distribution of suffixation and prefixation among the languages of the world. If head-final structures are always derived by phrasal movement, the prediction is that there will be no prefixation in OV languages, rather than just a strong preference. In fact, there are cases of prefixation in OV languages. These prefixes, it turns out, fall into a class of heads that are exceptional in relation to FOFC in other contexts, too.

Assuming the Single Engine Hypothesis, effects of FOFC may be expected in compounding and derivational morphology, too. It is shown that FOFC does constrain synthetic compounding.

2 Empirical Evidence for the Final-over-Final-Condition

Theresa Biberauer, Anders Holmberg, Ian Roberts,
and Michelle Sheehan

2.1 Introduction

In this chapter, we present a variety of cases from a variety of languages that provide empirical evidence for the Final-over-Final Condition (FOFC). The data have mostly been presented elsewhere: Biberauer, Newton, and Sheehan 2009b, Biberauer, Sheehan, and Newton 2010, Sheehan 2011, 2013a,b, Biberauer, Holmberg, and Roberts 2014. The goal here is neither to provide an exhaustive empirical overview, nor to provide an analysis of what FOFC might follow from; here the point is to provide a basic introduction to the core phenomena with a view to facilitating the later discussion.

To recapitulate, FOFC rules out a configuration where a head-initial phrase is immediately dominated by a head-final phrase, in the same projection line (Holmberg 2000a). It is well-known (since Greenberg 1963, Dryer 1992) that there is a preference for consistency, or harmony, when it comes to direction of the head-complement relation. (1a,b) are therefore found abundantly among the languages of the world. (1c) is considerably less common, but still found in a variety of languages and phrase types. (1d), however, is either very uncommon or nonexistent.

(1)

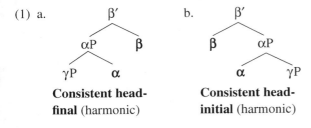

a. β' dominating αP and β, with αP dominating γP and α

Consistent head-final (harmonic)

b. β' dominating β and αP, with αP dominating α and γP

Consistent head-initial (harmonic)

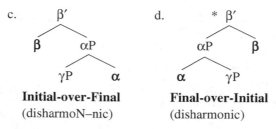

c. β′

β   αP

γP   α

Initial-over-Final
(disharmoN–nic)

d. * β′

αP   β

α   γP

Final-over-Initial
(disharmonic)

A head-final phrase can only dominate a head-final phrase, in the same projection line, while a head-initial phrase can dominate a head-initial phrase or a head-final phrase. As Kayne (1994) discusses, syntax is fundamentally asymmetric (or "antisymmetric"). FOFC is another example of this. The example mentioned in chapter 1 was (2):

(2) *[$_{AuxP}$ [$_{VP}$ V XP] Aux]

The proviso "in the same projection line" is required to allow, for example, the possibility of a head-initial subject dominated by a head-final TP, a not uncommon configuration:

(3) [$_{TP}$ [$_{DP}$ D NP] [$_{T'}$ VP T]]

V and Aux in (2) are in the same (extended) projection line. T and D in (3) are not. In the following sections, we will review a number of case studies all showing effects of FOFC.

2.2 *(S)-V-O-Aux

The initial observation comes from comparative Germanic. Looking across Germanic varieties, both synchronically and diachronically, one can observe a great variety of word orders, particularly at the clausal level and in VP. If we consider the three elements Aux,[1] V, and O, we find all possible permutations of these, with one very striking exception: the order V-O-Aux is not found. This fact has often been noted (see, e.g., Travis 1984:157–158), Den Besten 1986, Pintzuk 1991, 1999, Kiparsky 1996:168–171, Hróarsdóttir 1999, 2000, Fuss and Trips 2002). Let us look at these orders one by one.

First, O-V-Aux (*(John) the book read has*) is readily found. (4) illustrates this from German (extrapolating from main clauses, in order to avoid the confound introduced by the verb-second phenomenon):

(4) …dass Johann das Buch gelesen hat.   [German]
       that Johann the book read   has
    '…that Johann has read the book.'

This order is found, primarily in subordinate clauses, in German, Dutch, Afrikaans, all German, Dutch/Flemish, and Afrikaans dialects, Old English (OE), and Old Norse (ON). It is usually thought to derive from head-final order in TP and VP (and vP, if this is assumed).

Second, we find the order O-Aux-V (*(John) the book has read*). This corresponds to what has been known, since Evers 1975, as "verb-raising" order in Dutch:

(5) a. ...dat Jan het boek wil   lezen.   [Dutch]
        that Jan the book wants read.INF
        '...that Jan wants to read the book.'
    b. ...þe   æfre on gefeohte his handa wolde afylan.   [OE]
        who ever in battle   his hands would defile
        '...whoever would defile his hands in battle.'
    (*Ælfric's Lives of Saints* 25.858; Pintzuk 1991:102)

This order is also found in Standard Afrikaans and many nonstandard West Germanic varieties, but not in Standard German.

Third, we observe the order Aux-O-V (*(John) has the book read*). Since Haegeman and Van Riemsdijk 1986, this order has been known as "verb projection raising":

(6) a. ...da Jan wilt   een huis   kopen.   [West Flemish]
        that Jan wants a   house buy.INF
        '...that Jan wants to buy a house.'
        (Haegeman and Van Riemsdijk 1986:419)
    b. ...das de Hans wil   es huus   chaufe.   [Zürich German]
        that the Hans wants a house buy.INF
        '...that Hans wants to buy a house.'
        (Haegeman and Van Riemsdijk 1986:419)
    c. ...þæt hie mihton swa bealdlice Godes geleafan bodian.   [OE]
        that they could so boldly   God's faith   preach
        '...that they could preach God's faith so boldly.'
        (*The Homilies of the Anglo-Saxon Church* I 232; van Kemenade
        1987:179)

This order is also found in Middle Dutch (Hoeksema 1993), in Old High German (Behaghel 1932), ON (Hróarsdóttir 1999:203ff.), and in numerous nonstandard varieties of Flemish, Swiss and Austrian German, and Afrikaans (see Schmid 2005 and Wurmbrand 2006 for discussion and overview). Note that these examples appear to show the mirror image of the FOFC configuration, in that they plausibly have a head-initial TP (with the order Aux-VP) and, as complement to the Aux in T (or v), a head-final VP. Initial-over-final orders are readily attested, then, while final-over-initial order, schematized in (1d), is not. This is the central asymmetry that we observe.

A rarer but still attested order is V-Aux-O (*(John) read has the book*). This has often been described as "object extraposition." Here we illustrate with "PP-extraposition" in Dutch and a DP in final position in OE:

(7) a. ...dat het lijk   gevonden werd   in de kast.   [Dutch]
       that the corpse found   become in the closet
       '...that the corpse was found in the closet.'
       (Zwart 1997:39)

    b. ...þæt ænig mon atellan mæge ealne þone demm.   [OE]
       that any man relate can   all   the   misery
       '...that any man can relate all the misery.'
       (*Orosius* 52.6–7; Pintzuk 2002:283, (16b))

To the extent that the "extraposed" element is a PP, a CP, or (more marginally) a heavy DP, this order is also found in German, as well as many German and Dutch dialects, and in ON (Hróarsdóttir 1999:201–202). It is also found in Finnish, as will be discussed in chapter 10.

Finally, we find Aux-V-O (*(John) has read the book*). This is of course the head-initial order, different variants of which are found in Modern English and throughout Modern North Germanic. It is also found in Dutch and OE (where it has been analyzed as "verb raising" combined with "object extraposition"):

(8) a. ...dat het lijk   werd   gevonden in de kast.   [Dutch]
       that the corpse become found   in the closet
       '...that the corpse was found in the closet.'

    b. ...þæt he mot   ehtan   godra manna.   [OE]
       that he might persecute good men
       '...that he might persecute good men.'
       (*Wulfstan's Homilies* 130.37–38; Pintzuk 2002:282, (13b))

At first sight, then, it seems that all possible word orders are found—that, across the range of varieties, synchronically and diachronically, anything goes. But this is not the case. The crucial observation is that V-O-Aux is not attested. The missing order is the one that instantiates the schema in (1d) for α = V and β = Aux. In other words, the missing configuration is that in (9):

(9)   *   AuxP

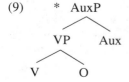

Moreover, this word order limitation is not restricted to Germanic. The same gap exists in Basque (Haddican 2004:116), in Kaaps, a dialect of Afrikaans heavily influenced by English, and in Finnish (Holmberg 2000a:128) and other Finno-Ugric languages that exhibit both head-initial and head-final orders, including North Saami (Marit Julien, pers. comm.). See Biberauer, Holmberg, and Roberts 2014 for illustration and discussion.

Crosslinguistically, therefore, a mix of patterns involving V, O, and Aux is found, and, notably, disharmonic orders of the "verb projection raising" (Aux-O-V) type are attested; but the mirror image of verb projection raising seems to be entirely missing. This kind of typological gap is striking, especially when attested in unrelated families, and calls for an explanation. FOFC is not intended as an explanation; rather, it is a broader generalization that includes this case.

2.3   The Crosslinguistic Distribution of Complementizers

The second piece of evidence for FOFC also concerns clause-level syntax. This is the observation, originally due to Hawkins (1990:223–261), that sentence-final complementizers are not found in VO languages (see also Dryer 1992:102, 2009b:199–205, Hawkins 2004, Kayne 2000:320–321). Crosslinguistically, we find OV languages with both initial and final complementizers. Latin is generally taken to be an OV language (see Vincent 1988, Salvi 2004, Clackson and Horrocks 2007, Ledgeway 2012, and the references given there), and it has initial complementizers, as the following examples show (taking *ut* and *quod* to be complementizers):

(10) a. Ubii   Caesarem   orant   [CP ut sibi   parcat].   [Latin]
Ubii.NOM Caesar.ACC beg.3PL   C selves.DAT spare
'The Ubii beg Caesar to spare them.'

b. Accidit   perincommode [quod eum nusquam vidisti].
happened.3SG unfortunately   C   him nowhere saw.2SG
'It is unfortunate that you didn't see him anywhere.'
(see Roberts 2007b:162–163 for sources and discussion)

On the other hand, Japanese is an OV language with final complementizers:

(11) Bill-ga   [CP [TP Mary-ga   John-ni   sono hon-o   watasita] [Japanese]
Bill-NOM   Mary-NOM John-DAT that book-ACC handed
to] itta (koto).
that said (fact)
'Bill said that Mary handed that book to John.'
(Fukui and Saito 1998:443)

And of course VO languages with initial complementizers are readily found, English being a good example.

But the fourth logical possibility, VO languages with final complementizers, appears not to be attested. The *World Atlas of Language Structures (WALS)* (Dryer and Haspelmath 2015) does not have a specific map for the order of general clausal subordinators in relation to the clause they introduce, and so we cannot directly look for evidence there. However, *WALS* does cover the order of "adverbial subordinators" such as *although, when, while,* and *if,* in relation to the clauses they introduce (Map 94A; Dryer 2015e). It is possible that some, if not all, of these elements are complementizers; however, Dryer (2015e) is explicit on the point that "care was taken not to include general markers of subordination"—that is, the clearest cases of complementizers. Nonetheless, the skewing is evident: 305 languages have VO and initial subordinators and 91 have OV and final subordinators. Placing the subordinators in C, then, we observe cross-categorial harmony in the majority of cases. More importantly for our purposes, there is a very clear asymmetry in the disharmonic orders: 61 languages have OV and initial subordinators, but *only* 2 are said to show the combination of final subordinators with VO: Buduma (Afro-Asiatic) and Guajajara (Tupi-Guaraní). Newton (2007), however, shows that final Cs in both languages appear to introduce OV rather than VO clauses; that is, both in fact exhibit the more generally attested disharmonic order rather than the FOFC-violating one in this context. Dryer also notes that subordinating suffixes are found, particularly in OV languages. In fact, there is only 1 VO language with subordinating suffixes (the Australian language Yindjibarndi), as against 56 OV languages with subordinating suffixes. Moreover, there are no subordinating prefixes (see section 11.4 for a possible account of this). In this respect, then, the data are significantly skewed.[2] The vanishingly small number of counterexamples clearly requires closer investigation, but the overall asymmetry in the distribution of logically possible combinations of orders is very clear.[3]

In terms of the schema in (2), there are two ways of ruling out final Cs in VO systems. On the one hand, we could have a head-initial VP inside a head-final TP and CP, as in (12a). This instantiates the schema in (1d) for $\alpha = V$ and $\beta = T$, and so constitutes a FOFC violation of the same type as the V-O-Aux orders considered in section 2.2. Alternatively, we could have a head-initial TP inside a head-final CP, as in (12b). This structure instantiates (1d) and hence violates FOFC, for $\alpha = T$ and $\beta = C$:[4]

(12) a. $*[_{CP} [_{TP} [_{VP} V O] T] C]$
      b. $*[^{CP} [^{TP} T [^{VP} V O]] C]$

Coordinating conjunctions are another kind of clause introducer. Zwart (2005) investigates 214 languages and finds no "true" final coordinating conjunctions in head-initial languages (see his table 3, and also Zwart 2009b).

In sum, the absence (or extreme rarity) of VO…C orders crosslinguistically is the second piece of evidence for FOFC.

2.4   FOFC Compliance: The Distribution of CP?

The third example of a FOFC effect comes from the distribution of CP-complements in OV languages. It is well-known that, unlike all other kinds of objects (DPs, PPs), C-initial complements in languages like German and Dutch surface in an "extraposed" postverbal position in the unmarked case (see Stowell 1981, Vanden Wyngaerd 1989, Lutz and Pafel 1996, Beerman, Leblanc, and Van Riemsdijk 1997, Büring and Hartmann 1997):

(13) …weil   er gesagt hat [$_{CP}$ **dass** Schnapps gut   schmeckt]. [German]
      because he said   has   that Schnapps good tastes
      '…because he said that Schnapps tastes good.'
      (Büring and Hartmann 1997:32)

Interestingly, as Biberauer and Sheehan (2012a) show, citing Hawkins (1994, 2004), Cinque (2008), and Dryer (2009a), this is a very general crosslinguistic effect, also observed in Persian (Aghaei 2006), Hindi-Urdu (Mahajan 1990a), and Afrikaans, as well as in OV languages with both initial and final complementizers: Turkish (Kornfilt 1997, 2001, Özsoy 2001), Bengali/Bangla (Bayer 2001), Marathi (Pandharipande 1997, Nayudu 2008), and Indic more generally (Masica 1991, Marlow 1997, Davison 2007). On the surface, at least, this appears to be a simple FOFC effect, as a head-initial CP cannot be immediately dominated by a head-final VP, as in (1d):

(14)   *   VP

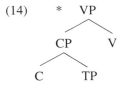

Biberauer and Sheehan (2012a) argue at length that this is indeed a FOFC effect and that extraposition can, in fact, be considered to be a FOFC-compliance strategy that languages employ to avoid a FOFC violation.

Crucially, in the case of Turkish, Bengali/Bangla, and Marathi, only C-initial complement clauses get obligatorily "extraposed" (CF = classifier):

(15) a. chele-Ta Sune-che   [cp **je** [or baba aS-be]].   S V CP [Bengali/
         boy-CF hear-PAST.3SG   C his father come-FUT   Bangla]
         'The boy has heard that his father will come.'
     b. *chele-Ta [cp **je** [or baba aS-be]] Sune-che.   *S CP V
     c. *[cp **je** [or baba aS-be]] chele-Ta Sune-che.   *CP S V
         (Bayer 1999:245)

C-final clauses can occur in the immediate preverbal position, be optionally
fronted to a topic position, or even (more marginally) be extraposed:

(16) a. chele-Ta [cp or baba aS-be   **bole**] Sune-che. S CP V [Bengali/
         boy-CF   his father come-FUT QUOT hear-PAST   Bangla]
     b. [cp or baba aS-be   **bole**] chele-Ta Sune-che. CP S V
             his father come-FUT QUOT boy-CF   hear-PAST
         'The boy has heard [that his father will come].'
     c. %chele-Ta Sune-che [cp or baba aS-be **bole**].   S V CP
         (based on Bayer 2001:14, 18)

A possible hypothesis is that this is an effect of (some version of) Stowell's
(1981) Case Resistance Principle: the preverbal position in SOV languages is
a Case position and therefore allows nominal clauses but not regular finite
clauses. That this is wrong can be clearly illustrated with data from Turkish.
Turkish has a number of different embedding strategies, one of which involves
an initial complementizer *ki*, borrowed from Persian. Whereas the normal
position for clausal complements is preverbal, *ki*-clauses always surface in
postverbal position:

(17) a. (Ben) [cp siz-in   Ankara-ya git-tig-iniz]-i   [Turkish]
         I   you-GEN Ankara-DAT go-NOM-POSS.2PL-ACC
         duy-du-m.
         hear-PAST-SG
         'I heard that you went to Ankara.'
         (Özsoy 2001:216)
     b. Anladım   [cp **ki** onun   bir derdi   var].
         understand.PAST.1SG   that 3SG.GEN a   problem.POSS.3SG exist.3SG
         'I realized that he had a problem.'
         (Haig 2001:201)

That this is a FOFC effect, rather than something regulated by Case, becomes
apparent when one considers that there are predicates that select reduced
"direct complements." These clausal complements *must* surface in preverbal
position, even though they lack nominal properties (e.g., genitive subjects and
nominal morphology) and are not marked with accusative Case:

(18) Biz [sen-Ø   Ankara-ya git-ti-n]   san-dı-k.   [Turkish]
     we   you-NOM Ankara-DAT go-PAST-2SG consider-PAST-1PL
     'We considered you had gone to Ankara.'
     (Özsoy 2001:217)

Similar effects can be observed in West Germanic languages, in which reduced
(head-final) clauses can surface in preverbal position, unlike head-initial
dass-clauses:

(19) a. ...dass Max mir empfohlen   hat [das Lexikon   zu   [German]
           that Max me recommended has the dictionary to
        kaufen].
        buy
     b. ...dass Max mir [das Lexikon   zu kaufen] empfohlen   hat.
           that Max me the dictionary to buy   recommended has
        '...that Max recommended I buy the dictionary.'
        (Bayer, Schmid, and Bader 2005:79)

In some cases, certain reduced clauses *must* surface in the canonical object
position without displaying nominal properties (see Biberauer and Roberts
2008):

(20) a. ...dass Hans [$_{TP}$ sich zu rasieren] schien.   [German]
            that Hans   self to shave   seemed
         '...that Hans seemed to shave himself.'
     b. *...dass Hans schien [$_{TP}$ sich zu rasieren].
            that Hans seemed   self to shave

   In sum, the placement of CP-complements in OV languages also seems to
be regulated by FOFC. Head-initial CPs simply cannot surface in preverbal
position and are forced into an "extraposed" position for FOFC compliance.
See Sheehan 2011 and Biberauer and Sheehan 2012a for an account of how
this might work. Note that the generalization that FOFC holds only within
extended projections requires a definition whereby embedded CPs do not
constitute separate extended projections from their selecting verb (see Biberauer, Holmberg, and Roberts 2014 for discussion).

2.5 Nominal Projections

A fourth piece of evidence for FOFC comes from nominal projections: NP,
DP, and also PP, if we take P to be the highest head in the nominal extended
projection (*pace* Grimshaw 2001, 2005; see Ledgeway 2012:chap. 5 for a very
elegant account of word order change in Latin/Romance on the basis of this

assumption). Finnish is a language that has prepositions as well as postpositions, where some adpositions can either precede or follow their complement
(see Manninen 2003). The noun in Finnish precedes its complement. In this
light, consider the paradigm in (21) (ELA = elative case, 'from'):

(21) a. ennen tuloa   [Finnish]
         before arrival
     b. tuloa ennen
         arrival before
         'before (the) arrival'
     c. ennen [tuloa   Amerika-sta]
         before arrival America-ELA
         'before arrival from America'
     d. *[tuloa   Amerika-sta] ennen
         arrival America-ELA before

The adposition *ennen* 'before' can take its complement DP either to the left
or to the right. If this complement DP itself contains a noun and a (postnominal) complement, the DP cannot precede P. (21d) is another instance of the
FOFC-violating disharmonic configuration (1d). See Holmberg 2000a and
Biberauer, Holmberg, and Roberts 2014 for discussion of other cases like this.
  Note also that a postnominal adjunct in the DP preceding the adposition has
the same effect as a postnominal complement (INE = inessive case):

(22) a. ennen [lomaa   (Espanja-ssa)]   [Finnish]
         before holiday Spain-INE
     b. [lomaa (*Espanja-ssa)]   ennen
         holiday Spain-INE   before
         'before the holiday (in Spain)'

The FOFC-violating configuration, therefore, is $[_{ZP} [_{XP} X^0 YP] Z^0]$, where X^0
and Z^0 are members of the same extended projection (e.g., N and P or V and
Aux), but where YP can be a posthead complement or a posthead adjunct (see
chapter 6 on adverbials and FOFC).
  The following is another case involving a nominal projection in Finnish.
The past participle occurs in construction with the auxiliary *ole* 'be', forming
the present perfect tense. The participle is initial in its phrase; however, like
other verb forms, it can optionally take its complement on the left under the
right circumstances (to be discussed in chapter 10; they include the case where
the sentence has a questioned subject):

(23) a. Poika on heittä-nyt   pallo-n.   [Finnish]
         boy   has throw-PAST.PTCP ball-ACC
         'The boy has thrown the ball.'

b. Kuka on pallo-n heittänyt?
who has ball-ACC throw-PAST.PTCP
'Who has thrown the ball?'

The same participial form is used in the prenominal participial relative construction (see Koskinen 1998). In this case, any complement (or adjunct) of the participle must precede it:

(24) a. [$_{NP}$ [pallo-n heittä-nyt] poika] [Finnish]
   ball-ACC throw-PAST.PTCP boy
   'the boy who threw the ball'
b. *[$_{NP}$ [heittä-nyt pallo-n] poika]

This, we contend, is another effect of FOFC. Further evidence of FOFC effects in the nominal domain involving demonstratives, quantifiers, and adjectives will be discussed in chapter 8.

2.6 Diachronic Evidence

FOFC makes strong predictions about the possible pathways of word order change. Essentially, it predicts that an overall change from head-final to head-initial order must proceed "top down," starting at the C-level and proceeding successively "downward" through the extended projection of V, affecting the projection of the lexical V itself (i.e., the order of V and the direct object) last. Schematically:

(25) [[[O V] T] C] → [C [[O V] T]] → [C [T [O V]]] → [C [T [V O]]]

Conversely, head-initial to head-final change must go "bottom up," starting at VP, then affecting TP, and then affecting CP:

(26) [C [T [V O]]] → [C [T [O V]]] → [C [[O V] T]] → [[[O V] T] C]

Any other sequence of changes in either case will lead to an intermediate synchronic system that violates FOFC at some stage. Consider, for example, what would happen if, starting from a uniformly head-final system like the first one shown in the series in (25), VP changed headedness first. This would give rise to a [[[V O] T] C] system; as noted above, such systems are not found. If they were possible outcomes of natural processes of change, presumably such systems would be found; FOFC explains their absence synchronically and, therefore, diachronically.

Biberauer, Sheehan, and Newton (2010:43–46) show that changes from head-final to head-initial order in TP and VP in both the history of English and the history of French conform to (25). As already mentioned, Ledgeway (2012:chap. 5) shows the same for the development of Latin to Romance, again a change from head-final to head-initial order.[5] In this connection, Ledgeway states, "[T]he first robustly head-initial structures to emerge in Latin involve the CP and the PP" (p. 225), and "once head-initiality becomes established in the topmost CP and PP layers, it is free to percolate down harmonically to the phrases that these in turn embed" (p. 228).

Word order change from head-initial to head-final is rarer, at least in Indo-European. However, Biberauer, Newton, and Sheehan (2009b:717–721) present data indicating that the Ethiopian Semitic languages may have undergone change in this direction. The oldest attested language of this group, Ge'ez, is VSO and has a basic head-initial typology; Tigré and Tigrinya are verb- and auxiliary-final, with mixed initial and final complementizers. Harari, on the other hand, has exclusively final Cs. These languages, then, offer some evidence in support of (26).

More generally, as Ledgeway's first-quoted remark suggests, the development (through grammaticalization or borrowing; on the latter, see again Biberauer, Sheehan, and Newton 2010) of an initial C, for example, may be enough to start a series of harmonic changes leading from general head-final to general head-initial order in the clause. FOFC does not explain the series of changes; chapters 3 and 4 will have more to say about the sources of harmony, synchronic and diachronic. But FOFC does predict the diachronic pathway that must be followed as one harmonic system eventually changes into the other.[6]

If FOFC is a hard universal, then it is predicted to constrain borrowing as well. Biberauer, Newton, and Sheehan (2009a,b) discuss one potential example of this in relation to the South Asian linguistic area. When Indo-Aryan and Dravidian first came into contact is controversial, but it is uncontroversial that they came to "structurally converge after multilingual contact extending over several millennia" (Hock and Joseph 1996:61). While many Indo-Aryan languages have developed a final complementizer from a quotative source, possibly through prolonged contact with Dravidian (Kuiper 1974, Meenakshi 1986), this is not true of all varieties (Masica 1991, Marlow 1997, Bayer 1999, 2001). Interestingly, it seems that exactly those languages that have an initial question particle have failed to develop a final complementizer (see Davison 2007 for a comprehensive overview of the data). Assuming that the question particle realizes a head that is structurally lower than a subordinating complementizer, the presence of a final complementizer in a language with a phrase-initial question particle would constitute a straightforward FOFC violation:

(27) *[[Q TP] C]

If borrowing of a FOFC-violating structure is ruled out, then the distribution of final complementizers in table 2.1 follows naturally.

Table 2.1
Distribution of final complementizers in Indo-Aryan (based on appendix A of Davison 2007)

No final C	Final C from 'saying'	Final C from demonstrative
Hindi/Urdu, Panjabi, Sindhi, Kashmiri, Maithili, Kurmali	Sinhala, Dhivehi, Marathi, Nepali, Dakkhini Hindi, Assamese, Bengali/Bangla, Oriya	Marathi, Gujarati

By way of illustration, compare Hindi-Urdu and Marathi. Hindi-Urdu has an initial question particle *kyaa* and lacks a final complementizer of any kind (the forms included here to illustrate this are equivalent to final complementizers found in related languages, which have been sourced from demonstratives and 'saying' verbs, respectively; see Bayer 2001):

(28) a. **kyaa** aap wahaaN aa-be-Ngii?   [Hindi-Urdu]
          Q   you there   go-FUT-2PL
          'Are you going there?'
          (Davison 2007:182)

   b. *usee   [[vee aa   rahee haiN] **yah/kah-kar**] maaluum hai.
       SG.DAT 3PL come PROG are   this/say-PART   known   is
       'He/She knows [that they are coming].'
       (Davison 2007:178)

Marathi, on the other hand, has a final question particle and both initial and final complementizers:

(29) a. [[to   kal   parat aalaa   **kaa(y)**]   [Marathi]
         he yesterday back come.PAST.3MSG Q
         mhaaNun/asa] raam malaa witSaarat hotaa.
         QUOT/such   Ram I.DAT ask.PROG be.PAST.3MSG
         'Ram was asking me [whether/if he came back yesterday].'

   b. raam maalaa witSaarat hotaa   **[ki** to kal   parat
      Ram I.DAT ask.PROG be.PAST.3MSG that he yesterday back
      aalaa   **kaa(y)**]].
      come.PAST.3MSG Q
      'Ram was asking me [whether/if he came back yesterday].'
      (Davison 2007:184; attributed to R. Pandharipande)

Biberauer, Newton, and Sheehan (2009a,b) show that this is a very general pattern both within and outside the Indian subcontinent, as the data in table 2.2 from Dryer 2005a,b illustrate (Q is labeled *POL*, short for for *Polarity*, in Biberauer, Newton, and Sheehan 2009a,b). Interestingly, all four apparent counterexamples to FOFC in this domain are languages in which embedded

Table 2.2
Typological positioning of question particles and complementizers

Type	Position of Q	Position of C	Number of languages (genera:families)
A	Initial	Initial only	72:35:13
B	Final	Initial	74:40:16
C	Final	Final only	45:33:20
D	**Initial**	**Final**	**4:3:3**

clauses appear to be nominalized (see Moore 1989 on Gavião, Allin 1976 on Resígaro, and de Ottaviano 1980 on Tacana). If FOFC fails to hold between nominal and verbal domains, for whatever reason, these counterexamples may thus be illusory.

2.7 Evidence from Language Acquisition

Interesting evidence for the relevance of FOFC to L2 acquisition comes from Lardiere and Schwartz's (1997) study of how Spanish-native L2 learners of English learn synthetic compounds such as *truck-driver*. A notable feature of the English compounds is that the notional verb in the compound (e.g., *drive*) follows the element it assigns its internal θ-role to (e.g., *truck*). FOFC can account for this: since the suffix *-er* is the head of the whole compound and is final, its complement cannot be head-initial, hence the ungrammaticality of *drive-trucker*. (See chapter 11 for more on FOFC in relation to synthetic compounds and other aspects of morphology.)

In Spanish, as elsewhere in Romance, English-style synthetic compounds are not found. Instead, root compounds such as *lavaplatos* (literally 'wash-dishes'; i.e., 'dishwasher') and *abrelatas* (literally 'open-cans'; i.e., 'can opener') are found. These compounds are head-initial and feature no nominal-izing suffix (the plural *-s* here attaches to the final noun, not to the whole compound, as is clear from the fact that these words refer to single dishwashers and can openers). These compounds are thus similar to English ones like *cut-throat* and *pickpocket*.

Adult L2 native-Spanish speakers learning English were tested by Lardiere and Schwartz on their ability to produce English synthetic compounds. The authors found that, largely as a function of general competence in English, various kinds of errors were produced. One class was "VO errors," of the general form *washer-dish(es)/washing-dish(es)*; forms of the type *dishes-washer* were also found. Another class was the "ING-error," that is, use of *-ing* for *-er*, as in *washing-dish(es)/dish(es)-washing*. Most important for our purposes, Lardiere and Schwartz observe that the subjects "do not produce compounds like *chase-micer* ...even though they hear *-er* as the last (linear) element of the compound in the input" (p. 342). This is the form that violates FOFC, which we predict to be unavailable to the L2 acquirers if it is ruled out by Universal Grammar (as will be argued in subsequent chapters).

Regarding L1 acquisition, Clark, Hecht, and Mulford (1986) have shown that children acquiring English go through a stage around age 4 where they make various errors with synthetic compounds, including producing forms like **dry-hairer*. However, these forms are in a minority and very short-lived compared with other "errors" the children produce. This can thus be seen as a further effect of FOFC.[7]

More generally, we can observe that, by ruling out a range of logically possible disharmonic word orders, FOFC facilitates the acquisition of word order. For example, acquisition of a final C alone is enough to guarantee that all the other categories in the clause are head-final (this is the obverse of Ledgeway's (2012) observation, noted earlier, that the innovation of an initial C is enough to make possible—although not to cause—word order change lower in the clause). The same will be true of the highest functional projection in the extended projection of N (D, or, if Ledgeway is correct, P, or perhaps K), and so on.

2.8 Conclusion

Although we have only touched upon the most important points, the foregoing gives some of the canonical evidence that has led to postulating FOFC as a generalization. Much more evidence is given elsewhere in this book and in the references cited. Like much fruitful recent work, the research on FOFC reported here builds on the two principal currents of research on universals that have emerged in the past fifty years or so: the Chomskyan tradition, in which the existence of language universals is deduced from the existence of an innate predisposition to language acquisition, and the Greenbergian tradition, in which universals, or at least strong tendencies to common patterning, are observed in increasingly wide-ranging surveys of crosslinguistic data. Therefore, this research has implications both for typology and for formal theories of syntax. In this book, we explore what these are.

3 Harmony, Symmetry, and Dominance in Word Order Universals

Ian Roberts

3.1 Introduction

The previous chapter gave the basic empirical motivations for postulating the Final-over-Final Condition (FOFC). The goal of this chapter is to set FOFC in a typological and theoretical background and to indicate its potential significance for both typology and linguistic theory. There are two key questions, which form the themes of this chapter. The first is how FOFC relates to, and challenges, both typologically and formally defined notions of symmetry and harmony. The second has to do with the consequences of the fact that FOFC concerns strong generative capacity: it is not a generalization about strings of formatives, but a generalization about hierarchical structure.

The chapter is organized as follows. Section 3.2 is devoted to a discussion of symmetry and harmony as originally put forward by Greenberg ([1963] 2007) and to how these notions relate (or not) to FOFC; section 3.3 looks at these concepts in relation to X-bar syntax, starting from the original proposals by Hawkins (1983), and section 3.4 looks at them in the light of Kayne's (1994) "antisymmetric" approach to phrase structure. This leads to a discussion of word order parameters in relation to markedness and the associated notion of parameter hierarchy, as put forward by Roberts and Holmberg (2010), Roberts (2012a), Biberauer et al. (2014), and Sheehan (2014). Finally, section 3.5 considers some more general implications of FOFC.

3.2 Greenberg [1963] 2007: Harmony, Symmetry, and Dominance

In (1), I give Greenberg's ([1963] 2007) Universals 2–4, 9, and 16 as stated in his appendix III:

(1) 2. In languages with prepositions, the genitive almost always follows the governing noun, while in languages with postpositions it always precedes.

3. Languages with dominant VSO order are always prepositional.
4. With overwhelmingly greater than chance frequency, languages with normal SOV order are postpositional.
9. With well more than chance frequency, when question particles or affixes are specified in position by reference to the sentence as a whole, if initial, such elements are found in prepositional languages and, if final, in postpositional.
16. In languages with dominant order VSO, an inflected auxiliary always precedes the main verb. In languages with dominant order SOV, an inflected auxiliary always follows the main verb.

Greenberg defined a general notion of harmony (or "harmonic and disharmonic relations among distinct rules of order" (2007:62)),[1] such that Universal 4 can be seen as stating that OV and postpositional orders are harmonic, and VO and prepositional orders are harmonic. Similarly, Universal 3 asserts a harmonic relation between VS and prepositions, and between SV and postpositions. We can thus build up relations of harmony such that prepositions, Noun-Genitive (NG), VS, and VO are harmonic, and postpositions, GN, SV, and OV are also harmonic.[2] To this we can add, on the basis of Universal 9, that initial question particles (QS) are harmonic with prepositions and final question particles (SQ) with postpositions. Finally, Universal 16 links Aux-V order to VS, VO, and so on, and V-Aux order to SV, VO, and so on.

The available evidence from the *World Atlas of Language Structures* (*WALS*) supports the idea that the harmonic systems Greenberg identified are more common than the disharmonic ones. Leaving aside V-Aux/Aux-V, for which evidence is unavailable in *WALS*, a pairwise comparison of each dyad with prepositional/postpositional orders yields the result that 75% of NG languages, 70.6% of VS languages, 64.7% of VO languages, and 56.9% of QS languages are prepositional, an average "harmony percentage" of 66.8%. So just about two-thirds of prepositional languages show the other harmonic properties identified by Greenberg. On the other hand, 64.5% of GN languages, 41.8% of SV languages (i.e., non-VS languages, including SVO and SOV), 66.2% of OV languages, and 40.9% of SQ languages are postpositional, an average of 54.1% harmony. The typological skewing can be seen from a comparison with disharmonic orders: just 7.9% of prepositional languages are GN, 25.3% are SV (i.e., non-VS languages, including SVO and SOV), 7.6% are OV, and 36.7% are SQ (note that the percentages for prepositions and postpositions among SQ languages are quite close, while among QS languages there is a big difference). Conversely, 2.8% of NG languages, 8.8% of VS languages, 6% of VO languages, and 20% of QS languages are postpositional (see Dryer

2015a,b,e,g,h). (See also the data and discussion in Bazalgette et al. 2012, which in fact provides further evidence for FOFC.)

Greenberg then clearly established the notion of cross-categorial harmony, which came to be a central concern in language typology and in comparative syntax more generally. We can also observe symmetry between the two sets of dyads: Pr, NG, VS, VO, QS vs. Po, GN, SV, OV, SQ. Each dyad appears to indicate a symmetric choice point: a language is either Pr or Po (if it has adpositions), and so on; the two orders are mirror images of one another (at the relevant structural level, at least). Thus, the notion of harmony is symmetric; there is apparently no particular bias in either direction.

On the other hand, Greenberg's notion of dominance is inherently asymmetric. The dominant order in a one-way implicational statement is the one that is allowed in both cases; in terms of material implication, it is the order referred to in the consequent. So, given a slightly restated version of Universal 3 as "If a language is VS, then it is prepositional," Pr is the dominant order since it occurs with both VS and SV, while VS is recessive. Another way to see this is in terms of a tetrachoric table, as follows:

| SV & Pr | SV & Po |
| VS & Pr | *VS & Po |

Here, the dominant order is the constant one in the left column; the harmonic orders are in the lower left and upper right.

Again, the crosslinguistic distribution of the orders, according to *WALS*, supports this. These are as follows (Dryer 2015a,e,g):

| SV & Pr (302 languages) | SV & Po (499 languages) |
| VS & Pr (137 languages) | *VS & Po (17 languages) |

Moreover, the dominant SV order is found in 1,194 languages, while the recessive VS order is found in 194 languages.[3]

In this connection, Greenberg links harmony and dominance as follows:

(2) "A dominant order may always occur, but its opposite, the recessive, occurs only when a harmonic construction is likewise present." (Greenberg [1963] 2007:62)

In our example, recessive VS order only occurs with the harmonic Pr order. The combination of recessive (VS) and nonharmonic (Po) is by far the rarest of the four. Greenberg ([1963] 2007:62) observes that, in a tetrachoric table like those above, "[t]he entry with zero [the ungrammatical/disfavored combination] is always the recessive one for each construction and the two constructions involved are disharmonic with each other." This is what we see with VS and Po here.

We can in fact see FOFC in terms of Greenberg's notions of dominance and harmony. Consider the following tetrachoric table:

$[_{\beta P}\ \beta\ [_{\alpha P}\ \alpha\ \gamma P]]$	$[_{\beta P}\ \beta\ [_{\alpha P}\ \gamma P\ \alpha]]$
$[_{\beta P}\ [_{\alpha P}\ \gamma P\ \alpha]\ \beta]$	$*[_{\beta P}\ [_{\alpha P}\ \alpha\ \gamma P]\ \beta]$

The harmonic head-initial and head-final orders are in the left-hand column. Now we can define the order where β is head-final as recessive, and we see that (2) predicts FOFC: that order only occurs with the harmonic order, that is, where α is also head-final. Equivalently, we can define the order where α is initial as recessive, with the same result. If, however, we had a way to independently characterize one of the two orders as marked in relation to the other, then we would be able to decide which is the recessive order. In section 3.4, we will see that the antisymmetric approach to phrase structure and word order proposed by Kayne (1994) gives us a way of doing this, with the consequence that head-final order emerges as recessive.

We can infer, then, that "high" head-final order and "low" head-initial order are both recessive: in this connection, we can note the widespread occurrence of a high left periphery (as opposed to the relative rarity of a high right periphery), on the one hand, and the preference for right-headed (suffixing) order in morphology, on the other; the latter follows if word-internal structure is the lowest level of phrase structure (see chapter 11 on this in relation to FOFC). Note also that, as Greenberg predicted, the FOFC-violating structure is both recessive (low head-initial, high head-final) and disharmonic. Clearly the notion of dominance/recessiveness is not symmetric, unlike harmony. Moreover, the two notions taken together are not symmetric, as (2) indicates. We will return to both of these concepts below.

A final comment on Greenberg's universals, and much subsequent typological work, is in order. Looking again at the universals listed in (1), we can observe that these generalizations are syntactically simplistic: they are made purely on the basis of linear order or grammatical function. The notion of strong generative capacity is not relevant to the formulation of these statements, since they do not refer to constituent structures (although they are construable as making statements defined in those terms): they simply refer to weakly generated strings. A related point is that they are stated over languages ("If a language L has property A, then it also has B"), rather than grammars. More detrimentally, they are not stated over constructions. A grammar can allow VO order and VP-Aux order (Finnish is a case in point; see Biberauer, Holmberg, and Roberts 2014 and chapter 10), but the combination of the two in a single extended projection in a given construction is ruled out.

FOFC is a different matter. FOFC does not simply rule out strings of a certain type, such as $Head_1 \frown complement \frown Head_2$; mirror-image cases of FOFC, such as verb projection raising in various West Germanic varieties (see chapter 2 and Biberauer, Holmberg, and Roberts 2014) illustrate the possibility of this order within a single extended projection. What is crucial for FOFC is the *hierarchical relationship* between the two heads, and between both of these and the complement: FOFC applies to the string $Head_1 \frown complement \frown Head_2$ just where $Head_1$ combines with the *complement* to form the derived complement of $Head_2$. In other words, FOFC is defined relative to the string *under a given structural description*, the classical notion of strong generative capacity (see Chomsky 1955/1975:5). FOFC also depends on the ability to state transitive relations among heads and/or complements (i.e., "The head of the complement of a final head must also be final"). It is the iteration of the notion of "head" that requires constituent structure, and, taking heads to be fundamentally elements of a similar kind, recursive constituent structure.

Two things follow from this. First, FOFC is a property of grammars, not of languages, although it can be stated as a generalization over languages. If FOFC holds universally, then it must be derivable from Universal Grammar (UG), or from UG in combination with other aspects of language design (see Chomsky 2005). Second, if FOFC does indeed hold as a universal, then it can be seen as a form of proof of the nature of the language faculty: the fact that that faculty depends on a generative grammar in the classical sense of a device that can produce recursive hierarchical structures. This is, clearly, by far the most important difference between FOFC and universals of the type discussed by Greenberg.

3.3 Hawkins 1983: X-bar Theory and Cross-Categorial Harmony

Hawkins (1983:134) proposed Cross-Categorial Harmony (CCH) as a generalization over many of Greenberg's implicational universals, as well as a number of exceptions to them. Hawkins states CCH as follows:

> There is a quantifiable preference for the ratio of preposed to postposed operators within one phrasal category ... to generalize to the others.

The term *operator* is taken from Vennemann's (1974) work: objects (along with main verbs, adjectives, relative clauses, etc.) are operators and verbs operands. It is important to note that CCH is stated as a preference, rather than as an absolute requirement, and so grammars tend to correspond to it but do not have to; I will return to this point in section 3.5. Furthermore, the principle makes reference to phrasal categories, explicitly acknowledging that phrase structure plays a role in accounting for these correlations (this could be taken as a recognition of the relevance of strong generative capacity for word order universals).

Hawkins (1983:179ff.) adopts X-bar theory as the prime structural explanation for CCH. The central idea of X-bar theory is that all syntactic categories conform to the same structural template. As Hawkins points out (p. 183), the basic advantage of X-bar theory is that, since it offers a category-neutral template for phrase structure, it is well-suited to the expression of cross-categorial generalizations like CCH. To see how this works, let us look again at the dyads defined by Greenberg's universals given in (1):

(3) a. Pr, NG, VS, VO, Aux-V, QS
     b. Po, GN, SV, OV, V-Aux, SQ

Leaving NG/GN and VS/SV aside,[4] the other dyads can all be unified under the general head-complement relation of X-bar theory. The dyads involve, respectively, the order of P and its (nominal) complement (Pr/Po), the order of V and its (canonically but not uniquely nominal) complement (VO/OV), the order of some functional projection(s) V^n in the extended projection of V and its complement $V^{n-1}P$ (Aux-V/V-Aux), and the order of C and its structural complement TP (QS/SQ). In these terms, a general Head Parameter of the kind in (4) would predict spectacular cross-categorial harmony:

(4) For all heads H, does the structural complement of a head H precede or follow H in overt order?

However, (4) is too strong to account for languages like German or Latin that show a certain degree of disharmony in their word order patterns (both are OV and Pr). Moreover, (4) cannot account for FOFC: as it stands, it rules out all kinds of disharmonic orders, those that violate FOFC and those that do not. If (4) is weakened so as to apply to individual categories, disharmonic systems of various kinds can be accounted for, but it does not seem possible to weaken the statement in anything like the form in (4) in such a way as to predict FOFC.

As already mentioned, Hawkins interprets CCH as a preference[5]. In fact, Hawkins suggests that CCH may derive from a preference for relatively simple grammars, since "the more similar the ordering of common constituents across phrasal categories at the relevant bar levels, the simpler are the word order rules of the grammar" (p. 205). If this is correct, and I believe it is, then cross-categorial harmony must derive from some higher-order factor determining interactions among formally independent parameter values, perhaps a simplicity metric of some kind. We will return to this idea in section 3.5.

So we see that, because of the category-neutral template it offers, Hawkins can use X-bar theory to state CCH. Greenberg's notion of harmony is thus captured directly and very interestingly. Moreover, the two basic sets of options—head-final and head-initial—are symmetric; there is no UG- or performance-based preference for one harmonic type over the other. For exactly these reasons, the account of word order variation put forward in Hawkins 1983 has no way of accounting for FOFC (but see Hawkins 2013 for a novel proposal).

Hawkins does not directly address the question of strong generative capacity, although he does point out that many of the universals he considered and refined, which derived from Greenberg, only involved two elements (p. 116). He then considers the question of "sequencing" of several elements, largely in relation to Greenberg's Universal 20 (on which, see chapter 8), and suggests an account of certain aspects of the constraints on the ordering of adnominal elements in terms of a binary-branching phrase structure (of the kind Kayne was starting to advocate for generative grammar at the time (see Kayne 1984), but was already assumed in various versions of Categorial Grammar; see Hawkins 1983:121 for references). This use of constituent structure clearly implies a need for strongly generated structures; it is noteworthy that this point arises as soon as one looks beyond universals involving simple dyads of the OV/VO kind. On the other hand, Hawkins does not discuss Greenberg's notion of dominance at all.

3.4   Kayne 1994, 2010: Antisymmetric Syntax

Kayne (1994) proposes an approach to phrase structure and linearization that leads to a very different view of the parameters governing word order variation. Kayne's central proposal is the Linear Correspondence Axiom (LCA), in his original exposition a principle of phrase structure (although, starting with Chomsky 1994, the LCA has been widely taken as a principle governing the mapping from an unordered narrow syntax to the linear ordering required by PF). The LCA can be stated as follows (this is an informal, simplified statement, based on Biberauer, Holmberg, and Roberts 2014; for the original, see Kayne 1994:5–6):

(5) A syntactic constituent α can precede a syntactic constituent β only if α asymmetrically c-commands β or is contained in a constituent γ that asymmetrically c-commands β.

We can see the implication of (5) for word order if we consider a simple verb-complement structure like (6), where for simplicity we assume that pronouns such as *I* are Ds, and vP is excluded:

(6)

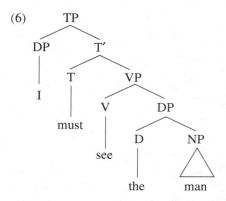

Here the subject DP asymmetrically c-commands T, VP, V, and DP and so, by the LCA, *must* precede those categories and the terminals they dominate; T asymmetrically c-commands V and DP and similarly must therefore precede those categories and the terminals they dominate. Further, V asymmetrically c-commands D and thus precedes *the* and *man*.[6] Given the LCA, there is no possibility of X-bar-determined parametric variation in underlying head-complement order of the type assumed by Hawkins (1983) and standardly assumed in much work in the 1980s. Instead, the natural assumption (although not the only logically possible one) is that all languages are underlyingly VO, and OV orders are derived by leftward movement of objects or a category containing the object. This idea extends to all cases where a complement precedes its head in surface order; it must have been fronted to that position from an underlying posthead position determined by the LCA.

Given Kayne's proposals just sketched, OV systems cannot differ from VO systems in terms of the first-merged order of elements. Instead, some functional category F structurally higher than, and hence to the left of, VP must attract the object, or a category containing the object. Following Biberauer, Holmberg, and Roberts (2014), I take this to involve complement-to-specifier movement. Schematically, OV order involves the following structure inside VP (the bracketed constituent is the copy of the moved element):

(7) [$_{VP}$ Obj [V (Obj)]]

Head-final order higher in the clause is derived by the iteration of complement-to-specifier movement. Consider then a Japanese sentence like (8):

(8) Bill-ga   [$_{CP}$ [$_{TP}$ Mary-ga   John-ni   sono hon-o   [Japanese]
    Bill-NOM   Mary-NOM John-DAT that   book-ACC
    watasita] to] itta (koto).
    handed   that said (fact)

'Bill said that Mary handed that book to John.'
(Saito and Fukui 1998:443)

Here we see OV order (*hon-o watasita*), T-final order (*-ta* is the past tense suffix on the verb) and the final C *to*. In terms of the type of "roll-up" derivation advocated here, the structure of the subordinate CP in (8) is as follows (abstracting away from scrambling possibilities):

(9)

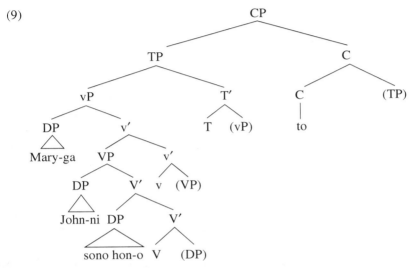

(The indirect object and the subject are both first-merged in specifier positions; in each case, the relevant specifier is targeted by roll-up movement of the complement before the argument is inserted.) Here the order O-V-T-C—that is, the harmonically head-final order of elements—emerges naturally from roll-up. If v contains "voice"-like elements such as passive *sase* and causative *rare*, these are correctly predicted to appear between the verb root and the tense marker. This type of analysis of head-final languages is discussed at length by Julien (2002:chap. 3) and in several of the chapters in this book.

I will not attempt a general justification of Kayne's approach here. However, it is useful to look at what this approach predicts for the notions of harmony and dominance. Since head-final order depends on the head's capacity to trigger movement of its complement to its specifier, and since in general the ability to trigger movement is an idiosyncratic, parameterized property of a head (which we can annotate using the ^ diacritic, following the practice in Biberauer, Holmberg, and Roberts 2014), one might be led to consider that this approach has no hope of capturing larger-scale implicational relations such as those discussed by Greenberg and Hawkins. But in fact it can do so. If we ally the antisymmetric approach to the idea that potential movement triggers (i.e., various (sub)classes of functional heads) tend to trigger or fail to trigger movement as classes—in unison, as it were—then we can in fact begin to understand the implicational relations shown above.

The tendency for "head-initial" and "head-final" patterns to hold across categories, as revealed by the typological work of Greenberg, Hawkins, and Dryer, would result from a preference for potential movement triggers to act together. So we could perhaps restate Hawkins's (1983) CCH as follows:

(10) There is a preference for the attraction property of a functional head
     $F^{\wedge}$ to generalize to other functional heads $G^{\wedge}$, $H^{\wedge}$, ...

(10) is intended to capture the idea that the preference for "harmonic" ordering seems to derive from an overriding tendency for independent parameters to conspire to produce a certain type of grammar. It can be seen as an approximation to a markedness convention of the type proposed for phonology by Chomsky and Halle (1968:chap. 9); see Roberts 2007b, 2012a.

To take a specific example, suppose, following the statements above about roll-up derivations, that OV orders—and more generally head-final orders in the clause—derive from iterated complement-to-specifier movement as shown in (9). In rigidly head-final languages like Japanese, many heads, perhaps all, will be able to trigger this type of movement. If movement is a marked option (as proposed, for example, in Roberts and Roussou 2003), such systems will emerge as very marked indeed, and less marked than "mixed" types like Latin, German, and so on. This does not appear to be a desirable outcome.

It is here that markedness conventions and the concept of the markedness of a whole system of parameters come in. Let us postulate, for concreteness, the following convention:

(11) The unmarked value of the $^{\wedge}$-feature for a given head H is $^{\wedge}$, just
     where V has $^{\wedge}$—that is, in an OV system.

This convention has the effect that, for all head-complement pairs that are subject to word order variation, head-final is the unmarked order in an OV system (and, conversely, head-initial order would be unmarked in a VO system since there will be a markedness constraint against associating $^{\wedge}$ with heads in this kind of system). In these terms, rigidly head-final languages are relatively unmarked, while rigidly head-initial languages are maximally unmarked, and "mixed" languages are relatively marked (and one can in principle quantify exactly how marked different types of mixed systems would be; see Biberauer et al. 2014). Furthermore, Dryer's (1992) observation that VO vs. OV order is the basic determinant of ordering among other head-complement pairs is directly captured.

This approach appears to disconnect markedness from a simple feature-counting simplicity metric of the kind put forward by Roberts and Roussou (2003), in that we are now claiming that systems where $^\wedge$ is present on all possible heads are relatively unmarked. Hence, a simple feature-counting approach to simplicity and markedness no longer suffices. However, we can think that the simplicity metric itself derives from a more general notion of conservatism of the learner, in that the learner will strive to assign the simplest representation or derivation possible to the primary linguistic data it is exposed to. In these terms, we can understand a markedness convention like (11) in terms of conservatism of the learner, assuming that another conservative aspect of the learner would be to exploit pieces of, perhaps marked, input to the full. So we could entertain something like (12):

(12) *Input Generalization*
     If acquirers assign a marked value to a head H, they will assign the
     same value to all comparable heads (F, G, ...).

(11) can naturally be understood in terms of (12), and both (12) and feature counting can be seen as different aspects of the overall conservatism of the learner, which is essentially trying to set parameters in the most efficient way possible; these ideas are developed in Roberts 2012a and Biberauer et al. 2014.

This idea in turn allows us to understand Baker's (1996, 2008) notion of macroparameter in terms of the idea that parameters are specified as the formal features of functional categories (e.g., presence or absence of $^\wedge$) by construing macroparameters as aggregates of microparameters. Apparent macroparametric variation appears when a group of functional heads are specified for the same properties: for example, if all heads implicated in determining word order variation have the same word-order-related property—namely, presence or absence of $^\wedge$—the system is harmonically head-initial or head-final. To repeat, this aggregate behavior is determined, not by UG, but by a conservative learning strategy (Input Generalization as in (12)); hence, the distinction between micro- and macroparameters is not part of UG, but is an emergent property of the interaction between the learner, the primary linguistic data, and UG.

In these terms, we can set up networks of parameters. (13) illustrates how this might work for word order, assuming that the default linearization option is head-initial, with head-final order derived by marking the relevant heads in some way, as we have seen:

(13)   Is the head-final feature
       present on any heads?

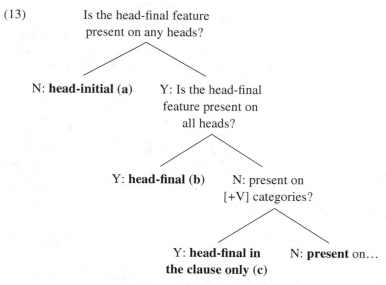

N: **head-initial (a)**   Y: Is the head-final
                             feature present on
                               all heads?

          Y: **head-final (b)**   N: present on
                                    [+V] categories?

                   Y: **head-final in**   N: **present** on...
                   the clause only (c)

Languages of type (a) are the harmonically, rigidly head-initial Celtic and Romance languages. Type (b) includes Japanese, Korean, Dravidian, and the like: the harmonically, rigidly head-final systems. Type (c) includes German and Dutch, to a close approximation, since they show head-final vP and VP but are (almost) head-initial in all other categories. At the "deepest right branch" (here this notion is just a notational choice, with no theoretical significance), the parameter breaks down into a series of increasingly specific microparameters. Roberts (2012a), Biberauer et al. (2014), and Sheehan (2014) sketch several parametric hierarchies of this kind.

True macroparameters sit at the top of the network, as here all relevant parameterized heads behave as one. As we move successively down, systems become more marked, and parameters become more "micro," behaving in a nonuniform, differentiated fashion that is inherently more complex than that of the systems higher in the tree (we can suppose that the options move from subsets of the set of formal features F to singleton features of heads $f \in F$, to increasingly context-sensitive environments, ultimately perhaps to single lexical items; see Biberauer and Roberts 2012). For language acquisition, each parameter hierarchy defines a learning path, much in the sense of Dresher (1999), with the higher options inherently preferred by the acquirer (see Biberauer 2011). More generally, we can think of the hierarchies as an epigenetic landscape (Waddington 1977), defined by incrementally more computationally complex options as the learner "moves down the tree." The acquisition device searches the space by looking for the "easiest" solution at each stage, where a solution is defined as a parameter setting compatible with available primary linguistic data. The device moves from a relatively easy to the next-hardest stage only when forced to by primary linguistic data incompatible with the current setting.

So we arrive at a position that largely preserves the basic insights behind Hawkins's CCH. This position is not incompatible with a feature-counting approach to markedness; it merely adds the further markedness convention of Input Generalization, which has the effect that certain systems with many occurrences of $^\wedge$ are less marked than systems with fewer occurrences of it. However, all other things being equal, there is nonetheless a cost associated with the occurrence of $^\wedge$, that is, with movement. For this reason, head-initial systems are less marked than head-final systems, as indicated in (13).

In the light of this, let us look again at Greenberg's notion of dominant and recessive orders, discussed in section 3.2. There, we noted that VS is recessive in relation to SV, and, from the Pr/Po, VS/SV table given there, we can also see that Po is recessive in this context. Moreover, Greenberg discusses Universal 25 ("If the pronominal object follows the verb, so does the nominal object"), and here we see that OV order is recessive (while VO order is compatible with V-Pro or Pro-V). As mentioned in note 4, VS orders are usually thought to be derived by V(P)-movement to a head or specifier position higher than the subject's surface position. We might be able to maintain the general idea that recessive orders involve more movement than dominant ones; they are more marked because they involve more occurrences of $^\wedge$. This implies that in an antisymmetric system head-final order is recessive, with the consequences for FOFC sketched above. Head-final is only recessive in a Kaynean system where these orders involve extra occurrences of $^\wedge$, being derived by movement. Indirectly, then, Kayne's system can tell us partially why FOFC is what it is, given Greenberg's definitions of dominance and harmony.

Kayne's approach, then, predicts asymmetry: all other things being equal, head-final orders will be more marked than (and hence recessive in relation to) head-initial orders. Input Generalization has the effect that all things are not otherwise equal, by making harmonically head-final orders relatively unmarked. In fact, Input Generalization is the one way to ensure harmony in a Kaynean system.

So this approach allows us to retain the basic ideas of harmony and dominance/recessiveness from Greenberg, relating them both to different kinds of markedness. In this connection, FOFC expresses a general asymmetry in a generally antisymmetric approach.

In fact, Kayne (2013:224ff.) gives a range of evidence in favor of the idea that syntax is inherently asymmetric. This evidence is as follows (page numbers refer to the pages of Kayne's paper where the asymmetry is discussed and illustrated in detail):

1. Hanging topics: A"hanging" topic in Cinque's (1977) sense only appears to the left of the sentence in which the topic originates, never to the right (pp. 224–225).
2. Greenberg's Universal 25: This universal (briefly mentioned above) states a general asymmetry in leftward movement of pronominal vs. nonpronominal objects (pp. 225–227).
3. Greenberg's Universal 33: "[W]hen number agreement between the noun and verb is suspended and the rule is based on order, the case is always one in which the verb precedes and the verb is in the singular" (Greenberg [1963] /2007:59) (pp. 227–229).[7]
4. Pre- vs. postnominal relatives: Prenominal relatives tend to lack complementizers and relative pronouns, and tend to be nonfinite (pp. 229–230).
5. Serial verbs: "[S]erial verb constructions differ crosslinguistically with respect to the relative position of verb and argument, but are crosslinguistically constant with respect to the relative order of the verbs themselves" (p. 230; observation due to Carstens (2002)).
6. Coordination: Coordinators invariably appear between the two conjuncts (p. 231; observation due to Zwart (2009b)).[8]
7. Backward pronominalization (as in *The fact that he's here means John is well again*) is not found in various languages, while forward pronominalization always is (pp. 231–232).

To these we can of course add FOFC. The conclusion that syntax is in some profound sense asymmetric seems clear.

Biberauer, Holmberg, and Roberts (2014) propose an account of FOFC that contains the following elements:

(14) a. Head-finality is a consequence of the movement trigger ^ being paired with the categorial feature [±V], which enters the derivation with the head of the extended projection.
   b. The movement trigger ^ can spread with [±V] from head to head up the spine of the extended projection, subject to parametric variation.
   c. C-selection relations are subject to Relativized Minimality.

(14a) is a refinement of the idea that head-final orders are derived by roll-up, stating that ^ is intrinsically associated (or not) with the head of the extended projection. (14b) states that $^\wedge$ can spread through the heads that make up the extended projection as a parametric option. Finally, (14c) goes back to the standard assumption, since Chomsky 1965, that c-selection/subcategorization is subject to a sisterhood condition. In terms of bare phrase structure, this can be implemented by taking c-selection to be a constraint on (external) Merge. Combined with Relativized Minimality, this guarantees the locality of c-selection: the relation cannot "skip" a sister. Since the extended projection is formed by c-selection relations among the successive heads that make it up, and since $^\wedge$ can only be introduced on the lexical head, the "spreading" mechanism is effectively c-selection. Hence, $^\wedge$ cannot "skip" a head; hence, FOFC is derived. Note that (14a) states that head-final and head-initial orders are not symmetric.

To see how all this works in practice, consider how Biberauer, Holmberg, and Roberts (2014) account for the absence of V-O-Aux order. Taking Aux to be a realization of v, this order presupposes the distribution of the movement trigger $^\wedge$ in (15), impossible if [$^\wedge$] can only enter the derivation as a property of the head of the extended projection (condition (14a)):

(15) [$_{vP}$ v   [$_{VP}$ V   O]]
          [V$^\wedge$]   [+V]

A configuration such as (16a) or (16b), where Aux is a higher auxiliary, realizing T rather than v, will also be ill-formed, a violation of FOFC, regardless of whether VP is head-initial or head-final:

(16) a. *v-V-O-Aux
       b. *v-O-V-Aux

(16a) would be ruled out as a case of (15), by condition (14a). (16b) would be the result of the following distribution of [+V$^\wedge$]:

(17) [$_{TP}$ T   [$_{vP}$ v   [$_{VP}$ V   O]]]
          [+V$^\wedge$]   [+V]   [+V$^\wedge$]

Given that a functional head can have [+V$^\wedge$] only by virtue of inheriting it from, ultimately, the head of the extended projection, this configuration violates Relativized Minimality, the intervening v blocking inheritance of $^\wedge$ by T from V. Biberauer, Holmberg, and Roberts (2014) show that parallel reasoning can explain all the cases of FOFC discussed in chapter 2.

This may not be the correct, or even an optimal, account of FOFC (see Sheehan 2013a,b and several of the chapters in this book for alternatives), but what is important here is that we observe the crucially asymmetric structure of the constraint and its explanation.

3.5 Conclusion

Two points emerge from the above considerations.

First, an account of crosslinguistic word order variation based on a version of the LCA, or at the very least one that contains an inherent asymmetry between head-initial and head-final order such that the former is (marginally) less marked, seems favored over the obvious alternative featuring a version of X-bar theory's Head Parameter. There are three reasons for this: (i) the former kind of theory can capture FOFC, as just sketched, following Biberauer, Holmberg, and Roberts (2014), while the latter cannot; (ii) there is reason to think that head-final orders are recessive in relation to their head-initial counterparts (e.g., Universal 25), as discussed above; (iii) Kayne has given evidence for a range of order asymmetries across languages, summarized in the previous section. Greenberg's notion of dominance can be captured in these terms, as can harmony, if Input Generalization is added as a markedness factor. Since Input Generalization is an acquisition strategy originating in the computationally conservative nature of the learner, it is not actually part of UG. Instead, it can be regarded as a third-factor optimization strategy in Chomsky's (2005) sense. If dominance/recessiveness is also defined in markedness terms (this time feature counting), it too derives from third-factor conservativity of the learner. Both of Greenberg's generalizations about word order universals may then have their roots in third-factor considerations, suggesting that, rather than being directly "coded" in UG, they, like parameters, emerge from the interaction of different factors in language design.

But the other thing that FOFC demonstrates is that strong generative capacity is necessary to understanding some kinds of typological generalization. In this, FOFC differs importantly from many of Greenberg's universals, as we saw (with the significant exception of Universal 20). If FOFC is indeed a universal, then it constitutes evidence concerning the nature of the language faculty: that faculty must include a generative grammar in the classical sense of a device that can produce recursive hierarchical constituent structure.

4 The Final-over-Final Condition and Linearization in Generative Grammar

Anders Holmberg

4.1 Linear Order in Early Generative Grammar

Linear order was not really seen as an issue in mainstream generative grammar until the publication of Kayne 1994 and subsequent developments in the Minimalist Program, including those in Chomsky 1994, 1995:chap. 4, which were in part a reaction to Kayne's proposals. In the early phase of generative grammar, when phrase structure rules were a component of the grammar, linear order was stipulated by the rules themselves: the rules generated strings. In a later phase, when phrase structure was generalized in the X-bar schema, word order was stipulated by word order parameter settings applied to universal X-bar structures. The way this was (and to some extent still is) conventionally represented is that the phrase structure tree, or the equivalent labeled bracket representation, encodes order as well as hierarchy. For example, the tree (1) is trivially mapped onto the linear order to the right of its arrow, and the tree (2), which in hierarchical terms is equivalent to (1), onto the linear order to the right of its arrow:

(1)

NP
|
N_1 V   NP $\rightarrow$ N_1 V N_2
|
N_2

(2)

          NP $\rightarrow$ V N_2 N_1
|
V   NP N_1
|
N_2

The mapping is trivial in that the linear order is derived simply by reading the terminal nodes in the tree from left to right. Thus, phrase structure encodes hierarchy as well as linear order. Matters get more complicated when functional heads spelled out as affixes or clitics are taken into account, but theoretical devices such as head movement are designed in part to accommodate such phenomena. The fact that such a straightforward theory with its conventional representation of structure and word order seems to work, up to a point, making possible more or less adequate descriptions of a wide range of complex constructions in languages investigated, is one reason for the success of generative grammar.

Consider what Chomsky (1965:123–125) has to say on this topic. After observing that the phrase structure rules carry out two separate tasks, defining the syntactic relations and ordering of elements in deep structures, he says:

It has been suggested several times that these two functions of the categorial component be more sharply separated, and that the second, perhaps, be eliminated completely. Such is the import of the proposals regarding the nature of syntactic structure to be found in Curry (1961) and Šaumjan and Soboleva (1963). They propose, in essence, that in place of such rules as (69), the categorial component should contain the corresponding rules (70), where the element on the right is a set rather than a string:

(69) S → NP^VP
      VP → V^NP

(70) S → {NP,VP}
      VP → {V, NP}

(Chomsky 1965:124)

He continues:

A priori, there is no way of determining which theory is correct; it is an entirely empirical question, and the evidence presently available is overwhelmingly in favor of concatenation-systems over set-systems, for the theory of the categorial component. In fact, no proponent of a set-system has given any indication of how the abstract underlying unordered structures are converted into actual strings with surface structures. Hence, the problem of giving empirical support to this theory has not yet been faced. (Chomsky 1965:125)

Since then, generative linguistic theory has undergone some quite radical changes, which will be sketched below. One result is that we now assume, within mainstream, Minimalist-oriented generative grammar, that syntactic structure is constructed by Merge, in Chomsky's (1993, 1995:chap. 4) sense, finally making phrase structure rules entirely superfluous. Another result is that we now have a theory for how to convert unordered structures into strings: the theory (or family of theories) based on Kayne's (1994) Linear Correspondence Axiom.

In 1965 and up until the mid-1970s, the formulation of transformations—the rules needed to derive passives, questions, relatives, and so on, from the deep structure generated by the phrase structure rules—crucially depended on linear order. The phrase structure rules generated strings of symbols (in fact, strings of words in the earliest versions, including Chomsky 1957). A transformation was a rule that took as input a string of symbols, a mix of terminal and non-terminal symbols and variables over symbols, and gave as output another string of symbols. Consider the English Dative Movement transformation, for example (adapted from Akmajian and Heny 1975:220):

(3) Input: V   – NP – to/for – NP
              1   2   3   4
    Output: 1 + 4   2   0   0

This rule could apply to any phrase marker that met the structural description of the input. The structure (4a) does, for example, so it will be transformed into (4b):

(4) a. [$_{VP}$ [$_V$ give] [$_{NP}$ a book] [$_{PP}$ to [$_{NP}$ Mary]]]
    b. give Mary a book

The terms of the rule are identified by linear order: they apply to an analyzed string, and they output another string. To apply to unordered structures (hierarchies of sets), the rules would have to be radically reformulated. As Chomsky put it:

[A] set-system such as (70) must be supplemented by two sets of rules. The first set will assign an intrinsic order to the elements of the underlying unordered Phrase-markers. … The second set of rules will be grammatical transformations applying in sequence to generate surface structures in the familiar way. (Chomsky 1965:125)

This formalism eventually became obsolete with the articulation of X-bar theory and the structure-preserving hypothesis—that is, the realization that deep structures and surface structures (input and output of transformations) all conformed to the same principles of phrase structure (Chomsky 1970, Emonds 1970, 1976, Jackendoff 1977). This meant that transformations could be formulated so as to apply to structurally defined constituents, moving them from one structurally defined position to another structurally defined position, or deleting them from structurally defined positions. Work by Chomsky (1973, 1976), building on Ross 1967, and by Rizzi (1990) further characterized the locality principles that govern movement and binding, making it possible to generalize and simplify the rules themselves, to the point where they could eventually be subsumed under the maximally general rule schema Move α (Chomsky 1981, 1982).

This should make it possible, in principle, to shift to a "set-system," where syntactic relations (θ-role relations, scope, movement, binding, modification,

Case, agreement, etc.) are defined in terms of hierarchical relations among constituents that form sets, not ordered multiples. The attraction of such a system is, primarily, that it appears to be empirically supported: syntactic relations *can* typically be characterized precisely and exhaustively without any reference to linear order. Linear order as such does not affect meaning—or, to put it more cautiously, does not add anything to aspects of meaning that are encoded at LF, including θ-roles, scope relations, binding relations, definiteness, tense, mood, aspect, and so on, and even (though much more arguably) relations such as topic and focus. What does affect, and determine, those aspects of meaning is structure: dominance, c-command, and structurally defined locality.[1] There is a small residue of syntactic relations or constructions for which linear order has been claimed to be crucial (see Kayne 2013). However, if the large majority of syntactic relations can be exhaustively characterized without reference to linear order, then it is reasonable to assume that *all* of them can be, and that the few apparent counterexamples have other explanations.

While it was widely accepted within generative linguistics in the 1970s and 1980s that structure, not order, was what mattered in syntax, it did not lead to factoring linear order out of syntax until a decade or two later, mainly because inclusion of ordering stipulations (implicit or explicit) in the syntax was seen as innocuous, and because there was no credible alternative. As Chomsky (1965) pointed out, dissociating linear order from hierarchy requires a theory of the mapping of hierarchical structure onto linear order.

4.2   Word Order Parameters

To recapitulate, prior to X-bar theory, the linear orders that were found in any given language depended on the phrase structure rules of the language and which transformations applied to the derived phrase-markers, and the transformations themselves were dependent on linear statements. Subsequent developments in the theory, including in particular X-bar theory, made it possible to generalize and simplify the phrase structure rules, and to formulate transformations without reference to linear order.

Finally, with the generalization of X-bar theory to all phrase types, including functional projections (Stowell 1981, Chomsky 1986), phrase structure rules became all but redundant, as they stipulated properties that followed, at least in part, from universal principles. Instead, the order of constituents in D-Structure became a matter of setting word-order-related parameters. This was made possible by the idea that syntactic variation across languages is a matter of a limited number of parameters, which are left open by Universal Grammar (UG) and are fixed in the course of language acquisition (Chomsky

1981). The order of constituents in the X-bar schema was one of the parameters. The order between specifier and X′ (including subject and predicate as a special case) seems to be almost universally specifier-X′. Assuming that this order is universal (Whitman 2008:234, 251), the only parameters would concern the order of head and complement and the order of head and modifier.[2] A highly attractive idea, which seemed to be supported by the findings of Greenberg (1963) and other research in Greenberg's footsteps, including Dryer's (1992), was that the head-complement (and head-adjunct) parameter settings were highly general; typically there would be one setting for nearly all types of heads within a language. The strongest position was that the setting *is* generalized to all heads: a complement precedes or follows the head, across all categories (see chapter 2). Apparent counterexamples would then be the result of movement, resulting from other parameter settings that had the effect of triggering movement. For example, one idea explored in work by Travis (1984, 1994) and Koopman (1984) was that the directions of θ-role assignment and Case assignment were parameterized, independently of each other and independently of the direction of the head-complement parameter. For example, a language could have head-complement order, but object Case assignment directed right to left. The result is that all the complements of a verb follow the verb, except DPs, which must precede the verb to be assigned Case (see Koopman 1984:120–130). A weaker theory is that languages have a default head-complement direction setting for all categories, but there can be exceptions acquired on a case-by-case basis, the system being more marked the more exceptions there are.

However, even at this point the grammar can still be seen as embodying a set of generalized phrase structure rules—XP → YP X′ (specifier-head), X′ → X ZP (head-complement), XP → WP XP (adjunction)—all subject to order parameterization, with the possible exception of the specifier-head rule. The notion "base order" or "D-Structure order" therefore makes sense: it is the order of words stipulated by the language-particular version of the phrase structure rules, once the terminal nodes have been replaced with lexical items (lexical insertion).

The D-Structure is typically modified by movement of heads and/or phrases, deriving S-Structure. With the possible exception of "affix hopping" (see Lasnik 2000), movement is always upward, but it can be either leftward or rightward, in the sense that, when the structure is spelled out from left to right, the moved constituent either precedes or follows its trace/original position. It was well-known that leftward movement is considerably more common, and that rightward movement, when it takes place, is considerably more constrained (Ross 1967; this was well-known but not well-understood).

Finally, at S-Structure the linear order is read off the structural representation by spelling the terminal nodes out from left to right, before any movement applies that affects the structure without affecting PF (covert movement). This is part of the derivation of PF.

Thus, the linearization aspect of the mechanics of the system was basically not an issue, at this point (the 1980s and early 1990s). Word-order-related issues concerned mainly how to combine a restrictive theory of parameterized phrase structure with a restrictive theory of movement to account for observed crosslinguistic variation regarding word order.

4.3 Narrow Syntax without Linear Order

The situation in current theory is quite different. Minimalist theorizing now favors a dissociation of hierarchy and linear order. In the most radical view, which is arguably the mainstream view at present, the narrow syntax (the derivation of LF) only recognizes hierarchy. Its only structure-building operation is binary Merge in the sense of *set-Merge*, combining categories successively pairwise, forming sets.[3] The so-formed sets are labeled, the label being equal to one of the merged categories (the head), but they have no order; the left-to-right order in the tree is just a notational convention forced upon us by the two-dimensional representation. The order only comes about in the derivation of PF, after spell-out (i.e., after the derivation splits into an LF and a PF branch). LF has no linear order.

This idea is closely connected with the radical idea that all linguistic variation is located in the derivation of PF. Narrow syntax—that is, the derivation of LF by Merge, Agree, and whatever other operations are required—is deemed to be completely uniform; for different implementations of this idea, see Chomsky 2001, Burton-Roberts and Poole 2006, Burton-Roberts 2009, Berwick and Chomsky 2011, Boeckx 2011, and Sigurðsson 2011a,b. The idea is attractive for several reasons. To begin with, we know there is a huge amount of variation in PF. Most if not all languages have words for things like eyes and ears and activities like walking and eating, and so on, but they are not pronounced the same (in sign languages they are not pronounced at all, but signed). Furthermore, the system of vowels and consonants varies across languages, intonation patterns vary, a functional morpheme can be a free word in one language but a suffix or a prefix in another language, and so on. Word order is another obvious point of much crosslinguistic variation. If word order variation (SVO vs. SOV, Adj-N vs. N-Adj, etc.) is also located in PF, then it may well be that all variation is.[4] We also know that there is not much variation that could be called semantic. It is, in fact, controversial whether there are any semantic parameters at all (see Chierchia 1998, von Fintel and Matthewson 2008, Ramchand and Svenonius 2008). If there are none, their absence supports the contention that narrow syntax is uniform across languages. (It should be noted that the works mentioned above all argue that there are at least some semantic parameters—or, more generally, variation that is semantic in nature.)

4.4 The Linear Correspondence Axiom

If Merge can only build hierarchically organized sets, and narrow syntax only recognizes relations that are based on hierarchy, then, as pointed out by Chomsky (1965), we need a theory of the mapping of syntactic structure onto linear order. The most influential theory proposed to date is the one based on Kayne's (1994) Linear Correspondence Axiom (LCA), an important milestone in generative linguistics. (5) is a simplified formulation of the LCA:

(5) Where α, β, and γ are terminal elements (lexical items), α precedes β if and only if α asymmetrically c-commands β, or α is dominated by γ, and γ asymmetrically c-commands β.

Given that syntactic constituents must be assigned a linear order (to be pronounceable and parsable), every linguistic expression consisting of more than one pronounced item must observe the LCA.

In the context of a theory assuming that narrow syntax does not recognize linear order, the LCA thus says that asymmetric c-command in narrow syntax maps onto precedence, hence linear order, in PF.[5] For Kayne, the motivation for the LCA was not to factor linear order out of syntax, though. In fact, Kayne explicitly distances himself from that view (Kayne 1994:48–49, 2013). Instead, the LCA was proposed to explain the pervasive left-right asymmetry of syntax, and to derive, instead of stipulating, the properties of X-bar theory. The asymmetries include these: almost all specifiers are on the left (including subjects), almost all movement is leftward, almost all head adjunction is on the left, and head-final order is not the mirror image of head-initial order but instead is more constrained than head-initial order. Another left-right asymmetry that the LCA can explain is Greenberg's Universal 20, discussed in chapter 8. The LCA entails that these asymmetries are universal and exceptionless, and any counterexamples only apparent. Under the LCA, specifiers are (always) on the left because a specifier, by definition (see note 5), asymmetrically c-commands, hence precedes, the head it is a specifier of. Movement is always upward (cf. the Extension Condition in Chomsky 1993, Freidin 1999); hence, the moved constituent asymmetrically c-commands its trace or copy and the sister of the trace or copy; hence, it precedes the trace or copy, and in this sense movement is always leftward.

Furthermore, Kayne (1994) notes that the LCA provides an explanation for X-bar theory. It follows from the LCA that a phrase cannot consist of two X^0 heads, or of two maximal XPs. Both types of phrases would be symmetric and therefore could not be linearized; linear order presupposes asymmetric c-command. That is to say, it follows from the LCA that a phrase must have one and only one head; endocentricity (hence, labeling of phrases) is thus a consequence of the LCA (see, however, Guimarães 2008).

Kayne (1994) argues that this means that the LCA, and hence linear order, must be a property not just of PF, but of every syntactic representation: "It follows that to declare the LCA inapplicable to some level of representation—say, LF—would be to declare inapplicable to that level of representation all the restrictions on phrase structure familiar from X-bar theory (existence of at least one and at most one head per phrase, etc.)" (p. 49). This does not follow, though, if the successful derivation of a linguistic expression requires that it *converge*, in Chomsky's (1995:chap. 4) sense: that is, it must satisfy the output conditions at PF *and* LF, the two interface levels. If a derivation crashes at one of the interfaces, it is ruled out. For example, if a small clause [DP AP] crashes at PF because it is too symmetric to be assigned a linear order (see Moro 2000), the derivation is thereby canceled; that is, the expression is underivable. This means that narrow syntax must provide the tools and building blocks required for phrases to observe the LCA at PF, even if these tools and building blocks would serve no purpose at LF. Phrases must have a structure such that they are linearizable at PF, even though the linearization is activated only after spell-out.[6]

One of the most notorious consequences of the LCA is that the underlying order of every phrase is specifier-head-complement. Take the case of the TP in (6):

(6)

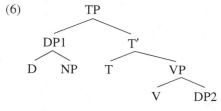

Since DP1 asymmetrically c-commands T, its daughter D and any terminal daughters of NP must precede T; moreover, T asymmetrically c-commands V and DP2, hence must precede them. This derives the specifier-head-comple-ment order. It follows that any other order must be the result of movement.

For example, the order specifier-complement-head, where it occurs, must be the result of movement of the complement to a position where it asymmetrically c-commands the head. "The LCA entails that all languages are underlyingly SVO languages" is a popular interpretation of this consequence of the theory. This consequence of the LCA has been the subject of much debate and is probably the one property of the theory that has caused the most resistance (see Svenonius 2000).

In a theory like that proposed in Chomsky 1995:chap. 4 where linear order is factored out of syntax, what does it mean to say that the underlying order of every phrase is specifier-head-complement? Can there be an "underlying order"? What it means is that, unless something happens to the phrase, such as movement of the complement to a position higher than the head, or movement of the head to a position higher than the specifier, the phrase will be spelled out as specifier-head-complement. In narrow syntax, the phrase is the result of Merge: first, Merge of head X^0 and a phrase YP forming a set {X^0, YP}, which is assigned the label X (call it X′); then Merge of another phrase ZP, forming a larger set {ZP {X^0, YP}}, again assigned the label X (call it XP); and so on. Constituents can be moved—that is, can be merged again (by internal Merge)—and can enter into various syntactic relations (Agree, binding, etc.) subject to locality conditions that only recognize structure. The LCA, as regarded here (not as regarded by Kayne (1994, 2013)), is activated only at spell-out, determining unequivocally the linear order of words and morphemes making up the terminal nodes of the hierarchical structures constructed by the narrow syntax.

It could be noted that the LCA-based theory of word order variation is not easily reconciled with the idea that all linguistic variation is a matter of externalization. This idea would seem to presuppose that all movement that creates chains and affects scope (i.e., has effects at LF) is universal, the crosslinguistic variation being a matter of which copies are pronounced (Groat and O'Neil 1996, Bobaljik 2002). For example, so called *wh*-in-situ would be a matter of pronouncing the lower copy in a *wh*-chain, in a theory where *wh*-movement is universal. Any movement that does not affect interpretation, including the movement of a complement around a head just to derive OV order (assuming the LCA), would then be postsyntactic (applying in the "PF component"). But then, if it is the case that OV order feeds operations that do have an effect on interpretation, there is a problem. For example, it is well-known that OV order in the VP is conducive to scrambling, a movement rule that has interpretive effects, on definiteness in particular and on information structure more generally (see chapter 10 for some discussion). This is not easily reconciled with the hypothesis that the derivation of OV order is postsyntactic (but see Richards 2004, Fox and Pesetsky 2005 for PF approaches to these problems).

4.5 The Bottom-Pair Problem

Incorporating the LCA into bare phrase structure (BPS) theory (Chomsky 1994, 1995) leads to a problem with regard to the "bottom pair"—that is, the two X^0 constituents merged first in any syntactic derivation. The problem is that they are, by definition, two nonbranching sister categories and as such will not be assigned a linear order by the LCA.[7] For example, the tree resulting from merging a definite article with a noun will look like (7) (the tree here representing a set consisting of the D *the* and the noun *book* labeled by the head D):

(7)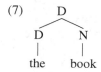

In terms of c-command, this is a symmetric structure, hence not linearizable. Any subsequently merged constituents will asymmetrically c-command the article and the noun and therefore can be linearized in relation to them, but the two cannot be linearized in relation to each other.

The problem did not arise in Kayne 1994, because (i) it does not adopt the BPS principle that Merge is the only structure-building operation, and therefore it does not rule out nonbranching nodes, and (ii) it adopts a definition of c-command based on first node, not first branching node. Thus, (7) can be analyzed as (8) in Kayne 1994, where D asymmetrically c-commands N, so that *the* will precede *book* when spelled out:[8]

(8)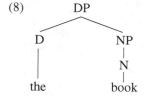

Various solutions to the bottom-pair problem have been proposed. Zwart (2011b) argues for a phrase structure theory that differs from the one proposed by Chomsky in that Merge does not derive sets, but ordered pairs: Merge is always an asymmetric process, not "merging a and b," but always "merging a with b," which avoids the bottom-pair problem—by reinstating linear order in narrow syntax.

Another possibility is that a structure like (7)—Merge of a functional X^0 and a lexical X^0—is never the bottom pair, because the lexical X^0 has the structure $[f, \text{root}]$, where f encodes lexical/syntactic category, following Marantz (1997) and Borer (2005). If f is n, for example, merging it with the root BOOK yields the noun *book*. This has the consequence that an article merged with $[n, \text{BOOK}]$ will asymmetrically c-command the constituents of $[n, \text{BOOK}]$ and therefore, given the LCA, will be spelled out preceding these constituents, unless they undergo movement, which will yield a postnominal article. Of course, this leaves the problem of how f and the root are linearized. We will return to this issue in the next section. Chomsky (2015), following the "Marantz-Borer conjecture," takes this line: the bottom pair is $[f, \text{root}]$. Chomsky (2015) is not concerned with linear order, though, but with projection and labeling: how is the label determined in the bottom pair where, apparently, two X^0 constituents are merged? He proposes that [root] does not qualify as a label, and therefore $[f, \text{root}]$ will always be labeled f.

4.6 Alternatives to the Linear Correspondence Axiom

Obviously, if the observed asymmetries that the LCA is based on are not universal, but at most tendencies, then alternatives have to be considered. One alternative is articulated by Abels and Neeleman (2009). They argue that the order of heads, complements, and specifiers is parameterized, in the sense that heads, complements, and specifiers can be externally merged (base-generated) in any order, fixed independently for each language. They discuss in particular Greenberg's (1963) Universal 20, a generalization concerning word order in noun phrases; see chapter 8. However, they argue, in line with Kayne (1994), that movement (internal Merge) is always leftward, which explains a number of asymmetries that are arguably universal, such as the absence of "verb-second-from-the-end languages" or rightward *wh*-movement languages. They also suggest that the ban on rightward movement is ultimately an effect of constraints on processing of syntactic dependencies (see chapter 5 for discussion).

Another alternative is articulated by Haider (2000, 2005, 2012). The core idea in Haider's theory is that given a highly restrictive, yet reasonably simple characterization of the relation between structure and word order, allowing for the variation observed, a model where head-final order is more basic than head-initial order (Haider 2000) gives a better account of the empirical facts when comparing head-final and head-initial systems. The theory is based on the universal Branching Constraint (9) and the parameterized direction of licensing of dependents by a head (10):

(9) *The Branching Constraint*
Projection-internal branching nodes on the (extended) projection line follow their sister node.

(10) Licensing to the left gives head-final order.
Licensing to the right gives head-initial order.

The projection of, say, a VP headed by a *put*-type verb will have the structure (11) in an OV language, that is, a language with licensing to the left:

(11)

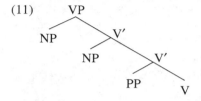

The projection-internal branching nodes here are the two V' nodes, which follow their sister—that is, the specifier. Here, because the bottom branching node is head-final, the licensing of the dependents is "harmonic" with the branching direction: all the heads (in the X-bar sense, that is, X^0 and X') license their dependents leftward. The VP can then be the complement of, for example, an auxiliary, forming another head-final phrase [VP Aux]. In a VO language, the structure will be (12):

(12)

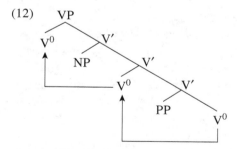

Here, the licensing direction is disharmonic with the branching direction: in order for the head to license the dependents, it must move, deriving a VP-shell structure. That is to say, this theory always derives head-initial order via head movement—in contrast with the LCA-based theory, which derives head-final order via complement movement. Haider provides arguments, in particular from the syntax of predicative modifiers, in favor of this theory.[9]

A related theory is articulated by Emonds (2013). As Emonds points out, if head-final order is the universal default, and if the X-bar theory notion that X'-level phrases are heads is adopted, then the fact that a specifier (apparently) always precedes its sister X′ would be a consequence of the universal head-final order. That is to say, one of the most powerful empirical arguments for the LCA (specifiers always precede heads) can be construed as an argument in favor of the view that head-final order is the universal "basic order."

Again we may ask, in a model where linearization is factored out of narrow syntax, what does it mean to say that head-final order is the basic order? The answer is essentially the same as in relation to the LCA in section 4.4: unless there is movement, the derived structure is spelled out as head-final. Embedding Haider's (2000) theory in such a model, with the crucial notion "licensing direction," "the head α licenses β to the right" (the marked option) requires that the head α move to a position where it c-commands β. When spelled out, this yields the order α-β. Licensing on the right does not require any head movement, so if no head movement occurs in the syntax or after (see Chomsky's (1995:chap. 4) suggestion that head movement is postsyntactic), the structure is spelled out as head-final in PF.

4.7 A Challenge for Linearization Theory: FOFC

This book is about a "word order condition" involving the relation between linear order and structure: the Final-over-Final Condition (FOFC) (see chapter 1):

(13) *The Final-over-Final Condition*
A head-final phrase αP cannot immediately dominate a head-initial phrase βP, if α and β are members of the same extended projection.

What are the implications of this condition for theories of linearization? We can note, first of all, that it cannot be stated just in terms of linear ordering specifications (directionality parameters), even if they are relativized to category (with different specifications for different categories). The issue does not arise in languages that are consistently head-initial or consistently head-final. It arises only in mixed-order languages—that is, languages where heads in the same extended projection may either precede or follow their complement. But, as shown in chapter 2, a language with mixed word order may well allow, for example, the linear order VO and the linear order VP-Aux, but still reject the combination of the two. This is the case, for example, in Finnish (see chapters 2 and 10 for more detailed discussion):

(14) a.   Anne on ostanut auton.   [V O]   [Finnish]
          Anne has bought car
          'Anne has bought a car.'

    b.   Milloin Anne tullut on?   [VP Aux]
        when   Anne come has
        'When did Anne come?'
    c. *Milloin Anne ostanut auton on?   [[$_{VP}$ V O] Aux]
        when   Anne bought car   has

See Biberauer, Holmberg, and Roberts 2014 for similar data from the Kaaps dialect of Afrikaans and Basque.

    The LCA has consequences for FOFC, though. To begin with, the LCA excludes a derivation where the structure (15a) is linearized as (15b):

(15) a. [$_{AuxP}$ [$_{VP}$ V O] Aux]
      b. V-O-Aux

Since Aux asymmetrically c-commands V and O in (15a), it will precede V and O according to the LCA. Instead, from the point of view of the LCA, the structure of the string (15b) could, a priori, be either (16a) or (16b) (where F is a phonetically null), with VP moved to a position where it asymmetrically c-commands Aux:

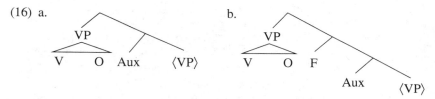

Since V and O are dominated by VP, which now asymmetrically c-commands Aux, V and O will precede Aux, by the LCA. However, this configuration is ruled out by FOFC formulated as in (13). It is ruled out in (16a), where α is Aux, a head in the extended projection of V (Grimshaw 1991, 2001). And it is ruled out in (16b), where α is F, also a head in the extended projection of V. The question is why (16a,b) are ruled out.

    Sections 4.8–4.11 will review four theories, all of which assume some version of the LCA, and all of which profess to explain FOFC in terms of some principle(s) of linearization. The first three theories are found in Holmberg 2000a (the first paper to address FOFC as a universal condition on the mapping of structure to word order); Biberauer, Holmberg, and Roberts 2014; and Sheehan 2011, 2013a,b. The fourth is presented here for the first time.

4.8   FOFC in Holmberg 2000a

Holmberg 2000a contains the original formulation of FOFC (without calling it that):

(17) If a phrase α is head-initial, then a phrase β which immediately
      dominates α is head-initial. If α is head-final, then β can be head-
      initial or head-final.

In other words, seen from the point of view of the dominating phrase, head-
final can only dominate head-final: hence the name *Final-over-Final* Condition. The paper focuses on Finnish sentential word order in particular, but
demonstrates that the condition is valid also in other languages and other types
of phrases. Sentential word order in Finnish is a telling example because,
although the unmarked order in Finnish sentences is uncontroversially head-
initial, head-final order occurs as well, systematically in certain syntactic
contexts, O preceding V, and VP preceding Aux. Head-final order occurs,
primarily, when some constituent is fronted to initial focus position—for
instance, a *wh*-phrase in a question (see chapter 10). We thus find Aux either
preceding VP or following it, and we find V either preceding its complement
O or following it. Given that the marked head-final alternative is always
optional, we would expect to find all the possible combinations of head-initial
and head-final VP and AuxP, given the right syntactic conditions. However,
one combination is judged unacceptable: a head-initial VP dominated by a
head-final AuxP (see chapters 2 and 10 for other examples):

(18) a. Milloin Jussi olisi   kirjoittanut romaanin?   [Finnish]
          when   Jussi would.have written   novel

                                                                      [Aux [V O]]

          'When would Jussi have written a novel?'
      b. Milloin Jussi olisi   romaanin kirjoittanut?   [Aux [O V]]
          when   Jussi would.have novel   written
      c. Milloin Jussi romaanin kirjoittanut olisi?   [[O V] Aux]
          when   Jussi novel   written   would.have
      d. *Milloin Jussi kirjoittanut romaanin olisi?   [[V O] Aux]
          when   Jussi written   novel   would-have

The explanation of FOFC in Holmberg 2000a is based on the following theoretical premises.

First, on the basis of a proposal by Svenonius (1994), it is assumed that
selection, specifically c-selection (or "strict subcategorization," in Chomsky's (1965) terms), is always accompanied by movement. More precisely,
c-selection *is* formally movement, or we might call it incorporation, of the
selected feature into the selecting head. The rationale is that the c-selection
is a strictly local phenomenon. This feature movement (or incorporation) has
three different realizations, subject to parametric variation (see also Julien
2002). Consider tree (19), where F c-selects G:

(19)

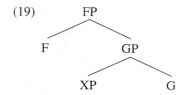

1. G can move by pure feature movement, which is always covert. The resulting structure is spelled out as F-XP-G.
2. G can move by head movement (overt incorporation of G into F). The resulting structure is spelled out as G-F-XP (typically with F a suffix on G).
3. G can move, pied-piping GP. The resulting structure, a harmonic head-final structure, is spelled out as XP-G-F.

Now assume that the tree is (20):

(20)

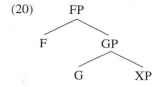

1. G can move by pure feature movement, which is always covert. The resulting structure is spelled out as F-G-XP.
2. G can move by head movement (overt incorporation of G into F). The resulting structure is spelled out as G-F-XP (typically with F a suffix on G), the same as in (19).
3. G can move, pied-piping GP. This will yield the FOFC-violating structure (21).

(21)

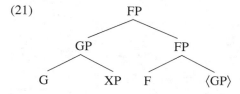

The theoretical device that rules this structure out is (22), taken to be a universal condition on c-selection (this is a simplification; see Holmberg 2000a for a more detailed formalization); see Richards 2010 for a more recent formalization and contextualization of this general idea, which is also applied to FOFC by Richards:

(22) C-selection requires adjacency between selector and selectee.

Feature movement and head movement will always yield adjacency. Phrasal movement will yield adjacency only if the pied-piped phrase is head-final.

While in the case of options 1 and 2 the adjacency is ensured in the (narrow) syntax by incorporation (overtly or covertly) of the selected head into the selecting head, in the case of (21) it is clearly a PF matter: a spelled-out phrase will intervene between selector and selectee. In the case of (19), it is assumed in Holmberg 2000a that GP is itself derived by phrasal movement of XP, as required if the LCA is assumed, as it is in that paper. It will thus have the structure (23), after movement of XP:

(23)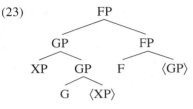

By hypothesis, the copy of XP does not intervene between G and F for the purposes of (22). That is to say, the required adjacency is a PF matter, a morphological issue.

The argumentation in favor of principle (22) in Holmberg 2000a begins with the observation that in the case where F is an affix (e.g., a suffixal tense head), adjacency is required because otherwise an "affix feature" (a morphological matter) remains unchecked. It proceeds to the suggestion that the affix feature is just a special case of the c-selection feature. It is, as it were, just a morphological accident that the selecting head is sometimes an affix (i.e., is spelled out as a bound morpheme) and sometimes a free morpheme: adjacency is a requirement in either case.

It is well-known that the heads in a head-final tree always line up adjacent to each other, while the heads in a head-initial tree often don't. FOFC has this effect: no complement can intervene between the heads in a head-final structure. But it is a more general condition, since typically adjuncts cannot intervene between the heads in a head-final tree, either (as mentioned in chapter 2 and further discussed in chapter 6). As an illustration, consider the following Finnish construction (based on Holmberg 2000a). (24) is the unmarked harmonic head-initial structure; here, the adverb can be inserted in various places, including between the auxiliary and the verb:

(24) Ei Jussi ole (vieläkään) hyväksynyt (vieläkään) sitä ajatusta [Finnish]
     not Jussi has yet   accepted   yet   that idea
     (vieläkään).
     yet
     'Jussi still hasn't accepted that idea.'

(25) is the head-final version. Here again, the adverb can be inserted in more than one place, but not between the verb and the auxiliary:

(25) Ei Jussi (vieläkään) sitä ajatusta (vieläkään) hyväksynyt   [Finnish]
     not Jussi yet   that idea   yet   accepted
     (*vieläkään) ole (vieläkään).
      yet   has yet
     'Jussi still hasn't accepted that idea.'

This is explained by (22). Consider the relevant part of the derivation of (25b) (simplified for ease of exposition): in (26), the object has moved to Spec,VP, and the auxiliary has been merged, c-selecting the verb meaning 'accepted':

(26) [$_{AuxP}$ ole [$_{VP}$ [$_{DP}$ sitä ajatusta] [$_{V'}$ hyväksynyt ⟨DP⟩]]]
           has   that idea   accepted

Now assume that prior to movement of V pied-piping the VP, the adverb is merged as an adjunct to AuxP, deriving (27a). Only then does the VP move, deriving (27b):

(27) a. [$_{AuxP}$ vieläkään [$_{AuxP}$ ole [$_{VP}$ [$_{DP}$ sitä ajatusta] [$_{V'}$ hyväksynyt ⟨DP⟩]]]]
             yet   has   that idea   accepted

     b. [$_{AuxP}$ [$_{VP}$ [$_{DP}$ sitä ajatusta] [$_{V'}$ hyväksynyt ⟨DP⟩] [$_{AuxP}$ vieläkään
                    that idea   accepted   yet
        [$_{AuxP}$ ole ⟨VP⟩]]]]
             has

This will yield the ungrammatical version of (25b). Principle (22), the principle explaining FOFC in Holmberg 2000a, will rule it out.

   (22) is still dubious as a principle of UG, though. C-selection is a narrow-syntax property (or operation), notoriously sensitive to features visible at the LF interface such as [±wh] or [±finite], and notoriously insensitive to morphological features such as whether a complement is actually pronounced or not (e.g., the VP-complement of Aux can be deleted in some contexts, in many languages). How can such a property (or operation) be subject to a PF adjacency condition? If we take this proposal seriously, it would seem to have radical architectural consequences. See Richards 2010, though, for a theory that does take that step.

   The alternative is that the adjacency does not in any sense drive the derivation (in a derivational model) or serve as an output condition (in a representational model), but is just an incidental consequence of how the derivation of head-final structure operates.[10]

4.9   FOFC in Biberauer, Holmberg, and Roberts 2014

The LCA is a crucial component in the theory articulated in Biberauer, Holmberg, and Roberts (BHR) 2014, as well. First, assuming the LCA, any string where VP precedes Aux (i.e., the constituents of VP precede Aux)—for instance, the well-formed substring *ein Auto gekauft hat* in (28)—must be derived by movement. The structure of (28a) will be roughly (28b):

(28) a. …dass Anne ein Auto gekauft hat.   [German]
     that Anne a   car   bought has
     '…that Anne bought a car.'

   b.
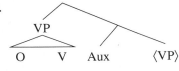

BHR explicitly assume that the relevant movement is movement of the sister of X^0 to Spec,XP, ignoring the more complex alternative where there is an additional abstract head above XP attracting the complement of X^0 to its Spec (see note 10), and ignoring the arguments in the literature against such very local movement.[11] Assuming the LCA, the order OV in the VP in (28b) must also be derived by movement; that is, the structure of the VP is, roughly, [$_{VP}$ O [$_{VP}$ V ⟨O⟩]]. In these terms, the contrast between the licit structure (23) and the illicit structure (21b) suggests the following generalization: a VP consisting of V and O cannot move around Aux unless O has moved around V (deriving OV order) (where the expression "YP moves around X^0" is shorthand for "the sister YP of X^0 moves to Spec,XP").[12] More generally, the movement required to derive an extended projection with head-final order must "start at the bottom": the sister of the lexical head L moves around L to a position where it asymmetrically c-commands L, before the phrase headed by L can move around the next head merged with LP, in the extended projection of L (why the notion "extended projection" is crucial here will be made clear below). Complex head-final structures are derived by iterated movement of successively larger complements, so-called snowball movement (Kayne 1994, Cinque 2005a, Jayaseelan 2009), but *always starting at the bottom of the tree*. Furthermore, the iterated movement of complements must be strictly successive: it cannot "skip" a head, or a FOFC violation will ensue. Consider the following example from Finnish:

(29) a. Kyllä minä nuotteja lukea osannut olen.   [Finnish]
          indeed I   notes   read could have [$_{AuxP}$ [$_{vP}$ [$_{VP}$ O V] v] Aux]
          'I have actually been able to read music.'

b. *Kyllä   minä lukea nuotteja osannut olen.

indeed I   read notes   could   have [$_{AuxP}$ [$_{vP}$ [$_{VP}$ V O] v] Aux]

c. *Kyllä   minä osannut nuotteja lukea olen.

indeed I   could   notes   read have [$_{AuxP}$ [$_{vP}$ v [$_{VP}$ O V]] Aux]

The extended projection of the verb here includes the restructuring verb *osata* 'know how to', labeled *v*, and the auxiliary *olla* 'have/be'. In the grammatical (29a), the object has moved around the verb (being spelled out as OV), the VP has moved around the v, and the vP has moved around the auxiliary. In (29b), O has not moved around V, but VP has moved around v, and vP around T. The result is ungrammatical, a FOFC violation. In (29c), O is moved around V, then VP is not moved around v, but vP is moved around T. The result is ungrammatical, another FOFC violation. This is not because the FOFC-violating restructuring verb must follow its complement as an inherent property: in other contexts, the verb *osata* can precede its complement:

(30) Kyllä minä olen osannut   nuotteja lukea.   [Finnish]

indeed I   have been.able.to notes   read [$_{AuxP}$ Aux [$_{vP}$ v [$_{VP}$ O V]]]

'I have actually been able to read music.'

BHR propose, following Chomsky 2000, 2001 and much subsequent work, that movement is triggered by a feature on the head that is the target of the movement. Chomsky refers to the feature as the *EPP-feature* (Chomsky 2000), *OCC* ("occurrence of"; Chomsky 2001), or the *edge feature* (Chomsky 2008). BHR use the symbol $^\wedge$ (caret) for the movement-triggering feature. This feature has different instantiations depending on which syntactic feature(s) it is associated with. Thus, A-movement is triggered by $^\wedge$ coupled with a φ-feature probe on T or v (i.e., a set of unvalued φ-features needing a matching valued set to assign values to it; Chomsky 2001). Ā-movement is triggered by $^\wedge$ associated with a head in the C-domain. The movement of the sister YP of X^0 around X^0, which has head-final order YP-X^0 as its principal effect, is triggered by $^\wedge$ associated with the categorial feature [±V] of X^0. This feature is introduced in a derivation with the lexical head. This is why the movement deriving head-final order starts at the bottom. Adapting the idea that the bottom pair results from Merge of a root and a categorial feature (see section 4.5), $^\wedge$ will be a property of the categorial feature. In fact, it is a parameterized property of the categorial feature; typically, a given lexical category (e.g., P) in a particular language consistently has $^\wedge$ or consistently lacks $^\wedge$ (the language is prepositional or postpositional). However, it is also possible for one class of P in the language to have $^\wedge$, while the complementary class lacks $^\wedge$, as in Finnish, where most adpositions are postpositions but there is a sizeable minority of prepositions (Manninen 2003; see chapter 1). There are also languages where $^\wedge$ can optionally accompany a given lexical category. Again, Finnish is an example. As shown in (14) and (18), and as will be discussed in more detail in chapter 10, VP, vP, and AuxP can be head-initial or head-final in Finnish.

An extended projection, in roughly Grimshaw's (1991, 2001) sense, is defined by the categorial feature of the lexical head. The extended projection of V is the sequence of functional heads sharing the categorial feature [+V] emanating from the verb, including at least v, Aspect, T, modals (in languages where they are verbal), and arguably C. The extended projection of N is the sequence of functional heads sharing the categorial feature [−V] emanating from the noun, including number, noun class, quantification, D, and arguably P. BHR propose that the movement trigger $^\wedge$ "spreads" or is copied from head to head along the spine of the extended projection. In (31), representing the structure of the bottom part of a head-final transitive sentence such as (29a), $^\wedge$ is introduced in the derivation as an accompaniment of [+V]. It triggers movement of the object DP to Spec,VP:

(31)

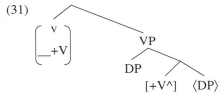

Subsequently, the transitivizing light verb v is merged. The light verb is marked as c-selecting [+V] (marked by a strict subcategorization feature), a condition for successful merger with VP. BHR propose that v is not itself inherently valued [+V]; rather, it "inherits" or copies this feature from its selected complement. In fact, the categorial feature copying can be seen as a necessary consequence of the selection relation: the selection feature is "checked" by copying the categorial feature of the complement (see Svenonius 1994, Holmberg 2000a, Julien 2002).[13] The result is (32), where $^\wedge$ is copied by v, triggering movement of VP around v. Following BHR, the presentation here ignores the subject, also merged with vP.[14]

(32)

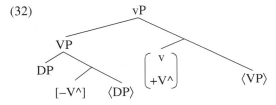

The movement trigger ^ can be, but need not be, copied along with the categorial feature it accompanies. This would be a point where UG is under-specified, thus allowing variation. And variation is what we find. In some languages, ^ is copied all the way up to the highest head of the extended projection of L. This yields a harmonically head-final extended projection of L. In other languages, ^ stops at some intermediate head along the projection line from L to the highest head in the extended projection of L. The stopping point is subject to parametric variation. Thus, we find SOV languages with the patterns in (33a) (^ copying goes all the way to C), (33b) (^ copying stops at T), and (33c) (^ copying stops at V):

(33) a. O > V > T > C   (Japanese)
     b. C > O > V > T   (Hindi)
     c. C > T > O > V   (Dutch)

Now, if copying of ^ is a consequence of selection, it follows that it is strictly local (a head-to-head relation). This locality is then what rules out (29c). To derive (29c), repeated here as (34a), ^ would have to be copied by Aux while skipping v, as shown in (34b):

(34) a. *Kyllä minä osannut nuotteja lukea olen.   [Finnish]
        indeed I   could   notes   read   have
     b. [$_{\text{AuxP}}$ [$_{\text{vP}}$ v   [$_{\text{VP}}$ O   V   ]] Aux   ]
                         [+V]   [+V$^{\wedge}$]   [+V$^{\wedge}$]

This, BHR argue, is ruled out by locality: Aux cannot c-select V, as required for feature copying. It can only c-select v—but v in (34b), although it has the right categorial feature [+V], does not have ^. Hence, Aux cannot have ^ trig-gering L-movement, and the system cannot derive (34a). BHR formulate the locality condition on selection in terms of Rizzi's (1990) Relativized Minimality:

(35) *Relativized Minimality*
    In a configuration X...Y...Z where X asymmetrically c-commands Z, no syntactic relation R can hold between X and Z if Y asymmetrically c-commands Z but does not c-command X, and R potentially holds between X and Y. (adapted from Rizzi 1990:7)

The notion "extended projection of L" is crucial for the following reason. BHR observe that FOFC appears not to apply to nominal complements to verbs, as (36a,b) show:

(36) a. Johann hat [$_{\text{VP}}$ [$_{\text{DP}}$ einen Mann] gesehen].   [German]
        Johann has   a   man   seen
        'Johann saw a man.'

b. Johann ist [$_{VP}$ [$_{PP}$ nach Berlin] gefahren].
   Johann is   to   Berlin gone
   'Johann went to Berlin.'

Here, by assumption, the complement of the main verb—a DP in (36a), a PP in (36b)—is moved around V, deriving a head-final VP. But the DP and the PP are head-initial, without any resulting FOFC violation. Consider again the formulation of FOFC in (13), repeated here:

(13) *The Final-over-Final Condition (FOFC)*
    A head-final phrase αP cannot immediately dominate a head-initial
    phrase βP, if α and β are members of the same extended projection.

The difference between (36a,b) and (14c)/(18b,c) is that α and β in the former are not heads in the same extended projection, while they are in the latter. In (36a,b), α is [+V] (the head of VP), while β is [−V] (the head of DP in one case, the head of PP in the other).

BHR present arguments that the crucial difference really is categorial feature value. In particular, they reject the idea that the crucial difference between (36a,b) and (14c)/(18b,c) is that the moved (prehead) complement is a referential expression, an argument of the verb, in (36b,c) but not in (14c)/(18b,c). This distinction is not crucial for two reasons: sentential complements to V are subject to FOFC (see section 2.3), and predicative noun phrase complements of V are not subject to FOFC. Consider the difference between (37a) and (37b):

(37) a. *...dass Johann niemals [$_{CP}$ dass er eigentlich ein   [German]
         that Johann never   that he actually   an
         angenommenes Kind sei]   besprochen hat.
         adopted   child be.SUBJ discussed has
   b. ...dass Johann niemals besprochen hat [$_{CP}$ dass er eigentlich ein
         that Johann never   discussed has   that he actually   an
         angenommenes Kind sei].
         adopted   child be.SUBJ
    '...that Johann has never discussed the fact that he is actually an
    adopted child.'

The embedded clause in (37a) is an argument of the verb. When this clause precedes the verb, the result is ungrammatical because it violates FOFC, according to BHR (see also chapter 2). When it is postposed to the verb, the result is grammatical. This follows if (i) FOFC only applies within an extended projection, and (ii) CP is a projection of [+V], part of the extended projection of the verb. An alternative hypothesis is that a CP-complement must be postposed because it is too "heavy" to be preposed. This hypothesis is falsified by (38), where the complement of V is even more complex, yet can be preposed:

(38) ...dass Johann niemals [$_{DP}$ den Verdacht [$_{CP}$ dass er   [German]
    that Johann never   the suspicion   that he
    eigentlich ein angenommenes Kind sei]]   besprochen hat.
    actually   an adopted   child be.SUBJ discussed   has
    '...that Johann has never discussed the suspicion that he is actually an adopted child.'

Under BHR's theory, (38) is well-formed, unlike (37a), because the preposed complement in (38) is a DP, not a projection of [+V].

Finally, (39) is an example of a nominal complement preposed to the verb that is not an argument, but a predicate:

(39) ...dat Johan [$_{NP}$ minister van buitelandse sake]   [Afrikaans]
    that Johan   minister of   foreign   affairs
    geword het.
    become has
    '...that Johan has become minister of foreign affairs.'

If BHR are right, FOFC is a consequence of how selection, feature projection, and movement work, in structure building. These are core processes in narrow syntax. In this model, where linear order is factored out of narrow syntax, FOFC's relation to linearization is that the structure that would yield the "FOFC-violating" word orders in (14c), (18b,c), and (37a) cannot be derived by the narrow syntax.

Summarizing, in BHR's model FOFC is a result of the following syntactic conditions:

(40) a. Head-finality is a consequence of the movement trigger $^\wedge$ being paired with the categorial feature [±V], which enters the derivation with the head of the extended projection.

    b. The movement trigger $^\wedge$ can spread with [±V] from head to head along the spine of the extended projection, subject to parametric variation.

    c. C-selection relations are subject to Relativized Minimality.[15]

4.10 FOFC in Sheehan 2011, 2013a,b

Another model providing a principled explanation of FOFC is articulated by Sheehan (2011, 2013a,b). Like BHR, Sheehan assumes a model where linear order is factored out of (narrow) syntax. Unlike BHR, Sheehan assumes that heads are marked for "direction" as part of their inherent c-selection features.

For instance, in a VO language V is marked, as an inherent property, to precede the category it selects when spelled out at PF (formally notated as V_P), while in an OV language it is marked to follow the category it selects when spelled out at PF (formally V_F).

A second distinctive property of Sheehan's model is that every terminal category must be linearized relative to every other terminal category within a certain domain without relying on dominance. For example, the structure [Aux [O V]] involves three linear relations, three linear pairs: OV, Aux-V, and Aux-O. Each must be unambiguously determined, though transitivity can be used to determine the order between heads that do not stand in a selection relation. The structure [Neg [Aux [O V]]] involves six linear pairs, which must be unambiguously determined: OV, Aux-V, Aux-O, Neg-Aux, Neg-V, Neg-O. And so on, for more complex structures. Some of these relations will be determined by the inherent directionality features, either directly or by transitivity. The remaining relations will be determined by the LCA. Sheehan (2013b) expresses the role of the LCA in the theory as follows:

(41) *Revised LCA*
   a. If a category A c-selects a category B, then A precedes/follows B at PF.
   b. If no order is specified between A and B by the sum of all precedence pairs defined by (a), then A precedes B at PF if A asymmetrically c-commands B.

That is to say, the LCA functions as a last resort for linearization. This immediately captures the fact that while heads seem to be able to precede or follow their complements, specifiers always seem to precede the rest of the phrase. In this model, the latter fact thus follows from the fact that specifiers are never selected (see section 4.8).

A third distinctive property of Sheehan's theory is that a head and its projection form a single multisegment category, distinct from the complement of the head. The technical device that Sheehan (2013b) proposes to achieve this effect is formalizing the projection of a categorial label as copying of the label. Consider the effect this has on the statement of linear relations in for example (42), the structure of *have read the book*:

(42)

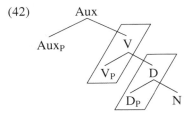

Note that this is a graphic representation of structure only, not order. Because (42) is a structure for English, Aux is marked to precede the category it selects. This means that Aux precedes the boxed category V. It does not entail that Aux also precedes D and N. V, in turn, is marked to precede the category it selects. This means that V precedes the boxed category D. It does not entail that V also precedes N. However, in this case, because V precedes D and D precedes N, V does precede N by transitivity. Likewise, because Aux precedes V, it also precedes D and N by transitivity. As a result, the total linear order in this case is Aux-V-D-N, and no recourse to asymmetric c-command is necessary.

Consider now how this accounts for FOFC. First, consider the permitted disharmonic "inverse-FOFC" order in (43a), with the structure in (43b):

(43) a. Kyllä Anne on auton ostanut.   [Finnish]
indeed Anne has car   bought
'Anne really has bought a car.'

b.

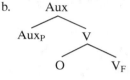

(43b) is strictly a representation of structure. Aux is marked to precede the category it selects at PF, while V is marked to follow the category it selects at PF. This yields the following ordered pairs:

(44) OV   (by selection)
Aux-V   (by selection)
Aux-O   (by the LCA)
Total order: Aux-O-V

There is no selection-determined order between Aux and O, either directly or by transitivity. Therefore, the LCA steps in to order these two categories on the basis of asymmetric c-command relations. Since Aux asymmetrically c-commands O, it will precede O at PF.

Now consider the ungrammatical, "FOFC-violating" order in (45a), with the structure (45b):

(45) a. *Kyllä Anne ostanut auton on.   [Finnish]
indeed Anne bought car   has

b.

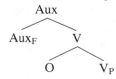

The structure is the same as in (43) (it could be graphically represented with V to the left of O and Aux to the right of V). The only difference is the linear selection features on Aux and V: Aux is marked to follow the category it selects (V), while V is marked to precede the category it selects (O). The linear pairs are as follows:

(46) VO   (by selection)
     V-Aux   (by selection)
     Aux-O   (by the LCA)
     Total order: V-Aux-O

Note that the total order resulting from this set of linear pairs is V-Aux-O, rather than V-O-Aux; since Aux asymmetrically c-commands O, it will precede it. The order seen in (45a) simply cannot be derived, given these selection features. Sheehan's (2011, 2013a,b) explanation of FOFC, then, is this: there is no narrow-syntax ban on "FOFC-violating structures"; it is just that these structures are never linearized with the complement intervening between the two heads in a head-final sequence.

One advantage of Sheehan's system is that it can account for the fact that FOFC seems to hold of both base-generated and movement-derived structures. Because the head and its projections constitute a single category, it follows that when a complex specifier is involved, only the projecting head c-commands into the main clausal spine. Thus, in (47) V asymmetrically c-commands v, but O does not:

(47)

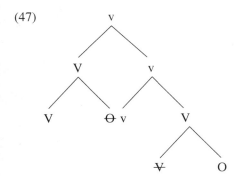

Sheehan argues that the only way to linearize FOFC-violating structures such as (47) is for O to be spelled out in its base position, yielding the order V-v-O. As there is fairly good evidence that movement of this kind is involved in some disharmonic languages, the fact that Sheehan's approach can derive the same linearization effect can be seen as a significant advantage. (For an example of this, see chapter 7.)

Moreover, Sheehan's approach predicts that FOFC is not sensitive to the complement/adjunct status of the material intervening between the two heads. Any XP that follows V in (47) or (45b) will pose the same linearization problem, whether it is a complement or an adverb. As adjuncts seem to behave like complements in this regard, linking FOFC only to selection as in Holmberg 2000a is problematic;[16] the prediction made by Sheehan's approach regarding FOFC is therefore an advantage (see chapter 6).

To explain the fact that DP complements of V are not subject to FOFC, whereas CPs (and arguably PPs; see chapter 5) are, Sheehan appeals to the fact that DPs are often strong islands. As FOFC is an effect only of linearization, the prediction is that atomized domains will not display the effect. As extraction is very generally possible from embedded CPs and PP, but not DPs, this seems to make the correct cut without the need to appeal to extended projections or categorial distinctness. The strong prediction is that any surface FOFC violations will involve an atomized phrase; see (48), where outline font indicates atomization:

(48)

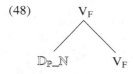

By hypothesis, then, the reason why N can precede V in (48) is that it is not part of the same linearization domain. N has already been linearized with respect to D when the two are merged with V, meaning that they behave like an atom. While this approach still faces challenges from the behavior of preverbal PPs in Germanic languages (as in (36b)), it seems promising as an explanation for certain kinds of FOFC exceptions.

As Sheehan (2013b) shows, the need for externally merged specifiers to be linearized with respect to the main clausal spine also provides a more nuanced PF explanation of Huang's (1982) Condition on Extraction Domain (CED). Externally merged head-initial specifiers will always pose a linearization problem, requiring them to be immediately atomized and hence to behave like strong islands. Externally merged head-final specifiers, on the other hand, will not pose the same problem. Consider the contrast in (49):

(49) a.   b.

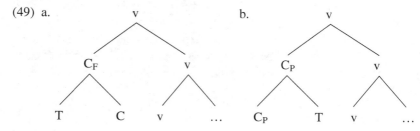

In (49a), a harmonically head-final CP is externally merged in a specifier position. C is specified to follow T because of c-selection. Because the C-projection is an externally merged specifier, it is not c-selected; and because it asymmetrically c-commands the category v, it must precede v. This gives the unambiguous linear order T-C-v by transitivity. Now compare (49b), where the externally merged specifier is harmonically head-initial. This time, C is specified to precede T by c-selection. Again, the C-projection is not c-selected, so its position with respect to v must be determined via asymmetric c-command. C again asymmetrically c-commands v and so must precede it. But these two orderings are not sufficient to order T with respect to v:

(50) C-T, C-v

Moreover, here asymmetric c-command will not help, as T and v do not stand in any c-command relation. As dominance is not used in linearization in this theory (for principled reasons), the only option is for the externally merged specifier in (49b) to be atomized upon being externally merged. Sheehan argues that this serves to explain the fact that many head-final languages fail to be subject to CED effects, something that other approaches to the CED have failed to explain.

Finally, Sheehan's approach predicts that extraposition will be observed wherever a FOFC structure is linearized. Rather than being a FOFC-compliance strategy, this is a simple effect of linearization. This provides a novel account of certain kinds of extraposition, which is empirically well-supported (see Sheehan 2011). A potential challenge is that extraposition does not always pattern exactly as expected. For example, instead of only the complement of C being extraposed, preverbal head-initial CPs are extraposed wholesale.

In Sheehan's terms, one way to capture what is special about Finnish is to say that it has dual specification of V and Aux: V_P and Aux_P but also V_F and Aux_F. The order V-Aux-O actually does occur in Finnish, albeit as a highly marked alternative; see chapter 10 for a detailed discussion. Note also the following consequence: if Aux in (45) is spelled out as a suffix on V (as is not uncommon for modal, aspectual, and temporal functional heads), then the linearization of (45b) will have the effect of head movement. This, too, will be discussed in chapter 10.

4.11 FOFC as an Effect of Incorporation and Pied-Piping

A background assumption in the theory sketched in this section concerns the nature of head movement or incorporation. The theory has some features in common with the theory in Holmberg 2000a (see section 4.8) but differs from it in a number of crucial respects. Roberts (2010a) proposes that incorporation of Y to X where X asymmetrically c-commands Y is triggered just where X and Y stand in an Agree relation, in the standard way, and Y's formal features are (properly) included in those of X. Let us refer to this as *Agree-driven incorporation*. According to Roberts, this kind of incorporation underlies many cases of cliticization, verb movement, noun incorporation, and so on.

A second assumption, from Roberts 2010a, is that the "core functional categories" that make up the basic functional hierarchy in both clauses and nominals (and probably elsewhere—for example, in the extended AP, although that case will not be addressed here) contain progressively more formal features as one moves up the hierarchy. For example, the lexical verb has (at most) one formal feature, the one that characterizes it as a verb—namely, the V-feature. The light verb v also has this feature, as well as φ-features. T also has a V-feature and φ-features, but in addition has its intrinsic T(ense)-features. Finally, C has V-features, φ-features (which may be shared in one way or another with T, following the suggestion in Chomsky 2008), T-features (see numerous analyses of tense and sequence of tense stemming from Enç 1987), and its intrinsic clause-typing features (Holmberg 1986, Cheng 1991). So we have the following picture:[17]

(51) *Basic clause structure*

$$[C_{[V, T, \varphi, \text{Clause Type}]} [T_{[V, T, \varphi]} [v_{[V, \varphi]} [V_{[V]}]]]]$$

Analogously, we can think of the basic structure of nominals as follows (see chapter 8):

(52) *Basic nominal structure*

$$[D_{[N, Q, \varphi, \text{Def}]} [Num_{[N, Q, \varphi]} [n_{[N, \varphi]} [N_{[N]}]]]]$$

If we now adopt Roberts's proposals regarding incorporation, each head will have to incorporate with the "next head up," which requires that the heads are in an Agree relation regarding these formal features. Let us suppose, however, that Agree in the standard sense is restricted to φ-features. Considering the clause structure in (51), this means that the only case where Agree-driven incorporation may take place is where T's φ-set is included in that of C. On standard assumptions (following Chomsky 1995:chap. 4), v also has a set of φ-features, but this set relates to the object and is therefore distinct from that of T/C.

At this point, we need to introduce a third assumption. Following Rizzi (2008), let us take c-selection to be external Search, while Agree is internal Search. C-selection, then, involves a head searching the numeration for another head bearing formal features of the relevant kind,[18] triggering external Merge with that head. We can now make a distinction between Agree-driven incorporation, defined and discussed in Roberts 2010a, and *select-driven incorporation*—that is, head movement of a selected category to its selector. Given the assumptions above, incorporation through the functional hierarchy is always possible. In fact, according to Roberts (2010a) Agree-driven incorporation is obligatory. On the other hand, we postulate that select-driven incorporation is always in principle optional, subject to parameterization.[19]

The final postulate necessary for a new account of FOFC is as follows:

(53) Where incorporation of X takes place, pied-piping of XP is a parametric option.

Pied-piping here refers to the movement of the category containing the goal, in this case the goal of external Search. Since the goal itself incorporates to the selecting head, the pied-piped XP must move to a position as close to that head as possible, internally merging with it to form a specifier.[20]

Now consider the order of operations as an extended projection is built. After the VP is built, v c-selects the lexical head V, and VP thus merges with v; this is a combination of external Search and external Merge. Next, we have the parametric option of incorporation of V to v (external Search and internal Merge). Then, and only then, comes the option of pied-piping of YP to Spec,X (internal Merge). From this, we can see that the basic cases of FOFC now follow; the basic FOFC-violating structure in (54a) is underivable, since, wherever αP moves to Spec,βP, α must have incorporated into β, as shown in (54b):

(54) a. *$[_{\beta P} [_{\alpha P} \alpha \gamma P] \beta]$
      b. $[_{\beta}^{P} [_{\alpha}^{P} (\alpha) \gamma P] \alpha + \beta]$

Consider once more the case of (S)-Aux-V-O and its permutations. Aux-V-O can be derived as in (55a), with no incorporation, the order following from the LCA (see section 4.5). The order V-Aux-O (see (7) of chapter 2 and (4)–(5) of chapter 10) is derived as in (55b), by incorporation of V into Aux with no pied-piping. The order O-V-Aux is derived as in (55c), by incorporation of V into Aux with pied-piping of VP:

(55) a. [Aux [V O]]
      b. [V+Aux [⟨V⟩ O]]
      c. $[_{AuxP}$ [⟨V⟩ O] [V+Aux ⟨VP⟩]]
      d. *$[_{AuxP}$ [V O] Aux]

The FOFC-violating structure/order (55d) cannot be derived if the system does not allow "comp-to-spec movement" (i.e., movement of the complement of a head H to the specifier position of H) except in conjunction with incorporation—that is, when realizing the option of pied-piping.[21]

In order to fully derive FOFC, more is needed. In particular, we must require that incorporation can only "start at the bottom" of the extended projection, with the lexical head. However, there are clear cases in the literature of head movement affecting only a relatively high position in an extended projection: for example, v-to-T movement (possibly the correct analysis of English "*have/ be* raising"; see Emonds 1976, 1978) and T-to-C movement as in English subject-aux inversion. See also chapter 11, where movement of higher heads in the clausal hierarchy is postulated without V-movement in analyses of Navajo and various other OV languages with tense/aspect prefixes.

Consider what would happen in a case of v-to-T movement associated with vP-pied-piping, but no V(P)-movement. The resulting structure for TP would be as follows:

(56) $[_{TP} [_{vP} (S) [_{v'} <v> [_{VP} \textbf{V O}]]] [_{T'} \textbf{v+T} <vP>]]$

Assuming that either v or T contains an auxiliary, (S)-V-O-Aux order results, contra FOFC. Furthermore, T could incorporate to C with pied-piping, giving VO...C.

As discussed in section 4.9 on the theory of FOFC in BHR 2014, given that select-driven head movement depends on categorial features defining extended projections, it makes sense that it must "start at the bottom," where the categorial feature defining the extended projection is introduced, however this notion is more precisely formalized (see section 4.9 and BHR 2014 for an attempt). Cases of head movement that start higher up are plausibly not cases of select-driven movement. T-to-C movement in English, for example, involves polarity and interrogativity. In Holmberg 2003, 2016, it is analyzed as Pol-to-C movement.

Note that this approach does not rely on a special movement trigger for linearization. The parametric options for linearization are as follows:

(57) a. Merge > Incorporate > Pied-Pipe   (head-final order)
     b. Merge > (Incorporate)   (head-initial order)

The operations Merge, Incorporate, and Pied-Pipe are all intrinsically ordered in relation to one another. Note further that, if incorporation is intrinsically linked to affixation, this also explains the greater incidence of affixation in OV languages, since these languages must feature incorporation on the view developed here.

A further interesting consequence of this approach is that it partially explains a generalization discussed in chapter 11, namely, that head-final languages rarely have any prefixes. Consider the derivation in (58):

(58) $[_{v'} X+V [_{XP} <X> YP]] \rightarrow [_{VP} [_{XP} <X> YP] [_{v'} X+V <XP>]]$

Here, XP is the complement of V. X incorporates to V, forming a prefix, followed by pied-piping of the remnant XP, deriving a head-final VP with a prefix on V. But in terms of the above proposals concerning the categorial structure of extended projections, X cannot be part of the same extended projection as V; instead, it is presumably in a high position in its own extended projection and therefore has either disjoint features in relation to V or a superset of V's features. Either way, incorporation of X is impossible under the present assumptions, and so (58) is not found. We do not, for example, find examples of D or C prefixed to V, with or without pied-piped NP or TP. This is because D and C have more or disjoint features in relation to V and so do not incorporate.

We have now derived FOFC in a novel and interesting way, but we are faced with a different problem: how is complement-head order possible where incorporation is impossible? This problem arises from the fact that the theory allows XP-movement for linearization only where incorporation takes place. Incorporation is always an option as an extended projection is being built, as we have seen, but is not possible "across" extended-projection boundaries, since either the relevant categories are disjoint or the lower head has more features than the higher one. For example, how can we derive OV order in a language like German, where it is clear that DP is head-initial and that D does not incorporate into V?

Here we have two options. The choice between them will be left open (it is possible, in fact, that individual languages choose between them). The first option is to reinstate the Head Parameter, but in a more restricted form than the traditional formulations (e.g., in Hawkins 1983). Under this view, along the lines proposed by Richards (2004), the parameter is relevant only for the relation between a lexical head and its complement. In fact, here a still narrower class of cases is relevant: the relation between a lexical head and a categorially distinct complement. In all other cases, word order is determined purely by movement. Thus, like Richards, we would adopt both the LCA and (a version of) the Head Parameter.

The second option is to modify the proposal made above regarding the featural makeup of categories in the extended projection and allow, perhaps as a parametric option, that the "higher" positions in certain extended projections are either absent or have fewer formal features than we have been assuming up to now. Such a hypothesis seems implausible for a language like German, which clearly has initial C and D, along with final V, and so here the Head Parameter may have to be invoked. On the other hand, Japanese has no clear examples of D and few really clear Cs, so perhaps the second option is at work in this language. More generally, given the relative paucity of clear

D-final and C-final languages, it may be worth considering the possibility that the second option is found in the more harmonically head-final languages, with the Head Parameter at work only in disharmonic ones.

4.12 Conclusions

Word order is obviously one aspect of syntax where there is much crosslinguistic variation. The big question is, what are the limits of this variation, if there are any limits? What are the limiting factors? Is the limiting factor UG?

This chapter has presented a brief history of the theory of linear order in generative Chomskyan linguistics, leading up to the currently widely accepted model where linear order is factored out of narrow syntax. In this model, narrow syntax builds hierarchies of sets of categories, by Merge, deriving syntactic representations (LF representations) that are semantically interpreted. Arguably these syntactic representations are universal, with no crosslinguistic variation possible. The hierarchies of sets of categories are assigned linear order as part of externalization, the post-narrow-syntax derivation of PF, subject to much crosslinguistic variation. As pointed out by Chomsky (1965:125), this model requires a theory of "how the abstract underlying unordered structures are converted into actual strings with surface structures." Such a theory was provided by Kayne (1994), including the LCA, which maps asymmetric c-command relations to linear order. The chapter also briefly discussed alternatives to Kayne's LCA-based theory, in particular Haider's (2000), based on a universal branching direction combined with a notion of "licensing direction," which is parameterized.

The chapter then addressed the structure-based condition on word order that is the topic of this book: FOFC. This condition, which is pervasive across languages, does not follow from established notions of the relation between structure and order and therefore presents a challenge for syntactic theory that must be met. The chapter reviewed four theories of the mapping of structure to word order purporting to explain FOFC, all compatible with the assumption that narrow syntax is order-free. The first theory, proposed in Holmberg 2000a, is based on the classical version of the LCA according to which head-final order is necessarily derived by phrasal movement, combined with the idea that selection in the syntax requires/is mapped to adjacency at LF (the head-initial case) or PF (the head-final case).

The second theory, articulated in BHR 2014, is also based on the version of the LCA according to which head-final order is necessarily derived by movement of the sister of the head and is, in this sense, the marked alternative. In BHR's theory, the mark of head-final order is a movement-triggering feature associated with the categorial feature [±V], defining extended projections. FOFC is an effect of how this movement feature "spreads," or projects, throughout an extended projection via c-selection, subject to Relativized Minimality.

The third theory reviewed, articulated in Sheehan 2011, 2013a,b, assumes that head-complement order is encoded as a lexically specified, inherent property of lexical categories. This lexical "directionality specification" determines the order of a head and its complement at PF. However, because the grammar is universally required to unambiguously determine the linear relation between every pair of terminals in a syntactic domain, the lexical linear specifications are typically not sufficient. Asymmetric c-command is also required to order specifiers and disharmonic combinations of heads, explaining why it is precisely these items that display Kaynean asymmetries. Sheehan assumes that the role of the LCA is to determine the linear relation between categories not ordered by virtue of these lexical specifications. One consequence of this system is that it explains FOFC, in that the FOFC-violating order cannot be derived.

The fourth theory is based on the theory of head movement in Roberts 2010a. As in Holmberg 2000a, the selection relation between a head α and its complement βP, where α and β are in the same extended projection, can be accompanied by head movement of β to α, or (unlike in Holmberg 2000a) by head movement of β to α with pied-piping of the remnant βP to Spec,αP. If the second option offers the only way a complement of α can end up as a specifier of αP, hence the only way it can end up immediately preceding α, then FOFC will always be observed, because a FOFC-violating structure is underivable.

In subsequent chapters, these theories—particularly the second and third— will be put to use in dissecting a variety of constructions exhibiting effects of FOFC, in a variety of languages. The four theories reviewed here are not the only ones in the literature purporting to explain FOFC. There are also proposals to the effect that FOFC can be explained in terms of conditions on speech processing; these are discussed in chapter 5. Another proposal is articulated in Philip 2012 in terms of an Optimality Theory–based theory of syntax; see BHR 2014 for some critical remarks on this proposal.

5 The Final-over-Final Condition and Processing

Michelle Sheehan

5.1 Introduction

It has often been claimed that word order universals lie beyond the remit of Universal Grammar (UG) and stem ultimately from parsing/processing principles or patterns of diachronic change rather than grammatical principles per se (see Hawkins 1994, 2004, Newmeyer 2005, Whitman 2008, Abels and Neeleman 2009, 2012). For this reason, it is worth assessing whether the Final-over-Final Condition (FOFC), too, might stem from processing pressures operative either synchronically or diachronically. Note that the FOFC asymmetry raises some interesting issues in this regard as it is an asymmetry concerning the ordering of *heads*, whereas most other word order asymmetries concern the ordering of *specifiers/phrases* (see Cinque 2005a, Richards 2008b, Abels and Neeleman 2009, 2012). Abels and Neeleman (2009) claim that all the word order asymmetries taken as evidence for the Linear Correspondence Axiom (LCA) can be reduced to a ban on rightward movement, which has a direct motivation from parsing: the need for fillers to precede gaps. FOFC, notably, seems to be different in this regard as it is not immediately clear how it could be derived from a ban on rightward movement. To this extent, then, FOFC appears to be crucial evidence that the ordering of heads is also subject to the same kind of left-right asymmetry associated with the ordering of phrases. This is not to say, though, that FOFC requires the LCA. It is of course possible that some other processing pressure is directly (or indirectly) responsible for FOFC. At least two such potential explanations have been proposed in the literature: Hawkins's (1994) Early Immediate Constituents and Cecchetto's (2013) restriction on backward dependencies. This chapter considers these two approaches and evaluates whether FOFC can be explained purely by processing pressures.

The remainder of the chapter is structured as follows. Section 5.2 introduces Hawkins's (1994) account of FOFC, which connects it to the more general preference for harmony in linguistic systems. Section 5.3 introduces a different approach developed by Cecchetto (2013), which attributes the effect to a restriction on backward Agree, assimilating FOFC to Ross's (1967) Right Roof Constraint. Section 5.4 considers the predictions of these accounts and argues that they face certain serious challenges. Section 5.5 considers the way that processing interacts with grammar in the approaches in question and argues that even the accounts in chapter 4 might ultimately be attributed to a processing effect, albeit indirectly. Section 5.6 broadens the discussion to include phonology, identifying a striking similarity between the Onset Maximization Principle and FOFC. Finally, section 5.7 concludes and outlines some matters for future research.

5.2   Hawkins 1994

One highly articulated processing-based account of word order is Hawkins's (1994, 2004) Performance-Grammar Correspondence Hypothesis (PGCH). While Hawkins's approach is well-known and highly influential as an account of the predominance of word order harmony in natural language, it is less well-known as an account of the FOFC asymmetry (but see Cecchetto 2013, Sheehan 2013a for discussion). Interestingly, though, Hawkins's (1994) Early Immediate Constituents, which gives rise to the preference for harmony, also provides an elegant account of (a statistical version of) FOFC.[1]

Hawkins (1994) proposes the following processing principle:

(1) *Early Immediate Constituents (EIC)*
    The human parser prefers linear orders that maximize the I[mmediate]
    C[onstituents]-to-non-I[mmediate]C[onstituents] ratios of Constituent
    Recognition Domains. (Hawkins 1994:77)

Immediate constituents (ICs) are the constituents required to identify a certain grammatical category/phrase. For example, a transitive VP consists of two ICs: the category V, which is constructed by the verb, and the category NP, which is constructed by the determiner or noun (assuming, as is standard in X-bar theory, that lexical items are distinct from category projections).[2] Hawkins defines *Constituent Recognition Domain* and *IC-to-non-IC ratio* as follows:

(2) *Constituent Recognition Domain (CRD)*
    The CRD for a phrasal mother node M consists of the set of terminal
    and non-terminal nodes that must be parsed in order to recognize M and
    all ICs of M, proceeding from the terminal node in the parse string that
    constructs the first IC on the left, to the terminal node that constructs

the last IC on the right, and including all intervening terminal nodes and the non-terminal nodes they construct. (Hawkins 1994:58–59)

(3) IC-to-non-IC ratio = $\dfrac{\text{Number of ICs in domain}}{\text{Number of non-IC nodes in domain}}$

As Hawkins acknowledges, the number of non-IC nodes in a given structure will vary depending on a number of independent syntactic assumptions (i.e., binary vs. ternary branching, heads and movements posited, and—more pertinently nowadays—X-bar theory vs. bare phrase structure, the vP-Internal Subject Hypothesis). To avoid entering into such issues, Hawkins also provides a simplified IC-to-word ratio, which factors out syntactic assumptions and gives results broadly similar to the IC-to-non-IC ratio:[3]

(4) IC-to-word ratio = $\dfrac{\text{Number of ICs in domain}}{\text{Number of words in domain}}$

Finally, Hawkins proposes that the ratio for a CRD is the average of the scores for all IC-to-word ratios calculated left to right:

(5) *Calculating left-to-right IC-to-non-IC ratios*
     The left-to-right IC-to-non-IC ratio for a nonoptimal CRD is measured by first counting the ICs in the domain from left to right (starting from 1) and then counting the non-ICs (or words alone) in the domain (again starting from 1). The first IC is then divided by the total number of non-ICs that it dominates (e.g., 1/2); the second IC is divided by the highest total for the non-ICs that it dominates (e.g., if this IC dominates the third through seventh non-ICs in the domain, then 2/7 is the ratio for the second IC); and so on for all subsequent ICs. The ratio for each IC is expressed as a percentage, and these percentages are then aggregated to achieve a score for the whole CRD. (adapted from Hawkins 1994:82)

According to Hawkins, these processing principles predict that harmonic head-initial and head-final constructions should be most common crosslinguistically, as these kinds of structures are optimal in terms of processing, with CRD and ratios as small as possible. Consider, by way of illustration, the harmonic orders for VPs containing an adpositional complement, with English words for illustration purposes (Hawkins 1994:96–97):

(6) [$_{VP}$ [$_V$ **go**] [$_{PP}$ [$_P$ **to**] [$_{NP}$ school]]]   IC-to-word ratio = 1/1, 2/2
          1   2   average = 100%

(7) [$_{VP}$ [$_{PP}$ [$_{NP}$ school] [$_P$ **to**]] [$_V$ **go**]]   IC-to-word ratio = 1/1, 2/2
               1   2   average =100%

In both (6) and (7), the NP-complement of P is not included in the CRD of VP because NP is an IC of PP but not of VP. In (6), the IC-to-word ratio of V (the first IC) is 1/1, as the word *go* serves to construct it (though at this point it remains unclear whether the V is transitive, intransitive, ditransitive, etc.). The IC-to-word ratio of PP is 2/2, as the second IC (PP) dominates only the second word contained in the CRD of VP, namely, *to*. The average IC-to-word ratio is therefore 100%, as the number of words is exactly equal to the number of ICs constructed. In (7), a similar effect holds, except that this time the head-final language is constructed "bottom up." Once again, the NP is not included in the CRD of VP. As a result, the CRD begins with *to*, which constructs the first IC of VP, namely, PP. Because NP is outside the CRD of VP, PP dominates only the first word in the CRD (*to*), giving it an optimal 1/1 IC-to-word ratio. Similarly, the word *go* constructs the second IC of VP, and V also dominates the second word in the CRD (*go*). Once again, the average of these two IC-to-word ratios yields a perfect 100%, as two adjacent words serve to construct the two ICs of VP. For this reason, Hawkins's approach means that harmonically head-final and harmonically head-initial structures are equally optimal in processing terms. If frequency correlates with processing efficiency, then Hawkins's EIC theory predicts that harmonic structures will be most frequent in the world's languages.

But EIC also yields more subtle predictions in relation to the two disharmonic combinations, as Hawkins (1994:255) notes, where NP-complements of P are necessarily included in the CRD of VP. He gives the following IC-to-word ratios, assuming that V and P are single words and that NP comprises a determiner and a noun:

(8) $[_{VP}$ $[_{V}$ **go**$]$ $[_{PP}$ $[_{NP}$ the shops$]$ $[_{P}$ **to**$]]]$ IC-to-word-ratio = 1/1, 2/4
      1   2   3   4   average = 75%

(9) $[_{VP}$ $[_{PP}$ $[_{P}$ **to**$]$ $[_{NP}$ the shops$]]$ $[_{V}$ **go**$]]$ IC-to-word ratio = **1/3**, 2/4
      1   2   3   4   average = 42%

In (8), the first word *go* constructs the first IC of VP, V, giving an IC-to-word ratio of 1/1. The second IC of VP (PP) is constructed by *to*. Now PP dominates the second through fourth words in the CRD, and so the IC-to-word ratio of PP is 2/4. The aggregate IC-to-word ratio is thus 75% for this word order. In (9), on the other hand, the first IC that is constructed is PP. In this case, PP dominates the first through third words in the CRD of VP (*to*, *the*, and *shops*). According to the definition in (5), then, the first IC-to-word ratio in (9) is 1/3. The IC-to-word ratio of the second IC (i.e., V) is 2/4 because the IC V dominates the fourth word in the CRD (*go*). Therefore, (9) has a substantially lower efficiency rate of 42%. Moreover, the greater the number of words in the intervening NP constituent, the larger the difference in efficiency between the two disharmonic word orders will be. In effect, the NP-complement of P is parsed twice in (9): once in the construction of the first IC (PP), and again in the construction of the second IC (V). Crucially, this makes the prediction that structures/orders like (9) will be less efficient to process, and hence less frequent than those in (8). As (9) is the FOFC-violating order, this version of the PGCH thus appears to derive a statistical FOFC from independently justifiable principles of efficient processing.[4]

In these terms, FOFC reduces to the fact that (i) CRDs are constructed left to right and (ii) higher heads are privileged in constructing more independent ICs. Another way to think of this is that, in a sequence head-phrase-head, the most economical way to parse it is head-[phrase-head] rather than [head-phrase]-head. The prediction, then, is that this parsing preference will be reflected in the linear orders of the world's languages. We will see below that these predictions seem to hold, though the numbers of FOFC violations are very small in all cases, arguably lower than Hawkins's account predicts. However, the PGCH also makes other predictions, which are not so well-supported. Crucially, it predicts that where two categories display a typological preference for harmony, they will also display a FOFC effect and vice versa.[5] This is because the same principle that gives rise to the preference for harmony (i.e., EIC) also gives rise to FOFC. While there might be additional (historical/sociolinguistic) factors that skew the typological sample away from harmony, where this happens, these same factors should also serve to rule *in* a FOFC-violating order. The prediction of EIC is therefore biconditional:

(10) The crosslinguistic preference for harmony between X and Y will hold if and only if FOFC holds between X and Y.

We will see below that there is suggestive evidence against such a biconditional relation. But first, we consider an alternative processing-based account of FOFC, proposed by Cecchetto 2013.

5.3 Cecchetto 2013

Cecchetto (2013) derives the FOFC asymmetry from the following grammatical principle, which he takes to be operative in the syntactic component, presumably universally, motivated by processing pressures:

(11) In a forward dependency, Agree can be cross-phrasal. In a backward dependency, Agree is phrase-bound. (Cecchetto 2013:77)

Assuming that Agree underlies all syntactic dependencies (see Chomsky 2000, 2001), it follows from (11) that any rightward dependency will have to be very local, whereas leftward dependencies can be cross-phrasal, hence longer-distance.[6] This, Cecchetto claims, serves to assimilate FOFC to the Right Roof Constraint, which states that rightward movement cannot cross a phrase boundary (12), as both involve a backward Agree dependency, if indeed selection, like movement, involves Agree. In order for this to work, it must be that selection is a relation between heads in the normal case:

(12) a. $[YP_i [_{ZP} \ldots t_i]]$
b. $*[[_{ZP} \ldots t_i] YP_i]^7$

(13) a. $[X [_{YP} Y\ldots]]$
b. $*[[_{YP} Y\ldots] X]$

The problem with FOFC, then, is that X in (13b) cannot backward-select a head in a lower phrase. In (13a), on the other hand, this is possible because the dependency is "forward" and so can be cross-phrasal. Despite the initial appeal of this parallel, a number of questions arise in relation to this account. First, there is a potential issue with the parallel itself. In filler-gap dependencies, the gap is dependent on the filler and not vice versa according to Cecchetto.[8] In selection, however, he argues that a head is dependent on its complement and not vice versa, on the basis that truncation is only possible at the top of a given structure. By way of example, Cecchetto (citing Belletti 1990) provides the following licit case of truncation from Italian absolute small clauses:

(14) Mangiata   la mela,   Gianni mori.   [Italian]
eaten   the apple   Gianni died
'Having eaten the apple, Gianni died.'

Although ellipsis of complements is of course also possible in many contexts, something that Cecchetto does not discuss, there is a sense in which the complement in ellipsis contexts like (15) is still present in the structure, and this is plausibly not the case where the upper portion of a sentence is missing as in (14):

(15) John ate an apple and Mary did too.

The elided VP is semantically present in (15) in that its content is recoverable from the antecedent VP in the preceding clause, whereas there is simply no tense information in the absolute clause in (14). There is a sense, then, in which the selection dependency can be argued to be unidirectional, like the filler-gap dependency, with a head being dependent on its complement and not vice versa. The particular parallel that Cecchetto draws in this instance, however, seems problematic. If filler-gap counts as a forward dependency because the gap is dependent on the filler, as Cecchetto proposes, and gap-filler, conversely, counts as a backward dependency, then comp-head should also count as forward dependency as it is the head that is dependent on its complement and not vice versa. This means that it should be head-comp that counts as a backward dependency. But this seems to make exactly the wrong predictions, as in this case head-comp selection relations would be restricted to phrase-internal contexts and FOFC would be left unexplained.

Even leaving this potential objection to one side, the approach faces other challenges. As Cecchetto (2013) acknowledges, one serious challenge is that (11), rather than ruling out [[head-complement]-head] orders per se, actually rules out selection between any two heads in a harmonic head-final sequence. In these terms, then, there is nothing especially bad about FOFC; head-finality more generally is incompatible with straightforward head-head selection. How then does Cecchetto address the fact that harmonic head-finality is an extremely common property of natural-language structures, arguably the most common word order (see Dryer 2015f)? Cecchetto notes that this ban on selection only applies as long as selection is conceived of as a relation between two heads, as in (13b), adapted here:

(16) *$[[_{YP} Y_{[F]}...] X_{[uF]}]$

According to (11), backward Agree must be phrase-internal and X is external to the phrase containing Y. Cecchetto claims, however, that in such cases a selection relation *is* possible between X and the entire phrasal complement YP. In such contexts, crucially, head movement—the usual means of creating fusional categories—is predicted to be banned as there is no head-head dependency. For this reason, it is predicted that head-final orders will be incompatible with head movement and/or fusional morphology. As evidence for this prediction, Cecchetto notes a statistical correlation between head-finality and agglutinating morphology.

A potential problem is that this solution appears to undermine Cecchetto's approach as an account of FOFC, as in such cases the selected phrase could be either head-final or head-initial, in the latter case violating FOFC:

(17) a. $[[_{YP [F]} ZP Y] X_{[uF]}]$
    b. $[[_{YP [F]} Y ZP] X_{[uF]}]$

As Cecchetto notes, the possibility of phrasal selection in such contexts appears to account for the fact that FOFC fails to hold across extended projections, if one assumes that verbs select DPs rather than Ds. If phrasal selection is generally available in harmonically head-final systems, though, why is it not always available in the FOFC-violating structure? What prevents an auxiliary verb from selecting VP, rather than V, ruling in *[[V O] Aux] structures? This problem seems particularly serious in systems displaying variable word order, such as Old English, Hungarian, Basque, and Finnish, where head-final sequences are perfectly possible and yet the FOFC-violating order is banned.

5.4   A Comparison of the Various Approaches to FOFC

5.4.1   On Statistical FOFC Effects
Both Hawkins and Cecchetto propose that the FOFC-violating order is ruled out because it is difficult to parse. For Hawkins, this is because it is an inefficient way to construct immediate constituents online: a phrase intervening between two heads is better parsed with the following head than the preceding one. For Cecchetto, the selection dependency, like all dependencies, must operate left to right as this is the order of the march of time, and only very local dependencies are possible in the opposite direction. For Cecchetto, though, FOFC arises because of a hard-wired principle of UG and so the effect is predicted to be absolute. For Hawkins, on the other hand, the FOFC order is dispreferred by the parser but not ruled out by UG. Therefore, the PGCH, unlike Cecchetto's approach and those discussed in chapter 4, does not completely rule out the possibility of FOFC-violating orders. Rather, it predicts that they will be infrequent and certainly less frequent than harmonic or inverse-FOFC orders. Presumably, over time such orders are predicted to die out, under the pressure for grammars to favor more efficient word orders.

Moreover, IC-to-word ratios are also influenced by the relative "heaviness" of the constituents involved, and the implication is that average relative weights might affect grammaticalization trends (see Hawkins 2013 for discussion). For this reason, the PGCH predicts that whether the structure [[Y ZP] X] is permitted may be (i) directly sensitive to heaviness of ZP or (ii) sensitive to the category of Z, where different categories have different average weights. For example, the FOFC-violating order would be expected to surface more frequently with lighter categories like DP and less frequently with heavier categories like CP (which typically contain more constituents/words).

5.4.2   Exceptions to FOFC
It remains to be seen, then, whether EIC can successfully account for apparent exceptions to FOFC. In their discussion of FOFC, Biberauer, Holmberg, and Roberts (2014) note certain kinds of counterexamples and propose that FOFC

holds only within extended projections. The reason they introduce this proviso is that DP complements of V, which surface in a preverbal position, are head-initial in some well-studied languages like German.

(18) Johann hat   das/ein Buch   ausgeliehen.   [German]
     Johann has   the/a   book   borrowed
     'Johann borrowed the/a book.'

In fact, there are relatively few OV languages with clear determiners in which DPs surface as the complements of V. Most OV languages either (i) lack determiners distinct from demonstratives (which are plausibly specifiers rather than heads) or (ii) have final determiners (see Dryer 1992:104). It is also noteworthy that it has been claimed that all OV languages permit scrambling (Kayne 2004; though the Ugric languages Khanti and Mansi seem to be rare counterexamples to this trend). Under one approach, scrambling, like differential object marking more generally, targets all DPs, with only structurally truncated NPs remaining in situ (Richards 2008a). If this analysis is along the right lines, then D-initial OV languages with the relevant DPs surfacing inside VP may not actually exist, making a more general version of FOFC possible. This raises the question of the status of indefinite articles. If, as argued in Sheehan 2011, they are specifiers rather than heads, then the indefinite in (18) may also fail to counterexemplify FOFC. In short, OV languages with initial articles are no less common (taking into account areal and genetic factors) than VO languages with final articles. Descriptively speaking, then, there is no FOFC effect between V and a DP complement. Depending on the status of indefinite articles and the position of DPs, this may or may not require additional restrictions to be built into formal accounts of FOFC. But what about processing-based accounts?

Hawkins's approach is concerned primarily with surface word order rather than syntactic structure, so the fact that DPs often scramble in OV languages will only be relevant to the extent that additional material between a verb and its complement creates longer CRDs. Hawkins (2013) rejects Abney's (1987) DP Hypothesis and assumes that NPs comprise Det and N in a flat structure, with either being sufficient to construct an NP. For this reason, N-initial and Det-initial nominals are equally efficient in processing terms, as both can effectively function as the head of NP.[9] As Hawkins notes, though, initial determiners will carry a processing advantage only in non-N-initial VO languages; in N-initial languages, they will make no difference, and in non-N-initial OV languages they will actually increase the CRD of VP. For this reason, the order D-NP-V *should* arguably be dispreferred compared with V-NP-D, as the former but not the latter carries a processing disadvantage. It seems, then, that EIC *does* predict a FOFC effect in this domain, despite the flat structure assumed for NP/DP. Recall, however, that EIC is sensitive to the relative heaviness of phrases. It therefore follows that DPs, tending to be light, might allow FOFC violations more often than other heavier categories like PP and CP from a crosslinguistic perspective.[10] Hence, the lack of a skewing between the two disharmonic combinations of article, NP, and V might not be a serious problem for EIC.

A complication for this view arises, however, from Dryer's (1992:103) observation that articles are nonetheless verb patterners, in that they tend to be phrase-initial in VO languages and phrase-final in OV languages. It is not clear why the lightness of a given phrase would be sufficient to render it immune to FOFC but not to the preference for harmony. Of course, the preference for harmony in this domain might have an independent (diachronic) motivation, but it is implicit in Hawkins's approach that diachronic processes should also be motivated by EIC. The facts seem to suggest, then, that FOFC and the preference for harmony might not stem from the same processing principle, contrary to the predictions of EIC. We will return to this issue below.

As noted above, Cecchetto (2013) proposes to accommodate the lack of a FOFC effect between V and DP by proposing that V selects for a DP rather than the head D. While this is a simple way to accommodate this kind of exception, some independent criteria are required regarding when and why a head selects for a phrase rather than a head (as also noted above). Without any such criteria, it is not clear what other predictions are made regarding where FOFC should fail to hold. Turning to PP-complements of V, for example, discussed next, it is not clear whether they are predicted to pattern with DP-complements or not. It is therefore difficult to assess how well Cecchetto's (2013) account can accommodate apparent exceptions to FOFC, and I do not discuss it further in this regard.

Biberauer, Holmberg, and Roberts (2007, 2008, 2014) do discuss this other kind of exception to FOFC involving prepositional phrases in OV languages. Once again, German provides a relevant example:

(19) Sie ist [$_{VP}$ [$_{PP}$ nach Berlin] gefahren].   [German]
      she is   to   Berlin   driven
      'She went to Berlin.'

Despite a small number of robust counterexamples, though, it appears that there is crosslinguistic evidence of a FOFC skewing between PP-complements and V. First, the raw data from Dryer 2015a,e indicate that there are more inverse-FOFC than FOFC-violating languages, and that the former occur in more macroareas and represent a more genetically diverse group than the small

Table 5.1
Languages with disharmony between the ordering of VP and the ordering of PP

	FOFC-violating P-NP and OV	Inverse-FOFC NP-P and VO
Languages	12[a]	38
Macroareas	3	5
Language families	5	16
Genera	8	22

[a]I have added German and Dutch to this category although they are categorized as having mixed order of verb and object in WALS because of their V2 property.

number of FOFC-violating languages (see table 5.1). These data seem to be consistent with the spirit of EIC, whereby FOFC is a statistical rather than a categorical effect, as there appear to be a number of languages that allow the FOFC-violating combination, though this order is dispreferred. Note, however, that WALS contains data about the directionality of PP and VP but does not consider the actual placement of head-initial and head-final PPs in otherwise OV and VO languages. An examination of the 12 P-NP OV languages reveals that many of them, despite being OV, require PPs to be postverbal, meaning that the surface FOFC-violating construction *[[P DP] V] does not actually occur.

Of the 12 languages, only the Indo-European languages (German, Dutch, Persian, Tajik, Kurdish, and Sorbian) and the Semitic language Tigré appear to allow the word order P-DP-V. The other languages all either lack true adpositions or are languages in which PPs appear in a postverbal position. Mangarrayi (Australian, Mangarrayi, Northern Territories) lacks true prepositions according to Merlan (1989:26); instead, it has "prepositional-like phrases consisting of an adverb followed by a noun appropriately case-marked to complement the combined meaning of the adverb and verb in the clause." Moreover, the order of the adverb and its complement is not fixed; both adv-comp and comp-adv are possible. Therefore, it is not clear that Mangarrayi is a true exception to FOFC. Moreover, in Päri (Nilo-Saharan, Nilotic, Sudan), Tobelo (West Papuan, North Halmaheran, Indonesia), Iraqw (Afro-Asiatic, Southern Cushitic, Tanzania), and Neo-Aramaic (Afro-Asiatic, Semitic, Israel), PP-complements to V seem to surface in a postverbal position (see Sheehan 2013a), as the following examples illustrate:

(20) á-lw'ʌʌr'   kí   kwàc   [Päri]
     1SG-fear   PREP   leopard
     'I am afraid of leopards.'
     (Anderson 1988:303)

(21) lăbulmunne   [ta-Bagdàd]   [Neo-Aramaic]
     take.me   to-Baghdad
     'Take me to Baghdad!'
     (Khan 1999:338)

(22) i-na   ta'⟨a'⟩ín   [ay dí-r   konkomo]   [Iraqw]
     S-PAST run⟨HAB⟩3SGM   to place.F-CON cock
     'He ran to the cock.'
     (Mous 1993:100)

In Päri, this is obligatory (Anderson 1988:303), as it is in all dialects of Neo-Aramaic (Geoffrey Khan, pers. comm.). There is insufficient information to say the same for Iraqw, though all examples suggest it to be the case.[11] Matters are slightly less clear in Tobelo.[12] This means that the number of languages displaying FOFC violations of this type is extremely small, so that [[P DP] V] is far rarer than the inverse-FOFC order [V [DP P]]. If this were not a FOFC effect, but merely an effect of the preference for harmony, then there would also be no explanation for the fact that postpositional phrases in VO languages are rarely preposed (see Dryer 1992:92).

These data can be accommodated by EIC, if they are taken to indicate a statistical FOFC effect. PP is a relatively "light" IC, so FOFC violations between V and PP are predicted to be typologically rare but not impossible. In these terms, Germanic, Persian, and Tigré are not optimal for processing purposes, but not ruled out by UG. Moreover, optional PP-extraposition is available to varying degrees in the languages in question, meaning that the problematic surface order P-NP-V may be avoided to a certain extent in usage. This raises the question, though, why German has not lost preverbal PPs over time.

Therefore, in a sense, a statistical FOFC asymmetry appears to be attested between PP and V, and this is potentially evidence against approaches that predict FOFC to be absolute and in favor of EIC as an analysis of FOFC. That said, the fact that the counterexamples are so small in number and largely genetically related means that an independent explanation for their exceptional behavior may well be possible, and the condition need not yet be abandoned as a hard condition. Whether this is plausible more generally depends on the status of counterexamples to the condition in other domains. Bazalgette et al. (2012) compare all the head-complement pairs from *WALS* pairwise, relative to their hierarchical rankings. As FOFC holds transitively through the clause, any head-initial phrase that is lower than a head-final phrase represents a FOFC violation. Inverse FOFC is the reverse disharmonic combination, and the two harmonic combinations speak for themselves. Figure 5.1 shows the results of this comparison regardless of extended projections. What these data seem to

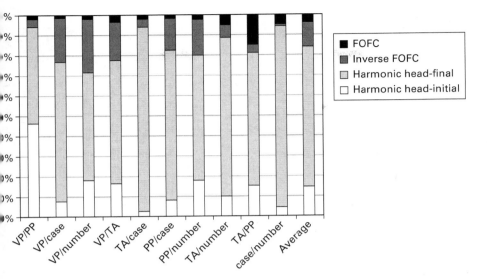

Figure 5.1
The four word order combinations across categories (from Bazalgette et al. 2012). TA = tense/
aspect marker

suggest is that there is a very general FOFC effect, with the exception of TA/
PP and case/number combinations. In all other cases, the harmonic head-final
combination is dominant and the inverse-FOFC order is strongly preferred to
the FOFC order. In most cases, the number of counterexamples is very small
indeed, but again, they require closer examination if one wants to maintain the
idea that FOFC is a hard condition. Note also that in some cases the inverse-
FOFC order is preferred over the harmonic head-initial order. For this reason,
these data present a different problem for Hawkins's approach: there appear
to be cases where FOFC holds between X and Y without X and Y displaying
any tendency toward harmony. This is problematic if both stem from the same
processing principle, an issue to which we now turn.

5.4.3   The Relation between FOFC and Harmony
According to the PGCH, harmony and FOFC are two effects of the same
processing principle (EIC). The clear prediction, given in (10), is that if two
categories show a preference for harmony, then they should also show a FOFC
skewing and vice versa. The other approaches to FOFC, including Cecchetto's
(2013), make no such prediction. Rather, they predict that the preference for
harmony between two categories may be neutralized for some independent
reason, but FOFC will always hold.

Table 5.2
Typological positioning of Polarity heads and complementizers (from Dryer 2015b,g)

Type	Position of Pol	Position of C	Number of languages (genera: families)
A	Initial	Initial	72: 35: 13 (78)
B	Final	Final	45: 33: 20 (46)
C	Final	Initial	74: 40: 16 (82)
D	Initial	Final	4: 3: 3 (4)

Some categories display both a preference for harmony and a FOFC effect. This is the case for Aux and VP, V and PP, C and VP, and V and CP (Dryer 1992). For this reason, these pairs of categories are well-behaved by the standards of EIC. Potentially more problematic for EIC is the fact that according to Dryer (1992), articles are also verb patterners, but not subject to FOFC effects crosslinguistically (see previous discussion). Polar question particles seem to display the opposite pattern. From a functional perspective, question particles (Pol) arguably serve to identify a polar question, and C serves to construct an embedded clause. For this reason, it is surprising that according to the data in table 5.2, the disharmonic inverse-FOFC combination of initial C and final Pol is more common than the harmonic combinations in terms of languages and genera and almost as common in terms of language families. There is thus no evidence of a preference for harmony between C and Pol. Crucially, though, FOFC appears to hold in this domain (see chapter 2). Once again, then, we witness the independence of harmony and FOFC: the same two categories display a FOFC effect but no preference for harmony. This is highly problematic for EIC, which attributes both FOFC and the preference for harmony to the same processing principle. Of course, it remains an open question why there is no harmonic preference between Pol and C.[13] What is clear, though, is that in such cases FOFC effects cannot straightforwardly be attributed to EIC.

5.4.4 Interim Conclusions
Given the previous discussion, it is arguably the case that Cecchetto's (2013) processing-based account of FOFC fares better empirically than Hawkins's (1994), as it does not tie the effect to a preference for harmony. On a deeper level, though, Cecchetto's approach faces many challenges. First, Hawkins captures the FOFC asymmetry without attaching any specific parsing cost to harmonically head-final systems, whereas Cecchetto is forced to assume a wholly distinct selection mechanism in head-final systems. While Cecchetto's observation that many head-final systems are agglutinating or lack head movement is interesting, the idea that head-finality might pose a parsing difficulty

seems unmotivated. The availability of this selection mechanism is thus suspect and actually undermines the approach as an account of FOFC. Second, Hawkins's attempt to assimilate the FOFC effect to the preference for harmony, while empirically problematic for the reasons discussed above, is still less problematic than Cecchetto's attempt to assimilate FOFC to the Right Roof Constraint. As discussed above, the Right Roof Constraint seems to be opposite to head-finality (and FOFC) in some respects, as it constrains when a filler can follow a (dependent) gap, whereas head-finality is a case where a head (dependent) follows its complement. Therefore, both processing-based accounts of FOFC discussed here face certain serious problems. This does not mean that no processing-based account of the effect is possible, however. Indeed, the fact that a statistical version of FOFC appears to hold across extended projections—and even, as we will see, at the level of phonology—strongly suggests that the ultimate explanation for FOFC may well stem from parsing. In the next section, we turn to this matter and to a proposal that the existing "formal" accounts of FOFC may be attributed at some level to the preferences of the parser.

5.5   The Effect of the Parser on Grammar

Another important difference between the two approaches to FOFC discussed here is the relationship they posit between the parser and the narrow syntax. For Cecchetto (2013), the restriction on backward dependencies is a (universal?) principle of grammar that "biologizes" a preference of the parser (to use Kiparsky's (2008) term). For Hawkins (1994), the relationship between the parser and the grammar (of a specific language) is actually more indirect; his claim appears to be that languages change over time according to the preferences of the parser, so that this relationship is always mediated by language use. For this reason, the innate component of grammar itself is not affected by parsing pressures; only the grammars of specific languages are (see also Newmeyer 2005, 2006). Of the two possibilities, Hawkins's seems the less problematic. The idea that principles of UG could be functionally motivated seems problematic and inconsistent with the apparent fact that language evolved very quickly, without intermediate stages of selection of the kind proposed by Pinker and Bloom (1990). But Hawkins's approach is not all that satisfactory either: if the relationship between the parser and the grammar of particular languages were always messily mediated by "language use," we might expect to find more counterexamples to FOFC than we actually do. More generally, we might expect asymmetries of the kind discussed by Kayne (1994) (see section 4.4) to be less striking and more statistical than absolute.

Of course, it is true that there are some apparent counterexamples to FOFC (see chapters 4 and 9, and above), but these seem to be fairly small in number and the condition seems to hold in several instances where languages otherwise have very free word order.

Biberauer et al. (2010b) and Biberauer, Roberts, and Sheehan (2014) propose a role for the parser that falls between these two extremes, whereby parsing preferences shape the grammar of a particular language within the limits imposed by UG by exerting a pressure during acquisition. This has the effect of creating a *no-choice parameter* whereby language learners are given "an offer they cannot refuse." As the authors observe, formal accounts of word order asymmetries that rely on the LCA face a problem: the form of the LCA itself seems to be a stipulation. Is it a principle of UG? It is easy to see why natural language would have to rely on syntactic relations such as c-command in the mapping from hierarchical structure to linear order. What does not follow from anything is why asymmetric c-command should map to precedence rather than subsequence. It is also easy to see that the fact that asymmetric c-command maps to precedence rather than subsequence (the two logically given options) might stem from parsing pressures (see Crain and Fodor 1985). However, making the LCA a principle of UG in this way effectively biologizes the requirements of the parser, as in Cecchetto's approach. Biberauer et al. (2010b) and Biberauer, Roberts, and Sheehan (2014) propose, as an alternative, that the LCA (or the revised LCA in Sheehan 2013a,b) is an emergent parameter of UG. Every language must get from hierarchical structure to linear order using syntactic dependencies. Whether these syntactic dependencies map to precedence or subsequence is simply not specified by UG, and the child must decide which option to take during acquisition, as a parametric choice. The parser, which exerts a pressure on language acquisition, strongly prefers the precedence option and so the LCA is effectively a nochoice parameter. Therefore, it could be argued that the preferences of the parser are the ultimate explanation for FOFC (and other word order asymmetries). The parser forces a linearization parameter to be set to precedence for parsing reasons, triggering a number of more arbitrary word order asymmetries as side effects, notably FOFC (see also Abels and Neeleman 2009, 2012 for a subtly different proposal).

5.6 The Onset Maximization Principle

Thus far, it has been argued that the two existing processing-based accounts of FOFC face certain problems but that "formal" accounts based on the LCA (discussed in chapter 4) might actually be ultimately grounded in the requirements of the parser.[14] An interesting parallel to FOFC found in the domain of phonology suggests that matters may be even more complex than this and that there may be more to say about the ultimate explanation for FOFC, an issue that is left open here.

If we assume that vowels/nuclei are equivalent to syntactic heads and consonants are equivalent to phrases, then a well-known proposed principle of phonology turns out to be very similar indeed to a linear version of FOFC. The Onset Maximization Principle prefers consonants to be grouped with a following rather than a preceding nucleus (as an onset rather than a coda, subject to partially language-specific prosodic/phonotactic constraints) (Blevins 1995:230):

(23) */...VC-V.../
      /...V-CV.../

The preference in (23) for consonants to form a constituent with a following vowel in such contexts seems analogous to the preference to parse a phrase with a following head rather than a preceding one. As Itô (1989) shows, things get more complex (and language-specific) where an intervening consonant cluster is involved; however, where a single intervening consonant is present, the effect is fairly robust, a fact reflected typologically by the observation that many languages require all syllables to have onsets but no known language requires all syllables to have codas (Itô 1989:222).[15] For this reason, the sequence VCCV can be syllabified as /V-CCV/ or /VC-CV/, but not *VCC-V (ibid.).

While onset maximization seems tantalizingly similar to the FOFC asymmetry, it is not clear whether a unified account of both effects is possible or desirable. This is true, in part, because of the many obvious differences between syntax and phonology. One obvious difference is that syntax, unlike phonology, is hierarchically structured and recursive (see Tallerman 2006 for discussion). Although the syllable has a constituent structure, the only sense in which syllables might be considered to be hierarchically structured in relation to each other is in terms of prosodic features such as stress. The parallel is thus not perfect, as there seems to be no requirement for the final V in (23) to dominate the initial V in any real sense. If a unified account is to be provided for Onset Maximization and FOFC, then, it would need to be a linear account— and it is not clear whether a linear account will work for the syntactic version of FOFC, for the reasons outlined above and in chapters 2, 3, and 4.

It might be insightful, nonetheless, to consider previous accounts of Onset Maximization and examine whether they can be extended as analyses of FOFC. Unfortunately, there are not many such accounts, as Onset Maximization has largely been taken to be directly encoded in UG—as, for example, in Steriade's (1982) Universal Core Syllable Rule, which requires all syllables to be of the type CV, or in a more nuanced parameter, Itô's (1989) Onset Principle, which states that languages either *avoid* or *ban* onsetless syllables. Even in more recent Optimality Theory approaches, Onset Maximization is simply encoded as a universal preference (Prince and Smolensky 1993). Of course, it might be that Onset Maximization stems from some deeper parsing principle, plausibly connected to salience, but I leave a full investigation of this possibility to future research.

5.7 Conclusions and Unresolved Issues

This chapter has considered two potential accounts of the FOFC asymmetry stemming from processing pressures. It was argued that while both have certain (different) merits, they nonetheless face certain (different) problems. Hawkins's (1994) account, based on EIC, faces the problem that there does not appear to be a biconditional relationship between the preference for harmony between two categories and a FOFC skewing between those two categories. Though it does not face this empirical problem, Cecchetto's (2013) approach faces certain other challenges, notably from the frequency of head-final orders and the existence of FOFC effects even in languages otherwise permitting head-final sequences. It was nonetheless argued that the ultimate explanation for FOFC might stem from parsing pressures, if some version of the LCA can be rethought as a no-choice parameter along the lines proposed by Biberauer et al. (2010b) and Biberauer, Roberts, and Sheehan (2014).

Nonetheless, some issues remain unresolved. The Onset Maximization Principle, it was noted, bears certain superficial similarities to FOFC, and this— coupled with the fact that FOFC effects can be observed between pairs of categories in distinct extended projections—suggests that a syntax-based approach to FOFC may not be general enough. Hopefully, future research can address these questions and shed new light on the differences and similarities between phonology, morphology, and syntax (see also chapter 11).

6   The Final-over-Final Condition and Adverbs

Michelle Sheehan

6.1   Introduction

Thus far, much of the evidence given in favor of the Final-over-Final Condition (FOFC) comes from instances of complementation. Evidence suggests, however, that the relevant asymmetry might actually be a more pervasive phenomenon, as both Holmberg (2000a) and Biberauer, Holmberg, and Roberts (2007, 2008a,b) note in passing. Thus, Holmberg (2000a:140) observes that Finnish and Germanic verb clusters cannot be interrupted by either complements or adjuncts, as the following examples from Finnish illustrate:[1]

(1) Matti ei   (koskaan) ole (koskaan) käynyt (koskaan) Pariisissa. [Finnish]
     Matti not ever   has ever   visited ever   in.Paris
     'Matti has never been to Paris.'
     (Holmberg 2000a:145)

(2) Milloin Jussi romaanin kirjoittaa olisi   [Finnish]
     when   Jussi novel   write   would.have
     (siinä   tapauksessa) ehtinyt?
     in.that case   had.time
     'When would Jussi, in that case, have had time to write a novel?'
     (Holmberg 2000a:130)

(3) Milloin Jussi romaanin kirjoittaa ehtinyt   (*siinä   [Finnish]
     when   Jussi novel   write   had.time   in.that
     tapauksessa) olisi?
     case   would.have
     (same)
     (Holmberg 2000a:130)[2]

Example (1) shows that adverbs can intervene in harmonically head-initial sequences of verbal heads in Finnish, which occur obligatorily in sentences lacking an initial focus (see Holmberg 2000a and chapter 10). Example (2) shows that when a disharmonic order is licensed by *wh*-movement to the left periphery (see chapter 10), an adverb can still intervene between two verbal heads in a head-initial sequence. However, as example (3) shows, the same is not true in a head-final sequence. This suggests that the *[[V O] Aux] gap discussed in chapter 2, and taken as core evidence for FOFC, might actually be better characterized as a ban on *[[V X] Aux], changing the nature of the FOFC generalization somewhat.

An apparent challenge to extending the generalization in this way comes from the widely held view that the indivisibility of head-final sequences is a property only of languages with variable word order (or nonrigid OV languages), and not of languages with obligatory head-final verb clusters (or rigid OV languages). Thus, Cinque (1999:57), citing Kayne (1994:53) and Mahajan (1989:225ff.), claims that Hindi differs from German in allowing head-final verbal sequences to be broken up "by the negation word, emphatics and some adverbials."[3]

(4) raam roTii khaataa nahiiN/to/roz   thaa.   [Hindi]
    Ram bread eat.MSG not/emphatic/every.day was.MSG
    'Ram was not eating bread/was eating *bread*/was eating bread every day.'
    (Mahajan 1989:225)

Likewise, in agglutinating languages such as Turkish, [[V O] Aux] is not permitted but a (very similar) small class of adverbials can nonetheless intervene in the head-final verb cluster. Data of this kind thus provide potentially crucial evidence in favor of stating FOFC as a generalization over complementation. The objective of this chapter is to inspect linear strings with the order V-Adv-Aux in certain well-studied languages so as to ascertain their underlying hierarchical structure and thus their relevance to FOFC (which is, it seems, a generalization over the connection between hierarchical structure and linear order, not linear order per se). It is proposed that, contrary to what has previously been claimed, there is a general ban on *[[$_{VP}$ V X] Aux], so that the apparent distinction between Germanic/Finnish and Hindi/Turkish in this respect is illusory. It is further claimed, however, that this ban does not derive directly from FOFC; rather, it derives from the interaction between FOFC and an independent word order constraint noted by Ernst (2003).

Section 6.2 notes that Hungarian and Germanic pattern like Finnish, whereas Basque, Turkish, and Hindi appear superficially to allow head-final verb sequences to be interrupted by a small class of adverbials. Section 6.3 argues that these surface strings fail to have the structure [[$_{VP}$ V Adv] Aux]. In Turkish and Hindi, almost all V-Adv-Aux orders plausibly involve a harmonically head-final structure whereby what has been classed as an adverbial is actually a projecting emphatic head. Therefore, the possibility that FOFC, whatever its explanation, holds of adjuncts as well as complements remains highly plausible. Section 6.4 argues that this gap actually falls out from the combination of existing approaches to FOFC and a further asymmetry noted by Ernst, which bans post-VP adverbials in OV languages. Section 6.5 returns to a different class of V-Adv-Aux orders in Basque, which have a different constituent structure but still fail to violate FOFC. Section 6.6 concludes.

6.2   The Adjunction Asymmetry

6.2.1   Head-Initial Verb Sequences
Nonbranching adjuncts (and subjects) can often intervene in head-initial sequences of auxiliaries/verbs. Consider, for example, the following SVO and VSO languages:

(5) Jean a   **toujours** joué   de la guitare.   [French]
    Jean has always   played of the guitar
    'Jean has always played the guitar.'

(6) kan   **dima** yaʕzef ʕal   gitar   [Libyan Arabic]
    was.3SG always play   on.the guitar
    'He always used to play the guitar.'

(7) Bhí na sealgairí **tamall fada** *ag*   amharc orthu.   [Irish]
    was the hunters time   long PROG look   on.them
    'The hunters were watching them for a long time.'
    (Harley and Carnie 1997:14)

In Cinque's (1999) influential analysis of adverbials, these kinds of effects are taken as crucial evidence for the existence of an articulated sequence of functional heads, each housing a particular class of adverbs (see also Alexiadou 1997). Cinque argues at length that these functional heads can be the target of verb movement (in potentially idiosyncratic language-specific ways), so that the following difference between English and French reduces to a difference in verb movement trajectories (as Pollock (1989) first proposed):

(8)   I (always) play (*always) the guitar.

(9)   Je (*toujours) joue (toujours) de la guitare.   [French]
      I   always   play always   of the guitar
      'I always play the guitar.'

Cinque and Pollock further propose that language-internal variation in the order of verbs and adverbs has the same status as the contrast in (8)–(9). Thus, in Italian an inflected main verb targets any one of a range of functional heads but can raise no higher than the head housing the adverbial specifier *solitamente* 'usually' (Cardinaletti 2011:507, citing Cinque 1999:31, 180n80, 214n7; see also Schifano 2015 for a very fine-grained study of verb movement across Romance):

(10) a. ...* 'probably' * 'usually' (V) 'again' (V) 'often' (V) 'quickly' (V) *mica* (V) 'already' ...

    b. Gianni **spesso** telefona / telefona **spesso** di sera   tardi.   [Italian]
       Gianni often   calls   / calls   often of evening late
       'Gianni often calls late in the evening.'

    c. Gianni **di nuovo** lo merita   / lo merita   **di nuovo**.
       Gianni of new   it deserves / it deserves of new
       'Gianni again deserves it.'

    d. Gianni **solitamente** lo merita   / *lo merita   **solitamente**.
       Gianni usually   it deserves / it deserves usually
       'Gianni usually deserves it.'

    e. Gianni **probabilmente** lo merita   / *lo merita   **probabilmente**.
       Gianni probably   it deserves / it deserves probably
       'Gianni probably deserves it.'

Although some objections have been raised to the head-movement account of the data in (10) (see Bobaljik 1999), the empirical facts are well-established: it is often possible to interrupt head-initial sequences of verbal heads with adverbials. Of course, this is not to say that an adverb can always intervene between two verbal heads in a head-initial sequence. In Persian, an OV language, adverbs cannot intervene in either V-Aux or Aux-V sequences, both of which occur in the language (the future auxiliary precedes V, whereas all other auxiliaries follow V):[4]

(11) ali (hamishe) gitâr zade   (*hamishe) ast   [Persian]
     Ali always   guitar play.PTCP always   be.3SG
     'Ali has always played the guitar.'

(12) ali (hamishe) gitâr xâhad (*hamishe) zad   [Persian]
     Ali always   guitar will   always   play
     'Ali will always play the guitar.'

Spanish, an Aux-V-O language, also displays such a restriction, not allowing adverbs to intervene between the perfective auxiliary *haber* and the past participle (see Ojea López 1994:409, Cinque 1999:147):[5]

(13) Juan (siempre) ha (*siempre) sido (siempre) amable.   [Spanish]
     Juan always   has   always been always   friendly
     'Juan has always been friendly.'

As Cinque notes, it is not clear how to account for this restriction in terms of verb movement. It seems more likely that there is an additional "adjacency requirement" associated with *haber*. Ojea López (1994:409) makes the same claim: "[*H*]*aber* no tiene autonomía como forma verbal" ('[*H*]*aber* does not have autonomy as a verbal form'). Note also that this is a fact about the particular auxiliary *haber*. The auxiliary *ser* 'to be', for example, which occurs in passives, need not be adjacent to a following passive participle (Cinque 1999:147, citing Lois 1989:34, 40). Therefore, the order Aux-Adv-V is generally, though not universally, possible. There are specific auxiliaries that must appear adjacent to a following verb, but there are also many examples of adverbs intervening in head-initial verbal sequences. A relevant question is whether the same is true in head-final sequences of auxiliaries and verbs.

6.2.2 Head-Final Verb Sequences

To give evidence for a general ban on [[V X] Aux], it is obviously not sufficient to show that the sequence V-Adv-Aux is blocked in *some* languages, as the same is also true of Aux-Adv-V (e.g., for certain auxiliaries in Spanish and Persian). Suggestive evidence for a genuine asymmetry between head-initial and head-final verb sequences is nonetheless available in languages with variable word orders. In many such languages, adverbs can intervene freely in head-initial but not head-final verbal sequences, even within mixed sequences. Thus, as in Finnish (discussed above), adverbs can interrupt Aux-V (but not V-Aux) sequences, as in "OV" Germanic languages and Hungarian (see Zwart 1996b, Koopman and Szabolcsi 2000, respectively):

(14) …dass er das Buch hätte (genau)   durchsehen   [High German]
      that he the book had   carefully through.look
      (*genau)   sollen.
      carefully shall
      '…that he should have looked through the book carefully.'
      (based on Zwart 1996b:237, 1 (Adv) 3 (*Adv) 2)

(15) a. PÉTER fogja (XP) akarni   (XP) kezdeni   (XP)   szét [Hungarian]
         Peter will   want.INF   begin.INF   apart
         szedni a   rádiót.
         take.INF the radio
      b. PÉTER fogja (XP) akarni   (XP) szét szedni   (*XP)
         Peter will   want.INF   apart take.INF
         kezdeni a   rádiót.
         begin.INF the radio

c. PÉTER fogja (XP) szét szedni (*XP) kezdeni (*XP)
Peter will apart take.INF begin.INF
akarni a rádiót.
want.INF the radio
'It is Peter who will want to begin to take apart the radio.'
(based on examples in Koopman and Szabolcsi 2000, 1 (Adv) 4
(*Adv) 3 (*Adv) 2)

This strongly suggests that an asymmetry exists here, but leaves open the possibility that the ban on V-X-Aux holds only in languages with variable word orders, as Cinque (1999) in fact has claimed (as discussed above).

Another language with variable word order is Basque (see Arregui 2002, Haddican 2004). In Basque, some adverbs have the ability to either precede or follow verbs and auxiliaries.[6] Despite this, Basque also appears to be subject to the same kind of restriction as OV Germanic, Hungarian, and Finnish with respect to head-final verb clusters:

(16) (Askotan) Mirenek (askotan) liburuk irakurten [Basque]
often Miren.ERG often book.ABS.PL read.IMP
(*askotan) dau (askotan).
often AUX.PL often
'Miren often read books.'
(Arregui 2002:127)

Where the auxiliary precedes the verb, however, the Aux-V sequence can be interrupted by arguments and adverbs (see Haddican 2004). In this respect, then, Basque appears to pattern with Finnish/Germanic. However, as Arregui (2002:148n41) also notes, unlike other adverbs/arguments certain modal evidential particles such as *ete* 'evidently' and *omen* 'apparently' can intervene between the verb and the auxiliary in the V-Aux order (see also Haddican 2004:97, Etxepare 2009). We will return to the status of these surface V-Adv-Aux orders in section 6.5, as they appear to have a different hierarchical structure from the V-Adv-Aux sequences observed in other OV languages.[7]

6.3 Apparent Counterexamples to the Asymmetry

6.3.1 Three Types of Head-Final Languages

Thus far, then, there appears to be suggestive evidence that the ban on *[[V O] Aux] that lies at the heart of the FOFC generalization might actually be a more general ban on *[[V X] Aux]. Why, then, has FOFC often been stated only in terms of complementation? The reason is that in languages with stricter head-final orders a small class of adverbs can freely surface between the verb and the auxiliary. On the basis of this observation, Cinque (1999:58) posits three different classes of head-final verbal structures:

1. verb-clustering languages with mixed word orders (e.g., German);
2. strictly head-final agglutinating languages (e.g., Turkish);
3. strictly head-final inflectional languages (e.g., Hindi).

By hypothesis, a crucial difference between types 1–2 and type 3 is that it is possible for material to intervene in a head-final sequence in type 3 languages. In Cinque's terms, this reduces to a difference in the kind of movement operations used to derive surface head-finality in a Linear Correspondence Axiom (LCA)–compliant framework. In German (type 1), what is at stake is head movement "with the non-head subparts of IP raising leftward over the verb cluster, either individually ... or within a single constituent" (Cinque 1999:58). (17a) shows the former case, (17b) the latter:

(17) a. [$_{FP}$ **Obj** F [$_{vP}$ **V+v** [$_{vP}$ t$_V$ t$_{Obj}$]]]
      b. [^{FP} [^{VP} t^V **Obj**] F [^{vP} **V+v** t^{VP}]]

The strict adjacency between V and Aux follows from the fact that they form a complex head structure. In type 2–3 languages, on the other hand, head-final verbal sequences are derived via phrasal movement. Although Cinque is equivocal on this matter, he suggests that type 2 agglutinating languages such as Turkish might be derived via local comp-to-spec movement of the kind proposed by Kayne (1994), Julien (2002), and Biberauer, Holmberg, and Roberts (2014) (where Aux is located in v):

(18) [$_{vP}$ [$_{VP}$ **Obj** V t$_{Obj}$] v t$_{VP}$]

Type 3 languages, on the other hand, would involve nonlocal movement of their complement to the specifier of some higher functional head.[8] This kind of movement allows for the possibility that an adverb might intervene in a head-final sequence in type 3 languages. Another property of these kinds of structures is the possibility of Ā-movement of a lexical verb via phrasal Ā-movement:

(19) [$_{GP}$ [$_{FP}$ [**Obj**] F [$_{VP}$ **V** t$_{Obj}$]] G [$_{vP}$ v t$_{FP}$]]

The apparent prediction of this three-way split is that agglutinating languages should pattern with type 1 languages in requiring strict adjacency between verbs and auxiliaries. This should be the case, as Cinque (1999:57–58) notes, if one follows Kayne (1994) in assuming a single specifier per phrase, as the latter is the target for roll-up movement in a head-final structure, meaning that it cannot house an adverb. Interestingly, though, as we will see, Turkish (a type 2 language) and Hindi (a type 3 language) actually pattern very similarly in that both allow the same kinds of adverbs to surface inside the verbal cluster.[9]

6.3.2 Hindi

Kayne (2004:9n18) points out that the restriction on adverbs between V and a following Aux does not apply to emphatics and morphemes corresponding to words like *even*. Thus, Hindi allows "the negation word, emphatics and some adverbs" to intervene between the verb and an auxiliary (Kayne 1994:53), citing Mahajan 1989:225:

(20) raam roTii khaataa nahiiN/to/roz   thaa.[10]   [Hindi]
     Ram bread eat.MSG not/emphatic/every.day was.MSG
     'Ram habitually did/did not eat bread/ate bread every day.'
     (Mahajan 1989:225)

6.3.2.1 Emphatic Markers

The emphatic markers *bhii* 'also' and *to* (a topic marker) can surface in the position between V and Aux when they are associated with a focused VP:

(21) aur vah paise letaa   bhii hai.   [Hindi]
     and he   money take.MSG also PRES.3SG
     'And he takes money too.'
     (Agha 1998:118)

As Cinque (1999:30–31) notes, however, these focusing adverbs are special in that they are not situated in the universal functional hierarchy but instead can occur adjacent to any phrase they modify (see also Bayer 1996).[11] Thus, *bhii/to*, like *nahiiN* 'not' in instances of constituent negation, can occur to the right of any maximal projection of a lexical category (see Kidwai 2000:41 on *to*, Koul 2008:144 on *bhii*, Dwivedi 1991 on *nahiiN*):[12]

(22) amar **bhii** gaya.   [Hindi]
     Amar also go.PAST
     'Amar also went.'
     (Koul 2008:145)

The fact that these modifiers form a constituent with the phrase preceding them is reflected not only by their semantics but also by the fact that they can undergo topicalization along with the modified phrase:

(23) kitaab **to** raam layega.   [Hindi]
     book TO Ram bring.FUT
     'The book, Ram will bring.'
     (Kidwai 2000:47)

This is consistent with Cinque's (1999:31) proposal, citing Bayer (1996:chap. 2), that these adverbials are actually projecting heads that take the phrases they modify as complements. Further evidence for this analysis comes from the fact that *bhii/to* cannot occur between a postposition and a noun, even when only the noun is focused (see Kidwai 2000, Koul 2008):

(24) *sita nur-**to**-ke   paas gɔy.   [Hindi]
     Sita Noor-TO-GEN near go.PAST
     'Sita went to Noor.'
     (Kidwai 2000:42)

(25) *ghar **bhii** meN garmii hai.   [Hindi]
     house also in   hot   is
     'It is hot in the house as well.'
     (Koul 2008:138)

More generally, it has been proposed that emphatic markers such as *even/also* can never intervene between an adposition and a DP-complement (Sichel 2007:24). This is true, for example in English and Hebrew:

(26) I gave the book to (??only) John.

This is the same restriction noted by Cable (2007:94) in relation to the distribution of question particles. He proposes to account for this gap via his Q[uestion] P[hrase] Intervention Condition (Cable 2007:122), which states that "a QP cannot intervene between a functional head and a phrase selected by that functional head," the idea being that the presence of a projecting question particle blocks selection in such cases. This account can be extended to the Hindi facts discussed above only if *bhii* and *to* are also projecting heads that would likewise block selection between P and DP.[13] This raises the question of the status of auxiliary verbs in Hindi. Since *bhii* and *to* can intervene between lexical verbs and certain auxiliaries, it follows that the latter cannot be functional heads in the extended projection of V; instead, they must be lexical heads. We will return to this issue below.[14] According to Cable (2007:122), the presence of an intervening QP does not block selection between a lexical head and its complement. If this is the case, then the emphatic markers *bhii* and *to* project head-final phrases in Hindi, meaning that V-Adv-Aux sequences are actually harmonically head-final structures.[15]

6.3.2.2 Constituent Negation

Instances of (V(P)) constituent negation plausibly fall under the same analysis. Dwivedi (1991) observes that *nahiiN* can be used for constituent negation in Hindi, in which case it usually immediately follows the negated phrase:

(27) [raam ke nahiiN] sita ko kitaabe diyaa, shyaam ne.   [Hindi]
Ram ERG NEG   Sita DAT books gave Shyaam ERG
'Ram didn't give the books to Sita, Shyaam did.'
(Dwivedi 1991:90)

Thus, (28) is a felicitous conversation involving constituent negation of the verb with the surface V-Neg-Aux order:[16]

(28) a. kyaa raam roTii khaa-taa thaa?   [Hindi]
Q   Ram bread eat-hAB was.MSG
'Did Ram eat bread?'

b. ji nahiiN, raam roTii khaa-taa nahiiN thaa
no   Ram bread eat-HAB not   was.MSG
raam roTii banaa-taa thaa!
Ram bread make-HAB was.MSG
'No, Ram didn't use to EAT bread, he used to MAKE bread.'

In such cases, *nahiiN*, like *bhii/to*, modifies only the focused constituent (VP or V) and projects. Dwivedi (1991) argues explicitly that *nahiiN* is a head in such cases. First, she notes that negated constituents always receive the main pitch accent of the sentence. She claims that as intonation patterns are not sensitive to adjuncts (see Selkirk 1984:chap. 5), negation cannot be an adjunct in instances of constituent negation. This leaves the option of *nahiiN* being a specifier or head. The basic word order facts of Hindi strongly suggest that it is a head rather than a specifier. Whereas other modifiers in Hindi (demonstratives, adjectives, quantifiers) all precede the phrase they modify, constituent negation always surfaces to the right. This follows if the former are specifiers/adjuncts whereas the latter is a head. However, the strongest support that Dwivedi gives for the claim that *nahiiN* is a head comes from the fact that a negated constituent can move, stranding the negation:

(29) raam ne   kitaab$_i$ supriya ko [t$_i$ nahiiN] dii, ...   [Hindi]
Ram ERG book Supriya DAT NEG   give
'It was not a book that Ram gave Supriya, ...'
(Dwivedi 1991:92)

Crucially, (29) can, but need not, have a reading whereby the direct object, which has scrambled out of VP, is constituent-negated. If the negation were an adverb or specifier here, such movement would be impossible according to standard assumptions.[17] Therefore, there is reason to believe that in instances of constituent negation the V-Neg-Aux sequence is also a harmonic head-final structure, compliant with FOFC.

6.3.2.3 Sentential Negation

Crucially, though, not all instances of V-Neg-Aux order in Hindi involve constituent negation. As Kumar (2004, 2006) shows, like preverbal negation and unlike unambiguous constituent negation, immediately postverbal negation can license negative polarity items (NPIs):[18]

(30) a. maiN kisii   ko bhii   nahiiN dekh sak-aa.   [Hindi]
         I   anyone to EMPH NEG   see   MODAL-PERF.MSG
         'I could not see anyone.'
     b. maiN kisii   ko bhii   dekh nahiiN sak-aa.
         I   anyone to EMPH see NEG   MODAL-PERF.MSG
         'I could not see anyone.'
     c. */?[maiN   nahiiN] kisii   ko bhii   dekh sak-aa.
         I   NEG   anyone to EMPH see MODAL-PERF.MSG
         (Kumar 2004:182)

Bhatt (2007:3) shows that the adverbial quantifier *thorii* 'little', which also has a negative meaning as indicated by the gloss, can also occur in this position:

(31) timur manu-ko Dã:T-taa   thoRii thaa.   [Hindi]
     Timur Manu-to scold-HAB little be.PAST
     'Timur didn't used to scold Manu.'
     (Bhatt 2007:3)

If *nahiiN* can be a head in constituent negation, it is possible that it might also be a head in instances of sentential negation. If this is the case, then the position of *nahiiN* in (30b) is as expected if the head-final NegP projection occupies a position between VP and AspP as in (32), as Dwivedi (1991) proposes (where *thaa* occupies Asp):[19]

(32)   AspP

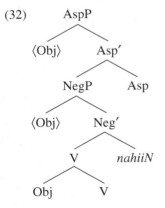

A complication with this analysis is that, as Mahajan (1989) notes, the position of negation in (30b) is not the most neutral position in Hindi. Rather, the unmarked position for negation is between the direct object and the lexical verb (see also Dwivedi 1991 and (30a) above):

(33) raam roTii nahiiN khaa-taa thaa.   [Hindi]
     Ram bread NEG   eat-HAB was.MSG
     'Ram didn't eat bread.'
     (Mahajan 1989:224)

To account for these two options (Neg-V-Aux and V-Neg-Aux), Mahajan (1990b) proposes that negation is adjoined to the right of the VP and that the verb optionally moves past Neg:

(34) a. [$_{AuxP}$ [$_{VP}$ Obj V] nahiiN] Aux]
     b. [$_{AuxP}$ [$_{VP}$ Obj t$_V$] nahiiN] V+Aux]

If this is the case, then the variability in Hindi is equivalent to the variability noted by Cinque (1999) for head-initial languages like Italian with respect to verb/adverb ordering, except that the negation is right-adjoined here, something that is ruled out under Kayne's (1994) LCA. There are two objections one could raise to this early proposal in the light of subsequent research. First, if it were the case that right-adjunction and rightward head movement of this type were possible, then it is surprising that we see this variability only with respect to negation, and not with respect to adverbs. Indeed, as discussed in section 6.4, there appear to be no OV languages with postverbal adverbs of the kind subject to Cinque's functional sequence. As illustrated above, the adverbs that can occur inside the verbal complex are exactly those that do *not* have a place in the Cinquean hierarchy, instead being focus-related or variable in placement. Moreover, following Pollock (1989) and Zanuttini (1997), it is widely held that negation is located in any of a number of functional projections with fixed hierarchical positions, so the idea that it is an adjunct seems problematic.

This raises the question of whether these two word orders can be accounted for if *nahiiN* is in fact a head. Deriving either of these orders from the other is not straightforward if *nahiiN* is always a head. It cannot be the case, for example, that the verb raises past the negation marker (see (35)), as this kind of movement violates Travis's (1984) Head Movement Constraint (as well as the LCA):[20]

(35)

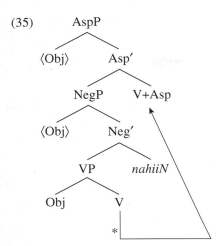

If the verb first moves to adjoin to Neg and then the V+Neg complex raises to Asp, roughly as proposed by Kumar (2004), then there is no ultimate explanation for the resulting word order (as Kumar (2004:15n6) acknowledges), as we would expect such movement in a head-final language to be string-vacuous. If, on the other hand, *nahiiN* can be either a head *or* a specifier, then it is predicted to be able to surface either to the right or to the left of V as (36) shows (assuming, regardless of the LCA, that a specifier always occurs to the left of its phrase):

(36)

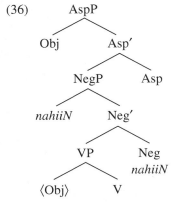

Provided the object also moves to a position above NegP, then, this derives the correct unmarked word order in Hindi. I propose that the two positions of *nahiiN* in (30a) and (30b) stem from its dual status as either a specifier or head of NegP (note that this may well be parallel to English, where *not* behaves like a specifier while *n't* behaves like a head).

This analysis accounts for the basic distribution possibilities of the negation marker across all tense and aspect combinations in Hindi (see Bhatt 2003, 2007, Kumar 2004):

(37) O   **I. Neg** V_{LEX} **II. Neg**   Aux   **III. *Neg**   Aux

Thus, *nahiiN* can intervene between the verb and the object or between a lexical verb and the inflected progressive marker, but never between two auxiliary verbs:

(38) ?maiN skuul jaa (nahiiN) rahaa   (*nahiiN) huuN/thaa.   [Hindi]
       I   school go NEG   PROG.MSG   not   am.1SG/was.MSG
       'I am/was not going to school.'
       (based on Kumar 2004:176)

This follows if *nahiiN* can only be the head or specifier of NegP, a phrase that occurs in a fixed position immediately dominating VP, as proposed above. Whether we have an instance of constituent or sentential negation, then, the order V-Neg-Aux arguably does not have the hierarchical structure that violates FOFC: [$_{AuxP}$ [$_{VP}$ V Neg] Aux]. Rather, it has the harmonically head-final order [$_{AuxP}$ [$_{NegP}$ V Neg] Aux].

6.3.2.4   Intervening Arguments
A final problem arising in Hindi is that objects can also surface between V and a following Aux in Hindi, in apparent violation of FOFC (see Mahajan 1990b):

(39) raam kha-taa sabzii   thaa.   [Hindi]
      Ram eat-HAB vegetables was.MSG
      'Ram used to eat vegetables.'[21]
      (Mahajan 1990b:338)

As Bhatt and Dayal (2007) note, indirect objects can also surface in this position (40), as can *wh*-phrases (41):

(40) sita-ne   kitaab   bhej-ii   raam-ko thii.   [Hindi]
      Sita-ERG book.FSG   send-PFV.FSG Ram-DAT be.PAST.FSG
      'Sita had sent the book to Ram.'
      (Bhatt and Dayal 2007:288, (3))

(41) sita-ne   dhyaan-se dekh-aa kis-ko   thaa?   [Hindi]
      Sita-ERG care-with see-PFV who-ACC   be.PAST
      'Who had Sita looked at carefully?'
      (Bhatt and Dayal 2007:291, (9))

Bhatt and Dayal (2007:291n6) also note that nonfinite clauses cannot occur in this position, though they can occur in either a preverbal or a postauxiliary position. Interestingly, moreover, the order V-O-Aux is not possible where preverbal negation is present:

(42) */???raam nahiiN kha-taa sabzii   thaa.   [Hindi]
       Ram   NEG   eat-HAB vegetables was.MSG
       'Ram used to eat vegetables.'
       (Mahajan 1990b:338)

One possible explanation for these facts is that (39) is derived via remnant VP-movement to some position higher than that housing the scrambled object and all auxiliary verbs, as in (43):

(43)

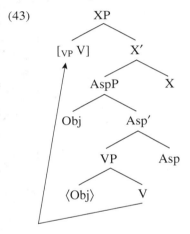

This movement, by hypothesis, is blocked by the presence of a negative speci-fier, which creates a negative island in Ross's (1967) sense. If V-O-Aux orders in Hindi are derived in this way, then they fail to involve a FOFC violation according to any of the approaches to FOFC explored in this volume (see chapter 4). For Biberauer, Holmberg, and Roberts (2014), remnant VP-movement in such cases would be Ā-movement (hence the sensitivity to nega-tion), which is not subject to FOFC. For Sheehan (2013b), such movement does not create a linearization problem, hence does not trigger a FOFC effect. In all cases, then, Hindi data that at first blush appear problematic for FOFC, on closer examination turn out not to be.

6.3.3 Turkish

In Turkish, an SOV agglutinating language, the unmarked position for adverbs is preverbal:

(44) Ahmet hızlı   koş-uyor-du.   [Turkish]
     Ahmet quickly run-PROG-PAST.3SG
     'Ahmet was running quickly.'
     (Wilson and Saygın 2001:413)

In fact, morphologically simple adverbs *must* surface to the immediate left of
the verb, even when modified by another adverb (as in Basque):

(45) Hasan çok yavaş konuş-ur.   [Turkish]
     Hasan very slow talk-AOR
     'Hasan talked very slowly.'
     (Kornfilt 1997:404)

(46) *Çok   yavaş Hasan konuş-ur.   [Turkish]
     very slow Hasan talk-AOR
     (Kornfilt 1997:404)

These adverbs clearly cannot surface between V and Aux. Other (morphologically complex) adverbs can appear in other positions, not immediately adjacent
to the verb, however.

    An obvious difference between Hindi and Turkish is that the usual way to
express tense, mood, and aspect in the latter is via agglutinating suffixes on
the verb. This alone, then, might serve to prevent any adverb from intervening
between V and Aux, assuming adjunction between a root and a suffix or
between suffixes is independently banned. Wilson and Saygın (2001:416)
point out, though, that "sometimes an auxiliary *ol-* 'be' needs to be inserted,
because only the past *-DI* and *-mIş* in its evidential sense can attach directly
to already-suffixed verbs." This means that, in practice, Turkish does have
auxiliary verbs in addition to suffixation:

(47) Cüneyt yarın   oku-yor   ol-acak.   [Turkish]
     Cüneyt tomorrow read-PROG be-FUT.3SG
     'Tomorrow Cüneyt will be reading.'
     (Wilson and Saygın 2001:416)

It is therefore these contexts that are the most likely to permit the order
V-X-Aux in Turkish.

    Unlike in Hindi (see section 6.3.2.4), it is impossible for arguments to
surface between V and Aux in Turkish. As is well-known, it is possible, in
Turkish, for a "backgrounded" object to surface in postverbal position (see
Kural 1997):

(48) Cüneyt yarın oku-yor ol-acak kitab-ı. [Turkish]
Cüneyt tomorrow read-PROG be-FUT.3SG book-ACC
'Tomorrow, Cüneyt will be reading the book/a specific book.'
(Jaklin Kornfilt, pers. comm.)

It is not possible, however, for an argument to surface between the main verb
and the epenthetic auxiliary *ol-*:

(49) *Cüneyt yarın oku-yor kitab-ı ol-acak. [Turkish]
Cüneyt tomorrow read-PROG book-ACC be-FUT.3SG
(Jaklin Kornfilt, pers. comm.)

To this extent, Turkish differs from Hindi and presumably lacks remnant
VP-fronting.

Interestingly, though, in Turkish too certain adverbial-like "particles" *can*
occur either between V and its suffixes or between V and the auxiliary verb
ol-: notably the question particle *mI* and the focus particles *bile* ('even'—in
main clauses only) and *dE* ('also'—in main and relative clauses) (see Kornfilt
1997:191–192, Göksel 2001:162):

(50) Hatta bu bölüm-ü anal-mış **bile** ol-du-k. [Turkish]
in.fact this section-ACC understand-PERF even AUX.PAST.1PL
'In fact, it even turns out that we have understood this section.'
(Kornfilt 1997:191–192)

(51) Gid- e- **de**- bil- ir- iz. [Turkish]
go- ABIL- also- ABIL- AOR- 1PL
'We can also GO there.'
(Göksel 2001:162)

Note that, as in Hindi, the kinds of adverbs permitted in this position are again
focus-related adverbs that fall outside Cinque's (1999) functional hierarchy.
Again as in Hindi, it appears that these particles can be associated with and
follow any focused phrase:

(52) BEN **de** iç-me-yeceğ-im. [Turkish]
I also drink-NEG-FUT-1SG
'I am not going to have any either.'[22]
(Göksel and Kerslake 2005:116)

(53) Hasan kitab-ı Ali-yé **bile** oku-du. [Turkish]
Hasan book-ACC Ali-DAT even read-PAST
'Hasan read the book even to Ali.'
(Kornfilt 1997:192)

As in Hindi, focused phrases associated with such emphatic particles can be fronted along with the particle (Kornfilt 1997:193). There is also suggestive evidence that these particles are projecting heads in Turkish too. *Bile*, for example, cannot occur between an adjective and suffixal tense inflection, which are plausibly in the same extended projection; rather, it must occur following the tense inflection:

(54) Komşu-nuz şirin-di **bile**.   [Turkish]
neighbor-2PL cute-PAST even
'Your neighbors were even cute.'
(Kornfilt 1997:194)

As Erguvanlı (1984:26) notes, these are also the only adverbials that can intervene between an unscrambled object and a selecting verb in Turkish (see also Göksel and Kerslake 2005:393):

(55) Murat kitab **da/bile** ok-ur.   [Turkish]
Murat book also/even read-AOR
'Murat also/even read a book.'
(Erguvanlı 1984:26)

Again, this follows if (i) these particles are actually projecting heads and (ii) they do not act as interveners between lexical heads and their complements but do block selection by functional heads, as Cable (2007) proposes. Finally, note that two of these particles can appear as suffixes on the verb and undergo vowel harmony, further suggesting that they are heads (the exception is *bile*, which is invariant). It seems to be the case that no full adverb can appear inside the verb cluster in Turkish. As in Hindi, all instances of the surface order V-X-Aux in Turkish plausibly involve harmonically head-final structures.

6.3.4 Summary

In many OV and variable VO/OV languages, it appears that adjuncts as well as arguments trigger a FOFC effect, implying that the structure *[$_{AuxP}$ [$_{VP}$ V Adv] Aux] is universally banned. The few cases of adverbials (typically 'even', 'also', 'too') that can intervene in V-Aux sequences are projecting heads that give rise to harmonic head-final sequences.[23] The question, then, is whether existing accounts of FOFC can handle this more general version of the FOFC effect. The following section argues that they can, when taken in conjunction with an independent asymmetry noted by Ernst.

6.4 Ernst's (2003, 2004) Asymmetry

Ernst (2003, 2004) observes a different asymmetry concerning the distribution of adverbs. He claims that nonbranching adverbs can either precede or follow head-initial phrases but must precede head-final phrases. Thus, in OV languages adverbs must precede V (though, because of scrambling, need not precede O). In VO languages, on the other hand, adverbs can either follow O or precede V or, in a subset of such languages, occur between V and O (see Pollock 1989):

(56) a. (Adv) V (Adv) O (Adv)
   b. (Adv) O (Adv) V (*Adv)

When taken in combination with FOFC, this asymmetry serves to explain the lack of [$_{AuxP}$ [$_{VP}$ V Adv] Aux]. In order for a language to allow postverbal adverbs, that language would have to have VO order, and final auxiliaries are ruled out by FOFC in VO languages (see chapter 2). A crucial question, then, is whether Ernst's asymmetry can be derived from anything, notably Kayne's (1994) Antisymmetry.

It is not immediately clear whether it can be. In Kayne's (1994) terms, there is no adjunct/specifier distinction. Following Cinque (1999), adverbs are usually taken to be specifiers of functional heads subject to a universal sequence, as discussed above. The immediate (naïve) prediction of the LCA, then, is that adverbs should precede the phrases they modify. However, as movement is available, by hypothesis, to alter the base-generated order of constituents, this naïve prediction unsurprisingly does not hold. In Kaynean terms, then, the asymmetry in (56) must derive from restrictions on movement. Interestingly, it seems to imply a restriction on movement of exactly the opposite kind from FOFC.

(57) *[$_{GP}$ [$_{VP}$ Obj V$^{\wedge}$] G$^{\wedge}$ [$_{FP}$ Adv [t$_{VP}$] F$^{\wedge}$]]

(58) [$_{GP}$ [$_{VP}$ V Obj] G$^{\wedge}$ [$_{FP}$ Adv [t$_{VP}$] F$^{\wedge}$]]

According to Biberauer, Holmberg, and Roberts's (2014) approach to FOFC described in chapter 4, (58) should be banned whereas (57) should be well-formed, contrary to fact. Rather, in (57), where all heads in the extended projection bear $^{\wedge}$, yielding OV order, the result is ungrammatical, whereas in (58), where the lexical head V lacks $^{\wedge}$, yielding VO order, the result is V-O-Adv, which is apparently attested. This is a problem for FOFC on two counts. First, and less problematically, FOFC fails to rule out (57), meaning that some additional constraint on movement is needed. But second, and more seriously, FOFC predicts (58) to be ungrammatical, apparently contrary to fact.

It is easy to provide examples from VO languages illustrating that Ernst's asymmetry holds as a surface constraint. In many VO languages, adverbs can follow V(P), though they are more marginal after CP complements, as the following examples show:

(59) a.   The children walked out of the room silently.
     b.   The children ate the cakes quickly.
     c.   ??He said that he's leaving yesterday.

(60) a.   Los niños   salieron de la sala   silenciosamente.   [Spanish]
          the children exited   of the room silently
          'The children left the room silently.'[24]
     b.   Los niños   comieron los pasteles rápidamente.
          the children ate   the cakes quickly
          'The children ate the cakes quickly.'
     c.   ??Dijo   [que se iba]   ayer.
          said.3SG that SE was.going   yesterday
          'He said that he was leaving yesterday.'
          (Jorge Cortina López, pers. comm.)

(61) a.   Les enfants sont sortis de la   pièce silencieusement.   [French]
          the children are left   of the room silently
          'The children left the room silently.'
          (Bonami, Godard, and Kampers-Manhe 2004:155)
     b.   Les enfants ont   mangé les gâteaux rapidement.
          the children have eaten the cakes   quickly
          'The children ate the cakes quickly.'
     c.   ??Il m' a   dit qu' il viendra   hier.
          he me has said that he will.come yesterday
          'He told me that he will come yesterday.'
          (Caroline Cordier, pers. comm.)

This might be taken as evidence that the linearization of adverbs is simply not subject to FOFC, presumably because adverbs do not select and are not selected for (in the normal case). Nonetheless, if one assumes both the LCA and FOFC, deriving clause-final adverb orders is no trivial task, as the functional heads housing adverbs in their specifiers are presumably subject to FOFC.

If the linearization of adverbs is determined by the LCA, then for a VP-adverb to follow VP, the material contained in VP must necessarily have raised higher than said adverb. Assuming, as Cinque (1999) has argued, that adverbs are merged as the specifiers of functional heads, the simplest way to derive the correct word order is via phrasal movement of VP past Adv, as mentioned above:

(62) [$_{FP}$ [$_{VP}$ V Obj] F$^\wedge$ [$_{XP}$ Adv X ~~VP~~]]

Cinque proposes that this "low" VP-fronting is Ā-movement, which may overcome the FOFC problem if there is independent evidence that Ā-movement is involved.[25] If this movement is A-movement, then movement of a head-initial VP past the null head X to the specifier of FP violates FOFC on both of the accounts of FOFC given in chapter 4. According to Biberauer, Holmberg, and Roberts (2014), F in (62) could only bear $^\wedge$ if it were a lexical head, beginning a new extended projection. Biberauer, Holmberg, and Roberts need to assume that auxiliaries, which are located higher than F, are in the extended projection of V in order to account for the lack of V-O-Aux. By implication, then, F must also be part of that same extended projection.[26] For Sheehan (2013b), movement of a head-initial VP within its phase is expected to require discontinuous spell-out of VP, giving rise to the order V-Adv-O rather than V-O-Adv.

There are at least three ways to circumvent this problem. The first is to reject the LCA and reformulate an alternative analysis of FOFC. For example, Biberauer, Holmberg, and Roberts's $^\wedge$-percolation account could be restated without the LCA, if the $^\wedge$-feature signaling head-finality signals only head-finality, rather than movement in the narrow syntax. Adjunct placement would then fall outside FOFC, being regulated by some other mechanism (see Ernst 2003, Abels and Neeleman 2009). The second option is to weaken the LCA and claim that it linearizes only argument structure, adjunct placement being regulated by some different mechanism. We will not explore either of these possibilities here. Finally, it might be claimed that the structure *[[V O] Adv] is, in fact, banned and that the data that appear to falsify it (in English, French, and Spanish) actually have a different hierarchical structure. We will briefly explore this last possibility here.

One possible analysis of V-O-Adv order is that the object and the verb do not move past the adverb as a constituent, but rather in separate movements (see Johnson 1991, citing Postal 1974, Koopman 1989). Johnson gives convincing evidence that both the verb and the DP-object vacate VP in English, whereas PP- and CP-complements remain in situ. Adapting his analysis slightly, I propose that V raises to v and that both DP- and PP-objects vacate VP, with DPs raising to a higher position than PPs. First, note the full range of adverb placement facts with DP-, PP-, and CP-complements in English:

(63) a. John {quickly} ate   {*quickly} his toast   {quickly}.
   b. John {quickly} walked {quickly} to school   {quickly}.
   c. John {quickly} said   {quickly} that he was late {??quickly}.

Assuming there are at least three relevant adverb positions here, the data can be summarized linearly as follows:

(64) ...T Adv_1 V DP Adv_2 PP Adv_3 CP

In these terms, the well-known adjacency condition that bans an adverb from intervening between a verb and a direct object in English reduces to the fact that there is no adverb position between the landing site of DP and V.[27] Johnson's proposal is that the DP has raised from its base position in VP to a position above the second adjunction position for *quickly*. Updating his proposal slightly, we get the following (simplified) clause structures for English and French/Spanish, abstracting away from the finer positions of the adverbs, and the fact that the verb actually raises higher in French than in Spanish:

(65) *English*

[$_{TP}$ Subj T [Adv_1 [$_{vP}$ V+F+Asp+v [$_{AspP}$ DP t_{Asp} [Adv_2 [PP t_F [Adv_3 [$_{VP}$ t_V CP]]]]]]]]

(66) *French/Spanish*

[$_{TP}$ Subj V+F+Asp+v+T [Adv_1 [$_{vP}$ t_v [$_{AspP}$ DP t_{Asp} [Adv_2 [PP t_F [Adv_3 [$_{VP}$ t_V CP]]]]]]]]

Johnson gives evidence that verbs move out of VP in English from coordination facts, attributed to Larson (1988:345n11):

(67) Chris ate [$_{VP}$ t_{ate} the meat slowly] but [$_{VP}$ t_{ate} the vegetables quickly].

Let us suppose that this analysis is along the right lines, so that V-O-Adv orders are derived not by VP-movement but by separate movement of the verb and its arguments past Adv. This derivation does not violate FOFC, as from the perspective of both Biberauer, Holmberg, and Roberts and Sheehan, FOFC is a condition on the movement/linearization of head-initial phrases. In (65)/(66), the object and the verb move separately, not as a head-initial phrase.

   Crucially, the same derivation could *not* derive V-O-Aux order: because of the Head Movement Constraint, the verb could never undergo head movement past the auxiliary:

(68) [$_{XP}$ V+F+X [$_{FP}$ Obj t_F [$_{AuxP}$ Aux [$_{VP}$ t_V t_{Obj}]]]]

Inasmuch as this account can be extended to all final adverbs in VO languages, it provides a FOFC-compliant derivation for V-O-Adv orders.

It is by no means clear, though, what rules out O-V-Adv orders, as these could be derived by either phrasal or separate V- and O-movements. I leave this matter open for future research (see Ernst 2003 for one proposal).

6.5 Basque Evidential Particles: A Different Challenge

In Basque, modal evidential particles such as *ete* 'evidently' and *omen* 'apparently', unlike other adverbs/arguments, *can* intervene between the verb and auxiliary in the V-Aux order (Arregui 2002:148n41; see also Haddican 2004:93–97):

(69) Bazkal-du-ko   bide   zue-n.   [Basque]
     lunch-ASP.PERF-FUT MOD.EVID AUX-PAST
     'Apparently he was going to have lunch.'
     (Haddican 2004:93)

(70) Lagun-tzen (*Miren/*maiz)   omen   zintu-en.   [Basque]
     help-ASP.IMP Miren/often   MOD.EVID AUX-PAST
     'Apparently she (often) helped (Miren).'
     (Haddican 2004:97)

These examples present an additional surface violation of the ban on *V-X-Aux. Once again, though, it appears that these examples do not have the structure *[[V Adv] Aux]. Haddican (2004) argues, partly on a semantic basis, that these examples involve phrasal movement. He shows that in nonnegative clauses in Basque, the whole verbal complex V!P (including the verb, modals, and preverbal interval arguments) raises to Spec,PolP. In negative contexts, the negative marker *ez* raises instead and VP remains in situ:

(71) Ez   al   zio-n   galde-tu-ko?   [Basque]
     NEG speech.act AUX-T.PAST ask-ASP.PERF-T.FUT
     'Wasn't she going to ask him (that)?'

Etxepare (2009) gives evidence that whether *omen* is a head or a specifier varies dialectally. In what he terms Eastern II dialects, *omen* is the specifier of a functional head in a different extended projection from TP. In central dialects, however, he argues that *omen* is a head that projects a head-initial ModP above the projection of the auxiliary (T). As such, phrasal movement of V!P past this head-initial phrase gives the following structure:

(72) [$_{PolP}$ [$_{V!P}$ O-V] Pol [$_{ModP}$ omen [$_{TP}$ T t$_{V!P}$]]]

Whether this is a violation of FOFC under Biberauer, Holmberg, and Roberts's (2014) account depends on the nature of the trigger for V!P-movement in such cases. If such movement is Ā-movement, then it plausibly falls outside FOFC. A potential problem with this is that the movement operations that give rise to disharmonic word orders in languages such as Finnish also look like Ā-movements in certain respects, yet they still give rise to FOFC effects. Under the PF-interface account, FOFC reduces to a linearization problem triggered by the movement of a nonatomic *head-initial* phrase. For this reason, the structure in (72) is unproblematic for that approach, as V!P, the moved phrase, is head-final.

6.6 Conclusions

This chapter has considered to what extent there is an asymmetry between head-initial and head-final sequences of verbs. While it is true that, in some languages, head-final verbal sequences can be interrupted by certain adverbials, the elements that can surface in this position are very limited in scope and do not usually, and perhaps never, have the structure *[[V Adv] Aux]. This means that a more general version of FOFC holds, whereby no phrase can occur between V and a following Aux. It has been noted that this gap is actually predicted by existing accounts of FOFC in conjunction with Ernst's (2003, 2004) asymmetry, which bans an adverb from following a head-final VP. As all V-Aux languages will necessarily be OV languages, the ban on V-Adv-Aux follows. The ultimate explanation for Ernst's asymmetry, though, remains elusive.

7 The Final-over-Final Condition and the Head-Final Filter

Michelle Sheehan

7.1 Introduction

There is a tantalizing similarity between the Final-over-Final Condition (FOFC), which bans a right-branching phrase as the complement of a left-branching phrase (in certain contexts; see chapter 2) and the ban on right-branching prenominal modifiers in English and many other languages (as noted in Biberauer, Holmberg, and Roberts 2007). (Example (2), but not structure (1), is from Abney 1987:326.)

(1) *Basic FOFC*
   $*[_{\gamma P} [_{\alpha P} \alpha \beta] \gamma]$

(2) *John is a $[_{NP} [_{AdjP}$ proud of his son] man].

Sentence (2) exemplifies Greenberg's (1963) Universal 21, later extended as Emonds's (1976) Surface Recursion Restriction and Williams's (1982) Head-Final Filter (HFF). The HFF bans anything from intervening between the head of a prenominal modifier and the phrase it modifies. Despite superficial similarities, however, there are apparent structural differences between (1) and (2), which make a reduction of (2) to (1) far from straightforward. The aim of this chapter is to consider how real these differences are and to argue that (2) should nonetheless fall under (1), making FOFC even more general than previously thought.

The chapter is structured as follows. Section 7.2 gives an overview of the HFF from the work of Greenberg and Williams and then compares it with FOFC. Section 7.3 gives evidence for the HFF from a number of languages, also discussing the "compliance strategies" employed in these languages to avoid violations. Section 7.4 discusses languages that do not seem to be subject to the HFF, notably a number of Slavic and Balkan languages. Section 7.5 raises some objections to previous accounts of the HFF and argues that the gap actually falls under FOFC, once certain independently motivated assumptions are made about adjectival modification. Finally, section 7.6 concludes and raises some questions for future consideration in the light of this new evidence for FOFC.

7.2   Evidence for the Head-Final Filter

7.2.1   Greenberg's Universal 21

Greenberg ([1963] 2007:70) notes that of the four possible word-order combinations of AdjP and N, (3d) alone is unattested in his representative sample of languages:

(3) a.   [N [Adv Adj]]
  b.   [N [Adj Adv]]
  c.   [[Adv Adj] N]
  d.   *[[Adj Adv] N]

He further notes that while there are N-Adj languages allowing both Adj-Adv and Adv-Adj orders, there are no Adj-N languages allowing both orders of Adv and Adj. This asymmetry is given as his Universal 21:

(4) *Universal 21*
  If some or all adverbs follow the adjective they modify, then the
  language is one in which the qualifying adjective follows the noun and
  the verb precedes the object as its dominant order. (Greenberg [1963]
  2007:70)

As is well-known, English fairly uncontroversially adheres to this universal, disallowing the order Adj-Adv in prenominal position (see Sadler and Arnold 1994):

(5) a.   *a [dressed in blue] man
  b.   *the [navigable by boat] rivers
      (Sadler and Arnold 1994:187)
  c.   *a [running smoothly] meeting
  d.   *a [long for such a late hour] journey
  e.   *a [skillful for a novice] surgeon
  f.   a [polite in manner] person
      (Sadler and Arnold 1994:190)

Where adverbials precede the adjective in this prenominal position, however, the result is fully grammatical:

(6) a.   a [smartly dressed] man
  b.   the [easily navigable] rivers

c. a [smoothly running] meeting
d. a [most extremely long] meeting
e. a [highly skillful] surgeon
f. a [very polite] person

A further similarity between Universal 21 and FOFC, then, is the fact that both also hold in languages with variable word orders.

7.2.2 Williams's Head-Final Filter

Without being aware of Greenberg's universal, Williams (1982:161) observes that the restriction on prenominal modification is actually more general and claims that it equates to "a constraint barring post-head material in prenominal modifiers" (p. 160; his Head-Final Filter). As he notes, postadjectival adverbial modifiers are banned as in (5), but so too are complements, as in (7):

(7) a. *a [bored of French] student
    b. *a [sick of waiting] patient
    c. *an [afraid of his contemporaries] writer
    d. *a [sporting a mackintosh] man
    e. *an [in the corner] chair[1]

Note that in (7e), the prenominal modifier is a PP rather than an AdjP, suggesting that the restriction is also not category-sensitive.

Beyond the examples in (5) and (7), however, there is some controversy about which other word order effects fall within the remit of the HFF. Grosu and Horvath (2006), for example, argue at length that the obligatory extraposition seen with comparatives and degree modifiers in many languages is directly attributable to the HFF (English examples are given here by way of illustration):

(8) a. *John is [more than Bill (is)] tall.
    b. *John is [more than he is fit] tall.

(9) a. *John is [too to be honest] kind.
    b. *John is [as as Mary] smart.

Grosu, Horvath, and Trugman (2007:13) further claim that the ban on right-hand modifiers inside comparative DPs has the same explanation:

(10) a. *John is a [more intelligent than Bill] man.
     b. *John is a [more unusually than any of you] dressed student.

For this to be the case, the underlying structure of comparatives and degree modifiers must be basically as follows, as they note:

(11) a. [$_{AdjP}$ [$_{DegP}$ more [$_{CP}$ than Bill (is tall)]] tall]

b. [$_{DP}$ a [$_{NP}$ [$_{AdjP}$ [$_{DegP}$ more [$_{CP}$ than Bill (is tall)]] tall] man]]

The HFF then forces the complement of the Deg head (*more*) in (11a) and (11b) to be extraposed.

There are several reasons to favor this explanation of extraposition in comparatives and degree modifiers over the semantic explanation proposed by Bhatt and Pancheva (2004). First, there is good evidence that the CP in such structures forms a constituent with the Deg head at some level of representation; in fact, even Bhatt and Pancheva argue at length for this, though they claim that the CP is late-merged in this position.[2] The main evidence that CP is the complement of Deg comes from the fact that there are selectional restrictions between the Deg head and C (as Bresnan (1973) noted).[3] Second, as Grosu, Horvath, and Trugman (2007) note, and as discussed in section 7.4, Russian allows superficial violations of the HFF with both comparatives and AdjPs, making a semantic explanation of extraposition in comparatives suspect.[4] Third, as Grosu, Horvath, and Trugman also note, other languages employ the same kinds of compliance strategies in both contexts. Thus, Hungarian, which is also subject to the HFF, permits the complements/modifiers of both attributive adjectives and comparatives to be fronted rather than extraposed (see section 7.3.2 on HFF compliance strategies):[5]

(12) Mari [Jánosnál] kevésbé magas.   [Hungarian]
       Mary John.at   less   tall
       'Mary is less tall than John.'
       (Grosu, Horvath, and Trugman 2007:22)

Finally, Grosu, Horvath, and Trugman (2007) point out a more general problem with Bhatt and Pancheva's (2004) semantic trigger for extraposition (via late merger). According to Bhatt and Pancheva (2004:39), it is the fact that *-er* is *nonconservative* that forces late merger of its complement, once it has undergone rightward quantifier raising (in the manner proposed in Fox and Nissenbaum 1999).[6] As Bhatt and Pancheva note, whereas most quantifiers in natural language are conservative, *-er* is nonconservative in that its first argument is a proper subset of its second. The problem is that many degree modifiers that also require obligatory extraposition are *conservative*, meaning that the late-merger analysis "misses what seems to be a significant generalization" (Grosu, Horvath, and Trugman 2007:14). It is, thus, reasonable to assume that the word order in comparatives can be attributed to the HFF.

The pattern with degree modification more generally is more complex, as all degree modifiers except those containing *enough* surface in a left-peripheral position in English. In all cases, though, complements are obligatorily extra-posed, presumably because of the HFF:

(13) a. *John is [$_{DP}$ [as smart as Pete] a guy].
     b. John is as smart a guy as Pete.

(14) a. *John is [$_{DP}$ [too smart to argue with] a guy].
     b. John is too smart a guy to argue with

(15) a. *John is [$_{DP}$ a [tall enough to play basketball]] guy.
     b. John is a tall enough guy to play basketball.

Finally, consider the behavior of *tough-* and other adjectives selecting a clausal complement, which are also subject to the HFF:[7]

(16) a. *a difficult for anyone to read book
     b. *an easy to persuade someone to read book

(17) a. *a pretty for anyone to look at flower
     b. *an unlikely to choose film
     c. *a willing to help out receptionist

The ungrammatical examples in (16), named *tough-nuts* by Berman (1974), can be ruled out by the HFF under the assumption that they share a basic structure with clausal *tough*-constructions. Hicks (2009) argues for the follow-ing structure for clausal *tough*-constructions whereby the nonthematic subject of a *tough*-construction is base-generated inside the null operator as the object of the most embedded verb. Once this operator has moved to the edge of CP, the DP becomes visible for raising to the matrix subject position, as per the following slightly simplified structure:

(18) [[This book]$_k$ is [$_{AdjP}$ difficult [$_{CP}$ [$_{DP}$ Op t$_k$]$_j$ C [$_{TP}$ PRO to read t$_j$]]]].

If the *tough*-nut structure is parallel, then in instances of indirect adjectival modification the nominal merged with the null operator (*books*) will raise to Spec,CP, as per Kayne (1994), with the reduced relative clause then free to front or remain in situ:

(19) a. [$_{CP}$ [books]$_k$ C [$_{AdjP}$ difficult [$_{CP}$ [$_{DP}$ Op t$_k$]$_j$ C [$_{TP}$ PRO to read t$_j$]]]]
     b. [$_{DP}$ D [$_{FP}$ [$_{AdjP}$ difficult [$_{CP}$ [$_{DP}$ Op t$_k$]$_j$ C [$_{TP}$ PRO to read t$_j$]]]$_m$ F [$_{CP}$ [books]$_k$ C t$_m$]]]

Where AdjP moves to the prenominal position (Spec,FP), the fact that its CP-complement is obligatorily extraposed would thus be a further effect of the HFF.[8]

There is thus considerable evidence that the HFF applies to several different kinds of prenominal modifiers in English (AdjPs, PPs, DegPs). The following section briefly considers the relationship between the HFF and FOFC before turning to broader crosslinguistic patterns of prenominal modification.

7.2.3   FOFC and the HFF

The superficial similarity between FOFC and the HFF has already been noted; see (1)–(2), repeated here:

(20) *Basic FOFC*
$$*[_{\gamma P} \ [_{\alpha P} \ \alpha \ \beta] \ \gamma]$$

(21) *HFF*
  *John is a $[_{NP} \ [_{AdjP}$ proud of his son] man].

As noted above, the fact that the HFF, like FOFC, holds both crosslinguistically and in languages with variable word orders (as illustrated in (5)–(6)) makes this similarity even greater. An important difference between the HFF and FOFC (in its simplest form), however, is that most examples of the latter involve complementation between γ and αP, whereas in (21) AdjP is a modifier of NP. It is argued in chapter 6 that FOFC effects are also observed where β is an adjunct, so that V-Aux sequences cannot generally be interrupted by either arguments or adjuncts; this suggests that FOFC may be sensitive to sisterhood rather than complementation. For the HFF also to fall under FOFC, it would have to be the case that the same structure is ruled out even where αP is an adjunct:

(22) a. $*[_{\gamma P} \ [_{\alpha P} \ \alpha \ \beta] \ \gamma]$ where αP and β are complements (basic FOFC)

   b. $*[_{\gamma P} \ [_{\alpha P} \ \alpha \ \beta \ \gamma]$ where αP is a complement and β is an adjunct (chapter 6)

   c. $*[_{\gamma P} \ [_{\alpha P} \ \alpha \ \beta] \ \gamma]$ where αP is an adjunct (HFF)

In the account of FOFC developed by Biberauer, Holmberg, and Roberts (2014) (see chapter 4), the condition is relativized to sisterhood relations within extended projections, meaning that (22c) would violate FOFC only if γ were a head in the extended projection of α. In Sheehan's (2013b) account (again see chapter 4), the condition holds wherever αP is externally merged as a complement lower than γ and moved without being atomized. In neither approach is it immediately obvious that (22c) can be analyzed in the same way as (22a,b).

  While it is fair to say that there is no general consensus regarding the structural status of (the various kinds of) adjectives (Adjs), with many different possibilities being entertained in the literature, certain possibilities can nonetheless be ruled out quite uncontroversially. As is well-known, the argument/

adjunct distinction is far from clear-cut, both empirically and theoretically. Nonetheless, there seem to be strong reasons to reject the idea that adjectival phrases are the complements of N.[9] Introductory textbooks often assert that complements are obligatory whereas adjuncts are optional: Adjs are clearly not complements in this sense, as they are never obligatory in DPs. There are well-known challenges to this generalization in both directions, though, making the diagnostic potentially problematic.[10]

   Another well-known diagnostic concerns iteration, the claim being that adjuncts (unlike complements) can be iterated. While there are restrictions on AdjPs containing complements in English, it is possible for two to cooccur, especially if one of them is spelled out discontinuously (see section 7.3.2.2):

(23) I know a customer annoyed with the service ??(and) aware of his rights.

(24) I know a younger man than John allergic to peanuts.

Thus, (23), where both the AdjPs are postposed, is rather awkward without the coordination marker, but (24), where *younger man than John* requires extraposition because of the HFF, is fully grammatical (see Grosu, Horvath, and Trugman 2007 and the discussion in section 7.2.2). Note that (23) also improves if one of the adjectival modifiers is embedded in a full relative clause, suggesting that the sentence might be marginal for processing reasons:

(25) I know a customer annoyed with the service who is aware of his rights.

More than two AdjPs are also possible, as in (26):

(26) I know a younger man than John allergic to peanuts ?(who is) sick of the food here.

   Other syntactic tests distinguishing adjuncts from complements also suggest that these AdjPs are adjuncts. The familiar *do so*- and *one*-replacement tests are standardly taken to indicate whether an XP associated with VP or NP (respectively) is a complement of that head or not. By this criterion, adjectival phrases (AdjPs) of the kind in (21) again do not pattern with complements of N:[11]

(27) a. ?John may not be a good parent but he is one proud of his son.[12]
    b. *Mary may not be a historian of ideas but she is one of science.

   Semantic diagnostics can also be applied with some degree of reliability. In the most basic terms, whereas adjunction often gives rise (semantically) to predicate modification, complementation gives rise to saturation via functional application. Thus, a red car is something that is both red and a car, whereas a historian of science is not someone who is both a historian and of science.[13] By this criterion too, then, AdjPs like *proud of his son* do not pattern with complements of N (a man proud of his son is someone who is both a man and proud of his son). For this reason, while the syntax of adjunction remains a highly complex issue that will be discussed at length below, it is fairly uncontroversial that example (21) does not straightforwardly fall under FOFC as stated in (22a). Nonetheless, this chapter will ultimately argue that (22a–c) should be taken as instantiations of the same deep condition. Let us begin by looking at the crosslinguistic status of the HFF in some detail, first considering languages where it appears to hold (section 7.3) and then turning to apparent counterexamples (section 7.4). We then consider how to derive the effect from FOFC.

7.3 Languages Subject to the HFF

7.3.1 Crosslinguistic Evidence for the HFF

The HFF can be seen to hold in (at least) English, German, Dutch, Swedish, Finnish, Hungarian, French, Spanish, Portuguese, Italian, Romanian,[14] Czech, Slovak, Sorbian, Bosnian/Croatian/Serbian, Slovene, and Persian (see Abney 1987, Sadler and Arnold 1994 on English; Williams 1982, Haider 2004 on German; Zwart 1996a, Hoekstra 1999 on Dutch; Platzack 1982, Delsing 1993 on Scandinavian; Grosu and Horvath 2006 on Hungarian; Bouchard 1998, 2002, Abeillé and Godard 2000 on French; Luján 1973 on Spanish; Giorgi 1988, González Escribano 2004:1n2 on Italian; Grosu and Horvath 2006 on Romanian; Siewierska and Uhlířová 1998 on Slavic; and Cinque 2010:44–49 for a brief overview). In all such languages, prenominal adjectives cannot be followed by a complement CP/PP:[15]

(28) de [trotse (*op zijn vrouw)] man   [Dutch]
      the proud of his wife   man
      Intended: 'the man proud of his wife'
      (Zwart 1996a:85n3)

(29) ein [unzufriedener (*damit)] Syntaktiker   [German]
      an unsatisfied   it.with syntactician
      Intended: 'a syntactician unsatisfied with it'
      (Haider 2004:783)

(30) une [facile (*à remporter)] victoire   [French]
      a   easy   to win   victory
      Intended: 'a victory easy to win'
      (Abeillé and Godard 2000:344)

(31) uma [boa   (*a matemática)] aluna   [Portuguese]
     a   good   at math   student
     Intended: 'a student good at math'

(32) o [interesantă (*pentru noi toți)] propunere   [Romanian]
     an interesting   for   us all   proposal
     Intended: 'an interesting proposal for us all'
     (based on Grosu and Horvath 2006:480)

Although comparative DPs are not generally discussed in relation to the HFF,
at least Dutch, Spanish, French, Portuguese, and Hungarian show the same
restriction in this domain too. The effect is therefore a pervasive property of
a number of natural languages, whatever its explanation.

   Note that this ban applies even in languages that only allow restricted classes
of prenominal adjectives, where its salience as a filter would be less manifest,
making it difficult to acquire. In Persian, adjectives usually follow the noun, which
bears *ezafe* marking (Samiian 1994). One exception to this comes from superla-
tives, which precede the noun and do not require *ezafe* (Mahootian 1997:259):

(33) kûechek-tarin mive   [Persian]
     small-est   fruit

Interestingly, in such contexts Persian also bars a complement from occurring
between the prenominal superlative adjective and the noun:

(34) *[vafadar-tarin be shohar-am] zan[16]   [Persian]
      loyal-est   to husband-my woman

Because of such cases, there is suggestive evidence that the ban results from
a synchronically active condition, rather than a historical idiosyncrasy, as it
holds even in hidden pockets of some languages. It has also been noted,
however, that a small number of Slavic/Balkan languages appear to permit
violations of the HFF. We will consider these languages in some detail in
section 7.4. First, though, let us examine the compliance strategies employed
in connection with the HFF.

7.3.2   Compliance Strategies

Another feature that the HFF shares with FOFC is that languages appear to
use repair or compliance strategies to avoid violations (see chapter 4 on extraposition and FOFC).

7.3.2.1   Preposing

In German, Dutch, Scandinavian, Finnish, Hungarian, Czech, Slovak, Sorbian,
Bosnian/Croatian/Serbian, and Slovene, it is possible to prepose a PP

complement/modifier of Adj to a preadjectival position (see Haider 2004 on German; Zwart 1996a, Hoekstra 1999 on Dutch; Platzack 1982, Delsing 1992, 1993 on Scandinavian; Grosu and Horvath 2006 on Hungarian; Siewierska and Uhlířová 1998 on Slavic):

(35) een [op Marie] verliefde jongen   [Dutch]
     an of Marie in.love boy
     'a boy in love with Marie'
     (Hoekstra 1999:180)

(36) ett [sedan i går]   välkänt   faktum   [Swedish]
     a   since yesterday well.known fact
     'a fact well-known since yesterday'
     (Delsing 1992:25)

(37) na [svého syna] pyšný muž   [Czech]
     of his   son proud man
     'a man proud of his son'
     (Siewierska and Uhlířová 1998:135)

(38) A [fizetésükkel]   elégedetlen munkások   nem   [Hungarian]
     the salary.their.with dissatisfied workers.NOM NEG
     dolgoznak jól.
     work.3PL well
     'Workers dissatisfied with their pay don't work well.'
     (Grosu and Horvath 2006:474)

This strategy is also marginally available in Macedonian, a language that has been claimed not to be subject to the HFF (but that actually displays a weak version of it, according to the informant who supplied this example):

(39) ?od svoite roditeli zavisno   momche[17]   [Macedonian]
     on his   parents dependent boy

Interestingly, the languages I have been able to test (English, Bosnian/Croatian/Serbian, Slovene, Afrikaans, and Swedish) do not readily permit this compliance strategy with CP complements of Adj.[18] It is at the very least much more marked than with PPs and is judged ungrammatical in Swedish and Slovene:[19]

(40) *da je vojna zavesten otrok   [Slovene]
     that is war.F aware.M child.M
     'a child aware that there is a war'

(41) ?(?)da je rat   svijestno dijete   [Bosnian/Croatian/Serbian]
     that is war.M aware.N child.N
     'a child aware that there is a war'

FOFC provides a potential explanation for why CPs behave differently from PPs in this way. As described in chapter 2, C-initial clausal complements cannot surface in a preverbal position even in otherwise OV languages, whereas PPs in some such languages can.[20] These data suggest that the same appears to hold of complements to Adj.

Hungarian allows the same preposing strategy with phrasal comparatives. In predicative position, the PP-complement of a comparative can either follow or precede Deg, but when DegP is preposed, it must precede it:

(42) a. Mari kevésbé magas [Jánosnál].   [Hungarian]
        Mary less   tall   John.at
     b. Mari [Jánosnál] kevésbé magas.
        Mary John.at   less   tall
        'Mary is less tall than John.'
        (Grosu and Horvath 2006:479)

(43) a. *Egy kevésbé magas [Jánosnál] lány lépett   be.   [Hungarian]
         a   less   tall   John.at   girl stepped in
     b. Egy [Jánosnál] kevésbé magas lány lépett   be.
        a   John.at   less   tall girl stepped in
        'A girl less tall than John walked in.'
        (Grosu and Horvath 2006:479)

Assuming that CPs also cannot be preposed in Hungarian, these facts lend support to Wunderlich's (2001) claim that true phrasal comparatives exist in addition to clausal comparatives.

This compliance strategy again makes the HFF appear similar to FOFC, as preposing the PP complement/modifier in such cases removes the offending right-branching structure. Interestingly, this compliance strategy coexists with alternative strategies in the languages in question, as discussed in the following sections.

7.3.2.2   PP/CP-Extraposition

Another compliance strategy is available in English, Dutch, Afrikaans, Swedish, Bosnian/Croatian/Serbian, Slovene, and more marginally German and Macedonian. This involves the extraposition of a CP/PP-complement/modifier from an AdjP/DegP.

In Slovene and Macedonian, the strategy appears to be generally available, regardless of the categorial status of the head or modifier, and regardless of whether the latter is a complement/adjunct and whether it is involved in stage- or individual-level modification:

(44) a. zavesten otrok, da je vojna   [Slovene]
         aware.M child.M that is war.F
         'a child aware that there is a war'
     b. odvisen   mladenič   od   svojih   staršev
         dependent.M young.man.M from REFL.POSS.ACC parent.PL.ACC
         'a youth dependent on his parents'
     c. pričakovano vplačilo   čez trideset dni
         expected.N payment (in).N in thirty   days.QUANT.GEN
         'a payment expected in thirty days'

In English, Swedish, Dutch, and to a lesser extent German and Afrikaans, this strategy is also available but more constrained and sensitive to (i) whether the head of the modifier is Adj or Deg; (ii) whether the PP/CP is a complement or an adjunct; (iii) whether prenominal adjectives are interpreted as stage- or individual-level modifiers in a given language. Extraposition is possible only with CP/PP-complements of Deg and with CP-complements/PP-modifiers of individual-level predicates (see González Escribano 2005, building on work by Bernstein (1995), for extensive discussion of the English data on which the following examples are based). Hence, CP-complement extraposition is banned from stage-level but not individual-level AdjPs, as González Escribano (2005) shows:

(45) a. a difficult book for anyone to read
     b. an easy book to persuade someone to read
     c. a pretty flower for anyone to look at
     d. an unlikely film to choose

(46) a. *an anxious foreigner to make himself understood
     b. *a bound marriage to fail
     c. *a condemned prisoner to be shot at dawn
     d. *a disinclined colleague to cooperate
     e. *a due book to appear soon
     f. *an eager yuppie to succeed

(47) a. *an aware child that there is a war
     b. *a conscious woman that she has no chance
     c. *a convinced teacher that he is always right
     d. *a glad mother that her children are well off
     e. *a happy girlfriend that he is a bachelor
         (González Escribano 2005:567–568)

Extraposition of PP-complements is not generally possible:

(48) a. *a proud man of his son
    b. *an angry teacher with her student
    c. *a satisfied customer with the service
    d. *a capable man of murder
    e. *a dependent youth on his parents
    f. *a familiar teacher with our problem[21]

Adjunct PP-extraposition from AdjP, however, *is* permitted, again as long as the adjective in question is individual-level:

(49) a. a long journey for such a short distance
    b. a skillful surgeon for a novice
    c. a fat man around the waist
    d. a lucky woman in matters of love
    e. a popular guy with girls
    f. a respected woman in her field
      (based on González Escribano 2005:568)

(50) a. *a blue man in the face
    b. *a due payment in thirty days
    c. *a restless child in her seat
    d. *a suffering patient from early childhood
    e. *a tired woman in the evenings
    f. *a yellow book with age
      (González Escribano 2005:567–570)

The same pattern holds in Dutch, Swedish, Afrikaans, and German.[22] At present, I have no clear understanding of why the stage-/individual-level distinction should affect extraposition possibilities or indeed why extraposition of complement PPs should be banned, and I leave these matters to future research, but note that the parallels across (Germanic) languages suggest that these are principled distinctions.

In the case of DegP, CP/PP-extraposition is much less constrained. Thus, CP-extraposition appears to be fully productive in comparative and degree modifier constructions regardless of the stage-/individual-level distinction:

(51) a. a bigger problem [$_{CP}$ than Op we had first anticipated]
    b. a bigger fool [$_{CP}$ than Op John (...)]
    c. too smart a guy [$_{CP}$ to argue with]
    d. a tall enough guy [$_{CP}$ to play basketball]
    e. a more restless child [$_{CP}$ than I had imagined]

(52) een meer intelligente student dan Wim   ,   [Dutch]
     a   more intelligent   student than Wim
     'a more intelligent student than Wim'
     (Hoekstra 1999:180)

The same is true in English, German, Afrikaans, and Swedish, but not Dutch,
with what González Escribano calls symmetric or comparative modifiers of
the following kind:

(53) a. an alternative view to Chomsky's
     b. an analogous hypothesis to Abney's
     c. a comparable situation to ours
     d. a different view from yours
     e. an equivalent idea to that
     f. a parallel theory to Frege's
     g. a separate room from ours
     h. a similar car to mine

I assume that these modifiers are also degree modifiers, hence the fact that
they can also surface with a *than*-CP complement and with an overt *wh*-phrase
(in nonstandard dialects), both properties they share with comparative
constructions:

(54) a different one than (what) I'm used to

For this reason, these examples are not counterexamples to the ban on PP-
complement extraposition from AdjP, as the extraposed material is a complement of Deg. Again, I have no clear understanding of why PP-complements
of Deg should pattern differently from PP-complements of Adj, and I leave
this matter to future research.

7.3.2.3 Wholesale Extraposition of AdjP

Finally, it is crucial to note that in all the languages I tested (English, German,
Swedish, Dutch, Afrikaans, Slovene, Bosnian/Croatian/Serbian, Polish, Macedonian, Portuguese, and French), in all HFF contexts right-branching modifiers
can simply be postposed wholesale to a postnominal position. In languages
that lack the other compliance strategies, this is the only option available; this
is the case, for example, in Spanish, Portuguese, and French, as it is with
PP/CP-complements/modifiers of stage-level AdjPs in English. In the other
Germanic and Slavic languages, this strategy coexists with the other available
strategies, though it is marginal in Afrikaans in the absence of a relative
marker:

(55) une victoire [facile à remporter] [French]
a   victory easy   to win
'an easy victory to win'
(Abeillé and Godard 2000:339)

(56) uma aluna   [boa (a matemática)][23] [Portuguese]
a   student good at math
'a student good at math'

(57) a. a student bored of French
     b. a patient sick of waiting
     c. a chair in the corner

(58) a. a man blue in the face
     b. a payment due in thirty days
     c. a child restless in her seat

This compliance strategy is reminiscent of the FOFC-compliance strategy observed with head-initial CP complements in OV languages, as discussed in chapter 2. These CPs are always extraposed wholesale in otherwise OV languages (see Biberauer and Sheehan 2012a for a potential analysis).

The data in table 7.1 show that all the languages that have more than one compliance strategy also permit wholesale extraposition of phrasal modifiers. (Spanish, Portuguese, and French are not included in the table as they *only* permit wholesale extraposition.) In addition to this compliance strategy, the languages in the table differ in the extent to which they employ the two additional strategies.

Table 7.1
Compliance strategies

	Slovene	German, Swedish, Dutch, Afrikaans	Bosnian/ Croatian/ Serbian	Macedonian	English	Polish
Preposing PP/CP-extraposition	PP, *CP unrestricted	PP, *CP restricted	PP, *CP *	? unrestricted	* restricted	* *
Wholesale extraposition	unrestricted	unrestricted	unrestricted	unrestricted	unrestricted	unrestricted

7.3.3 Similarities between the HFF and FOFC

The data discussed above, including the three compliance strategies, strongly suggest that the restriction on prenominal modifiers is sensitive to word order.[24]

This much is also obvious from Greenberg's (1963) observation that left-branching prenominal modifiers are readily acceptable in the same languages that block right-branching prenominal modifiers:[25]

(59) a. an [only recently posted] letter
     b. a [most extremely loyal] husband
     c. *a [running smoothly] meeting
     d. a [smoothly running] meeting

As expected, this means that more strongly head-final languages trivially conform to the HFF. The following are well-formed in Turkish, for example:[26]

(60) [ben-im kadar   yorgun] bir insan   [Turkish]
     I-GEN as.much.as tired   a   person
     'a person as tired as me'
     (Kornfilt 1997:96)

(61) [koca-sın-a   çok sadık] bir kadın   [Turkish]
     husband-GEN-DAT very loyal a   woman
     'a woman loyal to her husband'
     (Kornfilt 1997:96)

In Japanese, likewise, left-branching prenominal modifiers are fully acceptable, and indeed are the only available option:[27]

(62) chocolate daisuki josei[28]   [Japanese]
     chocolate love   woman
     'a woman fond of chocolate'

(63) kuroi fuku   o   kiteiru josei   [Japanese]
     black clothes ACC wearing woman
     'a black clothes wearing woman'

Thus far, the data from a range of Indo-European languages, Finnish, Hungarian, Turkish, and Japanese reveal the HFF to be more than a language-specific idiosyncrasy. The question remains open, though, whether it is a universal constraint, or a pervasive trait of Standard Average European (in the sense of Haspelmath 1998). The existence of apparent counterexamples even within the European area, in English as well as certain Balkan/Slavic languages, might appear to suggest that the HFF is not universal. As argued in the next section, however, these often only marginally acceptable counterexamples do not undermine the potential universality of the constraint, as there is independent evidence that prenominal modifiers involve considerable hidden structure at least in some of these languages.

7.4   Apparent Counterexamples to the HFF

7.4.1   Counterexamples from English

Although the effect of the HFF is pervasive, it is apparently not absolute. Even in English, for example, *tough*-adjectives with nonfinite clausal complements can often surface in the preverbal position:

(64) a. an easy-to-understand book
      b. a hard-to-refute argument
      c. some difficult-to-reach places
          (corpora examples from Leung and van der Wurff 2012)

The usual explanation for these kinds of counterexamples is that the AdjPs in question are "complex lexical items" or "atomic units," hence the tendency for hyphenation (see Nanni 1980:574, citing Roeper and Siegel 1978). This is also arguably the case with other apparently right-branching prenominal modifiers, which certainly have a lexical "frozen" flavor and are also often hyphenated:

(65) a. his holier-than-thou attitude
      b. the Final-over-Final Condition
      c. his down-to-earth demeanor

Note that this is also possible in some restricted cases with comparatives and, as O'Flynn (2008, 2009) notes, a small group of adjectives that cannot appear in *tough*-constructions:

(66) a. Mary is a [taller than average] player.
      b. There are [more than six] players in our team.
      c. an eager-to-please boyfriend

Crucially, these structures share certain properties with compounds. For example, regular plural morphology is blocked inside complex prenominal modifiers, as Sadler and Arnold (1994:189) note, just as it is inside compounds. In a postnominal position, however, such morphology is required:

(67) a. more than ten mile(*s) long walk
      b. a walk more than ten mile*(s) long

(68) a. a bug(*s)-catcher
      b. a catcher of bug*(s)

Another indication that these examples are frozen lexicalized structures is that they cannot contain adverbial modifiers, as Nanni (1980:575) observes:

(69) a. *an easy to quickly clean room
      b. *a hard to find in the attic manuscript
      c. *a simple to neatly sew pattern

Note that overt experiencers are also banned in these lexicalizations (Nanni 1980:575), as are parasitic gaps and multiple embeddings:

(70) a. *a difficult for anyone to read book
     b. *a difficult to read without buying book
     c. *an easy to persuade someone to read book

The construction is also limited in its productivity, being highly marginal with most *tough*-adjectives that are not on the easy-hard scale:

(71) This is an *unpleasant/*annoying/??amusing/?fun to read book.

This idiosyncratic restriction and the ban on internal syntactic structure are the hallmarks of a lexical phenomenon. Moreover, Leung and van der Wurff (2012) observe that examples like (64a–c) are only attested in corpora since the 1920s, suggesting that they are part of a recent trend toward heavy prenominal modification. The alternative *tough*-nut construction in (72) is attested from Old English onward, however, and is fully productive (Leung and van der Wurff 2012):[29]

(72) a. a tough nut to crack
     b. a difficult person to please
     c. a difficult place to reach

I therefore propose that these apparent counterexamples to the HFF in English are atomic lexical units, which do not represent a genuine counterexample to the HFF. That such atomized chunks are not subject to FOFC is unsurprising given the account of FOFC put forth by Sheehan (2013b) (see chapter 4) and extended to the HFF in section 7.5. Crucially, in these terms FOFC is a condition governing the relationship between hierarchical structure and linear order and so atomic units with no internal structure are immune to it.

7.4.2 Counterexamples from Balkan Languages

As is well-known, a number of Balkan languages appear to permit surface violations of the HFF. Cinque (2010:chap. 4) notes that apparent exceptions to the HFF are found in Russian, Bulgarian, Macedonian, Polish, Ukrainian, and Greek. These languages all allow right-branching AdjPs to appear prenominally (see also Babby 1975, Grosu and Horvath 2006, and Pereltsvaig 2007 on Russian, Siewierska and Uhlířová 1998 on Slavic, and Androutsopoulou 1995 on Greek). Grosu and Horvath (2006) further note exceptions from Romanian comparatives:

(73) a. [dovol'nyi vyborami]   prezident   [Russian]
        satisfied   elections.INSTR president
        'the president satisfied with the elections'
        (Cinque 2010:46, citing Bailyn 1994:25)

b. [mnogo gordiyat săs svoeto   dete] bašta   [Bulgarian]
   very   proud.the with SELF.the child father
   'the father very proud of his child'
   (Cinque 2010:46, citing Tasseva-Kurktchieva 2005:285)

c. i   [perifani ja to jos tis] mitera   [Greek]
   the proud   of the son her mother
   'the mother proud of her son'
   (Cinque 2010:46, citing Androutsopoulou 1995:24)

In fact, it seems that Bosnian/Croatian/Serbian and Slovene also permit slightly marginal surface violations of the HFF, arguably more so even than Macedonian.[30]

There are three possible ways of dealing with such counterexamples. First, in the worst-case scenario they might force one to abandon the HFF as a deep property of grammar and to posit it as a fairly superficial though recurrent language-specific rule. Second, it might be the case that the HFF is parameterized to hold only in certain languages. Third, the HFF might still reveal a deep property of grammar, with some other language-specific factor serving to give rise to apparent surface violations in some languages. The first two interpretations of the counterexamples are the most common in the literature, but I argue tentatively for the final possibility here.

7.4.3 Counterexamples from Russian and Polish

Polish permits surface violations of the HFF, though in many contexts such orders are slightly marginal, and wholesale extraposition is strongly preferred for the speaker I consulted:

(74) a. ??[ubrany w czern] mezczyzna[31]   [Polish]
        dressed in black man
     b. mezczyzna [ubrany w czern]
         man   dressed in black
         'a man dressed in black'

(75) a. ?[starszy od   Johna] przyjaciel   [Polish]
        older   than John   friend
        'an older friend than John'
     b. przyjaciel [starszy od   Johna]
         friend   older   than John
         'a friend older than John'

In Polish, nonbranching nonclassificational adjectives must precede the noun (Rutkowski 2002, 2007, Rutkowski and Progovac 2005). Extraposition of

AdjP therefore appears to be triggered only where AdjP is right-branching, in violation of the HFF. These data appear to suggest that prenominal AdjPs in Polish can be right-branching, but that this is only a marginal possibility; and, in fact, the awkwardness serves to make the postnominal position possible, even preferred. Polish is, therefore, subject to a weak form of the HFF.

In Russian, too, such word orders are stylistically marked according to Grosu, Horvath, and Trugman (2007), and wholesale extraposition is preferred. It is not clear, therefore, whether Russian and Polish differ from Bosnian/Croatian/Serbian and Slovene with respect to the HFF. All four languages marginally permit surface violations of the HFF, but Bosnian/Croatian/Serbian and Slovene have additional word orders available via preposing and CP/PP-extraposition that are not possible in Polish or Russian.

7.4.4 Counterexamples from Greek

In Greek, likewise, the HFF-violating order is actually slightly marginal for some speakers (as Grosu, Horvath, and Trugman (2007) also note and as my informant confirms), which I represent here with (?) in (76a), which repeats (73c).[32] Once again, the prenominal order alternates with wholesale extraposition. However, as is more generally the case with postnominal adjectives, this is only possible where the AdjP is also marked for definiteness (see Androutsopoulou 1995):

(76) a. (?)i   [perifani ja to   jos tis] mitera   [Greek]
           the proud   of the son her mother
           'the mother proud of her son'
           (Cinque 2010:46, citing Androutsopoulou 1995:24)
     b.   i   mitera *(i) [perifani ja to   jos tis]
           the mother the proud   of the son her
           'the mother proud of her son'

Therefore, Greek also displays a weak sensitivity to the HFF, though the marginal acceptability of (76a) remains problematic.

7.4.5 Counterexamples from Bulgarian

In Bulgarian, the HFF-violating order appears to be fully acceptable, though CP-complements in comparatives can still surface in an extraposed position. There is reason to believe, though, that complements of Adj might raise separately from Adj to a prenominal position. If so, then Bulgarian only superficially violates the HFF as it does not have head-initial prenominal AdjPs either.

In Bulgarian (which has enclitic determiners), when an AdjP is fronted, any material preceding the adjective is obligatorily pied-piped along to the predeterminer position, whereas any material following it is left behind (see, e.g., Dimitrova-Vulchanova and Giusti 1995, 1998, Embick and Noyer 2001, Bošković 2005, Dost and Gribanova 2006):

(77) a. mnogo xubavi-**te** knigi   [Bulgarian]
      very   nice-the   books
      'the very nice books'
    b. *mnogo-**te** xubavi knigi
      (Dimitrova-Vulchanova and Giusti 1995:47)

(78) a. kupena-**ta** ot Petko kniga   [Bulgarian]
      bought-the by Petko book
      'the book bought by Petko'
    b. *kupena ot Petko-**ta** kniga
    c. vernij-**at**   na Vera muž
      truthful-the to Vera husband
      'the husband truthful to Vera'
    d. *veren na Vera-**ta** muž
      (Bošković 2005:31n39)

Note that in (78), PP-complements/modifiers of Adj also surface in a prenominal position in apparent violation of the HFF. However, they do not surface adjacent to Adj; instead, they follow the enclitic determiner. One way to analyze these word orders, based on Kayne's (1994) analysis of relative clauses (79), is to posit two separate phrasal movements in such cases. First the PP-complement of the adjective vacates AdjP, possibly moving to Spec,CP (see (80a)); then the AdjP remnant moves to Spec,DP, where it serves as host to the enclitic D (see (80b)):[33]

(79) [$_{DP}$ the [$_{CP}$ [$_{XP}$ yellow]$_j$ C [$_{IP}$ [book] I [e]$_j$]]]

(80) a. [$_{FP}$ F [$_{CP}$ [$_{PP}$ na Vera]$_i$ C [$_{IP}$ [$_{NP}$ muž] I [$_{Adj}$ vernij t$_i$]]]]
    b. [$_{DP}$ [$_{Adj}$ vernij t$_i$]$_j$ -at [$_{CP}$ [$_{PP}$ na Vera]$_i$ C [$_{IP}$ [$_{NP}$ muž] I t$_j$]]]

In the case of definite DPs, this gives rise to overt discontinuity of AdjP. In the case of indefinite DPs, however, D is covert and so the adjective and its complement will be string-adjacent, giving the surface appearance of an HFF violation. Because of the facts in (77) and (78), this analysis seems empirically superior to either a straight head-movement or phrasal-movement account as well as to a nonsyntactic account. Plausibly, FOFC rules out movement of a right-branching AdjP to Spec,DP.

Although there is no direct evidence for such an analysis in the other Slavic and Balkan languages that (more marginally) permit HFF violations (with the exception of Macedonian, which has a determiner system similar to that of

Bulgarian), it might nonetheless be the case that a similar derivation applies in these other cases. For this reason, it seems reasonable to maintain the HFF as a universal in the belief that an independently motivated explanation for apparent violations in Russian, Polish, and Greek will emerge, possibly also based on remnant movement.

The following section examines and rejects previous accounts of the HFF, some of which adopt a weaker parameterized stance, and assimilates the HFF to FOFC.

7.5 The HFF as a FOFC Effect

7.5.1 Previous Accounts of the HFF

In an early approach to the HFF, Abney (1987) proposes an analysis whereby prenominal adjectives are heads in the extended projection of N, as mentioned in note 9:

(81) $[_{DP}$ D $[_{AdjP}$ Adj $[_{NP}$ N]]]

Bošković (2005) proposes that this structure is available only in languages with determiners. His basic proposal is that in such languages, the DP-projection serves to make AdjPs into arguments, whereas in languages lacking determiners no such possibility exists. As AdjPs cannot function as arguments, it follows that, in determinerless languages, only an NP-over-AdjP construction is possible (whereby the adjective is adjoined to NP). The attraction of this proposal concerns the other seemingly unrelated parametric effects that Bošković attributes to this NP-over-AdjP structure, notably the possibility of left-branch extraction. From such a perspective, the prediction is that determinerless languages should *not* be subject to the HFF as, in these languages, adjectival modifiers are phrasal. Compare the structure in (82) with that in (81):

(82) $[_{NP}$ $[_{AdjP}$ Adj $[_{PP/CP}$ ...]] N]

As also mentioned in note 9, Abney's account of the HFF, if correct, renders the effect wholly distinct from FOFC, despite their surface similarities. The crucial fact about (81) is that the adjective takes the NP as its complement and so can take no other complements (assuming binary branching), hence the HFF. It will be argued below, however, that both Abney's account of the HFF and Bošković's parameterization of it are empirically problematic.[34]

While Bošković's parametric account is highly elegant, it suffers from some obvious empirical problems. One concerns the predicted correlations between having/not having determiners and being/not being subject to the HFF. The

Table 7.2
The Head-Final Filter (HFF) and NP vs. DP languages

Class	Languages	NP language	Obeys the HFF
A	Russian, Polish	Y	N
B	Czech, Slovak, Sorbian, Bosnian/ Croatian/Serbian, Slovene, Finnish	Y	? (Y in Finnish)
C	English, German, Dutch, Swedish, Spanish, Portuguese, Italian, French	N	Y
D	Bulgarian, Macedonian, Greek, Romanian (in comparatives)	N	N

prediction is that languages without determiners will not be subject to the HFF, whereas those with determiners will be. This predicts two classes of languages, when in fact all four possible combinations of the two properties seem to be attested, as table 7.2 shows. Classes A and C in table 7.2 conform to expectations, putting to one side the fact that both Russian and Polish do show a sensitivity to the HFF. Russian and Polish are NP languages and hence fail (strongly) to adhere to the HFF, whereas English, German, and so on are DP languages and obey the HFF. Classes B and D, however, are not expected to exist. The NP/DP parameter does not explain why Bulgarian, Macedonian, and Greek should fail to adhere to the HFF, as they are all DP languages (as Pereltsvaig (2007) also notes). Of course, some of these languages might be only superficial counterexamples, as proposed in section 7.4.2. More problematic are the Class B languages—that is, the many NP languages which are apparently at least weakly sensitive to the HFF. Bošković notes that Czech, Slovak, Sorbian, Bosnian/Croatian/Serbian, and Slovene do freely permit phrasal prenominal modifiers, but with left-branching complements (see also section 7.3.2.1 and Cinque 2010:chap. 4n9, citing Siewierska and Uhlířová 1998:135–136). The problem with this explanation is that the same is also true of German and Swedish, which are DP languages and are thus predicted to pattern differently. In fact, the availability of preposed complements appears to be a compliance strategy for the HFF, as argued above.

As Svenonius (1994) and Hankamer and Mikkelsen (2005) point out, there are serious problems with Abney's (1987) original analysis of the HFF, which are retained in Bošković's account. For one thing, prenominal adjectives fail to block N-to-D movement in many languages that nonetheless adhere to the HFF, suggesting that they cannot be heads (see Longobardi 1994). Moreover, as both Greenberg (1963) and Williams (1982) note (see section 7.2), it is not the case that prenominal adjectives must be heads bearing no complements or modifiers; simply, they cannot bear right-branching complements/modifiers (as Hankamer and Mikkelsen (2005:96) note). In essence, Greenberg's Universal 21, which clearly states that word order is the crucial factor here, indicates that Abney's account cannot be the whole story (see Cinque 2010:chap. 4 for further problems).

7.5.2 Kayne's (1994) Discussion

Kayne (1994) does not directly discuss the HFF, but he does provide an explicit account of prenominal adjectival modification. Kayne (1994:97–101) proposes the following derivation for preverbal AdjPs, based on his raising analysis of relative clauses and drawing on a long tradition of raising prenominal adjectives from a postverbal position (following Chomsky 1957):

(83) [$_{DP}$ the [$_{CP}$ [$_{AdjP}$ yellow]$_j$ C [$_{IP}$ [book] I [e]$_j$]]]

In his terms, after the head noun *book* has raised to Spec,IP to satisfy the Extended Projection Principle, the AdjP *yellow* raises to Spec,CP, giving the surface word order. The implication is that much adjectival modification involves a covert relative clause. As evidence for this derivation, Kayne cites the fact that prenominal adjectives, like relative clauses and reduced relative clauses, render it possible for a definite determiner to surface with indefinite nominals, which otherwise reject *the*:

(84) *The sweater of John's is beautiful.

(85) The sweater of John's that was lying on the sofa is beautiful.

(86) ?The yellow sweater of John's is beautiful.

(87) ?The recently arrived sweater of John's is beautiful.

In Kayne's terms, (84) is ungrammatical because the definite determiner *the* simply cannot select an indefinite NP such as *sweater of John's*. In (85), the presence of a relative clause attenuates this incompatibility, in his terms, because in such cases D selects CP rather than NP:

(88) [The [$_{CP}$ [$_{NP}$ sweater of John's]$_i$ that t$_i$ was lying on the sofa]] is beautiful.

If (at least some) prenominal AdjPs result from covert relative clauses, then (86)–(87) can be explained in the same way.

Kayne's approach to adjectival modification offers no account of the HFF, as it stands. It does, however, offer the basis of a FOFC-based explanation. If all prenominal AdjPs are derived relative clauses, then the lack of head-initial prenominal AdjPs is also a ban on derived head-initial specifiers, making the effect look much more akin to a FOFC violation, as construed by Sheehan

(2013a,b) (see chapter 4). There is a serious problem, though, with assuming that all prenominal modifiers are base-generated as relative clauses: namely, the well-known fact that not all adjectives can participate in indirect modification (i.e., function predicatively and surface in relative clauses; see Emonds 1976, Cinque 2010:chap. 4). I address this problem in the next section, before offering an account of the HFF in section 7.5.4.

7.5.3   Direct/Indirect Modification

In discussions of AdjPs, a distinction is often made between "direct" and "indirect" modification. Cinque (2010), following Sproat and Shih (1988, 1990) and many others, makes this distinction along the following lines:[35]

Direct (attributive) modification
- obeys the universal adjective hierarchy
- permits only a nonintersective reading

Indirect (predicative) modification
- need not obey the universal adjective hierarchy
- permits only an intersective reading[36]

Sproat and Shih posit this distinction to deal with the two kinds of modification observed in Mandarin, but the distinction also exists in English and many other languages.[37]

Cinque (2010) pursues the idea that the two readings result from distinct syntactic configurations.[38] Direct modification involves an AdjP being externally merged as the specifier of a dedicated functional head, whereas indirect modification involves a (reduced) relative clause construction.[39] If the HFF reduces to a FOFC effect occasioned by movement of a head-initial modifier from a covert relative clause, it follows that only indirect modifiers should be subject to this condition. Direct modifiers, being externally merged as specifiers, should be immune to FOFC. Unfortunately, deciding which adjectives function intersectively and which do not is far from straightforward. At the two extremes, it is fairly clear that *former* can only function as a subsective/direct modifier whereas *red* can only be intersective, hence indirect:

(89) a. a red door = a door which is red
     b. a former colleague ≠ a colleague who is former

Clearly, *former* complies with the HFF in that it cannot surface with a posthead complement/modifier. This is, however, perhaps irrelevant to the HFF, as *former* and other clear direct modifiers do not readily accept any kind of modification:[40]

(90) a. *more former/alleged than John
      b. *a very former/alleged colleague
      c. *a more former/alleged colleague than John

Therefore, these adjectives may be amenable to an analysis like that proposed by Abney (1987), as discussed in section 7.5.1, whereby they are heads in the extended nominal projection, if the additional problems raised above can be addressed.

A crucial question, then, is whether there is any evidence of direct modifiers employing any of the compliance strategies discussed in section 7.3.2. According to the account provided by Cinque (2010), the two potential meanings of *old* can be attributed to the direct/indirect contrast:

(91) a friend who is old

(92) an old friend

While (91) can have only a pure intersective reading, where *old* denotes absolute age, (92) is ambiguous between this reading and another reading, whereby *old* denotes length of friendship (see Larson 1998, citing Siegel 1976, for discussion).

Cinque (2010:chap. 2) also notes that adjectives like *old* can be followed by a *than*-clause when used comparatively and that, in such contexts, the two meanings of *older* are made more explicit (though his English examples use the adjective *beautiful* and he actually claims that the equivalent to (93b) is ambiguous; see Cinque 2010:chaps. 2, 5):

(93) a. John is a friend older than Mary/the legal age.
      b. John is an older friend than Mary/#the legal age.

In (93a), only the absolute-age reading is possible, as expected if this example involves a reduced relative clause. In (93b), however, only the length-of-friendship reading is possible. If the length-of-friendship reading involves direct modification, then (93b) provides evidence that direct modification is also subject to the HFF.

It is not clear, though, that the contrast under discussion involves direct vs. indirect modification. According to Larson (1998), the distinction here does not concern intersectivity per se; rather, it concerns the variable that the AdjP modifies. The noun *friend* contains an event variable that can also be intersectively modified by an adjective, giving rise to the length-of-friendship reading in (92).

Recall also the following facts discussed by Bresnan (1973):

(94) a. I know a man taller than my mother.
      b. #I know a taller man than my mother.

Given that phrasal comparatives in English are covert clausal comparatives (Lechner 1999), one way to account for the infelicity of (94b) is to posit the following elided material:

(95) a. I know a man taller [than Op$_i$ my mother ~~is t$_i$ tall~~]
     b. #I know a taller man [than Op$_i$ my mother ~~is a t$_i$ tall man~~]

This explains why (93b) and (94b) strongly favor the readings they do, without the assumption that they involve direct modification.

In sum, it seems to be the case that the HFF applies only trivially to direct modifiers, as the latter cannot generally be modified. In instances of indirect modification, however, complements/modifiers are possible and languages make use of the various compliance strategies discussed in section 7.3.2. It is thus plausible that the HFF reduces to a restriction on the spelling out of head-initial phrases raised from a complement to a specifier position: that is, to a FOFC effect.

7.5.4 Assimilating the HFF to FOFC

If all prenominal indirect modifiers result from phrasal movement from a reduced relative clause, then the HFF can be assimilated to the PF account of FOFC proposed by Sheehan (2013b) (see chapter 4). In this analysis, FOFC is an effect of the linearization algorithm that relies only on c-command relations between *categories* (not between *phrases*) and uses asymmetric c-command only as a last resort when selection-based relations are not sufficient to order all categories in a given domain. For this reason, a difference emerges between right-branching and left-branching specifiers: only the latter can be linearized. As a simple illustration, consider the following structures (with some categories omitted and assuming that the PP functions as an atomized chunk for simplicity's sake):

(96) a. [$_{NP}$ [$_{AdjP}$ [$_{PP}$ PP] Adj] N [$_{AdjP}$ [$_{PP}$ ...]]
     b. [$_{NP}$ [$_{AdjP}$ Adj [$_{PP}$ PP]] N [$_{AdjP}$ Adj [$_{PP}$ ...]]]

In (96a), the category Adj, which does not enter into a selection relation with N, asymmetrically c-commands and so must precede the category N, and the atomic category PP must precede Adj (based on selection), giving the unambiguous order PP-Adj-N. For this reason, preposing PP serves to avoid the HFF, as noted in section 7.3.2.1. In (96b), on the other hand, the category Adj, which again does not enter into a selection relation with N, must still precede N, as it asymmetrically c-commands it, and PP must follow Adj. This means, however, that the c-command relations between PP and N must be inspected for them to be ordered. Interestingly, N asymmetrically c-commands PP, based on the definition of c-command in Sheehan 2013a,b (see chapter 4). For this reason, the prediction is that AdjP should be spelled out discontinuously, yielding Adj-N-PP. In fact, this possibility is not attested with complement PPs (though it is with complement CPs and adjunct PPs). I assume that this results from a fairly superficial processing constraint that requires Adj and its complement to be string-adjacent lest PP be construed as the complement of N. The only option, then, is wholesale extraposition, whereby Adj and PP are spelled out in their base positions, effectively meaning that movement is undone at PF.

Interestingly, whenever extraposition of PP/CP *is* available in a given language, wholesale extraposition is also possible (see section 7.3.2). This must mean either that two distinct linearization mechanisms operate optionally in such cases or, more likely, that movement of relative clauses is optional and is preferably avoided where they are heavy.

Note finally that the HFF applies to what are clearly fronted reduced relatives. As Cinque (2010) notes, the languages that permit surface HFF violations also do so with reduced relatives:

(97) a. Sidjaščaja okolo pal'my devuška (očen' krasiva). [Russian]
      sitting   near palm girl   (very pretty)
      'The girl sitting near the palm (is very pretty).'
      (Cinque 2010:46, citing Babby 1973:358)

    b. ta prósfata sideroména me   prosohi pukámisa   [Greek]
      the recently ironed   with care   shirts
      'the shirts recently ironed with care'
      (Cinque 2010:46, citing Melita Stavrou, pers. comm.)

Kayne (1994:98–99) gives other reduced prenominal relative clauses that, with the exception of incorporated prepositions, are subject to the HFF:

(98) a. the recently sent (*to me) book
    b. the much referred to hypothesis
    c. the little slept in bed

These facts make it all the more plausible that fronted AdjPs are reduced relatives, subject also to the same condition: FOFC.

7.6 Conclusions

This chapter has considered the HFF and argued that it reduces to an instance of FOFC applying to derived prenominal modifiers. Apparent counterexamples in some languages arguably involve hidden structure, which becomes apparent in definite DPs in Bulgarian. Complications arise from the fact that the same effect is observed with adverbial modifiers more generally, at least in many languages (Haider 2004; and see De Clercq, Haegeman, and Lohndal 2011, for an overview). Thus, Jackendoff (1977) notes that PP-adverbials in English have more limited placement possibilities than atomic adverbs:

(99) a. Bill {*with a crash} dropped the bananas {with a crash}.

b. Bill {(very) noisily} dropped the bananas {(very) noisily}.

At this point, it is not clear whether the account of the HFF proposed here extends to these kinds of examples, and the investigation of such cases is left to future research.

8 The Final-over-Final Condition in DP: Universal 20 and the Nature of Demonstratives

Ian Roberts

8.1 Introduction

In this chapter, we will turn our attention to nominals, the extended projection of N. For reasons that will become apparent, we will concentrate on topics relating to the syntax, and to one aspect of the semantics, of demonstratives. Section 8.2 focuses on Greenberg's Universal 20 and the role of the Final-over-Final Condition (FOFC) in excluding some of the illicit orders of adnominal modifiers as characterized by that universal. This leads to a discussion in section 8.3 of the typology of "low-demonstrative" languages, in connection with which I suggest a parameter specifying, in the unmarked case, a connection between overt low demonstratives and verb-initial clausal word order. Section 8.4 makes a novel proposal regarding the general nature of demonstratives based on ideas in Williams 1980, 1981a: the essential idea is that demonstratives are among a very small class of elements—in fact, possibly the only elements—able to overtly realize the referential external argument of n. Section 8.5 briefly looks at implications of these ideas for other aspects of DP-structure. Finally, section 8.6 compares the approach to Universal 20 adopted here with those in Cinque 2005a and Abels and Neeleman 2009, 2012. Section 8.7 concludes with a speculation about the fundamental differences between verbal/clausal extended projections and nominals.

Greenberg (1963:87) stated his Universal 20 as follows: "When any or all of the items (demonstrative, numeral and descriptive adjective) precede the noun, they are always found in that order. If they follow, the order is either the same or its exact opposite." Thus, Greenberg stated that these adnominal elements appear in the following orders in relation to each other and to N:

(1) a. Dem Num A N
    b. N Dem Num A
    c. N A Num Dem

Cinque (2005a:315) observes that, since Greenberg's original proposal was put forward, "[(1a)] remains virtually unchallenged, while [(1b,c) have] proven both too restrictive and too permissive." He discusses the various counterexamples in detail, and we will not linger over them here as, for the most part, they are not directly relevant to our concerns (except two classes, showing unexpectedly "low" demonstratives; see sections 8.2, 8.6). Cinque then proposes an analysis based on the Linear Correspondence Axiom (LCA) and certain assumptions about constraints on movement; the most important of these for our purposes is that no DP-internal category can move that does not contain the lexical projection NP. We will see that this is where FOFC has a role to play in the account of Universal 20.

8.2   Deriving Greenberg's Universal 20

I will discuss the ordering of the adnominal elements falling under Universal 20 in two parts. First, I will present a simplified version of Cinque's analysis, leaving aside certain technical complexities and, notably, leaving aside APs (section 8.2.1). This will permit us to see clearly the role FOFC plays in accounting for the possible and impossible orders. I will then reintroduce APs and look more closely at the four orders FOFC appears to exclude (section 8.2.2). Of these four, only two are clearly attested, one of them being much more common than the other. This demonstration, in turn, will set the scene for proposals regarding the nature and position of demonstratives (section 8.3.2).

8.2.1   Universal 20 without APs

In this section, I disregard adnominal APs and hence the relative order of A and N. One reason for this, in the context of FOFC, is that APs are modifiers and the core cases of FOFC seem to apply to head-complement relations (but see Biberauer, Holmberg, and Roberts 2014 and chapter 4 on this). Furthermore, as Cinque (2005a:315–316n2) points out, AP is probably not a unified category and, in particular, many putative APs in many languages may really be reduced relatives (see also Cinque 2010:chap. 6).

Cinque (2005a:321) assumes the following universal external-Merge order (see also Shlonsky 2004:1482):

(2)   [...[$_{WP}$ Dem...[$_{XP}$ ...Num...[$_{YP}$ A Y [$_{NP}$ N]]]]]

Cinque assumes that DemP, NumP, and AP are specifiers of functional categories he labels WP, XP, and YP. Interspersed among these are AgrPs into whose specifiers lower elements may move, as Cinque (2005a:326) proposes.

For now, I simplify this structure as follows:[1]

(3) [$_{DP}$ DemP D [$_{QP}$ NumP Q [$_{NP}$\{N (A)\}]]]]

Here, I take Dem and Num to be phrasal categories, as does Cinque.[2] On the relationship between Dem and D, see below. Weak quantifiers appear in Q (see section 8.5.1). I briefly comment on the locus of grammatical number (singular/plural/dual) in section 8.6. Very much in the spirit of Cinque 2005a, the attested orders now follow from (3) combined with the possibility of NP-movement, either to Spec,QP or to Spec,DP, and the further option of QP-movement, along with standard conditions on movement such as the A-over-A Condition and the Strict Cycle. As we will see, FOFC accounts for a gap in the set of possible derivations.

Consider the various surface orders that can be derived from (3). The first possibility is the very simple one in which nothing moves, giving a surface harmonic head-initial order (*these three boys*):

(4) Dem Num NP

This order is found in "very many languages" according to Cinque (2005a:319), among them English. There is nothing further to say about this order here, although see the discussion of first-merged orders in section 8.6.

The second possible order involves NP-movement, but only as far as Spec,QP. I will assume throughout this chapter that roll-up movement targets the outer specifier position where Num and Dem are present—that is, that Num and Dem are externally merged prior to internal Merge of the moving category. This is a standard assumption in cases such as object shift or *wh*-movement in relation to the external argument in Spec,vP (note that this replicates Cinque's assumption of single specifiers and interspersed AgrPs briefly discussed above). Then NP-movement to Spec,QP gives rise to surface Dem-N-Num order (*these boys three*):

(5) [$_{DP}$ **Dem D** [$_{QP}$ **NP** [$_{QP}$ Num [Q ⟨NP⟩]]]]]

According to Cinque (2005a:320), this order, with the adjective preceding the noun, is found in "few/very few languages" (see Cinque 2005a:320n13 for details). With the adjective following the noun, it is found in "many languages" (see Cinque 2005a:320n14). Dryer (2009c) lists 3 languages from 3 genera with the order Dem-N-Num-A, 0 languages with the order A-Dem-N-Num, 11 languages from 6 genera with the order Dem-A-N-Num, and 28 languages from 22 genera with the order Dem-N-A-Num.

The third possible order involves a further step of NP-movement to Spec,DP, giving the surface order N-Dem-Num (*boys these three*):

(6) [$_{DP}$ **NP** [$_{DP}$ **Dem** [$_{QP}$ ⟨NP⟩ Num [**Q** ⟨NP⟩]]]]

Again, this order is attested in "few/very few languages" (see Cinque 2005a:319nn11, 12). Dryer (2009c) lists 4 languages from 3 genera with the order N-Dem-Num-A, 19 languages from 11 genera with the order N-A-Dem-Num, 4 languages from 2 genera with the order A-N-Dem-Num, and 6 languages from 4 genera with the order N-Dem-A-Num. As Cinque (2005a:321) suggests, this paucity may be due to the markedness of NP not pied-piping at all, but merely undergoing successive-cyclic movement through QP to DP.

The fourth possible order involves "roll-up"—that is, pied-piping at each step, giving NP-movement followed by QP pied-piping. This derivation creates a surface order that is the mirror image of the first-merged order of elements, namely, N-Num-Dem (*boys three these*):

(7) [$_{DP}$ [$_{QP}$ **NP** [**Num** ⟨NP⟩]] [**Dem** ⟨[$_{QP}$ NP [Q ⟨NP⟩]]⟩]]

This order, with AP intervening between NP and Num (possibly derived by NP rolling up around AP on the lowest cycle, not shown in (7)), is very common, as Greenberg originally observed.

FOFC is relevant to a fifth order: namely, the derivation where NP does not move within QP, but QP raises to Spec,DP. This gives the surface order Num-N-Dem (*three boys these*):

(8) [$_{DP}$ [$_{QP}$ **Num NP**] [**Dem** ([$_{QP}$ Num ⟨NP⟩])]]

Recall that the basic structural schema that violates FOFC is as follows:

(9) *[$_{\beta P}$ [$_{\alpha P}$ α γP] β]

The structure in (8) instantiates the schema in (9) for α=Num, β=Dem, and therefore violates FOFC. So we see that FOFC underlies the observation that, if NumP moves in our simplified structure for DP, NP must first move to its Spec. Cinque's derivations (see Cinque 2005a:321–324) are all such that if anything moves, NP moves (Cinque allows for nothing at all to move, giving the order Dem-Num-A-N). In present terms, this observation can be explained by FOFC, since a configuration like (8) will inevitably result from moving XP ≠ NP without prior roll-up of NP and any YP containing NP and contained in XP (this corresponds to what Cinque calls "*picture-of-whom*" pied-piping).

So we see that FOFC predicts that Num-N-Dem order should not be found—or, more precisely, that if it is found, it will not instantiate the structure in (8). Let us now investigate this prediction, reviewing the possible examples of the FOFC-violating order in (8) and bringing the position of adnominal adjectives back into consideration.

8.2.2   Universal 20 with APs

If we bring adnominal adjectives back into the picture, the putative FOFC-violating order Num-N-Dem in (8) has four instantiations, as follows:[3]

(10) a. A Num N Dem   (unattested; Cinque/Dryer order (v))
     b. Num N A Dem   (attested; Cinque/Dryer order (s))
     c. Num A N Dem   (attested; Cinque/Dryer order (r))
     d. Num N Dem A   (attested; Cinque/Dryer order (g))

Let us look at these orders in turn. (10a) is clearly unattested. Cinque (2005a:320), citing Greenberg (1963) and Hawkins (1983), mentions no examples. There are no clear cases in the *World Atlas of Language Structures* (*WALS*), although the evidence in *WALS* is somewhat equivocal, since information is provided on each pair N-G ("Noun-Genitive"; see section 8.3.2 for a brief discussion of this order), N-A, N-Dem, and N-Num for very many languages, but not directly on the relative order of the adnominal elements themselves; moreover, this information is not always provided in grammars.[4] Dryer (2009c) says (10a) is unattested.

The order in (10b) is by far the most common of those in (10), being attested in a fair number of languages. Notably, it is found in all the Celtic languages:

(11) a. y   pum llyfr newydd hyn   [Welsh]
         the five book new   these
         'these five new books'
         (Roberts 2005:92)
     b. na   trì   leabhraichean mòra seo   [Scottish Gaelic]
         the.PL three books   big.PL this
         'these three big books'
         (David Adger, pers. comm.)
     c. an bheirt fhear mhóra seo   [Irish]
         the two   man   big.PL this
         'these two big men'
         (Jim McCloskey, pers. comm.)
     d. ar plac'h paour mañ[5]   [Breton]
         the girl   poor this
         'this poor girl'

According to *WALS* maps 87A, 88A, 89A (Dryer 2015a,e,h), this order is found in 77 languages altogether. Table 8.1 gives a breakdown by language family and information regarding the order of subject, object, and verb in the relevant languages. As the table shows, languages with order (10b) in DP have a far higher incidence of VS order than generally (approximately 50% as

Table 8.1
The 77 languages with Num-N, N-A, N-Dem order (*WALS* maps 87A, 88A, 89A; Dryer 2015a,c,d)

Language	Family	Causal word order
Zapotec (Zoogocho)	Oto-Manguean	VSO
Zapotec (Yatzachi)	"	VS
Mixtec (Jicaltepec)	"	VSO
Mixtec (Yosoudúa)	"	VSO
Chatino (Yaitepec)	"	VSO
Zapotec (Mitla)	"	VSO
Chinantec (Palantla)	"	VSO
Trique (Copala)	"	VSO
Zapotec (Isthmus)	"	VSO
Chinantec (Comaltepec)	"	VSO
Chatino (Lealao)	"	VSO
Mixtec (Ocotepec)	"	VSO
Mixtec (Chalcatongo)	"	VSO
Chatino (Sierra Occidental)	"	VSO
Tlapanec	"	VSO
Hoava	Austronesian	VSO
Ulithian	"	SVO
Tatana'	"	VS
Taiof	"	SVO
Tungak	"	SVO
Nehan	"	SVO
Gela	"	VOS
Roviana	"	VSO
Sisiqa	"	SVO
Halia	"	SVO
Longgu	"	VOS
Timugon	"	VSO
Tboli	"	VSO
Puluwat	"	SVO
Manggurai	"	SVO
Arosi	"	SVO
Lampung	"	SVO
Minangkabau	"	No dominant order
Woleaian	"	SVO
Iban	"	SVO
Kwaio	"	SVO
Sundanese	"	SVO
Muna	"	SVO
Tigak	"	SVO
Acehnese	"	SVO/VS
Kiribati	"	VOS

Table 8.1 (cont.)

Language	Family	Causal word order
Batak (Koro)	"	SVO/VSO
Rapanui	"	VSO
Fijian	"	VS
Indonesian	"	SVO
Bajau (West Coast)	"	SVO/VSO
Tuvaluan	"	OVS
Teop	"	SVO
Yapese	"	VSO
Kilivila	"	SVO/VOS
Berber (Chaouia)	Afro-Asiatic	SVO/VSO
Berber (Rif)	Afro-Asiatic	SVO
Hebrew (Modern)	"	SVO
Tamashek	"	VSO
Gelao	Tai-Kadai	SVO
Yay	"	SVO
Dong	"	SVO
Nung (Vietnam)	"	SVO
Hlai (Baoding)	"	SVO
Punu	Hmong-Mien	SVO
Hmong Njua	"	SVO
Cornish[a]	Indo-European	SVO[a]
Gaelic (Scottish)	"	VSO
Breton	"	SVO (*sic*); see note a
Welsh	"	VSO
Irish	"	VSO
Garifuna	Arawakan	VSO
Goajiro	"	VSO
Sre	Austro-Asiatic	SVO
Chrau	"	SVO
Sedang	"	SVO
Semelai	"	VSO/VOS
Vietnamese	"	SVO
Katu	"	SVO
Wolof	Niger-Congo	SVO
Basque	Isolate	SOV
Wichi	Metacoan	SVO

[a] Cornish is a special case, in that it is unclear whether the earlier typically Brythonic clausal order XP-Part-V-S-O, found in Middle Welsh and almost all modern dialects of Breton, was reanalyzed as SVO in Late Conish (with XP being consistently analyzed as the subject, the loss of the particles and the loss of the verb endings distinguishing a preverbal pronominal subject from a postverbal one). If it was, then Cornish is misclassified as SVO in *WALS*. On this basis, it seems that Breton is also misclassified. George (1993:457–458) argues that a change of this kind did in fact take place.

opposed to 6.89% (95) of the 1,377 languages in *WALS* map 81A; Dryer 2015b).This is a striking fact, which we will return to in section 8.3. Order (10b) is also found in the Oceanic language Sisiqa, which according Ross (2002d) exhibits a form of verb-second (V2) order. It is found in the following SVO languages: the Austronesian languages Arosi (Lynch and Horoi 2002), Bati-Vitu (Ross 2002a), Kwaio (Keesing 1985), Mussau (Ross 2002c), and Nakanai (Johnston 1980), as well as Nung (Tai-Kadai; Saul and Wilson 1980), Sre (Austro-Asiatic; Manley 1972), and the Hmong-Mien language Hmong Njua (Harriehausen 1990).[6] Haddican (2002) lists the following creoles as having this order: Haitian, Papiamentu, Angolar, Le Tayo, St. Lucian, and Louisiana Creole. Finally, Cinque (2005a:320n16) also cites certain Mon-Khmer languages (Dryer 2001) and the Australian language Watjarri (Douglas 1981:241).

Looking again at the Celtic languages in (11), there is reason to think that a morphosyntactic relation holds between the initial determiner and the low demonstrative. Such a relation seems particularly clear in some Semitic languages, where the demonstrative appears preceding the (otherwise) initial determiner as well as in the final position, as in the Moroccan Arabic example (12a), or where the definiteness marking "spreads" to N, A, and the final demonstrative, as in the Hebrew example (12b):[7]

(12) a. had ar rajeel haada   [Moroccan Arabic]
        this the man   this
        'this man'
        (Kaye and Rosenhouse 1997:300)
     b. ha-kufsa ha-gdola ha-zot   [Hebrew]
        the-box   the-big   the-this
        'this big box'
        (Berman 1997:327; see also Benmamoun 2000, Shlonsky 2004)

Moreover, a number of the other languages listed above show initial articles or determiners (Arosi, Nakanai, and Sisiqa). This evidence motivates the choice of D as the label for the category above QP.

We now face two questions:

(13) a. What is the first-merged position of Dem in DP in the order in (10b)?
     b. What is the relation between Dem and D?

In section 8.3, I will propose answers to these questions, which will allow (10b) to be derived without a FOFC violation. First, though, let us briefly consider the other orders in (10).

Concerning order (10c), Dryer (2009c) gives four languages from three genera. The languages listed in note 6 may have this order, but the crucial evidence, usually concerning the relative order of A and Dem, is either ambiguous or unavailable. Ndyuka, a Suriname creole, has the order Num/Quantifier-A-Article-N-Dem (Hutter and Hutter 1994:203–220), so this may be an example; Dryer (2009c) lists it as having this order. Cinque (2005a:320n15) cites Lynch (2002:769–770, 781, 809) for Xârâcùù, Iai, and Puluwatese (Dryer (2009c) also lists the former two); however, according to Tryon (1971:81) Iai has Num-N-Dem-A order (i.e., order (10d)). Cinque further cites Haddican (2002) and Rijkhoff (2002) for Berbice Dutch Creole, Sranan, and Bislama, an Indian Ocean creole; interestingly, the first two are also spoken in Suriname. Dryer (2009c) also lists Coast Tsimshian. Given these considerations, I will take this order to be either very rare or nonexistent.

(10d) is rare, but is attested in Kilivila, an Austronesian Oceanic language spoken by the Trobriand Islanders (Senft 1986).[8] Cinque (2005a:322n26) points out that the (10d) order "would only cease to be a problem if the adjective there derived from a relative clause, which is higher than Num, with Num N moved past the relative clause and Dem." It seems then that Cinque is proposing a derivation just like that in (8), with the single difference that [Num NP] moves over AP/RelCl:

(8′) [$_{DemP}$ [$_{NumP}$ **Num NP**] [**Dem** AP/RelCl ⟨[$_{NumP}$ Num NP]⟩]]

Clearly, this derivation leads to a FOFC violation, just like (8). So Cinque's suggested account of this order is not available here. I will suggest an alternative analysis of this case below, but first let us look more closely at the general case of putative "low-demonstrative" languages, particularly the questions raised in (13).

8.3   The Nature of "Low" Demonstratives

8.3.1   The D-Dem Relation

Guardiano (2010) makes a number of interesting proposals concerning the crosslinguistic relation between determiners and demonstratives, and argues that demonstratives are universally first-merged in a "low" position. When we see them in a "high" position, they have undergone raising to Spec,DP. This proposal was first made by Giusti (1993) for Romanian and by Brugè (1994) for Spanish (see also Brugè 1996, 2000, 2002:33–42, Brugè and Giusti 1996, Giusti 1997, 2002, Panagiotidis 2000, Rosen 2003, Shlonsky 2004, Grohmann and Panagiotidis 2005).

Guardiano's initial observations are (i) that demonstratives are universal (this is also pointed out in Lyons 1999:107 and Alexiadou, Haegeman, and Stavrou 2007:95), (ii) that definite articles are not, and (iii) that languages vary as to the cooccurrence possibilities of these two elements. As far as I am aware, these are all empirically correct observations. Observation (ii) is well-known (although, *pace* Bošković (2008, 2010), we are assuming that D is present even when not overtly realized; this is necessary in order to assimilate to the Celtic pattern those languages with the order (10b) that lack overt articles). Observation (iii) is precisely what we will discuss below, and observation (i) appears to be a substantive universal, with an obvious functional/communicative motivation (and, if the proposals in sections 8.4 and 8.5 are right, a semantic/conceptual motivation). On the basis of these observations, Guardiano goes on to distinguish six types of language, according to the position of the demonstrative in relation to other DP-internal elements, and according to the ability of demonstratives to cooccur with definite determiners.

Type 1 languages are represented by English and Italian, among many others. In these languages, Dem precedes nearly all other adnominal elements in DP (except quantifiers like *all/tutto*) and is in complementary distribution with D. In Type 2 languages, Dem is likewise initial in DP, but it systematically cooccurs with overt definite articles, as in Hungarian:

(14) a. ez   a   négy férfi   [Hungarian]
        this the four men
        'these four men'
     b. az   az   ötödik szimfónia
        that the fifth   symphony
        'that fifth symphony'

Type 3 languages include Welsh, where Dem cooccurs with D but follows it, with most other adnominal modifiers being postnominal. Type 4 languages, represented by Hebrew, are like Welsh as regards the position of Dem and definite D, but display "spreading" of definiteness marking in DP. Type 5 is exemplified by Modern Greek, where we find *aftos o anthropos* 'this.NOM the.NOM man.NOM' ('this man (nominative)'), but also *o anthropos aftos*, as well as, with adjectives, orders such as *o kalos aftos anthropos* 'the.NOM good.NOM this.NOM man.NOM' ('this good man (nominative)'). Finally, Type 6 includes languages like Spanish and Romanian where both a Welsh-type order and an English-type order seem to be options:

(15) a. este profesor/el   profesor este   [Spanish]
        this professor/the professor this
        'this professor'
     b. el   profesor este alemán/alemán   este
        the professor this German/German this
        'this German professor'

It is clear then that UG makes available at least two Dem/D positions, one initial in DP and one in a low postnominal position. As mentioned above, Guardiano proposes that there is a single universal first-merged position for demonstratives, in a relatively low position in the DP (Alexiadou, Haegeman, and Stavrou (2007) make a very similar proposal). This is the position in which demonstratives always surface in the Celtic languages. In languages like Spanish and Greek, demonstratives optionally raise to Spec,DP, and in languages like English, Italian, and Hungarian, this raising is obligatory (in fact, Greek appears to have a further "partial raising" option, which I will leave aside). We could add to this that French examples like *cette voiture-ci/là* 'this car here/there' may feature demonstrative elements in both positions (cf. Bernstein 2001:552).

The important conclusion from this brief summary of Guardiano's proposals is that, if Dem is able to appear either in Spec,DP or lower in the nominal, then the Num-N-(A-)Dem order of (10b) does not have to derive from QP-movement into Spec,DP. Hence, this order does not violate FOFC. However, if this approach to demonstratives is to be maintained, more must be said regarding both the first-merged position and (where appropriate) the nature of the trigger for movement of demonstratives.

8.3.2 Demonstratives as Subject of nP

Let us now return to the two questions raised in (13), repeated here:

(13) a. What is the first-merged position of Dem in DP in the order in (10b)?

b. What is the relation between D and Dem?

The best way to answer (13a) is in terms of the general structure of the DP. On analogy with the biphasal structure of the clause in (16a), proposed by Chomsky (2000, 2001), I propose the structure for DP given in (16b) (see also Julien 2005:4, Alexiadou, Haegeman, and Stavrou 2007):

(16) a. *Clause structure (Chomsky 2000, 2001, etc.)*
$[_{CP}$ C $[_{TP}$ T $[_{vP}$ v$[_{VP}$ V$]]]]$

b. *Nominal structure*
$[_{DP}$ D $[_{QP}$ Q $[_{nP}$ n $[_{NP}$ N$]]]]$

In these terms, we can think of C and D as the *external* phase heads, interfacing with higher categories and with the discourse context. Those functional heads that are not phasal, T and Q, arguably have the basic property of quantifying over the lower phasal category (this is also true of more elaborate "cartographic" functional structures for both CP and DP, where T and Q are split into sequences of heads of different quantificational types; see Cinque

1999:112, 2005a:328). The "little" v and n categories are the *internal* phase heads, determining nonlexical properties of the lexical root (case, agreement, perhaps category, etc.). V and N are lexical roots.

Focusing on the Celtic DP, and illustrating just with Welsh, a further point to be made is that PP-arguments of the noun appear following the demonstrative:

(17) a. y   llyfr hwn am forfilod   [Welsh]
        the book this on whales
        'this book on whales'

    b. y llun   hwn o'r   dyn gan Picasso
       the picture this of-the man by Picasso
       'this picture of the man by Picasso'
       (Rouveret 1994:221)

The same observation is made for Scots Gaelic by Adger (2013:110).

Similarly, sentential (CP) complements to nouns are always the absolute last item in the nominal in Welsh:

(18) a. posibilrwydd cryf   y   bydd y   Lib Dems yn   [Welsh]
        possibility   strong that will.be the Lib Dems PART
        colli eu   seddi gwledig yng Nghymru
        lose their seats rural   in Wales
        'a strong possibility that the Lib Dems will lose their rural seats in Wales'

    b. gobeithion mawr gan bawb   y   bydd hyn yn   datrys y
       hopes   big by everyone that will.be this PART solve the
       broblem
       problem
       'great hopes on the part of everyone that this will solve the problem'

    c. y syniad newydd trawiadol hwn bod modd trosglwyddo ynni
       the idea   new   striking this that can transfer   energy
       drwy'r   awyr
       through-the air
       'this striking new idea that it's possible to transfer energy through the air'
       (David Willis, pers. comm.)

(Brugè (2002:41) shows the same for Irish.)

We can now posit the following structure for the Celtic DP:

(19) $[_{DP} \text{ D } [_{QP} \text{ Q } [_{FP} \text{ (AP*) F } [_{nP} \text{ DemP } \mathbf{n} \text{ } [_{NP} \text{ N (PP) (CP)}]]]]]$

In (19), adjectives and demonstratives occupy a low position. N-to-Q raising (see Cinque 1994, Rouveret 1994, Duffield 1996), or perhaps NP-raising to the outer Spec,FP (we will opt for this possibility in section 8.6), then allows us to account for the Celtic orders without violating FOFC. It also captures the fact that demonstratives and adjectives intervene between N and its complements (the AP* notation glosses over the tricky question of adjective hierarchies in Welsh and the general possibility of a cartographic analysis of these; on which, see Willis 2006).

Adger (2013:107–113) argues against an analysis of this type on two grounds (on the basis of data from Scottish Gaelic, but the overall similarities in DP-internal syntax across Celtic are such that the discussion would apply, as far as I am aware, to the other languages too). His first point is that positing a definiteness-marking head (e.g., D), as in (19), runs into difficulties with the fact that both pronouns and proper names can cooccur with demonstratives:

(20) a. iad   sin   [Scottish Gaelic]
        they that
        'those (guys)'
     b. Daibhidh ud
        David   that
        'that David'

Adger says that in order to capture these facts we would need, in addition to postulating a D-Dem definiteness-checking relation, "to further stipulate another feature to ensure that any definite D obligatorily projected above Dem would be null if the complement of Dem were to be a pronoun or proper name" (p. 108). But all that is required here, given the structure in (19), is N-to-D raising of the kind familiar since Longobardi 1994 applying to proper names and pronouns. In other cases, we simply posit that definite D has an uninterpretable definiteness feature while Dem has an interpretable one.

Adger's second argument comes from coordinate structures. He points out that the definite article must appear in both conjuncts if the demonstrative has scope over both conjuncts (McCloskey (2004:4) makes the same observation for Irish):

(21) a. na dealbhan agus na h-ìomhaighean sin   [Scottish Gaelic]
        the pictures and the images   that
        'these pictures and images'
     b. *na dealbhan agus ìomhaighean sin
        the pictures and images   that

We can treat (21a) as a case of nP-coordination, combined with raising of this category to Spec,FP. This idea entails two complications of what we have said up to now: first, we have to raise Dem in any case, to a further functional position below FP and, second, we must treat the article *na* as first-merged in n rather than D. Concerning the first complication, in this respect Dem actually further parallels what is known about clausal external arguments in Celtic, in that these have been shown to undergo "short" raising from Spec,vP to a position whose status is unclear, but is additional to the standard clause structure given in (16) (see McCloskey 1996 on Irish, Roberts 2005 on Welsh, and Schafer 1994 on Breton). Concerning the second, we can treat *na* as first-merged in n and generally raising to D; this raising is blocked in coordinate structures like (21) owing to the Coordinate Structure Constraint.

The structure deriving from movement of the coordinated nP may itself appear to violate FOFC. However, Biberauer, Holmberg, and Roberts (2014:201–202) argue that coordination never gives rise to FOFC violations; neither conjunct violates FOFC in relation to the coordinating head, and the coordinate phrase itself does not violate FOFC either. This follows from the fact that FOFC is relativized to extended projections of categories, and conjuncts are acategorial.

A final consequence of nP-raising relates to the fact that complements of N always follow Dem in Celtic, as we have seen. We can treat this as a form of "obligatory extraposition" triggered by the need to avoid a FOFC violation (at the level of NP). Leaving aside the details of the extraposition operation, which would take us too far afield here, this is exactly analogous to the account of obligatory extraposition of head-initial CPs in OV languages put forward by Biberauer, Holmberg, and Roberts (2014:198).

Here are further examples of the order in (10b) from some non-Celtic languages:

(22) a. duwa droe ureueng nyang-sakit nyoe   [Acehnese]
         two   CL   person   REL-sick   this
         'these two sick people'
         (Durie 1985:108)

      b. a:^{M}i la:^{L} tiê^{L}i ki,á:^{H}-ʔi^M-ni^{LM}i   [Lealao Chinantec]
         three mule white of-1SGREL-that
         'those three white mules of mine'
         (Rupp 1989:63)

      c. uu   ndá ndīkā   náhnú ñúkwán   [Ocotepec Mixtec]
         two PL   banana big.PL that
         'those two big bananas'
         (Alexander 1988:220)

We can transpose the analysis of Celtic fairly straightforwardly to all of these cases, although the presence of a classifier in (22a) and the plural marker in (22c) create a complication. We can assume, as for Celtic, that the numerals occupy Spec,QP, and the classifier or plural marker is in Q, with AP in Spec,FP and DemP in Spec,nP. We can then posit either NP-movement to Spec,FP or (as just sketched for Celtic) "short" DemP-movement to a further low position, in combination with "remnant" nP-movement to Spec,FP. It has been proposed several times that classifiers appear in languages without plural inflection on nouns (see Chierchia 1998, Borer 2005:chap. 4, Huang 2015),[9] and so it seems natural to locate both properties in Q, in crosslinguistic complementary distribution (see in particular Borer 2005:92ff. on this last point, and see Huang and Ochi 2010 for a different view). So, the general approach sketched for order (10b) for Celtic can carry over in essence to the other languages showing this order.[10]

Interesting support for this approach comes from a typological observation regarding low-demonstrative (LD) languages. As mentioned in connection with table 8.1, there seems to be a link between verb-initial clausal order and LD order. In many cases, LD languages have VSO or VOS order: this is true of all the Celtic languages and of Moroccan Arabic, and was true of Biblical Hebrew (Modern Hebrew retains certain residual verb-initial constructions). In fact, examples of VS order in the clause and LD order in the nominal are to be found in all the major groups of VS languages: Austronesian (Raviona, Tinrin, Seediq, Karo Batak, Acehnese); Meso-American (Isthmus Zapotec, Ocotepec Mixtec, Chalcatongo Mixtec, Lealao Chinantec, Comaltepec Chinantec), and Salishan (Hisgha); see table 8.1. Moreover, all the languages that show VSO order and LD order also have QN order (Dryer 2015c,d,f). Given the nonexistence of (10a), and the apparent rarity of (10c) and (10d), this suggests that order (10b) is connected to verb-initial clausal order. Finally, of the other languages considered by Guardiano (2010), Spanish, Greek, and Romanian optionally have LD order and allow VSO order quite productively at the clausal level (unlike Italian, for example). This suggests a connection.

The most widely accepted analysis of VSO clausal order is that proposed by McCloskey (1996). He argues that this order is derived by a combination of V-raising to T and a lack of subject raising to Spec,TP (although, as already mentioned, it is fairly clear in many VSO languages that the subject does raise out of vP; on these assumptions, it must move to a position lower than Spec,TP). Schematically, this analysis posits the derived clause structure in (23):

(23) $[_{TP} [_{T}V]...SU...[_{vP} \langle V \rangle O]]$

The most important feature of this analysis for our purposes is that nothing is attracted to Spec,TP. Perhaps somewhat simplistically, we can say that there is no EPP-feature on T here; this is then a major parametric property that contributes to the derivation of VSO order (of course, V-raising is another, but this is clearly independent of VSO in principle, since many non-VSO languages feature V-to-T movement).

Now, we can generalize the LD structure of the DP in (19), and suppose that D bears some feature F that varies parametrically in its ability to attract Dem:

(24) $[_{DP}$ $D_{[F]}$ ... $[_{nP}$ Dem [n $[_{NP}$ N...]]]]

This idea has been independently put forward by Brugè and Giusti (1996), Brugè (2000, 2002), Alexiadou, Haegeman, and Stavrou (2007), and Guardiano (2010). For Guardiano, F is a person feature; for Brugè and for Brugè and Giusti, it is [+REF]; and for Panagiotidis (2000), Grohmann and Panagiotidis (2005), and Alexiadou, Haegeman, and Stavrou (2007:124), it is deixis. Also, Henry (2010) proposes a similar movement in varieties of English that allow both *this here book* and *this book here* (see also the discussions of nonstandard English in Alexiadou, Haegeman, and Stavrou 2007:117–118 and Kayne 2008). In order to pursue the parallel with clauses, I propose that the movement-triggering feature on D is the EPP-feature. Hence, we have (25):

(25) $[_{DP}$ $D_{[u\varphi, (EPP)]}$ ... $[_{nP}$ $Dem_{[i\varphi]}$ [n $[_{NP}$ N...]]]]

Here, the presence or absence of the EPP-feature on D is a parameter controlling the crosslinguistic variation in attraction of Dem (and other elements, as we will see in section 8.4). Note that D has uninterpretable φ-features here and Agrees with Dem's interpretable φ-features; we will return to this point below.[11]

We can generalize this account in an interesting way and make the link to VS order explicit. Let us suppose that there is a general parameter that applies to both clauses and nominals, as follows:[12]

(26) Does a functional head F in a higher phase attract the external argument of its phasal complement?

If we treat Dem as the external argument of n (an idea I will discuss at length in section 8.4), then (26) regulates subject raising in TP/CP and Dem-raising in DP. English and Italian set this parameter to the positive value, being SVO and "high-demonstrative" languages. The Celtic languages and other VSO languages set it to the negative value, having both VSO and LD orders. Greek, Spanish, and Romanian allow the EPP-feature under specific discourse or other conditions, which we need not go into here.

Kilivila, the language with the order schematized in (8′), appears to have alternating VSO/VOS word order. On analogy with Massam and Smallwood's (1997) analysis of clausal VSO/VOS order in Niuean as involving a combination of (possibly remnant) VP-fronting and object shift, we could posit NP-movement to Spec,FP, with AP in a lower position than that suggested by Cinque (2005a). This would give rise to the following structure (still thinking of the AP as being potentially a reduced relative):

(27) ...Num [$_{FP}$ NP [$_{F'}$ F [$_{nP}$ Dem A/RelCl n (NP)]]]

As mentioned in section 8.2, other languages that show this order, according to Dryer (2009c), are Katu (a Mon-Khmer language of Vietnam), Teop, Drehu (both Oceanic), and Yapese. Of these, we have no information on clausal word order in Katu, while Teop is SVO, Drehu is SVO/VOS, and Yapese is VSO.[13]

The parameter in (26) predicts a rigid VS-LD correlation. At first sight, this does not seem correct (see again table 8.1). Following Cinque's (2005a) discussion of exceptions to Greenberg's Universal 20, there certainly appear to be both SV-LD languages (e.g., Modern Hebrew, Wolof, Indonesian, and others given in table 8.1) and VS-HD languages. *WALS* lists 76 languages in the latter category and 448 in the former (I return to these briefly below).

It appears, then, that the relation between VS and LD orders has counterexamples in both directions. Therefore, it may be better to regard this as a preference. What the VS and LD orders share is lack of movement of the external argument to the relevant "high" specifier position, as (26) states. Given that this is not a categorical requirement, as the counterexamples show, let us formulate two more specific parameters as subcases of (26), as follows:

(28) a. Does F in the higher clausal phase attract the external argument?
      b. Does F in the higher nominal phase attract the external argument?

In a VS-HD language, then, (28a) is negative while (28b) is positive. Conversely, in an SV-LD language, (28a) is positive and (28b) is negative. Both of these settings represent relatively marked systems in relation to VS-LD or SV-HD, since the latter two options represent settings of (26). The parameter in (26) is less specific than those in (28); hence, it determines less marked systems than those in (28). Note that, in (26), movement of the external argument in nominals and movement of the external argument in clauses pattern together, while (28) allows them to pattern distinctly. Hence, the parameters in (28) are less general than that in (26), and so potentially give rise to more marked systems.[14] Since they allow more specific, and therefore more marked, options, the options in (28) represent a lower portion of the relevant parameter hierarchy than (26) in terms of the proposals for parameter hierarchies put forward in Roberts 2012a,b. See also Biberauer et al. 2014 and Biberauer and Roberts 2015b.

In this section, I have proposed that demonstratives may function as the external argument of n, and have looked at the typological support, as well as problems, for this idea. Accordingly, I have proposed the parameters (26) and (28a,b), suggesting that they may be related in terms of a hierarchy.

Let us now explore further the idea that demonstratives function as the external argument of n, before returning, in section 8.6, to a general discussion of Universal 20 and how the structure in (19) allows us to account for almost exactly the orders accounted for by Cinque (2005a). There, we will also discuss proposals made by Abels and Neeleman (2009, 2012).

8.4   The Demonstrative as the External Argument of n

We have posited the following structures for the DP and the CP:[15]

(29) a. $[_{DP} D_{[u\varphi,\ (EPP)]}...[_{nP} Dem_{[i\varphi,\ (uCase)]} [n [_{NP} N...]]]]$

   b. $[_{CP} C/T_{[u\varphi,\ (EPP)]}...[_{vP} DP_{[i\varphi,\ uCase]} [v [_{VP} V...]]]]$

Assuming the mechanism of Agree as proposed by Chomsky (2000, 2001) (i.e., pairing of interpretable and uninterpretable formal features in a local configuration), and assuming that DPs typically have interpretable φ-features, while finite V (more precisely, T) has uninterpretable features, we could propose that the D-Dem Agree relation is what renders D's φ-features interpretable and therefore able to Agree with clausal heads. The nature of Dem is then central to the functioning of DP in the Agree system. This idea could be extended to the uninterpretable Case feature of Dem, although any Case agreement with D would have to be vacuous in the sense that D's Case feature would not be thereby valued, since it is standardly assumed that structural Case features are uninterpretable (see note 11).

This proposal appears to face a serious problem, however: while it is thought that clauses always have an external argument (or at least they can always make a DP available in Spec,vP, perhaps through raising—passives, unaccusatives—or through expletive insertion; see Richards and Biberauer 2006 for arguments that expletives are first-merged in Spec,vP and Legate 2003 for arguments that A-movement in unaccusatives and passives transits through Spec,vP), it certainly does not appear to be the case that DPs always contain demonstratives. Here I will argue that, once we take a particular view of the way in which argument structure (in a rather general sense) is realized in nP, this problem disappears and, in fact, a very interesting, essentially Russellian picture of the syntax-semantics mapping in nominals emerges.

The leading idea was originally put forward by Williams (1981a). In addition to developing his (1980) proposal that the basic asymmetry in argument structure is between the external argument of a predicate and all other arguments, with the concomitant idea that the canonical external argument of a verbal predicate bears the Agent θ-role, Williams proposed that the external argument of the nominal was its reference. Thus, using Williams's notation for underlining the external argument of a predicate, we have something like this:[16]

(30) a. *hit* ($\underline{x}$, y), *run* ($\underline{x}$), *fall* (x)
     b. *dog* ($\underline{x}$), *father* ($\underline{x}$, y)

The single argument of a nonrelational noun such as *dog* is its external argument, and this argument bears the Reference role of the noun. In other words, the values of *x* in (30b) are referents of the noun *dog*. Thus, in a predicative clause such as *Fido is a dog*, *Fido* can be seen as bearing this θ-role: the relevant part of the logical form is *dog(f)* (Williams 1994:34).

In these terms, the proposal regarding Dem that is being developed here can be stated as follows:

(31) Dem can occupy the *x*-position in nP, as Dem is able to form a "logically proper name."

In other words, Dem is able to directly establish the reference of NP without the intermediary of a propositional function (i.e., some form of quantification)—what Russell (1905) called a "description." In this connection, it is worth quoting Russell:

We may even go so far as to say that, in all such knowledge as can be expressed in words – *with the exceptions of "this" and "that"* and a few other words of which the meaning varies on different occasions – no names, in the strict sense, occur, but what seem like names are really descriptions. (Russell 1919, in Ludlow 1997:332; emphasis added)

In this connection, we can think that what can be the external argument of nP is inherently restricted by the nature of n (alternatively, we could think of this restriction as definitional of n, and perhaps of nominals more generally, but I will not speculate further on this here). Arguably the only other elements that can appear in Spec,nP are pronouns (or perhaps more precisely, bundles of interpretable φ-features) and variables (note that pronouns are precisely "words of which the meaning varies on different occasions" in Russell's terms).[17] Fox (2002:67–68) proposes that variables arise at the semantic interface thanks to the operation of Trace Conversion, which applies to copies of Ā-moved DPs, as follows:

(32) a. *Variable Insertion*

   (Det) Pred → (Det) [Pred λy ($y = x$)]

   b. *Determiner Replacement*

   (Det) [Pred λy ($y = x$)] → the (Det)[Pred $\lambda y(y = x)$]

For example, these conventions convert *which boy Mary visited which boy* to *which boy λx [Mary visited the boy x]*. Fox observes (2002:67n6) that these operations are designed to apply to copies of Ā-bound DPs, leaving open the question of how they may generalize to other categories. In fact, if we posit quantifier movement inside DPs (on which, see below), a simpler convention suffices, which we can state as follows:

(32′) The chain (Q, Q), where Q is a strong quantifier, is interpreted as (Q, x), where x is a variable bound by Q.

The operation introduces a variable ranging over possible denotations of a predicate, which I take to be N; hence, it defines the restriction of the quantifier, Qx_N.

Aside from demonstratives, arguably the only other elements that can appear in Spec,nP are variables (see note 17). The latter include copies of quantified elements, as just described, and underspecified pronouns. Given that the interpretable features of Dem value those of D, which in turn value the clausal functional heads, we see that the referential property of demonstratives has the formal correlate of contributing a fully specified φ-set to the formal-feature system and thus making the probe-goal Agree system work. Let us now investigate the consequences of this proposal regarding demonstratives for DPs that do not contain demonstratives and for the general DP-clause relation.

8.5   Further Speculations on DP

8.5.1   Definite and Indefinite Articles

The ideas just outlined imply that we must rethink the nature of all (apparently) demonstrative-less DPs. Here, I will sketch how I see the principal DP-types, leaving much for future research.

Let us begin with *definite* DPs. Here, the central idea is that the definite article is a clitic Dem. Thus, from a structure like (33a), Art (to use a neutral term) cliticizes to D by incorporation, giving (33b) (see also Giusti 2001, Borer 2005:160–161, Corver and Van Koppen 2010):

(33) a. $[_{DP} D_{[u\varphi, EPP]} \dots [_{nP} Art_{[i\varphi]} [n [_{NP} N \dots]]]]$

   b. $[_{DP} Art_{[i\varphi]} + D_{[u\varphi, EPP]} \dots [_{nP} (Art_{[i\varphi]}) [n [_{NP} N \dots]]]]$

The cliticization operation here is in line with the general approach to cliticization/incorporation as syntactic head movement in Roberts 2010a. There, the central notion is that of a defective goal, defined as follows:

(34) Goal G is defective in relation to probe P iff G's formal features are properly included in those of P.

The condition on incorporation is (35):

(35) Defective goals must incorporate into their probes.

In (33), Art incorporates with D in virtue of having a subset of D's formal features. On the other hand, in (29), Dem does not incorporate with D because it has a feature not shared with D, presumably related to deixis (see Alexiadou, Haegeman, and Stavrou 2007:96–97). Hence, Dem in (29) is not a defective goal in relation to D while Art in (33) is.

As shown in (33), I assume that D is first-merged with uninterpretable/ unvalued φ-features. On the other hand, definite articles (indicated in (33) as Art) have a full set of interpretable φ-features, which gives rise to the "uniqueness/exhaustivity" interpretation associated with definiteness. Raising these features from Spec,nP to D endows D with interpretable features, making D in turn able to value the features of a clause-level category such as C/T or v. It also satisfies D's EPP-feature.[18] In this way, we see how the clausal Agree system depends on DP-internal relations that are intimately connected with the referential properties of DP. This idea is connected with the proposals developed extensively by Longobardi (1994, 1996, 2010) to the effect that certain features of N or NP must raise to D in order for DP to be licensed as an argument. There is a parallel here with T's φ-set in a fully null-subject language, which has the same property and licenses a definite pronominal interpretation of the subject (see Biberauer et al. 2010a). Lyons (1999:282–283) argues that person and definiteness should be conflated; see also the proposals in Biberauer et al. 2010a to the effect that a fully specified φ-set is equivalent to a D-feature, and Longobardi 2008 and Richards 2014 on the relation between D and Person.

Enclitic definite articles most clearly illustrate the cliticization of Art to D. Romanian, for example, displays the following paradigm:

(36) a. lup-ul   [Romanian]
         wolf-the
         'the wolf'
     b. batrân-ul lup
         old-the   wolf
         'the old wolf'

c. *lup   batrân-ul
   wolf   old-the
d. *batrân lup-ul
   old   wolf-the
   (Longobardi 2010)

Here, we see that the noun or adnominal adjective must raise to a position preceding the enclitic definite article -*ul*. We can account for this in terms of the general approach to second-position clausal enclitics in Roberts 2012b. There, it is proposed that second-position effects arise where a clitic incorporates to a phase head bearing an edge feature (EF) of the kind discussed in Chomsky 2008. Incorporation, by its nature, cannot satisfy EF and so some further category must move to the phase edge. This category can be a head or an XP. As Longobardi (2010) points out, it is very difficult to tell whether N- and A-raising inside DP is head movement or XP-movement. But we can account for the difference between the Romanian article, which is obligatorily enclitic, and its English or Italian counterpart, in terms of the presence vs. absence of EF associated with D. The order in (36c) is ruled out if we continue to assume that APs appear in the edge of the nP phase, and if we assume that Romanian has the "VSO-like" option of NP-fronting here, rather than NP- (or nP-) movement to Spec,FP and FP-movement to the pre-D position.[19]

Art-incorporation leaves a copy in Spec,nP that is interpreted as a variable at the semantic interface by (32′). If we identify the full set of interpretable φ-features, with the associated interpretation of uniqueness and exhaustivity, with the ι-operator, then we can see how *the NP* is interpreted as ιx [NP(x)].[20]

A major advantage of this approach is that it naturally captures the common diachronic relation between demonstratives and definite Ds. In many languages, the definite article derives from an earlier demonstrative (e.g., all the Romance definite determiners derive from the Latin demonstratives *ille* and *ipse*, and Modern English *the* derives from Old English *se, seo, þæt*, and so on; see Vincent 1997, Lyons 1999:331–332, Giusti 2001, Roberts and Roussou 2003:131–136, Alexiadou, Haegeman, and Stavrou 2007:96–97). On the view just sketched, definite articles simply lack one formal feature borne by demonstratives (the deictic feature). It has often been observed that feature loss is a common diachronic process (see in particular Roberts and Roussou 2003). The loss of the deictic feature on Art creates the conditions for incorporation of Art to D, since once this feature is lost, Art's formal features are a subset of those of D. Art thus becomes a D-clitic. See also C. Roberts 2002 and Elbourne 2008 for semantic arguments for a close relation between demonstratives and definite articles.

In languages like Hungarian, Greek, and Spanish, where articles and demonstratives can cooccur (see the discussion in section 8.3.1), the article simply spells out φ-features of D where Dem is also present (since Dem expresses definiteness; see the references just given). Where Dem is absent, the article may or may not cliticize; it is probable that a further distinction is to be made between languages where Art is always just a spell-out of φ-features of D and those where it can but does not have to be n's external argument, but exploring this would take us too far afield here.

Turning now to *indefinites*, I take these to feature a variable in Spec,nP (cf. Holmberg's (2010) analysis of generic null subjects as underspecified null pronouns). In that case, the indefinite article can be regarded as an existential quantifier first-merged in Q, which binds the variable (and, again, cliticizes to D). The structure of an indefinite DP would thus be as follows (see Lyons 1999:286, 301):[21]

(37) $[_{DP} D_{[u\varphi, EPP]} [_{QP} [_Q a] [_{nP} x [n [_{NP} N...]]]]]$

More generally, *weak quantifiers*, like the indefinite article, may be merged in Num and license the variable in Spec,nP by binding it (and, again, cliticize to D in English-style languages):

(38) $[_{DP} D_{[u\varphi, EPP]} [_{QP} [_Q some] [_{nP} pro/x [n [_{NP} N...]]]]]$

8.5.2 Strong Quantifiers and the "Definiteness Effect"

Strong quantifiers, on the other hand, raise from Spec,nP to Spec,DP, leaving a copy interpreted as a variable (see Borer 2005:140–141 for a very similar proposal):[22]

(39) $[_{DP} every D_{[u\varphi, EPP]} [_{QP} Q [_{nP} \text{every} = x [n [_{NP} N...]]]]]$

Clearly, this satisfies D's EPP-feature.

This leads to an interesting account of the definiteness effect (the basic syntactic difference between weak and strong quantifiers; Milsark 1974):

(40) There is a/*every fly in my soup.

We could think, along the lines proposed by Kayne (2008:185–186), that *there* is merged inside DP, let us say in Spec,nP:

(41) $[_{DP} D_{EPP} [_{QP} [_Q a] [_{nP} there [n [_{NP} N...]]]]]$

From this position, *there* raises successively to Spec,DP and on to Spec,TP:

(42) $[_{TP} there...[_{DP} \text{there} D_{EPP} [_{QP} [_Q a] [_{nP} \text{there} = x [n [_{NP} N...]]]]]]$

(Kayne proposes that the constituent [a N] raises, followed by remnant DP-movement of [*there* (a N)] after merger of V.) This is possible in the presence of a weak quantifier, as shown in (41) and (42), but *there* would compete with the first-merged position of strong quantifiers in Spec,nP. Hence, the definiteness effect emerges as an effect of the complementary distribution of *there* and strong quantifiers in Spec,nP. Note that D has no φ-features here; if it had them, *there* would cliticize to it. Arguably, *there* has a person feature but not a number feature (see Chomsky 2001), so *a* appears as a default element in Q, if this head has the feature [sg] and no weak quantifier is present. Hence, *there* can check with T. It cannot check with D as D has no features at all except EPP. Phonologically null D in English always has a default existential interpretation (see Longobardi 1994:641); this is true unless D is bound by a generic or negative operator in C, as in certain bare plurals or negative contexts. Note that *there* cannot bear the R-role, as it has no denotation; instead, this role is assigned to the variable left by *there* bound by the existential D. This is possible in the absence of a level of D-Structure requiring θ-roles to be all and only assigned to first-merged elements.

8.5.3 Generalized Quantifiers

The approach taken here also has interesting consequences in relation to generalized quantification. Consider the following simple example:

(43) Every boy thinks.

After DP-internal raising of *every*, variable insertion as in (32′) and raising of the subject to Spec,TP, the representation for (43) at the C-I (conceptual-intentional) interface is as follows:

(44) $[_{TP} [_{DP} [_D \text{ every}] [_{QP} Q [_{nP} x_1 [_N \text{ boy}]]]] T [_{vP} [_{DP} [_D \text{ every}]$
$[_{QP} Q [_{nP} x_2 [_N \text{ boy}]]]] [v [_{vP} \text{ thinks}]]]]$

Assuming that copy deletion can apply freely in LF as long as a well-formed interpretation results (as in standard accounts of reconstruction since Chomsky 1993), the D-phase of the DP-copy in Spec,vP deletes at the C-I interface to avoid vacuous quantification; otherwise, there will be two quantifiers and two nuclear scopes, but just one restriction. So we get (45) from (44):

(45) $[_{TP} [_{DP} [_D \text{ every}] [_{QP} Q [_{nP} x_1 [_N \text{ boy}]]]] T [_{vP} [_{\overline{DP}} [_{\overline{D}} \overline{\text{every}}]$
$[_{\overline{QP}} \overline{Q} [_{nP} x_2 [_N \text{ boy}]]]] [v [_{vP} \text{ thinks}]]]$

The interpretation of (45) is of course (46):

(46) $\forall(x) [\text{boy}(x) \rightarrow \text{think}(x)]$

(46) can be almost directly derived from (45) in a fully compositional fashion, aside from two apparent anomalies. The first is the insertion of the implicational connective, which has no syntactic counterpart. Following standard

conventions since Montague 1973, I take this to be directly stipulated in the interpretation of universal quantifiers. The other anomaly is more interesting: the two occurrences of [$_N$ boy] in (45). But this apparent anomaly actually gives us the conservative interpretation. If we interpret (45) with a direct one-for-one mapping from syntactic to logical expressions, we have:

(46') $\forall(x)$ boy(x) [boy$(x) \rightarrow$ think(x)]

This is 'every boy is a boy that thinks', the conservative interpretation (Barwise and Cooper 1981). Conservativity is thought to be a universal property of determiner quantification (see Keenan 1997:54–55 for more discussion); note that it does not hold of adverbial quantification, as can be seen from the interpretation of *Only birds fly*. This interpretation follows from the structure proposed here for DPs and the fact that just the D-phase is deleted in (45), which derives from free minimal deletion up to crash at the C-I interface, very much in the spirit of Fox 2000; what is deleted here is just enough to save the structure from crashing due to vacuous quantification (see also Fox 2002:67n7, for discussion of a different possible way to link the copy theory to conservativity).

8.5.4 Proper Names and Pronouns

Still pursuing this general approach, we can treat *proper names* largely following Longobardi (1994).[23] Longobardi observes the following paradigm for Italian and English:

(47) a. Gianni mio
     b. il mio Gianni
     c. John

Longobardi treats (47a) as involving N-to-D raising over the possessive pronoun *mio*, while (47b) features an expletive D, an option unavailable in English. N-raising is best seen as NP-raising through Spec,nP (as required by the Phase Impenetrability Condition) to Spec,DP, giving the following representation at the C-I interface:

(48) [$_{DP}$ Gianni D$_{[u\varphi, \; EPP]}$ [$_{QP}$ Q [$_{nP}$ [$_{AP}$ (mio)] [$_{nP}$ ~~Gianni~~ = x [n [$_{NP}$ ~~Gianni~~]]]]]]

If the copy of the proper name is interpreted as a variable, the DP emerges as a Russellian description ('the x such that x is Gianni'). The Italian expletive determiner, like the English expletive *there* discussed above, raises from Spec,nP, leaving a variable, and we get the same interpretation (note that *il* cliticizes to D, as its features are a subset of D's):

(49) [$_{DP}$ il-D$_{[u\varphi, \; EPP]}$ [$_{QP}$ Q [$_{nP}$ [$_{AP}$ (mio)] [$_{nP}$ ~~il~~ = x [n [$_{NP}$ ~~Gianni~~]]]]]]

Longobardi originally treated English article-less, unraised proper names as undergoing LF movement to D. If such operations are not available in the current versions of syntactic theory, then we have a representation like the following at the C-I interface:

(50) [$_{DP}$ D$_{[u\varphi, EPP]}$ [$_{QP}$ Q [$_{nP}$ x [n [$_{NP}$ John]]]]]

Here, the null D must have interpretable φ-features, in order to bind x in Spec,nP through Agree with D. This again creates a bound variable interpretation, again giving the Russellian interpretation. The same must be true of the null D of *bare plurals*, which have either an existential or a generic interpretation (the latter determined by an Agree relation with a sentential operator either in T or in C; the former possibly a default, as mentioned above for null D in English).

8.6   Universal 20 Once More

Here, we return to the basic Universal 20 facts. We saw in section 8.2 how Cinque (2005a) accounted for the observed legitimate orders of Dem, Num, A, and N in terms of a broadly Kaynean approach. Abels and Neeleman (2009, 2012) adopt a different approach, in which they reject what they refer to as the Specifier-Head-Complement Hypothesis (SHCH)—that is, the idea, which Kayne (1994) claims to follow from the LCA, that specifier-head-complement is the only admissible order of those elements in XP. In effect, Abels and Neeleman (2012) replace Cinque's assumptions, given in (51), with the assumptions in (52) (henceforth I focus my discussion on Abels and Neeleman 2012 rather than Abels and Neeleman 2009):

(51) a. The underlying hierarchy in the extended projection of the noun is Agr$_W$>W>Agr$_X$>X>Agr$_Y$>Y>N, where ">" indicates c-command and where Y hosts AP in its specifier, X hosts NumP in its specifier, and W hosts DemP in its specifier.
   b. All (relevant) movements move a subtree containing N.
   c. All movements target a c-commanding position.
   d. All projections are modelled on the Spec-Head-Complement template.
   (Abels and Neeleman 2012:30)

(52) a. The underlying hierarchy of Dem, Num, A and N in the extended nominal projection is Dem>Num>A>N, where ">" indicates c-command.
   b. All (relevant) movements move a subtree containing N.

c. All movements target a c-commanding position.

d. All movements are to the left.

(Abels and Neeleman 2012:33)

Assumptions (51b)/(52b) and (51c)/(52c) are the same; (51c)/(52c) is of course standard, and we will briefly speculate on (51b)/(52b) below. Assumptions (51a)/(52a) are effectively the same, if we abstract away from Cinque's postulation of the various AgrPs (as we did in section 8.2; see Abels and Neeleman 2012:47–51 for discussion). Since Abels and Neeleman drop the SHCH, they are free to postulate a range of base-generated orders, while still respecting their assumption (52a), as in (53):

(53)

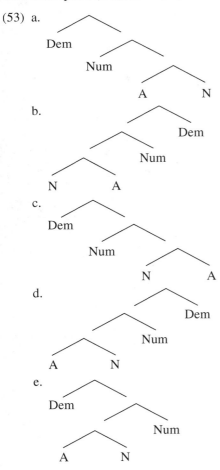

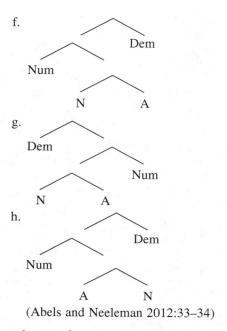

(Abels and Neeleman 2012:33–34)

As can be seen from these representations, "the nonterminals in the extended projection of the noun are left unlabelled and the demonstrative, numeral and adjective are not introduced by dedicated functional heads" (Abels and Neeleman 2012:34). Although these representations (and those given in (54)) suffice for their argument, at no point in their exposition do Abels and Neeleman commit themselves to a position on the labels of any of the nonterminals, or on the status of N, A, Num, and Dem as heads or phrasal categories. This makes it impossible to evaluate these structures in relation to FOFC. For example, if the lowest branching category—that immediately dominating N and A—is NP in (53b), then this structure violates FOFC; similarly in (53g), and, if the node immediately dominating the [N A] constituent is NumP, (53f). The situation is slightly clearer in the case of the derivations that Abels and Neeleman propose to involve movement, as in (54):

(54) a.

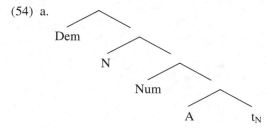

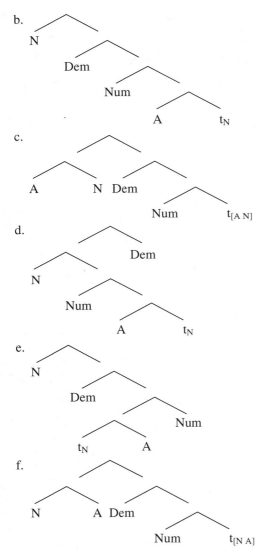

b.
N
Dem
Num
A t_N

c.
A   N Dem
Num $t_{[A\ N]}$

d.
Dem
N
Num
A t_N

e.
N
Dem
Num
t_N A

f.
N   A Dem
Num $t_{[N\ A]}$

Here, (54f) is likely to violate FOFC, if [N A] is NP. If [N A] is not NP, in fact, it is unclear what it is. It clearly cannot be a head (more generally, the N-movements postulated in (54a,b,d) are unlikely to be head movement, as they are not sufficiently local, given standard assumptions concerning the Head Movement Constraint). Therefore, if [N A] is not NP, it is N′, but it is standardly assumed that intermediate-level categories do not move (and are in general "inert" to the computational system). If [N A] is NP, Abels and

Neeleman must account for what has happened to the complements of N (see Cinque 2005a:326n34 and the discussion in section 8.3.2). (54e) looks like both a FOFC violation and a violation of the Condition on Extraction Domain. For these reasons, Abels and Neeleman's approach cannot be adopted here. Instead, we will adopt a variant of Cinque's approach (slightly "shrunken," in the terminology of Abels and Neeleman 2012:47–48), as we did in section 8.2. Given what we have seen above, the proposed account of Universal 20 must try to keep to the close clausal-nominal isomorphism adopted above, in particular in that Dem is the external argument of NP.

We will see, in fact, that certain marginally or dubiously attested orders do create difficulties, but it is possible to derive the main generalizations from a structure like (19).

First, here are the 24 logically possible orders, with a rough guide to their crosslinguistic distribution as described by Cinque (Dryer (2009c) gives a more fine-grained picture of the gradations of frequency, particularly among the rarer orders, but we will not linger over those potentially important details here):

(55) a. Dem Num A N   (very many languages)
     b. Dem Num N A   (many languages)
     c. Dem N Num A   (very few languages)
     d. N Dem Num A   (few languages)
     e. *Num Dem A N   (no languages)
     f. *Num Dem N A   (no languages)
     g. *Num N Dem A   (no languages)
     h. *N Num Dem A   (no languages)
     i. *A Dem Num N   (no languages)
     j. *A Dem N Num   (no languages)
     k. A N Dem Num   (very few languages)
     l. N A Dem Num   (few languages)
     m. *Dem A Num N   (no languages)
     n. Dem A N Num   (very few languages)
     o. Dem N A Num   (many languages)
     p. N Dem A Num   (very few languages)
     q. *Num A Dem N   (no languages)
     r. Num A N Dem   (very few languages)
     s. Num N A Dem   (few languages)
     t. N Num A Dem   (few languages)
     u. *A Num Dem N   (no languages)
     v. *A Num N Dem   (no languages)

w. A N Num Dem   (very few languages)

x. N A Num Dem   (very many languages)

(adapted from Cinque 2005a:319–320)

The structure for DP put forward in (19) is repeated here, with the first-merged positions of Num, A, and Dem indicated (and without the possible complements to N, which were given in (19)):

(56) $[_{DP}$ **D** $[_{QP}$ NumP Q $[_{FP}$ AP F $[_{nP}$ DemP **n** $[_{NP}$ N…$]]]]]$

Here, F might correspond to a position for classifiers, along the lines of proposals by Chierchia (1998, 2015:165–166), Borer (2005:86ff.), and Huang (2015:12), and hence a possible position for grammatical number features (as opposed to numeral expressions), at least in some languages (see also the comments in Abels and Neeleman 2012:56n30).

Order (55a) is derived by raising DemP to Spec,DP, as described in section 8.3. Order (55b) combines raising of DemP with NP-movement to Spec,FP. Order (55c) is the same except that NP raises a further step to Spec,NumP. Order (55d) involves raising NP to Spec,DP. Note that in all these cases of NP-movement, the movement targets an outer specifier.

The next four orders, (55e–h), are all unattested. They all feature illicit DemP-movement. We can account for them if we assume that the only movement option available for DemP (in neutral orders, without focus, etc.) is A-movement to Spec,DP, triggered by the φ- and EPP-features of D. Here there may be a further parallel with external arguments in clauses, which arguably can only A-move to Spec,TP (again leaving aside topicalization and focusing).

Similarly, (55i) and (55j) are ruled out by the general impossibility of (non-focusing) AP-movement, an assumption shared by Cinque and Abels and Neeleman.

On the other hand, order (55k) is problematic. It can be derived by combining the familiar DemP-raising to Spec,DP with further raising of FP to an outer Spec,DP. However, the derived structure, which is shown in (57), violates FOFC:

(57) $[_{DP}$ $[_{FP}$ AP F $[_{nP}$ NP ⟨DemP⟩ n ⟨NP⟩$]]$ Dem D $[_{QP}$ NumP Q ⟨FP⟩$]]$

(Here, NP-movement to Spec,nP is indicated, although the surface order would be the same without this operation; the lack of it would create a further FOFC violation.) (57) instantiates the general schema for FOFC given in (9) and repeated here for α=F, γ=nP, and β=D. As noted earlier, Cinque says this order is found in very few languages. According to Dryer (2009c), it is found in just 4 languages from 2 genera, and it ranks 14th out of 17 possible orders in his system. So we can be confident that this is a rare order, but clearly more needs to be done in order to establish what is really going on in these languages, and whether we really have a FOFC violation here, as we seem to.

Order (55l) contrasts minimally with (55k). It differs from (55k) just in that nP has rolled up inside FP, thereby avoiding the FOFC violation. Interestingly, according to Cinque, this order is attested in "few languages," as opposed to "very few languages" for (55k). Dryer (2009c) states that this order is found in 19 languages in 11 genera.

Order (55m) again features illicit AP-movement. Order (55n) is a further apparent FOFC violation, involving FP-movement to Spec,QP (combined with the usual DemP-raising) without FP-internal roll-up. The derived structure is like that in (57), except that FP occupies Spec,QP rather than Spec,DP. Clearly, then, the same kind of FOFC violation ensues. Once again, though, it is worth pointing out that this order is rare: Dryer (2009c) says it is attested in 11 languages from 6 genera. Again, order (55o) contrasts minimally, in that this order features FP-internal roll-up and hence avoids the FOFC violation. This is a much more common order, being found, according to Dryer (2009c), in 28 languages from 22 genera.

Order (55p) can be derived like (55o), but with an extra operation raising NP or nP to the outer Spec,DP, with the remnant FP, containing just AP, raising to Spec,QP. This order appears to be quite rare (rarer than (55n), according to Dryer) and highly marked. Cinque (2005a:323n27) suggests that the order may be "spurious." Abels and Neeleman (2012:61–62), on the other hand, provide evidence that this is indeed the neutral order in the Australian language Pitjantjatjara and in Nkore-Kiga, a Bantu language of Uganda.

We rule out order (55q) as a case of Alexiadou and Anagnostopoulou's (2001) "in-situ generalization" applying in the nominal. This is the order in which nothing moves from the first-merged positions shown in (56). As Alexiadou and Anagnostopoulou point out, there appears to be a requirement that some element raise from vP in the clause. Typically of course this is the external argument, but not always. The same seems to hold in the nominal; in all the other orders we have looked at, some element, and often more than one, moves out of nP. This order can only arise if nothing moves. Here, then, is another important parallel between the nominal and clausal extended projections.

Orders (55r,s,t) all involve NP-movement combined with the absence of DemP-movement. In (55r), NP raises to the outer Spec,nP. In (55s), it raises to Spec,FP (this is the "Celtic order" discussed in section 8.3.2). In (55t), it raises either to Spec,QP or to Spec,DP (in fact, both may well be possible, with this order disguising two distinct options).

Both orders (55u) and (55v) involve illicit AP-movement. Order (55w), on the other hand, is problematic. If we continue to rule out AP-movement, as we have needed to for (55i,j,m,u), then the A-N order must show FP-movement to a high position, at least Spec,QP. But this will clearly violate FOFC. Moreover, DemP appears not to move or at least to remain in a low position. But, aside from this one case, we have been able to assume either that DemP remains in situ in Spec,nP or that it raises to Spec,DP. Introducing a further option for DemP creates problems, especially in relation to (55e–h). But if DemP does not move here, then the A-N constituent is a nonconstituent. So this case is problematic independently of FOFC, given our assumptions. Once again, though, it is worth pointing out that this order is very rare; according to Dryer, it is found in just two languages, from the same genus, making it the second-rarest attested pattern of all.

Finally, order (55x) is very common, being one of the three Greenberg originally observed, as we have seen. This order involves the combination of DemP-raising and roll-up of (presumably) NP, nP, FP, and QP.

We are thus able to correctly account for 21 of the 24 patterns discussed by Cinque (2005a) and Abels and Neeleman (2012). The problematic cases are (55k), (55n), and (55w), each attested in only a small handful of languages, although clearly requiring further investigation. This is particularly true for (55k) and (55n), which appear to violate FOFC; we will leave the further investigation of these languages as an open problem.

It is also worth mentioning the three orders that are attested according to Dryer, but that Cinque rules out (as do Abels and Neeleman). These are (55g), (55m), and (55h). Of these, we briefly discussed (55g), found in Kilivila and 4 other languages, in section 8.2.2. Order (55h) would appear to require us to relax the restriction on DemP-movement, although that would create problems in relation to the nonattested (55e,f). Similarly, (55m) seems to pose a problem for the suggested ban on AP-movement. However, since these orders are both extremely rare (being attested in 2 languages and 1 language, respectively) and do not appear to pose any problems for FOFC, we will leave them aside.

To summarize, we have been able to derive almost all the attested orders and to rule out all the unattested ones in terms of the following assumptions:

(58) a. The first-merged order in (19)/(56)
      b. No AP-movement in neutral orders
      c. The LCA
      d. Roll-up movement

Clearly, the proposed account is close to Cinque's, but it differs from his regarding the question of the first-merged position of demonstratives. For the reasons outlined in the preceding sections, I consider this assumption to be well-motivated.

8.7 Conclusions

In this chapter, I raised three principal points. First, LD languages aren't a problem for FOFC, since they do not have to involve raising of a possibly head-initial low functional category along the lines proposed by Cinque (2005a).

Second, following Bruge and Giusti (1996), Alexiadou, Haegeman, and Stavrou (2007), and Guardiano (2010), I proposed that demonstratives are always first-merged in a low position, Spec,nP. Dem-raising to Spec,DP is subject to the parameters in (26) and (28), repeated here:

(26) Does a functional head F in a higher phase attract the external argument of its phasal complement?

(28) a. Does F in the higher clausal phase attract the external argument?
     b. Does F in the higher nominal phase attract the external argument?

The structural parallel between Dem and the external argument in Spec,vP in the clause led to the proposal of a typological link between LD and VS(O) orders; this prediction is partially fulfilled. In section 8.6, I developed an account of Universal 20 that is compatible with these ideas.

Third, and more speculatively, I suggested that demonstratives are among very few elements able to bear the R-role of n (a variable being, chiefly, the other such element). In turn, this led to a generally "Russellian" analysis of DPs, which has a number of attractive features.

I end with two conceptual points. First, the analysis of DPs involves a binding/Agree relation between D and Spec,nP in all cases. The result is that D must always have interpretable φ-features, which is of course also central to the functioning of Agree relations at the clausal level. So we see that DPs' general ability to license functional elements thanks to their interpretable φ-features can be traced back to the ways in which DPs refer. This provides an important conceptual justification for Agree theory.

Second, I have posited that n licenses the R-role of N, while assuming, standardly, that v licenses the external argument of V (if there is one, and allows expletives to be merged there if there isn't). This raises an interesting question in relation to examples like the following:[24]

(59) a. T [$_{vP}$ those [dance]]
     b. D [$_{nP}$ those [dance]]

Here, the innermost bracket could be v/n, with the root having raised there, or VP/NP without such raising. These structures are quite different things: the clause *those (ones) dance* vs. the nominal *those dances*. In both, *dance* is interpreted as *dance(x)*, and in both, *those* contributes interpretable (plural) φ-features. Yet in (59a), plurality relates to the external argument of *dance*, which with the contribution of T comes to something like 'there is/are event(s) of dancing, of which the Agent is plural' (assuming the "separation" interpretation of argument structure proposed in Parsons 1990, Schein 1992, and Herburger 2000). In (59b), on the other hand, the contribution of plurality is different: 'there are events of dancing'. In other words, in (59a), the syntactic external argument is interpreted as the Agent, but in (59b), it is interpreted as whatever the root denotes. As Milan Rezac (pers. comm.) observes, there are in fact two sources for this difference. One is that arguments of N in general do not have to be (overtly) realized, while the corresponding verbal argument structure must be projected into the syntax. Because of this, Spec,nP need not be interpreted as the Agent of *dance* in (59b). The other difference has to do with functional structure: in (59a), T is what establishes the "reference" of the "dance" eventuality, by embedding it in a tense/aspect matrix. On the other hand, in (59b) the reference of "dance" is established directly by the demonstrative in Spec,nP.

It seems clear that these differences between the intrinsic nature of v and n and the operations of their respective extended projections need to be reduced to a single property, but it remains unclear exactly how this is to be achieved.

9 The Final-over-Final Condition and Particles

Theresa Biberauer

9.1 Introduction

This chapter focuses on a diverse range of structures, all containing elements that have, in one context or another, been referred to as *particles*. As already noted in chapter 2, particle-containing structures superficially seem to be able to violate the Final-over-Final Condition (FOFC) rather readily. While V-O-Aux structures containing inflecting auxiliaries of the kind found in Germanic, Hungarian, Basque, and many other languages appear to be ruled out, V-O-Aux structures where Aux does not inflect do not seem to be subject to the same condition. The examples in (1) illustrate:

(1) a. Tā chī-le   fan **le**.   [Mandarin]
       3SG eat-PERF food PERF
       'He has eaten.'
       (Paul 2014:86)[1]
    b. Ego psis   dio avga   [Cappadocian Greek]
       1SG bake.1SG.PERF two eggs
       iton.
       PAST (= 3SG.IMPERF.BE)
       'I had baked two eggs.'
       (Español-Echevarría 1994:1)
    c. bɨs sa ja   tebɨre   **ga**.   [Bagirmi]
       dog eat meat yesterday COMPL
       'The dog has eaten the meat.'
       (Stevenson 1969:85)

That noninflecting auxiliaries do not behave like their inflecting counterparts has been well-known since Greenberg's groundbreaking typological work: in establishing his universals, he systematically excluded "uninflected auxiliaries," given the fact that they so clearly do not pattern like inflected ones (see

Greenberg 1963:85, 93). Similarly, Dryer (1992:99) pinpointed the ability to "bear all or some of the verbal inflections associated with the clause" as a difference between his categories of "auxiliary verb" and "tense/aspect particle," concluding that the former should therefore be regarded as heads ("verb-patterners") and the latter as modifiers ("object-patterners"). That the presence vs. absence of inflection is a relevant consideration in establishing why structures like (1a–c) are possible, whereas counterparts featuring inflected auxiliaries are not, is also strongly suggested by language-internal contrasts of the kind illustrated for Cappadocian Greek and Bwe-Karen below. Let us first consider Cappadocian Greek:

(2) a. Ego **iha**   psisi   dio avga.   [Standard Modern Greek]
       I   have.1SG bake.PTCP two eggs
       'I had baked two eggs.'
       (Español-Echevarría 1994:1)

   b. πῆγα   ἐτόν.[2]   [Cappadocian Greek]
      ˈpiɣa   eˈton
      go.PAST.1SG PAST (= 3SG.IMPERF.BE)
      'I had gone.'
      (Krinopoulos 1889:37)

   c. νίφτα   ἦτον.
      ˈnifta   ˈiton
      be.washed.PAST.1SG PAST (= 3SG.IMPERF.BE)
      'I had been washed.'
      (Archelaos 1899:141)

   d. πῆγαν   ’τόν.
      ˈpiɣan   don
      go.PAST.3PL PAST (= 3SG.IMPERF.BE)
      'They had gone.'
      (Alektoridis 1883:489)

As the contrast between Standard Modern (2a) and Cappadocian (2b–d) Greek shows, there is more than just a positional difference between the auxiliaries in these two varieties. Standard Modern Greek's preverbal auxiliaries exhibit the kind of finite inflection familiar from well-studied Western European languages: in compound tenses, the auxiliary exhibits agreement and tense inflection, while lower verbs surface without this inflection, instead being marked as nonfinite in some way. By contrast, Cappadocian Greek's final auxiliaries systematically fail to inflect: they are consistently third-person singular imperfect past forms, with the lexical verb instead bearing the full tense-aspect and agreement morphology that one would expect to find on a finite verb; as the examples above show, there can be both aspect and agreement discrepancies between the fully inflected lexical verb and the invariant clause-final auxiliary. This is a property of Pontic Greek varieties more generally (see Neocleous and Sitaridou in preparation). In these varieties, then, it is always a lexical verb that bears full finite inflection, with the BE-derived auxiliary interacting with neither the φ-/aspectual nor the argument-structure (see (1b) and (2a)) properties of the clause.

Let us now consider Bwe-Karen (Tibeto-Burman):

(3) a. ce-ɗɔ mi **jə-khɔ** phi má   nɔ (*jə-khɔ)?   [Bwe-Karen]
       3- say C 3- FUT take what   3- FUT
       'What did he say that he would take?'
       (Henderson 1997:187)

    b. yə- ca (*lɔ) dɛyo lɔ.
       1SG-see ASP picture ASP
       'I am looking at a picture.'
       (Henderson 1997:39)

As in the case of Cappadocian Greek, we see a clear distinction here between the placement of inflected and the placement of uninflected elements. As (3) shows, Bwe-Karen features clause-final aspectual markers that do not inflect and that must necessarily surface in clause-final position. In this case, however, it is important to note, as Philip (2012:115) points out, that the appearance of inflection does not actually point to the existence of inflected auxiliaries in Bwe-Karen; instead, the "agreement" in (3a) is a proclitic pronoun, which is therefore systematically absent in structures containing a full DP subject (see Swanson 2011:24 for an overview of the Bwe pronoun system). Nevertheless, the contrast between (3a) and (3b) is instructive in the wider context, as Bwe-Karen's final auxiliary elements differ strikingly from its numerous preverbal auxiliaries and also from its lexical verbs in being unable to host proclitic pronouns (see Swanson 2011 for detailed descriptive discussion of the Bwe verbal system). This renders these elements exceptional within the verbal system, as all other verbal elements—auxiliary, serial-verb, and lexical—can combine with person marking where they are the hierarchically highest verb in the structure. Acquirers, then, will have a very clear person-marking cue, parallel to that which acquirers of inflecting languages get, as to the formally quite distinct status of clause-final verbal elements. As will become clear in section 9.4, this cue is reinforced by numerous further indications in other parts of the grammar that a distinction needs to be drawn between heads that contribute directly to the extended projection (i.e., FOFC-relevant heads) and semantically related elements that do not (i.e., elements that do not "count" for FOFC purposes) (regarding extended projections, see Grimshaw 1991 et seq.). For the moment, I introduce just one of the latter, a recurring phenomenon in predominantly head-initial languages with an inventory of (apparently FOFC-violating) head-final functional elements:

(4) a. θɪɾd́okha d́ó   nu   yà   θí   [Bwe-Karen]
       rhinoceros animal.CLF DEM PROB step.on die
       lò   cɛ   (bé).[3]
       finished 3SG IRR
       'The rhinoceros might trample them to death.'
       (Swanson 2011:42)

   b. tʰan³ saa¹maat³ tʰam (daj³).   [Thai]
       3SG able   do   able
       'He can do it.'
       (Hanna 2010:17)

   c. too¹daj¹ baw² ʔaat² cak² kææ³ (daj³).   [Lue]
       anybody not able IRR solve able
       'Nobody could solve (the riddle).'
       (Hanna 2010:16)

In all of these examples, the element highlighted in grammatical descriptions as the auxiliary verb—irrealis *gɔ* 'might' in (4a), and ability *saa¹maat³* and *ʔaat²* in (4b,c)—may cooccur with a clause-final element associated with the same interpretation. In all cases, the final but not the initial element is optional, clearly signaling that the preverbal element is the "real" auxiliary (head).[4]

What we have established so far, then, is that there may be good reasons to think that auxiliary particles are formally distinct from the type of auxiliaries found in FOFC-respecting languages. What I will aim to achieve in the following sections is, first, to show that particles more generally do not constitute a threat to the universality of FOFC, interpreted (i) as a hierarchical universal (i.e., as a constraint on permissible narrow-syntax/narrow-syntax-internal phrase structure configurations; see Whitman 2008), and (ii) as a constraint that is relativized to extended projections in the manner stated in (5) (*pace* Abels 2013, Hawkins 2013, Sheehan 2013a, this volume, Whitman 2013, Etxepare and Haddican 2014, Erlewine to appear a,b, Zeijlstra 2015, Richards 2016; see chapter 1 for overview discussion):

(5) A head-final phrase αP cannot dominate a head-initial phrase βP where α and β are heads in the same extended projection.
    (cf. Biberauer, Holmberg, and Roberts (BHR) 2014)

Second, I will aim to explain why particles are such prolific apparent violators of this condition. In the course of this discussion, I will consider a wide range of particle types and demonstrate that there are various formal structures that would, on a narrow-syntax-internal, extended-projection-oriented interpretation of FOFC, be predicted *not* to produce a FOFC violation, all of which seem to be attested in the particle domain. This will lead directly to my third objective, which is to show how the FOFC-motivated investigation of particles reported here has led to what I believe to be a new discovery about the distribution of particle elements more generally: namely, that they are necessarily *peripheral* elements in a sense to be made precise. In other words, their distribution, like the distribution of disharmonic word order more generally, is more regular than has previously been thought.

The rest of this chapter is structured as follows. Section 9.2 presents an overview of the types of apparently FOFC-violating structures that are found in the particle domain. Section 9.3 introduces the formal configurations that would give rise to superficially FOFC-violating structures without actually violating the version of this condition presented in (5). Section 9.4 shows that all of these configurations exist. Section 9.5 discusses the consequences of this fact and concludes.

9.2 Apparently FOFC-Violating Particles: The Empirical Facts

The objective of this section is to illustrate the kinds of particle-containing constructions that have led to doubts concerning the universality of FOFC.

9.2.1 Final Auxiliary Particles

We have already considered some examples of VO structures featuring a final auxiliary (see (1)–(4)). This pattern is particularly widespread in East Asian languages and it also surfaces, though to a lesser extent, in certain Central African languages (see Dryer 2009b:344–345).[5] Worth noting in relation to the latter is that it always seems to be the case that V-O-Aux in languages that permit it is a minority pattern *alongside* Aux-V-O and/or inflectional tense/aspect/mood (TAM) marking (see Dryer 2015e). Consider the case of Bagirmi (Bongo-Bagirmi, Nilo-Saharan; Chad). This language features (prefixal) aspect marking on the lexical verb (6a,b), preverbal (agreeing) mood markers (6c), and a single[6] clause-final completive particle, *ga* (6d) (and a clause-final question marker (6b); see also below):

(6) a. ŋgab **kä**-pa   kag(a).   [Bagirmi]
         man IPFV-split wood
         'The man splits the wood.'
         (Stevenson 1969:102)

b. Q: boukar **tád**   djùm téŋ   làbà **sà**   *ksàa*   wà?
       boukar PFV.do gruel millet or   PFV.eat INF.eat Q
       'Did Boukar cook millet gruel or did he eat it?'
     A: boukar **tád**   djùm téŋ   *tádà.*
       boukar PFV.do gruel millet INF.do
       'Boukar COOKED millet gruel.'
       (Jacob 2010:129)
c. (née) **nɔ́**   **ndugo**   kìtàb kɛdɛ̀.
    3SG   3SG.FUT IPVF.buy book INDEF
    'She/He will buy a book.'
    (Jacob 2006:31)
d. bɨs **sà** ja   tebɨre   **ga.**
    dog eat meat yesterday COMPL
    'The dog ate the meat yesterday.'
    (Stevenson 1969:85, cited in Dryer 2009b:344)

As these examples show, there are clear formal distinctions between finite and nonfinite verbs in Bagirmi, with finite verbs systematically preceding the object (and nonfinite verbs), and post-object verb placement being possible only in verb-doubling constructions (6b) (see Jacob 2013 for discussion of the focus-backgrounding conventions that account for this placement). Completive *ga*, then, evidently does not occupy a position associated with either finite verbs or nonfocused verbs more generally.

A similar pattern emerges in Ngambay (Bongo-Bagirmi, Nilo-Saharan; Chad, Central African Republic):

(7) a. **m- îsī́/ m-ār m-ùsà** dā.   [Ngambay]
       1SG-PRES/1- PRES 1- eat meat
       'I am eating meat.'
       (Heine and Reh 1984:126, Vandame 1963:94–96)
   b. **m- îsi/ m-ár** mbā **k- ùsà** dā.
       1SG-PRES/1- PRES for NOM-eat meat
       'I am eating meat.'
       (Heine and Reh 1984:126, Vandame 1963:94)
   c. **m- ā k- ào** àl **ngà.**
       1SG-FUT NOM-go NEG REPEATED
       'I will not go again.'
       (Vandame 1963:118, cited in Dryer 2009b:344)

Here we see that Ngambay makes use of inflected auxiliaries that systematically occupy a preverbal position.[7] Strikingly, agreeing auxiliaries may either cooccur with agreeing lexical verbs (7a) or select for a nominalized complement, which, in the progressive, is introduced by a preposition (7b); *k-* marks the infinitive in (7b,c).[8] The formal and distributional differences between the finite and nonfinite Ngambay verbal forms and clause-final aspect-marking *ngà* are thus again evident. And similar observations can be made about Mbaye, another of the VO Bongo-Bagirmi languages that Dryer (2009b:344) identifies as featuring at least one clause-final auxiliary (see note 5; see Keegan 1997 and Anderson 2011 for discussion).

Three final Central African V-O-Aux languages highlighted by Dryer (2009b) that I will comment on here are Mumuye (Adamawa-Ubangi, Niger-Congo; Nigeria), Dholuo (Nilotic, Nilo-Saharan), and Ma'di (Moru-Madi, Nilo-Saharan). Dryer (2009b:356) presents the following data showing that Mumuye has both clause-final aspect (8a) and mood (8b) particles:

(8) a. znàsọ baasé ranti **yé**.   [Mumuye]
      Znaso mimic Ranti PERF
      'Znaso has mimicked Ranti.'
      (Shimizu 1983:107)

   b. znàsọ **dé**   baasé ranti **ni**.
      Znaso PERF mimic Ranti IMMED.FUT
      'Znaso is about to mimic Ranti.'
      (Shimizu 1983:112)

The discussion in Krüsi 1978 further reveals that this language has numerous other final particles, expressing meanings relating to aspect, mood, negation, interrogativity, and discourse-connectedness. Particularly important for our purposes is, first, the fact that Mumuye again appears to have auxiliary(-like) elements that surface in the clause-medial position that one would expect for a VO language, *dé* in (8b) being a case in point (see also *na* in (9a) and in Krüsi's illustrative narrative text). Second, closer consideration of the elements discussed in Krüsi 1978 shows (i) that the elements occurring in final position seem to be quite numerous and (ii) that at least some final elements appear to be multifunctional, having considerable positional freedom. A notable case in point is *ne*, which serves as a (partly discourse-oriented) continuative marker (9a), coordinator (9b), and general linker (9b):

(9) a. ɓayeh na   wa'n **ne**.   [Mumuye]
      Bayeh PAST sit   CONTINUATIVE
      'Bayeh was sitting.'
      (Krüsi 1978:271)

   b. **ne** tó **ne** wu ti ɓeehsan do yu.
      LINK say LINK he fix friend   still hair
      'And he said that he was still fixing his friend's hair.'
      (Krüsi 1978:272)

Patterns of this sort are also very evident in both Dholuo and Ma'di, much-better-studied languages on Dryer's V-O-Aux list. Descriptions of Dholuo consistently refer to medial TAM particles, surfacing in preverbal position, in front of a lexical verb that may, under the relevant circumstances, inflect for both subject and object agreement and aspect (see, e.g., Omondi 1982, Tucker 1994, Ojwang' 2008, Cable 2012). Strikingly, the TAM markings employed in Dholuo-English code-switching are consistently and exclusively of the preverbal type (Ochola 2006), suggesting that these are the core TAM elements in the system (see also notes 4 and 9, and the discussion of primary and secondary TAM marking below). This impression is reinforced by the observations in the literature querying the formal status of Dholuo TAM elements more generally: Cable (2012:657n10), for example, notes that the preverbal TAM elements form a closed class, with meanings reflecting those of the (inflectional) tense paradigms of surrounding languages (e.g., Kikuyu; Schwartz 2003);[9] following Omondi (1982) and Tucker (1994), among others, he raises the possibility that some of these particles may in fact be adverbs, citing their apparent positional freedom in support of this idea. (Omondi and Tucker note that many of the medial T-elements are homophonous with post-verbal adverbs; see also Cable's note 10. As we will see in later sections, this type of apparent homophony, which could equally be multifunctionality involving underspecified elements (see, e.g., Biberauer 2011 et seq., Duffield 2013a, 2014a,b, Wiltschko 2014), is a recurring theme in the particle domain, not only in Central Africa but also more generally.)

Blackings and Fabb's (2003:chap. 18) discussion of adverbial placement possibilities in Ma'di shows clearly why an adverbial analysis needs to be carefully considered where elements expressing TAM-related semantics surface clause-finally, and also why this is particularly important when dealing with languages that do not overtly mark TAM on lexical verbs. Ma'di features both free and fixed-position adverbial elements. The example in (10) illustrates the placement options available to free adverbials, many of which express temporal and also discourse-related meanings (see also sections 9.2.2–9.2.4;[10] @ in each case marks a possible placement option); (11) gives some examples of adverbials that obligatorily surface clause-finally:

(10) *drìádrū* 'now'   [Ma'di]
      @ má @ lὲ   @ mū-lé   @ ē6ù   gá   @
      1SG   want   N- go.SB   work LOC[11]
      'Now I want to go to work.'
      (Blackings and Fabb 2003:479)

(11) a. ópí odū   ízí   **gbù.**   [Ma'di]
Opi 3.take woman before
'Opi has married before.'
(Blackings and Fabb 2003:509)

   b. dʒì mī **lí**   ***gbírí**
close eye completely/completely
'shut eye completely/tightly'

   c. kɔ̄ ōdū **lí**   ***gbírí**
fall asleep completely/completely
'fall fast asleep'

   d. dʒì tī   **gbírí/**   ***lí**
close mouth completely/completely
'close mouth completely'
(Blackings and Fabb 2003:504)

The absence of overt TAM marking on the verb combined with the presence of obligatorily final TAM-related elements[12] readily creates the impression that there may be clause-final TAM positions in Ma'di.[13] Importantly, though, closer investigation reveals the semantically specific nature of these final elements. Consider, for example, the lexical restrictions on the use of the completives in (11b–d), which are representative of a more general pattern: Ma'di completives are numerous and have highly specific lexical requirements (Blackings and Fabb 2003:504–505). Taking into account what is now known about grammaticalization (see, e.g., Heine and Kuteva 2002, Hopper and Traugott 2003, Roberts and Roussou 2003, van Gelderen 2004, Roberts 2007b, and Narrog and Heine 2011 for overviews), it is clear that Ma'di's completives do not have the semantic profile typically associated with functional heads (Asp, T, M, etc.). They also do not have the formal profile of such heads, being amenable to "nominalization with *rì* [glossed *DEF*]" and also, in this case, to left-dislocation (Blackings and Fabb 2003:499). This is a property they share with other final adverbials, and with modals and negative elements, to which we will return in section 9.2.2. Crucially, this is very different from what we see in the context of languages in which auxiliaries cannot occur in V-O-Aux configurations: in these languages, auxiliaries resist independent fronting (e.g., topicalization and/or focalization operations) or, in systems permitting these operations, Stylistic Fronting (Holmberg 2000b, 2005) and predicate doubling (see, e.g., Güldemann 2010, Biberauer 2013). The completive and, more generally, auxiliary elements that surface finally in Ma'di appear to differ from FOFC-respecting auxiliaries, then, not only morphologically, by virtue of being consistently uninflected, but also in semantic and syntactic terms.

Looking beyond Central African languages, patterns strikingly similar to those highlighted above repeatedly emerge. First, East Asian VO languages, for example, feature both initial and final auxiliaries (12). Second, in these languages a range of elements at different points along the grammaticalization spectrum and with varying s-selection requirements are available to express the meanings associated with some of these elements (13)–(14). Third, many of the apparently FOFC-violating auxiliary particles are superficially homophonous with elements able to surface in other positions (15)–(16):

(12) a. Zhāng Sān **néng** qù Táiběi **le**.   [Mandarin]
       Zhang San can   go Taipei PERF
       'Zhang San can go to Taipei.' [✓*le* > ABLE TO, *ABLE TO > *le*]
   b. Zhāng Sān **kěnéng** qù Táiběi **le**.
       Zhang San may   go Taipei PERF
       'Zhang San may have gone to Taipei.' [*le > MAY, ✓MAY > *le*]
       (Erlewine to appear a:9)

(13) a. se2- **zo2** go2- fung1 seon3.   [Cantonese]¹⁴
       write-PERF DEM-CL   letter
       '… have/has written that letter.'
   b. se2- **jyun4** go2- fung1 seon3.
       write-finish DEM-CL   letter
       '… have/has finished writing that letter.'
   c. se2- **jyun4-zo2** go2- fung1 seon3.
       write-finish- PERF DEM-CL   letter
       '… am/is/are done with writing that letter.'

(14) a. Tuō sā   fēnzōng lìtóu huaǐ qiè   [Yixing Chinese]¹⁵
       he three minute in   can eat
       le/ guāng/wuě   sā   ge pǐngguò.
       PERF/finish/ empty three CL apple
       'He can eat three apples to the core in three minutes.'
   b. Tuō sā   fēnzōng lìtóu huaǐ qiè **guāng le/ wuě**   **le**   sā
       he three minute in   can eat finish PERF/empty PERF three
       ge pǐngguò.
       CL apple
       'He can eat three apples to the core in three minutes.' (= (14a))
   c. Tuō sā   fēnzōng lìtóu xíng **dǎo/ *guāng/wuě**   éng ge
       he three minute in   find arrive/finish/ empty five CL
       pòngyòu.
       friend
       'He found five friends in three minutes.'

d. Tuō sā   fēnzōng lìtóu xíng **dǎo**   **le**   éng ge pòngyòu.
he   three minute in   find arrive PERF five CL friend
'He found five friends in three minutes.' (= (14c))

(15) a. Ông Quang **được** mua cái nhà.   [Vietnamese]
PRN Quang GET   buy CL house
'Quang was allowed to buy a house.'   Deontic (permission)

b. Ông Quang mua **được** cái nhà.
PRN Quang buy GET   CL house
'Quang was able to buy a house.'   Aspectual (accomplishment)

c. Ông Quang mua cái nhà   **được**.
PRN Quang buy CL house GET
'Quang may possibly buy a house/Quang is able to buy a house.'
Abilitative/Epistemic(alethic)
(Duffield 2001:101–102, 2013a:128)

(16) a. laaw vaw   phaasaa   laaw **daj**.   [Lao]
3SG speak language Lao GET
'She/He can speak Lao.'

b. *daj^4*
1. *V.tr.*: come to have; obtain; acquire; gain; win; get
   V.tr.: have a procedural ability with regard to something owing to knowledge of that thing; can; know how to
2. *V. intr.*: succeed, win
3. *preverbal modal*: happen to; get to; have the opportunity to; be able to; have to
4. *postverbal modal*: can; okay; fine
(adapted from Enfield 2003:78)

(13)–(16) are worth commenting on in more detail. (13)–(14) illustrate some of the lexical options available to Cantonese and Yixing Chinese speakers for expressing perfect aspect. In addition to a highly grammaticalized particle (*zo* and *le*, respectively, which correspond to verbal *le*; see Soh and Gao 2006, Soh 2009), both varieties have at their disposal a number of less grammaticalized forms, which may surface either independently or together with *zo/le*; where these markers cooccur, *zo/le* is necessarily the outermost marker, as one might expect from a more grammaticalized form in the context of upward-grammaticalization theories like that of Roberts and Roussou (2003). (14) further illustrates the varying extents to which perfect-marking elements undergo semantic bleaching: picking up on their full-verb meaning, partly grammaticalized *guāng* 'finish' and *wuě* 'empty' are only compatible with contexts in which they can convey "complete consumption/disappearance" of some object, thus ruling them out in structures like (14c) (Xuhui Hu, pers. comm.); *dao* 'arrive', by contrast, would be compatible with the structure in (14a,b), but its presence would necessarily alter the structure's meaning to 'He *managed* to eat three apples to the core in three minutes', an adjustment that again reflects the fact that *dao* brings more specific semantics to the structure than verbal *le*. For our purposes, these examples highlight two key points: first, that the formal status of final auxiliaries in the languages we are concerned with needs to be carefully evaluated, and, second, that there appears to be systematically available evidence in V-O-Aux languages of ways in which potentially FOFC-violating auxiliaries contrast with truly verbal elements (see again note 4, and also Kuteva 1994, among others; see Anderson 2011 for a discussion focused specifically on African languages). We will return to this point in section 9.4.

(15)–(16) highlight two instances of the remarkable apparent homophony patterns encountered in East Asian languages (see Duffield 2013a, 2014a,b for detailed discussion). (15) illustrates the more general areal phenomenon, in terms of which an initially acquisitive verb meaning roughly 'get' takes on a range of modal meanings that, at least in Vietnamese, are systematically distinguished in positional terms (see, e.g., Cheng and Sybesma 2003, 2004, Enfield 2003, Duffield 2007, 2013a, 2014a,b, van der Auwera, Kehayov, and Vittrant 2009, J.-Y. Chung 2012, and Lam 2016 for discussion). Strikingly, immediately postverbal *được* bears a completive interpretation of the kind also seen in the Cantonese and Yixing examples in (13)–(14) (see also (16a)) and familiar from Chinese varieties more generally, while deontic *được* occupies the position most commonly occupied by modals more generally in Vietnamese and also other languages in the region (cf. (12) in this connection); finally, clause-final *được* occupies the position most directly associated, in languages of the region and also beyond, with speaker-oriented perspectives (see also sections 9.2.4 and 9.4.4.2). We will return in section 9.4.4.2 to the significance of these distributional facts and of the apparently extensive homophony that many final auxiliary particles exhibit. Importantly, very similar patterns appear to be possible in some of the African VO languages under discussion here, Ma'di being a case in point; see Blackings and Fabb 2003:chap. 17 for a discussion of the "modals" *rá* (expressing completion, necessity, and affirmation) and *wà* (expressing possibility; see also section 9.2.2).

Outside of Africa and East Asia, it also seems to be the case that final auxiliary elements in VO languages always cooccur with larger numbers of initial auxiliaries; consider again Cappadocian Greek ((1c), (2)). Tenetehára (Tupí-Guaraní), which has been argued by Bonfim Duarte (2012) to violate FOFC, represents an interesting contrast to this general trend. Said to be neutrally

VSO in main clauses,[16] but head-final in dependent clauses and also in non-clausal XPs (notably, nominals and PPs), this language features four final auxiliaries: the recent completives *kwez* (homophonous with the distal demonstrative) and *ra'e*, imperfective *iko*, and future *nehe*. Strikingly, it does not appear to have any initial auxiliaries. Bonfim Duarte (2012:368ff.) does, however, highlight three adverbial particles—*zekwehe* (unattested distant past), *zekaipo* (unattested distant past with significant speaker uncertainty), and *kakwez* (attested past)—which obligatorily surface clause-medially. The examples in (17)–(18) illustrate:

(17) a. Teko   w- apy ko   **kwez** kury.   [Tenetehára]
          people 3SG-burn farm IPAST now
          'The people have burned the field.'
          (Bonfim Duarte 2012:360)

      b. Awa w- ekar   tapi'ir **iko**.
          man 3SG-look.for tapir be
          'The man is looking for tapir.'
          (Bonfim Duarte 2012:374)

      c. Ma'e pe Zuze w- enu tazahu **ra'e**.
          what at John 3SG-hear big.pig IPAST
          'Where did John just hear the big pig?'
          (Bonfim Duarte 2012:374)

      d. A'e ae u- mu- me'u- putar wa- n- emiapo-kwer **nehe**.
          he EMP 3SG-CAUS-speak- want 3PL-ABS-make- PAST FUT
          'He will tell what they have made.'
          (Bonfim Duarte 2012:374)

(18) a. W- exak **ze- kwehe** zawar- uhu tapixi memyr   [Tenetehára]
          3SG-see EVID-UDPAST jaguar-big rabbit son
          a'e   pe no.
          there at also
          '(They say that) the big jaguar also saw the rabbit's son there.'

      b. U- m- ur **ze- kaipo** i- hy   i-   zupe.
          3SG-CAUS-come EVID-UDPAST his-mother him-to
          'His mother apparently gave (it) to him.'

      c. A- exak **kakwez**   ka'i   ihe.
          1SG-see DPAST.ATTESTED monkey I
          'I saw the monkey.'
          (Bonfim Duarte 2012:369)

That the TAM elements in (17) and (18) cannot occur in one another's positions is convincingly shown in Bonfim Duarte's discussion, thus establishing them as distinct from the forms we have considered above. A property that these elements share, however, and that, importantly, distinguishes them from verbal elements in Tenetehára more generally—consider the agreement marking on the lexical verbs in (17) and (18)—is their lack of verbal inflection. This is the more striking when we contrast Tenetehára with another VSO language that has been said to feature postverbal auxiliaries, the Arawakan language Garifuna (Iñeri, Maipurean):

(19) a. Ru- **tu**   Maria fein 1-   un John.   [Garifuna]
        give-3SG.F Maria bread 3SG.M-to John
        'Maria gives John bread.'
     b. Ariha 1-   umu-**tu**   John Maria.
        see   3SG.M-AOR-3SG.F John Maria
        'John sees Maria.'
        (Kaufman 2010:2)

As (19) shows, Garifuna postverbal auxiliaries immediately follow the verb; while this language therefore does not challenge FOFC, it does seem to violate the first component of Greenberg's (1963) Universal 16: "In languages with dominant order VSO, an inflected auxiliary always precedes the main verb." Kaufman (2010) offers detailed argumentation against this conclusion, which is not directly relevant here. What is crucial for present purposes is the contrast between Garifuna's inflecting postverbal auxiliaries and Tenetehára's consistently uninflected final forms: as we have seen repeatedly, apparently FOFC-violating final auxiliaries never seem to exhibit the inflectional marking associated with clearly finite verb-forms in the VO systems they occur in, and this is also true for Tenetehára.

Greenberg's original intuition regarding the "otherness" of uninflected auxiliaries therefore seems to be vindicated in the FOFC context. More generally, this section has also highlighted at least two further distinctive properties that apparently FOFC-violating particles frequently seem to show: (i) a degree of semantic specificity that contrasts with that associated with fully grammaticalized auxiliaries (to an extent that is likely to be (very) striking system-internally, where particles cooccur with other auxiliary elements), and (ii) homophony with elements surfacing in different positions and serving at first sight (quite) different functions. Further, we have seen that superficially FOFC-violating auxiliaries typically contrast with one or more semantically related elements exhibiting the "expected" head-initial and thus FOFC-conforming distribution. As we will see in the following sections, these properties recur to a conspicuous extent in other domains featuring final particles.

9.2.2 Final Negation Particles

Dahl (1979), Dryer (1988, 1992, 2007, 2009b), and LaPolla (2002) all mention negative particles as "outliers" that contrast with negative adverbs and verbal negatives, thereby constituting a classificatory challenge. As Dryer (1992:98) notes, for example, negative particles are not verb-patterners (*pace* Dryer 1988, which only considered verbal negatives). To the extent that verb-patterners can be interpreted as projecting heads and that analyses can be upheld within which negation is assumed to project a NegP contributing to the clausal extended projection (see, e.g., Pollock 1989, Ouhalla 1990, Zanuttini 1997, Zeijlstra 2004), they are FOFC-relevant elements. This section will therefore consider final negation elements in VO languages.

Dryer (2009b) observes that V-O-Neg patterns are crosslinguistically uncommon, with two notable exceptions: Central Africa (spread across the Niger-Congo, Nilo-Saharan, and Afro-Asiatic (Chadic branch) families) and Austronesia (Papuan and Austronesian languages; see Reesink 2002). In the former, 18/23 genera studied have V-O-Neg; in the latter, 9/18. Obligatory negative concord systems featuring multiple negative markers are left aside in Dryer's study, although optional negative concord systems in which the obligatory element follows VO are included. (20)–(21) illustrate with Bagirmi (Nilo-Saharan), Bongo (Bongo-Bagirmi, Nilo-Saharan), Buru (Austronesian), and Tidore (Papuan):

(20) a. deb-ge   tol kobio **li**.   [Bagirmi]
         person-PL kill lion   NEG
         'The people didn't kill the lion.'
         (Dryer 2009b:317)

   b. ma (**nja**) ami a'ji **wa**.   [Bongo]
         1SG NEG make thing NEG
         'I am not doing anything.'
         (Dryer 2009b:316)

(21) a. Sira   hapu lafa-t   la yako   langina **moo**.   [Buru]
         3PL.ACT tie   food-NOM for 1SG.BEN earlier NEG
         'They didn't tie up trailfood for me earlier.'
         (Reesink 2002:245)

   b. Ona (**kama**) hoda mansia tobo   **ua**.   [Tidore]
         3PL NEG   see   people bathe.in.sea NEG
         'They did not see the people bathe in the sea.'
         (Reesink 2002:254)

Significantly, Dryer (2009b:329–331) notes that some of the African V-O-Neg patterns actually surface in mixed OV/VO languages: 8 languages in his sample exhibit this pattern.[17] One of these is Ma'di, which we have already encountered in section 9.2.1 (recall that *N* signifies 'nonpast'):

(22) a. má è6ī ɲā   rá.   [Ma'di]
     1SG fish N.eat AFF
     'I will (certainly) eat fish.'
     (Blackings and Fabb 2003:157)
   b. m̄- āwí dʒótī **kōrù**.
     1SG-open door NEG.PAST
     'I did not open the door.'
     (Blackings and Fabb 2003:469)
   c. ídrέ ɔ́-ɲā ìzá   **kō**.
     rat 3-eat meat NEG.N
     'Rats don't eat meat.'
     (Blackings and Fabb 2003:470)

A striking aspect of the Ma'di V-O-Neg structure is that the negation element appears to be inflected (see also Dryer 2009b:337). Closer inspection, however, reveals that this is a misleading characterization of the data. As mentioned in note 13, Ma'di tense[18] is in fact encoded via the morphological form of the lexical verb and the manner in which the verb interacts with other elements in the sentence. More specifically, *inflected* verbs, marked by a floating low-tone prefix and OV order, express nonpast tense meanings (i.e., present and future); and *uninflected* verbs, which lack the low-tone prefix, but uniquely permit a prefixal subject paradigm alongside that available for inflected verbs[19] (see (23d)) and VO order, typically express past tense. These patterns—which are suspended in negative contexts, where only the uninflected VO structure is possible (see (22))—are illustrated in (23):

(23) a. *Inflected verb, OV order, present meaning*
     ká è6ī ɲā   [Ma'di]
     3SG fish N.eat
     'He is eating fish.'
     (Blackings and Fabb 2003:157)
   b. *Inflected verb, OV order, future meaning*
     má è6ī ɲā   **rá**.   (= (22a))
     1SG fish N.eat AFF
     'I will (certainly) eat fish.'
     (Blackings and Fabb 2003:157)

c. *Uninflected verb, VO order, past meaning*
   má ɲā gbándà.
   1SG eat cassava
   'I ate cassava.'
   (Blackings and Fabb 2003:140)
d. *Uninflected verb, VO order, past meaning*
   (ɔ́pí) ɔ́- ɲā èbī.
   Opi 3SG-eat fish
   'Opi, he ate fish/Opi was the one who ate fish.'
   (adapted from Blackings and Fabb 2003:139)

Worth noting here is that *rá* in (23b) should not be interpreted as the direct source of the future meaning distinguishing otherwise near-identical (23a) and (23b) (comparison of (23b) and (23c) shows that the difference in the person of the subject is immaterial); as noted in section 9.2.1, *rá* is an apparently multifunctional modal element (otherwise, there would need to be three distinct homophonous *rá*s; we will return to this in section 9.4.4), signaling completion, necessity, and affirmation (see again Blackings and Fabb 2003:chap. 17). As Blackings and Fabb (2003:167) note, the future interpretation of (23b) should be understood as the consequence of *rá*'s potential interpretations all being incompatible with a present interpretation: as a completive, it conflicts with the Ma'di present's imperfectivity, and as a necessity or affirmation marker, it implicates the future in different ways, in the latter case because an affirmation marker is felt to be redundant where a sentence relates to an action (etc.) that is visibly underway at the time of speech. What this shows is that tense in Ma'di is compositionally encoded via a range of devices (presence vs. absence of (tone-based) inflection on the lexical verb, final particles, adverbs, etc.). For our purposes, the crucial points are these. First, the language's clause-final modals never inflect for tense; tense inflection is exclusively a property of lexical verbs. Second, the final position in which modal—Blackings and Fabb (2003:451) identify *wà* (possibility) and *kpɛ́* (nonpossibility) alongside *rá* as modals—and negative elements surface cannot be viewed as a T-position in the standard generative sense, that is, as a position fundamentally associated with (a) [tense] (feature); if these elements do indeed target a single position—a point to which we will return in section 9.4.5—a modal position of some kind would seem more likely.[20] Regardless of the specifics here, though, it is clear that there is no meaningful sense in which the negators *kōrò* and *kō* can be said to be inflected; therefore, they do not constitute a counterexample to the generalization that is in place so far regarding the uninflected nature of the elements that appear to be able to violate

FOFC. Further evidence that *kōrʋ̀* and *kō*, like the other modals that can
surface clause-finally, cannot straightforwardly be viewed as heads contributing to the extended projection of the clause is the fact that all of these elements
can combine with the nominalizing definite marker, *rì*, and undergo fronting;
(24) illustrates, highlighting the fact that this option means that final modal and
negation particles are treated in the same way as the final adverbials discussed
in section 9.2.1 (see section 9.4.3 for further discussion of the significance of
this fact):

(24) a. **kō   rì**   má èɓī ɲā.[21]   [Ma'di]
        NEG.N DEF 1SG fish N.eat
        'The one that I don't eat is fish.'
        (Blackings and Fabb 2003:467)
     b. **kōrʋ̀   rì**   má ɲā èɓī.
        NEG.PAST DEF 1SG eat fish
        'The one that I didn't eat was fish.'
        (Blackings and Fabb 2003:469)
     c. **rá rì** ópí kò-ɲā- ā   nì.
        AFF DEF Opi 3- N.eat-OBJ FOC
        'The one who will eat it is Opi.'
        (Blackings and Fabb 2003:586)
     d. **tʃé tʃé rì** ópí ō-mū nì.
        slowly DEF Opi 3-go FOC
        'The one who went slowly is Opi.'
        (Blackings and Fabb 2003:500)

That negation can front like adverbials is familiar from Stylistic Fronting (see
again Holmberg 2000b, 2005); strikingly, though, the relevant negation elements are usually viewed as XPs rather than heads (see, e.g., Zeiljstra
2004:160ff.). All in all, then, it would seem that Ma'di V-O-Neg, despite initial
appearances to the contrary, exhibits properties very similar to the other apparently FOFC-violating structures we have considered so far in this chapter.

As one might expect given the areal nature of the V-O-Neg distribution that
we are considering here, contact appears to have played a role in creating some
of the V-O-Neg patterns (see Reesink 2002 and Dryer 2009b for discussion).
This, of course, represents another departure from what we have observed in
relation to FOFC-violating structures that might conceivably have arisen under
contact situations (see Biberauer, Newton, and Sheehan 2009a,b and Biberauer, Sheehan, and Newton 2010 for discussion). That V-O-Neg patterns are
different from those adduced as evidence in support of the universality of
FOFC is strongly suggested by the fact that these structures again exhibit

properties very similar to those that distinguish the uninflected-auxiliary-containing V-O-Aux structures discussed in section 9.2.1 from unattested V-O-Aux patterns. We have already seen in connection with Ma'di that final negators can pattern with adverbials and modals, which appear to be elements carrying enough semantic content to be frontable (see the discussion of perfect aspect markers in section 9.2.1). We have also observed in passing the apparent homophony of some of the elements Ma'di negators pattern with, *rá* being a case in point. This also affects negation elements themselves in other V-O-Neg systems. In certain bipartite negation systems, both the "real" negator and its reinforcer take the same form (see Bell 2004a,b). This is illustrated in (25):

(25) a. Ek verstaan   **nie₁** die probleem **nie₂**.   [Afrikaans][22]
        1SG understand NEG the problem   NEG
        'I don't understand the problem.'

     b. Yo **no₁** sé   nada   que se   llama   [Dominican Spanish]
        1SG NEG know nothing that REFL call
        así **no₂**.
        this NEG
        'I don't know anything that has this name.'
        (Lipski 2001:2)

     c. Eu **não₁** tô achando minha gatinha **não₂**. [Brazilian Portuguese]
        1SG NEG   am finding my   cat.DIM NEG
        'I can't find my pussycat.'
        (Biberauer and Cyrino 2009:16)

     d. **No₁** lagar-lo davert **no₂**.   [Lisignano]
        NEG leave-it open   NEG
        'Don't leave it open.'
        (Zanuttini 1997:97)

     e. Lāmí **bà₁** tà ci àbinci à   kāsuwā **ba₂**.   [Hausa]
        Lami NEG he eat food PREP market NEG
        'Lami didn't eat food at the market.'
        (Newman 2000:358)

In all of these cases, the "real" negator, which cannot be omitted in a well-formed negative, is the first one (on Brazilian Portuguese (BP), where the first negator can be omitted under certain circumstances, see below). These structures are therefore not V-O-Neg in Dryer's terms, but they do all feature a final concord element in VO structures, and this element is therefore of interest in the FOFC context.[23] Also of interest is the fact that the "real" negators are all located clause-medially, in positions where they could plausibly be interpreted as the initial heads of a NegP; in these systems, we therefore again see the contrast between "well-behaved" initial and apparently FOFC-violating final elements highlighted in the previous section (this is also very evident in the Bantu negative concord systems with final concord/reinforcing negation elements discussed in Devos and van der Auwera 2013).

Returning to the languages illustrated in (25): they notably differ with regard to the formal characteristics of the final element. While nie_2 in Afrikaans cannot be independently stressed or modified, unlike nie_1 (Biberauer 2008), and final ba_2 in Hausa is toneless, unlike $bà_1$ (Newman 2000), the final $não$ in BP at first gives the impression that it is a "strong" element of the sort that one might expect—bearing Jespersen's cycle in mind—to "reinforce" the original negator, $não_1$, which is typically realized as a clitic, num (see Biberauer and Cyrino 2009). These differences again point to differences in the extent to which superficially similar structures in fact contain similar elements. More specifically, they highlight the need to investigate the properties of individual apparently FOFC-violating elements very carefully. Let us consider the BP case in a little more detail. Here, closer investigation has shown that the final negator in (25c)-type doubling structures is not, in fact, the same element as the one that may surface independently without $não_1/num$. Consider the data in (26), where the final $não$s are respectively glossed as $não_2$ and $não_3$:

(26) A: O   João é   rico!   [Brazilian Portuguese]
          the John is rich
          'John is rich!'

     B: O   que? Ele **num/ não₁** tem um tostão furado!
          the what he   NEG.CL/NEG has a   cent with.a.hole
          'What?! He doesn't have a red cent!'

     B': O   que? Ele **num/ não₁** tem um tostão furado   **não₂**!
          the what he   NEG.CL/NEG has a   cent with.a.hole NEG
          'What?! He doesn't have a red cent!'

     B'': #O que? Ele tem um tostão furado   **não₃**!
          the what he has a   cent with.a.hole NEG

     B''': Ele tem um tostão furado   **não₃**; ele tem um inteiro!
          he has a   cent with.a.hole NEG he has one whole
          'He DOESN'T have a cent with a hole; he has a WHOLE one!'
          (i.e., the literal meaning)

Here we see that both the standard single- and the more emphatic double-$não$-containing structures (i.e., (26B) and (26B')) deliver a well-formed structure containing a negative-polarity-item (NPI) idiom. By contrast, the structure featuring only the final $não$ ($não_3$) does not produce a well-formed answer (26B''), at least not under the intended idiomatic reading: as (26B''') shows, independently occurring clause-final *não* (*não₃*) necessarily gives rise to a reading that would be felicitous if it were preceded by an utterance in which the speaker made a claim about the relevant male having a holed cent in his possession (i.e., a statement in which *um tostão furado* has its literal meaning), to which B can then respond by correcting that literal meaning. *Não₃*, then, evidently expresses presuppositional negation, which *não₂* does not do, and it also cannot license NPI idioms in the manner one would expect an integrated negation element to do. See Biberauer and Cyrino 2009, Biberauer 2012, 2015b, and the references cited there for detailed discussion of a wide range of evidence that converges on the conclusion that *não₂* and *não₃* are formally distinct final negation elements: like the final negators in Dominican Spanish (25b) and Lisignano (25d), both originally derive from the anaphoric negator, but whereas *não₂* and the negators in (25b,d) have grammaticalized into clause-peripheral negation elements, *não₃* still represents an element that is quite loosely adjoined to the main clausal spine, which can thus not serve as a licensor for polarity-related elements the clause contains. The latter fact recalls the behavior of "sealed-off" *kōrò* and *kō* in Ma'di (see note 21).

Afrikaans *nie₂* poses both similar and completely different challenges. On the one hand, it appears to contrast with BP *não₃* in having become highly grammaticalized, to the point where it is so semantically and formally bleached that its occurrence in the modern spoken language is not restricted to strictly negative contexts (see Oosthuizen 1998, Biberauer 2008, 2009, 2012, 2015b for discussion):

(27) a. Hy vertrek **sonder** dat ek agterkom (**nie₂**).   [Afrikaans]
     he leaves without that I realize   NEG
     'He leaves without me realizing it.'

   b. Hy kon   **nouliks** staan (**nie₂**).
     he could barely   stand NEG
     'He could barely stand.'

These structures point to the dubiousness of characterizing *nie₂* as a negation element; as argued in Oosthuizen 1998 and Biberauer 2008 et seq., an analysis as an element associated with Laka's (1990) Pol(arity) head (Sigma) would seem more illuminating.[24] Moreover, *nie₂* also serves as an optional further negative reinforcer in a range of nonclausal contexts:

(28) a. **Nie₁** die GELD (**nie₂**), maar die TYD pla   [DP] [Afrikaans]
     not the money NEG but   the time worry
     hom.
     him
     'Not the MONEY, but the TIME worries him.'

b. Ek is [nooit (nie$_2$)] moeg nie$_2$.   [Q/nP]
   I   am   never NEG   tired POL
   'I am NEVER tired.'

c. Moeder Natuur het   vir nie$_1$ minder (nie$_2$)   [AP]
   Mother Nature have for NEG less   POL
   as   drie beskermende lae   gesorg.
   than three protective   layers cared
   'Mother Nature provided no less than three protective layers.'
   (Donaldson 1993:410)

d. Hy gee dit nie$_1$ vir sy suster nie$_2$, maar   [PP]
   he give it NEG for his sister POL but
   vir sy niggie.
   for his niece
   'He gives it not to his sister, but to his niece.'

Nie$_2$, then, is a negative-related element that surfaces finally not only in (superficially) VO clauses (see note 23), but also as part[25] of a range of further XP-types, all of which are head-initial. If it can be shown to be part of all the extended projections that it combines with, located suitably high in the structure, it will be a FOFC-violating element. Given its likely origins as an emphatic tag negator (Roberge 2000)—that is, as an element that would initially have been adjoined to the CP-domain, much like BP *não$_3$* still appears to be—the structural-height condition appears to be met. As shown in Biberauer 2008, 2009, 2012, 2015b, the height requirement is indeed met. What will be crucial, then, is establishing what kind of lexical item *nie$_2$* is, a matter to which we will return in section 9.4.5. For the moment, note that *nie$_2$* and *não$_2$/não$_3$* all raise a question about the analysis of apparently homophonous items within a system: *nie$_1$* and *nie$_2$* appear to be rather distinct, with distinct semantic, positional, and more general formal properties, and this can also be shown to be the case for the various *não*s in BP, thus apparently justifying a distinct-homophones analysis for these elements. The possibility that these elements may in fact involve just a single underspecified multifunctional form also exists, however, raising the question of how we are to distinguish these analytical possibilities. As will become clear in later sections, the same question arises in other final-particle domains (including that already discussed in section 9.2.1).

A further lexicon-oriented question that also arises in other domains is that of the number of items that a system has to express negation, sentential and otherwise. As we have already observed, there are languages like Ma'di and Mumuye (see note 20) that employ distinct negation-elements under what appears to be tense-conditioning. Many African languages have even more

elaborate negation-element inventories, with fine-grained clausal considerations determining the choice of negator. For example, Hausa (Chadic, Afro-
Asiatic) uses the system schematized in (29), which is quite usual in Chadic
languages (Newman 1971, 2000, Jaggar 2001):

(29) a. Equative, nonverbal (constituent), and wide-focus ('It is not the case
        that …') negation: *bàa … bá/ba*
     b. Verbal negation, except continuous and subjunctive forms: *bà…bá/
        ba*
     c. Continuous forms: *báa*
     d. HAVE-possessives: *báà*
     e. Negative existentials: *báabù*
     f. Subjunctives and imperatives: *káddà*
        (Newman 1971:2–3)

Significantly, barring final *bá/ba*, all of these negative forms are initial, surfacing either at the start of the clause or in postsubject position, that is, in the
kind of position where one would expect to find a negative marker in a VO
language.

   To conclude this negation-oriented section, I highlight the fact that investigation of this domain has revealed properties that also played a role in the
V-O-Aux context: (i) absence of inflection (even where this has been recorded
in grammars); (ii) evidence of less grammaticalized and potentially nonhead
status (e.g., independent frontability); (iii) homophony with other elements in
the system, with which they may (Hausa *ba*) or may not (Afrikaans *nie₂*) have
a direct diachronic connection; and (iv) where there are multiple negation elements in a system, a contrast between (expected) initial and potentially FOFC-
violating final elements.

9.2.3   Final Interrogative and C-Particles

This section will consider both the specific matter of final interrogative (Q-)
particles and the more general question of final elements that have been construed as C-particles.

9.2.3.1   *Final Interrogative (Q-) Particles*

Q-particles are often viewed as clause-typers (see, e.g., Cheng 1991, 1997)
and are thus readily associated with the C-domain. (Rizzi (2001) explicitly
distinguishes Int(errogative)P as a projection within the articulated CP; and
Richards's (2010) account of overt *wh*-movement crucially relies, as Richards
(2016:175) explicitly notes, on elements like Chinese *ma* being a complementizer, and thus a C-head.) From a FOFC perspective, then, the expectation
would be that final Q-particles, like final complementizers, should be absent

Table 9.1
Position of polar question particle in relation to VO/OV. (This table was constructed by combining *WALS* Features 92A (Position of Polar Question Particles; Dryer 2015g) and 83A (Relationship between Order of Object and Verb; Dryer 2015e).)

Q-particle and OV/VO relation	Number of languages
Initial Q and VO	81
Initial Q and OV	37
Final Q and OV	140
Final Q and VO	154

from VO languages. In reality, though, this combination is an extremely common one; witness the distributional facts recorded in *WALS* (Dryer and Haspelmath 2015). As table 9.1 shows, V-O-Q is the most commonly attested pattern in the 312-language sample extracted from *WALS*,[26] being significantly more common than the reverse disharmonic order. We seem, then, to have an empirical scenario within which V-O-C is never attested where C is a subordinating complementizer, but within which it is extremely common where C is a Q-particle. Given the robustness of the former gap (Dryer 2009b), more detailed consideration of the formal properties distinguishing complementizers and Q-particles seems warranted (*pace* Paul 2014, 2015, Pan and Paul 2017). This will be our next objective.

VO languages featuring both (interrogative) complementizers and final Q-particles might be expected to be particularly informative regarding the similarities and differences between these two types of element. Fortunately, numerous languages display this profile. We will focus on Marshallese, given the range of insights that it offers (see Willson 2002, 2005, 2008).

The examples in (30) illustrate matrix and embedded clauses containing what appears to be a final Q-particle, *ke*:

(30) a. Herman e-   ar   lukkuun kōnan men in   [Marshallese]
        Herman 3SG-T(PAST) really   love   thing of
        mour **ke**?
        life Q
        'Did Herman really love animals?'
        (Willson 2005:424)
     b. I   jaje   e- j   **ke** likjikin.
        1SG don't.know 3SG-T(PRES) Q   make.up.stories
        'I don't know if she's making up stories.'
        (Willson 2005:423)

In being compatible with both matrix and embedded interrogatives, *ke* differs from Q-particles in the Chinese varieties (see, e.g., Chan 2013, Paul 2014,

2015) and in many other languages featuring final Q-particles (see, e.g., Bailey 2012, Biberauer and Sheehan 2012b, and Biberauer, Haegeman, and van Kemenade 2014 for further discussion and references; and see Cable 2010 for discussion of OV languages with the reverse pattern, a point we will return to in section 9.4.4). Closer investigation, however, reveals that *ke* cannot straightforwardly be equated with (interrogative) complementizers, and that its status as a final Q-particle requires qualification. Consider the following data:

(31) a. I   jaje   **ñe**   e   bed imweo imen.   [Marshallese]
        1SG don't.know COMP 3SG stay house his
        'I don't know if he's at his house.'
        (Willson 2002:48)

   b. Ij   kōjatrikrik **bwe** enaj   etal.
        1SG.PRES hope   COMP 3SG.FUT go
        'I hope that she/he will go.'

   c. Ij   kōjatrikrik **ke**   enaj   etal.
        1SG.PRES hope   COMP 3SG.FUT go
        'I hope (and I know for sure) that she/he will go.'
        (Willson 2002:47)

(32) a. Herman e- n   (**ke**) bajjik (**ke**) kōmmon   [Marshallese]
        Herman 3SG-should Q   just   Q   make
        (**ke**) pade eo   (**ke**) ñan ir   (**ke**)?
        Q   party DET.SG Q   for 3PL Q
        'Should Herman just throw the party for them?'
        (Willson 2005:421)

   b. Kwo-j   (****ke**) jab (****ke**) etal (****ke**) ñan Rita **ke**?
        2SG- T(PRES) Q   NEG Q   go   Q   to   Rita Q
        'Aren't you going to Rita?'
        (Willson 2005:424)

(31a) shows that Marshallese has an element corresponding to 'if' and that this element (*ne*) surfaces at the start of the embedded clause, as one would expect in a head-initial language. (31b) shows that the language also features an initial declarative complementizer, *bwe*. The contrast between (31b) and (31c) reveals that *bwe* is an evidentiality-sensitive complementizer, signaling the speaker's uncertainty regarding the truth of the proposition in the embedded clauses; a further complementizer, *ke*, marks speaker-certainty (Willson (2002:47) refers to *bwe* and *ke* as reportive and presuppositional complementizers, respectively). The latter is, of course, homophonous with the Q-particle in (30). In (32), we see that the Q-particle can, under the right circumstances, occur in other than clause-final positions; in fact, clause-final position is only absolutely required where *ke* cooccurs with negation. The former fact might lead one to conclude, as researchers working on other Polynesian languages have, that the Marshallese Q-particle is in fact an adverb (see, e.g., Mosel and Hovdhaugen 1992 on Samoan, Besnier 2000 on Tuvaluan, and Starks and Massam 2015 on Niuean, to which we will return in section 9.4.4). The latter fact, however, suggests that closer consideration might be warranted.

The necessarily final placement of *ke* in negative structures calls to mind the negative intervention effects discussed since Rizzi 1982 (see in particular Beck 1996a,b, Hagstrom 1998, Cheng and Rooryck 2000, Sauerland and Heck 2003). These take on a particularly clear form in languages such as Quechua that employ particles of various kinds to distinguish indefinites of different kinds (see, e.g., Haspelmath 1997:310–311, Sánchez 2010). In languages of this type, it is possible to establish more precisely which *wh*-indefinite-contained features are subject to the intervention effect. Consider the Southern Quechua data in (33)–(36):

(33) a. ima   b. ima- ta   [Southern Quechua]
        what   what-ACC
        'what'   'what (case-marked)'
     c. ima- pis   d. ima- ta- pas
        what- ADD   what-ACC- ADD
        'something'   'anything'

(34) a. **Ima- ta- *(m)**   Mariya yacha-n?   [Southern Quechua]
        what-ACC- FOC/EVID Mariya know- 3SG
        'What does Mariya know?'
     b. Mariya **ima-ta-(m)** yacha-n?
        (Sánchez 2010:134)

(35) a. **Ima- ta- m**   mana muna-n-chu?   [Southern Quechua]
        what-ACC-FOC/EVID NEG   want-   3SG-NEG
        'What doesn't she want?'
     b. *Mana **ima-ta-m** muna-n-chu?
        (Sánchez 2010:140–141)

(36) a. Mana **ima- ta- pas** muna-ni- chu.   [Southern Quechua]
        NEG   what-ACC- ADD want- 1SG-NEG
        'I do not want anything.'
     b. ***Ima-ta-pas** mana muna-ni-chu.
        (Sánchez 2010:141)

Here, we see that *ima* constitutes the base for all indefinite expressions ((33); see Haspelmath 1997 for detailed discussion). We also see that *wh*-movement is not generally obligatory (34b), except in negative *wh*-questions (35), where the composite *wh*-element must move to outscope the negator; NPIs, by contrast, necessarily remain in situ, within the scope of the negator (36).[27] Significantly, in Quechua varieties a range of focus and (contrastive) topic-oriented particles may cooccur with *wh*-elements, but not with NPIs, with *wh*-movement necessarily requiring the presence of a particle of this kind. One of these, *-taq*, has frequently been labeled a Q-particle (see Cable 2010 for discussion and references), although Sánchez (2010:35) identifies it as a contrastive focus marker. For our purposes, the key importance of the Quechua data is that they reveal these facts: (i) Negative features specifically interact with formal features associated with the *periphery* of *wh*-elements. (ii) Q-particles do not necessarily have to be clause-level elements; they can also associate with subclausal XPs. (iii) Q-particles may not in fact be specified as *question*-particles; they may be focus or other Ā-related particles (see, e.g., Horvath 1986, Kratzer 1991, Herburger 2000, Kim 2002, 2006, Beck 2006, and Ginsburg 2009 on the connection between *wh*- and focus; see also below, and section 9.2.4, on this "recycling" of features in natural-language grammars).

Against this background, a Q-particle analysis of Marshallese *ke* no longer seems so obvious. Instead, given its distribution, it is tempting to connect it in some way to focus, at least in its interrogative uses ((30) and (32)). Depending on whether wider Marshallese-internal evidence points to homophony or underspecification (see section 9.4.4), this analysis might also be extendable to its initial complementizer-type use in (31c); for example, if, as would be plausible on the basis of the data given here, all the uses of *ke* involve presupposition marking, it could be that *ke* is in fact a presupposition marker (see much work since Horn 1969 on the connection between focus and presupposition, and Van der Wal 2016 on the diagnosis of different types of focus). Marshallese, then, once again highlights the need to look very carefully at the overall distribution of elements that appear to serve as Q-particles: it instantiates another case where there is a contrast between initial C-elements and an allegedly final one, with apparent homophony in play.

One or both of these observations can also be made in relation to the final Q-particles that have been identified for Italian (Munaro and Poletto 2003, 2009, Penello and Chinellato 2008; see Cardinaletti 2011 for discussion), and, as Bailey (2012) observes, for Afro-Asiatic languages like Mina (Cameroon) and Zaar (Nigeria); Niger-Congo languages like Supyire (Mali; though see below), Fyem (Nigeria), and Ogbronuagum (Nigeria); the Austronesian language Tetun (East Timor); and numerous East Asian languages, including the Chinese varieties and the Karen languages. Particularly striking in this context are languages like Lagwan (Afro-Asiatic, Cameroon), Mupun (Afro-Asiatic,

Nigeria), and Lele (Afro-Asiatic, Chad), all of which have both initial and final
Q-related elements, with the possibility or even requirement that these elements cooccur. Consider (37)–(38):

(37) a. G- a   mma ì   gha ɗa?   [Lagwan]
        2SG-PERF leave her.ACC house Q
        'Did you leave it at home?'
        (Philip 2012:92)

    b. Mɨ ghɨn ɗɨkɨmi (ɗa)?
        1PL do   how   Q
        'What do we do?'
        (Philip 2012:117)

    c. Ndalu   ngwa fɨne,   ki bɨle=a   shi   a
        1SG.PROG look.at outside LINK man=LINK.M some 3SG.M.PERF
        s-   o   gha ɗa.
        enter- VENT house Q
        'I'm looking outside, (to see) whether someone has entered the
        house.'
        (Philip 2012:93)

(38) a. a   man nalep-e?   [Mupun]
        2SG know Nalep-Q
        'Do you know Nalep?'
        (Frajzyngier 1993:360)

    b. n- tal pə   wur a   nə ket gwar kat kə   nalep-e.
        1SG-ask PREP him COP that if he meet prep Nalep-Q
        'I asked him whether he met Nalep.'
        (Frajzyngier 1993:364)

In Lagwan, the matrix Q-particle cooccurs with an obligatory subordinating
complementizer, *ki*, which Philip (2012) analyzes as a linker, that is, a semantically vacuous functional head that serves as a syntactic means of marking
subordination and coordination relationships. Significantly, the Q-particle surfaces in both *yes/no* and *wh*-interrogatives, being optional in the latter. Mupun
exhibits a similar pattern, differing only in that the final Q-particle is accompanied by two initial complementizer-type elements, general-subordination *nə*
and specifically interrogative *ket*. Languages featuring double complementation markers in interrogative complements are more widely attested crosslinguistically and always seem to exhibit the same pattern, with a general
subordinator most directly linking the selected embedded interrogative clause
to the matrix predicate. In formal terms, this would seem to correspond to a

structure in which the generalized subordinator/linker dominates the interrogative complementizer, meaning that these elements are disharmonic in a FOFC-compliant way:

(39) a. (Man) nemīdānam   [(**ke**) [(**āyā**) (ū)   zabānšenāsī   [Persian]
1SG – NEG.know.1SG   SUB   if   3SG linguistics
mīxānad]].
study.3SG
'I don't know if she/he studies linguistics.'
(Korn and Öhl 2007:1)

   b. us- nee puuc-aa   [**ki** [**kyaa** tum aa-   oogee]].   [Hindi-Urdu]
3SG-ERG ask- PERF SUB POL you come-FUT
'He asked whether you will come.'
(Davison 2007:183)

   c. [[to kal   parat aalaa   **kaa(y)**]]   [Marathi]
he yesterday back COME.PAST.3SG.M POL
mhaaNun/asa] raam malaa   witSaarat hotaa.
QUOT   such Ram 1SG.DAT ask.PROG be.PAST.3SG.M
'Ram was asking me whether/if he came back yesterday.'
(Davison 2007:184, attributed to R. Pandharipande)

Estonian presents a further option, with the standard language featuring an initial Q-particle (40a) that also serves as the interrogative complementizer (40c). Strikingly, though, the dominant Q-particle in colloquial Estonian is clause-final *või/vä* (40b), which is also optionally available, alongside initial *kas*, in embedded interrogatives (40c):

(40) a. **Kas** homseni   ei   anna oodata?   [Estonian]
Q   TOMORROW.TER NEG let   wait.INF
'Can't it wait till tomorrow?'
(Keevallik 2009:146)

   b. Mtsa p:ilve   ei   jää   **vä**?
but   CLOUD.ILL NEG become Q
'But don't (you) become high?'
(Keevallik 2009:165)

   c. Ma küsisin,   et **kas** ta tuli   (**või/vä**).
1SG ask.1SG.PAST that Q   she COME.3SG.PAST Q
'I asked if she came.'
(Bailey 2012:60, citing personal communication from Anne Tamm)

A more radical case of a language "recycling" a matrix Q-particle is Yosondúa Mixtec (Oto-Manguean, Mexico):

(41) a. Káhnū tī   **nú**?   [Yosondúa Mixtec]
       big   3SG.AML Q
       'Is it (the animal) big?'
       (Farris 1992:36)

    b. Kīhīn ná ndéhé **nú** tu nīhi ná īso.
       go   1SG look Q NEG get 1SG rabbit
       'I'll go see if I can't get a rabbit.'
       (Farris 1992:42)

All the cases where a Q-particle cooccurs with one or more other C-related markers raise the question of what formal analysis we are to ascribe to the particle. That it might be the spell-out of an articulated CP-head such as Int is in principle possible where we are dealing with a second element that appears to be functioning as a subordinator (i.e., (37c) and (40c)); this subordinator could be analyzed as a Force head:

(42) [$_{ForceP}$ Initial C ... [$_{IntP}$ ... Q-particle]]

This analysis becomes less appealing when we consider the nature of the initial subordinators, however: in the languages in question, they serve as general subordination markers and do not have a clause-typing function. This is even more clearly the case in languages where general subordination markers (*linkers* in Philip's (2012) terms) cooccur with initial clause-typing complementizers, as in (38b) and (39). A more appropriate analysis, then, would seem to be one drawing on the proposals of Bhatt and Yoon (1992), Haegeman (2006, 2012), and others, in terms of which embedded clauses are introduced by Sub(ordinate)P, which dominates ForceP:

(43) [$_{SubP}$ Initial C ... [$_{IntP}$ ... Q-particle]]

In these cases, however, we would expect the Q-particle to be obligatory, as it, and not the initial complementizer, functions as the clause-typer. The fact that final Q-particles do not appear to be obligatory therefore runs counter to the predictions of this analysis. Further, (40c)-type structures do not seem readily amenable to this type of analysis: in this case, the initial C appears to be the "real" interrogative subordinator and not just a generalized subordinator, with the final Q-particle again being optional. It would appear, then, that final Q-particles may not be formally identical in all the (VO) languages that have them.

Further evidence of this fact comes from Chinese varieties possessing multiple Q-particles. Consider the following Yixing data:

(44) a. Ní huāxi yīngguo **fè**?   [Yixing Chinese]
       2SG like   Britain Q
       'Do you like Britain?'

b. Ní zuònie   xièhào **me**?
2SG homework finish Q
'Have you finished your homework?'

c. Ní huāxi yīngguo **à**?
2SG like   Britain Q
'Do you really like Britain? (I'm so surprised!)'
(Biberauer and Hu 2014:11–12)

(45) a. Tuō fè xiàoze ní huāxi yīngguo **fè**.   [Yixing Chinese]
3SG not know 2SG like   Britain Q
'He/She does not know whether you like Britain.'

b. Ní huāxi yīngguo **fè/à/fà**?
2SG like   Britain Q/Q/Q
'Do you like Britain?'

c. Ní zuònie   xièhào **me/ma**?
2SG homework finish Q/Q
'Have you finished your homework?' (impatient question)
(Biberauer and Hu 2014:11–12)

Yixing has two Q-particles: the basic *yes/no* Q-particle *fe*, and *me*. Both of these elements are derived from negation markers. Additionally, it has *a*, which typically marks speaker-surprise/agitation. Strikingly, these markers may cooccur, with one of the *yes/no* markers preceding surprise-marking *a* (45b,c) in strictly this sequence. The ordering restrictions suggest that these particles may be exponents of hierarchically organized CP-internal heads, although the precise nature of these heads is again unclear: *fe/me*, which cannot cooccur, could plausibly spell out either Int or Force, with *a* seeming to have more of a speaker-orientation, suggesting the possibility of merger within a Speech-Act-associated leftmost periphery (see, e.g., Speas and Tenny 2003, Sigurðs-son 2004, 2010, Speas 2004, Hill 2007, 2013a,b, Coniglio and Zegrean 2010, Giorgi 2010, Haegeman and Hill 2013, Haegeman 2014, Heim et al. 2014, Lam 2014, Heim 2016, Wiltschko and Heim 2016, Yang and Wiltschko 2016, and Wiltschko to appear on this possibility in general, and Paul 2014, 2015 for consideration of the form it may take in Mandarin specifically).

Languages with multiple Q-particles do not always require these to occur in a fixed sequence, however. Consider Dholuo in this connection:

(46) a. **Be(nde)** Arum ringo?   [Dholuo]
Q   Arum run.PROG
'Is Arum running?'

b. Arum **be(nde)** ringo.
Arum Q   run.PROG
'Is Arum running?' or 'Arum too is running.'

    c. Arum ringo   **be(*nde)**?
       Arum run.PROG Q
       'Is Arum (really) running?'
       (Ojwang' 2008:63–64)

(47) a. **Donge** Kamau biro?   [Dholuo]
       Q   Kamau come.PROG
       'Is it not true that Kamau is coming?'
    b. Kamau biro,   **donge**?
       Kamau come.PROG Q
       'Kamau is coming, is that not true?'
       (Ojwang' 2008:66)

(48) a. Nyako **be donge** idho   yien?   [Dholuo]
       girl Q Q   climb.PRES tree
       'Is it not true that the girl also climbs the tree?'
    b. Onyoso **donge be** o-   hero tugo?
       Onyoso Q   Q 3SG-like playing
       'Is it not true that Onyoso too likes playing?'
    c. Waseka nyalo ywak **be, donge?** ***donge, be**
       Waseka ADV   cry   Q Q
       'Waseka can also cry, can't she?'
    d. Waseka nyalo ywak **bende, donge?** ***donge, bende**
       Waseka ADV   cry   Q   Q
       'Waseka can also cry, can't she?'
       (Ojwang' 2008:67–68)

Here, we see that Dholuo appears to have at least three Q-particles—*be*, its more emphatic counterpart *bende*, and *donge*—which may surface in a number of different positions. Clause-initially (46a), *be(nde)* can also be interpreted interrogatively, but clause-medially (46b), either an interrogative or an additive interpretation is possible, the latter clearly showing *bende*'s origins as an additive particle. This is significant, as additives are crosslinguistically common sources for focus particles (see, e.g., Haspelmath 1997, Jayaseelan 2014, Zimmermann 2015), with the connection between focus and negation already having been highlighted in section 9.2.2, and that between negation and interrogative marking having emerged in this section. (46c) represents the "challenge" use of *be*, which Ojwang' (2008:64) describes as involving a grammaticalized form of *be(nde)*. Crucially, this clause-final use is a discourse-marked one; the initial use is the neutral one. (47) shows that Dholuo also has a tag Q-particle (*donge* means 'I confirm that it is true'), which can, again, be used either initially or finally. Lastly, (48) shows that these particles may combine, with variable order being possible clause-internally; at the right edge, however, *donge* must always be right-peripheral, as we might expect of a tag element. Dholuo, then, highlights three important points. First is the importance of looking closely at the functions of final Q-particles in the context of the wider system they interact with, a point that has already come up several times in our discussion. Second, additive elements (here, plausibly adverbs) and tag elements are further sources of Q-particles. Third, Q-particles differ in the extent to which they have been grammaticalized, which one would expect to have implications for how they integrate with the clausal spine, and which also raises challenging questions about how to determine the number of separately stored lexical items in play: completely distinct source and Q-particle elements vs. nondistinct, underspecified elements vs. a mixture of these options, depending on the nature of the particle, and so on.

Just how important the latter two considerations (source and degree of integration; see also section 9.2.2 on BP *não*) are becomes clear when we consider languages like Babungo (Niger-Congo; Cameroon) and Bwe-Karen (Tibeto-Burman):

(49) a. à   yàa ɔ́   tɨ tɨ fáŋ ŋkɔ́ nɔ́ dù' **mū?**   [Babungo]
        2SG P3 tell.IMPF to he as it   P4 SIT.PF Q
        'Did you tell him how it was?'

    b. ŋwɔ́ yì- jwí **mē?**
        3SG PFV-come Q
        'Has he come?' (expected answer: yes)

    c. sɨ́ gɔ́ shɔ́ **mu** lèe?
        1PL go there Q   EMPH
        'We shall go there, shall we?'
        (Schaub 1985:8, 9)

(50) a. nə= phú   ɔ   dɔ́ hi   **a?**   [Bwe-Karen]
        2SG=grandfather exist LOC home Q
        'Is your grandfather at home?'
        (Swanson 2011:53)

    b. dɛ   ladùlaʃá mi nu mɪ má   **nɔ?**
        thing strange CL NU is what Q
        'What is this strange thing?'
        (Swanson 2011:54)

    c. ɔ   nu mɪ dɑ́kú   tə ɓe, **nɔ a?**
        exist NU is winnowing.tray one flat Q Q
        'That is a "daku," isn't it?'
        (Swanson 2011:56)

d. nə= le ɔ̀   dɔ́   chíbúchígì lɛ́   nə=   pʊa   ɔ̀   dɪphodà
   2SG=go just LOC stream   and 2SG= catch.food just fish
   pho tə 6ɔ́ 6ɔ́ **nɔ nɔ nɔ?**
   small one long long Q Q Q
   'WHY don't you go to the river and catch some fish?'
   (Swanson 2011:57)

Babungo final Q-particles behave like tag elements, with *mē* replacing *mū*
where a positive response is expected, and the latter also being independently
reinforceable and prosodically separable from the main clause where the
speaker intends a stronger question (49c). Evidently, then, Babungo Q-particles combine interrogativity with speaker-perspective, syncretizing two
meaning components that are represented via independent particles in Dholuo
(48) and sometimes, though not always, in Yixing Chinese (45b,c). Importantly, this is the case whether there is a "common intonation"-marked tag
(49c) or not (49a,b). Bwe-Karen, in turn, has a basic Q-particle, which derives
from the disjunction marker and is also used to mark both *either/or* questions
and conditionals (Swanson 2011:53–54). Further, it has a distinct Q-particle
reserved for use in *wh*-questions, *nɔ* in (50b), and these two particles may
combine in the sequence *a nɔ* (basic Q-particle – *wh*-particle) to produce
prosodically marked tag questions (50c). Interestingly, it is also possible to
reduplicate the *wh*-related particle as shown in (50d) to produce a very
emphatic question. Taken together, these facts suggest that Q-particles, like
their negation counterparts, vary with respect to their degree of integration into
the main clausal structure, and that the extent to which they encode speaker-
hearer-oriented perspectives (i.e., Speech Act projection- (SAP) related information) needs to be taken into account (see Speas and Tenny 2003 on SAP).
As Enfield, Brown, and de Ruiter (2012) show on the basis of what they argue
to be a crosslinguistically representative discussion of Dutch (Indo-European),
Lao (Tai-Kadai), and Tzeltal Mayan (Mayan), the sentence-final particles
employed in polar questions are always more than "a mere question mark"
(Enfield, Brown, and de Ruiter 2012:239).

Both of these points connect to the question of the size of the Q-particle
inventory. In some cases, this is very extensive indeed. Supyire (Niger-Congo;
Mali) and Thai (Tai-Kadai) are two cases in point. For Supyire, Carlson
(1990:321) highlights the following clause-final Q-particles:

(51) a. *la, bɛ́: yes/no* Q-particle
     b. *mɛ́:* negation marker
     c. *mà:* negative Q-particle
     d. *yɛ:* constituent Q-particle

e. *kɛ́*: locative Q-particle

f. *dɛ́, sá, kɛ̀*: exclamative Q-particle (loans from neighboring Bambara)

g. *yò, yoò*: particles signaling politeness (e.g., attenuation, listening)

The basic Q-particle derives from the disjunction marker ('or'), a very common source of final Q-particles (Estonian *või*, Persian *(a)ya*, and Bwe-Karen *a* are also cases in point; see Jayaseelan 2001, 2008, Bailey 2012), while a further element is negation-derived, another very common source (see also, e.g., Yixing *fe* and *me*, discussed above). The existence of distinctive constituent and locative Q-particles points to the presence of nonclausal Q-particles (see the discussion of Marshallese above, and see section 9.4.4), while the exclamative and politeness-oriented particles again point to the often close connection between Q-particles and SAP meanings. Since Supyire Q-particles are always optional—as they also are to varying extents in the languages already discussed—it is expected that their inclusion will bring about an interpretive difference of some kind (cf. Chomsky's (2001) so-called *Fox-Reinhart intuition about optionality*); more specifically, their optionality leads us to expect an "extra" meaning/formal consequence/other effect *not* directly associated with the (potentially covert) obligatory interrogative force-marking element in interrogative structures. This expectation seems to be borne out, although it is often extremely difficult to specify what meanings/other effects Q-particles add (see again Enfield, Brown, and de Ruiter 2012 for discussion).

The same is true for many of the 25 or so *yes/no* Q-particles available in Thai (see Bailey 2012:chap. 7, Yaisomanang 2012). *Mǎy* 'not' and *rʉ̌ʉ* 'or' are the basic Q-particles, but these combine with other elements to produce the observed large inventory of Q-particles. In some cases, the resulting Q-particles are clearly tag elements or alternative-marking adverbials, that is, elements that seem more appropriately classified as clausal adjuncts, as their English translation-equivalents would be:

(52) a. tɛ̀ɛ kháŋ-thíi-lɛ́ɛw kin sǐi-khǐaw   dii   **khûn**   [Thai]
       but last.time   eat color.green good ascend(=ASP)
       chây-máy?
       Q
       'But last time, you took the green (medicine), and you got better, right?'

   b. mây rúu   **wâa** looŋbaan cà pìt   **rʉ́-plàaw.**[28]
      NEG know COMP hospital CM close Q- empty
      'I didn't know whether the hospital would be closed (or not).'
      (Iwasaki and Ingkaphirom 2005:288)

What our consideration of some of the languages featuring multiple elements that have been labeled Q-particles shows, then, is that these elements vary considerably in terms of their interpretive and formal properties, some seeming to be highly grammaticalized and others significantly less so. Therefore, as with the auxiliary and negative particles considered in previous sections, we cannot straightforwardly assume that final Q-particles will necessarily be spell-outs of relevant functionals heads—here, CP-related heads like Int or Force.

The attested diversity of final Q-particles allows us to understand Dryer's (2009b:350) observations about the worldwide and Africa-specific distribution of V-O-Q and V-O-Neg structures: the former type is much more widespread, both worldwide and within Central Africa, than the latter. This is what we would expect given standard generative assumptions about the locus of clause-typing (within the outermost layer(s) of the clausal structure) and given the empirical fact that a very wide range of elements are harnessed by the world's languages to serve interrogative-related functions; in the negative domain, by contrast, there is no specific clause-hierarchy reason to expect final Neg, nor do the sources of negation markers necessarily have any connection with an external periphery.[29] In light of this discrepancy, the following observations require further attention:

...VONeg languages tend to be VOQ, and ... the use of VONeg order may be in some sense "mimicking" the VOQ word order. ... Another, less common, phenomenon that may be associated with VO-Neg word order is VO-Aux order, where Aux is a particle indicating tense or aspect. A number of languages from central Africa also have such clause-final tense-aspect particles. (Dryer 2009b:361–362)

We will return to the matter of languages that seem to be "serial offenders" in the FOFC context in section 9.4.4.

Here, I will conclude by summarizing the Q-particle patterns that have emerged in this section. To begin with, final Q-particles do not appear to be subordinators (i.e., complementizers). In many languages, this is clearly signaled by the presence of one or more initial complementizers, which surface in the expected initial position; in others, the interpretive contribution suggests a noncomplementizer element. Q-particles also tend to be optional, though not typically in the way that complementizers can be optional in familiar languages (e.g., English). In the latter case, complementizer omission does not produce interpretive effects; in the Q-particle case, by contrast, it typically does, although the precise nature of the difference between Q-particle-containing and -lacking structures is often difficult to articulate. As we saw with auxiliary and negative particles, Q-particles vary as to how grammaticalized they are, some—notably the tag-type elements—evidently still being independently stressable and often also prosodically marked off from the rest of the structure, suggesting clausal adjunction. Some characteristic sources for Q-particles were identified, notably negation and disjunction, and, as in earlier sections, we observed that Q-particles may be (apparently) homophonous with other elements in the system.

9.2.3.2 Final C-Particles

Turning to C-particles more generally, we observe many of the same properties. That noninterrogative C-particles cannot straightforwardly be equated with complementizers is very clear in languages like Vietnamese (Duffield 2013a, 2014a,b), Taiwanese (Simpson and Wu 2002), Thai (Jenks 2011), and Shupamem (Nchare 2012), to name but a few. First, consider the following data:

(53) a. Tôi mong-ước **rằng/là** mình có thể có ngọn đèn   [Vietnamese]
         1SG wish   COMP   self can   possess lamp
         như th.
         like so
         'I wish that I had a lamp like that.'
         (Duffield 2013a:141)

  b. Phải nói **rằng là**   thế hệ   trẻ   của chúng ta
      MODAL say COMP COMP generation young of PL   3PRN
      rất   tài năng.
      very talented
      '(I) have to say that our young generation is very talented.'
      (Duffield 2013a:142)

  c. *Phải   nói **là**   **rằng** thế hệ   trẻ   của chúng ta
      MODAL say COMP COMP generation young of PL   3PRN
      rất   tài năng.
      very talented

(54) a. A●[30]-hui siong● **kong●** A●-sin m● lai.   [Taiwanese]
         A-   hui think COMP A-sin NEG come
         'A-hui thought that A-sin was not coming.'

  b. A●-hui siong● A●-sin m● lai   **kong●**.
      A- hui think   A-sin NEG come KONG
      'A-hui thought that A-sin was not coming.'

  c. A●-hui siong● **kong●** A●-sin m● lai   **kong●**.
      A- hui think   COMP A-sin NEG come KONG
      'A-hui thought that A-sin was not coming.'
      (Simpson and Wu 2002:296)

What these examples show is that both Vietnamese and Taiwanese have initial subordinators. *Rằng* is the standardly used declarative subordinator in Vietnamese, while *là*, which is also (homophonous with) the copula and the topic marker, is very common in the colloquial language. Taiwanese *kong* has grammaticalized from a 'saying' verb into an initial complementizer.[31] Although *là*, in colloquial Vietnamese, surfaces in apparently the same initial position as *rằng*, it is clear that the relationship between *là* and *rằng* is not one of simple formal equivalence; as (53b,c) show, these elements may occur in the same structure, with *rằng* necessarily preceding *là* in this case. Taiwanese provides a striking example of how grammaticalization can target the same element (here, the verb of saying, *kong*) twice to produce what appear to be formally distinct (homophonous) elements—here, what look like an initial and a final C-element, the latter evidently a matrix element, given that it can occur in monoclausal structures (see Simpson and Wu 2002 for discussion).[32] Significantly, these elements may again cooccur, making it very clear that multiple positions are in play, and also that these homophonous elements require some form of distinct formal analysis (see section 9.4.4).

Shupamem (Grassfields Bantu) also features obligatorily cooccurring elements in subordinate clausal contexts of various kinds. As (55a–d) show, the elements most closely resembling English complementizers—*júó* 'that' (also originally derived from the demonstrative) in (55a), the agreeing relative form of *júó* in (55b,c), and *nəká* 'if' in (55d) (see also Nchare 2012:337–339 for illustration of *kù* 'if.PRES' and *kú* 'if.PAST')—are initial; by contrast, the invariant particle glossed 'COMP' by Nchare (2012) is necessarily clause-final. As the examples show, this particle is obligatory in indicative embedded contexts, but barred in subjunctives introduced by initial *mí*, regardless of their matrix (56a) or embedded (56b) status. In the latter case, then, the question of homophony arises once more.

(55) a. ŋvŭɣóŋ   ná n- ʒŭ pàyú **júó**   [Shupamem]
        2^{33}.chimpanzees IRR PTCP-eat 3.food that
        púɣὲ   n-   ʒŭ **nə**.
        2.humans PTCP-eat COMP
        'Chimpanzees eat food that humans eat.'
        (Nchare 2012:333)

     b. mɔ́n   Ø-**wó** í   ʃéʃé   **nə** pà: rànì.
        1.child 1-REL 3SG commission COMP be smart
        'The child that he commissioned is smart.'
        (Nchare 2012:188)

c. pɔ́n **p-wó** í ʃéʃé   **nɔ́** pà: rànì.
2.child 2-REL 3SG commission COMP be smart
'The children that he commissioned are smart.'
(Nchare 2012:188)

d. **nɔ̀ká** mɔ́n   mbúí ʃi   jánkɔ̀ lèrwà **nɔ̀**...
if   1.child IPFV NEG learn lesson COMP
'If the child does not revise his lessons ...'
(Nchare 2012:263)

(56) a. **mí** wù twó   (*nɔ̀)!   [Shupamem]
that 2SG come.SUBJ   COMP
'Come!'
(Nchare 2012:339)

b. mɔ̀ pí kèn ì **mí** í mà twò (*nɔ̀).
1SG P3 forbid 3SG COMP 3SG NEG come COMP
'I forbade him to come [lit. that he not come].'
(Nchare 2012:418)

Udmurt (Uralic) represents a particularly interesting further instance of a language in which two complementizers seem to be able to cooccur.[34] It is generally assumed that Proto-Uralic lacked finite subordination (Collinder 1960), and modern Uralic languages still favor nonfinite subordination (Anderson 2005). However, under influence from Russian, since the 19th century Udmurt has developed a finite subordination pattern involving not just one but apparently two C-elements. Strikingly, one of these—*shto* 'that', borrowed from Russian—is initial, while the other—*shuysa*, a participial/gerundial form, which has grammaticalized from Udmurt *shuyny* 'to say'—is final. Further, contact with Russian since the 12th century has resulted in a shift from head-final to head-initial in many domains (Tánczos 2014). In FOFC terms, the expectation is that this kind of word order change will run "top-down" (Biberauer, Newton, and Sheehan 2009a,b, Biberauer, Sheehan, and Newton 2010)— in other words, that initial complementizers will be introduced before changes within TP and VP occur. Tánczos (2014) shows that the internally grammaticalized final *shuysa* became established prior to borrowing of Russian *shto* (deriving from the *wh*-word 'what'): initially restricted to infinitival purpose clauses—a context in which it is obligatory in Modern Udmurt—*shuysa* was subsequently extended to all types of subordination, and today surfaces in both adverbial and complement clauses. The source form, participial *shuysa* 'saying', is also still available in the modern language. *Shto* was borrowed after the development of *shuysa*, and the Udmurt corpus (19th–21st century, as Udmurt does not have a long written tradition) indicates that it initially alternated with *shuysa* in all subordination contexts, before becoming possible alongside *shuysa*. As shown in (57), all three options—*shuysa* only, *shto* only, and *shto…shuysa*—are available in Modern Udmurt:

(57) a. Mon malpas'ko, **shto** ton gozhtod [Udmurt]
I.NOM think.PRES.3SG COMP you.NOM write.FUT.2SG
umoj kn'iga.
good book.NOM
'I think that you will write a good book.'
b. Mon malpas'ko, ton gozhtod umoj
I.NOM think.PRES.3SG you.NOM write.FUT.2SG good
kn'iga **shuysa**.
book.NOM COMP
c. Mon malpas'ko, **shto** ton gozhtod umoj
I.NOM think.PRES.3SG COMP you.NOM write.FUT.2SG good
kn'iga **shuysa**.
book.NOM COMP
(Orsolya Tánczos, pers. comm.)

All the complements in (57) are extraposed, which is what we would expect for at least the subset of clauses featuring an initial complementizer: as discussed in chapter 2, [$_{VP}$ [$_{CP}$ C [$_{TP}$ …]] V] is a FOFC-violating structure, and it is a striking fact that preverbal *shto*-clauses are not attested in the Udmurt corpus (Tánczos 2014).[35] By contrast, preverbal *shuysa*-clauses are possible:

(58) Ta malpanez ulon-e pycha- loz **shuysa**, [Udmurt]
this.NOM dream.DET life- ILL naturalize-FUT.3SG that
nokin öz ockyly.
nobody.NOM NEG.AUX.PAST.3 believe.SG
'Nobody believed that this dream will come true.'
(Tánczos 2014:9, citing the newspaper *Udmurt dunne*, 2 February 2009)

This, combined with the fact that *shto* is used significantly less frequently than *shuysa* (447 vs. 12,478 uses in the 2.6-million-word corpus that Tánczos investigated; *shto…shuysa*, in turn, surfaces only 16 times), is unexpected in the FOFC context: a final C in a VO language constitutes a FOFC violation. Closer consideration, however, reveals that the more widespread use of *shuysa* is in part also due to its generally wider distribution. Recall that *shuysa* is obligatory with infinitival purpose clauses (59a). Additionally, it is also compatible with finite adverbial clauses (59b), and it can occur with embedded interrogatives (59c); by contrast, *shto* is only possible in declarative contexts, as shown in (60):

(59) a. So   ujani   **shuysa** vetliz.   (= preposed *shuysa-*   [Udmurt]
        3SG SWIM.INF COMP   went   clause)
        'He/She went to swim.'
     a′. So   vetliz ujani   **shuysa**.   (= postposed *shuysa-*
        3SG went   SWIM.INF COMP   clause)
     b. So   vetliz med ujaloz **shuysa**.
        3SG went   PART swim   COMP
        'He/She went to swim.'
     c. Mon juas'ko kytyn ton ulis'kod **shuysa**.
        1SG ask   where you live   COMP
        'I am asking, where do you live.'
        (Orsolya Tánczos, pers. comm.)

(60) a. *So   vetliz   **shto** ujaloz.   [Udmurt]
        3SG SWIM.INF COMP   went
     b. So   vetliz **shto** med ujaloz (**shuysa**).
        3SG went   COMP PART swim   COMP
        'He/She went to swim.'
     c. *Mon juas'ko **shto** kytyn ton ulis'kod (**shuysa**).
        1SG ask   COMP where you live   COMP

(59)–(60) show that *shuysa* must be less specified than *shto*; it has more of the
character of a Bhatt and Yoon (1992)–type pure subordinating C-element,
while *shto* still seems to require a declarative complement. That [finiteness]
cannot be part of *shto*'s featural specification is clear from the way it integrates
with infinitival clauses: as the contrast between (60a) and (60b) shows, the
infinitival particle *med* is obligatory in purpose clauses introduced by *shto*
(contrast (59a)).[36] Both of the Udmurt complementizers that we have been
discussing, then, differ from *that*-type complementizers. See section 9.4.4 for
further discussion.

   Languages with apparently FOFC-violating C-elements do not always
feature doubling structures of the kind we have discussed so far. Consider, for
example, the data in (61):

(61) a. [vɛ̃^{42} tse^{21} tsa^{42} **no^{33}**] sɣ55 xã55 ɣo^{42}.[37]   [Bai (Sino-Tibetan)]
        write tidy   COMP word read easy
        'Words that are written tidily are easy to read.'
     b. [zuotian   chi yurou **de**]   ren   [Mandarin]
        yesterday eat fish   COMP person
        'the people who ate fish yesterday'
        (Philip 2012:115)

Superficially, these examples appear to instantiate FOFC-violating V-O-C structures. Importantly, however, no^{33} and *de*—sometimes described as "association markers" (Li and Thompson 1981)—can be shown to be linkers in Philip's (2012) sense—that is, semantically vacuous functional heads that serve as a syntactic means of marking subordination relationships within a wide range of phrase-types. Consider (62), for example:

(62) a. si⁵⁵ɣɯ³³ ˡɯ³¹ ᵗsɯ³¹ xɛ̃⁵⁵ [**no³³** tuĩ⁵⁵].   [Bai]
      willow this CL grow LINK straight
      'This willow has grown straight.'

   b. [zhuyao **de**] daolu   [Mandarin]
      main LINK road
      'main road'

   c. Ni keyi [manman **de**] zou.
      2SG can slow LINK walk
      'You can walk slowly.'

   d. Wo-men [kexue **de**] yanjiu nei-ge wenti.
      1- PL science LINK research that-CL problem
      'We will research that problem scientifically.'
      (Philip 2012:33)

As they are generalized linkers, we might expect Bai no^{33} and Mandarin *de* to be highly grammaticalized elements, significantly more so than familiar clausal complementizers, and also more so than clause-specific subordinating (SUB) heads of the kind initially proposed by Bhatt and Yoon (1992). Interestingly, Zhang (1999, 2012) proposes that Mandarin *de* should in fact be analyzed as an even more grammaticalized element, namely, as a nominalizing n; particles of this type will be discussed in section 9.4.3.

To conclude this section, let us briefly consider a final type of apparently FOFC-violating C-element: the sentence-final particles (SFPs) so abundantly attested in, among other languages, the Chinese varieties. Consider the following examples:

(63) a. Ni-men zou **ba**!   [Mandarin]
      2- PL go SFP (order)
      'You leave (now)!'
      (Huang, Li, and Li 2009:35)

   b. I ma bo huantui **ma honn**?   [Taiwanese Southern Min]
      3 too NEG objection SFP SFP
      '(You know), he (or she) did not have any objection either, right?'
      (Hsieh and Sybesma 2007:7)

c. gam³ ngok³ gau² **ge² haa²**?   [Cantonese]
   so   hard do   SFP SFP
   'Why is it so hard, huh?'
   (Fang 2003:147)

d. keoi⁵ lo²- zo²   dai⁶-jat¹ ming⁴ **tim¹ ge³ laa³ wo³**.
   3   take-PERF first   place SFP SFP SFP SFP
   'And she got first place too, you know.'
   (Matthews and Yip 1994:345)

(64) a. ngo⁵ dim² dou¹ wui² bong¹ nei⁵ **gaa³**!'   [Cantonese]
        1   how all will help you SFP
        'I will surely help you under all circumstances (as you should know)!'
     b. ngo⁵ dim² dou¹ wui² bong¹ nei⁵ **gaak³**.
        1   how all will help you SFP
        'I will surely help you under all circumstances (contrary to what
        you seem to think).'
        (Fang 2003:60)

As the examples show, the SFPs, all of which are optional elements whose
presence is not required to produce a grammatical structure, contribute speaker-
and/or hearer-oriented information that is typically hard to pin down in precise
terms. Analyses that have interpreted them as C-heads (see, e.g., Sybesma and
Li 2007, Chan 2013, Lam 2014, Paul 2014, 2015, and Pan and Paul 2017 for
discussion and references) thus seem very natural: in clausal tripartition terms,
CP is the discourse domain. More recently, however, the arguments for distinguishing between the Rizzian articulated CP (Rizzi 1997 et seq.) and a higher,
specifically Speech-Act-oriented domain have mounted (see the works already
mentioned below (45); work like that of Frascarelli and Hinterhölzl (2007)
and Frascarelli (2008) partially bridges these proposed domains). In the present
context, therefore, the questions that arise are (i) whether attested SFPs belong
to the CP-domain "proper" or whether they are in fact more peripheral, and
(ii) to what extent these elements can be said to form part of the verbal
extended projection—that is, can these elements be thought of as contributing
projecting heads that integrate with the lower verbal functional structure?
Prosodic evidence suggests that the Chinese particles, at least, *are* formally
integrated since they are part of the same intonation unit as the main clause
(see, e.g., Simpson and Wu 2002, Sybesma and Li 2007, Yap, Wang, and Lam
2010, Zhang 2014).

The discussion in this section has shown that final particles in the C-domain
seem to share the properties that emerged from our consideration of auxiliary
and negation particles in previous sections. First, these elements lack

inflectional marking and may sometimes contrast with elements that exhibit this marking (Shupamem was one case in point). Second, they very frequently occur in systems that also include initial elements serving similar or related functions. Third, they frequently seem to be homophonous with other elements serving different functions. Fourth, they are often optional, thus not contributing centrally to the grammaticality of the structures they combine with, sometimes seemingly being "secondary" to an initial element in the system. Finally, they vary in the degree to which they have been grammaticalized, and some, particularly those exhibiting great positional freedom, seem amenable to analysis as adverbs.

9.2.4 Final Particles in Nonclausal Domains

The discussion here will be briefer than what has gone before, as space considerations preclude similarly detailed discussion of all the attested nonclausal final-particle facts. My objective here will simply be to confirm (i) that final particles surface in head-initial nominal and adpositional structures, and (ii) that, as in the clausal domain, these particles seem to occur both XP-internally and at the outermost XP-periphery.

I have already mentioned in passing (i) that Q-particles may combine with subclausal constituents and (ii) that the elements serving as Q-particles may actually be focus, contrastive, or emphatic (i.e., information-structurally relevant) particles that also serve in noninterrogative contexts (recall the discussion of Quechua, Marshallese, and Supyire in section 9.2.3.1). Here, I note that VO languages do not appear to employ Q-particles in combination with *wh*-elements to anything like the extent that OV languages do (see, e.g., Cable 2010 and Slade 2011 on Tlingit and Sinhala, respectively). The Syntactic Structures of the World's Languages (SSLW; http://sswl.railsplayground.net) database gives only 8 VO languages in which the "Q-marker follows narrow focus": Chickasaw (Muskogean), Finnish (Finno-Ugric), Kom (Niger-Congo), Malagasy (Malayo-Polynesian), Russian (Slavic), Tagalog (Austronesian), (Ancient) Tupí (Tupí-Guaraní), and Zamboanga Chabacano (a Spanish-based creole spoken in the Philippines). Of these, Finnish can be disregarded for current purposes, given its head-final nominals (Dal Pozzo 2007; see Holmberg 2014 for detailed discussion). The relevant Russian and Malagasy elements are particularly well-studied, so I will focus on these here.

Like Finnish *-ko*, Slavic *-li* can (in many languages) adjoin both to verbs and to XPs. Schwabe (2004) proposes that *-li* in Russian and Bosnian/Croatian/Serbian is the clitic spell-out of Force (i.e., a CP-related element), while *-li* in Bulgarian and Macedonian has two attachment options: (i) to V, and (ii) to an XP marked with a [focus] feature (see also Holmberg 2014 on Finnish *-ko*).[38] Crucially, then, the proposal is that what seems to be a shared lexical item is in fact not; while Russian and Bosnian/Croatian/Serbian have a *clausal* particle *-li* spelling out one of the heads of the CP-domain, Bulgarian and Macedonian have a non-CP-related *li* that adjoins to subclausal constituents of different kinds. The latter *-li* is of interest here since a subset of its XP-adjunction options produce final-over-initial structures, for example, [[PP P [DP D NP]]-*li*]. The contrast between the two types of *-li* is schematized in simplified form in (65):[39]

(65) a.   ForceP   b.

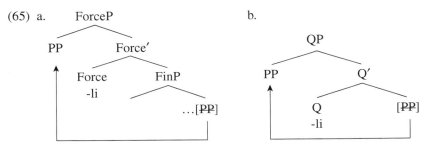

As the diagrams show, Force-head *-li* (65a) will not produce FOFC violations, as it contributes to the verbal extended projection (being specified [+V] in BHR's terms), while the fronted XP is [−V]. (The case where the fronted element is V evidently does not produce a FOFC violation; therefore, we will leave it aside here. We will return to the case where VP fronts in section 9.4.1.) XP-adjoined *-li* can, however, create a FOFC-violating structure if its specification is [+N] and the XPs in its specifier are also [+N].[40] On interpretations of P that view it as an extension of the nominal EP (see Asbury et al. 2008 and Cinque and Rizzi 2010 for discussion), this would also apply to PP, and not just to nominals.

Although *-li* is a polarity particle, fundamentally associated with *yes/no* questions, it may also surface with *wh*-elements in both Bulgarian and Bosnian/Croatian/Serbian:[41]

(66) a. Kavko **li** nameri?   [Bulgarian]
         what   Q found.3SG
         'What, if she has found anything, has she found?'
     b. Sta **li** si   mi   to   kupio?   [Bosnian/Croatian/Serbian]
         what Q AUX.2SG ME.DAT PART buy.PTCP
         'What, if you have bought anything for me, have you bought?'
         (Schwabe 2004:389)

As the translations show, *wh-li* gives rise to a very particular reading—one that overrules the existential presupposition initially introduced by the *wh*-interrogative (Schwabe 2004). As we will see, this type of reading is typical of languages whose *wh*-elements do not require a Q-particle for licensing purposes (contrast Tlingit, Sinhala, and Japanese, on which, see Cable 2010, Slade 2011; we will return to Malagasy below). Also typical of (65b)-type Q-particles (broadly construed; Finnish *-ko* is also a case in point) is that they do not seem to select for specific categories. Any category bearing [focus] may combine with *-ko* and Bulgarian/Macedonian *-li*, [focus] being potentially associated with an element embedded quite deeply within the *-ko/-li*-bearing XP; that is, it is not simply the case that *-ko/-li* select for a peripheral FocP associated with nonclausal XPs or verbs. We will return to this (non)selection point in section 9.4.3.

Malagasy *no* is another particle that seems to combine directly with *wh*-words. It forces the relevant *wh*-elements to undergo movement that would not otherwise take place, *wh*-in-situ being available for nonsubjects in the language (see Potsdam 2006:2158[42]). As Potsdam (2006:2159–2160) notes, *no* combines not only with (promoted-to-) subject *wh*-words (*pace*, among others, Keenan 1976, 1995, Pearson 2001, Paul 2002, Sabel 2002), but also with adverbial *wh*-words, which, unlike arguments, can be extracted regardless of the voice of the verb (68a–c) (being a focus marker, *no* also surfaces in clefts (Paul 2001), a significant fact, as we will see):

(67) a. Iza **no** nividy ny akoho?   [Malagasy]
         who FOC buy.ACT the chicken
         'Who bought the chicken?'   (✓Agent-subject *wh*)

     b. Inona **no** novidin' i Bao?
         what FOC buy.PASS Bao
         'What was bought by Bao?'   (✓Patient-subject *wh*)

     c. *Inona **no** nividy   i Bao?
         what FOC buy.ACT Bao
         ≠ 'What did Bao buy?'   (✓Patient nonsubject *wh*)

     d. *Iza **no** novidina ny akoho?
         who FOC buy.PASS the chicken
         ≠ 'Who was the chicken bought
         by?'   (✗Agent nonsubject *wh*)
         (Potsdam 2006:2159)

(68) a. Taiza **no** nanafina ny lakileko ny zaza?   [Malagasy]
         where FOC hide.ACT the key.1SG the child
         'Where did the child hide my key?'

b. Taiza **no** nafenin' ny zaza ny lakileko?
   where FOC hide.PASS the child the key.1SG
   'Where did the child hide my key?'

c. Taiza **no** nanafenan' ny zaza ny lakileko?
   where FOC hide.CIRC the child the key.1SG
   'Where did the child hide my key?'
   (Potsdam 2006:2160)

It is possible but not necessary to circumvent what appears to be a *wh*-fronting FOFC violation (69a) by extraposing the PP (69b) (see Sheehan 2013a,b and Biberauer to appear b for discussion of a parallel pattern in OV languages featuring head-initial PPs):

(69) a. [Iza tamin' ireo boky ireo] **no** novakin- dRabe? [Malagasy]
        which PREP DEM book DEM FOC read.PASS-Rabe
        'Which of these books were read by Rabe?'

     b. [Iza] **no** novakin- dRabe [tamin' ireo boky ireo]?
        which FOC read.PASS-Rabe PREP DEM book DEM
        'Which of these books were read by Rabe?'
        (Potsdam 2006:2171)

Significantly, *no* can again be shown not to constitute a clausal Q-particle, but instead to combine directly with the XPs (here, *wh*-phrases) it appears with. Like Finnish *-ko*, too, it can in fact be shown to be a determiner (see again Holmberg 2014 on the Finnish analysis, which, barring this determiner-parallel, is rather different from the one that seems most plausible for Malagasy). As the facts pointing to this analysis effectively illustrate the care that needs to be taken to establish the structure underlying what superficially appears to be a final-over-initial string, we will look at them briefly here.

Malagasy *no*, like Finnish *-ko*, is part of a larger particle system. More specifically, Malagasy features a class of so-called *postpredicate particles* including the quantifiers *daholo* 'all' and *avy* 'each' and the exclamative *anie*, which consistently mark the right edge of the (fronted) VP and, more generally, pattern like VP-adverbs (Keenan 1976, 1995):

(70) a. Manapaka bozaka (**anie**) Rasoa!   [Malagasy]
        cut.ACT grass EXCL Rasoa
        'Rasoa is really cutting the grass!'

     b. Mihomehy (**foana**) Rasoa.
        laugh.ACT always Rasoa
        'Rasoa is always laughing.'
        (Potsdam 2006:2163)

Crucially, in *wh*-questions, postpredicate particles obligatorily surface directly after the *wh*-word and before *no*:

(71) a. Iza (**anie**) **no** manapaka bozaka (*****anie**)?   [Malagasy]
      who EXCL FOC cut.ACT grass EXCL
      'Who is really cutting the grass?'
  b. Iza (**foana**) **no** mihomehy (*****foana**)?
      who always FOC laugh.ACT always
      'Who is always laughing?'
      (Potsdam 2006:2163)

If Malagasy *wh*-structures are pseudoclefts, as they are in many other Austronesian languages, including Tagalog, Seediq (Aldridge 2002), and Palauan (Georgopoulos 1991), the data in (71) follow readily: because the *wh*-elements are not fronted XPs as illustrated in (72a) (as suggested by Sabel (2002, 2003), among others) but nonverbal predicates first-merged with the VP, the subject being a headless relative clause containing an operator (Op$_j$), as illustrated in (72b), we expect postpredicate particles to surface in the immediately post-*wh* position (72b) rather than clause-finally (72a):

(72) a. *Fronting analysis*

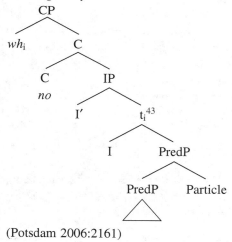

(Potsdam 2006:2161)

b. *Clefting analysis* (roughly *[It was] who that laughed?*)

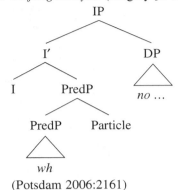

(Potsdam 2006:2161)

In light of (72b), even phrasal *wh*-elements will not violate FOFC, as *no* and the *wh*-element do not form a constituent (we will return in section 9.4.4.2 to the matter of (69)-type structures, in which a head-initial phrase is dominated by a potentially head-final element within its extended projection). What these examples show, then, is (i) that care is required to determine whether a Q-particle (or related element) is directly associated with the clause or with a subclausal XP; (ii) that subclausal particles may combine with a range of X(P)-types, raising questions about their selectional requirements; and (iii) that subclausal particles may not be as directly connected with (apparently) fronted constituents as seems to be the case at first sight.

Before leaving Q-particles aside, let us briefly consider a FOFC-relevant type described by Bayer and Obenauer (2011) (see also Bayer and Trotzke 2015, Bayer 2016a,b, Bayer, Häussler, and Bader 2016):

(73) a. [Von wem **schon**] kann man das sagen? [German]
  from whom MP can one that say
  'Of whom can one say that?! (Nobody!)'
 b. [Für wen **nur**] hat Holland dieses Stück Kitsch gemacht?
  for who FOC has Holland this piece kitsch made
  'Who on earth did [Agnieszka] Holland make this piece of kitsch for?!'
 (Bayer and Obenauer 2011:481)

Questions like these instantiate what Bayer and Obenauer (2011) call *special questions*, that is, questions that reflect certain speaker attitudes such as irritation or surprise (also see, e.g., Obenauer 2004; and see McCoy 2001 and Parrott 1997 on Russian *že*, which behaves in the same way as the German elements discussed here). In German, (eliminative) focus particles like *nur* 'only' and *bloß* 'only' (originally, 'naked') and modal particles like *denn* (originally, 'then') and *schon* (originally, 'already') surface in questions of this type. In examples like (74a,b), they can be shown to form a constituent with the *wh*-phrase, but they are also possible in the clause-medial position more generally associated with modal particles in German (see Struckmeier 2014 for discussion and references):[44]

(74) a. [Von wem] kann man das **schon** sagen?   [German]
         from whom can   one that MP   say
         'Of whom can one say that?! (Nobody!)'
         (Bayer and Obenauer 2011:472)

     b. [Für wen] hat Holland **nur** dieses Stück Kitsch gemacht?[45]
         for who has Holland FOC this   piece kitsch made
         'Who on earth did [Agnieszka] Holland make this piece of kitsch for?!'
         (Bayer and Obenauer 2011:481)

Both as part of the *wh*-XP and in clause-medial position, these particles may also stack, with the ordering of the particles within the stack being fixed:

(75) a. [Warum **denn nur**] kann AMD ihre CPUs billiger   [German]
         why   MP   FOC   can AMD its CPUs cheaper
         anbieten als Intel???
         offer   than Intel
         'How on earth can AMD offer their CPUs cheaper than Intel (I am wondering)?'
         (Source: http://3dfusion.de/forum/archive/index.php/t-1152.html)

     b. [Wie **denn bloß**] kann ich sie fangen?
         how MP   FOC   can I   her catch
         'How on earth can I catch her (I am wondering)?'
         (Source: http://www.e-stories.de/gedichte-lesen.phtml?70420)

These data thus once again raise the question of how many lexical items we are dealing with—underspecified elements with numerous selection options or distinct pairs of clausal and subclausal elements with more restricted selection options?—and of how they integrate with the structures they appear in (the same question arises in relation to Russian *že*; see again McCoy 2001 for discussion).

As we have seen, focus particles may optionally combine with *wh*-elements (including head-initial *wh*-phrases) in some languages to create apparently FOFC-violating structures. Additionally, focus particles may combine with focused XPs more generally, producing further apparently FOFC-violating structures:

(76) a. Ny mofo **no** novidin- dRasoa.[46]   [Malagasy]
the bread FOC buy.PASS-Rasoa
'It was the bread that was bought by Rasoa.'
(Potsdam 2006:2169)

    b. Ao ambanin' ny fandriana **no** nanafina ny lakile-ny zaza.[47]
there under the bed FOC hide.ACT the key- the child
'It's under the bed that the child hid my key.'
(Potsdam 2004:247)

(77) a. Inti **muntu** me kubwa.   [Kituba]
tree FOC PERF fall.INF
'It's the tree that has fallen.'
(Maniacky and Van der Wal 2015:3)

    b. Ngáí **moto** nazalí koloba.   [Lingala]
1SG FOC 1SG.be.PERF 15.talk
'It's me who is talking.'

    b'. Ngáí **ndé** nazalí koloba.
1SG FOC 1SG.be.PERF 15.talk
'It's me who is talking (rather than someone else).'

    b''. Ngáí **ndé moto** nazalí koloba.
1SG FOC FOC 1SG.be.perf 15.talk
'It's me who is talking (rather than someone else).'
(Maniacky and Van der Wal 2015:30–31)

The Kituba and Lingala examples illustrate a phenomenon also attested in other Bantu languages (particularly within Guthrie's (1948) B, C, and H classes), in terms of which a grammaticalized version of the noun meaning 'person' has become specialized as an exclusive and/or exhaustive-focus marker, which surfaces in nominal-final position (Bantu nominals are consistently head-initial). If this focus marker is indeed part of the nominal and not a clausal head (see Maniacky and Van der Wal 2015 for arguments that at least the Kituba and Lingala *moto* constructions involve a DP *moto*-constituent), and if it occupies a high position within the nominal extended projection, it will violate FOFC. Significantly, Lingala possesses a second postnominal (and therefore potentially FOFC-violating) focus marker, *ndé*. This element can be shown to be older than *moto* (Maniacky and Van der Wal 2015:31; see also Epée 1976 on the same form in Duala) and, being combinable with focused XPs of all kinds (DPs, PPs, etc.), to have a wider distribution than *moto*. Serving the same function as *moto*—the marking of exclusive focus—it is interchangeable with *moto* (77b,b') and, more surprisingly, combinable with *moto* (77b″). In the latter case, speakers prefer the sequence *ndé moto*, as in (77b″), although the addition of *moto* apparently does not result in any change of meaning. What is important for our purposes is that this case once again involves a final particle that, like many of the clause-final particles considered in earlier sections, may cooccur with an element that one might have expected it to be in complementary distribution with, thus raising questions about the nature of both elements.

Apparently FOFC-violating topic particles can also be identified. What is very interesting here, however, is how difficult it is to establish whether post-nominal topic particles in languages with head-initial nominals are in fact *clausal* or *subclausal* (i.e., directly topic-associated) heads.[48] Malagasy *dia* is a case in point. Consider first the data in (78):

(78) a. Rasoa **dia** tokony manoroka an- dRabe.   [Malagasy]
        Rasoa TOP should kiss   ACC-Rabe
        'Rasoa, she should kiss Rabe.'

    b. Ny fiaramanidina **dia** (tena) hovidin' ny zaza.
        the aeroplane   TOP EMPH buy.PASS the child
        'The aeroplane, the child will indeed buy it.'
        (Potsdam 2006:2167)

    c. [Itỳ radara itỳ] **dia** [ny Rosiana] **no** nanao   azy.
        this radar this TOP DET Russian FOC PAST.AT.do 3.ACC
        'As for this radar, it was the Russians who made it.'
        (Keenan 1976:273)

None of these examples clearly signals whether *dia* is a clausal Topic head or a Topic head associated with the fronted Topic: *tena* in (78b) is a prepredicate particle (Potsdam 2006:2165) with properties resembling Laka's (1990) Pol and Klein's (1998, 2006) Assertion; that is, it is an element we would expect to follow material topicalized into the CP-domain. Similarly, given the pseudocleft analysis of Malagasy focus constructions noted in the discussion surrounding (72), there would be space for a Topic domain dominating the focused XP in (78c). Even Pearson's (2001:237) framing-demonstrative diagnostic, in terms of which identical demonstratives mark the left and right edge of the DP—thereby producing another superficially FOFC-violating (doubling) structure (see (81))—does not help, as we would expect a DP-associated topic particle to be external to the usual boundaries of the DP. Paul (2008) argues for a clausal analysis of *dia*, and this also appears to be the consensus view on Austronesian topic particles more generally.

Final demonstratives and specificity markers also surface in apparently FOFC-violating structures, as shown in (79)–(81):

(79) a. di titi **dida** [Berbice Dutch Creole]
      the time that
      'that time'

   b. di hɛl weki **di**
      the whole week this
      'this whole week'
      (Kouwenberg 1993:156)

(80) a. **este** libro [Colloquial Spanish]
      this book
      'this book'

   b. el libro **este**
      the book this
      'this book'

   c. No podré comer de la tarta **esa**.
      NEG be.able eat.INF of the tart that
      'I won't be able to eat (from) that cake.'
      (Carla Bombi-Ferrer, pers. comm.)

   d. la televisión **esta** que tenemos
      the television that which 1PL.have
      'the television that we have'
      (Alexander 2007:111)

(81) a. **itỳ** boky **itỳ** [Malagasy]
      this book this
      'this book'

   b. **itỳ** boky mena **itỳ**
      this book red this
      'this red book'

   c. **itỳ** boky novakin'- ny mpianatra tany an- tokotany **itỳ**
      this book PAST.AT.read-DET student PAST.there OBL-garden this
      'this book which the student was reading in the garden'

   d. *****itỳ** boky **itỳ** novakin'- ny mpianatra tany an- tokotany
      this book this PAST.AT.read-DET student PAST.there OBL-garden
      (Pearson 2001:237)

Importantly, demonstratives are obligatorily final in Berbice Dutch, but only optionally so in colloquial Spanish (see (80a,b)) and Malagasy. In the case of Berbice Dutch and colloquial Spanish, final placement requires the presence of the initial determiner (the same is true in Celtic; see Guardiano 2010 and chapter 8). In the Spanish case, final demonstratives clearly play a speaker-oriented function, communicating that speakers believe themselves to be referring to hearer-old information from which they may be wanting to distance themselves (Bombi-Ferrer 2014). Crucially, this final demonstrative, unlike its initial counterpart, cannot be focused (Bombi-Ferrer 2014). Colloquial Spanish also differs notably from Malagasy in that the postnominal demonstrative must precede relative clauses, as in (80d), which is the order that is ungrammatical in Malagasy (see (81d)).

The final apparently FOFC-violating structure that we will briefly look at here involves postpositions in (circumpositional) PP structures of the West Germanic type, as in (82) (see Biberauer to appear b for more detailed discussion):

(82) a. Die bottel dryf **onder** die brug   **deur**.   [Afrikaans]
        the bottle float under the bridge through
        'The bottle floats through underneath the bridge.'
     b. Hulle hardloop (**in**) die bos   **in**.
        they   run   in the bush in
        'They run into the bush.'

Given that the postpositional elements consistently express directional meanings that seem to be universally associated with a higher hierarchical position than the locative meanings expressed by their prepositional counterparts (see Cinque and Rizzi 2010), it seems reasonable to assume that we are dealing with a final-over-initial structure here.

In sum, then, we have seen that there are many clausal and subclausal structures in which final particles seem to combine with head-initial structure in the manner proscribed by (5). As we will see in sections 9.3 and 9.4, consideration of the structures that might potentially underlie these superficially FOFC-violating structures renders this profusion readily understandable.

9.2.5 Borrowed Final Particles

Final discourse particles appear to be readily borrowable into VO languages. Consider the following examples from English contact varieties:

(83) a. Have some more food **lah**.   [Singaporean Colloquial English]
        (Wee 2004:117)
     b. It doesn't matter when the first time I do   [Hong Kong English]
        Philosophy **le**^{1},I met the same problem with you **gaa**^{3}.
        'It doesn't matter when I first did philosophy; when I did, I
        encountered the same problem as you did.'
        (Gibbons 1987:83)

Further, as we have already seen in connection with Udmurt (section 9.2.3), it is also known that complementizers differing in headedness from those already in the system may be borrowed. Probably the most well-known borrowed complementizer is Persian *ke*, which has been borrowed into languages belonging to six different families: Indo-European (Asia Minor Greek), Indo-Aryan (e.g., Hindi-Urdu, Bengali; Meenakshi 1986, Bayer 1999, 2001), (northern) Dravidian (e.g., Brahui; Haig 2001), Turkic (e.g., Turkish), Kartvelian (e.g., Laz), and Nakh-Daghestanian (e.g., Lezgian). As noted earlier in connection with Hindi-Urdu (39b) and Udmurt (57), and as shown for Uzbek (Karluk, Turkic) in (84), borrowing of an initial complementizer always entails taking on the postverbal distribution of the borrowed complementizer:

(84) Men ishonman **ki** siz tilagingiz-ga   [Uzbek]
     1SG believe.1SG that you desire-   2PL.POSS.DAT
     yetasiz.
     reach.2PL
     'I believe that you will reach [the object of] your desire.'
     (Bodrogligeti 2003:1222)

An in part similar pattern can be found in Jambi-Teochew, a strongly Malay-influenced variety of Southern Min spoken in Jambi City, Sumatra. Consider (85):

(85) a. [RC (**Yang**) pha? Aling **kai** nongkyā] khao.   [Jambi-Teochew]
              that   hit Aling that child   cry
         'The child that Aling hit cried.'
     a'. *[RC Nongkyā (**yang**) pha? Aling **kai**] khao.
     b. [Nongkyā **yang** pha? Aling (**kai**)] khao.
         child   that hit Aling that cry
         'The child that Aling hit cried.'
     b'. *[**Yang** pha? Aling (**kai**) nongkyā] khao.
         (Peng 2011:1)

Kai is the head-final Chinese relative complementizer, while *yang* is its head-initial Malay counterpart, which has been borrowed into the Jieyang variety of Teochew Chinese spoken in Jambi City (see Peng 2012 for more detailed discussion of this variety and related ones). As the examples show, Malay *yang* may optionally surface in prenominal relatives (85a). Similarly, Teochew *kai* may optionally surface in postnominal relatives (85b). What is not possible, however, is for a structure featuring *only* Teochew *kai* to be postnominal (85a') or, conversely, for one featuring only *yang* to be preverbal (85b'). To an extent, then, we see the pattern familiar from clausal complementation contexts:

wherever only a single relative complementizer is present, pre- and postnominal placement is as predicted, a finally headed relative clause having to precede the head noun and an initially-headed one having to follow it. Precisely how the additional complementizer is integrated into the structure such that it does not disrupt the relationship between the head noun and the placement-determining complementizer is an unanswered question at this point, however, as is how a final element that would normally be analyzed as a C-head—*kai*—is able to combine with a head-initial clause without falling afoul of FOFC. The first question—the integration matter, which the discussion of Brazilian Portuguese *não* in section 9.2.2 has already shown to be relevant in the FOFC context—cannot be addressed here in any definitive way owing to the unavailability of the kind of data needed to establish an empirically motivated analysis (though see section 9.4.2.2 for a theoretically motivated speculation). The second—how head-final *kai* may combine with a head-final clause to create a relative—will receive attention in section 9.4.3 (see also note 84, as the same question arises in relation to *de*-relatives in Mandarin and other more familiar varieties).

9.3 FOFC-Compliant Final-Particle Structures

Section 9.2 has shown that there are a great many superficially FOFC-violating structures involving final particles. In some cases, it is possible to see quite readily why a seemingly problematic structure is not so, but there are also many cases where matters are not so clear. The objective of this short section is to set out the formal circumstances that might give rise to a superficially FOFC-violating structure—[[Head-Complement] … Particle] (henceforth, *H-C … Part*)—without FOFC actually being violated. As will become clear, the characterization of FOFC given in (5) leaves room for a number of formal scenarios that will produce superficially FOFC-violating structures that are in fact FOFC-compliant; and, strikingly, all of these seem to be attested.

(5) crucially excludes structures in which final heads belonging to a given extended projection (EP) dominate initial heads belonging to the same EP in the sense of Grimshaw (1991 et seq.). Appealing to formal categorial features, this amounts to saying that final heads with a given categorial specification (e.g., [+V] or [−V]) cannot dominate initial heads with the same categorial specification. This formulation of the condition means that the following formal configurations will not give rise to FOFC violations:

(86) *FOFC-compliant H-C … Part configurations*
   a. The particle heads a projection to which a *noncomplement* head-initial XP has A- or Ā-moved.

b. The projection hosting the particle is *structurally lower* than the projection of the head-initial structure.

c. The particle is *categorially distinct* from the head-initial structure, bearing a *distinct categorial feature*.

d. The particle is *categorially distinct* from the head-initial structure in *lacking a categorial specification*. Here there are two possibilities:

    i. It does bear one or more other formal features ([F]s), alongside semantic features ([S]s) (Chomsky 1995).

    ii. It lacks [F]s altogether and is syntactically inert; it may or may not bear [S]s.

e. The particle is an *agreement-realizing* element not present in the Numeration as an element bearing an independent headedness specification; that is, it is the PF reflex of a narrow-syntax-internal Agree relation.

In the following section, I will show that each one of these structures exists, and, more specifically, that every one of the potentially FOFC-violating particle-containing structures discussed in section 9.2 appears to instantiate one of the above FOFC-compliant structures.

9.4   Reconsidering the Final-Particle Data

9.4.1   Final Particles in A- and Ā-Movement Configurations

BHR's analysis of head-final order entails that it is necessarily the consequence of (leftward) movement. More specifically, head-final order is assumed to result from *("roll-up") comp-to-spec* movement (*pace* Abels 2003, 2012, Grohmann 2003).[49] A FOFC violation, then, entails comp-to-spec movement of a head-initial XP, in other words, one that has not itself undergone internal comp-to-spec movement. This is crucially distinct from the spec-to-spec movement involved in canonical A- and Ā-movement, which cannot give rise to FOFC violations. This is an important outcome for the kind of "deep" universal approach to FOFC advocated by BHR, in terms of which FOFC bans the generation of final-over-initial structures during the syntactic derivation (see, e.g., Sheehan 2013a, Etxepare and Haddican 2014, and chapter 5 for "shallow" approaches that permit the generation of final-over-initial structures in the syntactic derivation but then "undo" these at PF). If the spec-to-spec movement resulting in (87) (repeated from note 41) were to "count" as a final-over-initial structure in the same way as the comp-to-spec movement generating (88)'s *V-O-Aux structure, we would not have any account of the difference in grammaticality between the two: in both cases, a head-initial XP (DP_1 and

VP) has moved into the specifier of a YP (DP$_3$ and AuxP) whose head Y is spelled out to the right (i.e., finally) in relation to XP.

(87) a. [$_{DP3}$ [$_{DP1}$ the-D$_1$ [$_{NP}$ people [$_{PP}$ down [$_{DP2}$ the-D$_2$ [$_{NP}$ road]]]]] 's-D$_3$ [$_{nP}$ n [$_{NP}$ magnolia tree]]]

b.

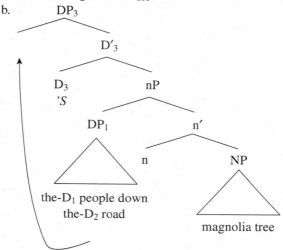

(88) a. [$_{AuxP}$ [$_{VP}$ read [$_{DP}$ the [$_{NP}$ book]]] has]

b.

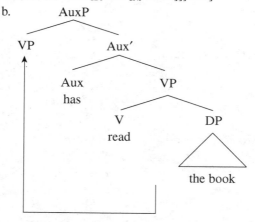

We would also not be able to account for Ā-movements like VP- (or vP-) fronting in head-initial languages like Swedish and Sardinian, or, indeed, for VP- (or vP-)fronting in any language in which C is [+V], as assumed by Grimshaw (1991). As the examples in (89) show, this type of movement would always result in a FOFC-violating configuration if FOFC were simply a matter of a head-initial XP of a given type being spelled out (overtly or covertly) to the left of a head of the same type:[50]

(89) a. [CP [VP **Åt pajerna**] såg-C [TP vi att han gjorde]]. [Swedish]
ate pies.DET saw we that he did
'Eat the pies we saw that he did.'
(Anders Holmberg, pers. comm.)

b. [CP [VP **Tunkatu su barkone**] C [TP pro asa-T]]. [Sardinian]
shut the window have.2SG
'It's shut the window you have!'
(Jones 1988:339)

c. They said they would support the cause and [CP [VP **support** [DP **the cause**]] C [TP they did]].

That Ā-type V-O-Aux of the kind illustrated in (89) is fundamentally different from "basic"/neutral V-O-Aux is strikingly illustrated by the contrast in colloquial German (90a,b). (The structural representations are simplified for expository convenience. This contrast is also readily replicated in Dutch and Afrikaans, both of which permit extraposition more readily than German.)

(90) a. [CP [VP Gesprochen mit ihr] hat-C [TP er [Colloquial German]
spoken with her has he
nicht mehr t_VP]].
not more
'As for speaking with her, he no longer did that.'

b. *... dass er nicht mehr gesprochen mit ihr hat.
that he not more spoken with her has

c. ... dass er nicht mehr gesprochen hat mit ihr.
that he no more spoken has with her
'... that he didn't talk to her anymore.'
(Haider 2012:80)

Evidently, then, FOFC only applies to structures in which the specifier is occupied by the categorially identical head-initial XP that constitutes the complement of its head—that is, where the EP-sister of a head X has "rolled up" into its specifier. This means that none of the final Topic- and Focus-particle structures that can be shown to involve clausal Topic and Focus heads into which a subclausal XP (i.e., a clearly noncomplement XP) has raised are FOFC-violating; the same would be true for clausal Topic and Focus heads located in vP (see the work arising from Belletti 2004), and for clausal Q-particles that can be shown to attract interrogative elements into their specifier, and, more generally, left-peripheral, discourse-oriented particles attracting subclausal XPs to their specifier.

Before this section concludes, a comment on the Finnish case that formed the basis of Holmberg's (2000a) postulation of the forerunner of FOFC—which did not make reference to EPs and therefore did not account for the acceptability of head-initial DPs and PPs—is in order. Holmberg shows that Finnish, which is fundamentally a VO language, permits both VO and OV orders. The latter arise in cases where O is focused, and, in this case, final Aux is also possible. Crucially, though, *V-O-Aux is ruled out. Since VO orders are the neutral orders in Finnish, this instantiates the same pattern as that illustrated for German in (90b); that is, the two gaps appear to be parallel. We will return to the question of precisely what rules out neutral V-O-Aux in section 9.4.6.

9.4.2 Final Particles Located below a Head-Initial XP

When the final particle is structurally *lower* than the head-initial XP, it will not violate FOFC, as this is in fact (a version of) the inverse-FOFC, initial-over-final structure. BHR highlight Germanic negation structures as one case of this type of superficially problematic but in fact FOFC-compliant structure. In (91), V and O have in fact undergone independent movement to positions higher than the low vP-internal domain associated with Germanic negation (see Haegeman 1995 for detailed discussion):

(91) a. Du verstehst   mich (einfach) **nicht.**   [German]
        you understand me   simply   not
        'You (simply) don't understand me.'

     b. Jag såg den **inte**.   [Swedish]
        I   saw it   not
        'I didn't see it.'
        (Anders Holmberg, pers. comm.)

This structural-height factor also seems to be relevant outside Germanic—for example, in evaluating the clause-final negation markers found in numerous Bantu languages (Devos and van der Auwera 2013). On the standard assumption that Bantu verbs raise at least as far as the Asp-domain and possibly beyond (see, e.g., Demuth and Harford 1999, Seidl 2001, Baker 2005b, Henderson 2007, Zeller 2013), V-O-Neg structures with negative elements that can be shown to be structurally low in these languages will be FOFC-compliant in the same way as the examples in (91). Devos and van der Auwera (2013) cite numerous Bantu languages featuring an optionally or obligatorily concording final negation element derived from 'nothing'-cognates (3 languages) and from a locative form (27 languages). As is clear from consideration of Jespersen Cycle–type developments crosslinguistically (see van Gelderen

2011 and Willis, Lucas, and Breitbarth 2013 for overview discussion) and from Poletto's (2008a,b) consideration of the etymology and formal characteristics of negation elements in Italian dialects specifically, the source of initially non-negative elements determines the domain within which they will grammatical-ize. For our purposes, this is important because it supports the idea that 'nothing'- and locative-derived concord markers are located within the vP-domain, which, in turn, means that V-O-Neg structures in the relevant (V-to-Asp-raising) Bantu languages do not challenge FOFC. The same argumentation carries over to the subset of Austronesian V-O-Neg languages that can be shown to feature both verb movement and low negation elements (Kabola, in which the final concord element, *nene*, alternates with the adverb meaning 'still, yet', which would be housed in a low Aspect head in Cinque's (1999) system, seems a likely candidate).

A different case involves Q-particles that can be shown to be lower than the clause they associate with (Aldridge 2011, Bailey 2012). As noted in section 9.2.3, the disjunction element is a very common source of Q-particles in the world's languages. Aldridge (2011) argues that the structure giving rise to disjunction Q-particles is that in (92):

(92)

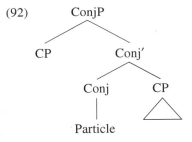

Here, Q-finality is the consequence of the elision of the second CP. The struc-ture is clearly FOFC-compliant. This type of analysis seems correct for lan-guages in which a disjunction element has not fully grammaticalized to become the main or default Q-particle (see again Aldridge 2011 for detailed discussion of an example from the history of Chinese, which included a stage of this kind). On the analysis of disjunction-sourced Q-particles in languages like Bwe-Karen, Estonian, and Thai, where the disjunction element constitutes the neutral Q-particle, which also exhibits signs of grammaticalization, see section 9.4.4.

The centrality of structural height as a consideration in determining the availability of an H-C ... Part structure is also strikingly illustrated in a C-oriented borrowing case study presented in Biberauer, Newton, and Sheehan

Table 9.2
Distribution of final complementizers in Indo-Aryan (Biberauer, Newton, and Sheehan 2009b:11)

No final C	Final C from 'saying'	Final C from demonstrative
Hindi/Urdu, Panjabi, Sindhi, Kashmiri, Maithili, Kurmali	Sinhala, Dhivehi, Marathi, Nepali, Dakkhini Hindi, Assamese, Bangla, Oriya	Marathi, Gujarati

2009a,b and Biberauer, Sheehan, and Newton 2010. Consider table 9.2 and the data below ((94) is repeated from (39b,c)):

(93) a. (**kyaa**) aap wahaaN aa-   ee- Ngii?   [Hindi-Urdu]
         Q   you there   coming-FUT-2PL
         'Are you coming there?'
         (Davison 2007:182)

     b. to kal   parat aalaa   **kaa(y)**?   [Marathi]
        he yesterday back COME.PAST.3SG.M Q
        'Did he come back yesterday?'
        (Davison 2007:182, citing Pandharipande 1997:8)

(94) a. us- nee puuc-aa   [**ki** [**kyaa** tum aa-   oogee]].   [Hindi-Urdu]
        3SG-ERG ask- PERF SUB Q   you come-FUT
        'He asked whether you will come.'
        (Davison 2007:183)

     b. [[to kal   parat aalaa   **kaa(y)**)]   [Marathi]
        he yesterday back COME.PAST.3SG.M Q
        mhaaNun/asa] raam malaa   witSaarat hotaa.
        QUOT   such Ram 1SG.DAT ask.PROG be.PAST.3SG.M
        'Ram was asking me whether/if he came back yesterday.'
        (Davison 2007:184, attributed to R. Pandharipande)

As table 9.2 shows, many Indo-Aryan languages have developed or borrowed a final complementizer. Strikingly, the languages that have not done so share a property that is absent from those that have: they have an initial Q-particle (described as initial Pol in the relevant papers; see also (39)[51]), whereas languages that have a final complementizer have final Q-partices. Regardless of whether, in the clausal case, this particle lexicalizes Int (Rizzi 2001) or Force (Rizzi 1997), it is clear that the kind of subordinating complementizer that has been borrowed or developed in the relevant languages would need to spell out a *higher* projection than the Q-particle—either Force (where Q is Int) or Bhatt and Yoon's (1992) Sub (where Q is Force). The fact that languages with initial Q-particles have resisted borrowing a final complementizer can therefore be understood as a response to FOFC: acquirers cannot postulate an analysis that would require the integration of a final element into the EP of a projection containing a lower head-initial XP.

A further case where a potentially FOFC-violating structure turns out to be innocuous because it involves the inverse disharmonic order, with the final element dominated by an initial one, is found in the PP-domain in Gungbe. The relevant structure is illustrated in (95):

(95) a. Mì fón   hàɖòkpólɔ́   sɔ́n zàn lɔ   jí!   [Gungbe]
2PL stand immediately P_1 bed DET P_2
'Get out of the bed immediately!'
(Aboh 2010:229)

b. P_1P (= direction/goal/path) > P_2P (= **AxPart**)
(Aboh 2010)

c. DirP > PathP > LocP > **AxPartP** > KP > DP
(adapted from Svenonius 2006, 2010, Pretorius 2017)

As Aboh (2010) demonstrates, the prepositional Ps (P_1) behave consistently differently from the postpositional Ps (P_2). The former evidently constitute a small closed class of five members all expressing direction/goal/path. All derive from verbs (possibly via serial constructions), seem to assign Case, and, rather unusually given the crosslinguistic trend, must necessarily be stranded. The latter are all derived from nouns and closely resemble the elements Jackendoff (1996) originally designated *axial parts*.[52] There are about 30 of them, they do not assign Case, and they must be pied-piped. Following Svenonius's (2006) characterization of Ax(ial)PartP as a nominal-peripheral ("light noun") projection located below the P-layers expressing location- and directed-motion-related meanings, Gungbe circumpositions will be initial-over-final structures (95b,c), the finality of the high nominal layer being unproblematic in view of Gungbe's more generally head-final nominal system (see also Aboh 2004).

At first sight, the West Germanic PP case introduced in section 9.2.4 is very different. Consider Afrikaans (96) (repeated from (82)):

(96) a. Die bottel dryf **onder** die brug **deur**.   [Afrikaans]
the bottle float under the bridge through
'The bottle floats through underneath the bridge.'

b. Hulle hardloop (**in**) die bos **in**.
they   run   in the bush in
'They run into the bush.'

In this case, the prepositional P is clearly locative, while the postpositional P is directional. Viewed in terms of (95c), then, West Germanic circumpositions of this type appear to be FOFC-violating. In fact, however, the West Germanic PPs are unproblematic for reasons in part similar to those that hold for Gungbe. Crucial here is the fact that both *deurdryf* 'drift through' and *inhardloop* 'run in' exist as (directional) particle verbs in Afrikaans (see Pretorius 2017 for detailed discussion). Drawing on the further observation that both Dutch and Afrikaans have silent GO, which surfaces in structures like (97a,b) (see Van Riemsdijk 2002, Biberauer and Oosthuizen 2011), a (simplified) structure of the kind in (98) suggests itself to account for (82)/(96):

(97) a. Hy is dorp toe [GEGAAN].[53]   [Afrikaans]
        he is town to GO
        'He has gone to town.'
     b. Sy moet lughawe toe [GAAN].
        she must airport to GO
        'She must go to the airport.'

(98)

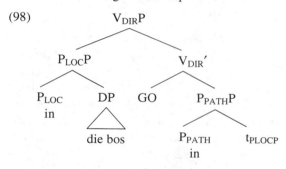

In (97), we see directionally interpreted structures that superficially lack a lexical verb. Van Riemsdijk (2002) provides convincing argumentation that this is only apparently the case and that a silent motion verb, GO, is in fact present in the structure. If this silent verb is also present in directional circum-positional structures like (82)/(96) and in directional postpositional structures more generally, we can understand why the "postpositions" in both types of directional structures are not in fact postpositions at all. Consider (98) to see why this is so. This simplified structure follows Den Dikken (2010a,b) in assuming a PP-structure in which $P_{LOC}P$ is selected by $P_{PATH}P$, which is, in turn, potentially dominated by $P_{DIR}P$ (see also Koopman 2010 for a variant of this proposal). The presence of silent GO, however, raises the possibility of structures in which the directionality component is represented not by a full-fledged $P_{DIR}P$ but by a V that incorporates $_{DIR}$, the silent V_{DIR} GO—that is, a structure in which the PP-component is defective, with part of what PPs can contribute to directional meaning being contributed by the verbal entity with which they combine rather than by the PP itself.[54] Significantly in the current context, this is a structure in which the directional postposition is in fact lower than the locative preposition, with the two PP-components additionally no longer forming a contiguous PP (importantly, the premovement PathP-structure— [$_{PATHP}$ *in* [$_{LOCP}$ *in* [$_{DP}$ *die bos*]]]. Contrary to appearances, then, West Germanic–type circumpositional structures are doubly FOFC-compliant: they involve initial-over-final structures, and a categorially distinct element separates their potentially troublesome components, head-final P$_{DIRP}$ and head-intial P$_{LOCP}$.

A final, rather different illustration of the way in which structural-height considerations can allow us to understand the availability of apparently FOFC-violating structures comes from Cardinaletti's (2011) analysis of the behavior of Italian SFPs. Cardinaletti specifically considers Venetan modal particles like *poi* (originally, 'later') and *ciò* (originally, 'it/that'), which can surface not only finally, but also also clause-internally, and, in the case of *ciò*, initially. Consider the following data (see also Penello and Chinellato 2008):

(99) a. Che beo el   film, **ciò**!   [Venetan]
         how nice the film CIÒ
         'What a nice movie (isn't it? I'm surprised)!'
         (Cardinaletti 2011:516)
     b. Parcossa, **ciò**, se   comporte-o cosita?
         why   CIÒ REFL behave-3SG so
         'Why does he behave like that?'
         (Cardinaletti 2011:517)
     c. **Ciò**, cossa i   vol?
         CIÒ what 3PL want
         'Well, what do they want?'
     d. Cossa i   vol, **ciò**?
         what 3PL want CIÒ
         'What do they want? (They shouldn't require anything …)'
         (Cardinaletti 2011:519)

As (99c,d) clearly show, initial and final *ciò* introduce very different speaker perspectives. Further, Cardinaletti (2011:520) highlights the fact that SFPs are associated with the same intonation contour as right-dislocated constituents like that in (100b) (these examples are from Standard Italian, but the patterns are the same in Venetan):

(100) a. Mi   sembra   strano che la macchina glie- la   [Italian]
          to.me 3SG.seem strange that the car   to.him- it
          presti.
          2SG.lend
          'It seems strange to me that you lend your car to him.'

a'. Mi sembra strano [$_{CP}$ che [$_{FamTopicP}$ [$_{DP}$ la macchina] FamTopic
[$_{IP}$ gliela presti ~~la macchina~~]]]

b. Mi   sembra   strano   che glie-   la presti,   la   macchina.
to.me 3SG.seem strange that to.him-it 2SG.lend the car

b'. Mi sembra strano [$_{CP}$ che [$_{TopicP}$ [$_{IP}$ gliela presti la macchina] Topic
[$_{FamTopicP}$ [$_{DP}$ la macchina] FamTopic [$_{IP}$ ~~gliela presti la macchina~~]]]]

Further, they behave like weak XPs, being uncoordinatable, unmodifiable, and
not contrastively stressable, while nevertheless containing segments that can
only occur in stressed syllables, with the result that they can bear word stress
(see Cardinaletti and Starke 1999, Cardinaletti and Repetti 2008). Taken
together, these facts lead Cardinaletti to conclude that Venetan modal SFPs are
weak adverbs—that is, deficient XPs that necessarily occupy the specifier of
a particular functional projection within the IP-domain. Importantly, then,
Cardinaletti's analysis entails that the relevant Italian SFPs are not merged
within the CP-domain, despite their interaction with speaker-oriented meanings (see also section 9.4.4, and see, e.g., Bayer and Obenauer 2011, Batllori
and Hernanz 2013, Biberauer 2013, 2016a, Kandybowicz 2013, Struckmeier
2014, and Biberauer and Roberts 2015c for further discussion of CP-oriented
elements located within a lower clausal domain). These SFPs surface clause-
finally as a consequence of further XP-movement around an IP-internal weak
adverb, as schematized in (101) (note the parallel with the right-dislocation
structure in (100b)):

(101) a. è   venuto, poi?   [Venetan]
3SG.have come   POI
'Has he arrived (I'm wondering)?'
(Cardinaletti 2011:516)

b. i. [$_{YP}$ poi [$_{Y'}$ Y [$_{ZP}$ è venuto]]]
where YP is within the IP-field

ii. [$_{XP}$ [$_{ZP}$ è venuto] [$_{X}$ X [$_{YP}$ poi [$_{Y'}$ Y ~~[$_{ZP}$ è venuto]~~]]]]

This structure clearly does not violate FOFC. Moreover, while it is compatible
with clause-internal uses of modal particles (see (99b)) and with right-dislocated elements that follow the final particle—as they indeed do—it requires
us to assume that there is a fundamental difference between initial and final
particles: as (99c) shows, initial particles precede elements that have moved
into the CP-domain and therefore must be located within this domain. For
colloquial Italian and varieties like Venetan, this seems correct, as Cardinaletti
(2011:526–528) shows on the basis of semantic and morphological evidence.
More generally, this proposal seems promising as an account of some of the
final-auxiliary, final-negation, and final-Q-particle data discussed in sections

9.2.1–9.2.3. Where languages feature a large inventory of final elements marking aspect, tense, mood, negation, or interrogativity, particularly where these are viewed as "secondary" to initial elements drawn from a smaller inventory of elements expressing these notions, a weak-adverb analysis of the final particles seems particularly appealing. Consider again the discussion of Mumuye, Ma'di, Dholuo, Tenetehára, and the less grammaticalized auxiliary elements in Bwe-Karen, Lue, Cantonese, and Yixing in section 9.2.1; Ma'di in section 9.2.2; Lagwan, Mupun, Lele, Dholuo, Babungo, Mina, Zaar, Supyire, Fyem, Ogbronuagum, Tetun, and the Chinese and Karen languages in section 9.2.3; and at least German in section 9.2.4. Similarly, Malagasy's postpredicate particles (70) give the appearance of being weak adverbs, particularly when contrasted with its prepredicate particles (78b). We will return to the significance of this contrast between initial and final elements in section 9.4.4.1.

Here, we conclude that there are a variety of ways in which final particles can actually be lower than the initial XP they occur with, and also that we have empirical evidence that these possibilities are implemented.

9.4.3 Categorially Distinct Final Particles

If a final particle belongs to a different syntactic category than the initial XP, there will, again, be no FOFC violation. We have already seen that this consideration is relevant in understanding the Malagasy focus particle *no*, a nominal element that cannot therefore produce a FOFC-violating structure where it follows a fronted VP (see section 9.2.4). This scenario also arises quite frequently in the complementation context. Consider the Yom (Gur; Benin) data in (102):

(102) a. ma   ma   dafaasə saŋər   **nɛɛ.**   [Yom]
     1SG know boys   danced Nɛɛ
     'I know the boys danced.'

   b. ma   ma   **ka**   dafaasə saŋər   **nɛɛ.**
     1SG know COMP boys   danced Nɛɛ
     'I know that boys danced.'

   c. ma   yɛr   a   cɛn **ka** gbəna **nɛɛ.**
     1SG saw 3SG go that sleep Nɛɛ
     'I saw a sleepwalker.'
     (Morgan 2012)

On the basis of (102a,b), it is tempting to conclude that *nɛɛ* is the obligatory complementizer in Yom, with initial *ka* being a secondary element. Consideration of (102c), however, reveals that *nɛɛ* is in fact a nominalizer (i.e., it is [−V]/[+N]), while its complements are verbal, an unproblematic situation as

far as FOFC is concerned. The same analysis carries over to Shupamem (see
the discussion around (55)–(56)). Importantly, it also seems to account for both
of the languages that appear to run counter to the generalization that CPs with
initial complementizers surface postverbally (and postnominally), namely,
Harar Oromo and Old Akkadian (see Dryer 2009b, Biberauer and Sheehan
2012a, Philip 2012). Let us consider Harar Oromo first:

(103) a. Inníi [**akka** deem-u]   good'-ám- é.   [Harar Oromo]
           he   COMP go-   DEP order- PASS-PAST
           'He was ordered to go.'
           (Owens 1985:145)
       b. [**Akka** na árk-aníi(=**f**)]   d'uf- an.
           COMP me see-PL=LINK.DAT came-PL
           'They came to see me.'
           (Owens 1985:146)

Here, we see that *akka* introduces preverbal complement clauses. Significantly,
it is said in reference grammars to have a very wide distribution, being trans-
latable as 'according to, just as, like, how, manner, way, (in order) to/that, (the
fact) that' (see Hodson and Walker 1922 and Owens 1985, cited in Philip
2012:87). Owens (1985:114) refers to the clauses introduced by *akka* as "noun
clauses," a characterization that seems to be morphologically confirmed in
cases like (103b), where dative marking is optionally possible, as shown. *Akka*,
then, appears to be a [−V]/[+N] C-element. Consequently, Harar Oromo no
more violates FOFC than Persian, where the nominalized nature of preverbal
C-initial clauses is very transparent:[55]

(104) a. Man midānam (**ke**)   gorbehā šir   dust dārand.   [Persian]
           1SG know   COMP cats   milk like have
           'I know that cats like milk.'
       b. Man [*(**in**) **ke**   gorbehā šir   dust dārand *(**ra**)] midānam.
           1SG   this COMP cats   milk like have   ACC know
           'I know that cats like milk.'
           (Lofti and Öhl 2004:1)

Franco (2012) argues that clausal complementation in fact *always* involves
two elements, even though only one or even neither may be overt: a high
nominal element, which he labels λ, and a lower verbal element that combines
directly with the lower clause, that is, Grimshaw's EP of V or CP.[56] This is
schematized in (105):

(105)   V_{ROOT}

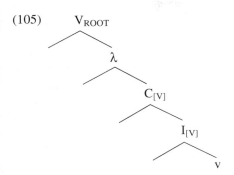

Importantly, only the lower element is part of the EP of the embedded clause,
while the higher element does not, in categorial terms, belong to either the
embedded or the matrix XP; in Panagiotidis's (2015) terms, the higher element
would be a so-called SWITCH-element, that is, one that changes the existing
category of the element with which it combines. Franco's proposal successfully accounts for complementation and relativization patterns such as those
observed in Shupamem (55)–(56) (on Udmurt, see section 9.4.4.2) and sheds
very interesting light on the Vietnamese dual-complementizer structures discussed in section 9.2.3. Recall that Vietnamese permits structures in which two
(declarative) complementizers cooccur ((106a,b) = (53b,c)):

(106) a.   Phải   nói **rằng là**   thế hệ   trẻ   của   [Vietnamese]
           MODAL say COMP COMP generation young   of
           chúng   ta   rất   tài năng.
           PL   3PRN   very   talented
           '(I) have to say that our young generation is very talented.'
           (Duffield 2013a:142)

      b.   *Phải   nói **là**   **rằng** thế hệ   trẻ   của chúng ta
           MODAL say COMP COMP generation young   of   PL   3PRN
           rất   tài năng.
           very   talented

Importantly, *là* also serves as the copula in Vietnamese, being in complementary distribution with the existential and assertion markers associated with the
vP-domain (Duffield 2013a:141). It could thus instantiate Franco's C_V, with
rằng constituting the SWITCH-element. Similarly, Chinese relative-marking
de—a final marker, which dominates a head-initial clause, paralleling the use
of Jambi-Teochew *kai* in (85)—has also been argued by Zhang (1999, 2012)
to effectively serve as a SWITCH-element: in terms of Zhang's analysis, relative-marking *de* is an n-head, which would therefore instantiate Franco's

higher λ and not constitute a challenge to FOFC (see also notes 83 and 84 on this proposal regarding n).

Now let us consider Old Akkadian. This originally SOV language featured an initial C, *kīma*—derived from a preposition *kī* with a fuzzy semantic range combined with an emphatic element, *ma*—that originated as an adverbial complementizer introducing (among others) comparative, purpose, and cause clauses. As documented in Deutscher's extensive work, *kīma*-clauses nearly always preceded the matrix V, also in cases where *kīma* apparently served to introduce complement clauses. Consider the following data:

(107) a. [**kīma**   tupp- ī   annī- am tammur-   [Old Akkadian]
         as.soon.as tablet-1SG.POSS DEM- ACC 2SG.M.see-
         u] nēmetta-ka   ana Bābili šubil-   am.
         SUB levy-   2SG.M.POSS to Babylon SG.M.send.IMP-VENT
         'As soon as you see this letter of mine, send your levy to me to Babylon.'
         (Deutscher 2009:63)

   b. [**kīma** udammiqak-   kunūš- **i**] dummikā-   nim.
         as   1SG.do.favors.PAST-to.you.PL-SUB do.favors.IMP.PL-to.me
         'As I have done you favors, do me favors.'
         (Deutscher 2000:40)

   c. [**kīma** še'- am   lā   imur-   **u**]
         COMP barley- ACC NEG.DEP 3SG.received-SUB
         [atta   tīde].
         2SG.M-NOM 2M.SG-know
         'You know that he didn't receive the barley.'
         (Deutscher 2000:58)

As the examples show, *kīma* always cooccurs with subordination marking on the verb, either *-u* or *-(n)I*; this is C_V in Franco's terms. In fact, this marker surfaces in all subordinate clauses and, in older Akkadian, it served as the only subordination marker in relative and complement clauses (Deutscher 2000, 2001).[57] Significantly, the complement clause in (107c) is not in fact in immediately preverbal position; this is a(n SOV) clausal-fronting structure of the kind also discussed by Bayer (1999, 2001) in relation to Bengali, another language with both initial and final complementizers, and in which C-initial clauses can undergo topicalization-type fronting. A more accurate translation of (107c) might then be '(The fact) that he didn't receive the barley, you know' (the neutral complementation structure would lack *kīma*, relying exclusively on the verbal subordinator as outlined above). This is significant in light both of recent work on nominal complementation (see, e.g., Arsenijević 2009, Kayne 2009, 2010b) and Franco's (2012) proposal. More specifically, (107c)-type structures can be viewed as CPs associated with a silent light noun that takes the *kīma*-clause as its complement (see also note 58 in this connection). Deutscher (2006) shows that, during Akkadian's more general OV > VO shift, complement-clause-associated *kīma* underwent a grammaticalization process that entailed not only semantic but also morphophonological bleaching, ultimately producing initial *ki*, which consistently headed *post*verbal and thus FOFC-compliant complement clauses.[58] In Franco's terms, we can think of a more complex nominal domain at the top of fronted *kīma*-clauses having undergone formal reduction to leave only a light nominal, *ki* (see section 9.4.4 for a further possible interpretation of *ki*'s ultimate formal status). For our purposes, the key point is that Old Akkadian's preverbal head-initial CPs also do not seem to violate FOFC because there is a categorial distinction between the initial complementizer and both the selecting predicate and *kīma*'s complement. Again, then, a FOFC-compliant structure that gives rise to a superficially FOFC-violating structure is shown to exist.

9.4.4 Acategorial Final Particles

In the previous section, we discussed final particles whose categorial status is distinct from that of the head-initial XP they appear with. In this section, we will consider two further types of categorially distinct final particles, both of which count as categorially distinct by virtue of lacking a categorial specification, that is, by virtue of being acategorial. We will first discuss acategorial elements that do contain formal features ([F]s) and then take up acategorial elements that completely lack [F]s and are thus formally inert.

9.4.4.1 Acategorial Final Particles Bearing Noncategorial Formal Features

The Marshallese Q-particle *ke*, the Bulgarian and Macedonian Q-particle *-li*, and the German *wh*-final modal particles discussed in section 9.2.3 are all good examples of elements that appear to be categorially unspecified, yet bear non-categorial [F]s. In the former case, *-li* may adjoin to XPs of any category and to verbal heads without altering the categorial specification of the elements it attaches to: a *-li*-bearing nominal can be selected as an argument just like a *-li*-less nominal. Unless the required number of categorially distinct *-li*s is postulated, entailing considerable homophony, these elements must be acategorial; and the same is true for focus elements that combine with a wide range of XPs, like Lingala *ndé* discussed in section 9.2.4, and for all-purpose negators like English *not* and Moi (West Papuan) *dau*, illustrated in (108):

(108) a. Nee   Moi yi-   sik **dau** y-   e-   sin-   [Moi]
      person Moi 3PL.HUM-take NEG 3PL.HUM-POSS-knife-
      keelik.
      machete
      'The Moi people did not take their machetes (but they left them
      behind).'
   b. Nee   Moi **dau** yi-   sik y-   e-   sin- keelik.
      person Moi NEG 3PL.HUM-take 3PL.HUM-POSS-knife-machete
      'Not the Moi people (but some other people) took their machetes.'
   c. Nee   Moi yi-   sik y-   e-   sin- keelik   **dau**.
      person Moi 3PL.HUM-take 3PL.HUM-POSS-knife-machete NEG
      'The Moi people did not take their machetes (but they took
      something else).'
      (Reesink 2002:255)

That these elements do, however, bear [F]s is clear from the distributional
constraints that they are subject to. Recall, for example, that Marshallese *ke*
is limited to clause-final position in negative structures (32b), despite its positional freedom in affirmative structures. As discussed in section 9.2.3, this
points to the kind of intervention effect familiar from negative contexts more
generally, and, hence, to the presence of [F]s. See Gagnon and Wellwood 2008
for an analysis of the Marshallese data that accordingly appeals to the features
[focus] (on Neg(ation)) and [polarity] (on *ke*).

Significantly, Holmberg (2014) independently harnesses exactly the same
features in his analysis of the distribution of Finnish -*ko*, which, as noted in
section 9.2.3, behaves in a way strikingly similar to Bulgarian and Macedonian
-*li* (Schwabe's (2004) analysis is completely compatible with Holmberg's
Finnish analysis): in all cases, the Q-particle -*ko* must be assumed to bear both
a [polarity] and a [focus] specification, allowing it to combine with [focus]-
bearing elements, while interacting with the clausal Pol-head (see again Laka
1990). Lingala *ndé*, in turn, evidently requires at least a [focus] specification
so that it can be probed by the relevant C-head and undergo movement to the
left edge. The same is true for movement-inducing focus particles more generally, and, where in-situ intervention effects are found (e.g., from negation),
also for in-situ focus particles.[59]

German's modal particles seem to require [F]s that allow them to interact
with what we might think of as the Speech Act domain (see, e.g., Speas and
Tenny 2003, Sigurðsson 2004, 2010, Speas 2004, Hill 2007, 2013a,b, Coniglio
and Zegrean 2010, Giorgi 2010, Haegeman and Hill 2013, Haegeman 2014)
or the Grounding and Response domains of, among others, Heim et al. (2014),

Lam (2014), Heim (2016), Wiltschko and Heim (2016), Yang and Wiltschko (2016), and Wiltschko (to appear). As noted above, modal particles prototypically—that is, in their clausal as opposed to *wh*-related use—surface clause-internally, plausibly at the left edge of vP (see Bayer and Obenauer 2011, Cardinaletti 2011, Struckmeier 2014 for discussion and references[60]). However, they interact with the Speech Act–/Grounding-associated domain in ways that suggest the need to postulate [F]s. This will particularly be the case if proponents of the idea that a Grounding domain constitutes a distinct domain located above CP (i.e., a further phase) are correct: in this case, a composed Agree relation of the kind sometimes assumed in Minimalist approaches to binding (see, e.g., Reuland 2005a,b, 2011; see also, e.g., D'Alessandro and Roberts 2010 and Roberts 2010a for other applications) will be required to allow elements located at the vP-edge to value probes located in the two left-peripheral subdomains. The reasoning here is that the mismatch between the location of modal particles—outside the outermost discourse-related domain(s)—and their interpretive function—exclusively discourse-related—will result in the postulation of suitable [F]s (see Biberauer 2015a). I leave the details of this matter to future research; for present purposes, the key point is that these particles, like the Q-, negation, and focus particles discussed above, appear to be FOFC-compliant by virtue of lacking a categorial specification. In all cases, they combine with a wide range of elements, whose categorial status they do not alter; nevertheless, they do not entirely lack [F]s, as clearly shown by their interaction with other [F]-bearing elements in the system.

Before we turn to completely [F]-less particles, let us briefly consider further explanatory advantages of the type of analysis suggested above. In connection with Q-particles, Cable (2010) shows that the way in which these combine with their XP-hosts plays a role in determining their distribution. More specifically, he suggests that Q-particles that take their hosts as complements will, by virtue of the QP-Intervention Condition in (109), not be available in matrix contexts, while those combining via adjunction will, in principle, be possible in both matrix and embedded contexts.

(109) *QP-Intervention Condition*
    A QP cannot intervene between a functional head F and a phrase selected by F.

The reasoning here is that a complement-taking Q-particle will project as part of a functional spine (i.e., an EP), with the result that a higher *functional* head will be unable to select its usual complement; *lexical* heads, by contrast, are unaffected by intervening QPs (see Cable 2010:57ff. for discussion, and see note 64 for an attempt at explaining this discrepancy, which Cable stipulates). By contrast, Q-particles that adjoin to their hosts will not affect the projecting functional structure, with the result that usual selection relations will not be disrupted. (110) schematizes the crucial difference (see Cable 2010:87):

(110) a. F_2P b. F_2P

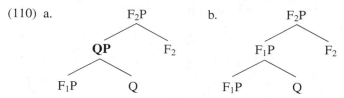

Cable predicts that Q-complementation languages (the (110a)-type) will bar Q-particles from matrix contexts, as the QP-dominating F_2-head will not be able to select F_1P in the lower functional structure in this case. By contrast, (110b)-type structures will not pose this difficulty, with the result that we expect matrix Q-particles to be available. Cable's focus is on the contrast between (head-final) Tlingit and Sinhala (Q-complementation languages without matrix Q-particles) and (likewise head-final) Japanese and Korean (Q-adjunction languages with matrix and embedded Q-particles).

As the languages we have been concerned with systematically exhibit matrix Q-particles, these should, at first sight, all be Q-adjunction particles on Cable's analysis. This analysis would, of course, render them FOFC-compliant on essentially the grounds set out by Cardinaletti (2011). That is, the relevant particles could be weak adverbs—phrasal elements occupying a specifier or phrasal position, depending on one's theoretical assumptions. And this is certainly a possibility for some of the Q-particles in the relevant languages. Recall that many of the languages we considered have multiple Q-particles, some of which are very evidently less grammaticalized than the basic/neutral Q-particle; tag elements are a case in point (see below and section 9.4.2.2 for further discussion).[61] For the grammaticalized particles, however, I would like to pursue a different analysis. Specifically, I would like to draw on the insights derived via the present FOFC-driven investigation of these particles to propose that these elements integrate via Q-complementation and that, in fact, they point to respects in which Cable's Q-particle typology can be further articulated.

Recall that, in terms of Cable's analysis, Q-complementation will be unproblematic wherever the Q does not have to be selected by a further *functional* head, that is, by another head within its EP. Selection by a *lexical* element aside, this condition is met where a Q-particle is the highest head merged with an EP, that is, where no further selecting functional head belonging to the same

EP has to be merged. Where Q spells out Force, this condition will be met, at least in languages lacking a higher SAP (Grounding) phase—if this possibility exists—or where the SAP-elements are simply adjoined to the existing clausal structure and therefore do not need to select; if a Q-particle is able to spell out the highest SAP-head, Q-complementation should, likewise, be available. The scenario where Q spells out Force seems correct for Hindi-Urdu and Marathi: as noted in section 9.4.2, FOFC considerations lead to the conclusion that the Q-particle (Pol) in these languages is a Force head rather than Int. As we have also seen that this Q-particle can combine with Sub-instantiating complementizers (like *ki*), however, a question arises about its availability in embedded clauses (see (94)). On Franco's (2012) analysis, this is readily understood, as *ki*—the higher complementizer head, λ—is not part of the verbal EP, with the result that it will not be selecting in the same way as other clausal heads, which are all functional heads sharing a [+V] specification (see section 9.4.4.2 for a further possibility).

The CP-peripheral analysis of Q-particles also seems right for the Chinese varieties, for which Paul (2014, 2015) has independently shown that they are high C-heads (her C_2 or Force C-heads).[62] The structural height of these elements can then be understood as the reason why they, unlike the particles Cable considers, are unavailable in embedded clauses (see, e.g., Bailey 2012, Haegeman 2014, and Paul 2014 for reasoning along these lines). A further benefit of this type of analysis is that we can understand the phenomena documented by Zhang (2014): although Chinese Q-particles are typically described as being optional, suggesting the feasibility of an adjunction analysis, Zhang shows that there is always some manifestation of the presence of Q—lexical or prosodic—in neutral interrogatives. This is precisely what we would predict if Q projects as depicted in (110a). As Wiltschko (2014) argues, projecting features (her *head features*) are necessarily ascribed a value, even when there is no overt lexical evidence of their presence. By contrast, nonprojecting features (her *modifying features*) do not exhibit this behavior; they are associated with optional elements, whose presence or absence does not impinge on the grammaticality of the structure in which they occur. What I propose for grammaticalized Q-particles and other grammaticalized particles exhibiting the acategorial but [F]-sensitive properties discussed in this section is the kind of structure illustrated for Q-particles in (111) (*[+Q]* here signifies the formal specification associated with the Q-particle, which is assumed to project onto the clausal spine, while *CP*, *TP*, *vP*, and *VP* are all to be understood as cover terms for potentially more elaborate fields; see Biberauer and Roberts 2015a,c for discussion and references):

(111)

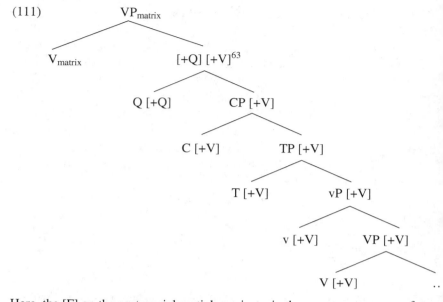

Here, the [F] on the acategorial particle projects, in the manner we assume for heads merged with phrasal structures more generally (see below, the discussion in section 9.4.4.2, and note 87), with the result that it is genuinely contributing to the clausal spine in [F] terms and can thus be said to be taking a *complement*. Where the particle is a Q-particle as in (111), then, it is accurate to apply Cable's Q-complementation classification to the resulting structure. As we will see in section 9.4.4.2, [F]-less acategorial particles cannot integrate with the clausal EP in this way, as they are syntactically inert and must therefore merge as adjuncts; [F]-less acategorial Q-particles—which also includes tag markers like English *hey*, *huh* and Canadian *eh* (see Wiltschko and Heim 2016)— thereore give rise to Q-adjunction structures like those in (110b), modulo the headedness of the clausal spine. Importantly, the [+V]-property, signaling that the clausal spine is an EP of V, will also project on the feature projection mechanism assumed here, which is essentially that argued for by Neeleman and Van de Koot (2004), with the additional, though rather natural, assumption that categorial features have a special status in defining EPs.[64] This structure does not violate FOFC, however, since it is clear that [+V] is not projecting from the Q-particle, a head that does not bear this feature; the same will apply uncontroversially to the [F]-less particles to be discussed below, as the combination of a syntactically inert element and an [F]-bearing one will necessarily result in the projection of the relevant [F](s).

What this discussion has shown, then, is that superficially FOFC-violating data have the potential to lead us to a more fine-grained understanding not only of the makeup of EPs, but also of matters such as the considerations determining whether a given projection and/or [F] will be visible to a higher head. If we are to preclude the need for undue postulation of lexical homophony where focus, negation, interrogative, topic, and similar particles are concerned, while still accounting for the absence of category-changing effects when these elements combine with their diverse XP-hosts, *and* for the fact that these elements appear to enter into long-distance Agree relations, it must be the case that they are acategorial, but nevertheless [F]-bearing. In other words, the particles discussed in this section and others sharing their properties are underspecified elements lacking a categorial specification. This means that a single lexeme can, in each case, be stored in the Lexicon and that a single element can combine with XPs of different kinds without altering the categorial specification of those XPs, while the fact that it features noncategorial [F]s makes it visible for syntactic operations like Agree.

9.4.4.2 *Acategorial Final Particles Lacking Formal Features*

Assuming selection—both the functional type just discussed, and the lexical type that has dominated generative discussion of so-called *c(ategorial)-selection*—to turn on the presence of [F]s, acategorial particles completely lacking [F]s cannot be selected, nor can they intervene for selection (see (109) again). Some of the apparently FOFC-violating structures considered in section 9.2 seem to involve exponents of elements of this type, and they will be our focus in the immediately following discussion.

Particles in systems that, upon closer inspection, turn out to feature multiple instances of apparent homophony are cases in point. Duffield (2007, 2013a, 2014a,b, 2015) provides illuminating discussions of the way in which Vietnamese represents a system of this type, and similar observations can be made about other East Asian languages. We have already considered the Vietnamese modal *được* (discussion surrounding (15); see also Lao *daj* (16)) and *là* (discussion surrounding (53)), both of which represent elements that may surface in a range of clausal positions, also available to other elements in the system, with their meaning/function depending on their position.

Let us look at *được* in more detail. As Duffield (2015) shows, this element is not alone in being able to surface, with interpretive implications, in different clausal positions; the modals *nên* 'should' and *phải* 'must' exhibit partly overlapping behavior:

(112) a. Họ **nên** làm việc lớn.   [Vietnamese]
       PRN should do job big
       'They should do great things.'

b. Cô ấy **được** kiếm việc.
PRN DEM GET seek job
'She is/was allowed to look for a job.'

c. Cô ấy **phải** kiếm việc.
PRN DEM must seek job
'She must look for a job.'   Deontic (permission)
(Duffield 2015:20)

(113) a. Họ làm **nên**   việc lớn.   [Vietnamese]
PRN do should job big
'They did (made) great things.'

b. Cô ấy **được** kiếm việc.
PRN DEM GET   seek job
'She is/was allowed to look for a job.'

c. Cô ấy   kiếm **phải** việc.
PRN DEM seek must job
'She found a job.'   Aspectual (accomplishment)
(Duffield 2015:20)

Here, we see that preverbal modals systematically receive a deontic interpretation (see also (15a)), while postverbal modals consistently receive a completive aspectual interpretation, often likened to Travis's (2010) "inner aspect." Unlike *được,* preverbal *nên* 'should' and *phải* 'must' may also be interpreted epistemically, meaning that (112a) and (112c) are in fact ambiguous, unlike (112b), a point to which will we return. As Duffield (2015:20) observes, one could, on a standard lexicalist approach, "assign different lexical features to the homophones of each modal element" to ensure that each element surfaces in the observed position;[65] this would, however, be "missing a crucial generalization about the complete class of modal auxiliaries, namely, that specific modal meanings are completely predictable from the structural context in which they appear. It could be argued that this is exactly the kind of predictable information that the lexicon should be free of" (Duffield 2015:20).[66] Duffield therefore proposes that Vietnamese and, more generally, East Asian items exhibiting this type of distribution should be analyzed as underspecified elements, lacking the formal featural specifications that would tie them to specific functional positions, for example, v, Asp, T, or Fin; instead, a rich (universally given) functional structure should be assumed to which these underspecified lexical items can be adjoined, and in combination with which they can be (compositionally) interpreted (see also Lam 2016).[67] In other words, the elements participating in what appears to be system-defining homophony of the kind seen not only in Vietnamese but also in many of the East Asian and African languages discussed in earlier sections do not themselves project to form part of an EP. The FOFC-relevant consequence of this is that superficially FOFC-violating elements that can be shown to be underspecified—by virtue of their apparent multifunctionality (see also Wiltschko 2014)—and not to contribute to an EP do not in fact violate FOFC (this was also the conclusion we reached for the [F]-bearing acategorial particles in section 9.4.4.1, as these particles, crucially, do not have a categorial feature to project). What is not yet clear, however, is how underspecified elements come to be *final* in the relevant structures. This is the matter to which we now turn.

Recall that *được*, uniquely, surfaces clause-finally when it is interpreted epistemically, as opposed to deontically (112) or aspectually (113). As noted in section 9.2.1, the same pattern is observed for the 'get/obtain' verb in many other East Asian languages. Not observed so far, but a point that will become significant here, is that this specialized regional use of 'get' is also associated with an abilitative meaning.[68] The full paradigm from (15), indicating all the meanings that are in play, is repeated here:

(114) a. Ông Quang **được** mua cái nhà.   [Vietnamese]
      PRN Quang CAN buy CL house
      'Quang was allowed to buy a house.'   Deontic (permission)
  b. Ông Quang mua **được** cái nhà.
      PRN Quang buy CAN CL house
      'Quang was able to buy a house.'   Aspectual (accomplishment)
  c. Ông Quang mua cái nhà **được**.
      PRN Quang buy CL house CAN
      'Quang may possibly buy a house/Quang is able to buy a house.'
                     Abilitative/Epistemic (alethic)
    (Duffield 2001:101–102, 2013a:128)

That the specific modal meaning of *được* is, indeed "completely predictable from [its] structural context," and, moreover, that its behavior and that of other Vietnamese modals mirrors what is observed in other languages is demonstrated very clearly by the following example:

(115) Cô ấy **nên** *được* kiếm việc.   [Vietnamese]
     PRN DEM should obtain find job
     'She should be allowed to find a job.' Epistemic interpretation of *nên*

Here we have cooccurring modal elements, *nên* and *được*, with the former, crucially, taking on an epistemic reading. Whereas *nên* can be interpreted both epistemically and deontically in single-modal structures like (112a), it is necessarily interpreted epistemically in double-modal structures like (115). As

(116a–c) illustrate, this is an effect that is familiar from languages like English, where "the same" modals can express both deontic and epistemic meanings:

(116) a. She **may/should/ought to** look for a job (now that she has a work permit). Ambiguous deontic/epistemic

b. She **may** *have to* look for a job (now that she has a work permit). Only epistemic reading

c. She **should/ought to** *be able to* find a job (now that she has a work permit). Epistemic reading strongly preferred

In (116a), where *may/should/ought to* select a lexical verb (*look for*), they may be interpreted either deontically or epistemically; in (116b,c), where they precede another modal element, they must be interpreted epistemically, with the lower element receiving a deontic interpretation. This is what we expect if Vietnamese, like English, respects the functional sequence mapped out by Cinque (1999): $Mod_{Epistemic}$ is higher than $Mod_{Necessity}$. Since Vietnamese is consistently head-initial in the clause (Duffield 2001, 2007, 2013b) and epistemically used modals also surface in initial position, as shown in multiple-modal-containing (112), it is not feasible to postulate a head-final Epist(emic) P—a welcome outcome from the FOFC perspective as EpistP would presumably be part of the EP of the verb.

One possibility, given the height of this head—Mod_{Epist} is very high in Cinque's (1999) functional hierarchy (see also below)—and also taking into account Vietnamese's status as a topic-prominent language, which systematically requires topic movement into the left periphery (see Paul and Whitman to appear for overview discussion), would be to analyze final *được* as a weak adverb, along the lines suggested by Cardinaletti (2011). In terms of this type of analysis, *được* would occupy a lower specifier than the fronted Topic, which would itself have to be fronted from within a fronted non-Topic XP, in the manner typically assumed in remnant movement analyses (see, e.g., Grewendorf 2015). The difficulty in the bare phrase structure context would be clarifying how it is possible for *được* not to head-adjoin or incorporate (in)to EpistP, as it presumably does in cases where it is spelled out head-initially, but instead to merge as the specifier of EpistP. The technicalities of this option may prove challenging, so I leave it aside here.

A more appealing option, which also facilitates insight into the behavior of final particles more generally, would be to capitalize on the location of EpistP. Given recent advances in our understanding of the way in which speaker-/hearer-oriented perspectives are grammaticalized (see the Speech-Act-related references given earlier), it seems plausible to expand the traditional clausal tripartition (see Grohmann 2003 and subsequent literature) along the lines depicted in (117):

(117) [$_{SAP}$ [$_{CP}$ [$_{IP}$ [$_{vP}$ ···

Here, *vP* represents the thematic domain, *IP* what Wiltschko (2014) designates the anchoring domain (often, but not exclusively, instantiated by TenseP), *CP* the content-oriented discourse domain, and *SAP* the speaker-oriented discourse domain, whose internal structure does not concern us here (see the ongoing work of Wiltschko and colleagues for detailed consideration). For Speas and Tenny (2003), EpistP is the sister of Evid(ential)P, itself the sister of Eval(uative)P, two clearly speaker-oriented projections (see (118a)); these fit into Cinque's (1999) hierarchy as indicated in (118b):

(118) a.

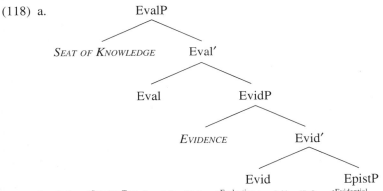

b. [Mood$^{\text{Sentence Type}}$ frankly [Mood^{Evaluative} luckily [Mood^{Evidential} allegedly [Mood^{Epistemic} probably [T^{Past} once [T^{Future} then ...

Although Mood$_{\text{Sentence Type}}$ at first sight suggests something like Rizzi's (1997 et seq.) ForceP, which would imply a CP-internal location for the SAP-projections, contra what is depicted in (117), the diagnostic adverbs associated with this projection, like those associated with Mood$_{\text{Evaluative}}$ and Mood$_{\text{Evidential}}$, rather clearly fit with the types of speaker-oriented meaning that has now convincingly been shown to *dominate* CP (see again the work by Wiltschko and colleagues).[69] Mood$_{\text{Epistemic}}$ again clearly encodes speaker-perspective (epistemological certainty), but it is also known to be part of what is encoded in complementizers, suggesting that it may usefully be thought of as a phase edge element not dissimilar to Rizzi's (1997) FinP. For our purposes, the key point is that the projection associated with epistemicity (EpistP) is plausibly located at the edge of a phasal domain. Drawing on Wiltschko's (2014 et seq.) ideas regarding the interpretation of the lower phase head (v) as being connected to event-related point of view, a similar argument could be made for the abilitative functional head—plausibly, Cinque's Mod$_{\text{Volition}}$—the second functional head with which *được* is associated.

This is significant in the context of a problem that we have not considered until now: namely, how acategorial elements that are completely devoid of [F]s are merged into a derivation. Assuming Merge to operate on the basis of [F]s (see, e.g., Pesetsky and Torrego 2006, 2007, Wurmbrand 2014), it might initially seem that [F]-less elements would be unmergeable. Assuming the existence of lexical arrays (LAs), however, one solution would be for such elements to be merged once all elements that can be merged on the basis of their [F]s have been merged. This predicts that elements of this type will always be spelled out at the *peripheries* of phasal domains—and therefore serve as useful acquisition cues, something that would be particularly important if the dynamic approach to phases turns out to be correct (see, e.g., Bobaljik and Wurmbrand 2013, Harwood 2013, 2015, Bošković 2014, and see the overview discussion in Citko 2014).

But how does this account for the observed Vietnamese facts? Let us first consider epistemically interpreted *được*. Recall that epistemic *được* surfaces clause-finally (15b)/(114c), while other epistemic modals surface initially (115), and that *được* additionally surfaces both pre- and postverbally ((15a)/ (112b)/(115) and (15c)/(113b)/(114b), respectively). Since Marantz 2001, there has been some consensus that both "words" and XPs may define LAs. Thus, for example, the components of V—a root and a verbalizing v, say— constitute an LA, in the same way that the components of the vP-domain do (see also Marantz 2008). Building on this idea, I propose that [F]-less—and, in fact, acategorial, more generally (see below)—elements may form part of both "word-" and phrase-level LAs. Where they are part of word-level LAs, they could be the last element to be merged from at least two different types of word-defining LA: (i) an LA containing a root and a categorizer alongside the particle (this holds in the case of postverbal particles like those in (15b) and (113), delivering aspectual interpretations; see Song 2016 for an analysis of "inner aspect" compatible with this idea) or (ii) an LA featuring a functional head (e.g., Mood or Epist; see again Duffield's (2015:18) partial cartography of Vietnamese) and the particle.

Let us first consider (i), the case of immediately postverbal (15b)/(113)/ (114b)-type particles. As noted above, these are part of LAs containing a root, a verbalizer, and a particle. If the root has a minimal featural specification, as assumed by Harley (2014), among others, the root and the verbalizer will merge first, leaving the featureless particle to be merged last, that is, at the edge of the structure produced by this LA. This is illustrated in (119), where v is the verbalizer, and √R and PRT are [F]-less elements:

(119)

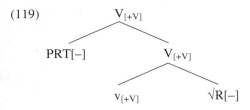

If both the root and the particle are featureless (see e.g., De Belder and Van Craenenbroeck 2014, 2015), either could in principle be first-merged with the verbalizer, creating V; in this case, we might appeal to Chomsky's (1995 et seq.) convergence-as-gibberish proposal where the particle is incorrectly merged first, thus permitting this option in principle, but ruling it out as a derivation that will give rise to the interpretations at issue here. Alternatively, it could just be the case that it is not possible to merge a completely [F]-less particle from a word-level array, so that the complication highlighted here is avoided. This may be correct if we consider phenomena such as verb focus, which in many focus-particle-containing systems seems to require a novel mechanism such as predicate doubling (see Aboh 2004 for discussion in relation to the Gbe languages). I leave the details of this matter to future research, assuming featureless roots for expository purposes.[70] What is clear from (119) is that [F]-less particles, if they *are* able to combine with categorized lexical heads, will do so as adjuncts.

(ii), the case where an [F]-less particle is part of an LA alongside a functional head Epist, is straightforward: the functional head will be [F]-bearing, presumably including a [+V] specification, while the particle is [F]-less, giving an adjunction structure as in (120):

(120)

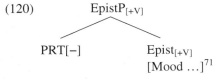

But how does linearization proceed? Here, the acategorial nature of the particles under discussion in this section and the previous one comes into play. Recall that these elements are identified as acategorial on the basis of (i) their superficially promiscuous selection behavior—they may combine with a range of XPs—and (ii) the fact that they evidently do not alter the category of the element they combine with. Taking categorial specification to mean the kind of specification that is able to define EPs and thus to involve [+/−V] specifications, particles can be said to lack this specification, whereas the elements they combine with—like the verbal categories in (119) and (120)—possess it.

Capitalizing on the fact that basic VO/OV word order is acquired very early (see, e.g., Wexler 1998, Tsimpli 2014), potentially on the basis of prosodic cues that have already been registered before birth,[72] it is plausible to assume that headedness information is an intrinsic part of "what it means to be a verb/ noun." In the context of (119) and (120), the [+V] specification associated with the heads the particle merges with thus includes the information that V is head-initial—in BHR's terms, it lacks the head-finality-creating movement diacritic ^. We therefore expect it to precede its complement, which, in both cases, results in the particle being spelled out finally. Where a particle combines with an overtly spelled-out verb, as in (119), it will surface postverbally, thus accounting for the postverbal position of được in (15c)/(113b)/(114b). Where it combines with a null head like Epist in (120), it will again be spelled out after this null head; since Epist is null, though, we have the impression of head-initiality, as seen in (15a)/(112b)/(114a).

This leaves only one further case, the one that is our central concern: clause-final and apparently FOFC-violating được. As noted above, this modal exhibits the same behavior as 'get'-derived epistemic modals in the East Asian region more generally, being amenable to both an epistemic and an abilitative reading (see again (15c)/(114c)). Accepting the earlier argument that functional heads associated with epistemic and abilitative interpretations—$Mood_{Epistemic}$ and $Mood_{Volitional}$ in Cinquean terms—are merged at the edge of phasal domains, it is possible to see how the proposal regarding the linearization of head-adjoined được may carry across to the case under consideration here. More specifically, if the relevant functional heads are the last [F]-bearing *heads* to be merged from their LA, we expect acategorial được to be merged as soon as any further elements in the relevant LA specifically selected by $Mood_{Epistemic}$ or $Mood_{Volitional}$ have been merged, that is, at the edge of the respective phasal domains. Final linearization then follows if acategorial particles are linearized, as they were in the head adjunction scenarios depicted in (119) and (120), on the basis of the headedness specification of the last-merged head, here $Mood_{Epistemic}$ or $Mood_{Volitional}$, which are both, as [+V]-bearing elements, head-initial. This linearization proposal is one that allows the grammar to make maximal use of minimal means (see Biberauer 2011 et seq.): it incorporates ordering information, which is available to the child from the earliest acquisition stages, into the formal specification of lexical categories, uses this categorial specification to define EPs—[+V]/[−V] are therefore effectively cover terms—and further exploits the information available via the EP in cases where an independent linearization algorithm (e.g., the Linear Correspondence Axiom; Kayne 1994) cannot apply.[73] Abilitative được is therefore final because it is last-merged from the clause's lower phasal domain, and epistemic được because it is last-merged from the clause's higher phasal domain. As there is no head-final structure in the syntax, neither case violates FOFC. And the same is true for acategorial particles—those lacking an EP-specification—more generally.

What is predicted here, then, is that acategorial particles in head-initial systems will always be spelled out finally—either in relation to given heads (V, and null or overt functional heads) or in relation to phasal domains (vP, CP, nP, DP, etc.): the last-merged categorially specified (and thus EP-defining) head, whose categorial specification will be visible on the head or maximal projection with which the particle combines, will dictate this. These particles, then, never project (i.e., they never contribute to EPs) and therefore do not challenge FOFC. Importantly, initial particles in head-initial systems may be nonprojecting (see the discussion of the preverbal uses of *được* above), but the way in which they combine with the functional head in relation to which they are interpreted differs from the way in which final particles in head-initial systems combine with these heads: the former combine directly with the functional head in question, whereas the latter combine with its maximal projection.[74]

The proposals made here, then, may also facilitate insight into Cardinaletti's (2011) discussion of the discrepancy between initial and final uses of what superficially appear to be "the same" particles in final and initial position. Likewise, the analysis proposed here predicts these elements to be formally quite different. Initial modals are part of a complex head containing [F]s in addition to any they may themselves bear (see (120)). The same is true of postverbal particles, which form a complex head including at least V's [+V]-feature (see (119)). XP-/clause-final particles, by contrast, do not combine directly with a functional head and are therefore [F]-deficient compared with initial and content-word-associated particles. This mirrors Cardinaletti's proposal in that it predicts that initial particles will look more like "normal" (i.e., projecting) functional heads, while final particles will look different, lacking both a direct connection to the EP (cf. Cardinaletti's spec-analysis) and [F]s (a point Cardinaletti does not specifically address). The proposals initially seem different regarding their expectations about the distributional properties of the two particle types: for Cardinaletti, initial particles are higher than their phonologically identical final forms, and there is no necessary connection to phasal domains; under the proposal made here, initial elements are predicted to surface anywhere where there is evidence of a functional head,[75] while final elements are predicted to occur only at phase edges. Both particle types, then, serve as diagnostics for formal structure, namely, the presence of functional heads (see also note 76) and the locus of phase edges. Despite the initial incompatibility between these predictions, there may be ways to unify them.

If we adopt phase-sliding (Gallego 2006, 2010, Den Dikken 2007), the two approaches might, however, not be so distinct: in that case, the IP-domain with which Cardinaletti associates the weak adverbs in Italian might constitute the expanded vP-phase edge.[76] If a unification is possible—clearly a topic for future research—the distinct weak-adverb type of FOFC-compatibility argument presented in section 9.4.2 may be dispensable, potentially a desirable outcome, given that it requires an independent motivation for remnant movement past the specifier bearing the weak adverb.[77]

The present proposal, then, makes a number of specific predictions about initial vs. final particles. We have already noted that the former combine directly with functional heads, whereas the latter combine with a maximal projection, rendering final particles in head-initial languages defective in relevant senses with respect to their head-initial counterparts (see also note 75). Furthermore, we may, in head-initial languages, observe initial particles that do *not* give evidence of acategorial behavior (e.g., apparently promiscuous selection behavior, and lack of effect on the categorial specification of the element they combine with) and that are evidently highly grammaticalized in the sense of Roberts and Roussou (2003); these plausibly constitute projecting functional heads, an option that is never available to final particles, if the definition of FOFC given in (5) is on the right track.[78] Final particles in head-final languages, by contrast, may be either projecting or nonprojecting. Interestingly, this mirrors the conclusion Cable (2010) reaches on the basis of his consideration of final Q-particles in head-final languages (see again the QP-Intervention Condition in (109) and surrounding discussion).

One question we have not yet addressed is how particle clusters such as those illustrated in (63)–(64), which frequently seem to involve acategorial particles of the kind considered in this section and the previous one, can be accounted for. On the account constructed so far, we expect that acategorial particles will be linearized in accordance with their hierarchical positions, with XP-final particles surfacing phase-peripherally because they were last out of the LA to which they belong. At first sight, this proposal would seem to rule out or at least impose very tight constraints on particle clustering. One phenomenon we might not expect, for example, would be the appearance of selectional relationships between multiple particles within a cluster in a given structure. But particles have been said to be subject to strict ordering relations cluster-internally (see Paul 2014, 2015, Erlewine to appear a,b; also see Pan 2016 for recent discussion and references). Consider, for example, (121):

(121) a.   Tā   bù   chōuyān **le**   **ma**?   [Mandarin]
           she/he NEG smoke   PERF   Q

'Does she/he no longer smoke?'
(Paul 2015:264)

a′. *Tā bù chōuyān **ma le**?

b. Jin lái **ba ou**!
enter come IMP gentle warning[79]
'Hurry, come in!'
(Paul 2015:253)

b′. *Jin lái **ou ba**!

Paul (2014, 2015) classifies all of the SFPs illustrated in (120) as C-elements. If these particles are indeed all associated with the CP-phase, the analysis we have been considering in this section clearly faces a challenge. Significantly, however, an existing tradition, which Paul picks up on and formalizes, distinguishes three subtypes of SFP: low C (C_1), Force (C_2), and Attitude (C_3) particles (see table 9.3). Against the background of our earlier discussion of the formalization of Speech Act meanings, this more fine-grained classification suggests how we might understand the ordering restriction exemplified in (121b/b′) without directly having to appeal to selection. In terms of the earlier discussion, it is plausible to view the Attitude and Clause Type SFPs as being associated with different phasal domains, namely, the SAP- and CP-domains depicted in (117) and repeated here:

(122) $[_{SAP}$ $[_{CP}$ $[_{IP}$ $[_{vP}$ …

If *ou* is last out of the SAP-defining LA and *ba* is last out of the Clause Type–defining LA, we can understand the ordering restriction illustrated in (120b/b′). *Ba* must precede *ou*, as it is merged first with the clausal EP, a head-initial structure; since *ba* does not project, head-initial [+V] will continue to project, thereby accounting for the absolutely final placement of *ou* once it is merged upon completion of the CP-phase.

Table 9.3 does not, however, allow us to understand the ordering restrictions in (121a/a′): here, two SFP types that Paul (2014, 2015) analyzes as belonging to the CP-domain cooccur in a fixed order, with SFP_1 preceding SFP_2. Closer consideration of the elements Paul classifies as low-C SFPs (SFP_1s), combined

Table 9.3
Typology of Mandarin sentence-final particles

SFP_1 (Low)	SFP_2 (Clause Type)	SFP_3 (Attitude)
le – currently relevant state	*ma* – interrogative	*ou* – gentle warning
láizhe – prior knowledge	*ba* – imperative	*(y)a* – astonishment
éryǐ – only	*ne* – follow-up question	*ne* – exaggeration
…	…	…

with what we have learned about the speaker/hearer relevance of phase edges (recall note 77, Wiltschko's (2014) interpretation of vP as the locus of event-related point of view, etc.), points to a route via which this complication may be circumvented: if SFP$_1$ elements can be shown to instantiate perspective-related elements associated with the edge of the lower clausal phase (vP), the order is as expected. Significantly, Erlewine (to appear a) argues precisely that sentence-final *le*, the element at issue here,[80] and also *éryĭ* 'only' and SFP$_1$ elements more generally are merged at the vP-edge. He provides detailed scope-based argumentation, showing that the observed scope interactions between *le* and *éryĭ* on the one hand and elements that are uncontroversially located in the IP-domain on the other are as expected if the former are in fact merged at the edge of vP. This leads him to the following reclassification of the SFPs initially considered by Paul (2014, 2015):[81]

(123)

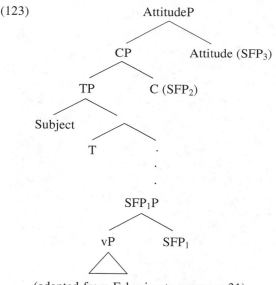

(adapted from Erlewine to appear a:31)

The examples we have considered here, then, do not fall afoul of the non-selection-based analysis of final particles argued for in this section: in each case, the elements of the final cluster derive from different LAs, leading us to expect that they will be linearized in accordance with the sequence in which these LAs feed into the derivation. This approach clearly makes some strong predictions, which initial investigations suggest are correct. As already noted, the current proposal predicts that particles exhibiting strict cluster-internal ordering effects will derive from different LAs. In the case we have considered, there are potentially four distinct phasal domains (V, vP, CP, and SAP), meaning that we may (in the absence of postverbal objects) expect up to four final particles in Sinitic SFP clusters, with the ordering reflecting the Merge order of the relevant domains: V > vP > CP > SAP. It is therefore not necessary for these particles to select each other or for them to be the spell-out of hierarchically organized heads in a tightly constrained functional sequence, as is commonly argued.

Further, the current proposal predicts that particles deriving from the same LA and competing for combination with the same functional head will not be able to cooccur, the usual complementary-distribution prediction, which is, of course, not unique to the present analysis. A prediction that is unique to this analysis is that acategorial particles deriving from the same LA will exhibit some ordering flexibility, leading to potentially quite small, but nevertheless scope-related interpretive differences. Taking into account that acategorial particles seem to vary as to whether they are completely [F]-less or bear a minimal [F]-specification, another possibility is that the latter acategorial type will be merged prior to the former type. I leave these and other matters to future research.

In the most general terms, then, the analysis of acategorial particles sketched here leads us to expect (apparently homophonous) multifunctional particles of this sort—and, by analogy, possibly others (see Biberauer 2015a, 2016a,b, to appear a on the effect of Input Generalization in this regard)—to be located in two distinct kinds of positions: (i) at word- and XP-level phase edges, and (ii) adjoined to independently available functional heads. Only the former will give rise—at PF—to head-finality in systems of the type we are concerned with here. In other words, we expect acategorial particles specifically to be phase-peripheral (as we will see in section 9.4.6, a peripherality prediction also arises in relation to the categorially distinct final particles discussed in section 9.4.3).

Strikingly, the peripherality prediction associated with these elements appears to fit well with some well- and lesser-known particle distributions. We have already seen the case of Mandarin and related Sinitic varieties, and also of Vietnamese, suggesting that final clausal particles in the East Asian region more generally may be amenable to the kind of analysis proposed here. Some of the predicate-final particles in Malagasy (see section 9.2.4) may also be vP-peripheral, if these turn out not to be adverbs, and the same applies to the inventory of particles in Niuean (Starks and Massam 2015). In the more general Polynesian and VOS/VSO context, Holmer's (2005) typological observation that final particles in V-initial languages appear to be confined to Niuean-type predicate-fronting—as opposed to Celtic-type verb-raising—languages may also be interesting, but I leave this to future research.

Looking beyond the verbal domain, similar peripheral possibilities are predicted and seemingly attested in nonclausal phasal domains, the demonstrative and PP-doubling structures in (79)–(81) and (82), respectively, being cases in point. Importantly, the XP-peripheral linkers discussed by Philip (2012) are not necessarily best analyzed as acategorial elements, although some of them may be. As noted in section 9.4.3, Zhang (1999) argues convincingly that Mandarin relative-marking *de* is best analyzed as (a predicative) n.[82] Further, we have noted in connection with clausal complementation that the higher λ-element assumed by Franco (2012) (see (105), which constitutes a linker for Philip, may likewise sometimes be n (on why nominal linkers should nevertheless surface peripherally, see section 9.4.6). Franco's complementation structure (105) is repeated here for ease of reference as (124):

(124)

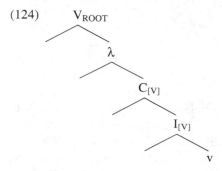

λ, then, may be nominal. Where a complementation marker is not sensitive to the nature of the complement introduced, an acategorial analysis does seem plausible, however, meaning that Franco's λ may not always be nominal, as he suggests; more-grammaticalized linkers may in fact be acategorial.[83] As noted in section 9.2.3, this may possibly also be the right analysis for Udmurt's (originally verbal and thus, in Franco's terms, C_V-instantiating) *shuysa*, which is now compatible with finite and nonfinite structures of all types. This element will therefore again not violate FOFC, even when combined with head-initial structures, as it does not bear the [+V]-feature it would initially have had (the prediction is, of course, that *shuysa* would have lost its [+V]-specification before VO ordering became possible in the relevant clausal complements, a prediction that seems to be correct). *Shto* may be either Franco's λ and thus nominal or, like *shuysa*, an acategorial element. In either case, being head-initial, it constitutes an unproblematic borrowing, the key point of interest here being its peripherality.[84]

To conclude this section, we will consider in more detail the relevance of (featurally underspecified) acategorial elements to our understanding of apparently FOFC-violating structures involving a borrowed or other "imported" element (see section 9.2.5). To the extent that the borrowing of clause-/XP-peripheral elements involves speakers taking over an element from another language *without an [F]-specification* and merging it into an existing [F]-based structure, the type of particle-final structure illustrated in (83), repeated here as (125), emerges as a very natural one in the context of the present analysis: as [F]-less elements, these borrowings must necessarily be merged phase-peripherally.

(125) a. Have some more food **lah**.   [Singaporean Colloquial English]
         (Wee 2004:117)

      b. It doesn't matter when the first time I do   [Hong Kong English]
         philosophy **le**[1], I met the same problem
         with you **gaa**[3].
         'It doesn't matter when I first did philosophy; when I did, I
         encountered the same problem as you did.'
         (Gibbons 1987:83)

If this is indeed what Singaporean and Hong Kong speakers are doing, these structures also clearly do not involve a FOFC violation. As we have just seen, Chinese SFPs appear at least to some extent to be acategorial and hence to lack [F]s, in which case borrowing of such elements—which already exhibit the placement properties typical of [F]-less elements—is predicted to be readily possible. On the analysis proposed above, the same would be true, language-internally, for the Italian final particles (see (99)), which have effectively been "internally borrowed" from another domain, and also, arguably, for cases like Brazilian Portuguese's own case of "internal borrowing," its clause-final harnessing of the anaphoric negator *não* illustrated in (26B″): as we saw in section 9.2.2, this element does not appear to be integrated with the verbal EP.

The case of Jambi-Teochew may possibly also involve underspecified complementizer elements of the kind under discussion here. Consider again (85), repeated here as (126):

(126) a. [$_{RC}$ (**Yang**) pha? Aling **kai** nongkyā] khao.   [Jambi-Teochew]
              that hit Aling that child   cry
         'The child that Aling hit cried.'

      a′. *[$_{RC}$ Nongkyā (**yang**) pha? Aling **kai**] khao.

      b. [Nongkyā **yang** pha? Aling (**kai**)] khao.
          child   that hit Aling that cry
         'The child that Aling hit cried.'

      b′. *[**Yang** pha? Aling (**kai**) nongkyā] khao.
          (Peng 2011:1)

Recall that the Chinese complementizer *kai* is described as being the Teochew counterpart of the Mandarin relative marker *de*. If this is correct, and if Zhang's (1999, 2012) analysis of Mandarin relative-marking *de* as n is correct, as we have been assuming (see section 9.4.3), *kai* should also be n. In this case, it could be Franco's higher complementizer-head, λ, and we would have an explanation for why the structures in (85)/(126) do not violate FOFC (see again the discussion in section 9.4.3). What would not be explained, however, is how borrowed initial *yang* is additionally possible in Jambi-Teochew relative clause structures already containing *kai*. The discussion so far has suggested that borrowed elements are frequently—possibly always?—integrated into syntactic structures via phase edges, that is, as peripheral elements in the phasal context (see also Biberauer 2016a, to appear a). If *yang* were to be the spell-out out of Franco's lower C_V complementizer position, Jambi-Teochew would constitute a counterexample to this hypothetical generalization. However, if *yang* behaves like other borrowed elements discussed in this section, being borrowed without [F]s and thus necessarily having to be the last element out of its LA, two possible scenarios suggest themselves.

On the first scenario, *yang* is part of the "standard" CP LA, meaning that it will be the last element merged from that array. In this case, crucially, it will already be part of the derivation when *kai*—which, recall, serves as a SWITCH-element in the sense of Panagiotidis (2015) and thus plausibly defines a (trivial) nominal LA—is merged. This derivation would deliver (85a)/(126a): the relative clause is headed by *kai*, as usual, and consequently exhibits the pre(head) nominal placement standardly observed with *kai* in all Teochew varieties. This structure is schematized in (127):

(127) [$_{nP[-V]}$ [$_{CP[+V]}$ **Yang** pha? Aling] **kai**] nongkyā khao.
           that   hit   Aling   that child   cry
     where CP is [+V] under the influence of the EP extending from *pha?*,
     yang itself being acategorial

On the second scenario, *kai* does not define a trivial nominal LA, as it did in the case just discussed; instead, *kai* and *yang* are both part of an LA that also includes the clausal CP constructed in earlier derivational steps. This proposal amounts to what Johnson (2003) calls *Renumeration* and Zwart (2011a,b, 2015) calls a *layered derivation*—that is, the idea that LAs consist of both simple and complex elements, the latter the output of earlier (LA-defined) derivational steps. In this case, *kai*, being formally specified as (head-final) [−V]/[+N], is the first element to be merged with the already constructed output of the earlier CP-derivation. *Yang*, as an [F]-less element, is again last out of this nominal array. As it is [F]-less, it is linearized in accordance with the headedness specification of its [−V]/[+N] sister, meaning that it will be linearized initially, as observed. Evidently, this is sufficient to dictate the placement of the head noun, which necessarily surfaces before the relative clause in the resulting structure, (85b)/(126b). The resulting structure is schematized in (128):

(128) Nongkyã [$_{nP[-V]}$ **yang** [$_{nP[-V]}$ [$_{CP[+V]}$ pha? Aling] **kai**]] khao.
       child   that   hit   Aling   that   cry
       where nP is [−V] under the influence of *kai*, which initially
       nominalized the clause that is relativized

Precisely why (128) should require postnominal placement, despite the featural specification of the relative clause, is unclear on the present proposal, a matter I leave to future research. What is hopefully clear is that the theoretical assumptions made here in order to account for the distribution of acategorial vs. categorially specified particles and for their innocuousness in the FOFC context also appear to go some way in helping us to understand the contact-induced patterns in Jambi-Teochew.

More generally, what section 9.4.4 as a whole has shown is that there are two respects in which acategorial final particles in head-initial systems are benign in the FOFC context. First, they seem quite uncontroversially to lack the formal categorial specification that would compromise the EP component of the condition in (5). Second, and slightly more controversially, it is also not so clear that structures containing these elements entail a *syntax-internal* structure that can straightforwardly be characterized as final-over-initial: if acategorial particles are (derivatively) linearized at PF, as suggested in this section, the final component of these structures arguably arises too late for it to impinge on FOFC.

9.4.5 Agreement-Realizing ("Late") Final Particles

In this section, we consider a final scenario in which a superficially FOFC-violating structure is in fact FOFC-compatible: that in which the final particle is an agreement-realizing element inserted at PF, in other words, where it is the PF reflex of a narrow-syntax-internal Agree relation. As with the acategorial particles we considered in the previous section, this scenario therefore involves an apparently FOFC-violating sequence that is not present in the syntax and only arises at PF. It is different from the cases we just considered, however, in that the ultimately final particle is not present in the Numeration and, thus, in any LA; this contrasts with the case of acategorial final Q-, focus, and other particles, which *are* assumed to be part of the initial Numeration. What is at stake here, then, is a distinction between elements that are merged in the syntax ("deep" elements) and those that are present as a consequence of spell-out ("surface/late" elements).[85]

Let us take the Afrikaans concord element, nie_2, by way of illustration. As the data in section 9.2.2 ((25) and (27)–(28); see also note 25) clearly show, this element must be acategorial, as it is able to combine with XPs of various kinds without altering their categorial specification. In Biberauer 2008 et seq., it has been analyzed as the spell-out of a negatively valued acategorial Pol-head, located at the periphery of the XPs it combines with, as illustrated in (129):

(129)

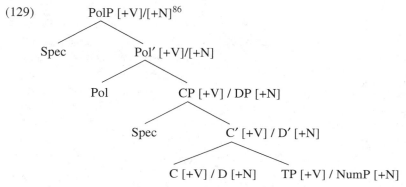

Here, the idea is that Numerations that will give rise to nie_2 will contain the acategorial Pol-head, bearing an unvalued Pol-attribute, [Pol:__]. In the presence of negative elements, which are assumed to bear a negatively valued Pol-feature [Pol:Neg], this Pol-head is then valued [Neg] under Agree. At the point of spell-out, Vocabulary Insertion takes place and [Pol:Neg] is spelled out as nie_2. This element then ends up in clause-/phrase-final position for the same reason as the acategorial particles discussed in section 9.4.2.2, namely, that it is located at the outermost periphery of a phasal domain and lacks [F]s, with the result that it is linearized finally under the influence of the consistently head-initial categorial specifications of the elements it combines with.[87]

Cases like (27), repeated as (130), in which nie_2 is spelled out despite the absence of a formal [Neg]-specification in its c-command domain, serve as further evidence that this element is not one that is initially present in the Numeration:

(130) a. Hy vertrek **sonder** dat ek agterkom (**nie₂**).   [Afrikaans]
          he leaves without that I realize   POL
          'He leaves without me realizing it.'
       b. Hy kon   **nouliks** staan (**nie₂**).
          he could barely   stand POL
          'He could barely stand.'

Here, nie_2 appears to be licensed by nonveridical rather than specifically anti-veridical operators (see Giannakidou 2005, 2011 on veridicality more generally). If one accepts the principle that spell-out always targets lexical items bearing at least the features present on a syntactic head and possibly a minimally extended set—the Superset Principle of Nanosyntax (Caha 2009), given in (131)—we can understand how a negatively specified Pol-head may be spelled out as the closest match (see Boef 2012) for a Pol-head of the kind that we might associate with structures containing nonnegative, nonveridical elements:

(131)   *The Superset Principle*
        Insert a tree in the Lexicon for a (sub)tree in the syntax if the tree in
        the Lexicon matches all the features of the (sub)tree in the syntax.
        Do not insert a tree from the Lexicon if it does not contain all the
        features in the syntax. When lexical items compete for insertion,
        insert the tree with the least unused features. (Caha 2009:55)

Nie_2 aside, Afrikaans has no other dedicated lexical items spelling out non-veridical Pol-heads, meaning that nie_2 will be the closest match for nonveridically specified Pol.[88]

Brazilian Portuguese, likewise introduced in section 9.2.2, also seems to give a particularly clear indication of the need to distinguish an agreement spell-out element—in this case, $não_2$—and an element that is already present in the narrow syntax—here, $não_3$. Consider the data in (132)–(133) ((133b,c) pick up on part of example (26), discussed in section 9.2.2):

(132) a. Ele **não**$_1$ comprou a   casa   (**não**$_2$).   [Brazilian Portuguese]
           he   not   bought the house POL
           'He has not/NOT bought the house.'
       b. Ele comprou a   casa   **não**$_3$.
           he bought   the house POL
           'He has not bought the house, contrary to what you were just
           saying.'
           (Biberauer and Cyrino 2009:2)

(133) a. Minha tia   disse que ele *(**não**$_1$)   [Brazilian Portuguese]
           my   aunt said that he   not
           comprou uma casa   (**não**$_2$).
           bought   a   house POL
           'My aunt said that he didn't buy a house.'
       b. Ele **não** tem *um tostão furado* (**não**$_2$!).
           he not   has a   coin   holed   POL
           'He doesn't have a red cent.' (i.e., he is poor)

c. Ele tem *um tostão furado* **não₃**! Um intero.
   he has a   coin   holed POL a   whole
   '*He is poor.' vs. 'He doesn't have a red cent; he has a blue one.'
   (literal meaning)
   (Biberauer and Cyrino 2009:16)

If *não* is an underspecified element of the kind discussed in section 9.4.4, we can understand the three *não*s illustrated above as follows:

1. *Não₁* is the result of underspecified *não* being part of a word-level LA along with the (clause-internal) Neg-head; combined with this head, it is interpreted as sentential- negation-marking 'not'.

2. *Não₃* is the result of underspecified *não* being part of the highest clause-level LA—that is, the highest phase, designated *SAP* in (122). Merged at the edge of this LA, it is interpreted as an anaphoric negator, which therefore cannot license NPIs—contrast **I have a red cent, no* with *I don't have a red cent*; hence (133c)).[89]

3. *Não₂* differs from *não₁* and *não₃* in that it is the result of [Pol:__] (i.e., unvalued Pol) being part of a clause-level LA (e.g., CP), where it is valued [Neg] on the basis of a [Neg]-bearing element in the lower clausal domain, for example, *não*+Neg (=*não₁*). This [Pol:Neg] is then spelled out as *não₂* at PF.

Não₂, then, like Afrikaans *nie₂*, is the reflex of an Agree relation, whereas *não₁* and *não₃* are the outcome of LAs containing underspecified *não* from the outset. In other words, *não₁* is a "deep" negation element; *não₂* is a "surface/late" negation element; and *não₃* is a "deep" negation element.

Further, this agreement-spell-out approach also offers an attractive way of making sense of the obvious connection between Ma'di's affirmative, negative, and Q-particles (recall the discussion in sections 9.2.2–9.2.3): the striking parallels between these elements and also their harmlessness in the FOFC context immediately become comprehensible if we view them as alternative spell-outs of an initially unvalued Pol-head, all of which are subsequently linearized at PF. In some cases, the same may be true for Q-particles that are formally identical to negation elements. More generally, the approach also offers a tempting possibility for understanding what one might think of as "generalized Jespersen" doubling structures involving a structurally high element—that is, those featuring a "real" element along with an agreeing/concording one, where the latter dominates the former and therefore potentially creates a challenge to FOFC. Simpson and Wu (2002), for example, discuss (i) definiteness agreement between Mandarin *de* and the demonstrative, a discussion that could potentially also carry over to the Malagasy "framing demonstrative" construction (see (81)); (ii) a discontinuous aspect construction involving preverbal progressive-marking *zai* and an additional (superficially FOFC-violating) VP-final aspect-marker, *ne*; and (iii) modal-final structures of the kind we have considered a different analysis for in the Vietnamese context (see (15c) and the discussion of clause-final *được* in section 9.4.2.2).

9.4.6 Interim Conclusions and Some Implications
This section has shown that the five major ways in which superficially FOFC-violating but nevertheless FOFC-compliant structures may be generated, listed in (86) and repeated here, all seem to be attested:

(134) *FOFC-compliant H-C...Part configurations*
 a. The particle heads a projection to which a *noncomplement* head-initial XP has A- or Ā-moved.
 b. The projection hosting the particle is *structurally lower* than the projection of the head-initial structure.
 c. The particle is *categorially distinct* from the head-initial structure, bearing a *distinct categorial feature*.
 d. The particle is *categorially distinct* from the head-initial structure in *lacking a categorial specification*. Here there are two possibilities:
     i. It does bear one or more other formal features ([F]s), alongside semantic features ([S]s) (Chomsky 1995).
     ii. It lacks [F]s altogether and is syntactically inert; it may or may not bear [S]s.
 e. The particle is an *agreement-realizing* element not present in the Numeration as an element bearing an independent headedness specification; that is, it is the PF reflex of a narrow-syntax-internal Agree relation.

In addition, it may be possible that some apparently FOFC-violating structures involve weak adverbs, merged in lower specifiers (Cardinaletti 2011), and that some, like the West Germanic circumpositions discussed in (95)–(98), involve nonovert structure that means that the overtly realized structure is in fact discontinuous. The fact that there is such a range of mechanisms via which elements that do not form part of a given head-initial EP can surface finally in relation to it allows us to understand why H-C...Part structures should be as frequent as they are. Crucially, it is precisely maintaining (5) as an exceptionless "deep" condition on the kinds of structure that may be created in the narrow syntax that allows us to formulate the kinds of circumstances under

which we would expect FOFC-respecting surface violations. Far from suggesting that this word order condition is tendential, the existence of so many
particle-containing apparent counterexamples is precisely what one would
expect, given the nature of the condition.

Further, the particle patterns discussed in this chapter do not receive a
natural explanation under the alternative accounts of FOFC that have been
proposed in the literature. Neither processing-/parsing- nor diachronically
oriented accounts offer any insight into the attestation discrepancy between
final-over-initial structures where the final and initial elements are part of the
same EP (seemingly unattested) and final-over-initial structures where the final
element does not contribute to the EP (copiously attested, as shown in this
chapter) (see Hawkins 2013, Philip 2013, and Mobbs 2015 for parsing
accounts, and Whitman 2013 for a diachronically oriented account). On "late"
PF-oriented accounts like Sheehan's (2013a,b), final-over-initial structures are
impossible to linearize owing to the complications that complex specifiers
introduce at the linearization stage (see also Uriagereka 1999); hence, these
structures may only be generated in the syntax if (i) this structure is "repaired"
via extraposition at PF (this reduces the specifier's complexity) or (ii) the
initial structure has already been spelled out (atomized), with the result that
the linearization challenge posed by complex specifiers is eliminated. In the
present context, extraposition is not a pattern we systematically see with final-
particle-containing structures: it is clearly unproblematic for particles that
combine with head-initial structures to surface finally. This leaves the atomization possibility, which is also what Sheehan (2013b) speculatively proposes to
deal with this case. As she notes, however, this option predicts that final-particle-containing head-initial structures will be islands from which it is not
possible to extract. This prediction is somewhat hard to test, but there are some
indications that it is too strong, as there are final-particle-containing structures
from which extraction is entirely unproblematic.[90] Afrikaans negative clauses
are a case in point, as (simplified) (135) shows (overstrike indicates the haplol-
ogy that targets the second of two adjacent *nie*s in Afrikaans; see Biberauer
2008):

(135) [$_{PolP}$ [$_{CP}$ Wie het sy nie gedink [$_{PolP}$ [$_{CP}$ t$_{wie}$ gaan   [Afrikaans]
          who has she NEG thought   go
     nie daar wees] nie$_2$]] ~~nie$_2$~~]?
     NEG there be   POL   POL
     'Who didn't she think would not be coming?'

The problems with Richards's (2016) part syntax–part PF approach, which
assumes that FOFC only applies internally to phasal spell-out domains (defined

in terms of the Phase Impenetrability Condition first proposed in Chomsky 2000), were already highlighted in note 82. Essentially, this approach gets the positioning of final particles in head-initial systems right (see also Erlewine to appear a,b), but appears to make the wrong predictions about the (non) defectivity of the elements that may surface finally: (strong) phase heads would not be expected to be formally defective in the ways that final particles in head-initial systems seem to be. Taking everything in this paragraph into account, then, the initially rather unlikely-seeming conclusion would seem justified that attested H-C...Part structures, far from undermining the generalization in BHR 2014, constitute a strong argument precisely *for* the "deep" interpretation of FOFC expressed in (5).

More specifically, taking the interpretation of FOFC in (5) as the point of departure appears to account successfully for the chief characteristics of the data presented in section 9.2, namely:

1. Final particles are typically defective in some sense, lacking inflection otherwise seen in the system and so on. This follows if they are the spell-out of formally defective heads/XPs that do not integrate with the EP in the manner of nondefective, EP-projecting elements (see also point 3 and section 9.5 on the correlation between lack of inflection and nonprojection/lack of [F]s).

2. Final particles often occur in systems with head-initial manifestations of "the same" grammatical category, the head-initial element being the obligatory one, the inflecting one, the one transferred in code-switching, and so on. To children seeking to analyze their input in a maximally economical way, drawing on Input Generalization and Feature Economy (see note 67), these properties signal the fact that the head-initial element, which is harmonic with the rest of the head-initial system, is the EP-projecting head, and that the final particle is to be distinguished from it in formal terms.

3. Final particles are often homophonous with elements surfacing in different positions and possibly even serving at first sight very different functions. This follows if the units of language (see Wiltschko 2014) spelled out as final particles are underspecified elements that do not themselves contribute to the projection of an EP, instead merging with a projecting head that also serves to modulate the interpretation of the underspecified particle in predictable ways, that is, in accordance with the hierarchical position in the structure where it is merged. Importantly, the fact that languages with system-defining homophony are, to the best of my knowledge, highly analytical systems like the relevant East Asian languages also follows from the proposals in section 9.4.4. This is very

clear for the syntactically inert particles discussed in section 9.4.4.2: an element without [F]s cannot enter an Agree relation with other elements in a given syntactic structure. For the acategorial yet [F]-bearing particles in section 9.4.4.1, we again do not expect to see inflection, as these elements may in fact be single-featured,[91] with the result that they can at most exhibit agreement reflecting the feature they encode, [focus], [topic], or [negative] agreement, for example.

4. Final particles are, in cases where we are genuinely dealing with a final-over-initial structure (i.e., not those discussed in sections 9.4.1–9.4.2), X(P)-peripheral elements with an apparent tendency to occur at phase edges. In the case of the categorially specified, categorially distinct particles discussed in section 9.4.3, they are necessarily peripheral because recategorizers must merge at the top edge of the XP they are recategorizing. Were the resulting recategorized XP to switch category again, the new recategorizer would, likewise, have to merge at the edge of the existing XP. As we will see in section 9.5, there is in fact a constraint on recategorization that exhibits the same general character as FOFC and prohibits multiple switches within a given structure. The rationale underlying the peripherality of [F]-less acategorial particles has been set out in section 9.4.4.2: these elements must be last out of their LA by virtue of their unselectability and inability to select. [F]-bearing acategorial particles, on the other hand, could potentially be merged in a more internal position, given that they have an [F] to project, but the particles we have identified do all seem to belong to naturally peripheral categories (Focus, Topic, Q, Negation, etc.), and it may be that their peripherality follows from a selection logic in terms of which categorially specified elements must select other categorially specified elements, leaving the acategorial [F]-bearing elements to last. This would certainly follow in terms of the Phrasal Coherence constraint that seems to apply in human language, which we will briefly consider in section 9.5. In general, though, the present investigation of final particles does suggest that these elements are prototypically phase-peripheral. As the relevant particles also include a great many spoken-language elements, this may be a very useful acquisition cue, signaling phase boundaries to acquirers.

5. VO languages with final nominal particles will have final nominals more generally. This seems correct for all the languages discussed in section 9.4.3.

6. Acategorial particles merged with head-initial phrases will surface finally, while those merged with head-final phrases will surface initially. The

German modal particles illustrated in (74)–(75) exemplify the correctness of this prediction.

7. Acategorial particles merged from word-level arrays—whether combining with roots (119) or with already-categorized functional heads (120)—will surface to the right of overtly realized heads in head-initial systems. Verbal *le*, which surfaces between V and the object, looks like a case in point; see the Yixing variant in (14a). In head-final systems, by contrast, these elements will surface to the left.

8. Finally, adopting an EP-based perspective on FOFC allows us to describe the difference between A- and Ā-moved superficially final-over-initial strings, which are evidently possible, and the basic linearization type, which is clearly not (see section 9.4.1). FOFC only applies to structures in which the specifier is occupied by the categorially identical head-initial XP that constitutes the complement of its head, that is, where the EP-sister of a head X has "rolled up" into its specifier. Where spec-to-spec movement has generated a structure in which a specifier is occupied by a head-initial XP of the same category as the head that has projected the specifier—an apparent final-over-initial structure—no FOFC violation results. Consecutively merged heads belonging to the same EP must therefore either exhibit the same headedness (initial or final), or, if the lower head is final, requiring comp-to-spec movement, the higher head could lack this movement; but comp-to-spec movement can never start EP-medially. A form of contiguity effect, affecting consecutive EP-projecting heads, therefore seems to be in play.[92]

Building on this last point, I would like to conclude this section by sketching the extent to which the particle-derived insights into FOFC considered in this chapter might explain why such structures are underivable.

Consider, first, VO languages that lack V-movement, that is, languages where V remains in situ in V.[93] Maintaining our assumptions about phasal spell-out—namely, that the complement of a phase head is sent to spell-out upon exhaustion of the LA associated with that phase head, in accordance with the Phase Impenetrability Condition (Chomsky 2000; see Richards 2004 for discussion)—we then expect V and O to be sent to spell-out upon completion of the vP phase. After this point, the VO constituent will only be available for combined movement and VP-level agreement. V and O may not be independently probed; the resulting structure is an island.[94] To generate a V-O-Aux or V-O-C structure in a language of this type, one would need to front the VP to the phase edge. Given the apparently emerging consensus that phase edges are discourse-sensitive domains (see, e.g., the references in note 77), we might expect that this type of (atomized) VO fronting would be discourse-marked rather than neutral. In other words, this would be the type of structure that we would usually characterize as Ā-moved—that is, a type of structure that is not subject to FOFC, as argued in section 9.4.1 (see in particular the discussion around (90), which illustrates the difference between a permitted Ā-structure and a banned neutral V-O-Aux structure in German). On this view, then, generating discourse-neutral V-O-Aux is independently ruled out, which therefore also accounts for the Finnish patterns initially highlighted by Holmberg (2000a).[95]

On an alternative perspective, where invariant obligatory movements of the same element are necessarily discourse-neutral (see, e.g., Biberauer 2016b), consistent movement of a VO constituent to a phase edge could produce a discourse-neutral VOS structure. Crucially, though, clausal heads in the higher phase (T, C, etc.) would not be able to interact with V (or O) via head-head (or head-DP) probing; both elements would only be accessible via the featural specification associated with the label of the dominating VP. This is how particle heads are assumed to interact with lower heads in the EP with which they combine (see again the discussion in section 9.4.2.2 and note 75; see also Biberauer and Roberts 2010, where, following Massam 2001 et seq., it is proposed that this type of derivation is found in VOS languages of the Niuean type). Assuming the existence of languages of this type, then, they would not be predicted to violate FOFC: they would necessarily be particle-containing systems of the type dicussed in this chapter.[96]

Next let us consider VO systems in which V raises. In these systems, V will never, in neutral structures, be sent to spell-out at the same time as O: O will be sent to spell-out upon completion of the vP-phase, while the height of V-movement will determine when it is sent to spell-out. For low-movement systems in which V moves only to v, V-O-Aux would therefore not be possible in systems where auxiliaries are v's (a plausible analysis of auxiliaries in argument-sensitive auxiliary-selection systems, and also for aspectual auxiliaries, among many others). By contrast, a structure that would be possible is V-Aux-O, which is indeed attested in many languages, including the well-studied Germanic languages (see BHR 2014 for discussion and references). For higher auxiliaries—for example, those in T—V-to-T movement would again deliver V-Aux-O order. But if V remains in v and vP raises to Spec,TP, V-O-Aux could result. Crucially, this would be V-O-Aux in which T is able to probe V-v in the usual manner, with vP-raising to Spec,TP—that is, the head-initial counterpart of the derivation that Biberauer and Roberts (2005 et seq.) propose for head-final Germanic. This structure could, then, raise to Spec,CP, giving a V-O-C structure. Just combining our particle-derived insights with a phasal spell-out system, then, will accurately account for the nonoccurrence of a great many potentially FOFC-violating structures; but it cannot account for the absence of these structures in short V-raising languages, as demonstrated here. Given the number of accurate predictions our assumptions have delivered, it seems worth considering whether this type of structure may be possible after all, but, in the manner of the H-C...Part structures that have been the focus of this chapter, nevertheless still not violate FOFC. I will conclude this section by considering a possibility that is also very much in keeping with the striking patterns to be discussed in section 9.5 and that makes an empirical prediction that appears to be borne out.

I start with this chapter's central insight that particles that can be shown to genuinely dominate initial XPs can also be shown not to combine with these XPs in the way that EP-defining heads do (see sections 9.4.3–9.4.5): they do not project onto the EP that they would need to be part of to violate FOFC. Why would this be so? The answer I will propose here takes acquisition as its point of departure. From an acquisitional perspective, the "specialness" of outlier-final elements in the head-initial systems to which they belong would be expected to be very striking. As noted in section 9.4.4.2, word order is a property children are sensitive to from very early on, plausibly because the basic headedness properties of their language have effectively been fixed from birth, making subsequent zeroing in on the ordering properties associated with different syntactic elements a more tractable task (see again the research by Mehler, Gervain, Nespor, and colleagues, note 73). In section 9.4.2.2, I proposed that headedness information—arguably the earliest formal property acquired by children and thus the first formal means at their disposal to begin construction of the syntactic system (see also Tsimpli 2013, 2014)—is an intrinsic part of "what it means to be a verb/noun."[97]

Verb vs. noun, in turn, is the central notion underlying the postulation of an "extended projection." As the term suggests, these are necessarily extensions of a particular projecting element, the element in question being assumed to be at the bottom of the EP, that is, the noun or the verb and, by extension, other genuinely lexical (content) categories that can be identified for the system in question (these may or may not include P and A, a matter I leave aside here; but see, e.g., Baker 2003 and S. Chung 2012 for discussion). Since we have been assuming that the formally represented features of lexical items project along the EP, head-finality ($V^\wedge$) will project along the EP of a clausal spine extending from a head-final lexical verb, while head-initiality (V) will do likewise in the case of a system in which lexical verbs are initial.[98] Since being part of the EP of a lexical category means sharing its categorial property (which, as just argued, includes the relevant headedness information), we can define a natural class of verbal (and, likewise, nominal) elements: those bearing [V^] or [V] in the verbal case, and [N^] and [N] in the nominal case.

Accepting this to be the case, a final T-element clearly cannot be part of the EP of a VO language (i.e., [V]).[99] This conclusion seems correct for the particle T-elements and more generally the auxiliary elements considered in this chapter: these elements provided varying types of evidence indicating that they are not normally projecting elements, notably lacking agreement and tense, mood, aspect inflection—basically, any indication of being specifically finite elements—and sometimes contrasting positionally with elements that are evidently the primary auxiliary elements in the relevant language (by virtue, for example, of being inflected in contrast to the uninflected final element, or being obligatory in contrast to the optional final particle, or being used exclusively in code-switching, and so on).

For the kind of derivable V-O-Aux system under discussion here—a V-to-v raising system with a final auxiliary—we might, then, predict similar properties; the only difference between this type and the type that has been the focus of most of our discussion would be the V-to-v raising component. Additionally, though, a language that gives its acquirers clear evidence of V-to-v raising might also be expected to be inflectionally richer than one in which v-elements are (final) particles. This brings to mind nonanalytic final-particle-containing VO languages of the kind illustrated in section 9.1 on the basis of Cappadocian Greek, for example. Consider again the example presented in (1b):

(136) Ego psis   dio avga **iton**.   [Cappadocian Greek]
       1SG bake.1SG.PERF two eggs PAST (= 3SG.IMPERF.BE)
       'I had baked two eggs.'
       (Español-Echevarría 1994:1)

As noted at the outset, the final auxiliary in this variety, and in all the other contact varieties in the region, systematically fails to inflect: it is always the same third-person singular imperfect past form that surfaces in this position. At the same time, the lexical verb bears all the tense and agreement morphology that we would expect to find on a finite verb in this language. This pattern repeats through the contact Greek varieties in the region, and a very similar pattern also seems to have arisen in copula contexts in Sason Arabic (Akkuş and Benmamoun 2016) and a number of other peripheral Arabic varieties that have been in contact with head-final systems and variously harnessed third-person forms of 'be' and pronouns to spell out the previously null copula. If the discussion here is on the right track, then, the fact that there is (on the assumptions entertained here) a derivation that can give rise to V-O-Aux structures in languages with V-to-v raising may be a further boon deriving from the

EP-oriented characterization of FOFC argued for in this chapter: it allows us to deepen our understanding of the typology of VO languages and to understand the (limited) circumstances under which final elements can be part of inflecting systems. The EP-oriented characterization of FOFC in (5), then, is not undermined by the possibility we have considered here; this will only be the case if an inflecting VO system with a final auxiliary that inflects in the normal manner is uncovered. And that, to date, has not been the case.

9.5   Conclusion: What Particles Tell Us about the Nature of FOFC

Given the unclarity surrounding the notion "particle" in generative syntax, as in linguistics more generally, the initial purpose of this chapter was to give an overview of the types of particle-containing structures that appear to challenge FOFC. The discussion has revealed that apparently FOFC-violating [[Head-Complement]...Particle] structures are very common, particularly in analytic languages of the sort that are less common in Europe. In fact, many of these languages feature multiple superficially FOFC-violating elements in distinct domains (consider, for example, Dryer's (2009b) observation about the way in which V-O-Neg, V-O-Q, and, to some extent, V-O-Aux cluster together in West African languages). Some of these phenomena (e.g., the very well-known V-O-Q- and, more generally, V-O-C-related particle data from Mandarin and Cantonese) have led researchers to conclude that FOFC is in fact a statistical tendency rather than an absolute universal (see, e.g., Whitman 2013, Paul 2014, 2015, Pan and Paul 2017). What the second half of this chapter has sought to show, however, is that this conclusion would result in some extremely rewarding questions not being asked. More specifically, sections 9.3 and 9.4 have demonstrated that pursuing the idea that FOFC is a "deep" syntactic universal—a hierarchical universal, in Whitman's (2008) terms—banning a particular configuration from narrow syntax is a very useful heuristic for developing insight, both into the (diverse) nature(s) of particle elements themselves and into the syntax of a range of, for the most part, understudied constructions. As with other surface-defined phenomena (SVO, SOV, null subjects, etc.), closer investigation has shown that Head-Comp...Part structures are underlyingly quite varied and that there is no meaningful sense in which such structures are structurally "the same." They do, however, share one property: on closer investigation, none of them seem to violate FOFC. Head-Comp... Part structures are common because there are so many harmless structural configurations that can give rise to a surface FOFC violation; they are not common because they signal the nonuniversality of FOFC or because the formulation of this condition given in (5) requires rethinking. The discussion in this chapter has supplied further evidence that EPs are central to the definition of FOFC; it has also supplied evidence that [F]-oriented consideration of the data is crucial in furthering our understanding both of FOFC and of matters of more general generative interest, such as how functional categories are detected and correctly identified, what domains constitute phasal domains, and what empirical phenomena enable acquirers to identify them.

Strikingly, however, we have also seen that considering the relevant phenomena in exclusively featural (syntactic) terms is insufficient: syntax-PF mapping considerations also come into play. This is important, given the current debate regarding the nature of FOFC. What particle-final structures seem to show is that discussion about whether FOFC is a "deep" syntactic *or* a surfacy PF phenomenon is misfocused; instead, it appears that FOFC is fundamentally an observation about the (permissible) makeup of EPs, conceived of, significantly, within a phasal approach to syntactic derivation, and that this has certain necessary consequences at PF. A "blind" PF approach to FOFC, in terms of which all heads (defective and otherwise) are equal and it is the output (i.e., the final string) that counts, would evidently undermine the insights FOFC has to offer in nontrivial ways.

To conclude this chapter, I will broaden the perspective by considering FOFC against the background of a small selection of at first sight unrelated linguistic phenomena that I will argue are, in fact, shaped by the same factors as FOFC. Viewed in very general terms, FOFC is clearly a harmony effect, applying to contiguous stretches of an EP, with the bottom of the EP having a privileged status in determining higher options. More specifically, FOFC requires that (i) head-finality must start at the bottom of an EP, and (ii) once a head-final sequence has "stopped," it cannot restart within the same EP. A remarkably similar contiguity effect emerges in the domain of categorization. As Panagiotidis (2015) points out, building on work by Bresnan (1997), Borsley and Kornfilt (2000), Malouf (2000), and Ackema and Neeleman (2004), among others (see also Baker 2005a), verbalization and nominalization are subject to the constraint of Phrasal Coherence, illustrated in (137):[100]

(137) a.

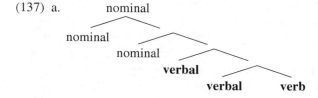

b. *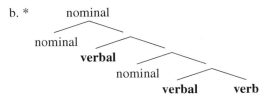

As (137) shows, an EP that starts off verbal can be recategorized, but recategorization is subject to the condition that it cannot subsequently be "undone" and "redone." Just as in the case of FOFC, then, no "on-off" patterns are permitted; in the words of Panagiotidis (2015:137–138), "the nominal and the verbal chunk in a mixed projection are distinct...; crucially, *they never intersperse* [emphasis original]," and "...in mixed projections there must always exist a cut-off point where verbal/clausal characteristics end and nominal ones begin" (see also Bresnan 1997, Malouf 2000, Ackema and Neeleman 2004:174, Baker 2005a). Further, crosslinguistic investigation of mixed-category projections has uncovered that these always involve structures with the external distribution of a nominal. In other words, EPs can start off either nominal or verbal, but the option of becoming mixed only exists for EPs that started off verbal. Again, this exactly parallels what we have seen for FOFC: the heads defining an EP can be either final or initial to begin with, but the option of changing the headedness of an EP only exists if it started out head-final.

Similarly, Pesetsky (2013) points to a constraint on agreement that exhibits what appears to be a remarkably parallel kind of contiguity effect. First, he observes that it is possible for Russian nominals to switch gender nominal-internally: a given nominal may start out masculine, but become feminine at a given point in its functional structure. The switch can be shown to be possible at varying heights within the nominal structure, although the very lowest adjectives are not able to make this switch. Importantly, Pesetsky shows that once the gender switch has taken place (i.e., once the initially masculine nominal is feminine), all higher DP-internal agreement *and* all external agreement must be feminine. The reverse switch—feminine to masculine—is not possible. A Russian nominal may therefore be consistently masculine or consistently feminine, but if there is a gender change at any point in the nominal structure, it has to be masculine to feminine. Masculine thus parallels head-finality and verbality in the earlier linearization and categorization examples, while feminine patterns with head-initiality and nominality.

An essentially identical pattern emerges in Lebanese Arabic (see Ouwayda 2012, 2014). Here, the options are for a nominal to be consistently singular or consistently plural throughout, or for it to start off singular but then become plural at varying points in the higher functional structure. Again, low adjectives fall below the threshold; again, once the conversion has taken place, all higher agreement and all external agreement must be plural; and, again, the switch may be from singular to plural, but never the reverse. Singular number therefore patterns with head-finality, verbality, and masculine gender in the earlier linearization, categorization, and agreement examples, and plural number with head-initiality, nominality, and feminine gender.

Finally, Puškar (2015) shows that the same kind of consideration holds in the determination of grammatical vs. semantic agreement in Bosnian/Croatian/Serbian: semantic agreement is possible at the bottom of a nominal, but once grammatical agreement has started, it must continue. In Bosnian/Croatian/Serbian, then, nominals may either exhibit consistent semantic agreement, consistent grammatical agreement, or mixed agreement, in terms of which semantic agreement becomes grammatical at some point in the functional nominal structure. In this language, then, semantic agreement patterns with head-finality, verbality, masculine gender, and singular number in the earlier linearization, categorization, and agreement examples, while grammatical agreement patterns with head-initiality, nominality, feminine gender, and plural number.

Taking just the first two cases into account, Pesetsky (2013) argues that there must be a threshold below which a null feminizing or pluralizing morpheme (Ж and #, respectively) cannot be merged, but above which it can be merged, at any stage, after which no return to the earlier gender or number is possible. The same analysis seems extendable to Puškar's (2015) data, and Panagiotidis (2015) in fact explicitly proposes a null SWITCH-element that produces the recategorizations observed in the categorization domain (see also Ackema and Neeleman 2004 on the obligatory nullness of this element). In each case, then, a specific null morpheme is assumed to mark the crossover point. An alternative, capitalizing on recent insights into the dynamic nature of phasal domains (see, e.g., Bobaljik and Wurmbrand 2005, Bošković 2014, Harwood 2013, 2015) and seeking to bring FOFC into the picture—a null-morpheme-based analysis does not seem obviously illuminating in this latter case—might be to ascribe all the crossover options discussed here to phase dynamics: switches can potentially be made at all the phase-internal points where a phase could in principle be well-formed, even if it has not reached its maximal extent (i.e., if the LA in question happens not to contain items spelling out the highest edge of the relevant domain). On this view, then, switches of the kind discussed here would serve as indicators of the internal makeup of phasal domains, something that ever more research seems to suggest is likely to be subject to language-specific variation; and final particles, being peripheral elements as argued above, would likewise serve as phase edge markers. The usefulness of a signal of this type will become clear in what is to follow. For the moment, the key point is not precisely what underlies the observed pattern, but the fact that we have a recurring pattern of the kind that we do, one that appears to extend the spirit underlying FOFC into other domains. In every case, we see contiguous harmony effects, precluding "on-off" patterns.

And the recurring pattern does not end there. Hierarchy effects such as those relating to the Animacy Hierarchy (Silverstein 1976), the Case Hierarchy (Caha 2009), the Auxiliary Hierarchy (Sorace 2004), the Agreement Accessibility Hierarchy (Bobaljik 2008), and the *ABA syncretism patterns highlighted by nanosyntacticians (see, e.g., Caha 2009) all seem to represent further instances of harmonic contiguity effects in human language. In other words, all the "splits" attested in human languages also seem to be subject to the constraint that a split will divide a given contiguous domain into harmonic subsections; the prediction is therefore that, as with FOFC, what we will not see once we have investigated the relevant phenomena carefully are "on-off" effects. Looking beyond splits, long-established formal principles like the Ban on Improper Movement (Chomsky 1973, May 1979) and Li's (1990) Generalization—in terms of which a lexical head cannot move into a functional head, followed by incorporation into another lexical head—have the same core character: movement operations can be differentiated into various types, depending on their formal properties, with the types having to take place in a designated sequence (A before Ā in the former case, and lexical-into-functional incorporation before functional-into-functional incorporation in the latter); once a switch has taken place from one type to the next, it is not "reversible." That a question of harmonic contiguity is at stake becomes clear if we consider the fact that the movement types discussed here map onto the clausal (and nominal) hierarchy in a very systematic way: in relation to the Ban on Improper Movement, clausal A-movement targets what we might designate the vP- and TP-domains, while clausal Ā-movement targets the higher CP-domain; for Li's Generalization, it is clear that lexical incorporation will target the bottom of an EP, while functional incorporation must target higher heads. Violations of the Ban on Improper Movement and Li's Generalization, then, entail structures in which a "lower" movement type has followed a "higher" one—in other words, the kind of reversal pattern that is also barred in the FOFC and other harmonic contiguity contexts discussed above. As Williams (2003) and Abels (2008) point out, independently and on the basis of very different empirical considerations, the Ban on Improper Movement can in fact be made both more fine-grained (see Abels's UCOOL in (138)) and generalized (see Williams's Generalized Ban on Improper Movement, and Abels's derivational counterpart):

(138) *The Universal Constraint on Operational Ordering in Language (UCOOL)*

θ > A-movement > Ā-/Operator movement

For our purposes, the key point is that the FOFC-type harmonic contiguity pattern, in terms of which contiguous sections of a given formally defined domain must be treated identically and changes are only possible at designated points where the lower structure is of the right type, seems to be a very general one in human language. In fact, the picture that has emerged from the discussion in this section calls to mind the fractal patterns that have been observed elsewhere in nature, for example, in snowflakes, proteins, and DNA. The key property of fractals is their repeating pattern, which emerges in the same form at different levels of magnification (scale); here, the repeatedly emerging basic pattern seems to be one that recurs in different aspects of morphosyntactic organization, requiring that structure be built and operated on in such a way that "higher" structure builds on/references "lower" structure, switches between "higher" and "lower" structure being possible, but not reversible: once "higher" structure is in place, no return is possible, within the same domain, to "lower" structure. The question, of course, is why patterns of this kind should recur as they seem to. This, and some of the related questions highlighted by the investigation of FOFC and particles reported in this chapter, is the topic of ongoing research.

10 The Final-over-Final Condition in a Mixed-Word-Order Language

Anders Holmberg

10.1 Introduction

Finnish is classified as an SVO language because the unmarked word order in transitive clauses is Subject (Aux) Verb Object, as in (1):

(1) a. Anne osti   auton.   [Finnish]
      Anne bought car
      'Anne bought a car.'
  b. Minä olen juonut kahvia.
     I   have drunk coffee
     'I've had coffee.'

But SOV and S-O-V-Aux are possible as well, as marked alternatives. The condition is, primarily, that a constituent is focused by movement to, or base-generation in, the C-domain (internal or external Merge in the C-domain), as in (2) (Vilkuna 1989, 1995, Holmberg 2000a, 2001):[1]

(2) a. Milloin Anne auton osti?   [Finnish]
      when   Anne car   bought
      'When did Anne buy a car?'
  b. Kyllä minä kahvia juonut olen.
     indeed I   coffee drunk have
     'I have indeed had coffee.'

The SOV and S-O-V-Aux order seen in (2a,b) is sharply ungrammatical in sentences without initial focus. The initial focus can be the subject:

(3) a. ANNE auton osti.   [Finnish]
      Anne car   bought
      'It was Anne that bought a car.'
  b. MINÄ kahvia juonut olen.
     I   coffee drunk have
     'I'm the one who has had coffee.'

I will assume that the explanation for this condition proposed in Holmberg 2001 is basically right: the effect of linearizing the complement of V, and other VP-internal constituents, to the left of V, is that they are defocused. In Vilkuna's (1995) words, the verb-final, XV-ordered V-field should not contain the Main News.[2] In the unmarked case, the information focus of a sentence is VP, or some constituent of VP. With SOV order, this is excluded in Finnish. But a sentence must have a focus; this is a universal of language (more specifically a universal of information structure).[3] There are two ways to express focus in Finnish: (i) focus in situ and (ii) focus in the C-domain. If (i) is not available, then (ii) is the only option.

In this chapter, I will discuss the basic facts concerning SOV order in Finnish and propose a formal account of them in terms of a version of the theory of the mapping between structure and word order articulated by Sheehan (2011, 2013a,b) and introduced in chapter 4. One reason for discussing Finnish in such detail here is that when head-final order is used in the clause, the syntax really looks like that of a head-final language; in particular, it conforms to the Final-over-Final Condition (FOFC). This has consequences for the theoretical explanation of the phenomenon, which I will explore in this chapter.

Finnish is a mixed-word-order language. There are, as it were, two grammars at work: an SVO grammar, with properties familiar from SVO languages such as English, Swedish, and Thai, and an SOV grammar, with properties familiar from SOV languages such as Turkish and German. Haider (2012) argues that, alongside VO and OV languages, there is a third type, characterized by allowing both VO and OV and therefore exhibiting properties of both the VO and the OV systems. For one thing, this means that the languages exhibit very "free word order" in sentential constructions (the extended projection of V). Haider's example of this third type of language is Russian, along with (some) other Slavic languages, known for exhibiting much word order variation in sentential constructions. Finnish would be another example. The question is how to account for this freedom of word order. Is it a matter of V, and other functional heads in the extended projection of V, having dual linearization instructions (or even lacking linearization instructions), or, in a model where there are no directionality parameters/linearization parameters, a matter of greater freedom of movement?

I will argue that Finnish does not exhibit any special movement properties. In particular, I will show that movement of V-complements is subject to Holmberg's Generalization. In terms of a model that assumes that heads are supplied with a linearization instruction, I will argue that Finnish V, which in the unmarked case is marked for linearization preceding its complement, can optionally be marked for linearization following its complement.

10.2 Object Position Facts

The following paradigm shows that in a sentence where there is initial focus, here a questioned *wh*-phrase, the constituents have considerable freedom of order in the presupposed part of the clause. The sentence in (4) is glossed in detail only once; thereafter, the glosses are simplified (PTCP = participle).

(4) a. Milloin hän   ol-i   osta-nut   auton-n?   [Finnish]
         when   she.NOM be-PAST buy-PAST.PTCP car-ACC
         'When would she have bought a car?'
    b. Milloin hän oli auton ostanut?
        when   she had car   bought
    c. Milloin hän auton oli ostanut?
        when   she car   had bought
    d. Milloin hän auton ostanut oli?
        when   she car   bought had
    e. *Milloin hän ostanut auton oli?
        when   she bought car   had
    f. ?Milloin hän ostanut oli auton
        when   she bought had car

(4a) is the straightforward S-Aux-V-O alternative, which is always grammatical, with or without initial focus. (4b–d) are all well-formed and are pragmatically equivalent. None of them would be well-formed without the initial focus. (4e) is the FOFC violation. (4f) may appear very marginal when taken out of context. However, Maria Vilkuna (pers. comm.) found quite a few examples when searching a corpus of dialects (*Syntax Archive Data/Lauseopin arkisto* Clarin). The following examples are adapted from that corpus. The order in (4f) seems to be particularly frequent in sentences introduced by the focal particle *kyllä* 'indeed, surely', common in spoken Finnish (PART = particle).

(5) a. Kyllä   minä ampunut olen useampiakin (mutta   [Finnish]
         indeed I   shot   have several   but
         ne   on   mennyt pohjaan).
         they have gone   bottom.to
         'I have shot several (but they have sunk to the bottom).'
    b. ...vaikka   kyllä mar te   nähnyt olette semmoisia
        although surely PART you seen   have   such
        vanhanaikaisia kraakkuja?
        old-fashioned   hooks
        '...but surely you have seen such old-fashioned hooks?'

c. Kyllähän   minäkin nähnyt olen karhut niin kuin tuolla
indeed.PART I.too   seen   have bears as   like there
Helsingissäkin.
Helsinki.in.even
'I've seen bears, too, like over there in Helsinki.'

It seems, therefore, that this word order cannot be ignored. Like (4b–d), it is impossible in the absence of initial focus.

Note that the FOFC-violating order (4f) is marginally possible when the verb is contrastive, as in (6):[4]

(6) Kyllä minä KUULLUT sen olen, mutta en koskaan   [Finnish]
    indeed I   heard   it   have but   not ever
NÄHNYT.
seen
'I have HEARD it, but never SEEN it.'

Following a suggestion by Maria Vilkuna (pers. comm.), I will propose below that the verb and the object do not form a constituent in (6); instead, the verb and the object have moved independently, the verb as a remnant VP. Consequently, the construction does not violate FOFC. See Biberauer, Holmberg, and Roberts 2014 for discussion of FOFC in the nominal extended projection in Finnish, where the word order is likewise quite free.

In the following section, we will go through the derivation of the various OV constructions, assuming a modified version of the model in Sheehan 2011, 2013a,b.

10.3 Sheehan's Model (Modified)

The theory articulated in Sheehan 2011, 2013a,b was presented in section 4.10, with some implementations discussed in chapters 5, 6, and 7. The following is a summary of the main points, although with one important difference in (7d):

(7) a. A head and its projections form a single category.
   b. Categories are lexically marked as either preceding or following the category they select, as part of their c-selection features. The notation is X_P for "the category X precedes the category it c-selects" and X_F for "X follows the category it c-selects."
   c. The total linear order among the categories in a linearization domain is determined without reference to dominance (i.e., phrases are not linearized relative to heads or other phrases).

d. Where the linear order is not given by the lexical directionality
   feature, either directly or by transitivity, it is determined by
   asymmetric c-command: if a copy A asymmetrically c-commands
   B and is not linearized in relation to B by virtue of (b), then A
   precedes B.

The difference reflected in (7d) is as follows. In Sheehan 2013b, what gets
linearized are categories, where a category is a set of copies, derived by projection (projection/labeling being regarded as copying) and by movement.
Thus, copies of a category A do not get independently linearized. The formulation in (7d) in Sheehan 2013b would be "If a *category* A asymmetrically
c-commands B and is not linearized in relation to B by virtue of (b), then A
precedes B." We will see below when it makes a difference which formulation
we adopt. I will refer to the model assumed here as *Sheehan(m)* (for *modified*)
and to the original model, articulated in greatest detail in Sheehan 2013b, as
Sheehan(o) (for *original*).

As an illustration of how the system works, consider how FOFC is derived
in this theory (both versions). Consider the tree (8), a representation of the
"inverse-FOFC" type of disharmonic structure:

(8)

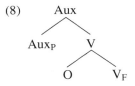

When linearized, this comes out as (8′):

(8′) a. Aux-V   (by virtue of c-selection, henceforth *selection*)
     b. O-V   (by virtue of c-selection, henceforth *selection*)
     c. Aux-O   (by virtue of asymmetric c-command, henceforth *a-cc*)

This yields the total order Aux-O-V. This shows the effect of (the residue of)
the Linear Correspondence Axiom (LCA), (7d): when the linear order between
two categories A and B is not determined by selection, directly or by transitivity, the LCA steps in, with asymmetric c-command deciding the order between
A and B.

Now consider (9), a FOFC-violating disharmonic structure:

(9)

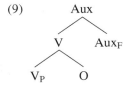

When linearized, this comes out as (9′):

(9′) a. V-Aux   (selection)
    b. V-O   (selection)
    c. Aux-O   (a-cc)

This yields the total order V-Aux-O. That is to say, the "FOFC-violating" order V-O-Aux is underivable. The structure is not ill-formed, even in combination with the linearization instructions, but it cannot be linearized with the order that we recognize as a FOFC violation.

An interesting property of Sheehan's theory is that suffixation, derived by head movement in standard generative grammar, following Travis (1984), Pollock (1989), and Baker (1988), can be modeled as an effect of linearization; this property will be made use of here. Consider, for instance, the Finnish participial VP in (10) (cf. (4a)):

(10) Hän   on   osta-nut   auto-n.   [Finnish]
    he/she has buy-PAST.PTCP car-ACC
    'He/She has bought a car.'

The structure of the participle phrase is (11) (quite uncontroversially, aside from the linearization diacritics, given that functional categories are syntactic heads):

(11)

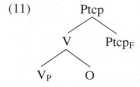

Linearization will yield the following relations:

(11′) a. V-O   (selection)
     b. V-Ptcp   (selection)
     c. Ptcp-O   (a-cc)

This yields the total order V-Ptcp-O. This is indeed the linear order seen in (11), with the participle head suffixed to the verb. Being a suffix is an additional morphological property of the participle head, but does not, by itself, determine the word order. Nor is any head movement or other syntactic operation involved in the formation of the inflected word; it is simply a consequence of how linearization works, in conjunction with the affixal property of the participle head. Note that (11) is the same configuration as (9), the "FOFC-violating" structure, well-formed as such but not linearizable as [[head complement] head].

As we will see, we still need to allow for some head movement in the theory. But we can dispense with very local affix-driven head movement, such as would apply in the participle phrase in (10), for example; this would instead be a linearization effect without any movement.

10.4   Finnish SOV: Derived by Movement or by Selection?

An important question is whether the order of O and V in the Finnish SOV constructions is a matter of V being optionally marked V_F instead of the unmarked value V_P, or whether it is an effect of movement applied to a harmonically head-initial base. In other words, is Finnish a mixed VO-OV language, with VO as the unmarked alternative, or is it a VO language with unusually free movement of complements? Are there any mixed VO-OV languages in this sense (as Haider 2012 would have it)?

We may note first that, for example, the orders (4b–d,f), repeated here, could be derived by movement applied to a "head-initial base," in Sheehan's model (both versions):

(4) a.   Milloin hän   ol-i   osta-nut   auton-n?   [Finnish]
         when   she.NOM be-PAST buy-PAST.PTCP car-ACC
         'When had she bought a car?'
    b.   Milloin hän oli   auton ostanut?
         when   she had car   bought
    c.   Milloin hän auton oli   ostanut?
         when   she car   had bought
    d.   Milloin hän auton ostanut oli?
         when   she car   bought had
    e.   *Milloin hän ostanut auton oli?
         when   she bought car   had
    f.   ?Milloin hän ostanut oli   auton?
         when   she bought had car

As movement always takes place upward, movement of a category A that is the complement of B will always put A in a position asymmetrically c-commanding B, hence preceding B by virtue of the (residue of the) LCA. In some of the constructions, (4b–d), the movement analysis would be relatively straightforward. In (4f), it would have to be more complex, including at least two movements and an additional abstract head.[5] Obviously, this level of complexity is not unheard of in recent generative grammar. As always, the challenge is to devise a theory that allows the complexity required to generate all well-formed constructions, yet does not allow generation of the ill-formed ones—in this case, a theory that can derive (4f) but not (4e).

Consider also the following word order facts (ALL = allative):

(12) a. Minä ole-n   pan-nut   kirja-t   hylly-lle.   [Finnish]
        I   have-1SG put-PAST.PTCP book-PL.ACC shelf-ALL
        'I have put the books on the shelf.'
     b. Kyllä minä olen kirjat hyllylle pannut.
        indeed I   have books on.shelf put
        'I HAVE put the books on the shelf.'
     c. Kyllä minä olen kirjat pannut hyllylle.
        indeed I   have books put   on.shelf
        'I HAVE put the books on the shelf.'

If a *put*-type verb, taking a complex two-part complement, is put in a context licensing OV order, either the whole complement is (optionally) preverbal, as in (12b), or only one of the two parts is, with no effect on the interpretation. This is not characteristic of "consistent SOV" languages (which typically allow just the order corresponding to (12b), with both parts of the complement preceding V), and it may suggest that the OV order in Finnish is derived by movement, which may affect the whole complement phrase or (if locality conditions on movement are met) a part of the complement.

Under a movement account of SOV order, the defocusing effect could be modeled as an effect of the movement: the domain between C and VP would be a nonfocus domain. Movement of a verb complement to that domain will mean that it cannot be assigned focal interpretation.[6] Matters are complicated, though, by the observation that in (12c), for example, not only is the fronted direct object necessarily defocused, but also the postverbal locative phrase and indeed the verb itself. Another complication is that the domain between C and VP is not a defocused domain for the *subject*. Instead, the subject has a high topic position, which is either the highest specifier position in the IP-domain or the lowest in the C-domain (see Holmberg and Nikanne 2002 for discussion). Below this position, the subject is assigned focal interpretation (Holmberg and Nikanne 2002, 2008).

Why do VO languages such as English, Swedish, French, Arabic, and Thai (to mention a few) resist object movement in the IP-domain, deriving SOV order? There is a well-known typological generalization according to which OV languages often display movement of the object within the IP-domain (so-called scrambling), with more or less free order in the IP-domain as a result, while VO languages display such movement much less often (Saito and Fukui 1998). There is another more specific word order generalization much discussed in recent literature that bears on this issue, Holmberg's Generalization (HG), according to which the object of a verb V cannot move across V into the IP-domain, unless V itself moves even higher. In OV languages, HG is trivially satisfied, since the object already precedes (thus, under an LCA-based theory, asymmetrically c-commands) the verb at the relevant point in the derivation.

If Finnish is essentially a VO language with SOV order derived by scrambling, this implies that HG is parameterized, holding in some languages but not in others. Alternatively, Finnish operates with two grammars, a VO and an OV grammar. In terms of Sheehan(m) or (o), V could be marked either V_P or V_F, and likewise other heads in the extended projection of the verb (up to negation, which always precedes its sister; Holmberg 2000a). In this sense, Finnish would belong to a third type of language, alongside the "pure" VO and OV types (in the spirit of Haider 2012).

To determine whether this is the case, we need to consider HG in more detail, particularly in the context of Finnish.

10.5   Object Shift and Holmberg's Generalization

Two versions of HG can be found in the literature (see Holmberg 1986, 1999, Holmberg and Platzack 1995:chap. 6, Vikner 1995, Fox and Pesetsky 2005). Where the distinction is crucial, I will refer to one as *HG(s)* (for *HG simplified*) and the other as *HG(r)* (for *the real HG*):

(13) *HG(s)*
     No V-movement → no object shift

(14) *HG(r)*
     No object shift across a phonologically spelled-out category in VP

In this section and the next, I will discuss the implications of HG(s) for linearization in a mixed-word-order language like Finnish. In section 10.8, I will return to HG(r) and make an amendment to the theory required to explain this generalization.

In the references mentioned, HG is discussed in particular in connection with object shift, as found in Scandinavian:

(15) *Object shift*
     Object shift constitutes movement of the object DP out of VP but within IP, across adjuncts and other constituents outside VP, but not across the subject.[7]

In Mainland Scandinavian, object shift applies to weak pronouns only; in Icelandic, it applies also to lexical DPs:[8]

(16) a. Elsa har tydligen   inte hittat **den**.   [Swedish]
         Elsa has apparently not found it
     b. *Elsa har **den** (tydligen inte) hittat.
     c. Elsa hittade **den** tydligen   inte.
         Elsa found   it   apparently not
         'Apparently Elsa didn't find it.'
(17) a. Ég hef   ekki lesið **þessa bók**.   [Icelandic]
         I have not read this   book
     b. *Ég hef **þessa bók** (ekki) lesið.
     c. Ég las **þessa bók** ekki.
         I read this   book not
         'I didn't read this book.'

The contrast between (16b) and (16c), and between (17b) and (17c), shows
that the object pronoun cannot move out of VP, across sentential adverbs
(including negation), unless the main verb has moved as well, as it does in
Scandinavian when it is the finite verb in a main clause, ending up in "second
position" (the verb-second condition; Holmberg 1986, 2015, Holmberg and
Platzack 1995:chap. 2, Vikner 1995). The adjuncts are in parentheses in (16b)
and (17b) to show that the word order with the object preceding the verb is
ungrammatical with or without adjuncts. Object shift is not a matter of VP-
movement taking along the object pronoun. This is shown by the fact that the
verb and the object are not necessarily contiguous, even when both are moved
out of VP:

(18) a. Hittade Elsa **den** inte?   [Swedish]
         found   Elsa it   not
         'Did Elsa not find it?'
     b. Elsa hittade tydligen   **den** inte.
         Elsa found   apparently it   not
         'Apparently Elsa didn't find it.'
     c. *Elsa tydligen hittade **den** inte.

In (18a), the verb has moved across the subject, and the object is left behind
in the shifted position preceding the negation. In (18b) (acceptable in some
but not all varieties of Scandinavian), the object has moved out of VP, but not
across all the sentential adjuncts, while, as (18c) shows, the verb must move
to the "second position" (to C, under the analysis in Holmberg and Platzack
1995, Vikner 1995).

Several authors, advocating partly different frameworks, have proposed that
HG is an "order preservation" or "shape conservation" phenomenon (Sells

2001, Fox and Pesetsky 2005, Engels and Vikner 2014). In these terms, the generalization is that the VO order established between the verb and the object at the VP-level must be preserved throughout the derivation, so the object can move but only if the verb moves higher, preserving their linear relation (with some systematic exceptions, notably if the object raises by Ā-movement to the C-domain, as with *wh*-movement). I will return to Fox and Pesetsky's implementation of the shape conservation idea in section 10.8.

Consider how shape conservation works in the theory assumed here. Consider (19), the structure of the Swedish participle-headed phrase of (16a):

(19)

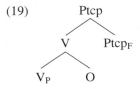

The linear relations are as in (19'):

(19') a. V-O   (selection)
     b. V-Ptcp   (selection)
     c. Ptcp-O   (a-cc)

This yields the total order V-Ptcp-O: *hitta-t den*. Now assume that the object moves to a position where it c-commands PtcpP, which is the case in (16b). The structure is (20), with linear relations as in (20'). We will ignore the adjuncts for the time being. The object has moved past the adjuncts in (16b), but this is of no direct consequence for HG, as the sentence is equally bad without the adjuncts.

(20)

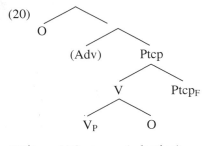

(20') a. V-O   (selection)
     b. V-Ptcp   (selection)
     c. Ptcp-O   (a-cc)
     d. O-V   (a-cc)
     e. O-Ptcp   (transitivity)

There are conflicting linear statements in (20′): (a) and (d), and (c) and (e). This, I propose, is what rules it out. The word order in (16b) and (17b), violating HG, is unlinearizable.

In (16c) and (17c), the object has moved. We can tell that it has, because it precedes the adjunct, but the verb is linearized preceding it and the sentence is well-formed. Assume that the verb has moved to a position c-commanding the moved object (to C in Holmberg 1986, Holmberg and Platzack 1995, and Vikner 1995). The linear relations are as in (21′), still ignoring the adjunct:

(21)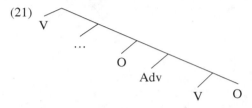

(21′) a. V-O   (selection)
      b. O-V   (a-cc)
      c. V-O   (a-cc)

This can be characterized as V-movement rescuing the linear conflict caused by object shift. The selection-based order is reestablished by V-movement. This is a case where we must assume head movement, after all. HG cannot be purely a linearization effect. This is because other categories than the verb and its selected object are involved as well, notably adjuncts. If the object moves across an adverb adjoined to VP or higher, an ordering conflict will arise between the verb and the adverb, resolved if the verb moves.

We can account for this formally by the following postulate:

(22) For the linear relation between two categories, the linearization
     algorithm ignores all but the selection-based relation and the final
     relation (final in terms of bottom-up derivation).[9]

That is to say, the relation (21′b) is ignored; hence, the structure is well-formed from a linearization point of view. (22) also explains why the adverb in (21) does not cause a linearization conflict, even though it both precedes and follows the object: the adverb has no selection-based relation to O, only two a-cc-based relations. Following the postulate (22), the lower one is ignored.

The difference between HG(s) and HG(r) shows up when constituents other than V appear in VP, being linearized along with the verb and the object. (23) is one such case. In Swedish, verb particles corresponding to *in, out, up, down,* and so on, obligatorily precede the object, even a pronominal object, as shown in (23a,b). V-movement, as in (23c), does not license movement of the object.

(23) a. Elsa har tydligen   inte skrivit **upp det**.   [Swedish]
         Elsa has apparently not written up   it
         'Apparently Elsa has not written it up.'
     b. *Elsa har tydligen inte skrivit **det upp**.
     c. *Elsa skrev **det** tydligen   inte **upp**.
         Elsa wrote it   apparently not up

The present model accounts for this pattern as follows. The structure of the
VP in (23) is (24), and the linear relations therefore are as in (24'). I ignore
the participial suffix, for ease of exposition. (PART = verb particle)

(24)   V

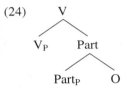

(24') a. Part-O   (selection)
       b. V-Part   (selection)
       c. V-O   (transitivity)

This yields the total order V-Part-O. (23b) has the (simplified) structure (25)
and the linear relations in (25'):

(25)

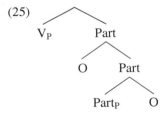

(25') a. Part-O   (selection)
       b. V-Part   (selection)
       c. V-O   (a-cc and transitivity)
       d. O-Part   (a-cc)

There is a conflict between (25'a) and (25'd), the linear relation caused by
movement of the object. In (23c), the verb has moved, as well as the object.
This does not alter the linear relations between the particle and the object,
though, so (23c) is ruled out just as (23b) is.

   In Danish, where the object can (and in fact must) precede the particle in
the PartP, which I assume is the case because the particle selects a preceding
object in Danish, the object can shift, provided the verb moves as well

(Holmberg 1999, Engels and Vikner 2014). As the particle selects the object on its left, there is no linear order conflict.

(26) a. Elsa har ikke skrivet **det op.**   [Danish]
      Elsa has not written it   up
    b. Elsa skrev **det** ikke **op.**
      Elsa wrote it   not up
      'Elsa didn't write it up.'

In fact, this is still not enough to fully account for HG(r). We will return to this issue in section 10.8. SOV languages do not show any effects of HG, because the object precedes the verb by virtue of selection. This explains, at least in part, the generalization that SOV languages have more or less free object scrambling, while SVO languages do not (Saito and Fukui 1998). Scrambling is movement of the object (or objects, in the case of ditransitive verbs) to a position outside VP but inside IP. That is to say, it is another name for object shift in SOV languages. In SVO languages, this movement is "blocked by the verb," by virtue of linearization of VP, unless the verb also moves, as in the Scandinavian languages. In SOV languages, where the object is linearized preceding the verb by selection, object shift/scrambling will preserve the selected linear order.[10]

10.6 Object Shift in Finnish

In Finnish, we can see the effect of HG in examples such as these:

(27) a. Anne on jo   heittänyt kukat/ne   pois.   [Finnish]
      Anne has already thrown   flowers/them away
      'Anne has already thrown the flowers/them away.'
    b. *Anne on kukat/ne   jo   heittänyt pois.
      Anne has flowers/them already thrown   away
    c. Anne heitti jo   kukat/?ne   pois.
      Anne threw already flowers/them away
    d. Anne heitti kukat/ne   jo   pois.
      Anne threw flowers/them already away

(27a) has the unmarked SVO order, compatible with wide focus or any narrow focus. (27b), where the object is outside VP, as if object-shifted (or scrambled), is ill-formed.[11] (27d), where the main verb has moved to T (see Holmberg et al. 1993, Holmberg and Nikanne 2002), is perfectly well-formed with the object moved out of VP, with wide focus. (27c) is included to show that movement of the object across the adverb is optional (although in this case weakly preferred with a pronominal object), as is characteristic of object shift of lexical objects in Icelandic, too:

The word order in (27), with a moved object, is fine if the sentence has initial focus, as when it is introduced by the focused adverb *kyllä* or a *wh*P:

(28) a. Kyllä Anne on kukat/ne   jo   heittänyt pois.   [Finnish]
      indeed Anne has flowers/them already thrown   away
      'Anne HAS already thrown the flowers/them away.'

  b. Miksi Anne on kukat/ne   jo   heittänyt pois?
      why   Anne has flowers/them already thrown   away
      'Why has Anne already thrown the flowers/them away?'

(29a–d) is another set demonstrating the same effect (ILL = illative).

(29) a. Kyy   oli heti   purrut poikaa jalkaan.   [Finnish]
      adder had immediately bit   boy   foot.ILL
      'The adder had immediately bit the boy in the foot.'

  b. *Kyy   oli poikaa heti   purrut jalkaan.
      adder had boy   immediately bit   foot.ILL

  c. Kyy   puri heti   poikaa jalkaan.
      adder bit immediately boy   foot.ILL
      'The adder immediately bit the boy in the foot.'

  d. Kyy   puri poikaa heti   jalkaan.
      adder bit boy   immediately foot.ILL

Again, the word order in (29b) is fine if the sentence has initial focus, as when it is introduced by the focused adverb *kyllä* or a *wh*P:

(30) a. Kyllä kyy   oli poikaa heti   purrut jalkaan.   [Finnish]
      indeed adder had boy   immediately bit   foot-ILL
      'The adder had actually immediately bit the boy in the foot.'

  b. Milloin kyy   oli poikaa heti   purrut jalkaan?
      when   adder had boy   immediately bit   foot-ILL
      'When had the adder immediately bit the boy in the foot?'

These examples demonstrate that there are two ways that an object can move out of the VP to a position in the IP-domain in Finnish. One is by the "SOV option," occurring in conjunction with initial focus. The other way, and the only possible way when the initial-focus condition is not met, is by object shift, respecting HG. The importance of this observation is that it is not the case that Finnish is insensitive to HG. We can thus maintain that HG is universal: movement of a complement across the selecting head will always yield an ungrammatical result, unless the head moves even higher, because of conflicting linearization instructions.[12] This, in turn, means that when Finnish exhibits SOV order, with the object or other verb complement preceding V, this is because the linearization instruction of V is set to V_F. What makes Finnish different from Swedish, English, French, Thai, and other more consistent SVO languages is that V can be set to either V_P or, as a marked alternative, to V_F.

Next, we will see how the various word orders are derived in Sheehan(m), including, in section 10.8, some word orders not derivable in Sheehan(m) or (o) without further modification. We will then return to the formal account of the initial-focus condition.

10.7   Deriving SOV Order in Sheehan(m)

Consider again the sentences in (4):

(4) a.   Milloin   hän   ol-i   osta-nut   auton-n?   [Finnish]
         when   she.NOM be-PAST buy-PAST.PTCP car-ACC
         'When had she bought a car?'
    b.   Milloin hän oli   auton ostanut?
         when   she had car   bought
    c.   Milloin hän auton oli   ostanut?
         when   she car   had bought
    d.   Milloin hän auton ostanut oli?
         when   she car   bought had
    e.   *Milloin hän ostanut auton oli?
         when   she bought car   had
    f.   ?Milloin hän ostanut oli   auton?
         when   she bought had car

Consider first the structure of the lower part of (4a):

(31)   Ptcp

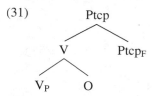

This tree will be linearized as follows:

(31′) a. V-O   (selection)
      b. V-Ptcp   (selection)
      c. Ptcp-O   (a-cc)

This yields the total order V-Ptcp-O, which is the order in (4a), with Ptcp attached as a suffix on V. When Aux is merged, marked Aux$_P$, as in (32), the linear relations will be as in (32′):

(32)

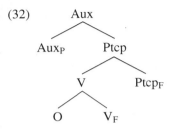

(32′) a. O-V   (selection)
       b. V-Ptcp   (selection)
       c. O-Ptcp   (transitivity)
       d. Aux-Ptcp   (selection)
       e. Aux-O   (a-cc)
       f. Aux-V   (a-cc)

This yields the total order Aux-O-V-Ptcp, where in Finnish, V and Ptcp form a single word.

Consider (4c). The structure is (33), which is equal to (32), except that O has moved and adjoined to Aux.[13] The linear relations are listed in (33′):

(33)

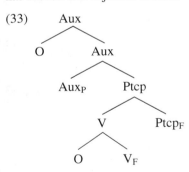

(33′) a. O-V   (selection and a-cc)
       b. V-Ptcp   (selection)
       c. O-Ptcp   (transitivity)
       d. Aux-Ptcp   (selection)
       e. Aux-O   (a-cc)
       f. Aux-V   (a-cc)
       g. O-Aux   (a-cc)

The only conflicting linear statements are (e) and (g). However, since Aux and O are not in a selection relation, the lower relation (e) is ignored.[14] This yields the total order O-Aux-V-Ptcp. The movement of the object does not yield any conflicting ordering statements, because the verb selects a preceding object.

Consider (4d), the consistently head-final structure. The structure is (34), with the linear relations in (34′):

(34)

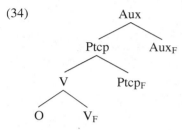

(34′) a. O-V   (selection)
       b. V-Ptcp   (selection)
       c. O-Ptcp   (transitivity)
       d. Ptcp-Aux   (selection)
       e. V-Aux   (transitivity)
       f. O-Aux   (transitivity)

The total order is O-V-Ptcp-Aux. Now consider (4e), the "FOFC violation," already dealt with in section 10.3. The structure is (35), with the linear relations (35′), which yield the total order (36). (36) is the order seen in (4f), which, as discussed in section 10.2, is highly marked, yet does occur in spoken Finnish, in the contexts that license OV order.

(35)

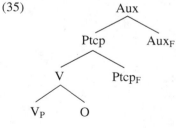

(35′) a. V-O   (selection)
       b. V-Ptcp   (selection)
       c. Ptcp-O   (a-cc)
       d. Ptcp-Aux   (selection)
       e. V-Aux   (transitivity)
       f. Aux-O   (a-cc)

(36) V-Ptcp-Aux-O

As noted in section 10.2, the FOFC-violating order (4f) is marginally possible
when the verb is contrastive, as in (37) (= (6)):

(37) Kyllä minä KUULLUT sen olen, mutta en koskaan   [Finnish]
     indeed I   heard   it   have but   not ever
     NÄHNYT.
     seen
     'I have HEARD it, but never SEEN it.'

As suggested by Maria Vilkuna (pers. comm.), this is presumably derived by
separate movement of the object and the verb. Assume that the tree (33), the
partial structure of (4c), is first derived. Subsequently, the remnant PtcpP is
moved to a position c-commanding the moved object, possible only if it is
accompanied by contrastive stress and interpretation. Under this analysis, (37)
is not a counterexample to FOFC.

Now consider the case of *put*-type verbs, where, as discussed, either the
whole complex complement can precede the verb, or just one part ((38a,b) =
(12b,c)):

(38) a. Kyllä minä olen kirjat hyllylle pannut.   [Finnish]
        indeed I   have books on.shelf put
        'I HAVE put the books on the shelf.'
     b. Kyllä minä olen kirjat pannut hyllylle.
        indeed I   have books put   on.shelf

I propose to describe this as follows: the complex complement of *put*-type
verbs has the structure in (39), with an abstract head, call it G, mediating
between the two constituents:[15]

(39)

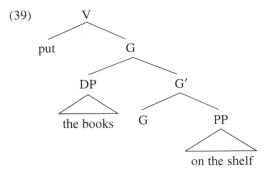

The variation between (38a) and (38b) can now be described as variation in
the selectional properties of G in Finnish (mirroring the variation in the selectional properties of other V-related heads), either G_P or G_F.[16] Consider first the
case of G_F, combined with V_F. (I refer to the specifier and the complement of

G as DP and PP, respectively, for ease of exposition, even though D and P would be formally more appropriate in the model under discussion.) The structure is (40), the linear relations are (40'a–f), and the total order is (41):

(40)

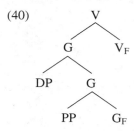

(40') a. PP-G   (selection)
    b. DP-G   (a-cc)
    c. DP-PP   (a-cc)
    d. G-V   (selection)
    e. PP-V   (transitivity)
    f. DP-V   (transitivity)

(41) DP-PP-G-V

This is the order in (38a), with G null. Now consider the case of G_P. The structure is (42) (= (40) except for the selection feature of G), and the linear relations are as in (42'):

(42)

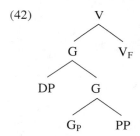

(42') a. G-PP   (selection)
    b. DP-G   (a-cc)
    c. DP-PP   (a-cc)
    d. G-V   (selection)
    e. V-PP   (a-cc)
    f. DP-V   (transitivity)

The only difference between (40') and (41') is (e). This yields the total order (43) for (42') (where G is null), that is, the order in (38b):

(43) DP-G-V-PP

10.8   HG(r) and the Linearization Algorithm

However, the construction (38), with the underlying structure (39), raises a problem for the theory as articulated so far. Consider the following construction, which manifests the problem even more obviously:

(44) a. Maria sjöng halsen   hes.   [Swedish]
Maria sang   the.throat hoarse
'Maria sang her throat hoarse.'
   b. Maria ... [$_{VP}$ sjöng [$_{IP}$ halsen [$_{I'}$ I [$_A$ hes]]]]

The embedded result clause is labeled *IP* to indicate that it has clausal structure but is not a full CP. Consider (45), testing the effect of object shift on the construction:

(45) a.   Maria har inte sjungit den hes.   [Swedish]
Maria has not sung   it hoarse
   b.   *Maria har den inte sjungit hes.
Maria has it   not sung   hoarse
   c.   Maria sjöng den inte hes.
Maria sang   it   not hoarse
'Maria didn't sing it hoarse.'
   c'. Maria sjöng den inte ⟨sjöng⟩ [$_{IP}$ ⟨den⟩ hes]

The point is that the subject of the IP undergoes object shift just like the direct object of a transitive verb would, even though there is no selection relation between the verb and the embedded subject. In this case the verb, being intransitive, does not select any part of the complement. (46) would be the schematic structure of the ungrammatical (45b):

(46)
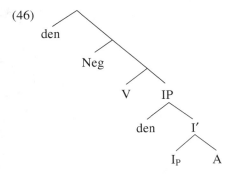

The problematic linearization relations here are (47a,b):

(47) a. V-den   (a-cc)
   b. den-V   (a-cc)

These are conflicting statements. We know that they are the source of the ungrammaticality, because the construction is saved by V-movement, as shown in (45c), with the structure (45c'). This is not predicted as the theory now stands, though, because neither of the relations (47a,b) is a selection-based relation. According to (22), only the final relation should count in this case; object shift across the verb is predicted to be as good as object shift across negation, in this case.

We find the same situation in all "small-clause-type" constructions, where a verb has a sister constituent with subject-predicate structure but no C; (39) is another such case. In this case, as is well-known, the embedded subject behaves like an object of the verb in some respects, most famously by being assigned object Case (Stowell 1981). In Scandinavian, it behaves like the direct object of the verb under object shift, as shown by (45). Not surprisingly, that is true of Finnish as well, exemplified here with a result clause (TRA = translative):

(48) a. *Marja on kurkkunsa varmaan laulanut käheäksi.   [Finnish]
        Marja has throat.her surely   sung   hoarse.TRA
     b. Marja lauloi kurkkunsa varmaan käheäksi.
        Marja sang   throat.her surely   hoarse.TRA
        'Marja surely sang her throat hoarse.'

Sheehan(o) and (m) is based on the idea that Universal Grammar characterizes one syntactic relation as privileged with respect to linearization, namely, the selection relation. Categories are lexically marked to precede or follow their c-selected complement, as formulated in (7b). Only if there is no selection relation between two heads does asymmetric c-command step in to fix their linear relation. Cases like (45) and (48) show that that cannot be right, or cannot be the whole story.

One way to accommodate cases like (45) and (48) would be to reformulate (22) as follows:

(49) When computing the linear relation between two chains A and B, the linearization algorithm ignores all but (a) the linear relation based on external Merge within the minimal lexical projection that contains A and B and (b) the final relation.

In the cases at hand, this means that when computing the linear order between the verb and the small-clause subject, the linearization algorithm will ignore all but the V-internal relation and the final relation. In the structure (46), we have the following relations:

(50) a. V-den   (a-cc, V-internal)
     b. den-V   (a-cc)

At this point, there is a linearization conflict, as the algorithm will count both relations. The situation can be resolved by V-movement to a position c-commanding *den*. In that case, the relation (50b) is demoted to an intermediate relation, and the final relation between the higher copy of the verb and the object pronoun will accord with the V-internal relation, the relation based on external Merge within V/VP. We still have to assume a selection relation between 'sing' in (44) and (48) and its complement, even though there is no θ-relation between them. We need this in order to account for the head-final version of the structure. In Finnish, it could be (51):

(51) Kyllä   minäkin kurkkuni   käheäksi laulanut olen.   [Finnish]
      indeed I.too   throat.my hoarse   sung   have
      'I, too, have sung my throat hoarse.'

The variation between the head-initial and head-final versions would be accounted for by a linearization feature P or F, which, by hypothesis, the verb would have even though it does not actually c-select the complement.

Small-clause subjects are not the only case where HG depends on syntactic relations that are not c-selection-based. Consider, for example, the following fact, argued to fall under HG(r) (Holmberg 1986, 1999, Holmberg and Platzack 1995, Fox and Pesetsky 2005): object shift cannot apply across a phonologically spelled-out category in VP. What (52) shows is that object shift of the direct object of a double-object construction across the indirect object is ruled out, even though the verb has moved. (52a) shows the order in the VP when the verb stays in situ. (52b) shows the order when the main verb moves, being the finite verb of a main clause. The lexical indirect object stays in situ and the pronominal direct object follows it.

(52) a. Jag har   inte givit Elsa den.   [Swedish]
       I   have not given Elsa it
       'I haven't given it to Elsa.'
    b. Jag gav   inte Elsa den.
       I   gave not Elsa it
       'I didn't give it to Elsa.'
    c. *Jag gav   den inte Elsa.
       I   gave it   not Elsa

Finally, (52c) shows that object shift of the pronominal direct object across the indirect object and the negation is ruled out. This is not predicted by the theory where only the selection relation is privileged, as there is no selection relation between the two objects. It is predicted by the theory incorporating (49), though: the linear order of the two objects based on external Merge (i.e., prior to any movement) is indirect object–direct object, on the basis of asymmetric c-command, so movement of the direct object across the indirect object yields a linearization conflict.

With this modification of the linearization principles, the theory moves closer to the one articulated by Fox and Pesetsky (2005). They propose a phase-based account of linearization, whose biggest virtue is an elegant explanation of HG(r) (see (14)). It is based on the following theoretical assumptions:

1. Syntactic derivation proceeds in phases (Chomsky 2001).
2. VP is a linearization domain, in the sense that once vP (the projection of the phase head that has VP as complement) is complete, VP is linearized.[17]
3. Linearization of A and B, in the course of the derivation of a sentence S, means that the linear order between A and B must be preserved at every subsequent stage of the derivation of S.

That is to say, unlike the model in Chomsky 2001, VP is not opaque to syntactic relations even after the vP-phase is constructed. A constituent A of VP can be moved to a position in the IP-domain; however, any such movement must respect the linear order between A and the other constituents of VP, established when VP is linearized. For example, once the linear relation between the verb and a direct object has been fixed as VO as part of the spell-out of VP (the spell-out domain of the vP-phase), movement of the verb is possible with no consequence for the object. Movement of the object is possible, too, but only if the verb moves higher, reestablishing the linear relation (which explains HG). Or once the linear relation of the direct and indirect objects of a double-object construction has been fixed as IO-DO as part of the spell-out of VP, the indirect object can move with no consequences for the direct object, but the direct object can move across the indirect object only if the latter moves even higher, reestablishing the IO-DO order. Compare (53) and the ungrammatical (52c). In (53), the indirect object has been topicalized, reestablishing the IO-DO order. In this way, Fox and Pesetsky's (2005) theory explains HG(r).

(53) Elsa gav jag den inte.   [Swedish]
     Elsa gave I it   not
     'I didn't give it to ELSA.'

However, the theory presented in this chapter has a number of empirical consequences that Fox and Pesetsky's (2005) theory does not have. In particular, their theory does not explain FOFC. Nor does it have the interesting consequence for head movement that the present theory has.

10.9 Formal Properties of the Initial-Focus Requirement

In a model where structures are built derivationally from the bottom up, how does the system know that the object cannot be focus (or Main News in Vilkuna's (1995) sense) when the verb is marked V_F? As discussed, this makes object movement out of VP possible (without V-movement), and by assumption VP is a focus domain for the object. But nothing in the system as described so far forces movement of the object out of VP. Instead, it seems that something prevents assignment of focus to VP, or any constituent of VP, making initial focus necessary, when V is marked F. As discussed in section 10.4, this explains why not just the preverbal object, but all other constituents of VP (including postverbal ones) and the verb itself, are defocused. A way to deal with this is to assume that Finnish has a rule of the information structure module that "defocalizes" the projection of V_F. The rule can be stated as follows:

(54) α is [–Foc] if dominated by the projection of V_F.

If we adopt Vilkuna's (1995) category Main News as an information-structural feature (primitive or derived), then the rule could be "α is [–Main News] if dominated by V_F." Since the constituents dominated by V_F can be moved out of VP, preserving their defocused property, it would be the case that (54) applies early, presumably at the point when the projection of V_F is complete, and [–Foc] is carried along under movement.

10.10 Conclusions

Finnish is a mixed-word-order language with VO as the unmarked order, but with OV as an option, typically in sentences with initial focus. Notably, when the initial-focus condition is met, the order of the sentential constituents in the TP is very free. For example, Aux-O-V, O-Aux-V, O-V-Aux, and even V-Aux-O all occur, but, predictably, the "FOFC-violating" order V-O-Aux does not. The big question this chapter has focused on is how to account for this freedom of word order. What is it that distinguishes Finnish from, for example, the neighboring Scandinavian languages, which makes the considerably greater freedom of word order in the lower part of the sentence possible in Finnish? Two possibilities have been considered. One is based on the traditional hypothesis that heads are lexically marked for linear order—specifically, whether they precede or follow their complement. In terms of this hypothesis, if Finnish verbs and auxiliaries are marked as allowing both options, the greater freedom of word order in Finnish is accounted for. The other possibility is based on the hypothesis that all word order variation is a matter of movement, following Kayne (1994). What is special about languages with more freedom of word order (in some domain) would then be that complement movement is, for some reason, freer (in that domain).

It was shown that object movement in Finnish is subject to Holmberg's Generalization, involving a restriction on movement of objects of verbs in VO languages. This was taken to imply that object movement is not freer in Finnish than in, for example, Swedish. In addition, it was shown that the defocusing effect of OV order cannot be explained as an effect of (just) object movement. Instead, it was hypothesized that verbs and auxiliaries in Finnish are marked to either precede or follow the category they select. This hypothesis was embedded in a version of the theory proposed by Sheehan (2011, 2013a,b) (see also section 4.10), referred to as Sheehan(m). This theory, enriched with the additional constraint (49) governing the computation of linear relations, was shown to predict correctly which permutations of the constituents in TP are grammatical and which are not. The initial-focus condition on OV order was taken to be a consequence of the defocusing effect of OV order (following Vilkuna 1995). The defocusing effect, in turn, can be expressed in terms of a rule, assuming Sheehan's theory.

11   The Final-over-Final Condition in Morphology

Ian Roberts

11.1 Introduction

In this chapter, we look at some possible effects of the Final-over-Final Condition (FOFC) below the word level, and at FOFC in relation to the interaction of the word and phrase levels. Although I will not adopt all the details of the Distributed Morphology framework, I will try to follow the leading idea that morphology is "syntax all the way down" (Marantz 1997). Specifically, I will adhere as far as possible to the Single Engine Hypothesis, the idea that complex morphological objects (i.e., derived words of various kinds) are constructed in the same way as complex syntactic objects, by the iteration of binary (internal or external) Merge. The principal focus will be on the extent to which head movement/incorporation (as well as phrasal movement; see Julien 2002 and below) plays a role in constructing complex words, and how FOFC interacts with these processes. Accordingly, the main focus will be on inflectional morphology.

More specifically, the empirical focus will be a striking typological generalization regarding suffixing morphology, put forward by Hawkins and Gilligan (1988; henceforth H&G): the suffixing preference. This states that OV/postpositional languages show a strong preference for suffixing, while VO/prepositional languages show no preference between suffixation and prefixation. I will suggest an account of this preference that combines FOFC and the Linear Correspondence Axiom (LCA; Kayne 1994), and look at some of the ramifications of this.

The chapter is organized as follows. In section 11.2, I introduce the suffixing preference, showing how recent evidence from the *World Atlas of Language Structures* (*WALS*) supports H&G's original observations. In section 11.3, I propose an account of the suffixing preference in terms of FOFC and the LCA. In section 11.4, I address derivation and compounding and offer a speculation regarding the relation between incorporation and FOFC. Section 11.5 concludes.

This chapter owes a particular debt to Neil Myler's University of Cambridge MPhil dissertation, which dealt with many of the same topics. *Myler 2009* refers to a revised and extended version of that dissertation, whose inspirational nature is hereby acknowledged.

11.2   The Suffixing Preference: Hawkins and Gilligan 1988

H&G present the evidence in favor of what they refer to as the *suffixing preference*. As they point out, the original observation was made by Greenberg ([1963]/2007), in the form of his Universal 27:

(1) *Greenberg's Universal 27*
    If a language is exclusively suffixing, it is postpositional; if it is exclusively prefixing, it is prepositional.

In this connection, Greenberg remarks, "Exclusively suffixing languages are fairly common, while exclusively prefixing languages are quite rare" ([1963] 2007:57). H&G elaborate as follows: "Languages with VO and/or Pr+NP word orders in their syntax regularly have prefixes and/or suffixes in their morphology. But in a suggestively large number of cases, languages with OV and/or NP+Po have suffixes only" (1988:219). Drawing on developments in morphological theory in the 1970s and 1980s, notably by Aronoff (1976) and Williams (1981a), which postulated that complex words are endocentric and that both inflectional and derivational affixes act as heads, they propose the Head-Ordering Principle (H&G 1988:227, (19)):

(2) *Head-Ordering Principle*
    The affixal head of a word is ordered on the same side of its subcategorized modifier(s) as P is ordered relative to NP within PP, and as V is ordered relative to a direct object NP.

H&G postulate 18 implicational universals based on a database of 16 morphological categories in approximately 200 languages, of the type "If a language has NP+Po, GENDER affixes on N (if any) are suffixed" (1988:223). From these implicational statements relating to specific affix-types, H&G derive the following generalization: "NP+Po and/or SOV always implies suffixing, never prefixing; and prefixing implies Pr+NP and/or VO, but never NP+Po and/or SOV" (1988:228). Moreover, they note the following prefixing-to-suffixing ratios (1988:230):

(3) VO languages: 52%:48%. Prepositional languages: 44%:56%.
    OV languages: 22%:78%. Postpositional languages: 22%:78%.

They also note that nominal and verbal suffixes differ somewhat in their cross-linguistic incidence, formulating the following implicational statement:

(4) "If a language has any prefixes on N, then any affixes on V will also include prefixes with more than chance frequency." (H&G 1988:224)

In other words, prefixes are more frequent on V than on N. The prefixing-to-suffixing ratios for nominal morphology are 34%:66% (VO languages), 33%:67% (prepositional languages) (i.e., roughly 2 to 1 in favor of suffixing in head-initial languages), and 13%:87% (OV languages), 16%:84% (postpositional languages) (i.e., between 5 to 1 and 7 to 1 in favor of suffixing in head-final languages).

WALS supports H&G's results. Dryer (2015h) looks at 10 affix types across a sample of 969 languages. The affix types, each of which is covered in a separate chapter in WALS, are as follows:

1. Case affixes on nouns
2. Pronominal subject affixes on verbs,
3. Tense/Aspect affixes on verbs
4. Plural affixes on nouns
5. Pronominal possessive affixes on nouns
6. Definite or indefinite affixes on nouns
7. Pronominal object affixes on verbs
8. Negative affixes on verbs
9. Interrogative affixes on verbs
10. Adverbial subordinator affixes on verbs

The affixation index for each language was calculated by looking at each of the affix types and, if the type is found in the language, adding one point to the suffixing index if it is mainly suffixing, one point to the prefixing index if it is mainly prefixing, and half a point to each if it is equally suffixing and prefixing. In the case of affix types 1–3 (case affixes on nouns, pronominal subject affixes on verbs, and tense/aspect affixes on verbs), the indices were doubled. Finally, the prefixation/suffixation index was calculated as the percentage of the overall affixation index (e.g., if a language has 4 affixation points and 2.5 prefixation points, then the prefixing index is 2.5/4 = 62.5%).

In these terms, a language is classed as having "little or no inflectional morphology" if it has 2 affixing points or fewer. A language is classed as "predominantly suffixing" if its suffixing index is greater than 80%, and as having a "moderate preference for suffixing" if its suffixing index is between 60% and 80%. The classes of "moderate preference for prefixing" and "predominantly prefixing" are likewise defined as those languages with a prefixing index of 60% to 80% and over 80%, respectively. Finally, languages with a

Table 11.1
Numbers and percentages of languages showing various prefixing and suffixing tendencies (based on Dryer 2015e, 969 languages)

Affixation type	Number of languages	Percentage of languages
Little or no inflectional morphology	141	14.6
Predominantly suffixing	406	41.9
Moderate preference for suffixing	123	12.7
Approximately equal amounts of prefixing and suffixing	147	15.2
Moderate preference for prefixing	94	9.7
Predominantly prefixing	58	6.0
Totals	969	100.1

Table 11.2
Numbers and percentages of OV and VO languages with different affixing patterns (based on Dryer 2015e, 969 languages, and Dryer 2015h, 1,519 languages)

	Number OV	% OV	Number VO	% VO
Little affixation	35	7.8	100	23.5
Mainly suffixing	339	75.0	136	31.9
Equal suffixing and prefixing	49	10.9	78	18.3
Mainly prefixing	29	6.3	112	26.3
Totals	449	100	426	100

suffixing or prefixing index of 40% to 60% are classed as having "approximately equal amounts of prefixing or suffixing." The results are given in table 11.1. Here, as Dryer observes, the suffixing preference is readily apparent. In particular, predominantly suffixing languages outnumber predominantly prefixing languages by almost 7 to 1. In fact, as Dryer observes, "[O]f the five types other than those with little affixation, those which are predominantly suffixing are about as frequent as the other four types combined (382 vs. 390)" (2015e:4).

The typological skewing with respect to suffixing becomes still more evident if the above figures are combined with those for OV and VO languages. This is shown in table 11.2. (In the table, I have combined predominantly suffixing/prefixing and moderately suffixing/prefixing. Only languages with data for both features are reported; hence, the total number of languages is 875.) Here, we see that OV suffixing languages outnumber OV prefixing languages by a factor of over 11, while suffixing and prefixing are just about equally distributed in VO languages. As H&G point out, there are two things to account for in these data: the very strong suffixing preference in OV languages, and the almost equal possibility of suffixing or prefixing in VO languages. Note that there is more going on here than a simple preference for harmony of head-complement order within the word and the phrase: this idea immediately accounts for the strong suffixing preference in OV languages, but it fails to account for the equal distribution of suffixing and prefixing in VO languages. If it were purely a matter of cross-categorial harmony across word and phrase, we would expect an equally strong prefixing preference in VO languages. But this is not observed; in fact, there is a very slight preference for suffixing (31.9% vs. 26.3%). So one way of phrasing the question is this: why do we observe harmony between word structure and phrase structure only in OV languages? As we will see, this is where FOFC has a role to play.

Three further questions also arise from the data presented in table 11.2. The first concerns the residue of prefixing in OV languages. We cannot treat the suffixing preference as categorical on the basis of the data we have here: 6.3% of OV languages do show a prefixing preference, and 10.9% have equal suffixing and prefixing. So this must also be accounted for. Finally, we should also try to account for what seems to be a preference for affixation in OV languages, as only 7.8% of these languages show little affixation, while 23.4% of VO languages fall into this category.

I now present three more illustrations of the suffixing preference, in relation to specific affixes. Tables 11.3, 11.4, and 11.5 give the percentages of suffixes vs. prefixes overall and then in OV and VO languages for case marking on nouns, tense/aspect marking on verbs and plural marking on nouns (the cases

Table 11.3
Numbers and percentages of suffixes vs. prefixes overall and in OV and VO languages for case marking on nouns (based on Dryer 2015a, 1,031 languages, and Dryer 2015h, 1,519 languages)

	Number overall	% overall	Number OV	% OV	Number VO	% VO
Case suffixes	452	43.8	286	56.4	91	22.6
Case prefixes	38	3.7	4	0.8	32	7.9
Other case marking[a]	162	15.7	116	22.9	25	6.2
No case marking	379	36.8	101	19.9	255	63.2
Totals	1,031	100	507	99[b]	403	99.9

[a] These include case tone (5 languages), case stem change (1 language), mixed morphological case (i.e., both prefixes and suffixes; 9 languages), postpositional clitics (123 languages), prepositional clitics (17 languages), and inpositional clitics (i.e., a case clitic attaches to a constituent inside the NP/DP, usually the first; 7 languages). The adpositional clitic languages include many instances that are commonly thought of as morphological case systems, for example, Japanese. If we collapse this class with case affixes, we obtain 575 case-suffixing languages, or 55.8%, vs. a combined total of 38+17 = 55 case-prefixing languages, or 5.3%. Suffixes then outnumber prefixes by a factor of more than 10. For OV languages, the combined total of case suffixes and postpositional clitics is 286+107 = 72.1%. There is only 1 VO language with postpositional clitics: Waray, a language of the Gunwinyguan subfamily spoken in Northern Australia.
[b] This is a rounding effect.

Table 11.4
Numbers and percentages of suffixes vs. prefixes overall and in OV and VO languages for tense/aspect marking on verbs (based on Dryer 2015b, 1,131 languages, and Dryer 2015h, 1,519 languages)

	Number overall	% overall	Number OV	% OV	Number VO	% VO
Tense/aspect suffixes	667	59	443	81.3	136	29.5
Tense/aspect prefixes	153	13.5	23	4.2	120	26
Other tense/aspect marking[a]	159	14.1	42	7.7	100	21.7
No tense/aspect marking	152	13.4	37	6.8	105	22.8
Totals	1,131	100	545	100	461	100

[a] These include tone (13 languages) and mixed types (i.e., both prefixes and suffixes; 146 languages).

Table 11.5
Numbers and percentages of suffixes vs. prefixes overall and in OV and VO languages for plural marking on nouns (based on Dryer 2015g, 1,066 languages, and Dryer 2015h, 1,519 languages)

	Number overall	% Overall	Number OV	% OV	Number VO	% VO
Plural suffixes	513	48.1	299	64.4	149	31.2
Plural prefixes	126	11.8	8	1.7	102	21.4
Other plural marking[a]	329	30.9	113	24.4	185	38.9
No plural marking	98	9.2	44	9.5	41	8.6
Totals	1,066	100	464	100	477	101[b]

[a] These include stem change (6 languages), tone (4 languages), mixed marking (i.e., combining prefixes, suffixes, tone, separate words, etc.; 60 languages), complete reduplication (8 languages), plural words (170 languages), and a plural clitic (81 languages).
[b] This is a rounding effect.

of affixation that Dryer (2015e) judges most significant). Table 11.3 confirms the basic observation of Greenberg's ([1963]/2007) Universal 41: "[I]f in a language the verb follows both the nominal subject and the nominal object in the dominant order, the language almost always has a case system" (if we take *almost always* to mean 'in 80% of cases'). On the basis of tables 11.3, 11.4, and 11.5, the average rate of suffixing in OV languages is 67.4% (this rises to 72.6% if we count "postpositional case clitics" as classified by *WALS* as case suffixes; see note a to table 11.3), while the average rate of prefixing is 2.2%. In VO languages, on the other hand, the average rate of suffixing is 27.8% and of prefixing is 18.8%. The overall suffixing preference is thus extremely clear, as is the fact that the preference holds much more strongly in OV languages than in VO languages.

I now turn to the investigation of the questions raised by the suffixing preference in relation to FOFC.

11.3   Accounting for the Suffixing Preference in OV Languages

11.3.1   The Suffixing Preference in OV Languages

We expect FOFC to be relevant for the suffixing preference, since it is in essence a constraint on head-final orders. Assuming suffixes to head the words they form, suffixed words are an instance of head-final order, and so FOFC should apply (if syntax and morphology are part of the same generative system, as in the Single Engine Hypothesis mentioned in section 11.1). Indeed, one simple formulation of FOFC is as follows (see chapter 2):

(5) A head-final category cannot immediately dominate a head-initial category in the same extended projection.

Assuming (5), along with the general idea that head-final orders are derived by complement movement to the left, which I take to be a consequence of the LCA (see Biberauer, Holmberg, and Roberts 2014 and chapters 2 and 3, for discussion and formulation of the LCA in relation to FOFC), then all structures are first-merged in head-initial order. Now, supposing F is a bound functional morpheme merged immediately above VP, we have five possibilities involving leftward movement of V, VP, both, or neither:

(6) a. $[_{FP}$ F $[_{VP}$ V O]]
    b. $[_{FP}$ $[_{VP}$ V O] [F (VP)]]
    c. $[_{FP}$ $[_{VP}$ O V (O)] [F (VP)]]
    d. $[_{FP}$ $[_F$ V+F] $[_{VP}$ (V) O]]
    e. $[_{FP}$ $[_{VP}$ (V) O] $[[_F$ V+F] (VP)]]

In (6a), nothing moves. The result is a head-initial structure in which F is a prefix (still assuming it is a bound morpheme).

In (6b), VP moves to Spec,FP. If VP is head-initial, this leads to a FOFC violation.

In (6c), a head-final VP moves; hence, there is no FOFC violation. Here, F suffixes to V. This is the structure that, according to Julien (2002), underlies the crosslinguistically common pattern of OV order combined with agglutinative morphology. Note that if we iterate the operations that derive (6c), merging a further functional head G, containing a bound morpheme, above FP, and moving FP into Spec,GP, we obtain (7):

(7) $[_{GP}$ $[_{FP}$ $[_{VP}$ O V (O)] [F (VP)]] [G (FP)]]

Here, V appears with two suffixes, F and G, in that order. We thus obtain the result that agglutinating affixes in head-final languages stack up in mirror-image order to their free-morpheme counterparts (auxiliaries, particles) in head-initial languages. Julien (2002:114ff.) shows that this kind of derivation works for a range of head-final agglutinating languages, including Japanese and Turkish (see also Cinque 1999:chap. 3). Most important for present purposes is the fact that it is impossible for F or G to surface as a prefix in (7). If this is the general way, or at least the commonest way, in which OV order is derived, then we can seemingly explain the suffixing preference in OV languages. (If this were the only way to derive OV order, we would falsely predict that there are no prefixes in OV languages; we will return to this point below.)

In (6d), it is just V that moves. Here, since the LCA requires V to left-adjoin to F, F is a suffix. (6d) gives VO order, and here we see how suffixing may be derived with this order, a point we will return to in the next section.

Finally, (6e) features the combination of VP- and V-movement. Again, V must left-adjoin to F, and hence F will be a suffix.[1]

Although the LCA does most of the work in deriving the suffixing preference here, FOFC still plays a crucial role in forcing the fronted VP to be head-final: this is what gives rise to verbal suffixing in OV languages. Hence, the suffixing preference results from the interaction of the LCA and FOFC.

However, there is a further option that should be considered, in addition to those in (6). This involves object shift alone, without V- or VP-movement, shown in (8):

(8)

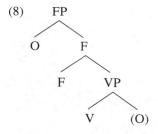

Since some OV languages have prefixes (see the discussion and examples in section 11.3.3), (8a) should not be ruled out completely. One important generalization is that the prefixes, where they occur, are typically "low" clausal heads: Voice or Aspect, but hardly ever Tense. It seems that Tense is not typically marked by prefixes (as indicated by H&G). That is explained if the prefixes are derived as in (8a) with O-movement across F to a rather low medial position outside FP. In a head-final system, FP then moves over the landing site of O (see Holmberg and Roberts 2013). FP-movement appears to create a FOFC violation, but phase-based spell-out operations may be relevant here. For example, if we introduce vP into the picture, then we have the structure in (9):

(9) [$_{FP}$ F [$_{vP}$ v [$_{VP}$ V O]]]

Here, F can be spelled out as a prefix on v/V, as part of the spell-out of the vP-phase, independently of O raising to Spec,vP.

Finally, let us briefly return to the case of FOFC inside complex heads, after two iterations of head movement. Here, there are two structures of interest:

(10) a. $[_G [_F V + F] + G]$

   b. $*[_G [_V F +V] + G]$

(10a) is a harmonically head-final (suffixing) word and as such is allowed by FOFC (and readily attested in languages with rich inflectional morphology). (10b), on the other hand, violates FOFC. We will return to this in section 11.3.3 and when we briefly discuss infixation in section 11.3.4.

To conclude, we can see how FOFC and the LCA together account for the suffixing preference in OV languages, as long as we assume that OV order must involve leftward VP-movement (and leaving aside the potentially problematic (10b) for now).

11.3.2   Suffixing in VO Languages

Here, we look at the second of the questions raised by H&G: why VO languages show the possibility of either suffixing or prefixing. Recall that this is unexpected in terms of the Head-Ordering Principle, since if the affix is the head of the derived word and if there is harmony between words and phrases with respect to head-complement order (as the very strong suffixing preference in OV languages suggests), then we expect VO languages to show a prefixing preference. All other things being equal, this preference should be as strong as the suffixing preference is in OV languages. As the data clearly show, however, this is not at all the case. In this section, I will outline how the assumptions adopted here, most importantly the LCA as it applies to both head movement and XP-movement, can explain the lack of a prefixing preference and can predict, to a good approximation, the distribution of suffixing and prefixing orders in VO languages.

To see how this works, let us again consider the options in (6):

(6) a. $[_{FP} F [_{VP} V O]]$

   b. $[_{FP} [_{VP} V O] [F (VP)]]$

   c. $[_{FP} [_{VP} O V (O)] [F (VP)]]$

   d. $[_{FP} [_F V+F] [_{VP} (V) O]]$

   e. $[_{FP} [_{VP} (V) O] [[_F V+F] (VP)]]$

Only options (6a) and (6d) are available in a VO language. (6b) is ruled out by FOFC, while (6c) and (6e) give OV order. (6a) gives rise to prefixing; (6d) gives rise to suffixing since the LCA requires head movement to create left-adjunction structures. As mentioned in section 11.2, these orders are roughly equally instantiated. Table 11.2 gives 31.9% suffixing and 26.3% prefixing. Averaging the figures for tables 11.3, 11.4, and 11.5 gives 27.8% suffixing, 18.8% prefixing, and 53.8% "other" or no prefixing. These last figures suggest that there is roughly a 50% chance that a functional morpheme will be realized as an affix in a VO language, and that there is a roughly equal chance that that affix will be a prefix or a suffix (the relatively low proportion of prefixes emerging from tables 11.3–11.5 is probably due to the extremely low proportion of case prefixes, something noted also by H&G and by Myler (2009), and for which neither they nor I have an explanation). If the presence of an overt affix in F triggers V-movement 50% of the time, we expect suffixing in VO languages to occur about 25% of the time (and prefixing about 25% of the time); this is approximately correct, as these figures show.

In fact, the situation is more interesting than this, once we take the nature of the functional hierarchy and the cyclic nature of movement into account. For each functional head H in the hierarchy, the probability of its being realized by an affix is chance, or 1 in 2. But the probability of a functional head H attracting the lexical head diminishes steadily as a function of the H's position in the hierarchy, given the cyclic nature of movement and the idea that head movement on any given cycle occurs at chance. If the appearance of an affix in H and lexical-head movement to H are completely independent variables, then the probability of V-movement to v is 1 in 2, while the probability of V-to-v movement followed by V-to-T movement is 1 in 4; in fact, for all functional heads H above v the probability of V-movement to H can be calculated as 1 in $2n$, where n is the number of heads in the extended projection c-commanded by H. For T, then, the probability of V-movement is 1 in 4, since T c-commands two heads in the extended projection, and the probability of V-movement to C is 1 in 6. But the probability of any of these heads being realized as an affix is constant at 1 in 2. It follows that, if suffixation is invariably a reflex of head movement, the probability of suffixal realization is 1 in $(2n \times 2)$, for all heads above v, for which it is 1 in 4.

It now follows that the probability of T being realized as a suffix should be in 1 in 8, or 12.5%. However, table 11.4 gives 29.5% suffixation in VO languages for tense/aspect heads. Assuming the WALS data are not historically or areally skewed, and assuming that "tense/aspect suffixes" uniformly appear in T,[2] then we appear to be faced, again, with a surprising suffixing preference.

The explanation for this lies in the nature of head movement: if we think that there is a 1 in 2 chance of a given functional head H being morphologically realized, and a 1 in 2 chance of that morpheme being bound, then there is a 1 in 4, or 25%, chance of a suffix, to which the 29.5% seen in table 11.4

approximates rather well. This means that the chances of a suffix in H, alone, dictate the chances of the lexical-head moving to H. In other words, as has frequently been suggested in the literature on head movement, if a given functional head is suffixal, it will attract the lexical head. In other words, the appearance of an affix in H and lexical-head movement to H are not independent variables: the latter is triggered by the former. The statistical evidence in table 11.3 can be seen as supporting this contention.

Moreover, the same can be said about plural marking. Suppose plural marking is located in Q, in a DP with the structure in (11) (see chapter 8 on FOFC in DPs):

(11) $[_{DP}$ D $[_{QP}$ Q $[_{nP}$ n $[_{NP}$ N...]]]]

Then the probability of N-movement to Q would be 1 in 4 and the probability of a suffixal plural 1 in 8. But table 11.5 shows that suffixal plurals appear 31.2% of the time, that is, at a rate of almost 1 in 3. If N-movement to Q is dictated purely by the chances of Q containing a suffix, then we predict a 25% instance of suffixal plural-marking. This is not quite right, but certainly much closer than 1 in 8. Again, then, we see the statistical case for suffixes triggering movement of the lexical head.

The same reasoning holds for case marking. If we take case morphemes to occupy a K head that takes DP as its complement, then the chances of K attracting N should be 1 in 8, since K c-commands 4 heads in the extended projection of N seen in (11). So the chances of suffixal case-marking should be 1 in 16, or about 6%. However, table 11.3 gives 22.6% case suffixes in VO languages. Again, this approximates much more closely to 1 in 4. So it appears that the suffixal nature of K alone is responsible for attracting N. (What remains anomalous is the very low proportion of case prefixes, as noted above.)

A final, and very intriguing, observation arises if we now look at the corresponding figures for suffixation in OV languages. Averaging the figures for tables 11.3, 11.4, and 11.5 for OV languages gives 67.4% suffixing, while averaging the figures for VO languages gives 27.8%. The figure for suffixing in OV languages is more than double that of VO languages. Now, if suffixing can arise either through the suffix attracting the lexical head or through XP-movement to the specifier of the head occupied by the suffix, and if these are chance parametric options, we expect twice as much suffixing in OV languages as in VO languages, since any given head has, as it were, two chances of being a suffix (and recall that it is possible that these are different kinds of suffix; see note 1). So this seems to be exactly right. Of course, if XP-movement is cyclic, its incidence should decline as a function of the position in the hierarchy. But this is not what we observe, and so again we see that affixes appear to play a triggering role in relation to both head movement and XP-movement.

In sum, there is no prefixing preference in VO languages. Instead, there is an approximately chance distribution of affixal functional heads, and an approximately chance incidence of incorporation into those heads. Once these probabilities are worked out, the figures obtained from *WALS* approximate quite closely to the expected possibilities.

11.3.3 Suffixing-Preference Violations in OV Languages

We have now accounted for the two basic observations made by H&G (1988): the very strong suffixing preference in OV languages, and the fact that VO languages do not show a corresponding prefixing preference. However, as it stands, the account given of the suffixing preference in section 11.3.1 is too strong, in that it does not allow for a significant residue of exceptions to the suffixing preference in OV languages. In this section, again inspired by the proposals in Myler 2009, I will propose an account of these exceptions.

H&G note that five types of affixes fall outside the general OV+suffixing pattern:

(12) possessive, subject marking, object marking, negation, voice

According to H&G (1988:225), with these suffixes "anything goes"; that is, there are no crosslinguistic generalizations to be made about the ordering of these elements. Similarly, on the basis of the survey of inflectional morphology in 530 languages in Julien 2002:app. 2, Myler (2009:13–14) finds 82 (16%) apparent cases of *[[F +V] + G], that is, what one could superficially characterize as "FOFC violations inside the words" (although on the view adopted by both Myler and Julien, these are syntactic FOFC violations like any other); this corresponds to (10b), briefly discussed in section 11.3.1. Myler argues quite convincingly that in the vast majority of cases the F or G is one of the following classes of elements: an argument-adding morpheme, usually causative (42 languages), a "high" mood marker (17 languages), negation (10 languages), or a discourse particle (7 languages). Aside from these cases, only 6 languages appear to violate FOFC in their inflectional system.[3] Finally, Julien (2002:235) observes that agreement morphemes are found in a very wide range of positions in the word.

There is a parallel here between the exceptions found by Myler and H&G, as well as Julien's observation regarding agreement morphemes. If we construe "subject marking" and "object marking" as agreement, and take "possessive marking" to be DP-internal agreement, then we can combine the three sets of observations as follows:

(13) *FOFC violators in inflection*
      Agr, negation, discourse markers/"high" mood markers, voice/
      causativizers

Since Chomsky 1995, it has been widely held that Agr-elements are not
autonomous categories, but φ-bundles associated with another head. Because
the φ-bundles can appear with various other heads (T, D, v, etc.), we expect
them to be able to appear in a wide range of positions in clause structure, as
observed by Julien (see also Cinque 1999:53ff.).

      Concerning negation and discourse markers (a category that may overlap
with "high" mood markers), Biberauer, Holmberg, and Roberts (2014) observe
that these elements frequently appear to violate FOFC at the clausal level, if
they are taken to be heads. The following examples illustrate for question
particles (one kind of discourse particle) and negation (see chapter 9 for extensive discussion and analysis of these clause-final particles):

(14) a. Ni   yao   kan zhe-ben shu   **ma**?   [Mandarin]
          you want read this-CL book Q
          'Do you want to read this book?'
          (Aldridge 2011:412)
      b. deb-ge   tol kobio **li**.   [Bagirmi; Nilo-Saharan]
          person-PL kill lion   not
          'The people didn't kill the lion.'
          (Dryer 2009b:317)

The categories in question have a special status as syncategorematic elements.
Such elements have the following properties:

(15) a. They are not c-selected.
      b. They do not c-select.
      c. They (therefore) occupy no fixed position in the clausal hierarchy.
      d. They have surface scope determined by their position.
      e. They may violate consistent word-order patterns of the language.
      f. They may violate FOFC.

Essentially, these elements function somewhat like "pure" logical constants,
in lacking any form of argument structure, hence c-selection properties. As
such, they can appear anywhere in the clause (or, we can add, the word),
subject only to the condition that the default interpretation is that they take
surface scope.[4]

      Finally, regarding Voice morphemes (e.g., passivizers) and causativizers, it
is possible that these categories head their own (verbal) extended projection.
If so, then apparent FOFC violations would be expected in their complement.

However, H&G list just five languages with causative prefixes. Of these, information concerning two was available to me (Khasi and Quiegolian Zapotec); in both of these languages, we find the order F-Caus-V, where F is an aspectual head. Here, there is no FOFC violation; instead, these appear to be systems where V does not move (or only moves to a rather low position) and F and Caus are directly merged into higher functional heads (see the discussion of Navajo and Slave below).

By and large, then, the systematic exceptions to the suffixing preference in OV languages can be accounted for. However, as we saw in section 11.2, there are still some exceptions to the general tendency regarding other affixes. Table 11.3 shows the very low incidence of case prefixes in OV languages (4 languages, 0.8% of the total). According to table 11.4, there are 23 OV languages with tense/aspect prefixes (4.2% of the total); and according to table 11.5, there are 8 OV languages (1.8%) with plural prefixes. Let us look at these languages in more detail.

The OV, case-prefixing languages are Burrara (an Australian language of the Northern Territories), Gapapaiwa (an Austronesian language spoken in Papua New Guinea), Prasuni (an Indic language of Afghanistan), and Takelma (an Amerind language spoken in Oregon).

In three of these languages (Gapapaiwa, McGuckin 2002:314; Prasuni, Morgenstierne 1949:220; Takelma, Sapir 1922:241), there is a small class of locative (pro)clitics, but these can hardly be regarded as constituting a system of case prefixes; the vast majority of nouns in Gapapaiwa and Takelma have no case marking at all, while Prasuni has a residual suffixal case system inherited from Indic (which seems to show split-ergativity). Burrara, on the other hand, has prefixes that are glossed as "acc" in Glasgow 1984:6–8, appearing between a descriptive prefix that characterizes one of four noun classes and the stem (e.g., *an-mu-jaruk* 'messenger' (lit. descriptive prefix – acc – story)). It is unclear whether there are any other case morphemes, or what the motivation was for referring to these morphemes as "accusative." If we leave Burrara aside as an unresolved instance, then we see that there are no really convincing examples of OV languages with case prefixes. This is a very interesting observation, which we can explain along the lines given in section 11.3.1. We could explain the difference between case marking and other forms of prefixation in this manner if we suppose that the complement of N is unable to move around the case head, perhaps because case is a very high head. But the complement of the case head can move around it by roll-up. Hence, if case is affixal at all, it is (almost) always a suffix.

Turning now to the data from table 11.4, the 23 OV languages with tense/aspect prefixes are as follows: Western Apache, Chipewyan, Gooniyandi,

Gumawana, Gyarong (Cogtse), Iduna, Iwam, Ket, Kiliwa, Maisin, Maklew, Marind, Navajo, Päri, Seri, Sinaugoro, Slave, Tanacross, Tawala, Toussian, Yaqay, Yelî Dnye, and Zimakani.

Of the languages in this group on which I was able to obtain further information, several appear to have functional systems where there is no roll-up and little or no head movement: for example, Ket (a Yenizeian language spoken in Siberia) has T-(Agr)-Asp-V, suggesting no V-movement (Werner 1997:154–155).[5] OV order must then be derived by object fronting or, if V incorporates with v, remnant VP-fronting. Boelaars (1950) describes three different Papuan languages. All three display some evidence for partial V-movement through the functional system, and some evidence that the prefixes are separate auxiliaries. Marind has Agr_S-T-Agr_O-(Num)-V except with a third person plural subject, where T (= future, aspect, negation, or perfect) precedes the subject, in which case it looks like a separate auxiliary (Boelaars 1950:5–8). Makleu has T-V-(Distant Past)/Agr_S (Boelaars 1950:20–21), suggesting partial V-movement through the functional hierarchy. Yaqay, related to Marind, has preterite, future, and evidential markers preceding the subject, but the subject preceding the Present marker. The former again look like separate auxiliaries rather than prefixes (Boelaars 1950:62–63). In all these languages, if V moves to v, then OV order can be derived by remnant VP-fronting.

Navajo shows the typical Athapaskan system involving a complex prefixal morphological template on the verb, featuring up to 10 prefixes (depending on the analysis); see Speas 1990:205ff. and the references given there. The basic word order is SOV. Speas argues that part of the prefixing system, the conjunct prefixes, is constituted by functional heads, as shown in (20) (from Speas 1990:279):[6]

(16) 1   2   3   # 4   5   6   7   8   9   V
     ADV ITER DIST PL DO DEIC SU   ADV   MODE   SUBJ   VOICE

The # between positions 3 and 4 marks a phonological boundary, which Speas suggests corresponds to the left edge of the functional system making up the inflected verb. Speas goes on to identify prefixes 4–8 with functional heads in a head-final version of the clause structure proposed by Chomsky (1991), as follows (she does not comment on position 5):

(17) 4   5   6   7   8   9   V
      DO DEIC SU ADV   MODE   SUBJ   VOICE
      ↑   ↑   ↑   ↑
     Agr_O Asp   Finite Agr_S

She then suggests that "the verb originates immediately to the left of the object-agreement morpheme and moves to the highest INFL position" (p. 280).

In other words, Speas assumes a left-branching clause structure with the heads V, Agr_O, Asp, F, and Agr_S therefore ordered left to right, followed by V-movement right-adjoining V to Agr_S. We can adapt the main elements of this analysis to the general assumptions made here—in particular, the head-initial configuration of functional heads and the general constraint that head adjunction is always left-adjunction—by assuming that V (and possibly Voice) do not raise, but that v=Agr_O (since it instantiates object φ-features) raises through Asp to T, which contains Finiteness and subject φ-features. In this way, despite the differences with Speas's analysis, we can concur with her conclusion that "the Pollock/Chomsky theory of the structure of S in English and French makes these languages look much more like Navajo than had previously been suspected" (p. 280).

Slave, like Navajo, shows the Athapaskan pattern of rich, templatic prefixation to the verb. According to Rice's (1989:425ff.) description, position 11 in the template is occupied by "mode," aspect, or tense, and this position precedes a subject marker, a voice/classifier morpheme, and the verb root. It thus seems similar to position 7 in (17), suggesting that perhaps an analysis similar to the one just sketched for Navajo could apply here. A further point of interest is that Slave has periphrastic past tense markers that follow the entire verbal complex:

(18) kǫ́é   ghóhtsį   yįlé   [Slave]
     house 3.PERF.build PAST
     'He had built a house.'
     (Rice 1989:1115)

(Navajo has a class of postverbal modal particles that may be comparable; see Speas 1990:276–277 and the references given there.) Clearly, we can treat this order as involving movement of the constituent containing the object and the inflected verb to the left of the Past morpheme. However, if one of the prefix positions instantiates T, then we are compelled to treat these structures as biclausal, with the past marker functioning somewhat like a restructuring trigger. On the other hand, if the prefixes represent a functional hierarchy below T, then we can treat this as iterated head movement of functional elements to Mode/Agr_S followed by phrasal movement of ModeP to Spec,TP. The position of the object reflects object movement. As a pronominal-argument language, Slave is quite freely able to place arguments in a variety of positions; in fact, the object may occupy an adjunct position here. The structure of (18) would thus be as follows:

(19) $[_{TP} [_{ModeP} O [_{ModeP} [_{Mode} [_{Asp} v Asp] Mode]] [_{AspP} (Asp) [_{vP} (v) [_{VP} V (O)]]]] T (ModeP)]$

Of course, many more details are required in order to support an analysis of this type, but it is certainly a possibility. Most importantly for present purposes, it does not involve any FOFC violation.

Finally, Tawala (an Austronesian language spoken in Papua New Guinea) has SOV order, with tense, subject-marking, and aspect prefixes, but object suffixes. Frequently, but not always, the subject and tense prefixes form a single syncretic element (Ezard 1991:112), suggesting that subject φ-features are associated with T:

(20) Awai' i   yam e-   an- an'-i?   [Tawala]
     what our(EXCL) food 3SG+PRES-DUR-eat- 3SG
     'What is eating our food?'
     (Ezard 1991:113)

Here, it looks as though V-to-v movement takes place (with the object φ-features instantiating v), combined with remnant VP-fronting to Spec,TP.

Turning next to table 11.5, the OV plural-prefixing languages are Bininj Gun-Wok, Cherokee, Eudeve, Lafofa, Nevome, Ngandi, Tunen, and Wedau.

Of these languages, Evans (2003) describes Bininj Gun-Wok (an Australian language spoken in the Northern Territories) as having completely free word order. As such there is no evidence that the language is OV, and so it need not be a counterexample. Nevome (an Uto-Aztecan language of Northern Mexico) forms plurals by reduplication (Shaul 1986:42); it is unclear that such markers need to be treated as syntactic prefixes. Ngandi (another language of the Northern Territories) has unclear word order and noun class prefixes for masculine singular, feminine singular, masculine dual and plural (which includes feminine dual and mixed /masculine-plus-feminine dual; Heath 1978:35). Again, it is unclear whether such prefixes represent autonomous functional heads or are manifestations of φ-features of the noun. Tunen (a Bantoid language of Cameroon) also has fairly typical Bantu-style noun class prefixes. No information was available regarding the other languages, but again, no clear counterexamples to FOFC are found here.

In general, then, we can account for the cases of prefixation in OV languages without having to allow for FOFC violations, and so our general account holds. What is quite common in the languages discussed here, especially those with tense/aspect prefixes, appears to be partial movement of functional heads, or in some cases v/V, through the functional system. This clearly supports the overall thesis proposed here concerning the role of FOFC in the suffixing preference.

11.3.4 A Note on Infixing and Other Possibilities

With respect to infixatioin, Greenberg's ([1963]/2007) Universal 26 is relevant: "If a language has discontinuous affixes, it has either prefixing or suffixing or both." Given this, and given that the present approach to affixation only allows suffixation of X to Y (derived by movement of X to Y) or prefixation of Y to X (derived by lack of movement of X to Y, where X and Y are adjacent and Y is specified as a bound morpheme), I regard infixation as resulting from the combination of suffixing and prefixing. We have seen that the combination of prefixing and suffixing in a given system is fairly rare (see tables 11.1 and 11.2); this is presumably a subcase of the general infrequency of disharmonic types. We thus expect infixing to be rarer still, since, given present assumptions, it can only take place in a system that allows both suffixing and prefixing, and it requires both operations in the same derivation.

Let us consider what the possibilities of infixing are, in terms of our basic assumptions. Let us start from a structure with a lexical head V and two functional heads F and G, as in (21):

(21) $[_{GP}$ G $[_{FP}$ F $[_{VP}$ V...]]]

Infixing of F can be directly derived from this structure, simply by specifying both F and G as bound here. Infixing of G can only be derived by raising F, giving the derived structure in (22), where, all else being equal, F+G can be a prefix to V:

(22) $[_{GP} [_G$ F+G] $[_{FP}$ (F) $[_{VP}$ V...]]]

The otherwise analogous XP-movement operation is not available, since FP does not form a constituent without VP, and so FP cannot be fronted over G without V also being fronted. The comparative rarity of this construction must be due to (i) the rarity of incorporation of a functional head without prior incorporation of the relevant lexical head (this would also account for the rarity of the prefix-dominant systems of the Athapaskan type, if the analysis in section 11.3.3 is right; note that this is an example of what Abels and Neeleman (2012), following Cinque (2005a), call a "Universal 20 effect"—see chapter 8), and (ii) the need for G to be specified as both hosting incorporation of F and being bound to V. Other conceivable structures include those in (23):

(23) a. $[_F$ F+G] + V
    b. $[_F$ F + $[_G$ G+V]]

(23a), which could be seen as a FOFC violation (if V is the head of the whole complex and F the head of F+G) can only be derived by lowering and right-adjunction of G to F, and both of these operations are ruled out by our general assumptions. (23b) could only be derived by lowering of G to V, again an impossible operation.

Ambifixing can be derived by raising V to F and no further. Cases of this involving Tense and Aspect (where Tense = G and Aspect = F) are documented by Myler's (2009:13ff.) summary of Julien's (2002:330–331) database of tense/aspect systems; these have the structure G $[_{FP}$ $V+F]$. The structure $[_G$ $G+V]$ + F is impossible, since it would have to involve right-adjunction of V to G (and a violation of the Head Movement Constraint, although that in itself may not be problematic; see in particular Roberts 2010a:chap. 5).

The other conceivable case is $[[$ $F+V$ $]$ + $G]$. This is impossible as a case of head movement, since it would have to feature right-adjunction of V to F (the heads V and F do not otherwise form a constituent that excludes other elements). It is a possible order derived from FP-movement; however, it then violates FOFC.

A further case that might be relevant is the root-and-template morphology characteristic of the Semitic languages. As is well-known, in these languages roots are expressed as triconsonantal morphemes, and much inflectional and derivational information is encoded in vowel sequences interpolated among the consonants; there are also suffixes and prefixes. A very partial illustration of this kind of system is given in (24), showing some of the forms based on the root *ktb* 'write' in Arabic:

(24) a. katab   (perfective active)
     b. kutib   (perfective passive)
     c. aktub   (imperfective active)
     d. uktab   (imperfective passive)
     (Spencer 1991:135)

In Distributed Morphology terms, this might be handled by means of fusion of the consonantal root and the vocalic melody (Bert Vaux, pers. comm.), suggesting a syntactic derivation of these forms involving head movement of V through various clausal projections; in fact, there is good independent motivation for V-to-T movement in Arabic (Fassi-Fehri 1993:19–20, Shlonsky 1997:7–8).

Most Semitic languages, including all varieties of Arabic and Hebrew, are VO. However, there is a group of OV Semitic languages spoken in Ethiopia, including Tigrinya (Kogan 1997) and Tigré (Raz 1997). These languages clearly both have root-and-template morphology, with some prefixing (e.g., Tigré imperfect *te-*). Probably the best analysis, then, would be a combination of V-movement and "roll-up" movement of the remnant VP, and so on, although of course the details remain to be worked out.

11.3.5 Conclusion

In this section, I have shown how FOFC combines with the LCA to give an account of the suffixing preference in OV languages. Regarding VO languages, suffixation occurs almost at chance, reflecting the parametric options of suffixal realization of functional heads and incorporation (the latter being triggered by the former, as we saw).

One important consequence of this conclusion is that we have evidence that FOFC applies in morphology, which in turn supports the Single Engine Hypothesis; these conclusions concur with Myler's (2009).

One question remains open: can we find evidence that FOFC applies in the other major areas of morphology, derivation and compounding? This is the topic of the next section.

11.4 Derivation and Compounding

Concerning derivational morphology, Myler (2009:40–41) observes that FOFC comes very close to deriving the Right-hand Head Rule (RHR), originally proposed by Williams (1981b:248), which states that "[i]n morphology, we define the head of a morphologically complex word to be the right-hand member of that word." Myler points out that the RHR can be broken into two parts, as follows:

(25) a. Where suffixes appear, they project.
      b. Where prefixes appear, they do not project.
         (Myler 2009:40, (5))

Myler observes that, given the LCA, which requires all structures to be head-initial (and in Distributed Morphology this includes the internal structure of words), a suffix must trigger movement of its complement. In order for this to happen, the suffix must project. Prefixes, on the other hand, do not trigger movement of their complements. One way to ensure this is to treat them as nonprojecting. In this case, FOFC is derived. Myler concludes, "The RHR is thus reconceptualized as one of many strategies for avoiding the possibility of FOFC-violations" (2009:41).[7]

There are, however, many cases of derivational morphology that appear to violate FOFC. Nominals derived from denominal and deadjectival verbs, where the verbalizing morphology is a prefix, are a case in point:

(26) a. [N [V be [N head]] ing]
      b. [N [V en [A noble]] ment]

In these cases the prefix projects, converting the noun or adjective into a verb (although it does not trigger movement of its complement, and hence surfaces as a prefix). Further suffixation of the nominalizing morphology creates a structure that violates FOFC. Cases like (26) can be admitted if we allow for a general Category Proviso on FOFC, stating that the constraint only applies to heads of the same category, or in the same extended projection. In that case, since derivational morphology almost exclusively involves category change, FOFC will in general not apply in the case of derivation.

Turning to compounds, we can immediately observe that productive synthetic compounding in English obeys FOFC:[8]

(27) a. [$_N$ [[$_N$ can] [$_V$ open]] er]
b. [$_N$ [[$_N$ rocket] [$_N$ scient]] ist]
c. [$_A$ [[$_N$ ear] [$_V$ split]] ing]

The affixes characteristic of synthetic compounds are suffixes, and so the complement to this affix must be head-final, given FOFC. We observe that English, although of course a head-initial language in VP, shows head-final order in these compounds; this can be seen as a necessary FOFC-compliance strategy, in that VO order (*open-canner, etc.) would violate FOFC. Other types of verb-object compound, which lack a suffix, can show VO order: *pick-pocket*, *cut-purse*, and so on (although this is not obligatory: for example, *corkscrew*, *fly-spray*). Also, verb-object compounds in Romance languages, although less productive than English synthetic compounds, lack a suffix and show VO order: French *ouvre-boîte* 'open-can' ('can-opener'), *tue-mouches* 'kill-flies' ('fly-killer'), *tire-bouchon* 'pull-cork' ('corkscrew'); Italian *gira-dischi* 'turn-records' ('turntable'). Finally, we can observe that, in certain semantic fields, English features both compounds involving head-initial phrasal expressions and ones involving head-final compounds: for example, *history of science* and *rocket science*. Only the latter can enter into synthetic compounds, as Ackema and Neeleman (2004:164ff.) observe; this is a further FOFC effect. Note further the contrasts in (28), also attributable to FOFC playing a role in compounding:

(28) a. the boy has red hair → he is [red-hair]ed
b. the boy is red of hair → *he is [red of hair]ed
c. gold-mining → gold-mining expert
d. mining of gold → *mining of gold expert

It appears, then, that FOFC plays a role in compounding.[9]

We can in fact say a little more about how synthetic compounds like those in (27) are derived. Let us assume that sub-word-level roots may a lack a lexical specification (cf. Marantz 1997). Then *can*$_\emptyset$ and *open*$_\emptyset$ merge to form *{{open*$_\emptyset$}, {open$_\emptyset$,can$_\emptyset$}}*. Incorporation is possible here since neither head has any formal features and so their features are nondistinct from each other.[10]

This structure incorporates into $-er_N$, since its features (none) are properly included in those of $-er$ (N). And here N must project: the order inside the root conforms to FOFC. This account predicts that root compounds can have either order in a VO language (this is correct, as the above examples from English and Romance show), but FOFC would require head-final order in an OV language.

Veenstra (2006) gives examples of V-O-affix order in synthetic compounds in the Dutch-English-based creole Saramaccan:

(29) a. bébe-daán-ma   [Saramaccan]
       drink-rum-AFF
       'drunkard' (i.e., 'rum-drinker')
    b. séi-kónde-ma
       sell-country-AFF
       'traitor' (i.e.,'country-seller')
       (Veenstra 2006:203)

These would appear to pose a problem for FOFC, but Veenstra (2006:215) in fact argues (i) that the notional verb and its object in these compounds form a VP and (ii) that Saramaccan has a null nominalizing affix (for which he provides independent evidence), which he suggests can attach to the compound, with $-ma$ attaching outside it. So the structure of (29a) is as in (30):

(30) $[_N [_N [_{VP}$ bébe-daán$]$ $\varnothing]$ ma$]$

There is no FOFC violation here, as the zero affix and the VP are categorially distinct (and hence different extended projections). The structure of (30) is almost exactly analogous to that of English *pizza delivery-man*, which we can analyze as *$[_N [_N [\varnothing$ pizza deliver] y] man]*; here, there is no FOFC violation, as the compound is consistently head-final. The ill-formed English compound *deliver-pizza(-y) man* is ruled out because there is no VP inside the English compound; as suggested above, the *can-open* subpart of *can-opener* in English is formed from two category-neutral roots (which may even be freely ordered, given the existence of both VO and OV root compounds, as we saw). We can see that this cannot be a VP precisely because it can be "head-final" (i.e., display the order θ-assignee–θ-assigner); there is no motivation for positing that English verbs either allow noun incorporation or trigger complement-to-specifier movement.[11]

11.5 Conclusion

In this chapter, the main theoretical question has been the extent to which FOFC applies to word formation. We have seen clear evidence that it applies to inflection and compounding, though the situation regarding derivational morphology is unclear. These conclusions do not differ significantly from those of Myler (2009) and, as Myler notes, are consistent with the Single Engine Hypothesis for morphosyntax; it's syntax all the way down.

The main empirical issue has been accounting for Hawkins and Gilligan's (1988) suffixing preference. We saw that FOFC, combined with the LCA, achieves this. Furthermore, an argument based on the crosslinguistic suffixing vs. prefixing patterns in OV and VO languages showed that the affixal nature of heads plays a direct role in triggering head movement.

Notes

1. Apparently semi-apocryphal, as documented by the quotation investigators at http://quoteinvestigator.com/2015/03/02/eureka-funn.
2. With some partial predecessors, as discussed in chapter 4.

2 Empirical Evidence for the Final-over-Final Condition

1. "Aux" may be either an auxiliary or a verb capable of triggering clause union/restructuring. Following Cinque (2004), we take both types of element to instantiate clausal functional heads.
2. There are several other combinations that are somewhat indeterminate in relation to present concerns. For example, Dryer (2015b) defines a "mixed" category for subordinators, which includes the combination of initial and final, as well as clause-internal (often second position) and suffixal. WALS lists 31 VO languages with mixed subordinators, and clearly these need to be investigated. Furthermore, some languages are taken to have no dominant order among OV and VO: 4 of these have mixed subordinators, 3 have suffixal subordinators, and 2 have final subordinators. The numbers are small in every case, but again these languages should be investigated more closely.
3. In the SSWL database (Syntactic Structures of the World's Languages; http://sswl. railsplayground.net/), there are as many as 14 languages with VO as a possible order and with (some) clause-final complementizers, as against 124 with VO but no clause-final complementizers. Of those 14, however, 9 also have OV order. The claim we make, following Biberauer, Newton, and Sheehan (2009a,b), Biberauer, Sheehan, and Newton (2010), and Biberauer, Holmberg, and Roberts (2014), is specifically that embedded verbal clauses cannot have a final subordinating complementizer; this is the FOFC-violating configuration. We do not claim that the grammar of a language could not allow VO order and have clause-final subordinating complementizers; the claim is that they cannot be combined in the same construction. We thus predict that in those 14 languages either the final complementizers are not subordinating complementizers of verbal clauses, or, if they are, the clauses they head do not have VO order. For example, Hungarian is one of the 14 languages, but its only final complementizer is a

question particle (in fact, a suffix on the verb), not a subordinating complementizer (see SSWL). Another of the 14 languages is Shupamem, a rigid VO language. It has a final complementizer only in relatives and clefts (see SSWL). Also among these languages is Titan, another rigid VO language with a final complementizer, which, however, is only found in counterfactual and conditional clauses, typically as an optional element (Bowern 2011:86–87, 147–148), and which may conceivably be an adverb. Unfortunately, information about the more precise nature of the final complementizers cannot be had from SSWL (at the time of writing), except in the few cases where a comment is added to that effect.

4. Question particles initially also appear to be good candidates for C-elements. As shown by Dryer (2015g) and discussed by Bailey (2012) and Biberauer, Holmberg, and Roberts (2014), VO languages quite readily allow final Q-particles. This case will be considered, along with clausal force-related particles more generally, in chapter 9.

5. See also Sigurðsson 1988, discussed in Holmberg 2000a, for the same point in relation to Scandinavian.

6. It should be emphasized that the overall change from head-initial to head-final or vice versa is not inevitable once the initial step is taken. The intention here is not to reintroduce the notion of typological drift, justly criticized in particular by Lightfoot (1979). What we are stating here is weaker: if there is an overall change from head-final to head-initial (or vice versa), the change must follow the pathways indicated here.

7. If FOFC violations are ruled out by Universal Grammar, as just suggested in the text, we would not expect them to occur at all in child language. Forms like *dry-hairer* would then be due to misanalysis of the word as, say, being headed by *hair*, which makes little sense semantically, explaining why such forms are rare and short-lived.

3   Harmony, Symmetry, and Dominance in Word Order Universals

1. The page numbers refer to the reprinted version of the paper in Roberts 2007a.

2. Greenberg included order of Noun and Adjective as a further harmonic dyad here, but I omit this since Dryer (1992) has demonstrated that these orders do not genuinely correlate with the others; this conclusion was instead an effect of the sample of languages Greenberg used.

3. The numbers of SV languages only sum to 801 as there is a residue of SV languages that either lack adpositions or for which the relevant data are unavailable.

4. If subjects and possessors occupy specifier positions, one could be tempted to parameterize specifier-X′ order. However, specifier-final order, giving VS and NG, would have to be harmonic with head-initial, which is difficult to state naturally in X-bar theory terms. Moreover, VSO order remains a problem. Partly for these reasons, these orders are usually analyzed in terms of V(P)-movement over the subject and N(P)-movement over the possessor (see in particular McCloskey 1996 and Carnie and Guilfoyle 2001 on VSO, and Bernstein 1991, Longobardi 1994, 1996, and Shlonsky 2004 on N(P)-movement to D). As Kayne (1994, 2010a) points out, there is a general dearth of evidence for rightward specifiers, notably in the crosslinguistic absence of unbounded *wh*-movement to the right and "reverse V2" (verb second-to-last). Therefore, I do not propose a parameterization of the order of specifier and X′, taking it to

be universally specifier-left. This of course raises a conceptual question regarding the Head Parameter: why should the order of head and complement be parameterized, but not that of specifier and X'? See Richards 2004 for a possible solution.

5. Dryer (1992:116) also formulates his Branching Direction Theory as a preference.

6. At the deepest level here, inside NP, I have followed Kayne (1994) for purely expository purposes in taking NP to be a nonbranching node. Given standard definitions of c-command relying on a "branching-node" clause, *man* symmetrically c-commands *the* here, making linearization of these two terminals impossible. If we adopt bare phrase structure, there will be no distinction between the nodes labeled N and NP here, giving rise to the same problem. This is a well-known problem if one attempts to combine the LCA with bare phrase structure; see Chomsky 1995 for discussion. One possibility, essentially that suggested by Chomsky, is that there is at least one silent category inside NP (concretely, there may be a silent n head of nP, taking NP as its complement; see chapter 8). Silent categories do not have to be linearized and so do not give rise to this problem. There may therefore always be a silent category at the deepest branch, as Chomsky suggests; see Watumull 2010 for a very interesting implementation of this idea in the context of a general formal theory of Merge.

7. The restatement of this universal in Greenberg's appendix III omits reference to precedence.

8. Latin *-que* and its counterparts elsewhere in the older Indo-European languages may be an exception to this; see Ledgeway 2012.

4 The Final-over-Final Condition and Linearization in Generative Grammar

1. C-command can be defined in terms of dominance (or containment) and sisterhood: α c-commands β if and only if β is α's sister, or β is dominated by γ that is α's sister (Chomsky 2000), implying that the primitive structural relations are dominance/containment and sisterhood.

2. Typically, complements and adjuncts occur on the same side of the head, although there are also many counterexamples (see Dryer 1992). This is consistent with the idea that there is one parameter for head and dependent, where complements and adjuncts are two types of dependents.

3. Chomsky (2000) argued that adjunction was a different type of Merge, pair-Merge, an inherently asymmetric process forming ordered pairs. While this idea has hardly been developed since, the notion that Merge is an inherently asymmetric process always building ordered pairs has been articulated in work by Jan-Wouter Zwart (see Zwart 2011b and the text below).

4. There is also lexical variation. Clearly, not all languages have a word for, say, *gooseberry* (if the speakers have never encountered or heard of gooseberries). More interestingly, not all languages have a word for *religion* (Boyer 2001), and not all languages have a definite article. A radical view is that all languages have a definite article and possibly, in some sense, words for *gooseberry* and *religion* as well, but these items happen not to have a pronounced form in some languages; see Ramchand and Svenonius 2008 for discussion (the authors do not take that position).

5. The notion of c-command assumed by Kayne is as follows (Kayne 1994:16):

(i) X c-commands Y iff *X and Y are categories* and X excludes Y and every category that dominates X dominates Y.

The notion "category" is crucial: while X^0 and XP are categories, X'-level phrases count not as categories but as segments. This means that an X'-phrase does not c-command its sister YP, the specifier (or adjunct), while the sister YP does c-command X'. This ensures asymmetric c-command between a specifier (or adjunct) and its sister, hence ensures that the specifier (or adjunct) necessarily precedes (the constituents of) its sister.

6. This is not to say that I concur with the view that labeling is required just to satisfy the LCA; labeling is crucial for the interpretation of any complex expression at LF as well (the semantic difference between, for example, *wallpaper* and *paper wall* is a difference in headedness, nothing else) and arguably is required for Merge to operate (i.e., if we reject Collins's (2002) label-free syntax and assume that c-selection requires labels). See also Chomsky 2013 and Sheehan 2013b.

7. See Sheehan 2013b for a summary of further symmetry problems raised by BPS.

8. In bottom-up derivational terms, building a nonbranching tree such as the NP in (8) requires an operation Grow or Sprout, whereby N grows into an NP; but the only structure-building operation in BPS is Merge.

9. Haider (2005, 2012) argues that there is a third type of language alongside VO and OV languages, namely, those that are underspecified for licensing direction and therefore allow both VO and OV orders, employed in a systematic fashion.

10. Svenonius (2006) suggests a way to reconcile these two hypotheses: the surface adjacency is not an output condition but a cue in the L1 acquisition of grammar (on "cues," see Lightfoot 1999) leading the learner to a particular analysis, which in Svenonius's terms is that there is an abstract head in the structure triggering movement. For example, in (i) (which would be the derivation of (18c)) that head would be above Aux, triggering movement of the complement of Aux.

(ii) F [$_{AuxP}$ Aux [$_{VP}$ O [$_{V'}$ V $\langle$O$\rangle$]]] $\rightarrow$ [$_{FP}$ [$_{VP}$ O [$_{V'}$ V $\langle$O$\rangle$]] [F [$_{AuxP}$ Aux $\langle$VP$\rangle$]]]

11. As argued by Abels (2003), if movement is triggered by the need to check a feature under locality, as in standard versions of Minimalist syntactic theory, then movement from complement to specifier cannot occur, since that would move a constituent from the most local relation possible (sisterhood) to a less local relation (specifier-head). However, in BHR 2014 the movement in question is not triggered by the need to check a feature. The only effect it has is to change the c-command relation between the head and its dependent, which in turn results in head-final order.

12. A more neutral definition is "the sister YP of X^0 undergoes the minimal movement allowed by UG required to place XP in a position where YP asymmetrically c-commands X^0." This definition is neutral between (28b), assuming movement from Comp,X^0 to Spec,XP, and a theory of phrase structure where such a movement is ruled out as being "too local" (see note 11).

13. The selection feature could be construed as an unvalued feature, being assigned a value by the complement (thus, categorial selection would be viewed as a special case of Agree; Chomsky 2001). If so, the value assigned would not be the categorial value

(since that is what is selected for), but the "value" of the root. In that way, the identity of the root of L would be carried along to the highest head in the extended projection of L.

14. As discussed by Sheehan (2013b), this is not an innocuous simplification: including the subject means allowing multiple specifiers, excluded by the standard formulation of the LCA in Kayne 1994, which relies on a category-based definition of c-command.

15. It is interesting to consider how a theory such as Haider's (2000), where head-final order is basic and head-initial order invariably involves head movement (see section 4.6), can deal with FOFC. In Haider's theory, the Head Parameter is expressed as a difference in "licensing direction": heads license complements to the right or to the left. Licensing to the left is the less marked option, being harmonic with the universal branching direction. Left-licensing can proceed in principle without any movement: the head licenses its sister complement, and the X'-projection of the head licenses *its* sister, the specifier or adjunct. If a head licenses to the right, on the other hand, it must move to a position where it c-commands the complement (or specifier or adjunct). The right-licensing property of a head is thus effectively a head movement–triggering feature (symbolized here by [→]). The left-licensing property is unmarked. (i) represents the base-generated structure of the FOFC-violating configuration:

(i) [$_{AuxP}$ [$_{VP}$ O V] Aux]
          [→]   A

The feature [→] triggers head movement of V, forming a VP-shell on top of VP, giving the typical FOFC-violating order (unless O moves even higher). In principle, a version of BHR's theory could be devised such that the marked [→] would be forced to "spread" up the tree, to the highest terminal node in the extended projection (it would have to be forced to spread, not just allowed to, as in BHR's system). The unmarked left-licensing property would not need to spread, which follows if it is the default, an effect of the absence of a directional feature. The desired outcome would result: wherever [→] was introduced in the tree, triggering head movement and thus head-initial order, any higher node in the spine of the extended projection would also be head-initial.

16. Note that unlike earlier versions of the theory (Biberauer, Holmberg, and Roberts 2007, 2008a,b), BHR's (2014) theory can accommodate the case of FOFC as an effect of adjunction. The L-movement-triggering feature triggers movement of the sister of L regardless of whether it is a selected complement or a nonselected adjunct.

17. The notion of a "cartographic field" can now be defined as a sequence of functional heads with the same set of formal features—more formally, the functional sequence $\langle F_1...F_n \rangle$ such that all F_j have identical formal features. See Roberts 2010a for the proposal that it is actually semantic features that distinguish, say, the sequence of aspectual heads that Cinque (1999) argues constitute the lower part of the clausal functional sequence. Similarly, we can define the notion of extended projection as follows: α and β form an extended projection where α c-selects β and α and β are nondistinct in lexical categorial features.

18. This can be stated, technically, by treating the selecting feature as uninterpretable; hence, v has an uninterpretable V-feature, while V has an interpretable one, and so on. More precisely, v has an uninterpretable Categorial feature, [Cat:__], which is valued

in the standard way by copying V's value for Cat. Interestingly, this appears to invert the more common view originating in Marantz 1997 that v "categorizes" the acategorial lexical root. But it does not really, since we can still assume that roots are acategorial and that each lexical head has the form [$_{Cat}$ Root Cat], quite visible in many languages although in English Cat is usually phonologically null. It may be the copying of this categorial feature that makes the fundamental difference between the two types of extended projection, entailing a different kind of external argument, different substantive features on the higher heads, and so on.

19. Compare (19) in section 4.8. In that theory, selection-driven incorporation is obligatory, but can be overt or covert.

20. This is a crucial difference between the theory advanced here and that of Holmberg (2000a) or BHR: there is no XP-movement as such from complement position of a head H to the specifier position of H. What there is, is incorporation of the head of XP into H, with pied-piping of the rest of XP as an option subject to parametric variation, where the pied-piped phrase ends up as the specifier of H.

21. The big advantage of this theory over Holmberg's (2000a), reviewed in section 4.8, is that the dubious condition (22) is not required. Adjacency between the two heads in a head-final configuration is an automatic consequence of incorporation.

5 The Final-over-Final Condition and Processing

1. The fact that Hawkins (2013) rejects FOFC as an empirical generalization is thus surprising, in one sense, and marks a change between Hawkins 1994 and Hawkins 2004. In personal communication, Hawkins notes that his 2004 approach could explain the asymmetry only if there were some preference for mother attachment over daughter attachment. Interestingly, this is reminiscent of the core idea behind the LCA whereby there is a requirement for higher categories to precede lower ones. See Walkden 2009 for further discussion of Hawkins 2004 in relation to FOFC.

2. Hawkins rejects the DP Hypothesis and uses NPs, and I follow his usage here for consistency.3. As far as I can see, Hawkins gives no definition of what a word is and instead uses the term *word* in an informal sense. This may of course prove problematic, especially if Julien (2002) is right and words have no real syntactic status. See also chapter 11 for discussion of FOFC effects below the word level, which supports Julien's general approach. Recall, though, that the technical statement of Hawkins's principle is in terms of ICs-to-non-ICs, so this problem may not be all that serious. Moreover, one might plausibly reformulate Hawkins's proposal, substituting *morpheme* for *word*. As shown in section 5.5, this may well be necessary on empirical grounds.

4. DP- and PP-complements to V are beyond the remit of FOFC for Biberauer, Holmberg, and Roberts (2008a,b, 2014) because of a category or extended-projection proviso. Nonetheless, as discussed below, there is a sense in which a kind of FOFC asymmetry is observed with PP-complements of V, suggesting that PPs should perhaps not be ruled out of FOFC. There is also a potential FOFC effect between V and truncated nominal NumP-complements, resulting in extraposition (see Sheehan 2011). See also chapter 4.

5. I am not concerned here with conceptual objections to Hawkins's general approach, but rather with teasing out its empirical predictions. For a conceptual critique of the PGCH, see Mobbs 2008.

6. See Carstens 2013 for an implementation of a very similar idea.

7. It is not totally clear how Agree can mediate extraposition. If the assumption is that all Ā-movements are licensed by Agree and extraposition is an Ā-movement, then the problem remains that the head "attracting" the extraposed phrase (v in (i)) can be seen to be initial in languages like English, but the Right Roof Constraint holds nonetheless:

(i)   I [$_{vP}$ met a man t yesterday] [who I used to know].

Even if the specifier of v is to the right, the Agree dependency is presumably between v and the trace and is hence a forward dependency.

8. For this reason, there are conceptual as well as technical issues with reducing extraposition to an Agree relation: the dependency goes in the wrong direction, as a trace is dependent on its filler, not vice versa.

9. Hawkins uses the label *Art* rather than *Det*.

10. Heaviness equates to number of words for the purposes of online reordering processes. According to the PGCH, though, grammars can develop categorical rules stemming from heaviness tendencies. Thus, the fact that PP always contains DP makes PP heavier than DP in general terms, even though both can have different heaviness values in different contexts. For this reason, an extraposition rule might be grammaticalized to apply only to PP and not to DP regardless of their relative online heaviness.

11. Following Kandybowicz and Baker's (2003) analysis of Nupe, we might take the position of PP as evidence that these languages are basically head-initial, with DP-V order derived via A-movement of DP objects.

12. The vast majority of the examples show PPs to be postverbal, as in (i):

(i)   ngohi-o to-modeke de   o-Matias   [Tobelo]
      I-also 1-agree PREP NM-Matias
      'I also agreed with Matias.'
      (Holton 2003:30)

However, Holton (2003:55) explicitly states that oblique arguments can occur "either before or after the verb." Unfortunately, he uses the term *oblique arguments* to refer to both PPs and DPs marked with a locative or directional case suffix. The only example he gives with PP-V order involves an instrumental PP that may be a topic in the CP layer:

(ii)   de   ma-kakatama n-a-lye-ino   [Tobelo]
       PREP NM-tongs   2-3-roll-ALL
       'Roll it up with the tongs.'
       (Holton 2003:55)

In the absence of further data, it is impossible to say for certain whether Tobelo PPs adhere to FOFC or not.

13. Ultimately, this might also shed light on the reason why final Q is so frequent in VO languages (see Dryer 2015e,g).

14. Many thanks to Bert Vaux and Francis Nolan for useful discussion of the issues in this short section. They should, of course, not be taken to endorse any of what follows.

15. Francis Nolan (pers. comm.) notes that there are empirical problems with Onset Maximization in its strongest form, even in English.

6   The Final-over-Final Condition and Adverbs

1. Biberauer, Holmberg, and Roberts (2008a,b) also discuss English prenominal APs, which appear to display a FOFC effect. These kinds of examples are discussed at length in chapter 7:

(i)   *John is a [$_{YP}$ [$_{AP}$ proud of his son] man].

2. It has subsequently come to light that Finnish does allow certain adverbs (including at least 'here' and 'there') to interrupt V-Aux sequences, where the verb is focused and stressed and the adverb unstressed:

(i)   Milloin minä laulanut täällä olisin?   [Finnish]
      when   I   sung   here would.have
      'When would I have sung here?'
      (Anders Holmberg, pers. comm.)

Unstressed pronominal complements can also occur in the same position:

(ii) Kyllä minä lukenut sen olen.   [Finnish]
      PART I   read   it   have
      'I have indeed read it.'
      (Anders Holmberg, pers. comm.)

These examples pose a potential problem for all existing accounts of FOFC. In chapter 10, it is suggested, however, that examples like (ii) involve separate movement of the (remnant) VP and the object.

3. As we will see, though, Hindi actually also allows V-O-Aux as a marked order, suggesting that the grammaticality of (4) might not be sufficient to indicate that FOFC is a generalization only about complementation.

4. Thanks to Yalda Kazemi Najafabadi for Persian judgments and Ali Algryani for Libyan Arabic judgments.

5. The Corpus del Español contains no examples of *ha siempre* + regular past participle, *ha ya* ('already') + regular past participle, or *ha *mente* (adverb ending in -*mente*) + regular past participle from the 20th century onward, but many genuine examples from the 13th to the 19th century. So this restriction appears to be fairly recent. These facts echo Ojea López's (1994:409) claim that examples where adverbs intervene between *haber* and the past participle "eran más frequentes en otras etapas de la lengua" ('were more frequent in other stages of the language').

6. Basque (like Turkish) places short manner adverbs like *gogor* 'hard' immediately preceding and adjacent to the verb (Arregui 2002, citing Elordieta 2001):

(i) Athletic Real Madriden   kontra **gogor** jolasten dau.   [Basque]
    Athletic Real Madrid.GEN against hard   play.IMP AUX.PRES
    'Athletic plays hard against Real Madrid.'
    (Arregui 2002:128)

Therefore, these adverbs cannot occur between V and a following Aux for independent reasons.

7. Consider also Pintzuk's (2005:121) observation that no constituent (argument or adjunct) can intervene between V and Aux in V-Aux orders in Old English. Perhaps relevant, though, is Pintzuk's (2005:121) other observation that the three attested examples of the V-X-Aux orders involve a PP or an adverb rather than a DP-complement.

8. Following Aboh (2004), this is sometimes known as *snowballing movement*.

9. In more recent work, Cinque has rejected these distinctions and now assumes that all head-finality is derived via snowballing (see Cinque 2005a, 2010, 2013).

10. Authors differ in capitalizing or not capitalizing proper names in Hindi examples. Here, we use capital letters in Hindi examples only to represent retroflex consonants.

11. Note that a similar set of adverbials fails to count for V2 (verb-second) in certain Germanic languages (Swedish *bara* 'only', *nästan* 'nearly', *till och med* 'even', *helt enkelt* 'simply'; Nilsen 2003, Holmberg 2015).

12. There are certain restrictions on the distribution of *bhii*, though. The particle *bhii* cannot intervene between the lexical verb and the future marker or between the progressive marker and the verb *hona* 'be' (Koul 2008:144):

(i) *vah khaa rahaa **bhii** hai.   [Hindi]
    he eat   PROG also is

13. A potential exception to this comes from instances where only the verb appears to be modified and fronted:

(i) khaataa **to** raam roTii thaa.   [Hindi]
    eat.MSG TO Ram bread was.3MSG
    'Ram was eating bread.'
    (Mahajan (1989:226)

This could potentially be remnant VP-fronting, given that Hindi allows scrambling.

14. This issue raises some challenges for the account of FOFC pursued by Biberauer, Holmberg, and Roberts (2014) as, for their account of the ban on V-O-Aux to go through, it must crucially be the case that auxiliary verbs are never lexical heads originating their own extended projection.

15. The only example of an adverb that Mahajan (1989) gives is *roz*, which he glosses 'every day'. Other adverbs in Hindi occur in preverbal positions. The status of *roz* requires further investigation.

16. Thanks to Pallavi Worah for Hindi judgments and discussion.17. Dwivedi (1991) gives further evidence from an Eastern dialect of Hindi spoken in Uttar Pradesh in which negation appears to incorporate into the verbal cluster. As it is not clear how

general these facts are, though, this does not imply that negation always undergoes head movement to T in Hindi.

18. Following Mahajan (1990b), it is generally accepted that Hindi NPIs are licensed not at S-Structure but at LF, meaning that no surface c-command is required between sentential negation and an NPI. Thus, an NPI-containing direct object need not be in the surface scope of negation here.

19. I assume that the habitual inflection on V in (31) is equal in status to the -*ing* on a progressive form in English.

20. But see Roberts (2010a:chap. 5) on the Head Movement Constraint.

21. This example seems to be wrongly translated as 'Ram did not (use to) eat vegetables' in Mahajan (1990b:338).

22. I have added glosses to these examples.

23. The Basque examples are of a different nature and are considered below.

24. A potential confounding factor is that -*mente* is arguably a separate word in Modern Spanish, as illustrated by the fact that it can modify coordinated adjectives:

(i) Subió   la   escalera   [triste y   lenta]mente.   [Spanish]
     climbed the stairway   sad   and slowly
     'He/She climbed the stairs sadly and slowly.'

Perhaps for this reason, -*mente* adverbs qualify as "heavy" (though left-branching) and can be extraposed. In fact, adverbs without -*mente* cannot appear in this post-PP/DP position:

(ii) *Habló con los chicos bajo.   [Spanish]
      spoke with the boys   low

(iii) Habló bajo con los chicos.   [Spanish]
      spoke low with the boys
      'He/She spoke quietly with the boys.'

A similar case could be made for French -*ment* adverbs. Note that time adverbials such as *ayer/hier* 'yesterday' can also appear in a post-PP/DP position, but these may perhaps be concealed PPs.

25. As is well-known, predicates behave differently from arguments when moved, so many of the usual diagnostics for Ā-movement are unavailable (see Huang 1993).

26. If auxiliaries are not part of the same extended projection as the verb, then the lack of V-O-Aux structures cannot be a FOFC effect.

27. As is also well-known, the adjacency condition fails to hold in Romance; this is often attributed to the fact that English, unlike Romance, lacks verb movement. The same effect obtains, however, if verb movement in Romance targets a higher position than in English, raising past the Adv_1 position.

7   The Final-over-Final Condition and the Head-Final Filter

1. A plausibly related phenomenon is the class of adjectives that derive historically from prepositional phrases and cannot surface prenominally (e.g., *asleep, aslant, ajar,*

atilt). Larson and Marušič (2004:270n2) propose that *a-* is still a head in such examples, meaning they have the same status as (7e).

2. This is not universally accepted, though. See Abney 1987 and Kennedy 1999 for analyses claiming that the CP and the Deg head do not form a constituent.

3. Thus, *as* requires an *as*-clause and *too* requires a nonfinite clause, whereas *-er* requires a *than*-clause.

4. However, as Grosu, Horvath, and Trugman (2007) also note, Romanian displays a mixed behavior, allowing violations of the HFF only in comparatives. Grosu and Horvath (2006) propose that atomization is possible in such contexts, but this is little more than a description of the facts.

5. We will return to other compliance strategies in section 7.3.2.

6. There are problems, also, with postulating rightward quantifier raising (see Sheehan 2011 for discussion and an alternative analysis of extraposition).

7. Interestingly, *tough*-adjectives do permit apparent surface violations of the HFF in restricted contexts, a point to which we will return in section 7.4.1:

(i) a. an easy-to-understand book
   b. a hard-to-refute argument
   c. some difficult-to-reach places

Moreover, there appear to be several classes of adjectives with distinct word order possibilities (see O'Flynn 2008, 2009 for a lengthy description). I put these additional complications to one side for reasons of space.

8. Actually, as Fleisher (2008) notes, citing Berman 1974, there are some surprising differences between *tough*-constructions and *tough*-nuts, notably regarding the thematic status of overt *for*-arguments:

(i) a. This is a tough building for there to be a riot in.
   b. July is an unusual month for it to snow (in).
   c. *This building is tough for there to be a riot in.
   d. *July is unusual for it to snow (in).

Fleisher concludes from this that whereas *for*-arguments are selected by the *tough*-adjective in *tough*-constructions, they are contained in CP in *tough*-nuts. In other respects, though, *tough*-nuts share many properties with *tough*-constructions.

Fleisher (2011) further discusses a superficially similar construction, which he calls the *nominal attributive-with-infinitive construction* (nominal AIC):

(ii) a. *Middlemarch* is a long book to assign.
    b. Bob is a short guy for the Lakers to draft.
       (Fleisher 2011:342)

On the surface, the AIC might be viewed as a further example of the HFF in action. Fleisher argues at length, however, that this construction has a wholly distinct structure, resulting from a nonfinite relative clause. Whereas only a limited class of adjectives can surface in *tough*-nut constructions (the same ones that can surface in clausal *tough*-constructions), many more adjectives can participate in nominal AICs. There are thus no paraphrases of (iia) equivalent to (iiia,b):

(iii) a. *It is long to assign *Middlemarch*.
    b. **Middlemarch* is long to assign.

While I do not find (iiib) fully ungrammatical, I agree that it is degraded compared with (iia). Fleisher (2011) argues convincingly that the CP in nominal AICs is a nonfinite relative clause rather than a complement of the adjective. This accounts for the fact that not all adjectives participating in this construction can select a clausal complement, as well as the fact that nominal AICs can only surface in predicative positions, like other nominals bearing nonfinite relatives.

9. Interestingly, the opposite possibility—that N is the complement of Adj—*has* been pursued, notably by Abney (1987). We will return in section 7.5.1 to this proposal and the problems it faces, but note immediately that under Abney's proposal, the HFF is *not* a FOFC effect, but a direct consequence of the fact that Adj can take only one complement (see Svenonius 1994 and section 7.5.1 for a critical discussion).

This is not to say that AdjPs have not been analyzed as *complements*. Under Kayne's (1994) influential analysis of relative clauses, certain kinds of intersective adjectival modifiers (reduced and full relatives) are taken to be complements of D. See section 7.5.4 for arguments supporting this approach and a demonstration that it serves to make the HFF a FOFC effect.

10. Consider, for example, adjectives functioning as secondary predications, which *are* obligatory in certain contexts:

(i)   John sneezed himself *(better).

11. But see Sheehan 2011, citing Schütze 1995, for some complications regarding the *one*-replacement test as a test for complementhood.

12. *Proud* is not actually the best adjective in these constructions despite its ubiquitous use to illustrate the HFF. Unlike other adjectives, it is not very good as a postnominal restrictive modifier:

(i)   ?The man proud of his son asked for him to be promoted.

(ii)   The man annoyed with the service asked for a refund.

This seems to be a semantic effect rather than a syntactic one, as the (in)definiteness of the DP also plays a role. This is possibly because modifiers in this postnominal position have a restrictive reading (without comma intonation) and there is a general assumption that all men are proud of their sons. Other AdjPs, which do not suffer from this drawback, are less awkward with *one*-replacement:

(iii)   Mary saw a customer pleased with his meal as well as one annoyed at the delay.

13. While this diagnostic seems to be a sufficient condition for adjuncthood, it is clearly not a necessary condition, given the existence of nonintersective adjectives such as *former*, to which we will return in section 7.4.3.

14. Romanian appears to permit violations of the HFF in comparative constructions, for unclear reasons.

15. In fact, as discussed in section 7.4.2, Bosnian/Croatian/Serbian and Slovene are subject to the HFF in a weaker form.

16. Thanks to Yalda Kazemi Najafabadi for all Persian judgments.

17. Thanks to Nino Nikolovski for the Macedonian judgments.

18. This is difficult to test in Dutch and German for independent reasons.

19. Thanks to Moreno Mitrović (Slovene and Bosnian/Croatian/Serbian) and Boban Arsenijević (Bosnian/Croatian/Serbian) for judgments.

20. The reason why PPs remain immune to FOFC in Germanic and Slavic remains opaque, however.

21. González Escribano (2005) also discusses certain marginal cases where it is unclear if the PPs in question are complements or adjuncts:

(i) a. ?a foolish man about money matters
    b. ?a fussy man about wine
    c. ?an invisible process to the naked eye
    d. ?a kind man to strangers
    e. ?a loyal soldier to his queen
    f. ?a particular man about food
    (González Escribano 2005:589)

He posits a processing explanation for the virtual acceptability of such examples, whereby the PPs in question are analyzed online as complements of N rather than A.

22. Thanks to Anders Holmberg (Swedish), Jenneke van der Wal (Dutch), Theresa Biberauer (Afrikaans), and Ulrich Reichard (German) for help with the data. Note that this strategy is slightly marked in German and Afrikaans.

23. Actually, the adjectives *boa/bom* 'good' and *mau/má* 'bad' also marginally allow PP-extraposition of the complements:

(i) ?uma boa aluna   a matemática   [Portuguese]
    a   good student at math
    'a student good at math'

This is a very restricted phenomenon, however, as extraposition is not possible with the PP-complements of *orgulhosa/o* 'proud', *chateada/o* 'annoyed', *farta/o* 'tired', *satisfeita/o* 'satisfied'.

24. This is a fatal flaw in Abney's (1987) account of the HFF, as discussed in section 7.5.1.

25. Abeillé and Godard (2000) note that certain Adv-Adj modifiers are also blocked in the preverbal position in French:

(i) *une politiquement importante décision   [French]
    'a politically important decision'

There must, therefore, be additional constraints on adjectival modification in French.

26. Note that in Turkish all adjectival modifiers of NP precede the indefinite article (see Tat 2010 for an account of this observation based on Kayne 1994).

27. In fact, as Larson and Takahashi (2007) show, prenominal relative clauses in head-final languages behave unlike postnominal relative clauses and like prenominal AdjPs in requiring a strict ordering, with direct (individual-level) modifiers occurring closer to N than indirect (stage-level) modifiers:

(i) a. [Watashi-ga kinoo   atta] [tabako-o   suu]   hito-wa   [Japanese]
        [1SG-NOM   yesterday met]   [tobacco-ACC inhale] person-TOP
        Tanaka-san desu.
        Tanaka-TOP COP
        'The person who smokes who I met yesterday is Miss Tanaka.'
    b. ?*[Tabako-o suu] [watashi-ga kinoo atta] hito-wa Tanaka-san desu.
        (Larson and Takahashi 2007:103)

(ii) a. the nonvisible visible stars (stage-level > individual-level)
     b. #the visible nonvisible stars (individual-level > stage-level)
         (Larson and Takahashi 2007:111)

In English, the strict ordering between stage-level and individual-level modifiers does not apply to postnominal relative clauses. This follows if Japanese relative clauses can occupy the specifier positions of dedicated functional projections in the extended nominal field. In languages with right-branching relative clauses, this will be blocked by the HFF.

28. Thanks to Makiko Mukai for the Japanese judgments.

29. Van Riemsdijk (2001) discusses other apparent counterexamples involving a superficially right-branching structure, but in which the rightmost Adj is semantically the head of AdjP:

(i)   a close to trivial matter

(ii) a far from trivial matter

These seem to be the adjectival equivalent of "measure" nouns, which, contrary to appearances, are not the heads of the DPs in which they are contained:

(iii) A load of people are/*is waiting outside.

They do not, therefore, represent robust counterexamples to the HFF.

30. A crucial difference between Bosnian/Croatian/Serbian and Slovene and Polish/Bulgarian, though, is that in the former languages HFF-violating orders are always highly marginal and significantly worse than other potential orders. From a sampling perspective, note that all of the languages that apparently fail to adhere to the HFF are either Slavic or from the Balkan Sprachbund, meaning that on a typological scale the scope of the counterexamples is quite limited (more so, it must be noted, than the scope of the languages adhering to the HFF).

31. Thanks to Malgorzata Krzek for Polish judgments.

32. Thanks also to Dimitris Michelidoukakis for discussion of the Greek data.

33. Giuliana Giusti (pers. comm.) notes that not all analyses of enclitic determiners posit movement. While Dimitrova-Vulchanova and Giusti (1998) give strong evidence against N-to-D movement, however, they fail to give compelling evidence against phrasal movement, so in the absence of evidence to the contrary, I tentatively pursue the idea that movement is nonetheless involved.

34. The debate over the relative merits of parameterizing nominal denotation and thus the presence of D is well-rehearsed. Some conceptual problems with Abney's general approach are discussed by Svenonius (1994) and Pereltsvaig (2007).

35. In this chapter, the discussion is limited to modification within DP. The possibility remains, however, that the same contrast exists in the clausal domain, giving rise to intersective vs. nonintersective readings. Moreover, as Emonds (1976) and Haider (2004) note, some version of the HFF is also observed in the clausal domain (see De Clercq, Haegeman, and Lohndal 2011) for recent discussion). I put this matter to one side here for reasons of space (see also Larson 1998).

36. There is disagreement in the literature about whether direct modification gives rise to ambiguity or only to a nonintersective reading. This stems from the fact that many adjectives can participate in both kinds of modification. Cinque (2010) advocates the stronger position whereby there is a closer syntax-semantics mapping and direct modification always gives rise to a nonintersective reading.

37. Not all languages have both kinds of modification, though. Cinque (2010:chap. 3) cites Slave (Athapaskan), Lango, Hixkaryana, and Tiriyó as languages lacking direct modification, citing Baker (2003:207), Noonan (1992:103), and Dixon (2004:28–29), respectively. He also discusses Yoruba and Gbaya Mbodómó (Niger-Congo) as languages lacking indirect modification, citing Ajíbóyè (2001:6) and Boyd (1997:sec. 3.1.3), respectively.

38. Reichard (2013) proposes that the intersective reading observed with relative clauses follows from the phasal architecture.

39. Cinque (2010) further assumes that relative clauses are also externally merged as specifiers, but I adopt the more conservative view that they are complements of D, as per Kayne (1994).

40. Cinque (2010), citing Tallerman (1998), does mention a few potential examples, but these all plausibly involve idioms or parenthesis:

(i)   I feel the most utter fool.

(ii) The main point in principle is that …

8   The Final-over-Final Condition in DP: Universal 20 and the Nature of Demonstratives

1. In section 8.6, I fully integrate AP into my proposals and compare my approach systematically both with Cinque's and with Abels and Neeleman's (2012), also taking into account the implications of the "low-demonstrative" hypothesis developed in section 8.3.

2. Actually, Dem and Num are typically both minimal and maximal in bare-phrase-structure terms, consisting just of a demonstrative and a numeral, respectively. I leave aside the question of complex demonstratives (e.g., *that there*) and numerals (e.g., *one thousand three hundred and twenty-seven*), as do Greenberg, Cinque, and other authors who have looked at Universal 20, such as Abels and Neeleman (2012). See Kayne 2008, Chierchia 2015.

3. Here and elsewhere, I refer to the various orders in DP by the letters given by Cinque (2005a:319–320) and followed by Dryer (2009c:4). What differs between the two is the empirical status of the existence of orders (g, h, m) and the frequency of certain other orders, questions somewhat tangential to the main concerns here.

4. Izin, Ogbronuagum (both Niger-Congo languages spoken in Nigeria), and Soonsorol-Tobi (an Oceanic Austronesian language) are possibilities, in allowing or requiring the orders Num-N, A-N, and N-Dem. However, partly owing to lack of sources, I have been unable to verify that the order in (10a) is actually possible in any of these languages.

An interesting case in this connection is the Oceanic language Mussau, which allows the order A-Num-N and normally has postnominal demonstratives. However, when a demonstrative is added to the A-Num-N order, it precedes N and a special preposition *tana* is added:

(i) a. ouna ateba ale   [Mussau]
       new SG   house
       'one new house'
    b. ouna ateba toko tana ale
       new SG   DEM PREP house
       'this new house'
    (Ross 2002c:155)

Whatever is going on here, we see that the order in (10a) does not appear, although the pairs A-N, Num-N, and N-Dem are all separately possible.

5. In http://makino.linguist.jussieu.fr/ARBRES/index.php/Demonstratif, accessed 10 January 2010 and 4 February 2011, the Breton demonstrative is referred to as an analytic demonstrative, in which the lower element is a "deictic adverb" ("adverbe déictique spatial"). In many of the Austronesian languages mentioned in the text where the same order shows up, it seems as though the lower element is also a deictic adverb of some kind. If we replace the term *adverb* with *modifier*, since it seems anomalous to speak of DP-internal adverbs, then we are dealing with a deictic modifier. I will continue to refer to these elements as *low demonstratives*, since their central property is that of allowing deictic reference, although the idea that demonstratives are formed from the combination of definiteness and locative features is quite widespread (see, e.g., Brugè and Giusti 1996) and would justify referring to these cases as *analytic demonstratives*. The full importance of the deictic nature of demonstratives will emerge in section 8.4. Thanks to Mélanie Jouitteau for discussion of these points.

6. Other languages that might show either this order or the one in (10c), but for which the crucial evidence is missing in the available sources, include Palantla Chinantec (Oto-Manguean; Merrifield 1968) and Ghat Berber (Afro-Asiatic; Nehlil 1909), Dong (Tai-Kadai; Yaohoung and Zheng 1998), Pwo-Karen (Sino-Tibetan; Kato 2003), Ogbronuagum (Niger-Congo; Kari 2000), Sedang (Austro-Asiatic; Smith 1979), and the Austronesian languages Arop-Lokup (D'Jernes 2002), Kaulong (Ross 2002b), Lampung (Walker 1976), Muna (van den Berg 1989), Puluwat (Elbert 1974), Sundanese (Hardjadibrata 1985), Taiof (Ross 2002e), Tigak (Beaumont 1979), and Timugon (Prentice 1971). Cinque (2005a:320n15) mentions Puluwat as having this order.

7. This is not true for Basque, where the determiner appears to be low, like the Celtic demonstratives. For this language, then, a "low-demonstrative" analysis seems to be required, with QP rolling up around the D. I will suggest below that a "low-demonstrative" analysis may be correct for Celtic too.

8. Other languages that may show the same order as Kilivila are Iai (Tryon 1971), Nengone (Tryon 1967), Sundanese (Hardjadibrata 1985), and Urak-Lawoi' (Hogan and Pattemore 1988), all Austronesian.

9. According to Borer (2005:86), this idea originated with Sanches and Slobin (1973:4).

10. Not all the languages with order (10b) have the Welsh order of Dem and complements/postmodifiers of N. In Nung, a Tai-Kadai language spoken in Vietnam, for instance, Dem follows a postnominal relative clause:

(i) dạ-mé mu'hu khà-còn thài té   [Nung]
     mother his   before   died that
     'his mother who had died before'
     (Saul and Wilson 1980:36)

Here we have to employ the Kaynean strategy of complement movement out of NP followed by remnant NP-movement to a higher position. I leave aside the question of how to connect this to the structure in (19). A perhaps related point is that several languages that display order (10b) have "low" possessors (lower than in Celtic, where they are probably in D), occurring between A and Dem. This is true of Sre, Isthmus Zapotec, Karo Batak, Comaltepec Chinantec, Lealao Chinantec, and Nung (Dryer 2015i).

11. If we apply Chomsky's (2001) Activity Condition and require the goal of Agree to also bear an (active) uninterpretable feature, then we could posit an uninterpretable Case feature on Dem, which perhaps Agrees vacuously with a similar feature on D. I will leave this possibility aside here, however, along with the more general question of the status of the Activity Condition. The Agree relation between D and Dem here has a parallel in the binding relation posited between (Spec)D and Dem in Lyons 1999:302.

12. In terms of the proposals in Chomsky 2008, F would have to be the head of the higher phase. This certainly appears to be the case for D, as we can see; in the clause, to the extent that McCloskey's (1996) analysis of VSO as summarized above is correct, we would have to consider the feature to be inherited by T from C.

13. There is in fact still a possibility of a FOFC violation in (27), if NP contains a complement to N and is head-initial. One option is that of "complement extraposition" of the kind found in Celtic, but the relevant evidence is unavailable. Clearly, more needs to be said about languages of the Kilivila type, and more data are also needed.

14. In Roberts 2007, 2012a, I suggest that relatively unmarked, more general parameter settings are always preferred owing to the action of an acquisition strategy I refer to as *Input Generalization*. This can be stated as follows:

(i) If a functional head F sets parameter P_j to value v_i, then there is a preference for similar functional heads to set P_j to v_i.

Taking the movement-triggering feature to be the marked value of a head in relation to the same head without a movement trigger (see Roberts and Roussou 2003), we can see that (26) specifies less marked systems than (28). For more on Input Generalization and parameter hierarchies, see Biberauer et al. 2014 and Biberauer and Roberts 2015a.

15. The *C/T* notation in (29b) is intended to indicate that, while according to Chomsky (2008) C is the true probe, T may inherit C's probing features.

16. I leave aside the question of whether there are "unaccusative nouns." Presumably, to the extent that the external argument of n is always and only the Reference role, then such nouns would not refer, so deciding this question depends on exactly what we would take that to mean, an issue I do not propose to go into here.

17. Although see Elbourne 2013 for arguments that pronouns are definite descriptions. If that is correct, then only variables and demonstratives can be first-merged in the external-argument position of nP.

18. In Roberts 2010a, I assume that cliticization to a head H cannot satisfy H's EPP-feature. Here, I take the view that cliticization can satisfy an EPP-feature, but not an edge feature.

19. Actually, a derivation comparable to that proposed for Kilivila in (27), with AP in Spec,nP and NP raised to Spec,FP, followed by FP-fronting to Spec,DP, could give this order. This suggests that Romanian has the more "VSO-like" option of fronting just N(P). See section 8.6 for more on FP in relation to the position of N and A and Universal 20.

The Scandinavian languages also have enclitic definite articles, but Longobardi (2010) shows that the N-D/A-D elements occupy lower positions in the DP in these languages than in Romanian. It appears, in fact, that the Art is a clitic in n in these languages, and that binding is effected purely by the Agree relation with D (as suggested for Scottish Gaelic in section 8.3.2). The order in (36d) could perhaps involve nP-movement, but then (32') would create an unbound variable in the fronted nP (assuming the order of operations Art-incorporation > (32b') > nP-raising, the former two taking place in the n-phase, the latter in the D-phase). See also the discussion of FOFC in relation to adjuncts in chapter 6.

20. The ι-operator, introduced in Russell and Whitehead 1910–13, is the description operator. From the predicate Fx it forms $(\iota x)Fx$, denoting the unique thing that is F, if there is such a thing. For example, if F is the predicate *king of France*, $(\iota x)Fx$ denotes the unique existing individual such that that individual is the king of France (i.e., no entity, in the actual world, hence the falsity of *The king of France is bald*).

21. Another possible way of assigning reference to this element is to bind it from outside DP; this amounts to a version of the Kamp/Heim approach to indefinites (see Kamp 1981, Heim 1982). Biberauer and Roberts (2011) develop a version of this idea in their analysis of negative clauses. The required binding is instantiated by the Agree relation between an operator in C (in declaratives, this is the veridical operator Op_{Decl}) and D. This gives a particular value to D—for example, in the case of Op_{Decl} the value of existential import, which allows this D to be interpreted as an existential quantifier. D is then able to bind the variable in Spec,nP. We can represent the relevant Agree relations as follows:

(i) $[_C Op_{Decl}]$ ... $[_{DP} D[\exists](x)$ $x]$
      |_____||_____|
      Agree$_1$ Agree$_2$

Agree$_1$ is the clausal $\bar{\text{A}}$-relation between Op_{Decl} and D, brought about by the inherently active nature of Op and an unvalued feature on D. Agree$_2$ is the binding of x in Spec,nP, brought about by D's intrinsic property as an operator combined with the nature of the underspecified *x*. The combined result of the two Agree relations is that the sentence is interpreted as veridical and the D is interpreted as existentially quantifying over a set of existing individuals (on nonveridical contexts, see Biberauer and Roberts 2011). On this view, the indefinite article itself would be merely a morphological marker of indefiniteness with no quantificational force of its own (see Lyons 1999, Borer 2005, Crisma 2011), occupying either Q or D. In fact, in English-type languages, I take it to be cliticized to D owing to its lack of feature content; this also satisfies D's EPP-feature.

22. A potential problem with this idea is that we have followed Fox's (2002) claim that only Ā-traces undergo Trace Conversion, but movement of *every* here seems to be A-movement in that it satisfies the EPP. However, it is not clear that A-movement is defined by EPP satisfaction. In particular, if XP-movement to Spec,CP in V2 clauses in V2 languages is also driven by an EPP-feature (as first proposed in Haegeman 1996), then clearly the EPP can trigger Ā-movement. So, however the distinction between A- and Ā-movement is to be defined, it is not in terms of EPP-features.

23. See Sheehan and Hinzen 2011 and Hinzen and Sheehan 2013:chap. 3 for a different implementation of Longobardi's basic approach.

24. I am indebted to Milan Rezac for raising these examples and for helping me see their full significance.

9 The Final-over-Final Condition and Particles

1. Paul (2014) glosses clause-final *le* as C_{Low}, reflecting her analysis of this element. The gloss given here instead prefigures the analysis to be presented in section 9.4.4.2, in terms of which this *le* and verbal *le* share certain meaning components, with clause-final *le* being a vP-internal element (see also Erlewine to appear a,b).

2. Thanks to Petros Karatsareas, Nicos Neocleous and Ioanna Sitaridou for discussion of the Cappadocian and, more generally, Pontic Greek data and for pointing me to the examples given in (2b–d). The variation in the realization of the final element is phonologically driven and thus left aside here.

3. The optionality-signaling brackets have been added to Swanson's (2011) original example here. Swanson does not explicitly mark optional elements, but the discussion of irrealis/epistemic markers makes it clear that the obligatory element is the preverbal one, many *bé*-less examples being cited in the course of this discussion.

4. Interestingly, as Haas (1964:xxii) notes, Thai grammatical tradition refers to verbal words preceding the main verb as *auxiliaries*, while those following the main verb are called *secondary verbs*. The practice of distinguishing between positionally distinct elements with related aspect, tense, and mood semantics in languages of this type is therefore well-established.

5. The languages that Dryer (2009b:355) lists as having "VOAux order, for at least some Aux" are Bimobo (Gur, Niger-Congo), Adioukrou (Kwa, Niger-Congo), Mumuye, Linda (Adamawa-Ubangi, Niger-Congo), Birom (Platoid, Niger-Congo), Kresh (Kresh, Nilo-Saharan), Baka, Bongo, Jur Mödö, Ngambay, Mbaye, Bagirmi (Bongo-Bagirmi, Nilo-Saharan), Dholuo (Nilotic, Nilo-Saharan), Moru, Avokaya, Logbara, Ma'di

(Moru-Madi, Nilo-Saharan), Kera (East Chadic, Afro-Asiatic), and Musgu (Biu-Mandara, Afro-Asiatic).

6. Peggy Jacob (pers. comm.).

7. That the auxiliaries in (7) are in fact inflected, rather than associated with clitic pronouns as in the Bwe-Karen case discussed in section 9.1, is clear from the discussion in Ndjerareou, Melick, and Moeller 2010: there are clear discrepancies between the realization of agreement (which is, for example, suspended in the second and third person singular) and the availability of clitic pronouns for all persons.

8. That the inflected tense-marking elements in (7b) are in fact auxiliaries and not copular elements is clear when one considers their overall distribution, and also when one considers the form of equative structures, which do contain a copula:

(i) kuˈnjaˈ toˈ   yelꜜꜜ.   [Ngambay]
     chicken 3SG.COP bird
     'A chicken is a bird.'

(Here, ˈ is a mid tone, ˈ a high tone, and ꜜꜜ a low to mid tone; see Ndjerareou, Melick, and Moeller 2010:38.)

9. Cable (2012:656) lists the preverbal tense particles in (i):

(i) a. *a(ye)* very recent past (just happened)
    b. *ne(nde)* recent past 1 (any time today)
    c. *nyo(ro)* recent past 2 (any time yesterday)
    d. *nyo(cha)* recent past 3 (any time more than two days ago)
    e. *ne(ne)* remote past tense 1 (at least several days ago)
    f. *yande* remote past tense 2 (at least several days ago)
    g. *ang'* near future tense 1 (later today)
    h. *kiny* near future tense 2 (some time tomorrow)
    i. *orucha* near future tense 3 (at least two days from now)

Of these, a small subset (e.g., *a(ye)*, *ang'*) cannot occur clause-finally. Importantly, many postverbal TAM-related forms cannot surface in the preverbal position occupied by TAM elements. There is therefore a partial overlap between medial and final elements, with most of the former being able to surface in final position, but many of the latter not being able to surface preverbally.

10. See Blackings and Fabb 2003:476 for discussion of constituents within which these adverbials may not surface. Essentially, these appear to be what we might think of in Givónian terms as satellite-internal positions; that is, adverbials may not surface internally to DPs and PPs.

11. Here, *N* signifies 'nonpast' and *SB* that the associated verb is a subordinate form. See section 9.2.2 for further discussion of Ma'di verb forms.

12. Ma'di also has an extensive inventory of temporal nouns whose default position is clause-final (Blackings and Fabb 2003:522–532).

13. We will see in section 9.2.2 that Ma'di tense is in fact encoded via the morphological form of the lexical verb (and/or its interaction with other elements in the structure): so-called *inflected* verbs express nonpast tenses (present and future), while *uninflected* verbs mark the past (see Blackings and Fabb 2003:chaps. 7 and 8).

14. Thanks to Chun Wai Leung, Joana Wat, and Cherry Lam for these data. It is worth noting that *zo* is the counterpart of postverbal *le*, and not of the clause-final *le* in (12). See section 9.4.4 for further discussion.

15. Thanks to Xuhui Hu for the Yixing data and for numerous discussions of the phenomena they illustrate.

16. Given the data presented in Bonfim Duarte 2012, it seems that Tenetehára makes extensive use of topic and focus fronting, and, consequently, also very readily allows SVO ordering.

17. There are also languages with mixed OV/VO word order that avoid superficial FOFC violations by combining their final negators with OV order. This pattern is common in Surmic languages, which exhibit VO order in affirmatives and OV in negatives:

(i) a. ɛdɛ or kobu- o.   [Me'en]
     3PL see chicken-PL
     'They see chickens.'
  b. ɛdɛ kobu- o or- **on.**
     3PL chicken-PL see-NEG
     'They don't see chickens.'
     (Dryer 2009b:342–343)

18. As Dryer (2009b:337) observes, whether tense or aspect is at issue is a matter of debate. Blackings and Fabb (2003) argue in favor of tense, a position I will also adopt for expository purposes here.

19. The prefixal paradigm creates the initial impression that *these* forms might best be described as "inflected." In addition to the examples discussed here, see (11a) and (22b,c).

20. Mumuye also superficially seems to have tense-conditioned negation, the form cited by Dryer (2009b:453) being the past form, and *kpa(n)*, cited by Krüsi (1978), being the nonpast form.

21. Here, the nonpast negator *kō* combines with an inflected verb, an option that is not available in unmarked nonpast negation contexts (cf. (22c)). Various considerations indicate that fronted elements are "sealed off" from the rest of the clause, with the result that it is structured independently of their featural properties. In the negative context, that *rì*-fronted negators are "sealed off" in this way is clear from the fact that they cannot license negative items like *kuwa* 'never' in the way they usually would (Ma'di is a negative concord language; see Blackings and Fabb 2003:484).

22. Unless otherwise indicated, Afrikaans data were constructed by the author, a native speaker. All unattributed Afrikaans data illustrate uncontroversial properties of the language.

23. Afrikaans is an OV verb-second (V2) language, like German. In the absence of finite auxiliaries, it readily permits VO-*nie* structures, though; hence its inclusion in the present discussion.

24. A Pol analysis more generally seems appropriate for the reinforcing/concording element in negative concord systems; as shown by Rooryck (2008), Breitbarth and Haegeman (2010, 2013), and Makri (2013), among others, concord elements frequently surface in nonnegative contexts.

25. Prosodic properties make it very clear that *nie$_2$* should be interpreted as constituting part of the XPs it reinforces. Consider the contrast between these examples:

(i) a. Ek is **nooit nie**   moeg **nie**.   [Afrikaans]
    I   am never NEG/POL tired POL
    'I am NEVER tired.' *or* 'I am never not tired.'
  b. Ek is [**nooit (nie$_2$)**] moeg **nie$_2$**. (=(28b))
    I   am never NEG   tired POL
    'I am NEVER tired.'
  c. Ek is [**nooit**] [**nie$_1$**] moeg **nie$_2$**.
    I   am never   NEG tired POL
    'I am never not tired.' (i.e., 'I am always tired.')

Without prosodic marking, (ia) is ambiguous between a negative-concord (ib) and double-negation (ic) reading. Wherever negative concord is intended, *nie* is produced as part of the prosodic phrase containing the negated element (see also the bracketing indicated in (28)); this *nie* is therefore the concord element, *nie$_2$*. Wherever double negation is intended, *nie* is prosodically marked off from the other negation element(s) in the structure; that is, it is the "real" negator *nie$_1$*. See Biberauer 2009 for further discussion.

26. For simplicity's sake, I have simply used the languages classified as OV and VO by Dryer (2015e), leaving aside the fact that some languages classified in other ways (e.g., "no dominant order") would also feature VO orders that are of interest here in the interrogative context, and the fact that some of these languages (e.g., German) would be specifically classified one way or another on a generative analysis.

27. See also Beck and Kim 1997 for well-known discussion of the obligatory scrambling of Korean *wh*-elements where they cooccur with NPIs, a further manifestation of this intervention constraint in an otherwise *wh*-in-situ language.

28. *Rú-plàaw* literally means 'or empty'. As Yaisomanang (2012) shows, *rú-plàaw* surfaces in the same type of question—an alternative question—as *rú-mǎy* 'or not'; more grammaticalized *mǎy* and less bleached *plàaw* are therefore in the same kind of relationship as the one we observed in relation to grammaticalized *le/zo* and less bleached completive markers in section 9.2.1.

29. In V-O-Neg and V-O-Q languages, the hierarchical discrepancy between these two elements is very evident in structures where the final Neg- and Q-particles cooccur. As (i)–(ii) show, Neg precedes Q (Dryer 2009b:350):

(i)   w-   átò   wái déŋgà **ù**   **rú**?   [Kanakuru (West Chadic; Nigeria)]
     NEG-FUT.3SG.FEM get pot   NEG Q
     'Can't she get a pot?'
     (Newman 1974:71)

(ii) dè   **kpã̀ mǫ̀ 6a   ya**?   [Mumuye]
     AORIST.NEG meet 2SG NEG Q
     'Did he not meet you?'
     (Shimizu 1983:103)

30. The dots in these examples indicate that the previous element has undergone tone-sandhi change.

31. See also innovative Mandarin *shuo*:

(i) Zhangsan xiang **shuo** Lisi bu   lai   le.   [Innovative Mandarin]
    Zhangsan think   that Lisi NEG come ASP
    'Zhangsan thinks that Lisi is no longer coming.'
    (Hwang 1998; see also Wang, Katz, and Chen 2003)

32. Initial *kong* is also possible in structures like (i), where it resembles insubordination markers like Spanish *que* (see Corr 2016a,b, for recent overview discussion):

(i) **Kong** u   cit   khuan lang   la!   [Taiwanese]
    KONG have this kind person SFP
    '[I can't believe] that there exist this kind of people!'
    (Hsieh and Sybesma 2007:8)

This conventionalized main-clause use of the innovated subordinating marker points to a further round of reanalysis in relation to *kong*, a significant fact in featural terms, as will become clear in section 9.4.4. Here, it is worth noting that "insubordination" *kong* can cooccur with the sentence-final particle (SFP) *la*, a further piece of evidence in favor of the conclusion that Taiwanese C-related elements do not all target the same position.

33. The numeral markings preceding noun glosses represent Bantu noun class membership: that is, Class 1 or 2, the (mostly) animate singular and plural classes, respectively.

34. Thanks to Orsolya Tánczos for most helpful discussion of the Udmurt data.

35. It is worth noting that *shto* is not the only initial complementizer in Modern Udmurt; more complex forms, deriving from Udmurt sources, also exist—for example, *maly ke shuono* 'because' (literally 'why (=what.DAT) if say.PTCP'). *Shuysa* is also not the only final complementizer; *ke* 'if', which also features in the complex complementizer illustrated in (ia), is also available. The following examples illustrate:

(i) a. Sasha   shunyt dis'jas'k- iz,   **maly ke shu-ono**   [Udmurt]
       Sasha.NOM warm   get.dressed-PAST.3SG why if say- PTCP
       pedlon kez'yt val.
       outside cold   was
       'Sasha dressed warmly because it was cold outside.'
    b. Shunyt dis'jas'ky, pedlon kez'yt **ke**!
       warm   get.dressed outside cold   if
       'Dress warmly if it is cold outside!'
    (Orsolya Tánczos, pers. comm.)

36. This parallels the pattern found in creoles, which in purpose (and some other irrealis) clauses feature a complementizer derived from a verb of saying *(tàa* in the partly English-influenced Surinamese creole, Saramaccan) that necessarily combines with an infinitive marker *(fu* in Surinamese; see Veenstra 1996, Aboh 2006, Demonte and Fernández Soriano 2009):

(i) I   taki **tàa** **fu**   a naki di   daga.   [Saramaccan]
    2SG said COMP PART he hits DET dog
    'You told/asked him to hit the dog.'
    (Veenstra 1996:156)

37. The numerals in this example indicate tones.

38. It is worth noting that some of the final Q-particles identified in *WALS* are in fact also final clitics. Fyem (Platoid, Niger-Congo) is a case in point:

(i) taa   won aré=   n=   a?   [Fyem]
    3SG.PERF wash clothes=DEF=Q
    'Did she wash the clothes?'
    (Nettle 1998:50)

39. No significance should be attached to the Force-Fin selection relationship depicted in (65a); the structure of the Russian and Bosnian/Croatian/Serbian CP may well include additional articulated structure, but this is not our concern here. Similarly, the comp-to-spec movement in (65b) does not signify rejection of the arguments for antilocality (Abels 2003, 2012, Grohmann 2003), though see Ledgeway to appear for a proposal in terms of which antilocality is in fact a parameterizable principle.

40. This configuration is, of course, the same as that usually assumed for English possessives—for example, *the [people down the road]'s magnolia tree*. We will return to this matter in section 9.4.1. On the assumption that possessors—and, more generally, elements that can be marked by the Saxon genitive in English—are first-merged within the thematic domain of the nominal (see, e.g., Alexiadou, Haegeman, and Stavrou 2007 for discussion), and that their surface location reflects a position in which they have subsequently been internally merged via A-movement, they do not violate FOFC. Only "roll-up" movements involving head-initial structure violate FOFC, and, in the case of possessor-raising, it is only the (head-initial) specifier of the lower nP that is raised; the possessum remains in situ (cf. *the people down the road magnolia tree's*).

41. Bošković (2001) observes that *wh-li* is the only XP-*li* option readily allowed by Bosnian/Croatian/Serbian native speakers; other options sound archaic. Interestingly, the Q-particle -*ko* can be combined with *wh*-words only in colloquial Finnish, producing emphatic focus:

(i) Mi-   stä- kö talo- sta hän tuli?   [Finnish]
    which-ELA-Q house-ELA he came
    'WHICH house did he come from?'
    (Holmberg 2014:286)

As Holmberg (2014) observes, some of the core *wh*-words in Finnish seem to contain a cognate of -*ko*: *mikä* 'what', *kuka* 'who', and *kuinka* 'how' are all cases in point. Colloquial Finnish therefore appears to be "reusing" -*ko* in a way familiar from discussion of Jespersenian developments in other domains, notably negation (see, e.g., Jespersen 1917, Kiparsky and Condoravdi 2006, van Gelderen 2009, 2011, Willis, Lucas, and Breitbarth 2013, Meisner, Stark, and Völker 2014).

42. Potsdam (2006:2158) supplies the following examples:

(i) a. Nividy **inona** ianao?   [Malagasy]
       buy.ACT what 2SG.NOM
       'What did you buy?'
    b. Novidin' **iza** ny omby?
       buy.PASS who the cow
       'Who was the cow bought by?'

c. Nividy vary **taiza** ianao?
  buy.ACT rice where.PAST 2SG.NOM
  'Where did you buy rice?'

43. I represent Spec,IP as Spec-final here, following the presentation in Potsdam 2006 and what was more generally assumed for VOS languages until the early 2000s (see the discussion in Carnie and Guilfoyle 2001, and see Carnie, Harley, and Dooley 2005 for convincing argumentation that these languages, too, feature initial specifiers). I adhere to the older convention simply for expository convenience, as the details of Spec,IP placement are not relevant to the discussion here.

44. Intriguingly, Antonelli (2015) shows that Late Latin fronted *wh*-elements other than *why* (which is plausibly first-merged within the CP-domain; see Rizzi 2001) typically cooccurred with connective particles like *enim* 'for', *ergo* 'therefore', *igitur* 'therefore', and *autem* 'but'. This calls to mind the behavior of *wh*-words in languages like Quechua, where *wh*-movement is obligatory when the *wh*-element is associated with certain focus and/or contrastive topic particles (recall the discussion earlier in this section).

45. Without intonational disambiguation, this structure is ambiguous between a reading in which *nur* 'only' associates with *dieses Stück* 'this piece'—thus, 'For which person did Holland make only this single piece (as opposed to lots of pieces)?'—and the one indicated in the text.

46. On the determiner incorporation found in (76a,b), see Travis 2006).

47. As noted in connection with (68), adjunct fronting does not require specific voice morphology on the verb; thus, (76b) would also be grammatical with passive or circumstantial voice marking on V.

48. It is worth noting that languages well-known for their final topic particles—for example, the Sinitic and many West African languages—do not constitute challenges to FOFC, as these languages have head-final nominals. The consistently head-initial Mayan languages, in turn, do not seem to have final nominal-related particles.

49. The parentheses around *"roll-up"* are important here. As numerous authors point out (see, e.g., Baker 2005b, Cinque 2005b, Biberauer 2008, Hawkins 2008, Broekhuis 2011, Biberauer and Sheehan 2013, Biberauer and Roberts 2015b, Biberauer to appear b), "head-final"/OV languages vary in the rigidity of their head-finality requirement. Biberauer and Sheehan (2013) distinguish three types:

1. rigidly head-final languages like Japanese and Malayalam, which consistently require "roll-up," that is, comp-to-spec movement;
2. intermediate head-final languages like Dutch and German, which feature few head-final categories and consequently permit CP-extraposition and, optionally, PP-extraposition; and
3. minimally head-final languages like Vata, Lok<u>aa</u>, and the S-O-V-X languages discussed in Hawkins 2008 and Biberauer 2016a, which are only OV where O is a DP.

In all cases, OV order is generated by comp-to-spec movement of some kind; but this is only "roll-up" movement in the case of Type 1 languages.

50. If we assume the wider, non-EP-based definition of FOFC initially proposed by Holmberg (2000a) and upheld by Hawkins (2013), Sheehan (2013a, chapters 5–7, this volume), and Etxepare and Haddican (2014), the potential problem highlighted here becomes even more serious: Topic/Focus-C, Subject-T, and Object-v configurations in a language with head-initial nominals would, for example, all violate FOFC.

51. For the idea that Q-particles may be viewed, alongside Neg(ative) and Aff(irmative), as a spell-out of Pol, see Biberauer 2013, 2015b, to appear a, Holmberg 2013, 2016, and the discussion in section 9.4.4.

52. Jackendoff clarifies the notion "axial part" as follows:

The "axial parts" of an object—its top, bottom, front, back, sides, and ends—behave grammatically like parts of the object, but, unlike standard parts such as a handle or a leg, they have no distinctive shape. Rather, they are *regions* of the object (or its boundary) *determined by their relation to the object's axes*. The up-down axis determines top and bottom, the front-back axis determines front and back, and a complex set of criteria distinguishing horizontal axes determines sides and ends. (Jackendoff 1996:14, emphasis added)

53. Since Afrikaans differs from Dutch in lacking HAVE vs. BE auxiliary selection in compound tenses, at first sight it might seem implausible to assume the presence of Van Riemsdijk's silent GO in structures like (97a), which contains a form of BE. However, given the systematic discrepancies between null and overt elements of "the same" kind (see, e.g., Nunes 2004, Kayne 2010a, Biggs 2014, Douglas 2015, 2016, Biberauer 2016a, to appear a) and the minimal specification associated with BE in Afrikaans, as in Dutch, this becomes less troubling.

54. In Pretorius 2017, these options are conceived of as the consequence of different "spanning" choices (see Svenonius 2011, 2016).

55. More generally, there is considerable crosslinguistic evidence that nominal features are added to elements that undergo fronting. Consider, for example, the nominalized forms that are a prerequisite for predicate doubling and VP-fronting in many languages (see, e.g., Aboh and Dyakonova 2009, Güldemann 2010, Buell 2012). If fronted VPs are always enclosed in "extra," nonverbal structure facilitating Ā-movement—as assumed, for example, in Biberauer and Roberts 2015b—we have an additional reason to understand why VP-fronting of head-initial VPs of the kind illustrated in (89) does not produce a FOFC violation.

56. This proposal clearly echoes Rizzi's (1997) Force-Fin take on complementation, but crucially differs from it in explicitly committing to the idea that only one of the complementizer positions is part of V's EP. As we will see, it is also not clear that λ should be equated with Force, or, indeed, that complementation structures always take the specific bipartite form that Franco proposes. To the extent that Franco's λ simply marks a relationship (subordination) that has already been marked by a lower element (by C_V), it acts as a linker in Philip's (2012) sense. We will return to this point in section 9.4.4.

57. In the context of Franco's (2012) analysis, these clauses would still feature a null higher λ. Being nominal, its headedness would be immaterial to our concerns here.

58. This brought factive complements into line with the other finite-complementation structures in Old Akkadian, namely, restrictive relative clauses. Like factive complements, relatives were initially only marked by means of the verbal subordination

marker, meaning that they were prenominal. However, introduction of an initially agreeing demonstrative, which became nonagreeing *ša*, resulted in the rise of a consistently postnominal relative construction:

(i) eql- am   [**ša** … nītiq-   **u**]   lišqi'ū.   [Old Akkadian]
    field-ACC   COMP 1PL.passed-SUB 3PL.should.water
    'They should water the field that we passed.'
    (Franco 2012:571)

59. I leave open the possibility that some focus particles may lack [F]s, being only semantically specified for focus (see Zeijlstra 2008, 2014, Biberauer 2011, 2015a, 2016b, and Wiltschko 2014 for general discussion of the difference and how to detect it).

60. Some of these authors (see, e.g., Cardinaletti 2011) propose an IP-internal location for modal particles. Consideration of the arguments in favor of this location suggest the low IP-domain, which does not seem incompatible with alternative conceptualization as the upper end of the vP-domain. As we will see in the text, the latter perspective is particularly appealing, given recent discoveries about the apparent parallelisms between the peripheries of phase heads.

61. To the extent that we might expect less grammaticalized elements to retain more of the structure of the elements they were originally grammaticalized from, it is reasonable to leave open the possibility that less grammaticalized particle elements may be phrasal rather than head categories. It is worth noting, though, that "more structure" need not mean "phrasal." If Cardinaletti and Starke's (1999) strong-weak-clitic typology is interpreted, not in phrasal terms, as it typically is, but as indicative of the relative complexity of the feature structure within, respectively, strong, weak, and clitic *heads*, we can also understand their typology in head terms. The latter possibility may also be more compatible with the assumptions of bare phrase structure (Chomsky 1994), assuming the Lexicon to consist mostly—with the exception of entries like idioms—of heads, and it is certainly what would emerge on a spanning approach (see Svenonius 2011, 2016). From this perspective, too, it may be that Cardinaletti's (2011) proposals and those in this section are not fundamentally different.

62. Higher speaker/hearer-related elements (expressing notions like surprise, annoyance, exaggeration, and warning) are possible in Chinese varieties, as Paul (2014) shows. These, however, have the appearance of nonintegrated, adjoined elements (see Biberauer and Hu 2014, Heim et al. 2014; see also the discussion of Brazilian Portuguese *não* in section 9.2.2).

63. Note that the projection of [+Q] here does not create any complementation difficulties, as the matrix predicate is a lexical category, which is therefore exempt from Cable's (2010) QP-Intervention Condition (109). In the specific case of Q-particles, it is also possible to imagine that a matrix predicate taking a Q-particle-containing complement will be selecting for an interrogative, so the Q-specification encountered on the matrix predicate's complement, alongside [+V] and other projecting features, will be appropriate to the predicate's selection requirements. Where [focus]- or [topic]-bearing particles project, one might imagine a complication, as [focus] and [topic] are not selected-for [F]s. But [focus]- and [topic]-marked constituents are most commonly subclausal, and we know that verbs also do not c-select for DPs and that non-*wh*-selecting

predicates do not select for [wh]-DP/PP objects of the kind they will combine with in *wh*-interrogatives; in both cases, selection is usually thought to be for N or a nominal more generally, that is, for the categorial specification emanating from the base of the EP and represented along the EP-spine (see, e.g., Baltin 1989, Payne 1993, Williams 2003, Sportiche 2005, Bruening 2009, Fowlie 2014; and see Bruening, Dinh, and Kim 2015 for discussion). To the extent that cross-categorial (i.e., inter-EP) selection can be shown to be more "myopic" than intracategorial (or EP-internal) selection, we may have an independent motivation for the discrepancy between lexical and functional selection encoded in the QP-Intervention Condition.

64. If [F]s are hierarchically organized, categorial features could, for example, be at the top of each [F] stack, a location that might be viewed as following from the early acquisitional stage at which these categories are identified and acquired. Alternatively, their prominence relative to other [F]s could simply follow from these features' having the distinction of being the only ones that are present from the very bottom of the EP—in other words, from another relational calculation of prominence, which would be very much in keeping with Minimalist thinking (consider also bare phrase structure (Chomsky 1994), for example).

65. The "lexical features" Duffield (2015) refers to evidently include the [F]s under discussion here; that is, 'features of items stored in the Lexicon' is the intended meaning, entailing all of the phonological, semantic, and formal features discussed in Chomsky 1995 et seq.

66. In the context of the emergentist approach to formal features and categories proposed by Biberauer (2011 et seq.) and Biberauer and Roberts (2015a,c, 2017), going the lexicalist route would fall afoul of both of the third-factor-imposed acquisition biases, Input Generalization ("Maximize the use of available [F]s," generalized from Roberts 2007b) and Feature Economy ("Postulate as few features as possible to account for the input," generalized from Roberts and Roussou 2003; see also van Gelderen 2004). In other words, this type of formal characterization of the relevant elements would not be acquisitionally plausible. See also note 68.

67. It does not in fact seem necessary to assume a rich, universally given functional structure for an underspecification approach of the kind Duffield envisages to work. See, among others, Biberauer 2011, 2015a,b, 2016b, Biberauer and Hu 2014, Cowper and Currie Hall 2014, Ramchand and Svenonius 2014, Wiltschko 2014, and Biberauer and Roberts 2015a,c for discussion of how non-UG-given (emergent) functional hierarchies may arise and supply the necessary spine for underspecified elements to attach to.

68. See Lam 2016 for some diachronic speculations, and Enfield 2003 on contact considerations.

69. That these adverbs are possible in certain *that*-clauses (e.g., *I think that, frankly, you should just care less about what other people think*) does not undermine the proposal that the SAP-related projections are located above the CP-domain: selected clauses that exhibit so-called *embedded main-clause phenomena* are known to be larger than those that do not, effectively instantiating a complete root clause, which, of course, has a full SAP (see, e.g., Heycock 2005, Aelbrecht, Haegeman, and Nye 2012, and Haegeman 2012 for recent discussion of embedded main-clause phenomena).

70. As the structure in (119) shows, [F]-less particles are formally identical to roots. This calls to mind Zwart's (2009a) proposal that head-finality in a head-initial language is "lexical." As the discussion in this chapter shows, this is partially correct: superficially FOFC-violating structures do often draw on root-like [F]-less lexical elements, and on lexical items lacking the specification associated with "full" functional categories. However, other facts are in play as well (see the discussion in sections 9.4.1–9.4.3, 9.4.5), and it is also anything but clear that head-finality generally is always "lexical" in Zwart's sense (see Biberauer and Sheehan 2013, Biberauer and Roberts 2015b).

71. The bracketing here is intended to indicate that the projecting Epist functional head will bear [F]s over and above the [+V]-feature it contributes to the EP. Following Neeleman and Van de Koot (2004), among others, it may well be at that *all* [F]s project along the EP. For our purposes, though, the only crucial EP-contained feature is the categorial one, which is argued to be directly implicated in FOFC (see (5)).

72. See much work by Jacques Mehler, Marina Nespor, Judit Gervain, and colleagues: Mehler et al. 1996, Nazzi, Bertoncini, and Mehler 1998, Christophe, Mehler, and Sebastián-Gallés 2001, Christophe et al. 2003, Nespor, Peña, and Mehler 2003, Gervain et al. 2008, Toro et al. 2008, Gervain and Mehler 2011, Gervain and Werker 2013.

73. Any specifiers merged with the last-merged functional head will, as usual, be spelled out to the left of this head, as a consequence of the Linear Correspondence Axiom (see Biberauer, Roberts, and Sheehan 2014 on the plausibly functional motivation for the precedence clause of this axiom).

74. This proposal calls to mind Cecchetto's (2013:71) speculation that particles, like lexical heads, differ from functional heads within an EP in not needing to "see" (probe) the formal features of any specific head, but that they instead "only look at the [X]P label with no need to access the features of the [X] head." As with my proposal and that of Zwart (2009a)—see note 71—a (partial) parallel between particles and lexical (as opposed to functional) elements emerges. As noted in the text, this parallel is also interesting in light of Cable's (2010) distinction between lexical and functional heads in the context of the QP-Intervention Condition (see (109) and surrounding discussion).

75. In the context of the emergent system proposed in Biberauer 2015a and Biberauer and Roberts 2015a,c, where languages do not share a universally given inventory of functional heads (*pace* Cinque 1999 et seq., Chomsky 2001), the contrast between phonologically initial and final elements with systematically different interpretations would, in head-initial languages of the kind under discussion here, itself constitute a vital cue to the existence of a functional head. In other words, particle placement can serve as a diagnostic for the existence of an EP-defining functional head. See sections 9.4.4.2, 9.4.6, and 9.5 for further discussion of the diagnostic value of final particles in head-initial systems.

76. This would also allow a potentially very interesting unification with analyses of German modal particles that locate them at the vP-edge (see Struckmeier 2014) and, more generally, with the idea that phase edges generally are associated with discourse- and possibly also speaker-related information (see, e.g., Poletto 2012, Biberauer 2013, Cognola 2013, Kandybowicz 2013, Biberauer and Roberts 2015c, Wiltschko to appear).

77. A further difference between the approach being considered here and Cardinaletti's (2011) proposal, of course, rests on the phrasal status of the particle. For Cardinaletti,

weak adverbs are deficient XPs, whereas the proposal here is that they are heads. In the context of a Marantz (2001)–type approach to "words," however, in terms of which heads are also phrasal at the earliest stages of structure-building, it is not clear that this discrepancy needs to be of any significance; in fact, the lack of categorial specification may contribute very directly to the absence of formal structure that Cardinaletti attributes to weak adverbs.

78. Importantly, if the present discussion is on the right track, nonprojection need not be a definitive property of elements designated *particles* in the literature (see, e.g., Duffield 1995, Toivonen 2003, Svenonius 2008). As Cardinaletti (2011) also suggests, particles seem to vary in their degree of defectiveness. What is crucial for the discussion here is that *final* particles are never fully projecting (i.e., categorial-feature-projecting) elements.

79. The glossing here follows the characterization in Paul 2014:78.

80. In addition to sentence-final *le*, Mandarin has what is usually described as perfective verbal-suffix *le* (see, e.g., Soh and Gao 2006). The two *les* are illustrated in (ia,b):

(i) a. Tāmen dàoda-**le**   shān-   dǐng.   [Mandarin]
       he.PL reach- PERF mountain-top
       'He reached the top of the mountain.'
    b. Tāmen dàoda-**le**   shān-   ding **le**.
       he.PL reach- PERF mountain-top LE
       'They reached the top of the mountain (which they hadn't done before, contrary to what one might expect).'
       (Soh 2009:625)

Le, then, appears to be amenable to an analysis somewhat paralleling what was suggested for Vietnamese *được*: it appears to be underspecified, with its placement depending on whether it combines with V (to deliver the 'complete-consumption' (Freddy Hu, pers. comm.) inner-aspect meaning in (ia); see (119)) or with vP (to deliver the point-of-view, current-relevance interpretation added by sentence-final *le* in (ib)).

81. For Erlewine, the conclusion that SFPs are found at the edge of both the vP- and CP-phases serves as further motivation for pursuing Richards's (2016) Contiguity-based analysis of FOFC, in terms of which this condition applies within the domain of the phase, but not across entire EPs, as proposed here (see Biberauer, Holmberg, and Roberts 2008a,b for an early attempt at formulating FOFC in phase-based terms). For Richards and Erlewine, the occurrence of final elements at the edges of head-initial phases reflects the fact that these edge elements will never be sent to spell-out and linearized at the same time as the head-initial elements within the phasal domain, meaning—in highly simplified terms—that the usual selection-based Contiguity requirement does not hold. This approach therefore makes the same prediction as the present analysis regarding the significance of phase edges: the key distributional aspect of final-particle behavior that also emerges from the present account is captured. Richards's analysis, however, has nothing to say about the striking fact that superficially FOFC-violating elements so consistently give evidence of defectivity (e.g., in being frequent in systems like those in East Asia with system-defining homophony, and in systems where the final element at first serves "the same" function as one or more head-initial elements, in being omissible in ways that meet Wiltschko's (2014)

nonprojection tests, etc.). All of these consistent properties would have to be accidental on Richards's analysis. In fact, in specifying phase heads as the elements that may superficially violate FOFC (modulo the effects of head movement, which are assumed to trigger "phase-sliding/extension" effects of the kind proposed in Gallego 2006, 2010, Den Dikken 2007, and Gallego and Uriagereka 2007; see also Trinh 2014), one might be led to the opposite expectation regarding the nature of the elements that could potentially constitute apparent FOFC violators: phase heads are typically regarded as privileged heads, which dictate the properties of elements in their domain, with some work additionally distinguishing between weak/defective and strong/nondefective phases (see Chomsky 2000 for the original proposal, and Gallego 2012 and Citko 2014 for overview discussion). Given the kinds of behavior discussed in this chapter, we might conclude that apparently FOFC-violating particles are simply weak/defective phase heads, but this would, on most definitions of *weak phase head*, undermine Richards's central predictions, as weak phase heads do not define their own phasal domains.

82. Recall that nominals in Mandarin are head-final; therefore, nothing special needs to be said to account for *de*'s head-finality. The fact that *de* is nominal does, however, allow us to understand why it does not create FOFC violations wherever it combines with a head-initial clause to form a relative clause (see the discussion in section 9.4.3). See note 84 on the likely predicative nature of n.

83. Where a Sub-head seems to be acategorial, it may, of course, still be associated with a silent noun. Note, however, that Jenks (2011) proposes that nominal complementation and, more generally, linking markers should be predicative, a proposal that is, in principle, compatible with Zhang's (1999) n-analysis of *de* and also compatible with Franco's (2012) proposals on the assumption that λ is a predicate n. An n- rather than D-nominal would also open up the way to understanding why complement clauses are not generally islands for extraction (see Biberauer and Sheehan 2012a for discussion of some relevant cases).

84. A similar case is the German-influenced Romance variety Cimbrian, which has borrowed the complementizer *az* (> German *dass*) and uses it alongside native *che* to mark complement clauses. As Grewendorf and Poletto (2009) and Bidese, Padovan, and Tomaselli (2012) show, *az* occupies a position above Force (the locus of *che*), with the result that it may effectively take matrix-style CPs as its complement. Again, then, we have borrowing of an element that is added on top of an existing structure as an extra layer, rather than being incorporated as a further member of an existing class of complementizer elements.

85. This "deep/surface" distinction undermines Berwick and Chomsky's (2011) proposal that "syntactic" variation must necessarily be located at PF, in other words, that syntactic variation is "surface/late" variation.

86. Recall that the categorial specification of the XP with which Pol merges (CP or DP) will project up the EP. That Pol itself is not projecting the EP-defining feature will be clear, as Pol has no categorial specification to project. In cases where the headedness of a categorially specified head is the opposite of the headedness of the XP with which it combines, it will project as usual, thus altering the headedness of the structure.

87. By contrast, *nie*₁, the real negator in Afrikaans, which is located clause-medially (low in the vP-domain) and also initially in negated subclausal constituents, may be spelled out superficially initially by virtue of its having adjoined to Neg in a word-level derivation, along the lines outlined for Vietnamese *được* in section 9.4.2.2 (see (120) in particular). Alternatively, since Afrikaans does not feature the level of systematic (in part, class-defining) homophony that Vietnamese and East Asian languages do, it may simply be the case that the "real" negator *nie*₁ is in fact a different lexical item; the alternative perspectives are presented in Biberauer 2008, 2009 and Biberauer and Zeijlstra 2011, 2012a,b. What is clear here is that the number of items involved in apparent homophony in a system will matter in determining how acquirers analyze its formal properties (cf. Yang's (2016) Tolerance Principle, which entails a "tipping point" determining whether acquirers will learn individual items or seek to establish a generalization, something that can clearly change over time).

88. As shown in Biberauer 2016a, the interrogative complementizer *of* 'if' in most varieties of Modern Afrikaans is a C- and not a Pol-head. There are speakers—seemingly only strongly monolingual ones, whose numbers are dwindling—who permit embedded V2 structures of the kind illustrated in (i):

(i) [PolP [CP Ek weet nie₁ [PolP **of** [CP **sal** daar werk vir my wees]]]   [Afrikaans]
        I know not   if   shall there work for me be
    nie₂].
    POL
    'I don't know if there will be work for me.'
    [Contrast English: *I don't know **if will** there be work for me.]
    (Feinauer 1989:30)

Even in varieties where *of* has been reanalyzed as Pol, it is presumably still specified for subordination, however, meaning that *of* does not constitute a suitable spell-out for nonveridical main-clause [Pol].

89. The cases where the anaphoric negator surfaces clause-initially rather than clause-finally—a less emphatic structure—may involve *não* merging directly with a CP-internal head like Topic or Focus; that is, *não* in this case may initially be part of a word-level LA, after which it is renumerated in Johnson's (2003) sense, becoming part of the CP LA.

90. This is, of course, also true for the head-initial nominals that surface preverbally in West Germanic. These entail a complex specifier on the Kaynean analysis Sheehan (2013a,b) assumes, leading us to expect that it should not be possible to extract from preverbal nominals, an option that is, however, available.

91. In the present system, these particles correspond to spell-outs of the single-featured heads assumed in Nanosyntax (see Starke 2009), spanning exactly one head (see Svenonius 2011, 2016). They realize heads bearing maximally scattered features in the sense of Giorgi and Pianesi (1997).

92. It should be clear from the formulation here, which references the EP rather than phasal domains, that the kind of contiguity I envisage should not be equated with that formulated in Richards 2016. See note 82.

93. At first sight, this might seem contrary to Chomsky 2001, which is often interpreted as suggesting that V-to-v movement is universal to ensure categorization of V (i.e., V

is in fact an acategorial root). Considerable subsequent research has clearly shown, however, that verbalizing v should be distinguished from external-argument-introducing v (see, e.g., De Belder and Van Craenenbroeck 2014, 2015, Harley 2014, Myler 2014).

94. The latter consideration suggests that this type of derivation will be impossible in ergative languages, a number of which are VOS (see, e.g., Aldridge 2004, Deal 2016).

95. Strikingly, a V-O-Aux structure derived via VP-fronting to the phase edge would also not involve comp-to-spec-type roll-up if an external argument is merged in the lower specifier of vP: roll-up of the kind that produces a FOFC-violating structure would require the complement of v—the VO VP—to move into v's innermost (derivationally first) specifier; movement from v's complement to a more peripheral specifier cannot be roll-up.

96. Worth noting here is that these V-O-Aux/V-O-C systems would meet Sheehan's (2013a) islandhood requirement on the head-initial constituent in particle-containing structures.

97. In the context of a more general framework where Maximize Minimal Means is a third-factor acquisition bias, it is natural to expect every bit of regular and thus predictable information in the system to be harnessed in this way. See Biberauer 2015a, 2016a,b for detailed discussion of the various kinds of departures from arbitrary and thus unpredictable patterning—classic Saussurean arbitrariness—that acquirers may utilize as cues to the formal structuring of the system they are acquiring.

98. As noted by BHR (2014) and Biberauer, Roberts, and Sheehan (2014) (see also section 9.4.4.2), there seem to be good reasons for assuming that head-finality is formally marked, while head-initiality is not: the FOFC skewing observed in the empirical domain gives one indication of this, and identifying the head-finality-marking property with the diacritic that triggers the leftward movement that appears to be universal in human languages (see, e.g., Kayne 1994, 2013, Abels and Neeleman 2009, 2012, Haider 2012) allows us to unify word order and movement and avoid the introduction of a linearization-specific diacritic (see Biberauer et al. 2010a and Biberauer, Roberts, and Sheehan 2014 for discussion). The unification entailed here is, of course, desirable from the perspective of a Minimalist program, attempting to establish how minimal the formal means required to regulate syntactic structure are (see note 97). Head-initiality/-finality could, in principle, have been marked by individual diacritics signaling initiality and finality (see Biberauer and Sheehan 2012a, Sheehan 2013a, and chapters 4 and 10 for discussion). This is, however, clearly less parsimonious than harnessing a diacritic that already seems to be independently required and is therefore available to be more maximally utilized. Naturally, it would be even more parsimonious to dispense with the diacritic altogether, something that is attempted in Biberauer and Roberts 2015b.

A point worth noting here is that the unification under discussion assumes that $^\wedge$ is associated with heads to signal leftward phrasal movement. It could, of course, also be associated with a head to signal that it will attract the (EP-internal) head that it selects to head-adjoin to it—essentially the proposal made in Haider 2012 and all the work leading up to this volume (see also chapter 4 for discussion). In view of the very striking harmonic contiguity patterns to be discussed in section 9.5, however, I reject this possibility: if head-initiality were to be the marked option, the lexical elements at the bottom of EPs would always be unmarked, regardless of the headedness of the system, meaning that it would not be possible to state a "harmony" pattern that appears to start from (i.e., include) the lexical head in the way that appears to be necessary. For proponents of the view that head movement is postsyntactic, this option would also not exist for independent reasons, and, likewise, for proponents of the view that head movement does not require a diacritic (e.g., Roberts 2010a). The issue does not arise in the context of the proposals in Biberauer and Roberts 2015b.

99. Neither, of course, can an initial T-element or any other clausal head in the context of an OV language. This might at first sight seem to be problematic, as the West Germanic languages, for example, all feature at least initial C (since auxiliaries surface finally, it is reasonable to assume that T at least bears $^\wedge$). Closer consideration, however, reveals that viewing West Germanic C as a head that is not *intrinsically* verbal—and thus [V$^\wedge$]—is potentially useful. Consider, for example, the fact that West Germanic C—like C in V2 languages more generally—has long been acknowledged to be a "hybrid" category, associated both with verbal/clausal and with nominal properties (see Vikner 1995 for overview discussion of this idea). If C itself is underspecified with respect to verbal/nominal specification—that is, in the context of the present proposal, if it is *not* itself specified [V$^\wedge$]—we can understand the nature of this hybridity similarly to the way we made sense of the behavior of acategorial elements in section 9.4.4. In other words, when the finite verb raises to C in West Germanic, its [V$^\wedge$] feature will project to CP, making the projection as a whole [V$^\wedge$]—and thus incapable of serving nominal functions like subjecthood, a well-known fact about V2 clauses. Likewise, when a subordinating complementizer merges with C, its nominal specification will project to CP, accounting for the fact that *dass/dat*-clauses in West Germanic are well-formed subjects. As C itself is null, just as the Epist head in Vietnamese (120) is null, the finite verb's [V$^\wedge$] requirement will be satisfied by spell-out to the right of the null C; there is no prediction that the finite verb will be spelled out in final position.

Looking beyond Germanic, work considering the fine-grained structure of C also suggests that unambiguous classification as verbal or nominal is too simplistic (see, e.g., Franco 2012, which has informed some of the discussion here). To the extent that C is (the cover term for) a category that (at least in part) interacts with clausal heads that are verbal, we expect it to be a head that may obtain verbal properties. Note also that what is being said here about West Germanic C does not rule out the possibility of languages in which C is intrinsically verbal ([V]-marked): languages in which C exhibits the same headedness as the lexical verb could all in principle be intrinsically [V]-marked, and it is striking that many final heads in head-final languages derive from verbs (e.g., *say* and its counterparts; Udmurt *shuysa*, discussed in section 9.2.3, is a case in point). Similarly, many initial Cs in head-final languages derive from operators (see Bayer 1999, 2001). Evidently, then, the question of the formal makeup of Cs is a complex one, deserving (continued) closer study—among other reasons, so that the precise nature of the ban on final complementizers in VO languages and the obligatoriness of CP-extraposition in OV languages can be properly understood.

100. For Baker (2005a), (137) falls out from his (2003) Reference-Predication Constraint:

(i) *The Reference-Predication Constraint*
     No syntactic node can have both a specifier and a referential index.

For Baker (2003), specifier projection is definitive of verbs (i.e., the "meaning" of Chomsky's (1970) [+V]), while the ability to bear a referential index is definitive of nouns (i.e., the "meaning" of [+N]).

10 The Final-over-Final Condition in a Mixed-Word-Order Language

1. There are certain other contexts where OV order is also found; see Vilkuna 1989, 1995 and Holmberg 2000a for discussion.

2. Main News in Vilkuna 1995 is information that "is New with respect to the immediate premise of the sentence" (p. 249).

3. This universal is not often discussed, perhaps because it is so self-evident that it tends to go unnoticed. Sentences can be very short and may have very little content, as in (i), a possible answer to the question *Isn't it cold in here?*

(i)   It is.

Yet there is always a focus. In (i), it is the polarity, the truth of the proposition 'It is cold in here', indicated phonologically by focal stress on *is*; (ii) is therefore not an option:

(ii)   *It's.

4. Thanks to Maria Vilkuna and Pauli Brattico for discussion of these data.

5. The object could first move to the specifier of an abstract head G, as in (i):

(i)   [GP auton G [PtcpP ostanut auton]]

Once Aux is merged, the remnant PtcpP could then move to Spec,AuxP:

(ii)   [AuxP [PtcpP ostanut ~~auton~~] [AuxP oli [GP auton G [PtcpP ~~ostanut auton~~]]]]

6. In Holmberg 2000a, I postulate a head labeled *New*, with the property that its c-command domain is the domain of new information (i.e., information focus). This is one way to formalize the idea in the text. Movement of the object out of VP, merging it with NewP, moves it out of the information-focus domain.

7. Some varieties also allow object shift across the subject, under more restricted conditions, so-called long object shift (Holmberg and Platzack 1995:chap. 6):

(i)   Varför gör   mej Helge alltid   irriterad?   [Swedish]
       why   makes me Helge always annoyed
       'Why does Helge always make me annoyed?'

8. Object shift across lower adverbs can apply to lexical DPs in Mainland Scandinavian as well, subject to dialectal variation (see Nilsen 2003, Bentzen 2007).

9. In Sheehan(o), this auxiliary hypothesis is not needed. There, copies of a category are not linearized independently. Instead, once the linear order between (in the case discussed) the verb and the object is determined by the lexical specification of V as V-O, this linear order is ensured wherever the object moves. The notion of V-movement applying to restore a linear relation does not play a part in that theory.

On the other hand, since it turns out that V-movement is called for anyway, for other reasons, and has the effect of restoring linear order by virtue of asymmetric c-command if copies are linearized independently, I have taken the step to assume that this is, indeed, how it works. As will be discussed in section 10.8, another reason for not adopting Sheehan(o) wholesale is that the impression that HG depends on a selection relation between verb and object is mistaken.

10. Another challenge for the present theory (and any other theory assuming shape conservation) is that some SOV languages allow V-movement to override the selection-based linear order between V and O; an example is the Germanic SOV languages, where main clauses have verb-second order, including SVO.

11. The ill-formedness in (27b) may not appear as striking as the violations of HG in Swedish and Icelandic in (16b) and (17b). The reason for this, I suggest, is that because Finnish has very free sentential word order, there is a tendency not to rule any word order variant out directly, without giving it a chance, so to speak. But on reflection, the word order is odd because it has no natural interpretation in terms of new vs. old information, focus or topicality, the features that are modified by word order variation. This is characteristic of ill-formed, unusable sentential word orders in Finnish.

12. The Slavic languages, notorious for their free word order, do not constitute counterexamples if the free order is a consequence of dual selection specifications, as argued by Haider (2012).

13. The structural representation is simplified, for ease of exposition; actually, T is merged at this point, and O adjoins to TP.

14. Given the definition of c-command in Sheehan 2013b, this structure would, in fact, give rise only to O-Aux.

15. Compare Den Dikken's (2007) Relator head, which, however, differs from the head proposed in the text in that it does not select its complement.

16. The notion that a head that is never actually spelled out may still have parameterized linearization properties is obviously not uncontroversial. How would such a head be learned? I assume that the head is universally present, though, for structural reasons. If so, it seems not implausible that it is automatically assigned the same structural and linearization properties as other verbal heads.

17. Constraint (49) could have been formulated in terms of phases rather than lexical projections. Fox and Pesetsky (2005) use the phase formalism in their account of *wh*-movement and other Ā-movement to the CP-domain, which presents a challenge for the shape conservation idea. Following Chomsky (1986, 2001), they postulate that an object *wh*-phrase moves first to the edge of VP, where it is linearized as preceding V, when VP is spelled out. This order is then preserved under further *wh*-movement. This solution is not open here, though, as intermediate structures are ignored by the linearization algorithm.

11 The Final-over-Final Condition in Morphology

1. One possibility is that where V adjoins to F by head movement, fusional morphology results. On the other hand, where V and F are merely contiguous thanks to VP-movement alone, agglutination results. I will not pursue this idea here, but see Bazalgette's (2011) interesting implementation of it in relation to the internal structure of

pronouns, and Neeleman and Szendrői's (2007) account of radical pro-drop. Julien (2002:136–142) argues against V-movement in Japanese (as proposed in Otani and Whitman 1991, Koizumi 1995, and Nakajima 1999). She concludes that "the verb does not move in head-final languages" (p. 142), but we are not forced to this conclusion purely on the basis of her discussion of Japanese. Indeed, in section 11.4 we will see a reason to suspect that V *always* moves in head-final languages.

2. Note that if we split tense and aspect, placing Tense above Aspect as we assumed in the discussion of (8) (see also Cinque 1999 on this), and if we maintain v, then the probability of suffixal Aspect is 12.5% and the probability of suffixal Tense is half of that (6.25%), still further removed from the 29.5% shown in table 11.4.

3. Igbo, Oromo (East Cushitic), Mokilese (Central-Eastern Malayo-Polynesian), Hua (East New Guinea Highlands), Russian, and North Puebla Nahuatl. See Myler 2009:32–34 for discussion of these cases.

4. Of course, sentential negation does not by any means always take surface scope, but this species of negation may be special in being bound up with both focus and finiteness for its interpretation, which may be determined in large part by abstract elements in the left periphery (see, e.g., Biberauer and Roberts 2011). Constituent negation, which is of course much freer in its distribution, tends very strongly to scope over just its surface c-command domain.

5. Werner (1997:167) makes the following comment:

Nach E.A. Krejnovič' Auffassung entstanden die verbalen Komposita aus Wortfügungen, die historisch in Wörter zusammengezogen wurden....Solche Gebilde, die man als Zusammenrückungen bezeichnen könnte, gibt es im Ketischen in der Tat; sie haben aber mit Inkorporation nichts zu tun, denn sie gehen auf analytischer Verbalformen zurück. ('According to E.A. Krejnovič's description, the compound verbs developed from sequences of words, which historically combined to form larger words....Such forms, which could be called *Zusammenrückungen*, do in fact exist in Ket; but they have nothing to do with incorporation, since they go back to analytic verb forms.')

This seems to support the analysis sketched in the text.

6. The abbreviations are as follows: ADV = adverbial, ITER = iterative, DIST PL = distributed plural, DO = direct object, DEIC SU = deictic subject (indefinite or fourth person), MODE "marks perfective, imperfective, progressive or optative" (Speas 1990:206), SUBJ = subject.

7. An alternative is to allow prefixes to project and treat them as not triggering movement, as in section 11.3.

8. These compounds involve bracketing paradoxes, in that morphophonological evidence indicates that their internal structure is not as given in (27); rather, the affix and the second element of the compound form a constituent excluding the first element of the compound. The bracketing in (27), however, is motivated by argument structure: it is clear that *can*, *rocket*, and *ear* are the internal arguments of *open*, *scient*, and *split*; and to the extent that internal arguments must first-merge with their predicates (a widely made assumption that might be seen as a residue of the Government-Binding notion of GF-θ), this structure is the one that must be seen by the narrow syntax and by the semantic interface. Presumably, the bracketing is adjusted at the PF interface, giving rise to the relevant morphophonological effects.

9. However, Myler (2009:54ff.) points out examples like the following, which appear problematic for the general thesis that FOFC constrains compounding:

(i) a. an [[I-couldn't-care-less] attitude]
     b. the [[man-of-the-match] award]
     c. an [[easy-to-please] customer]
     d. the [[Final-over-Final] Constraint] (!)
     e. the [[channel 4] news]

Myler suggests that the complex modifiers in these examples are able to undergo "Renumeration" in the sense of Johnson (2003) and Harley (2009), thus being structurally opaque ("spelled out" in the sense of Uriagereka 1999, Nunes and Uriagereka 2000) at the point at which they are combined with the element that becomes the head of the compound. I will not go into this question here (on Renumeration in relation to FOFC more generally, see the discussion and analysis in Biberauer and Sheehan 2012a).

10. Here, I am assuming that the root *open* projects, even though it has no formal features. An alternative is that roots are completely inert, as proposed in Chomsky 2013.

11. Veenstra (2006:208–209) notes some very interesting language acquisition evidence that supports FOFC. First, Lardiere and Schwartz (1997) show that Spanish-native L2 learners of English never produce synthetic compounds of the type *chase-micer*, although English-style synthetic compounds do not exist in Spanish, and they do produce a range of erroneous forms. Similarly, citing Clark, Hecht, and Mulford (1986), Veenstra observes that L1 acquirers of English go through a stage around age 4 where they make various errors in synthetic compounds, including producing forms like *dry-hairer*. However, these forms are in a minority and very short-lived.

References

Abeillé, Anne, and Danièle Godard. 2000. "French Word Order and Lexical Weight." In *The Nature and Function of Syntactic Categories*, ed. Robert Borsley, 325–360. San Diego, CA: Academic Press.

Abels, Klaus. 2003. "Successive Cyclicity, Anti-locality, and Adposition Stranding." PhD diss., University of Connecticut, Storrs.

Abels, Klaus. 2008. "Towards a restrictive theory of (remnant) movement." *Linguistic Variation Yearbook* 7:52–120.

Abels, Klaus. 2012. *Phases: An Essay on Cyclicity in Syntax*. Berlin: Mouton de Gruyter.

Abels, Klaus. 2013. "On 231." Unpublished ms., University College London.

Abels, Klaus, and Ad Neeleman. 2009. "Universal 20 without the LCA." In *Merging Features*, ed. José M. Brucart, Anna Gavarró, and Jaume Solà, 60–80. Oxford: Oxford University Press.

Abels, Klaus, and Ad Neeleman. 2012. "Linear Asymmetries and the LCA." *Syntax* 15:25–74.

Abney, Steven P. 1987. "The English Noun Phrase in Its Sentential Aspect." PhD diss., MIT.

Aboh, Enoch. 2004. *The Morphosyntax of Complement-Head Sequences*. Oxford: Oxford University Press.

Aboh, Enoch. 2006. "Complementation in Saramaccan and Gungbe: The Case of C-Type Modal Particles." *Natural Language and Linguistic Theory* 24:1–55.

Aboh, Enoch. 2010. "The P-Route." In *Mapping Spatial PPs*, ed. Guglielmo Cinque and Luigi Rizzi, 225–260. New York: Oxford University Press.

Aboh, Enoch, and Maria Dyakonova. 2009. "Predicate Doubling and Chains." *Lingua* 119:1035–1065.

Ackema, Peter, and Ad Neeleman. 2004. *Beyond Morphology: Interface Conditions on Word Formation*. Oxford: Oxford University Press.

Adger, David. 2013. *A Syntax of Substance*. Cambridge, MA: MIT Press.

Aelbrecht, Lobke, Liliane Haegeman, and Rachel Nye. 2012. *Main Clause Phenomena: New Horizons*. Amsterdam: John Benjamins.

Agha, Asif. 1998. "Form and Function in Urdu-Hindi Verb Inflection." In *The Yearbook of South Asian Languages and Linguistics*, ed. Rajendra Singh, 105–133. New Delhi: Sage Publications.

Aghaei, Behrad. 2006. "The Syntax of *ke*-Clause and Clausal Extraposition in Modern Persian." PhD diss., University of Texas.

Ajíbóyè, Ọládiípọ̀. 2001. "The Internal Structure of Yorùbá DP." Paper presented at Annual Conference on African Linguistics 32. University of California, Berkeley.

Akkuş, Faruk, and Elabbas Benmamoun. 2016. "Clause Structure in Contact Contexts: The Case of Sason Arabic." In *Perspectives on Arabic Linguistics XXVIII: Papers from the Annual Symposium on Arabic Linguistics, Gainesville, Florida, 2014*, ed. Youssef Haddad and Eric Potsdam, 153–172. Amsterdam: John Benjamins.

Akmajian, Adrian, and Frank Heny. 1975. *An Introduction to the Principles of Transformational Syntax*. Cambridge, MA: MIT Press.

Aldridge, Edith. 2002. "Nominalization and *Wh*-Movement in Seediq and Tagalog." *Language and Linguistics* 3:393–427.

Aldridge, Edith. 2004. "Ergativity and Word Order in Austronesian Languages." PhD diss., Cornell University.

Aldridge, Edith. 2011. "Neg-to-Q: The Historical Development of One Clause-Final Particle." In *Particles*, ed. Theresa Biberauer and Michelle Sheehan, special issue, *The Linguistic Review* 28:411–447.

Alektoridis, Anastasios S. 1883. Λεξιλόγιον τοῦ ἐν Φερτακαίνοις τῆς Καππαδοκίας γλωσσικοῦ ἰδιώματος. *Deltion Istorikis Ethnologikis Etaireias* 1:480–508.

Alexander, David. 2007. "The Spanish Postnominal Demonstrative in Synchrony and Diachrony." PhD diss., Ohio State University.

Alexander, Ruth Mary. 1988. "A Syntactic Sketch of Ocotepec Mixtec." In *Studies in the Syntax of Mixtecan Languages*, Vol. 1, ed. C. Henry Bradley and Barbara Hollenbach, 151–304. Dallas, TX: Summer Institute of Linguistics and the University of Texas at Arlington.

Alexiadou, Artemis. 1997. *Adverb Placement: A Case Study in Antisymmetric Syntax*. Amsterdam: John Benjamins.

Alexiadou, Artemis, and Elena Anagnostopoulou. 2001. "The Subject-in-Situ Generalization and the Role of Case in Driving Computations." *Linguistic Inquiry* 32:193–231.

Alexiadou, Artemis, Liliane Haegeman, and Melita Stavrou. 2007. *The Noun Phrase in the Generative Perspective*. Berlin: Mouton de Gruyter.

Allin, Trevor R. 1976. *A Grammar of Resígaro*. Horsleys Green, Buckinghamshire: Summer Institute of Linguistics.

Anderson, Gregory. 2005. *Auxiliary Verb Constructions*. Oxford: Oxford University Press.

Anderson, Gregory. 2011. "Auxiliary Verb Constructions in the Languages of Africa." *Studies in African Linguistics* 40(1/2):1–409.

Anderson, Torben. 1988. "Ergativity in Päri, a Nilotic OVS Language." *Lingua* 75:289–324.

Androutsopoulou, Antonia. 1995. "The Licensing of Adjectival Modification." In *Proceedings of the Fourteenth West Coast Conference on Formal Linguistics*, ed. José Camacho, Lina Choueiri, and Maki Watanabe, 17–31. Stanford, CA: CSLI Publications.

Antonelli, André. 2015. "Roots of V to C Movement in Romance: Investigating Late Latin Grammar." Paper presented at the Traces of History Workshop, Oslo. (http://www.hf.uio.no/ilos/english/research/projects/traces-of-history/abstracts/antonelli.pdf; last accessed 3 July 2016)

Archelaos, I. Sarantidis. 1899. Ἡ Σιναςός, ἤτοι θέσις, ἱστορία, ἠθικὴ καὶ διανοητικὴ κατάστασις, ἤθη, ἔθιμα καὶ γλῶσσα τῆς ἐν Καππαδοκίᾳ κωμοπόλεως Σιναςοῦ. Ἐν ἐπιμέτρῳ δὲ καὶ σύντομος περιγραφὴ τῶν ἐν ταῖς ἐπαρχίαις Καισαρείας καὶ Ἰκονίου Ἑλληνικῶν Κοινοτήτων ὡς καὶ τῶν ἐν αὐταῖς σῳζομένων ἑλληνικῶν διαλέκτων ἐν σχέσει πρὸς τὴν ἐν Σιναςῷ λαλουμένην. Athens: Ioannis Nikolaidis.

Aronoff, Mark. 1976. *Word Formation in Generative Grammar*. Cambridge, MA: MIT Press.

Arregui, Karlos. 2002. "Focus on Basque Movements." PhD diss., MIT.

Arsenijević, Boban. 2009. "Clausal Complementation as Relativization." *Lingua* 119:39–50.

Asbury, Anna, Jakub Dotlačil, Berit Gehrke, and Rick Nouwen. 2008. *Syntax and Semantics of Spatial P*. Amsterdam: John Benjamins.

Babby, Leonard H. 1973. "The Deep Structure of Adjectives and Participles in Russian." *Language* 49:349–360.

Babby, Leonard H. 1975. *A Transformational Grammar of Russian Adjectives*. The Hague: Mouton.

Bailey, Laura. 2012. "The Syntax of Question Particles." PhD diss., Newcastle University.

Bailyn, John. 1994. "The Syntax and Semantics of Russian Long and Short Adjectives: An X′-Theoretic Account." In *Formal Approaches to Slavic Linguistics: The College Park Meeting*, ed. Jindřich Toman, 1–30. Ann Arbor: Michigan Slavic Publications.

Baker, Mark C. 1988. *Incorporation: A Theory of Grammatical Function Changing*. Chicago: University of Chicago Press.

Baker, Mark C. 1996. *The Polysynthesis Parameter*. Oxford: Oxford University Press.

Baker, Mark C. 2003. *Lexical Categories*. Cambridge: Cambridge University Press.

Baker, Mark C. 2005a. "On Gerunds and the Theory of Categories." Unpublished ms., Rutgers University.

Baker, Mark C. 2005b. "On Verb-Initial and Verb-Final Word Order in Lokaa." *Journal of African Languages and Linguistics* 26:125–164.

Baker, Mark C. 2008. "The Macroparameter in a Microparametric World." In *The Limits of Syntactic Variation*, ed. Theresa Biberauer, 351–374. Amsterdam: John Benjamins.

Baltin, Mark. 1989. "Heads and Projections." In *Alternative Conceptions of Phrase Structure*, ed. Mark Baltin and Anthony Kroch, 1–16. Chicago: University of Chicago Press.

Barwise, Jon, and Robin Cooper. 1981. "Generalized Quantifiers and Natural Language." *Linguistics and Philosophy* 4:159–219.

Batllori, Montserrat, and Maria-Lluïsa Hernanz. 2013. "Emphatic Polarity Particles in Spanish and Catalan." *Lingua* 128:9–30.

Bayer, Josef. 1996. *Directionality and Logical Form: On the Scope of Focusing Particles and* Wh-*in-Situ*. Dordrecht: Kluwer.

Bayer, Josef. 1999. "Final Complementizers in Hybrid Languages." *Journal of Linguistics* 35:233–271.

Bayer, Josef. 2001. "Two Grammars in One: Sentential Complements and Complementisers in Bengali and Other South Asian Languages." In *The Yearbook of South Asian Languages: Tokyo Symposium on South Asian Languages - Contact Convergence and Typology*, ed. Peri Bhaskararao and Karumuri V. Subbarao, 11–36. New Delhi: Sage Publications.

Bayer, Josef. 2016a. "Criterial Freezing in the Syntax of Particles." Unpublished ms., University of Konstanz.

Bayer, Josef. 2016b. "Why Doubling Discourse Particles?" Unpublished ms., University of Konstanz.

Bayer, Josef, Jana Häussler, and Markus Bader. 2016. "A New Diagnostic for Cyclic *Wh*-Movement: Discourse Particles in German Questions." *Linguistic Inquiry* 47:591–629.

Bayer, Josef, and Hans-Georg Obenauer. 2011. "Discourse Particles, Clause Structure, and Question Types." *The Linguistic Review* 28:449–491.

Bayer, Josef, Tanja Schmid, and Markus Bader. 2005. "Clause Union and Clausal Position." In *The Function of Function Words and Functional Categories*, ed. Marcel den Dikken and Christina Tortora, 79–114. Amsterdam: John Benjamins.

Bayer, Josef, and Andreas Trotzke. 2015. "The Derivation and Interpretation of Left Peripheral Discourse Particles." In *Discourse-Oriented Syntax*, ed. Josef Bayer, Roland Hinterhölzl, and Andreas Trotzke, 13–40. Amsterdam: John Benjamins.

Bazalgette, Timothy. 2011. "A Crosslinguistic Investigation of *Wh*-Internal Structure: Morphology, Macroparameters and the Borer-Chomsky Conjecture." MPhil thesis, University of Cambridge.

Bazalgette, Timothy, Ian Roberts, Michelle Sheehan, and Jenneke van der Wal. 2012. "Two Statistical Typological Generalisations and Their Consequences." Paper presented at The Syntax of the World's Languages (SWL), Dubrovnik, 1–4 November.

Beaumont, Clive H. 1979. *The Tigak Language of New Ireland*. Canberra: Australian National University.

Beck, Sigrid. 1996a. "Quantified Structures as Barriers for LF-Movement." *Natural Language Semantics* 4:1–56.

Beck, Sigrid. 1996b. "*Wh*-Constructions and Transparent Logical Form." PhD diss., Tübingen University.

Beck, Sigrid. 2006. "Intervention Effects Follow from Focus Interpretation." *Natural Language Semantics* 14:1–56.

Beck, Sigrid, and Shin-Sook Kim. 1997. "On *Wh-* and Operator Scope in Korean." *Journal of East Asian Linguistics* 6:339–384.

Beerman, Dorothee, David Leblanc, and Henk van Riemsdijk. 1997. *Rightward Movement*. Amsterdam: John Benjamins.

Behaghel, Otto. 1932. *Deutsche Syntax: Eine geschichtliche Darstellung*. Vol. 4, *Wortstellung. Periodenbau*. Heidelberg: Winter.

Bell, Arthur. 2004a. "Bipartite Negation and the Fine Structure of the Negative Phrase." PhD diss., Cornell University.

Bell, Arthur. 2004b. "How N-Words Move: Bipartite Negation and 'Split-NegP.'" In *Triggers*, ed. Anne Breitbarth and Henk van Riemsdijk, 77–114. Berlin: Mouton de Gruyter.

Belletti, Adriana. 1990. *Generalized Verb Movement: Aspects of Verb Syntax*. Turin: Rosenberg and Sellier.

Belletti, Adriana. 2004. "Aspects of the Low IP Area." In *The Structure of CP and IP*, ed. Luigi Rizzi, 16–51. Oxford: Oxford University Press.

Benmamoun, Elabbas. 2000. *The Feature Structure of Functional Categories: A Comparative Study of Arabic Dialects*. Oxford: Oxford University Press.

Bentzen, Kristine. 2007. "Order and Structure in Embedded Clauses in Northern Norwegian." PhD diss., University of Tromsø.

Berman, Arlene. 1974. "Adjectives and Adjective Complement Constructions in English." PhD diss., Harvard University.

Berman, Ruth A. 1997. "Modern Hebrew." In *The Semitic Languages*, ed. Robert Hetzron, 312–333. London: Routledge.

Bernstein, Judith B. 1991. "DPs in French and Walloon: Evidence for Parametric Variation in Nominal Head Movement." *Probus* 5:5–38.

Bernstein, Judith B. 1995. "Adjectives and Their Complements." Paper presented at the annual meeting of the Linguistic Society of America, New Orleans.

Bernstein, Judith B. 2001. "The DP Hypothesis: Identifying Clausal Properties in the Nominal Domain." In *The Handbook of Contemporary Syntactic Theory*, ed. Chris Collins and Mark Baltin, 536–561. Oxford: Blackwell.

Berwick, Robert C., and Noam Chomsky. 2011. "The Biolinguistic Program: The Current State of Its Evolution and Development." In *The Biolinguistic Enterprise: New Perspectives on the Evolution and Nature of the Human Language Faculty*, ed. Anna Maria Di Sciullo and Cedric Boeckx, 19–41. Cambridge, MA: MIT Press.

Besnier, Niko. 2000. *Tuvaluan, a Polynesian Language of the Central Pacific*. London: Routledge.

Besten, Hans den. 1986. "Decidability in the Syntax of Verbs of (Not Necessarily) West Germanic Languages." *Groninger Arbeiten zur germanistischen Linguistik* 28:232–256. [Reprinted in *Studies in West Germanic Syntax*, 111–135. Amsterdam: Rodopi (1989).]

Bhatt, Rajesh. 2003. "Topics in the Syntax of the Modern Indo-Aryan Languages: Negation and Negative Polarity." Class handouts, MIT.

Bhatt, Rajesh. 2007. "Little or Nothing." Unpublished ms., University of Massachusetts, Amherst.

Bhatt, Rajesh, and Veneeta Dayal. 2007. "Rightward Scrambling as Rightward Remnant Movement." *Linguistic Inquiry* 38:287–301.

Bhatt, Rajesh, and Roumyana Pancheva. 2004. "Late Merger of Degree Clauses." *Linguistic Inquiry* 35:1–45.

Bhatt, Rakesh, and James Yoon. 1992. "On the Composition of COMP and Parameters of V2." In *Proceedings of WCCFL 10*, ed. Dawn Bates, 41–52. Stanford, CA: Stanford University, Stanford Linguistics Association.

Biberauer, Theresa. 2008. "Doubling and Omission: Insights from Afrikaans Negation." In *Microvariations in Syntactic Doubling*, ed. Sjef Barbiers, Margreet van der Ham, Olaf Koeneman, and Marika Lekakou, 103–140. Bingley: Emerald.

Biberauer, Theresa. 2009. "Jespersen Off Course? The Case of Contemporary Afrikaans Negation." In *Cyclical Change*, ed. Elly van Gelderen, 91–130. Amsterdam: John Benjamins.

Biberauer, Theresa. 2011. "In Defence of Lexico-centric Parametric Variation: Two 3rd Factor-Constrained Case Studies." Paper presented at the Workshop on Formal Grammar and Syntactic Variation: Rethinking Parameters, Madrid.

Biberauer, Theresa. 2012. "Competing Reinforcements: When Languages Opt Out of Jespersen's Cycle." In *Historical Linguistics 2009: Selected Papers from the 19th International Conference on Historical Linguistics, Nijmegen, 10–14 August 2009*, ed. Ans van Kemenade and Nynke de Haas, 1–30. Amsterdam: John Benjamins.

Biberauer, Theresa. 2013. "Predicate Doubling in (Germanic) Contact Varieties: Introducing the Case of Afrikaans." Paper presented at the 27th Comparative Germanic Linguistics Conference, Yale University.

Biberauer, Theresa. 2015a. "Macro- and Microvariation: An Emergentist Perspective." Paper presented at Formal Approaches to Morphosyntactic Variation, Vitoria-Gasteiz.

Biberauer, Theresa. 2015b. "*Nie sommer nie*: Sociohistorical and Formal Comparative Considerations in the Rise and Maintenance of the Modern Afrikaans Negation System." In *Studies opgedra aan Hans den Besten: Suider-Afrikaanse perspektiewe/Studies Dedicated to Hans den Besten: Southern African Perspectives*, ed. Theresa Biberauer and Johan Oosthuizen, 129–175. Stellenbosch: Sunmedia.

Biberauer, Theresa. 2016a. "Contact and Acquirers: The 'Exotic' Factors That Have Shaped Afrikaans V2." Paper presented at the 1st Workshop on the Determinants of Diachronic Stability, Ghent.

Biberauer, Theresa. 2016b. "Going beyond the Input: Three Factors and Variation, Change and Stability." Paper presented at Formal Ways of Analyzing Variation 3, New York.

Biberauer, Theresa. To appear a. "Optional V2 in Modern Afrikaans: Probing a Germanic Peculiarity." In *Verb-Second Languages: Essays in Honour of Ans van Kemenade*, ed. Bettelou Los and Pieter de Haan. Amsterdam: John Benjamins.

Biberauer, Theresa. To appear b. "Probing the Nature of the Final-over-Final Constraint: The Perspective from Adpositions." In *Order and Structure in Syntax*, ed. Laura Bailey and Michelle Sheehan. Language Science Press.

Biberauer, Theresa, and Sonia Cyrino. 2009. "Negative Developments in Afrikaans and Brazilian Portuguese." Paper presented at the 19th Colloquium on Generative Grammar, Vitoria-Gasteiz.

Biberauer, Theresa, Liliane Haegeman, and Ans van Kemenade. 2014. "Putting Our Heads Together: Towards a Syntax of Particles." *Studia Linguistica* 68:1–15.

Biberauer, Theresa, Anders Holmberg, and Ian Roberts. 2007. "Disharmonic Word-Order Systems and the Final-over-Final-Constraint (FOFC)." In *Proceedings of the XXXIII Incontro di Grammatica Generativa*, ed. Antonietta Bisetto and Francesco Barbieri, 86–105. Bologna: University of Bologna.

Biberauer, Theresa, Anders Holmberg, and Ian Roberts. 2008a. "Linearising Disharmonic Word Orders: The Final-over-Final Constraint." In *Perspectives on Linguistics in the 21st Century*, ed. K.-A. Kim, 301–318. Seoul: ICLK.

Biberauer, Theresa, Anders Holmberg, and Ian Roberts. 2008b. "Structure and Linearization in Disharmonic Word Orders." In *WCCFL 26: Proceedings of the 26th Western Coast Conference on Formal Linguistics*, ed. Charles B. Chang and Hannah J. Haynie, 96–104. Somerville, MA: Cascadilla Proceedings Project.

Biberauer, Theresa, Anders Holmberg, and Ian Roberts. 2014. "A Syntactic Universal and Its Consequences." *Linguistic Inquiry* 45:169–225.

Biberauer, Theresa, Anders Holmberg, Ian Roberts, and Michelle Sheehan. 2010a. *Parametric Variation: Null Subjects in Minimalist Theory*. Cambridge: Cambridge University Press.

Biberauer, Theresa, Anders Holmberg, Ian Roberts, and Michelle Sheehan. 2010b. "Reconciling Formalism and Functionalism: A Minimalist Perspective." Paper presented at the annual meeting of the Linguistics Association of Great Britain, Leeds, September 2010.

Biberauer, Theresa, Anders Holmberg, Ian Roberts, and Michelle Sheehan. 2014. "Complexity in Comparative Syntax: The View from Modern Parametric Theory." In *Measuring Grammatical Complexity*, ed. Frederick J. Newmeyer and Laurel B. Preston, 103–127. Oxford: Oxford University Press.

Biberauer, Theresa, and Xuhui Hu. 2014. "Chinese Particles Revisited: Implications for the Typology of Syntactic Categories." Paper presented at the 3rd Cambridge Comparative Syntax (CamCoS 3) Prequel Workshop.

Biberauer, Theresa, Glenda Newton, and Michelle Sheehan. 2009a. "The Final-over-Final Constraint and Predictions for Diachronic Change." In *Toronto Working Papers in Linguistics 31*, ed. Ruth Compton and Monica Irimia. (http://twpl.library.utoronto.ca/index.php/twpl/article/view/6091; last accessed 15 November 2015)

Biberauer, Theresa, Glenda Newton, and Michelle Sheehan. 2009b. "Limiting Synchronic and Diachronic Variation and Change: The Final-over-Final Constraint." *Language and Linguistics* 10:699–741.

Biberauer, Theresa, and Johan Oosthuizen. 2011. "More Unbearably Light Elements? Silent Verbs Demanding Overt Complementizers in Afrikaans." *Snippets* 24:5–6.

Biberauer, Theresa, and Ian Roberts. 2005. "Changing EPP-Parameters in the History of English: Accounting for Variation and Change." *English Language and Linguistics* 9:5–46.

Biberauer, Theresa, and Ian Roberts. 2008. "Phases, Word Order and Types of Clausal Complements in West Germanic Languages." Paper presented at the 23rd Comparative Germanic Syntax Workshop, Edinburgh.

Biberauer, Theresa, and Ian Roberts. 2010. "Subjects, Tense and Verb Movement." In *Parametric Variation: Null Subjects in Minimalist Theory*, ed. Theresa Biberauer, Anders Holmberg, Ian Roberts, and Michelle Sheehan, 263–302. Cambridge: Cambridge University Press.

Biberauer, Theresa, and Ian Roberts. 2011. "Negative Words and Related Expressions: A New Perspective on Some Familiar Puzzles." In *The Evolution of Negation: Beyond the Jespersen Cycle*, ed. Richard Ingham and Pierre Larrivee, 23–60. Berlin: de Gruyter.

Biberauer, Theresa, and Ian Roberts. 2012. "The Significance of What Hasn't Happened." Paper presented at Diachronic Generative Syntax Conference XIV, Lisbon.

Biberauer, Theresa, and Ian Roberts. 2015a. "The Clausal Hierarchy, Features and Parameters." In *Beyond Functional Sequence*, ed. Ur Shlonsky, 295–313. Oxford: Oxford University Press.

Biberauer, Theresa, and Ian Roberts. 2015b. "Movement without Diacritics: Getting Maximal Use out of Minimal Means." Paper presented at the 41st Incontro di Grammatica Generativa, Perugia.

Biberauer, Theresa, and Ian Roberts. 2015c. "Rethinking Formal Hierarchies: A Proposed Unification." In *Cambridge Occasional Papers in Linguistics 7*, ed. James Chancharu, Xuhui Hu, and Moreno Mitrović, 1–31. (http://www.ling.cam.ac.uk/COPIL/papers/7-BiberauerRoberts.pdf)

Biberauer, Theresa, and Ian Roberts. 2017. "Parameter Setting." In *The Cambridge Handbook of Historical Syntax*, ed. Adam Ledgeway and Ian Roberts, 134–162. Cambridge: Cambridge University Press.

Biberauer, Theresa, Ian Roberts, and Michelle Sheehan. 2014. "No-Choice Parameters and the Limits of Syntactic Variation." In *WCCFL 31: Proceedings of the 31st West Coast Conference on Formal Linguistics*, ed. Robert Santana-LaBarge, 46–55. Somerville, MA: Cascadilla Press.

Biberauer, Theresa, and Michelle Sheehan. 2012a. "Disharmony, Antisymmetry, and the Final-over-Final Constraint." In *Ways of Structure Building*, ed. Myriam Uribe-Etxebarria and Vidal Valmala, 206–244. Oxford: Oxford University Press.

Biberauer, Theresa, and Michelle Sheehan. 2012b. "Introduction: Particles through a Modern Syntactic Lens." *The Linguistic Review* 38:387–401.

Biberauer, Theresa, and Michelle Sheehan. 2013. "Introduction." In *Theoretical Approaches to Disharmonic Word Order*, ed. Theresa Biberauer and Michelle Sheehan, 1–46. Oxford: Oxford University Press.

Biberauer, Theresa, Michelle Sheehan, and Glenda Newton. 2010. "Impossible Changes and Impossible Borrowings." In *Continuity and Change in Grammar*, ed. Anne Breitbarth, Chris Lucas, Sheila Watts, and David Willis, 35–60. Amsterdam: John Benjamins.

Biberauer, Theresa, and Hedde Zeijlstra. 2012a. "Negative Changes: Three Factors and the Diachrony of Afrikaans Negation." In *Parameter Theory and Linguistic Change*, ed. Charlotte Galves, Sonia Cyrino, Ruth Lopes, Filomena Sandalo, and Juanito Avelar, 237–263. Oxford: Oxford University Press.

Biberauer, Theresa, and Hedde Zeijlstra. 2012b. "Negative Concord in Afrikaans: Filling a Typological Gap." *Journal of Semantics* 29:345–371.

Bidese, Ermenegildo, Andrea Padovan, and Alessandra Tomaselli. 2012. "A Binary System of Complementizers in Cimbrian Relative Clauses." *Working Papers in Scandinavian Syntax* 90:1–21.

Biggs, Alison. 2014. "Dissociating Theta-Roles and Case: A Comparative Investigation." PhD diss., University of Cambridge.

Blackings, Mairi, and Nigel Fabb. 2003. *A Grammar of Ma'di*. Berlin: Mouton de Gruyter.

Blevins, Juliette. 1995. "The Syllable in Phonological Theory." In *Handbook of Phonological Theory*, ed. John Goldsmith, 206–244. Oxford: Blackwell.

Bobaljik, Jonathan David. 1999. "Adverbs: The Hierarchy Paradox." *Glot International* 4(9/10):27–28.

Bobaljik, Jonathan David. 2002. "A-Chains at the PF-Interface: Copies and 'Covert' Movement." *Natural Language and Linguistic Theory* 20:197–267.

Bobaljik, Jonathan David. 2008. "Where's Phi? Agreement as a Post-Syntactic Operation." In *Phi-Theory: Phi Features across Interfaces and Modules*, ed. Daniel Harbour, David Adger, and Susana Béjar, 295–328. Oxford: Oxford University Press.

Bobaljik, Jonathan David, and Susi Wurmbrand. 2005. "The Domain of Agreement." *Natural Language and Linguistic Theory* 23:809–865.

Bobaljik, Jonathan David, and Susi Wurmbrand. 2013. "Suspension across Domains." In *Distributed Morphology Today—Morphemes for Morris Halle*, ed. Ora Matushansky and Alec Marantz, 185–198. Cambridge, MA: MIT Press.

Bodrogligeti, Andras. 2003. *An Academic Reference Grammar of Modern Literary Uzbek*. Munich: Lincom.

Boeckx, Cedric. 2011. "Approaching Parameters from Below." In *The Biolinguistic Enterprise: New Perspectives on the Evolution and Nature of the Human Language Faculty*, ed. Anna Maria Di Sciullo and Cedric Boeckx, 205–221. Cambridge, MA: MIT Press.

Boef, Eefje. 2012. "Doubling in Relative Clauses: Aspects of Morphosyntactic Variation in Dutch." PhD diss., Utrecht/Meertens Instituut.

Boelaars, J. H. M. C. 1950. *The Linguistic Position of South-Western New Guinea*. Leiden: E. J. Brill.

Bombi-Ferrer, Carla. 2014. "Spanish Postnominal Demonstratives." BA thesis, University of Cambridge.

Bonami, Olivier, Danièle Godard, and Brigitte Kampers-Manhe. 2004. "Adverb Classification." In *Handbook of French Semantics*, ed. Francis Corblin and Henriëtte de Swart, 143–184. Stanford, CA: CSLI Publications.

Bonfim Duarte, Fabio. 2012. "Tenetehára: A Predicate Fronting Language." *Canadian Journal of Linguistics/Revue Canadienne de Linguistique* 57:359–386.

Borer, Hagit. 2005. *Structuring Sense*. Vol. 1, *In Name Only*. Oxford: Oxford University Press.

Borsley, Robert, and Jaklin Kornfilt. 2000. "Mixed Extended Projections." In *The Nature and Function of Syntactic Categories*, ed. Robert Borsley, 101–131. San Diego, CA: Academic Press.

Bošković, Željko. 2001. "*Li* without PF Movement." In *Formal Approaches to Slavic Linguistics: The Indiana Meeting, 2000*, ed. Steve Franks, Tracy Holloway King, and Misha Yadroff, 57–75. Ann Arbor: Michigan Slavic Publications.

Bošković, Željko. 2005. "On the Locality of Left Branch Extraction and the Structure of NP." *Studia Linguistica* 59:1–45.

Bošković, Željko. 2008. "What Will You Have, DP or NP?" In *NELS 37*, ed. Emily Elfner and Martin Walkow, 101–114. Amherst: University of Massachusetts, Graduate Linguistic Student Association.

Bošković, Željko. 2010. "On NPs and Clauses." Unpublished ms., University of Connecticut.

Bošković, Željko. 2014. "Now I'm a Phase, Now I'm Not a Phase: On the Variability of Phases with Extraction and Ellipsis." *Linguistic Inquiry* 45:27–89.

Bouchard, Denis. 1998. "The Distribution and Interpretation of Adjectives in French: A Consequence of Bare Phrase Structure." *Probus* 10:139–183.

Bouchard, Denis. 2002. *Adjectives, Number, and Interfaces: Why Languages Vary*. Amsterdam: Elsevier.

Bowern, Claire. 2011. *Sivisa Titan: Sketch Grammar, Texts, Vocabulary Based on Material Collected by P. Josef Meier and Po Minis*. Honolulu: University of Hawai'i Press.

Boyd, Virginia Lee. 1997. "A Phonology and Grammar of Mbodómó." MA thesis, University of Texas at Arlington.

Boyer, Pascal. 2001. *Religion Explained: The Evolutionary Origins of Religious Thought*. New York: Basic Books.

Breitbarth, Anne, and Liliane Haegeman. 2010. "Continuity Is Change: The Long Tail of Jespersen's Cycle in Flemish." In *Continuity and Change in Grammar*, ed. Anne Breitbarth, Christopher Lucas, Sheila Watts, and David Willis, 61–76. Amsterdam: John Benjamins.

Breitbarth, Anne, and Liliane Haegeman. 2013. "The Distribution of Preverbal *en* in (West) Flemish: Syntactic and Interpretive Properties." *Lingua* 147:69–86.

Bresnan, Joan. 1973. "Syntax of the Comparative Clause Construction in English." *Linguistic Inquiry* 4:275–343.

Bresnan, Joan. 1997. "Mixed Categories as Head Sharing Constructions." In *Proceedings of the LFG97 Conference*, ed. Miriam Butt and Tracy Holloway King, 1–17. Stanford, CA: CSLI Publications.

Broekhuis, Hans. 2011. "A Typology of Clause Structure." *Linguistic Variation Yearbook* 10:1–31.

Bruening, Benjamin. 2009. "Selectional Asymmetries between CP and DP Suggest That the DP Hypothesis Is Wrong." In *Proceedings of the 32nd Annual Penn Linguistics Colloquium*, ed. Laurel MacKenzie, 26–35. University of Pennsylvania Working Papers in Linguistics 15.1. (http://repository.upenn.edu/pwpl/vol15/iss1/; last accessed 2 June 2016)

Bruening, Benjamin, Xuyen Dinh, and Lan Kim. 2015. "Selection, Idioms, and the Structure of Nominal Phrases with and without Classifiers." Unpublished ms., University of Delaware. (http://udel.edu/~bruening/Downloads/IdiomsClassifiers7.3.pdf; last accessed 2 June 2016)

Brugè, Laura. 1994. "Alcune considerazioni sulla sintassi del dimostrativo in spagnolo." Unpublished ms., Universities of Padua and Venice.

Brugè, Laura. 1996. "Demonstrative Movement in Spanish: A Comparative Approach." *University of Venice Working Papers in Linguistics* 6:1–53.

Brugè, Laura. 2000. *Categorie funzionali del nome nelle lingue romanze*. Milan: Cisalpino.

Brugè, Laura. 2002. "The Positions of Demonstratives in the Extended Nominal Projection." In *Functional Structure in DP and IP*, ed. Guglielmo Cinque, 15–53. Oxford: Oxford University Press.

Brugè, Laura, and Giuliana Giusti. 1996. "On Demonstratives." Paper presented at the 19th GLOW Colloquium, Athens. *GLOW Newsletter* 36:24–25.

Buell, Leston. 2012. "Ewe VP Fronting and Derivation by Phase." Unpublished ms., University of Amsterdam.

Büring, Daniel, and Katharina Hartmann. 1997. "Doing the Right Thing: Extraposition as a Movement Rule." *The Linguistic Review* 14:1–42.

Burton-Roberts, Noel. 2009. "The Grounding of Syntax – and More." *Newcastle Working Papers in Linguistics* 14:22–39.

Burton-Roberts, Noel, and Geoffrey Poole. 2006. "'Virtual Conceptual Necessity', Feature Dissociation and the Saussurean Legacy in Generative Grammar." *Journal of Linguistics* 42:575–628.

Cable, Seth. 2007. "The Grammar of Q: Q-Particles and the Nature of *Wh*-Fronting, as Revealed by the *Wh*-Questions of Tlingit." PhD diss., MIT.

Cable, Seth. 2010. *Q-Particles, Wh-Movement, and Pied-Piping*. Oxford: Oxford University Press.

Cable, Seth. 2012. "The Optionality of Movement and EPP in Dholuo." *Natural Language and Linguistic Theory* 30:651–697.

Caha, Pavel. 2009. "The Nanosyntax of Case." PhD diss., University of Tromsø.

Cardinaletti, Anna. 2011. "German and Italian Modal Particles and Clause Structure." *The Linguistic Review* 28:493–553.

Cardinaletti, Anna, and Lori Repetti. 2008. "The Phonology and Syntax of Preverbal and Postverbal Subject Clitics in Northern Italian Dialects." *Linguistic Inquiry* 39:523–563.

Cardinaletti, Anna, and Michal Starke. 1999. "The Typology of Structural Deficiency: A Case Study of the Three Classes of Pronouns." In *Clitics in the Languages of Europe*, ed. Henk van Riemsdijk, 145–235. Berlin: Mouton de Gruyter.

Carlson, Robert. 1990. *A Grammar of Supyire*. Berlin: Mouton de Gruyter.

Carnie, Andrew, and Eithne Guilfoyle. 2001. *The Syntax of Verb Initial Languages*. Oxford: Oxford University Press.

Carnie, Andrew, Heidi Harley, and Sheila Dooley, eds. 2005. *Verb First: On the Syntax of Verb-Initial Languages*. Amsterdam: John Benjamins.

Carstens, Vicki. 2002. "Asymmetry and Word Order in Serial Constructions." *Language* 78:3–50.

Carstens, Vicki. 2013. "Delayed Valuation: A Reanalysis of 'Upwards' Complementizer Agreement and the Mechanics of Case." Unpublished ms. (http://ling.auf.net/lingbuzz/001432)

Cecchetto, Carlo. 2013. "Backward Dependencies Must Be Short." In *Challenges to Linearization*, ed. Theresa Biberauer and Ian Roberts, 57–92. Berlin: Mouton de Gruyter.

Chan, Brian Hok-Shing. 2013. "Sentence-Final Particles, Complementizers, Antisymmetry and the Final-over-Final Constraint." In *Theoretical Approaches to Disharmonic Word Order*, ed. Theresa Biberauer and Michelle Sheehan, 445–468. Oxford: Oxford University Press.

Cheng, Lisa. 1991. "On the Typology of *Wh*-Questions." PhD diss., MIT.

Cheng, Lisa. 1997. *On the Typology of Wh-Questions*. New York: Garland.

Cheng, Lisa, and Johan Rooryck. 2000. "Licensing *Wh*-in-Situ." *Syntax* 3:1–19.

Cheng, Lisa, and Rint Sybesma. 2003. "Forked Modality." *Linguistics in the Netherlands* 2003: 13–23.

Cheng, Lisa, and Rint Sybesma. 2004. "Postverbal 'Can' in Cantonese (and Hakka) and Agree." *Lingua* 114:419–445.

Chierchia, Gennaro. 1998. "Reference to Kinds across Languages." *Natural Language Semantics* 6:339–405.

Chierchia, Gennaro. 2015. "How Universal Is the Mass/Count Distinction? Three Grammars of Counting." In *Chinese Syntax in a Cross-Linguistic Perspective*, ed. Audrey Li, Andrew Simpson, and Wei-Tien Dylan Tsai, 147–178. Oxford: Oxford University Press.

Chomsky, Noam. 1955/1975. "The Logical Structure of Linguistic Theory." 1955 ms. published in part with Chomsky's introduction, New York: Plenum Press (1975).

Chomsky, Noam. 1957. *Syntactic Structures*. The Hague: Mouton.

Chomsky, Noam. 1965. *Aspects of the Theory of Syntax*. Cambridge, MA: MIT Press.

Chomsky, Noam. 1970. "Remarks on Nominalization." In *Readings in English Transformational Grammar*, ed. Roderick A. Jacobs and Peter S. Rosenbaum, 184–221. Waltham, MA: Ginn.

Chomsky, Noam. 1973. "Conditions on Transformations." In *A Festschrift for Morris Halle*, ed. Stephen Anderson and Paul Kiparsky, 232–286. New York: Holt, Rinehart and Winston.

Chomsky, Noam. 1976. "Conditions on Rules of Grammar." *Linguistic Analysis* 2:303–349.

Chomsky, Noam. 1981. *Lectures on Government and Binding*. Dordrecht: Foris.

Chomsky, Noam. 1982. *Some Concepts and Consequences of the Theory of Government and Binding*. Cambridge, MA: MIT Press.

Chomsky, Noam. 1986. *Barriers*. Cambridge, MA: MIT Press.

Chomsky, Noam. 1991. "Some Notes on Economy of Derivation and Representation." In *Principles and Parameters in Comparative Grammar*, ed. Robert Freidin, 417–454. Cambridge, MA: MIT Press.

Chomsky, Noam. 1993. "A Minimalist Program for Linguistic Theory." In *The View from Building 20: Essays in Linguistics in Honor of Sylvain Bromberger*, ed. Kenneth Hale and Samuel Jay Keyser, 1–52. Cambridge, MA: MIT Press.

Chomsky, Noam. 1994. "Bare Phrase Structure." MIT Occasional Papers in Linguistics 5. Cambridge, MA: MIT, MIT Working Papers in Linguistics.

Chomsky, Noam. 1995. *The Minimalist Program*. Cambridge, MA: MIT Press.

Chomsky, Noam. 2000. "Minimalist Inquiries: The Framework." In *Step by Step: Essays on Minimalist Syntax in Honor of Howard Lasnik*, ed. Roger Martin, David Michaels, and Juan Uriagereka, 89–155. Cambridge, MA: MIT Press.

Chomsky, Noam. 2001. "Derivation by Phase." In *Ken Hale: A Life in Language*, ed. Michael Kenstowicz, 1–52. Cambridge, MA: MIT Press.

Chomsky, Noam. 2005. "Three Factors in Language Design." *Linguistic Inquiry* 36:1–22.

Chomsky, Noam. 2008. "On Phases." In *Foundational Issues in Linguistic Theory: Essays in Honor of Jean-Roger Vergnaud*, ed. Robert Freidin, Carlos Otero, and Maria Luisa Zubizarreta, 133–166. Cambridge, MA: MIT Press.

Chomsky, Noam. 2013. "Problems of Projection." *Lingua* 130:33–49.

Chomsky, Noam. 2015. "Problems of Projection: Extensions." In *Structures, Strategies and Beyond: Studies in Honour of Adriana Belletti*, ed. Elisa Di Domenico, Cornelia Hamann, and Simona Matteini, 1–16. Amsterdam: John Benjamins.

Chomsky, Noam, and Morris Halle. 1968. *The Sound Pattern of English*. New York: Harper and Row.

Christophe, Anne, Maria-Teresa Guasti, Marina Nespor, and Brit van Ooyen. 2003. "Prosodic Structure and Syntactic Acquisition: The Case of the Head-Direction Parameter." *Developmental Science* 6:211–220.

Christophe, Anne, Jacques Mehler, and Núria Sebastián-Gallés. 2001. "Perception of Prosodic Boundary Correlates by Newborn Infants." *Infancy* 2:385–394.

Chung, Jui-Yi Zoey. 2012. "Investigating the Syntax of Postverbal Modals in Hakka." *Taiwan Journal of Linguistics* 10:69–114.

Chung, Sandra. 2012. "Are Lexical Categories Universal? The View from Chamorro." *Theoretical Linguistics* 38:1–56.

Cinque, Guglielmo. 1977. "The Movement Nature of Left Dislocation." *Linguistic Inquiry* 8:397–412.

Cinque, Guglielmo. 1994. "On the Evidence for Partial N-Movement in the Romance DP." In *Paths towards Universal Grammar: Essays in Honor of Richard Kayne*, ed. Guglielmo Cinque, Jan Koster, Jean-Yves Pollock, Luigi Rizzi, and Raffaella Zanuttini, 85–110. Washington, DC: Georgetown University Press.

Cinque, Guglielmo. 1999. *Adverbs and Functional Heads: A Cross-Linguistic Perspective*. New York: Oxford University Press.

Cinque, Guglielmo. 2004. " 'Restructuring' and Functional Structure." In *Structures and Beyond: The Cartography of Syntactic Structures*, Volume 3, ed. Adriana Belletti, 132–191. New York: Oxford University Press.

Cinque, Guglielmo. 2005a. "Deriving Greenberg's Universal 20 and Its Exceptions." *Linguistic Inquiry* 36:315–332.

Cinque, Guglielmo. 2005b. "A Note on Verb/Object Order and Head/Relative Clause Order." *University of Venice Working Papers in Linguistics* 15:49–104.

Cinque, Guglielmo. 2008. "Two Types of Nonrestrictive Relatives." In *Empirical Issues in Syntax and Semantics 7*, ed. Olivier Bonami and Patricia Cabredo Hofherr, 99–137. Paris: CSSP.

Cinque, Guglielmo. 2010. *The Syntax of Adjectives: A Comparative Study*. Cambridge, MA: MIT Press.

Cinque, Guglielmo. 2013. "Deriving Word Order Types: A Change of Perspective." In *Theoretical Approaches to Disharmonic Word Order*, ed. Theresa Biberauer and Michelle Sheehan, 47–73. Oxford: Oxford University Press.

Cinque, Guglielmo, and Luigi Rizzi, eds. 2010. *Mapping Spatial PPs*. Oxford: Oxford University Press.

Citko, Barbara. 2014. *Phase Theory: An Introduction*. Cambridge: Cambridge University Press.

Clackson, James, and Geoffrey Horrocks. 2007. *The Blackwell History of the Latin Language*. Oxford: Blackwell.

Clark, Eve V., Barbara Frant Hecht, and Randa C. Mulford. 1986. "Coining Complex Compounds in English: Affixes and Word Order in Acquisition." *Linguistics* 24:7–29.

Cognola, Federica. 2013. "The Mixed OV/VO Syntax of Mòcheno Main Clauses: On the Interaction between High and Low Left Periphery." In *Theoretical Approaches to Disharmonic Word Order*, ed. Theresa Biberauer and Michelle Sheehan, 106–136. Oxford: Oxford University Press.

Collinder, Bjorn. 1960. *Comparative Grammar of the Uralic Languages*. Stockholm: Almqvist and Wiksell.

Collins, Chris. 2002. "Eliminating Labels." In *Derivation and Explanation in the Minimalist Program*, ed. Samuel David Epstein and T. Daniel Seely, 42–64. Malden, MA: Blackwell.

Coniglio, Marco, and Iulia Zegrean. 2010. "Splitting Up Force: Evidence from Discourse Particles." In *Main Clause Phenomena: New Horizons*, ed. Lobke Aelbrecht, Liliane Haegeman, and Rachel Nye, 229–256. Amsterdam: John Benjamins.

Corr, Alice. 2016a. "Structure beyond Force? Evidence for a 'Speech Act' Projection from Ibero-Romance." Paper presented at GLOW 39, Göttingen.

Corr, Alice. 2016b. "Ibero-Romance at the Syntax-Pragmatics Interface: The Clause and Beyond." PhD diss., University of Cambridge.

Corver, Norbert, and Marjo van Koppen. 2010. "(Dis)harmonic Variation, the Definite Article and NPE in the Dutch Dialects." Paper presented at the Workshop on Disharmony in Nominals at the annual meeting of the Linguistics Association of Great Britain, Leeds University, September 2010.

Cowper, Elizabeth, and Daniel Currie Hall. 2014. "*Reductio ad Discrimen:* Where Features Come From." *Nordlyd* 41:145–164.

Craenenbroeck, Jeroen van, and Marijke De Belder. 2014. "On Vocabulary Insertion." *Linguistic Analysis* 39:173–210.

Craenenbroeck, Jeroen van, and Marijke De Belder. 2015. "How to Merge a Root." *Linguistic Inquiry* 46:625–655.

Crain, Stephen, and Janet D. Fodor. 1985. "How Can Grammars Help Parsers?" In *Natural Language Parsing*, ed. David Dowty, Lauri Karttunen, and Arnold Zwicky, 94–128. Cambridge: Cambridge University Press.

Crisma, Paola. 2011. "On the So-Called 'Indefinite Article.'" Paper presented at the 21st Colloquium on Generative Grammar, Seville.

Curry, H. B. 1961. "Some Logical Aspects of Grammatical Structure." In *Structure of Language and Its Mathematical Aspects: Proceedings of the Twelfth Symposium on Applied Mathematics*, ed. by Roman Jakobson, 56–68. Providence, RI: American Mathematical Society.

Dahl, Östen. 1979. "Typology of Sentence Negation." *Linguistics* 17:79–106.

D'Alessandro, Roberta, and Ian Roberts. 2010. "Past Participle Agreement in Abruzzese: Split Auxiliary Selection and the Null-Subject Parameter." *Natural Language and Linguistic Theory* 28:41–72.

Dal Pozzo, Lena. 2007. "The Finnish Noun Phrase." MA thesis, University of Venice.

Davison, Alice. 2007. "Word Order, Parameters, and the Extended COMP Projection." In *Linguistic Theory and South Asian Languages*, ed. Josef Bayer, Tanmoy Bhattacharya, and M. T. Hany Babu, 175–198. Amsterdam: John Benjamins.

Dawkins, Richard. 1916. *Modern Greek in Asia Minor.* Cambridge: Cambridge University Press.

Deal, Amy Rose. 2016. "Syntactic Ergativity: Analysis and Identification." *Annual Review of Linguistics* 2:165–185.

De Clercq, Karen, Liliane Haegeman, and Terje Lohndal. 2011. "Clause Internal Scrambling in English and the Distribution of PP and DP-Adjuncts." Paper presented at the annual meeting of the Linguistics Association of Great Britain, Manchester, 7–10 September.

Delsing, Lars. 1992. "On Attributive Adjectives in Scandinavian and Other Languages." In *Papers from the Workshop on the Scandinavian Noun Phrase. Report 32*, ed. Anders Holmberg, 20–44. Umeå, Sweden: University of Umeå, Department of General Linguistics.

Delsing, Lars. 1993. "On Attributive Adjectives in Scandinavian and Other Languages." *Studia Linguistica* 47:105–125.

Demonte, Violeta, and Olga Fernández Soriano. 2009. "Force and Finiteness in the Spanish Complementizer System." *Probus* 21:23–49.

Demuth, Katherine, and Carolyn Harford. 1999. "Verb Raising and Subject Inversion in Comparative Bantu." *Journal of African Languages and Linguistics* 20:41–61.

Deutscher, Guy. 2000. *Syntactic Change in Akkadian: The Evolution of Sentential Complementation.* Oxford: Oxford University Press.

Deutscher, Guy. 2001. "On the Mechanisms of Morphological Change." *Folia Linguistica Historica* 22:41–48.

Deutscher, Guy. 2006. "Complement Clause Types and Complementation Strategies in Akkadian." In *Complementation: A Cross-Linguistic Typology*, ed. R. M. W. Dixon and Alexandra Aikhenvald, 159–177. Oxford: Oxford University Press.

Deutscher, Guy. 2009. "The Semantics of Clause Linking in Akkadian." In *The Semantics of Clause Linking*, ed. R. M. W. Dixon and Alexandra Aikhenvald, 56–73. Oxford: Oxford University Press.

Devos, Maud, and Johan van der Auwera. 2013. "Jespersen Cycles in Bantu: Double and Triple Negation." *Journal of African Languages and Linguistics* 34:205–274.

Dikken, Marcel den. 2007. "Phase Extension: Contours of a Theory of the Role of Head Movement in Phrasal Extraction." *Theoretical Linguistics* 33:1–41.

Dikken, Marcel den. 2010a. "Directions from the GET-GO: On the Syntax of Manner-of-Motion Verbs in Directional Constructions." *Catalan Journal of Linguistics* 9:25–55.

Dikken, Marcel den. 2010b. "On the Functional Structure of Locative and Directional PPs." In *Mapping Spatial PPs*, ed. Guglielmo Cinque and Luigi Rizzi, 74–126. Oxford: Oxford University Press.

Dimitrova-Vulchanova, Mila, and Giuliana Giusti. 1995. "Quantified Noun Phrase Structure in Bulgarian." *University of Venice Working Papers in Linguistics* 5:43–65.

Dimitrova-Vulchanova, Mila, and Giuliana Giusti. 1998. "Fragments of Balkan Nominal Structure." In *Possessors, Predicates and Movement in the Determiner Phrase*, ed. Artemis Alexiadou and Chris Wilder, 333–360. Amsterdam: John Benjamins.

Dixon, R. M. W. 2004. "Adjective Classes in Typological Perspective." In *Adjective Classes: A Cross-Linguistic Typology*, ed. R. M. W. Dixon and Alexandra Aikhenvald, 1–49. Oxford: Oxford University Press.

D'Jernes, Lucille S. 2002. "Arop-Lokep." In *The Oceanic Languages*, ed. John Lynch, Malcolm Ross, and Terry Crowley, 249–269. Richmond: Curzon Press.

Donaldson, Bruce. 1993. *A Grammar of Afrikaans.* Berlin: Mouton de Gruyter.

Dost, Ascander, and Vera Gribanova. 2006. "Definiteness Marking in the Bulgarian DP." In *WCCFL 25: Proceedings of the 25th West Coast Conference on Formal Linguistics*, ed. Donald Baumer, David Montero, and Michael Scanlon, 132–140. Somerville, MA: Cascadilla Proceedings Project.

Douglas, Jamie. 2015. "Unifying the *That*-Trace and Anti-*That*-Trace Effects." Unpublished ms., University of Cambridge. (http://ling.auf.net/lingbuzz/002793; last accessed 26 December 2015)

Douglas, Jamie. 2016. "The Syntactic Structures of Relativization." PhD diss., University of Cambridge.

Douglas, Wilfred H. 1981. "Watjarri." In *Handbook of Australian Languages*, Vol. 2, ed. R. M. W. Dixon and Barry J. Blake, 196–272. Canberra: Australian National University Press.

Dresher, Bezalel Elan. 1999. "Charting the Learning Path: Cues to Parameter Setting." *Linguistic Inquiry* 30:27–68.

Dryer, Matthew S. 1988. "Object-Verb Order and Adjective-Noun Order: Dispelling a Myth." *Lingua* 74:77–109.

Dryer, Matthew S. 1992. "The Greenbergian Word Order Correlations." *Language* 68:81–138.

Dryer, Matthew S. 2001. "Mon Khmer Word Order from a Cross-Linguistic Perspective." In *Papers from the 6th Annual Meeting of the Southeast Asian Linguistics Society 1996*, ed. Karen L. Adams and John Hudak, 83–99. Tempe: Arizona State University, Program for South-East Asian Studies.

Dryer, Matthew S. 2005a. "Order of Adverbial Subordinator and Clause." In *The World Atlas of Language Structures*, ed. Martin Haspelmath, Matthew S. Dryer, David Gil, and Bernard Comrie, 382–385. Oxford: Oxford University Press.

Dryer, Matthew S. 2005b. "Position of Polar Question Particles." In *The World Atlas of Language Structures*, ed. Martin Haspelmath, Matthew S. Dryer, David Gil, and Bernard Comrie, 374–377. Oxford: Oxford University Press.

Dryer, Matthew S. 2007. "Word Order." In *Language Typology and Syntactic Description*, ed. Terry Shopen, 61–131. Cambridge: Cambridge University Press.

Dryer, Matthew S. 2009a. "The Branching Direction Theory Revisited." In *Universals of Language Today*, ed. Sergio Scalise, Elisabetta Magni, and Antonietta Bisetto, 185–207. Berlin: Springer.

Dryer, Matthew S. 2009b. "Verb-Object-Negative Order in Central Africa." In *Negation Patterns in West Africa*, ed. Norbert Cyffer, Ewald Ebermann, and Georg Ziegelmeyer, 307–362. Amsterdam: John Benjamins.

Dryer, Matthew S. 2009c. "The Order of Demonstrative, Numeral, Adjective and Noun: An Alternative to Cinque." Paper presented at Theoretical Approaches to Disharmonic Word Orders, Newcastle.

Dryer, Matthew S. 2015a. "Order of Adposition and Noun Phrase." In *The World Atlas of Language Structures Online*, ed. Matthew S. Dryer and Martin Haspelmath. Leipzig: Max Planck Institute for Evolutionary Anthropology. (http://wals.info/chapter/85; accessed on 19 February 2015)

Dryer, Matthew S. 2015b. "Order of Adverbial Subordinator and Clause." In *The World Atlas of Language Structures Online*, ed. Matthew S. Dryer and Martin Haspelmath. Leipzig: Max Planck Institute for Evolutionary Anthropology. (http://wals.info/chapter/94; accessed on 19 February 2015)

Dryer, Matthew S. 2015c. "Order of Demonstrative and Noun." In *The World Atlas of Language Structures Online*, ed. Matthew S. Dryer and Martin Haspelmath. Leipzig: Max Planck Institute for Evolutionary Anthropology. (http: //wals.info/chapter/88; accessed on 19 February 2015)

Dryer, Matthew S. 2015d. "Order of Numeral and Noun." In *The World Atlas of Language Structures Online*, ed. Matthew S. Dryer and Martin Haspelmath. Leipzig: Max

Planck Institute for Evolutionary Anthropology. (http://wals.info/chapter/89; accessed on 19 February 2015)

Dryer, Matthew S. 2015e. "Order of Object and Verb." In *The World Atlas of Language Structures Online*, ed. Matthew S. Dryer and Martin Haspelmath. Leipzig: Max Planck Institute for Evolutionary Anthropology. (http://wals.info/chapter/83; accessed on 14 April 2015)

Dryer, Matthew S. 2015f. "Order of Subject, Object and Verb." In *The World Atlas of Language Structures Online*, ed. Matthew S. Dryer and Martin Haspelmath. Leipzig: Max Planck Institute for Evolutionary Anthropology. (http://wals.info/chapter/81; accessed on 19 February 2015)

Dryer, Matthew S. 2015g. "Position of Polar Question Particles." In *The World Atlas of Language Structures Online*, ed. Matthew S. Dryer and Martin Haspelmath. Leipzig: Max Planck Institute for Evolutionary Anthropology. (http://wals.info/chapter/92; accessed on 19 February 2015)

Dryer, Matthew. 2015h. "Prefixing and Suffixing in Inflectional Morphology." In *The World Atlas of Language Structures Online*, ed. Matthew S. Dryer and Martin Haspelmath. Leipzig: Max Planck Institute for Evolutionary Anthropology. (http://wals.info/chapter/26; accessed on 5 May 2016)

Dryer, Matthew S. 2015i. "Order of Genitive and Noun." In *The World Atlas of Language Structures Online*, ed. Matthew S. Dryer and Martin Haspelmath. Leipzig: Max Planck Institute for Evolutionary Anthropology. (http://wals.info/chapter/86; accessed on 11 January 2017)

Dryer, Matthew S., and Martin Haspelmath, eds. 2015. *The World Atlas of Language Structures Online*. Leipzig: Max Planck Institute for Evolutionary Anthropology. (http://wals.info/)

Duffield, Nigel. 1995. *Particles and Projection in Irish Syntax*. Dordrecht: Kluwer.

Duffield, Nigel. 1996. "On Structural Invariance and Lexical Diversity in VSO Languages: Arguments from Irish Noun Phrases." In *The Syntax of the Celtic Languages*, ed. Robert D. Borsley and Ian Roberts, 314–340. Cambridge: Cambridge University Press.

Duffield, Nigel. 2001. "On Certain Head-Final Effects in Vietnamese." In *WCCFL 20: Proceedings of the 20th West Coast Conference on Formal Linguistics*, ed. Karine Megerdoomian and Leora A. Bar-el, 101–114. Somerville, MA: Cascadilla Press.

Duffield, Nigel. 2007. "Aspects of Vietnamese Clause Structure: Separating Tense from Assertion." *Linguistics* 45:765–814.

Duffield, Nigel. 2013a. "Head-First: On the Head-Initiality of Vietnamese Clauses." In *Linguistics of Vietnamese: An International Survey*, ed. Daniel Hole and Elizabeth Löbel, 127–155. Berlin: Mouton de Gruyter.

Duffield, Nigel. 2013b. "On Polarity Emphasis, Assertion and Mood in English and Vietnamese." *Lingua* 137:248–270.

Duffield, Nigel. 2014a. "Minimalism and Semantic Syntax: Interpreting Multifunctionality in Vietnamese." Unpublished ms., Konan University. (http://ling.auf.net/lingbuzz/001919; last accessed 21 September 2015)

Duffield, Nigel. 2014b. "Shake Can Well." Unpublished ms., Konan University. (http://ling.auf.net/lingbuzz/002119; last accessed 21 September 2015)

Duffield, Nigel. 2015. "On What Projects." Unpublished ms., Konan University. (http://ling.auf.net/lingbuzz/002429; last accessed 21 September 2015)

Durie, Mark. 1985. *A Grammar of Acehnese on the Basis of a Dialect of North Aceh.* Dordrecht: Foris.

Dwivedi, Veena. 1991. "Negation as a Functional Projection in Hindi." In *Proceedings of the Western Conference on Linguistics*, ed. Katherine Hunt, Thomas A. Perry, and Vida Samiian, 88–101. Fresno: California State University.

Elbert, Samuel H. 1974. *Puluwat Grammar.* Canberra: Australian National University, Research School of Pacific Studies, Department of Linguistics.

Elbourne, Paul. 2008. "Demonstratives as Individual Concepts." *Linguistics and Philosophy* 31:409–466.

Elbourne, Paul. 2013. *Definite Descriptions.* Oxford: Oxford University Press.

Elordieta, Arantzazu. 2001. "Verb Movement and Constituent Permutation in Basque." PhD diss., Leiden University.

Embick, David, and Rolf Noyer. 2001. "Movement Operations after Syntax." *Linguistic Inquiry* 32:555–598.

Emonds, Joseph. 1970. "Root and Structure-Preserving Transformations." PhD diss., MIT.

Emonds, Joseph. 1976. *A Transformational Approach to English Syntax: Root, Structure-Preserving, and Local Transformations.* New York: Academic Press.

Emonds, Joseph. 1978. "The Verbal Complex V'-V in French." *Linguistic Inquiry* 9:151–175.

Emonds, Joseph. 2013. "Universal Default Right Headedness and How Stress Determines Word Order." In *Theoretical Approaches to Disharmonic Word Order*, ed. Theresa Biberauer and Michelle Sheehan, 139–161. Oxford: Oxford University Press.

Enç, Mürvet. 1987. "Anchoring Conditions for Tense." *Linguistic Inquiry* 18:633–657.

Enfield, Nick. 2003. *Linguistic Epidemiology: Semantics and Grammar of Language Contact in Mainland Southeast Asia.* London: Routledge Curzon.

Enfield, Nick, Penelope Brown, and J. P. de Ruiter. 2012. "Epistemic Dimensions of Polar Questions: Sentence-Final Particles in Comparative Perspective." In *Questions: Formal, Functional and Interactional Perspectives*, ed. J. P. de Ruiter, 193–221. Cambridge: Cambridge University Press.

Engels, Eva, and Sten Vikner. 2014. *Scandinavian Object Shift and Optimality Theory.* London: Palgrave.

Epée, Roger. 1976. "On Some Rules That Are Not Successive Cyclic in Duala." *Linguistic Inquiry* 7:193–198.

Erguvanlı, Eser Ermine. 1984. *The Function of Word Order in Turkish Grammar.* Berkeley: University of California Press.

Erlewine, Michael Yoshitaka. To appear a. "Low Sentence-Final Particles in Mandarin Chinese and the Final-over-Final Constraint." *Journal of East Asian Linguistics.*

Erlewine, Michael Yoshitaka. To appear b. "Sentence-Final Particles at the vP Phase Edge." In *Proceedings of the 25th North American Conference on Chinese Linguistics (NACCL 25)*.

Ernst, Thomas. 2003. "Adjuncts and Word Order Asymmetries." In *Asymmetry in Grammar*, ed. Anna Maria Di Sciullo, 187–208. Amsterdam: John Benjamins.

Ernst, Thomas. 2004. "Principles of Adverbial Distribution in the Lower Clause." *Lingua* 14:755–777.

Español-Echevarría, Manuel. 1994. "Auxiliary Selection in Greek Dialects." Paper presented at Western Conference on Linguistics 24, Fresno.

Etxepare, Ricardo. 2009. "Evidential Configurations in Basque." Paper presented at the Workshop on Clause Types, Paris.

Etxepare, Ricardo, and William Haddican. 2014. "Repairing Final-Over-Final Constraint Violations: Evidence from Basque Verb Clusters." Unpublished ms., CNRS (Bayonne) and CUNY.

Evans, Nicholas. 2003. *Bininj Gun-wok: A Pan-dialectal Grammar of Mayali, Kunwinjku and Kune*. Canberra: Australian National University.

Evers, Arnold. 1975. "The Transformational Cycle of Dutch and German." PhD diss., Utrecht University.

Ezard, Bryan. 1991. *Tawala Grammar: A Functional Approach*. Canberra: Australian National University.

Fang, Xiaoyan. 2003. *Sentence-Final Particles in Guangzhou Cantonese*. Guangzhou: Jinan University Press.

Farris, Edwin. 1992. "A Syntactic Sketch of Yosundúa Mixtec." In *Studies in the Syntax of Mixtecan Languages*, Vol. 4, ed. Henry Bradley and Barbara Hollenbach, 1–171. Dallas, TX: Summer Institute of Linguistics and the University of Texas at Arlington.

Fassi-Fehri, Abdelkader. 1993. *Issues in the Structure of Arabic Clauses and Words*. Dordrecht: Kluwer.

Feinauer, Ilse. 1989. "Plasing in Afrikaanse afhanklike sinne." *Suid-Afrikaanse Tydskrif vir Taalkunde* 7:30–37.

von Fintel, Kai, and Lisa Matthewson. 2008. "Universals in Semantics." *The Linguistic Review* 25:139–201.

Fleisher, Nicholas. 2008. "A Crack at a Hard Nut: Attributive-Adjective Modality and Infinitival Relatives." In *WCCFL 26: Proceedings of the 26th West Coast Conference on Formal Linguistics*, ed. Charles B. Chang and Hannah J. Haynie, 163–171. Somerville, MA: Cascadilla Proceedings Project.

Fleisher, Nicholas. 2011. "Attributive Adjectives, Infinitival Relatives, and the Semantics of Inappropriateness." *Journal of Linguistics* 47:341–380.

Fowlie, Meaghan. 2014. "Adjunction and Minimalist Grammars." In *Formal Grammar: 19th International Conference, FG 2014*, ed. Glyn Morrill, Reinhard Muskens, Rainer Osswald, and Frank Richter, 34–51. Dordrecht: Springer.

Fox, Danny. 2000. *Economy and Semantic Interpretation*. Cambridge, MA: MIT Press.

Fox, Danny. 2002. "Antecedent-Contained Deletion and the Copy Theory of Movement." *Linguistic Inquiry* 33:63–96.

Fox, Danny, and Jon Nissenbaum. 1999. "Extraposition and Scope: A Case for Overt QR." In *WCCFL 18: Proceedings of the 18th West Coast Conference on Formal Linguistics*, ed. Sonya Bird, Andrew Carnie, Jason D. Haugen, and Peter Norquest, 132–144. Somerville, MA: Cascadilla Proceedings Project.

Fox, Danny, and David Pesetsky. 2005. "Cyclic Linearization of Syntactic Structure." *Theoretical Linguistics* 3:1–46.

Frajzyngier, Zygmunt. 1993. *A Grammar of Mupun*. Berlin: Dietrich Reimer Verlag.

Franco, Ludovico. 2012. "Against the Identity of Complementizers and (Demonstrative) Pronouns." *Poznań Studies in Contemporary Linguistics* 48:565–596.

Frascarelli, Mara. 2008. "The Fine Structure of the Topic Field." In *The Bantu-Romance Connection: A Comparative Investigation of Verbal Agreement, DPs, and Information Structure*, ed. Cécile De Cat and Katherine Demuth, 261–292. Amsterdam: John Benjamins.

Frascarelli, Mara, and Roland Hinterhölzl. 2007. "Types of Topics in German and Italian." In *On Information Structure, Meaning and Form*, ed. Susanne Winkler and Kirsten Schwabe, 87–116. Amsterdam: John Benjamins.

Freidin, Robert. 1999. "Cyclicity and Minimalism." In *Working Minimalism*, ed. Samuel David Epstein and Norbert Hornstein, 95–126. Cambridge, MA: MIT Press.

Fuss, Eric, and Carola Trips. 2002. "Variation and Change in Old and Middle English: On the Validity of the Double Base Hypothesis." *Journal of Comparative Germanic Linguistics* 4:171–224.

Gagnon, Michaël, and Alexis Wellwood. 2008. "Interrogative Structures in Marshallese." In *Proceedings of the Canadian Linguistics Association Annual Meeting 2007*, ed. Susie Jones, 1–12. (http://homes.chass.utoronto.ca/~cla-acl/actes2008/CLA2008_Gagnon_Wellwood.pdf; last accessed 21 September 2015)

Gallego, Ángel. 2006. "Phase Sliding." Unpublished ms., Universitat Autònoma de Barcelona.

Gallego, Ángel. 2010. *Phase Theory*. Amsterdam: John Benjamins.

Gallego, Ángel. 2012. *Phases: Developing the Framework*. Berlin: de Gruyter.

Gallego, Ángel, and Juan Uriagereka. 2007. "Sub-extraction from Subjects: A Phase Theory Account." In *Romance Linguistics 2006*, ed. José Camacho, Nydia Flores-Ferrán, Liliane Sánchez, Viviane Déprez, and María José Cabrera, 149–162. Amsterdam: John Benjamins.

Gelderen, Elly van. 2004. *Grammaticalization as Economy*. Amsterdam: John Benjamins.

Gelderen, Elly van. 2009. *Cyclical Change*. Amsterdam: John Benjamins.

Gelderen, Elly van. 2011. *The Linguistic Cycle: Language Change and the Language Faculty*. Oxford: Oxford University Press.

George, Ken. 1993. "Cornish." In *The Celtic Languages*, ed. Martin J. Ball and James Fife, 410–468. London: Routledge.

Georgopoulos, Carol. 1991. *Syntactic Variables: Resumptive Pronouns and A' Binding in Palauan*. Dordrecht: Kluwer.

Gervain, Judit, and Jacques Mehler. 2011. "Speech Perception and Language Acquisition in the First Year of Life." *Annual Review of Psychology* 61:191–218.

Gervain, Judit, Marina Nespor, Reiko Mazuka, Ryota Horie, and Jacques Mehler. 2008. "Bootstrapping Word Order in Prelexical Infants: A Japanese-Italian Cross-Linguistic Study." *Cognitive Psychology* 57:56–74.

Gervain, Judit, and Janet Werker. 2013. "Prosody Cues Word Order in 7-Month-Old Bilingual Infants." *Nature Communications* 4:1490.

Giannakidou, Anastasia. 2005. "N-Words and Negative Concord." In *The Blackwell Companion to Syntax*, ed. Martin Everaert and Henk van Riemsdjik, 327–391. Oxford: Blackwell.

Giannakidou, Anastasia. 2011. "Negative Polarity and Positive Polarity: Licensing, Variation and Compositionality." In *The Handbook of Natural Language Meaning*, 2nd ed., ed. Klaus von Heusinger, Claudia Maienborn, and Paul Portner, 1660–1712. Berlin: Mouton de Gruyter.

Gibbons, John. 1987. *Code-Mixing and Code Choice: A Hong Kong Case Study*. Clevedon: Multilingual Matters.

Ginsburg, Jason. 2009. "Interrogative Features." PhD diss., University of Arizona.

Giorgi, Alessandra. 1988. "La struttura interna dei sintagmi nominali." In *Grande grammatica italiana di consultazione*, ed. Lorenzo Renzi, 273–314. Bologna: Il Mulino.

Giorgi, Alessandra. 2010. *About the Speaker: Towards a Syntax of Indexicality*. Oxford: Oxford University Press.

Giorgi, Alessandra, and Fabio Pianesi. 1997. *Tense and Aspect: From Semantics to Morphosyntax*. Oxford: Oxford University Press.

Giusti, Giuliana. 1993. *La sintassi dei determinanti*. Padua: Unipress.

Giusti, Giuliana. 1997. "The Categorial Status of Determiners." In *The New Comparative Syntax*, ed. Liliane Haegeman, 95–124. London: Longman.

Giusti, Giuliana. 2001. "The Birth of a Functional Category: From Latin *Ille* to the Romance Article and Personal Pronoun." In *Current Studies in Italian Syntax: Essays Offered to Lorenzo Renzi*, ed. Guglielmo Cinque and Giampaolo Salvi, 157–171. Amsterdam: North Holland.

Giusti, Giuliana. 2002. "The Functional Structure of Noun Phrases: A Bare Phrase Structure Approach." In *Functional Structure in DP and IP*, ed. Guglielmo Cinque, 54–90. Oxford: Oxford University Press.

Glasgow, Kathleen. 1984. *Burarra Word Classes*. Canberra: Australian National University.

Göksel, Aslı. 2001. "The Auxiliary *ol* at the Morphology-Syntax Interface." In *The Verb in Turkish*, ed. Eser Erguvanlı-Taylan, 151–182. Amsterdam: John Benjamins.

Göksel, Aslı, and Celia Kerslake. 2005. *Turkish: A Comprehensive Grammar*. London: Routledge.

González Escribano, José Luis. 2004. "Head-Final Effects and the Nature of Modification." *Journal of Linguistics* 40:1–43.

González Escribano, José Luis. 2005. "Discontinuous APs in English." *Linguistics* 43:563–610.

Greenberg, Joseph. 1963. "Some Universals of Grammar with Particular Reference to the Order of Meaningful Elements." In *Universals of Language*, ed. Joseph Greenberg, 58–90. Cambridge, MA: MIT Press. [Reprinted in *Comparative Grammar*, ed. Ian Roberts, 1:41–74. London: Routledge (2007)].

Grewendorf, Günther. 2015. *Remnant Movement*. Berlin: Mouton de Gruyter.

Grewendorf, Günther, and Cecilia Poletto. 2009. "The Hybrid Complementizer System of Cimbrian." In *Proceedings of XXXV Incontro di Grammatica Generativa*, ed. Vincenzo Moscati and Emilio Servidio, 181–194. University of Siena CISL Working Papers 3. Cambridge, MA: MIT, MIT Working Papers in Linguistics.

Grimshaw, Jane. 1991. "Extended Projection." Unpublished ms., Rutgers University.

Grimshaw, Jane. 2001. "Extended Projection and Locality." In *Lexical Specification and Insertion*, ed. Peter Coopmans, Martin Everaert, and Jane Grimshaw, 115–133. Amsterdam: John Benjamins.

Grimshaw, Jane. 2005. *Words and Structure*. Stanford, CA: CSLI Publications.

Groat, Erich, and John O'Neil. 1996. "Spell-Out at the LF Interface." In *Minimal Ideas*, ed. Samuel David Epstein, Höskuldur Thráinsson, C. Jan-Wouter Zwart, and Werner Abraham, 113–139. Amsterdam: John Benjamins.

Grohmann, Kleanthes. 2003. *Prolific Domains: On the Anti-locality of Movement Dependencies*. Amsterdam: John Benjamins.

Grohmann, Kleanthes, and Phoevos Panagiotidis. 2005. "An Anti-locality Approach to Greek Demonstratives." In *Contributions to the 30th Incontro di Grammatica Generativa*, ed. Laura Brugè, Giuliana Giusti, Nicola Munaro, Walter Schweikert, and Giuseppina Turano, 243–263. Venice: Ca' Foscari.

Grosu, Alexander, and Julia Horvath. 2006. "Reply to Bhatt and Pancheva's 'Late Merger of Degree Clauses': The Irrelevance of (Non)conservativity." *Linguistic Inquiry* 37:457–483.

Grosu, Alexander, Julia Horvath, and Helen Trugman. 2007. "DegPs as Adjuncts and the Head Final Filter." In *Bucharest Working Papers in Linguistics 8*, ed. Alexandra Cornilescu, 13–20. Bucharest: University of Bucharest Press.

Guardiano, Cristina. 2010. "Demonstratives and the Structure of the DP: Crosslinguistic Remarks." Paper presented at the Workshop on Disharmony in Nominals at the annual meeting of the Linguistics Association of Great Britain, Leeds University, September 2010.

Guimarães, Maximiliano. 2008. "A Note on the Strong Generative Capacity of Standard Antisymmetry Theory." *Snippets* 18:5–7.

Güldemann, Tom. 2010. "(Preposed) Verb Doubling and Predicate-Centered Focus." Paper presented at Workshop Project B7, Berlin, 21–22 November 2010. (http://www2.hu-berlin.de/predicate_focus_africa/data/B7.Workshop.2010-Güldemann-Verb.doubling.pdf)

Guthrie, Malcolm. 1948. *The Classification of the Bantu Languages*. London: Oxford University Press for the International African Institute.

Haas, Mary. 1964. *Thai-English Students' Dictionary*. Stanford, CA: Stanford University Press.

Haddican, William. 2002. "Aspects of DP Word Order across Creoles." Paper presented at the CUNY/SUNY/NYU Linguistics Mini-Conference, New York University, 20 April.

Haddican, William. 2004. "Sentence Polarity and Word Order in Basque." *The Linguistic Review* 21:87–124.

Haegeman, Liliane. 1995. *The Syntax of Negation*. Cambridge: Cambridge University Press.

Haegeman, Liliane. 1996. "Verb Second, the Split CP and Null Subjects in Early Dutch Finite Clauses." *GenGenP* 4:133–175.

Haegeman, Liliane. 2006. "Conditionals, Factives and the Left Periphery." *Lingua* 116:1651–1669.

Haegeman, Liliane. 2012. *Main Clause Phenomena and the Composition of the Left Periphery*. Oxford: Oxford University Press.

Haegeman, Liliane. 2014. "West Flemish Verb-Based Discourse Markers and the Articulation of the Speech Act Layer." *Studia Linguistica* 68:116–139.

Haegeman, Liliane, and Virginia Hill. 2013. "The Syntacticization of Discourse." In *Syntax and Its Limits*, ed. Raffaella Folli, Robert Truswell, and Christina Sevdali, 370–390. Oxford: Oxford University Press.

Haegeman, Liliane, and Henk van Riemsdijk. 1986. "Verb Projection Raising, Scope, and the Typology of Rules Affecting Verbs." *Linguistic Inquiry* 7:417–466.

Hagstrom, Paul. 1998. "Decomposing Questions." PhD diss., MIT.

Haider, Hubert. 2000. "OV Is More Basic than VO." In *The Derivation of VO and OV*, ed. Peter Svenonius, 45–68. Amsterdam: John Benjamins.

Haider, Hubert. 2004. "Pre- and Postverbal Adverbials in OV and VO." *Lingua* 114:779–807.

Haider, Hubert. 2005. "How to Turn German into Icelandic and Derive the VO-OV Contrasts." *Journal of Comparative Germanic Linguistics* 8:1–53.

Haider, Hubert. 2012. *Symmetry Breaking in Syntax*. Cambridge: Cambridge University Press.

Haig, Geoffrey. 2001. "Linguistic Diffusion in Present-Day Eastern Anatolia: From Top to Bottom." In *Areal Diffusion and Genetic Inheritance: Problems in Comparative Linguistics*, ed. Alexandra Aikhenvald and R. M. W. Dixon, 195–224. Oxford: Oxford University Press.

Hankamer, Jorge, and Line Mikkelsen. 2005. "When Movement Must Be Blocked: A Reply to Embick and Noyer." *Linguistic Inquiry* 36:85–125.

Hanna, William J. 2010. "Twenty Functional Categories Compared between Thai and Lue." *Payap University (PYU) Working Papers in Linguistics* 6:1–32.

Hardjadibrata, R. R. 1985. *Sundanese: A Syntactical Analysis*. Canberra: Australian National University, Research School of Pacific Studies, Department of Linguistics.

Harley, Heidi. 2009. "Compounding in Distributed Morphology." In *The Oxford Handbook of Compounding*, ed. Rochelle Lieber and Pavel Stekauer, 129–144. Oxford: Oxford University Press.

Harley, Heidi. 2014. "On the Identity of Roots." *Theoretical Linguistics* 40:225–276.

Harley, Heidi, and Andrew Carnie. 1997. "The EPP, PRO and Irish Clausal Architecture." Paper presented at Celtic Languages Conference, Dublin.

Harriehausen, Bettina. 1990. *Hmong Njua: Syntaktische Analyse einer gesprochenen Sprache mithilfe datenverarbeitungstechnische Mittel und sprachvergleichende Beschreibung des südostasiatischen Sprachraumes*. Tübingen: Niemeyer.

Harwood, Will. 2013. "Being Progressive Is Just a Phase." PhD diss., Ghent University.

Harwood, Will. 2015. "Being Progressive Is Just a Phase: Celebrating the Uniqueness of Progressive Aspect under a Phase-Based Analysis." *Natural Language and Linguistic Theory* 33:523–573.

Haspelmath, Martin. 1997. *Indefinite Pronouns*. Oxford: Oxford University Press.

Haspelmath, Martin. 1998. "How Young Is Standard Average European?" *Language Sciences* 20:271–287.

Hawkins, John A. 1983. *Word Order Universals*. New York: Academic Press.

Hawkins, John A. 1990. "A Parsing Theory of Word Order Universals." *Linguistic Inquiry* 21:223–261.

Hawkins, John A. 1994. *A Performance Theory of Order and Constituency*. Cambridge: Cambridge University Press.

Hawkins, John A. 2004. *Efficiency and Complexity in Grammars*. Oxford: Oxford University Press.

Hawkins, John A. 2008. "An Asymmetry between VO and OV Languages: The Ordering of Obliques." In *Case and Grammatical Relations: Essays in Honour of Bernard Comrie*, ed. Greville Corbett and Michael Noonan, 167–190. Amsterdam: John Benjamins.

Hawkins, John A. 2013. "Disharmonic Word Orders from a Processing Efficiency Perspective." In *Theoretical Approaches to Disharmonic Word Order*, ed. Theresa Biberauer and Michelle Sheehan, 391–406. Oxford: Oxford University Press.

Hawkins, John A., and Gary Gilligan. 1988. "Prefixing and Suffixing Universals in Relation to Basic Word Order." In *Papers in Universal Grammar*, ed. John A. Hawkins and Heather Holmback, special issue, *Lingua* 74:219–259.

Heath, Jeffrey. 1978. *Ngandi Grammar*. Canberra: Australian Institute of Aboriginal Studies.

Heim, Irene. 1982. "The Semantics of Definite and Indefinite Noun Phrases." PhD diss., University of Masschusetts, Amherst.

Heim, Johannes. 2016. "The Distribution of the Intersubjective Particle *gell*." Unpublished ms., University of British Columbia (http://syntaxofspeechacts.linguistics.ubc .ca/wp-content/uploads/2014/02/JHeim_intersubjective-gell-_ms.pdf; last accessed 3 July 2016)

Heim, Johannes, Hermann Keupdjio, Zoe Wai-Man Lam, Adriana Osa-Gómez, and Martina Wiltschko. 2014. "How to Do Things with Particles." In *Proceedings of the*

Canadian Linguistics Association. (http://syntaxofspeechacts.linguistics.ubc.ca/wp -content/uploads/2014/02/heim-et-al-cla-2014-proceedings.pdf; last accessed 3 July 2016)

Heine, Bernd, and Tania Kuteva. 2002. *World Lexicon of Grammaticalization*. Cambridge: Cambridge University Press.

Heine, Bernd, and Mechtild Reh. 1984. *Grammaticalization and Reanalysis in African Languages*. Hamburg: Helmut Buske.

Henderson, Brent. 2007. "Multiple Agreement and Inversion in Bantu." *Syntax* 9: 275–289.

Henderson, Eugenie. 1997. *Bwe Karen Dictionary. With Texts and English-Karen Word List*. London: School of Oriental and African Studies.

Henry, Alison. 2010. "Demonstratives in Belfast English: Microvariation and Externalization." Paper presented at the Workshop on Disharmony in Nominals at the annual meeting of the Linguistics Association of Great Britain, Leeds University, September 2010.

Herburger, Elena. 2000. *What Counts? Focus and Quantification*. Cambridge, MA: MIT Press.

Heycock, Caroline. 2005. "Embedded Root Phenomena." In *The Blackwell Companion to Syntax*, ed. Martin Everaert and Henk van Riemsdijk, 174–209. Oxford: Blackwell.

Hicks, Glyn. 2009. "*Tough*-Constructions and Their Derivation." *Linguistic Inquiry* 40:535–566.

Hill, Virginia. 2007. "Vocatives and the Pragmatics-Syntax Interface." *Lingua* 117: 2077–2105.

Hill, Virginia. 2013a. "Features and Strategies: The Internal Syntax of Vocative Phrases." In *Vocatives! Addressing the System and Performance*, ed. Barbara Sonnenhauser and Patrizia Noel Aziz Hanna, 79–102. Berlin: Mouton de Gruyter.

Hill, Virginia. 2013b. *Vocatives: How Syntax Meets with Pragmatics*. Leiden: Brill.

Hinzen, Wolfram, and Michelle Sheehan. 2013. *The Philosophy of Universal Grammar*. Oxford: Oxford University Press.

Hock, Hans Heinrich, and Brian D. Joseph. 1996. *Language History, Language Change, and Language Relationship: An Introduction to Historical and Comparative Linguistics*. Berlin: Mouton de Gruyter.

Hodson, Arnold W., and Craven H. Walker. 1922. *An Elementary and Practical Grammar of the Galla or Oromo Language*. London: Society for Promoting Christian Knowledge.

Hoeksema, Jack. 1993. "Suppression of a Word-Order Pattern in West Germanic." In *Historical Linguistics 1991, Papers from the 10th International Conference on Historical Linguistics*, ed. Jaap van Marle, 153–174. Amsterdam: John Benjamins.

Hoekstra, Teun. 1999. "Parallels between Nominal and Verbal Projections." In *Specifiers*, ed. David Adger, Susan Pintzuk, Bernadette Plunkett, and George Tsoulas, 163–187. Oxford: Oxford University Press.

Hogan, David W. and Stephen W. Pattemore. 1998. *Urak-Lawoi': Basic Structures and a Dictionary*. Canberra: Australian National University, Research School of Pacific Studies, Department of Linguistics.

Holmberg, Anders. 1986. "Word Order and Syntactic Features in the Scandinavian Languages and English." PhD diss., Stockholm University.

Holmberg, Anders. 1999. "Remarks on Holmberg's Generalization." *Studia Linguistica* 53:1–39.

Holmberg, Anders. 2000a. "Deriving OV Order in Finnish." In *The Derivation of VO and OV*, ed. Peter Svenonius, 123–152. Amsterdam: John Benjamins.

Holmberg, Anders. 2000b. "Scandinavian Stylistic Fronting." *Linguistic Inquiry* 31:445–483.

Holmberg, Anders. 2001. "The Syntax of *yes* and *no* in Finnish." *Studia Linguistica* 55:140–174.

Holmberg, Anders. 2003. "Yes/No Questions and the Relation between Tense and Polarity in English." In *Linguistic Variation Yearbook 3*, ed. Pierre Pica, 43–68. Amsterdam: John Benjamins.

Holmberg, Anders. 2005. "Stylistic Fronting." In *The Blackwell Companion to Syntax*, ed. Martin Everaert and Henk van Riemdsdijk, 530–563. Oxford: Blackwell.

Holmberg, Anders. 2010. "Null Subject Parameters." In *Parametric Variation: The Null Subject Parameter*, ed. Theresa Biberauer, Anders Holmberg, Ian Roberts, and Michelle Sheehan, 88–124. Cambridge: Cambridge University Press.

Holmberg, Anders. 2013. "The Syntax of Answers to Polar Questions in English and Swedish." *Lingua* 128:31–50.

Holmberg, Anders. 2014. "The Syntax of the Finnish Question Particle." In *Functional Structure from Top to Toe*, ed. Peter Svenonius, 266–289. Oxford: Oxford University Press.

Holmberg, Anders. 2015. "Verb Second." In *Syntax: An International Handbook of Contemporary Syntactic Research*, 2nd ed., ed. Tibor Kiss and Artemis Alexiadou, 343–384. Berlin: Walter de Gruyter.

Holmberg, Anders. 2016. *The Syntax of* Yes *and* No. Oxford: Oxford University Press.

Holmberg, Anders, and Urpo Nikanne. 2002. "Expletives, Subjects and Topics in Finnish." In *Subjects, Expletives, and the EPP*, ed. Peter Svenonius, 71–106. Oxford: Oxford University Press.

Holmberg, Anders, and Urpo Nikanne. 2008. "Subject Doubling in Finnish: The Role of Deficient Pronouns." In *Microvariation in Syntactic Doubling*, ed. Sjef Barbiers, Olaf Koeneman, Marika Lekakou, and Margreet van der Ham, 325–349. Bingley: Emerald.

Holmberg, Anders, Urpo Nikanne, Irmeli Oraviita, Hannu Reime, and Trond Trosterud. 1993. "The Structure of INFL and the Finite Clause in Finnish." In *Case and Other Functional Categories in Finnish Syntax*, ed. Anders Holmberg and Urpo Nikanne, 175–206. Berlin: Mouton de Gruyter.

Holmberg, Anders, and Christer Platzack. 1995. *The Role of Inflection in Scandinavian Syntax*. Amsterdam: John Benjamins.

Holmberg, Anders, and Ian Roberts. 2013. "The Syntax-Morphology Relation." In *Syntax and Cognition: Core Ideas and Results*, ed. Luigi Rizzi, special issue, *Lingua* 130:111–130.

Holmer, Arthur J. 2005. "Seediq: Antisymmetry and Final Particles in a Formosan VOS Language." In *Verb First: On the Syntax of Verb-Initial Languages*, ed. Andrew Carnie, Heidi Harley, and Sheila Dooley, 175–201. Amsterdam: John Benjamins.

Holton, Gary. 2003. *Tobelo*. Munich: Lincom Europa.

Hopper, Paul, and Elizabeth Traugott. 2003. *Grammaticalization*. Cambridge: Cambridge University Press.

Horn, Laurence. 1969. "A Presuppositional Approach to *only* and *even*." In *CLS 5: Papers from the Fifth Regional Meeting of the Chicago Linguistic Society*, ed. Robert I. Binnick, Alice Davison, Georgia M. Green, and Jerry L. Morgan, 98–107. Chicago: University of Chicago, Chicago Linguistic Society.

Horvath, Julia. 1986. *FOCUS in the Theory of Grammar and the Syntax of Hungarian*. Dordrecht: Foris.

Hróarsdóttir, Thorbjörg. 1999. "Verb Phrase Syntax in the History of Icelandic." PhD diss., University of Tromsø.

Hróarsdóttir, Thorbjörg. 2000. *Word Order Change in Icelandic: From OV to VO*. Amsterdam: John Benjamins.

Hsieh, Feng-fan, and Rint Sybesma. 2007. "On the Linearization of Chinese Sentence-Final Particles: Max Spell Out and Why CP Moves." Unpublished ms., MIT and Leiden University.

Huang, C.-T. James. 1982. "Logical Relations in Chinese and the Theory of Grammar." Ph.D. diss., MIT.

Huang, C.-T. James. 1993. "Reconstruction and the Structure of VP: Some Theoretical Consequences." *Linguistic Inquiry* 24:103–138.

Huang, C.-T. James. 2015. "On Syntactic Analyticity and Parametric Theory." In *Chinese Syntax in a Cross-Linguistic Perspective*, ed. Audrey Li, Andrew Simpson, and Wei-Tien Dylan Tsai, 1–48. Oxford: Oxford University Press.

Huang, C.-T. James, Y.-H. Audrey Li, and Yafei Li. 2009. *The Syntax of Chinese*. Cambridge: Cambridge University Press.

Huang, C.-T. James, and Masao Ochi. 2010. "Classifiers and Nominal Structure: A Parametric Approach and Its Consequences." Paper presented at the 8th GLOW in Asia, Beijing.

Hutter, George L., and Mary Hutter. 1994. *Ndjuka*. London: Routledge.

Hwang, Jya-Lin. 1998. "A Comparative Study on the Grammaticalization of Saying Verbs in Chinese." In *Proceedings of the 10th North American Conference on Chinese Linguistics*, ed. Chao Fen Sun. GSIL: USC, 585–597.

Hwang, Jya-Lin. 2000. "On Grammaticalization in Serial Verb Constructions in Chinese." PhD diss., University of Hawaii.

Itô, Junko. 1989. "A Prosodic Theory of Epenthesis." *Natural Language and Linguistic Theory* 7:217–259.

Iwasaki, Shoichi, and Preeya Ingkaphirom. 2005. *A Reference Grammar of Thai*. Cambridge: Cambridge University Press.

Jackendoff, Ray. 1977. *X-Bar Syntax: A Study of Phrase Structure*. Cambridge, MA: MIT Press.

Jackendoff, Ray. 1996. "The Architecture of the Linguistic-Spatial Interface." In *Language and Space*, ed. Paul Bloom, Merrill Garrett, Lynn Nadel, and Mary Peterson, 1–30. Cambridge, MA: MIT Press.

Jacob, Peggy. 2006. "Informationsstrukturelle Aspekte des Tar B'arma." MA thesis, Humboldt University Berlin.

Jacob, Peggy. 2010. "On the Obligatoriness of Focus Marking: Evidence from Tar B'arma." In *The Expression of Information Structure: A Documentation of Its Diversity across Africa*, ed. Ines Fiedler and Anne Schwartz, 117–144. Amsterdam: John Benjamins.

Jacob, Peggy. 2013. "Doubled Verbs: Principles of Distribution in Sara-Bagirmi." Paper presented at the Nilo-Saharan Linguistics Colloquium, Humboldt University Berlin.

Jaggar, Philip. 2001. *Hausa*. Amsterdam: John Benjamins.

Jayaseelan, K. A. 2001. "Questions and Question-Word Incorporating Quantifiers in Malayalam." *Syntax* 4:63–93.

Jayaseelan, K. A. 2008. "Question Particles and Disjunction." Unpublished ms., Hyderabad. (http://ling.auf.net/lingbuzz/000644; last accessed 21 September 2015)

Jayaseelan, K. A. 2009. "Stacking, Stranding, and Pied-Piping: A Proposal about Word Order." *Syntax* 13:298–330.

Jayaseelan, K. A. 2014. "Decomposition Coordination: The Two Operators of Coordination." Unpublished ms., Hyderabad. (http://ling.auf.net/lingbuzz/002389; last accessed 21 September 2015)

Jenks, Peter. 2011. "The Hidden Structure of Thai Noun Phrases." PhD diss., Harvard University.

Jespersen, Otto. 1917. *Negation in English and Other Languages*. Copenhagen: Høst.

Johnson, Kyle. 1991. "Object Positions." *Natural Language and Linguistic Theory* 9:577–636.

Johnson, Kyle. 2003. "Towards an Etiology of Adjuncts." *Nordlyd* 31:187–215.

Johnston, Raymond Leslie. 1980. *Nakanai of New Britain: The Grammar of an Oceanic Language*. Canberra: Australian National University, Research School of Pacific Studies, Department of Linguistics.

Jones, Michael. 1988. *Sardinian Syntax*. London: Routledge.

Julien, Marit. 2002. *Syntactic Heads and Word Formation*. Oxford: Oxford University Press.

Julien, Marit. 2005. *Nominal Phrases from a Scandinavian Perspective*. Amsterdam: John Benjamins.

Kamp, Hans. 1981. "A Theory of Truth and Semantic Representation." In *Formal Methods in the Study of Language*, ed. Jeroen Groenendijk, Theo Janssen, and Martin Stokhof, 277–322. Amsterdam: Mathematical Centre. [Reprinted in *Truth, Interpretation,*

Information, ed. Jeroen Groenendijk, Theo Janssen, and Martin Stokhof, 1–41. Dordrecht: Foris (1984) and *Formal Semantics: The Essential Readings*, ed. Paul Portner and Barbara H. Partee, 189–222. Oxford: Blackwell (2002).]

Kandybowicz, Jason. 2013. "Ways of Emphatic Scope-Taking: From Emphatic Assertion in Nupe to the Grammar of Emphasis." *Lingua* 128:51–71.

Kandybowicz, Jason, and Mark C. Baker. 2003. "On Directionality and the Structure of the Verb Phrase: Evidence from Nupe." *Syntax* 6:115–155.

Kari, Ethelbert E. 2000. *Obronaguam (the Bukuma language)*. Munich: Lincom Europa.

Kato, Atsuhiko. 2003. "Pwo-Karen." In *The Sino-Tibetan Languages*, ed. Graham Thurgood and Randy J. LaPolla, 632–648. London: Routledge.

Kaufman, Daniel. 2010. "Greenberg's 16th Slayed in the Bronx? Language Universals and Fieldwork in NYC." Unpublished ms., Endangered Language Alliance and CUNY. (https://www.academia.edu/1919323/Greenbergs_16th_slayed_in_the_Bronx; last accessed 21 September 2015)

Kaye, Alan S., and Judith Rosenhouse. 1997. "Arabic Dialects and Maltese." In *The Semitic Languages*, ed. Robert Hetzron, 263–311. London: Routledge.

Kayne, Richard S. 1984. *Connectedness and Binary Branching*. Dordrecht: Foris.

Kayne, Richard S. 1994. *The Antisymmetry of Syntax*. Cambridge, MA: MIT Press.

Kayne, Richard S. 2000. *Parameters and Universals*. Oxford: Oxford University Press.

Kayne, Richard S. 2004. "Antisymmetry and Japanese." In *Variation and Universals in Biolinguistics*, ed. Lyle Jenkins, 3–37. Amsterdam: Elsevier. [Reprinted in *Movement and Silence*, 215–240. Oxford: Oxford University Press (2005).]

Kayne, Richard S. 2008. "Expletives, Datives and the Tension between Morphology and Syntax." In *The Limits of Syntactic Variation*, ed. Theresa Biberauer, 175–218. Amsterdam: John Benjamins. [Reprinted in *Comparisons and Contrasts*, 95–145. Oxford: Oxford University Press (2010).]

Kayne, Richard S. 2009. "Antisymmetry and the Lexicon." *Linguistic Variation Yearbook* 8:1–31. [Reprinted in *Comparisons and Contrasts*, 165–189. Oxford: Oxford University Press (2010).]

Kayne, Richard S. 2010a. *Movement and Silence*. Oxford: Oxford University Press.

Kayne, Richard S. 2010b."Why Isn't *this* a Complementizer?" In *Comparisons and Contrasts*, ed. Richard S. Kayne, 190–227. Oxford: Oxford University Press.

Kayne, Richard S. 2010c. *Comparisons and Contrasts*. Oxford: Oxford University Press.

Kayne, Richard S. 2013. "Why Are There No Directionality Parameters?" In *Theoretical Approaches to Disharmonic Word Orders*, ed. Theresa Biberauer and Michelle Sheehan, 219–244. New York: Oxford University Press,

Keegan, John. 1997. *A Reference Grammar of Mbay*. Munich: Lincom Europa.

Keenan, Edward. 1976. "Remarkable Subjects in Malagasy." In *Subject and Topic*, ed. Charles Li, 247–301. New York: Academic Press.

Keenan, Edward. 1995. "Predicate-Argument Structure in Malagasy." In *Grammatical Relations: Theoretical Approaches to Empirical Questions*, ed. Clifford S. Burgess, Katarzyna Dziwirek, and Donna Gerdts, 171–216. Stanford, CA: CSLI Publications.

Keenan, Edward. 1997. "The Semantics of Determiners." In *The Handbook of Contemporary Semantic Theory*, ed. Shalom Lappin, 41–64. Oxford: Blackwell.

Keesing, Roger. 1985. *Kwaio Grammar*. Canberra: Australian National University.

Keevallik, Leelo. 2009. "The Grammar-Interaction Interface of Negative Questions in Estonian." *SKY Journal of Linguistics* 22:139–173.

Kennedy, Christopher. 1999. *Projecting the Adjective: The Syntax and Semantics of Gradability and Comparison*. New York: Garland.

Khan, Geoffrey. 1999. *A Grammar of Neo-Aramaic: The Dialect of the Jews of Arbel*. Leiden: Brill.

Kidwai, Ayesha. 2000. *XP-Adjunction in Universal Grammar: Scrambling and Binding in Hindi-Urdu*. Oxford: Oxford University Press.

Kim, Shin-Sook. 2002. "Intervention Effects Are Focus Effects." In *Japanese/Korean Linguistics 10*, ed. Noriko Akatsuka and Susan Strauss, 615–628. Stanford, CA: CSLI Publications.

Kim, Shin-Sook. 2006. "More Evidence That Intervention Effects Are Focus Effects." In *Proceedings of the 8th Seoul International Conference on Generative Grammar: Minimalist Views on Language Design*, ed. Changguk Yim, 161–180. Seoul: Hankuk University of Foreign Studies.

Kiparsky, Paul. 1996. "The Shift to Head-Initial VP in Germanic." In *Studies in Comparative Germanic Syntax II*, ed. Höskuldur Thráinsson, Samuel David Epstein, and Steve Peter, 140–179. Dordrecht: Kluwer.

Kiparsky, Paul. 2008. "Universals Constrain Change; Change Results in Typological Generalizations." In *Language Universals and Language Change*, ed. Jeff Good, 23–53. Oxford: Oxford University Press.

Kiparsky, Paul, and Cleo Condoravdi. 2006. "Tracking Jespersen's Cycle." In *Proceedings of the 2nd International Conference of Modern Greek Dialects and Linguistic Theory*, ed. Mark Janse, Brian Joseph, and Angela Ralli, 172–197. Mytilene: Doukas.

Klein, Wolfgang. 1998. "Assertion and Finiteness." In *Issues in the Theory of Language Acquisition: Essays in Honor of Jürgen Weissenborn*, ed. Norbert Dittmar and Zvi Penner, 225–245. Bern: Lang.

Klein, Wolfgang. 2006. "On Finiteness." In *Semantics Meets Acquisition*, ed. Veerle van Geenhoven, 245–272. Dordrecht: Kluwer.

Kogan, Leonid E. 1997. "Tigrinya." In *The Semitic Languages*, ed. Robert Hetzron, 424–445. London: Routledge.

Koizumi, Masatoshi. 1995. "Phrase Structure in Minimalist Syntax." PhD diss., MIT.

Koopman, Hilda. 1984. *The Syntax of Verbs: From Verb Movement Rules in the Kru Languages to Universal Grammar*. Dordrecht: Foris.

Koopman, Hilda. 1989. "The Structure of VP in Dutch." Paper presented at the Summer Syntax Workshop, University of California, Irvine.

Koopman, Hilda. 2010. "Prepositions, Postpositions, Circumpositions, and Particles." In *Mapping Spatial PPs*, ed. Guglielmo Cinque and Luigi Rizzi, 26–73. Oxford: Oxford University Press.

Koopman, Hilda, and Anna Szabolcsi. 2000. *Verbal Complexes*. Cambridge, MA: MIT Press.

Korn, Agnes, and Peter Öhl. 2007. "The Rise of *ke āyā* Constructions in Persian Interrogative Embedding." Paper presented at the Second International Conference on Iranian Linguistics, Hamburg.

Kornfilt, Jaklin. 1997. *Turkish*. London: Routledge.

Kornfilt, Jaklin. 2001. "Functional Projections and Their Subjects in Turkish Clauses." In *The Verb in Turkish*, ed. Eser Erguvanlı-Taylan, 183–212. Amsterdam: John Benjamins.

Koskinen, Päivi. 1998. "Features and Categories: Non-Finite Constructions in Finnish." PhD diss., University of Toronto.

Koul, Omar N. 2008. *Modern Hindi Grammar*. Springfield, VA: Dunwoody Press.

Kouwenberg, Silvia. 1993. *A Grammar of Berbice Dutch Creole*. Berlin: Mouton de Gruyter.

Kratzer, Angelika. 1991. "The Representation of Focus." In *Semantik: Ein internationales Handbuch der zeitgenössischen Forschung*, ed. Arnim von Stechow and Dieter Wunderlich, 825–834. Berlin: de Gruyter.

Krinopoulos, Socrates. 1889. Τὰ Φερτάκαινα ὑπὸ Ἐθνολογικὴν καὶ Φιλολογικὴν Ἔποψιν Ἐξεταζόμενα. Athens: Fexis.

Krüsi, Peter. 1978. "Mumuye Discourse Structure." In *Papers on Discourse*, ed. Joseph Grimes, 267–272. Dallas, TX: Summer Institute of Linguistics.

Kuiper, F. J. B. 1974. "The Genesis of a Linguistic Area." *International Journal of Dravidian Linguistics* 1:135–153.

Kumar, Rajesh. 2004. "Negation and the Clause Structure of Hindi." In *Proceedings of the Annual Meeting of the Chicago Linguistic Society 40*, ed. Nikki Adams, Adam Cooper, Fey Parrill, and Thomas Wier, 1:171–188. Chicago: University of Chicago, Chicago Linguistic Society.

Kumar, Rajesh. 2006. *The Syntax of Negation and the Licensing of Negative Polarity Items in Hindi*. London: Routledge.

Kural, Murat. 1997. "Postverbal Constituents in Turkish and the Linear Correspondence Axiom." *Linguistic Inquiry* 28:498–519.

Kuteva, Tania. 1994. *Auxiliation: An Enquiry into the Nature of Grammaticalization*. Oxford: Oxford University Press.

Laka, Itziar. 1990. "Negation in Syntax." PhD diss., MIT. Published as *Negation in Syntax*. New York: Garland (1994).

Lam, Cherry. 2016. "Unifying Polyfunctional Postverbal DAK: A Study of Four Chinese Varieties." Unpublished ms., University of Cambridge.

Lam, Zoe Wai-Man. 2014. "A Complex ForceP for Speaker- and Addressee-Oriented Discourse Particles in Cantonese." *Studies in Chinese Linguistics* 35:61–79.

LaPolla, Randy. 2002. "Problems of Methodology and Explanation in Word Order Universals Research." In *Dongfang yuyan yu wenhua* (Languages and Cultures of the East), ed. Pan Wuyun, 204–237. Shanghai: Dongfang Chuban Zhongxin.

Lardiere, Donna, and Bonnie Schwartz. 1997. "Feature-Marking in the L2 Development of Deverbal Compounds." *Journal of Linguistics* 33:327–353.

Larson, Richard K. 1988. "On Double Object Constructions." *Linguistic Inquiry* 19:335–391.

Larson, Richard K. 1998. "Events and Modification in Nominals." In *Semantics and Linguistic Theory 8*, ed. Devon Strolovitch and Aaron Lawson, 1–27. Ithaca, NY: Cornell University. (http://journals.linguisticsociety.org/proceedings/index.php/SALT/issue/view/101)

Larson, Richard K., and Franc Marušič. 2004. "On Indefinite Pronoun Structures with APs: Reply to Kishimoto." *Linguistic Inquiry* 35:268–287.

Larson, Richard K., and Naoko Takahashi. 2007. "Order and Interpretation in Prenominal Relative Clauses." In *Proceedings of the 2nd Workshop on Altaic Formal Linguistics*, ed. Meltem Kelepir and Balkız Öztürk, 101–120. MIT Working Papers in Linguistics 54. Cambridge, MA: MIT, MIT Working Papers in Linguistics.

Lasnik, Howard. 2000. Syntactic Structures *Revisited: Contemporary Lectures on Classic Transformational Theory*. Cambridge MA: MIT Press.

Lechner, Winfried. 1999. "Comparatives and DP-Structure." PhD diss., University of Massachusetts, Amherst.

Ledgeway, Adam. 2012. *From Latin to Romance: Morphosyntactic Typology and Change*. Oxford: Oxford University Press.

Ledgeway, Adam. To appear. "From Latin to Romance: The Decline of Edge-Fronting." In *Word Order Change*, ed. Adriana Cardoso and Ana Maria Martins. Oxford: Oxford University Press.

Legate, Julie Anne. 2003. "Some Interface Properties of the Phase." *Linguistic Inquiry* 34:506–516.

Leung, Cheong (Alex), and William van der Wurff. 2012. "Language Function and Language Change: A Principle and a Case Study." Unpublished ms., Newcastle University.

Li, Charles, and Sandra Thompson. 1981. *Mandarin Chinese: A Functional Reference Grammar*. Berkeley: University of California Press.

Li, Yafei. 1990. "X^0-Binding and Verb Incorporation." *Linguistic Inquiry* 21:399–426.

Lightfoot, David. 1979. *Principles of Diachronic Syntax*. Cambridge: Cambridge University Press.

Lightfoot, David. 1999. *How to Set Parameters: Arguments from Language Change*. Cambridge, MA: MIT Press.

Lipski, John. 2001. "Strategies of Double Negation in Spanish and Portuguese." Unpublished ms., Pennsylvania State University. (http://www.personal.psu.edu/jml34/negation.pdf; last accessed 21 September 2015)

Lofti, Ahmad, and Peter Öhl. 2004. "Nominalised CPs in Persian: A Parametric Account." Paper presented at the 2nd International Conference on Iranian Linguistics.

Lois, Ximena. 1989. "Aspects de la syntaxe de l'espagnol et théorie de la grammaire." PhD diss., University of Paris VIII.

Longobardi, Giuseppe. 1994. "Reference and Proper Names: A Theory of N-Movement in Syntax and Logical Form." *Linguistic Inquiry* 25:609–665.

Longobardi, Giuseppe. 1996. "The Syntax of N-Raising: A Minimalist Theory." Utrecht: OTS Working Papers.

Longbardi, Giuseppe. 2008. "Reference to Individuals, Person, and the Variety of Mapping Parameters." In *Essays on Nominal Determination: From Morphology to Discourse Management*, ed. Henrik Høeg Müller and Alex Klinge, 189–211. Amsterdam: John Benjamins.

Longobardi, Giuseppe. 2010. Lecture Series on DP-Structure. University of Cambridge, November 2010.

Ludlow, Peter, ed. 1997. *Readings in the Philosophy of Language*. Cambridge, MA: MIT Press.

Luján, Marta. 1973. "Pre- and Postnominal Adjectives in Spanish." *Kritikon Litterarum* 2:398–408.

Lutz, Uli, and Jürgen Pafel. 1996. *On Extraction and Extraposition in German*. Amsterdam: John Benjamins.

Lynch, John. 2002. "Xârâcùù." In *The Oceanic Languages*, ed. John Lynch, Malcolm Ross, and Terry Crowley, 765–775. Richmond: Curzon Press.

Lynch, John, and Rex Horoi. 2002. "Arosi." In *The Oceanic Languages*, ed. John Lynch, Malcolm Ross, and Terry Crowley, 562–572. Richmond: Curzon Press.

Lyons, Christopher. 1999. *Definiteness*. Cambridge: Cambridge University Press.

Mahajan, Anoop K. 1989. "Agreement and Agreement Phrases." In *Functional Heads and Clause Structure*, ed. Itziar Laka and Anoop K. Mahajan, 217–252. MIT Working Papers in Linguistics 10. Cambridge, MA: MIT, MIT Working Papers in Linguistics.

Mahajan, Anoop K. 1990a. "The A/A-Bar Distinction and Movement Theory." PhD diss., MIT.

Mahajan, Anoop K. 1990b. "LF Conditions on Negative Polarity Item Licensing." *Lingua* 80:333–348.

Mahootian, Shahrzad. 1997. *Persian*. Abingdon: Routledge.

Makri, Margarita. 2013. "Expletive Negation beyond Romance: Clausal Complementation and Epistemic Modality." MA thesis, York University.

Malouf, Robert. 2000. "Verbal Gerunds as Mixed Categories in Head-Driven Phrase Structure Grammar." In *The Nature and Function of Syntactic Categories*, ed. Robert Borsley, 133–166. San Diego, CA: Academic Press.

Maniacky, Jacky, and Jenneke van der Wal. 2015. "How 'Person' Got into Focus: Grammaticalization of Clefts in Lingala and Kikongo Areas." *Linguistics* 53:1–52.

Manley, Timothy M. 1972. *Outline of Sre Structure*. Honolulu: University of Hawaii Press.

Manninen, Satu. 2003. "Finnish PPs and the Phase Impenetrability Condition." In *Generative Approaches to Finnic and Saami Linguistics*, ed. Satu Manninen and Diane Nelson, 295–320. Stanford, CA: CSLI Publications.

Marantz, Alec. 1997. "No Escape from Syntax: Don't Try Morphological Analysis in the Privacy of Your Own Lexicon." In *Proceedings of the 21st Annual Penn Linguistics Colloquium*, ed. Alexis Dimitriadis, Laura Siegel, Clarissa Surek-Clark, and Alexander Williams, 201–225. Pennsylvania Working Papers in Linguistics 4.2. Philadelphia: University of Pennsylvania, Penn Linguistics Club.

Marantz, Alec. 2001. "Words." Unpublished ms., MIT.

Marantz, Alec. 2008. "Phases and Words." In *Phases in the Theory of Grammar*, ed. Sook-Hee Choe, 191–222. Seoul: Dong In.

Marlow, Patrick Edward. 1997. "Origin and Development of the Indo-Aryan Quotatives and Complementizers: An Areal Approach." PhD diss., University of Illinois, Urbana.

Masica, Colin P. 1991. *The Indo-Aryan Languages*. Cambridge: Cambridge University Press.

Massam, Diane. 2001. "VSO Is VOS: Aspects of Niuean Word Order." In *The Syntax of Verb Initial Languages*, ed. Andrew Carnie and Eithne Guilfoyle, 97–117. Oxford: Oxford University Press.

Massam, Diane, and Carolyn Smallwood. 1997. "Essential Features of Predication in English and Niuean." In *NELS 27*, ed. Kiyomi Kusumoto, 236–272. Amherst: University of Massachusetts, Graduate Linguistic Student Association.

Matthews, Stephen, and Moira Yip. 1994. *Cantonese: A Comprehensive Grammar*. New York: Routledge.

May, Robert. 1979. "Must Comp-to-Comp Movement Be Stipulated?" *Linguistic Inquiry* 10:719–725.

McCloskey, James. 1996. "The Scope of Verb-Movement in Irish." *Natural Language and Linguistic Theory* 14:47–104.

McCloskey, James. 2004. "Irish Syntax 1: Demonstratives." Unpublished ms., University of California at Santa Cruz. (http://ohlone.ucsc.edu/~jim/papers.html)

McCoy, Svetlana. 2001. "Colloquial Russian Particles *-to*, *že*, and *ved'* as Set-Generating ('Kontrastive') Markers: A Unifying Analysis." PhD diss., Boston University.

McGuckin, Catherine. 2002. "Gapapaiwa." In *The Oceanic Languages*, ed. John Lynch, Malcolm Ross, and Terry Crowley, 297–321. Richmond: Curzon Press.

Meenakshi, K. 1986. "The Quotative in Indo-Aryan." In *South Asian Languages: Structure, Convergence and Diglossia*, ed. Bhadriraju Krishnamurti, Colin Masica, and Anjani Sinha, 209–218. Delhi: Motilal Banarsidass.

Mehler, Jacques, Emmanuel Dupoux, Thierry Nazzi, and Ghislaine Dehaene-Lambertz. 1996. "Coping with Linguistic Diversity: The Infant's Viewpoint." In *Signal to Syntax: Bootstrapping from Speech to Grammar in Early Acquisition*, ed. James Morgan and Katherine Demuth, 101–116. Mahwah, NJ: Lawrence Erlbaum.

Meisner, Charlotte, Elisabeth Stark, and Harald Völker, eds. 2014. *Jespersen Revisited: Negation in Romance and Beyond*. Lingua 147.

Merlan, Francesca. 1989. *Mangarrayi*. London: Routledge.

Merrifield, William R. 1968. *Palantia Chinantec Grammar*. Mexico City: Museo Nacional de Antropología.

Milsark, Robert. 1974. "Existential Sentences in English." PhD diss., MIT. Published as *Existential Sentences in English*. New York: Garland (1979).

Mobbs, Iain. 2008. " 'Functionalism,' the Design of the Language Faculty, and (Disharmonic) Typology." MPhil thesis, University of Cambridge.

Mobbs, Iain. 2015. "Minimalism and the Design of the Language Faculty." PhD diss., University of Cambridge.

Montague, Richard. 1973. "The Proper Treatment of Quantification in Ordinary English." In *Approaches to Natural Language*, ed. Jaakko Hintikka, Judith M. E. Moravcsik, and Patrick Suppes, 221–242. Dordrecht: Reidel. [Reprinted in *Formal Philosophy: Selected Papers of Richard Montague*, 247–270. New Haven, CT: Yale University Press (1974) and *Formal Semantics: The Essential Readings*, ed. Paul Portner and Barbara H. Partee, 17–34. Oxford: Blackwell.]

Moore, Denny. 1989. "Gavião Nominalizations as Relative Clause and Sentential Complement Equivalents." *International Journal of American Linguistics* 55:309–325.

Morgan, Justin. 2012. "Fieldnotes on Yom." Unpublished ms., University of Cambridge.

Morgenstierne, Georg. 1949. "The Language of the Prasun Kafirs." *Norsk Tidsskrift for Sprogvidenskap* 15:186–334.

Moro, Andrea. 2000. *Dynamic Antisymmetry*. Cambridge, MA: MIT Press.

Mosel, Ulrike, and Even Hovdhaugen. 1992. *Samoan Reference Grammar*. Oslo: Scandinavian University Press.

Mous, Maarten. 1993. *A Grammar of Iraqw*. Hamburg: H. Buske.

Munaro, Nicola, and Cecilia Poletto. 2003. "Ways of Clausal Typing." *Rivista di Grammatica Generativa* 27:87–105.

Munaro, Nicola, and Cecilia Poletto. 2009. "Sentential Particles and Clausal Typing in Venetan Dialects." In *Dislocated Elements in Discourse*, ed. Benjamin Shaer, Philippa Cook, Werner Frey, and Claudia Maienborn, 173–199. London: Routledge.

Myler, Neil. 2009. "Form, Function and Explanation at the Syntax-Morphology Interface: Agreement, Agglutination and Post-Syntactic Operations." Extended version of MPhil thesis, University of Cambridge.

Myler, Neil. 2014. "Building and Interpreting Possession Sentences." PhD diss., New York University.

Nakajima, Heizo. 1999. *Locality and Syntactic Structures*. Tokyo: Kaitakushi.

Nanni, Deborah L. 1980. "On the Surface Syntax of Constructions with *Easy*-Type Adjectives." *Language* 56:568–581.

Narrog, Heiko, and Bernd Heine, eds. 2011. *The Oxford Handbook of Grammaticalization*. Oxford: Oxford University Press.

Nayudu, Aarti. 2008. "Issues in the Syntax of Marathi: A Minimalist Approach." PhD diss., Durham University.

Nazzi, Thierry, Josiane Bertoncini, and Jacques Mehler. 1998. "Language Discrimination by Newborns: Toward an Understanding of the Role of Rhythm." *Journal of Experimental Psychology: Human Perception and Performance* 24:1–11.

Nchare, Abdoulaye Laziz. 2012. "The Grammar of Shupamem." PhD diss., New York University.

Ndjerareou, Mekoulnodji, Christy Melick, and Sarah Moeller. 2010. "A Brief Grammatical Sketch of Ngambay." *GIALens: Electronic Notes Series* 4(2). (http://www.gial .edu/documents/gialens/Vol4-2/MelickMoellerMekoulnodj-Ngambay.pdf; last accessed 21 September 2015)

Neeleman, Ad, and Krista Szendrői. 2007. "Radical Pro Drop and the Morphology of Pronouns." *Linguistic Inquiry* 38:671–714.

Neeleman, Ad, and Hans van de Koot. 2004. "The Configurational Matrix." *Linguistic Inquiry* 33:529–574.

Nehlil, Mohammad. 1909. *Etude sur le dialecte de Ghat.* Paris: E. Leroux.

Neocleous, Nicos, and Ioanna Sitaridou. In preparation. "The Rise of Final Auxiliaries in Asia Minor Greek." Unpublished ms, University of Cambridge.

Nespor, Marina, Marcela Peña, and Jacques Mehler. 2003. "On the Different Roles of Vowels and Consonants in Speech Processing and Language Acquisition." *Lingue & Linguaggio* 2:203–229.

Nettle, Daniel. 1998. *The Fyem Language of Northern Nigeria.* Munich: Lincom Europa.

Newman, Paul. 1971. "The Hausa Negative Markers." *Studies in African Linguistics* 2:183–195.

Newman, Paul. 1974. *The Kanakuru Language.* Leeds: Institute of Modern English Language Studies.

Newman, Paul. 2000. *The Hausa Language: An Encyclopedic Reference Grammar.* New Haven, CT: Yale University Press.

Newmeyer, Frederick J. 2005. *Possible and Probable Languages: A Generative Perspective on Linguistic Typology.* Oxford: Oxford University Press.

Newmeyer, Frederick J. 2006. "A Rejoinder to 'On the Role of Parameters in Universal Grammar: A Reply to Newmeyer by Ian Roberts and Anders Holmberg.'" (http://ling .auf.net/lingbuzz/000248)

Newton, Glenda. 2007. "Complementizers and C Particles." Unpublished ms., University of Cambridge.

Nilsen, Øystein. 2003. "Eliminating Positions: Syntax and Semantics of Sentential Modification." PhD diss., Utrecht Institute of Linguistics.

Noonan, Michael. 1992. *A Grammar of Lango.* Berlin: Mouton de Gruyter.

Nunes, Jairo. 2004. *Linearization of Chains and Sideways Movement.* Cambridge, MA: MIT Press.

Nunes, Jairo, and Juan Uriagereka. 2000. "Cyclicity and Extraction Domains." *Syntax* 3:20–43.

Obenauer, Hans-Georg. 2004. "Nonstandard *Wh*-Questions and Alternative Checkers in Pagotto." In *The Syntax and Semantics of the Left Periphery*, ed. Horst Lohnstein and Susanne Trissler, 343–383. Berlin: Mouton de Gruyter.

Ochola, Eunita. 2006. "English Words and Phrases in Dholuo-English Codeswitching." In *Selected Proceedings of the 36th Annual Conference on African Linguistics*, ed. Oloaba Arasanyin and Michael Pemberton, 208–220. Somerville, MA: Cascadilla Proceedings Project.

O'Flynn, Kathleen. 2008. "Tough Nuts to Crack." Unpublished ms., UCLA.

O'Flynn, Kathleen. 2009. "Prenominal Adjective-Complement Constructions in English." Unpublished ms., UCLA.

Ojea López, Ana. 1994. "Adverbios y categorías funcionales en español." *Revista Española de Lingüística* 24:393–416.

Ojwang', Benson Oduor. 2008. "Encoding Polar Questions in Dholuo." *Studies in African Linguistics* 37:61–91.

Omondi, Lucia Ndonga. 1982. *The Major Syntactic Structure of Dholuo*. Berlin: Dietrich Reimer Verlag.

Oosthuizen, Johan. 1998. "The Final *nie* in Afrikaans Negative Sentences." *Stellenbosch Papers in Linguistics* 31:61–94.

Otani, Kazuyo, and John Whitman. 1991. "V-Raising and VP-Ellipsis." *Linguistic Inquiry* 22:345–358.

Ottaviano, Ida de. 1980. *Textos Tacana*. Riberalta, Bolivia: Instituto Lingüístico de Verano, en colaboración con el Ministerio de Educación y Cultura.

Ouhalla, Jamal. 1990. "Sentential Negation, Relativized Minimality and the Aspectual Status of Auxiliaries." *The Linguistic Review* 7:183–231.

Ouwayda, Sarah. 2012. "Where Plurality Is: Agreement and DP Structure." In *NELS 42*, ed. Stefan Keine and Shayne Sloggett, 423–436. Amherst: University of Massachusetts, Graduate Linguistic Student Association.

Ouwayda, Sarah. 2014. "Where Number Lies: Plural Marking, Numerals, and the Collective-Distributive Distinction." PhD diss., University of Southern California.

Owens, Jonathan. 1985. *A Grammar of Harar Oromo (Northeastern Ethiopia)*. Hamburg: Helmut Buske Verlag.

Özsoy, A. Sumru. 2001. "On 'Small' Clauses, Other 'Bare' Verbal Complements and Feature Checking in Turkish." In *The Verb in Turkish*, ed. Eser Erguvanlı- Taylan, 213–237. Amsterdam: John Benjamins.

Pan, Victor. 2016. "Mandarin Peripheral Construals at the Syntax-Discourse Interface." *The Linguistic Review* 33:819–868.

Pan, Victor, and Waltraud Paul. 2017. "What You See Is What You Get: Chinese Sentence-Final Particles as Head-Final Complementisers." In *Discourse Particles – Formal Approaches to Their Syntax and Semantics*, ed. Josef Bayer and Volker Struckmeier, 49–77. Berlin: Mouton de Gruyter.

Panagiotidis, Phoevos. 2000. "Demonstrative Determiners and Operators: The Case of Greek." *Lingua* 110:717–742.

Panagiotidis, Phoevos. 2015. *Categorial Features: A Generative Theory of Word Class Categories*. Cambridge: Cambridge University Press.

Pandharipande, Rajeshwari. 1997. *Marathi*. London: Routledge.

Parrott, Lillian. 1997. "Discourse Organization and Inference: The Usage of the Russian Particles *že* and *ved'*." PhD diss., Harvard University.

Parsons, Terence. 1990. *Events in the Semantics of English: A Study in Subatomic Semantics*. Cambridge, MA: MIT Press.

Paul, Ileana. 2001. "Concealed Pseudo-Clefts." *Lingua* 111:707–727.

Paul, Ileana. 2002. "On Extraction Asymmetries." In *Proceedings of the 8th Meeting of the Austronesian Formal Linguistics Association (AFLA 8)*, ed. Andrea Rackowski and Norvin Richards, 211–224. MIT Working Papers in Linguistics 44. Cambridge, MA: MIT, MIT Working Papers in Linguistics.

Paul, Ileana. 2008. "On the Topic of Pseudoclefts." *Syntax* 11:91–124.

Paul, Waltraud. 2005. "Adjectival Modification in Mandarin Chinese and Related Issues." *Linguistics* 43:757–793.

Paul, Waltraud. 2014. "Why Particles Are Not Particular: Sentence-Final Particles in Chinese as Heads of a Split CP." *Studia Linguistica* 68:77–115.

Paul, Waltraud. 2015. *New Perspectives on Chinese Syntax*. Berlin: de Gruyter.

Paul, Waltraud, and John Whitman. To appear. "Topic Prominence." In *The Blackwell Companion to Syntax*, ed. Martin Everaert and Henk van Riemsdijk, 2nd ed. Oxford: Blackwell. (http://crlao.ehess.fr/docannexe/file/1799/topic_prominence_final_public_february_2015.pdf; last accessed 21 September 2015)

Payne, John. 1993. "The Headedness of Noun Phrases: Slaying the Nominal Hydra." In *Heads in Grammatical Theory*, ed. Greville Corbett, Norman Fraser, and Scott McGlashan, 114–139. Cambridge: Cambridge University Press.

Pearson, Matt. 2001. "The Clause Structure of Malagasy: A Minimalist Approach." PhD diss., UCLA.

Penello, Nicoletta, and Paolo Chinellato. 2008. "Le dinamiche della distribuzione di *ciò* in Veneto: Breve saggio di microvariazione." In *L'Italia dei dialetti: Proceedings of the Dialectology Meeting of Sappada/Plodn – 2007*, ed. Gianna Marcato, 111–118. Padua: Unipress.

Peng, Anne. 2011. "Head-Final and Head-Initial Relative Clauses in Jambi Teochew." In *Online Proceedings of GLOW in Asia Workshop for Young Scholars*, ed. Koichi Otaki, Hajime Takeyasu, and Shin-ichi Tanigawa. (http://faculty.human.mie-u.ac.jp/~glow_mie/Workshop_Proceedings/WorkshopProceedings_WholeBook.pdf; last accessed 21 September 2015)

Peng, Anne. 2012. "Aspects of the Syntax of Indonesian Teochew." PhD diss., University of Delaware.

Pereltsvaig, Asya. 2007. "The Universality of DP: A View from Russian." *Studia Linguistica* 61:59–94.

Pesetsky, David. 2013. "Что дѣлатъ? What Is to Be Done?" Paper presented at the annual meeting of the Linguistic Society of America.

Pesetsky, David, and Esther Torrego. 2006. "Probes, Goals and Syntactic Categories." In *Proceedings of the 7th Annual Tokyo Conference on Psycholinguistics*, ed. Yukio Otsu, 25–60. Keio: Hituzi Syobo.

Pesetsky, David, and Esther Torrego. 2007. "The Syntax of Valuation and the Interpretability of Features." In *Phrasal and Clausal Architecture*, ed. Simin Karimi, Vida Samiian, and Wendy Wilkins, 262–294. Amsterdam: John Benjamins.

Philip, Joy. 2012. "Subordinating and Coordinating Linkers." PhD diss., University College London.

Philip, Joy. 2013. "(Dis)harmony, the Head-Proximate Filter, and Linkers." *Journal of Linguistics* 49:165–221.

Pinker, Steven, and Paul Bloom. 1990. "Natural Language and Natural Selection." *Behavioral and Brain Sciences* 13:707–784.

Pintzuk, Susan. 1991. "Phrase Structures in Competition: Variation and Change in Old English Word Order." PhD diss., University of Pennsylvania.

Pintzuk, Susan. 1999. *Phrase Structures in Competition: Variation and Change in Old English Word Order*. New York: Garland.

Pintzuk, Susan. 2002. "Verb-Object Order in Old English: Variation in Grammatical Competition." In *Syntactic Effects of Morphological Change*, ed. David Lightfoot, 276–299. Oxford: Oxford University Press.

Pintzuk, Susan. 2005. "Arguments against a Universal Base: Evidence from Old English." *English Language and Linguistics* 9:115–138.

Platzack, Christer. 1982. "Transitive Adjectives in Old and Modern Swedish." In *Papers from the 5th International Conference on Historical Linguistics*, ed. Anders Ahlqvist, 273–282. Amsterdam: John Benjamins.

Poletto, Cecilia. 2008a. "On Negative Doubling." *Quaderni di Lavoro ASIt* 8:57–84.

Poletto, Cecilia. 2008b. "The Syntax of Focus Negation." *University of Venice Working Papers in Linguistics* 18:181–202.

Poletto, Cecilia. 2012. *Word Order in Old Italian*. Oxford: Oxford University Press.

Pollock, Jean-Yves. 1989. "Verb Movement, Universal Grammar, and the Structure of IP." *Linguistic Inquiry* 20:365–424.

Postal, Paul M. 1974. *On Raising: One Rule of English Grammar and Its Theoretical Implications*. Cambridge, MA: MIT Press.

Potsdam, Eric. 2004. "*Wh*-Questions in Malagasy." In *Proceedings of AFLA 11*, ed. Paul Law, 244–258. Berlin: ZAS.

Potsdam, Eric. 2006. "More Concealed Pseudoclefts and the Clausal Typing Hypothesis." *Lingua* 116:2154–2182.

Potsdam, Eric. 2009. "Austronesian Verb-Initial Languages and *Wh*-Question Strategies." *Natural Language and Linguistic Theory* 27:737–771.

Prentice, D. J. 1971. *The Murut Languages of Sabah*. Canberra: Australian National University.

Pretorius, Erin. 2017. "Spelling out P: A Unified Syntax of Afrikaans Adpositions and V-Particles." PhD diss., Stellenbosch University and Utrecht University (Utrecht Institute of Linguistics and Netherlands Graduate School of Linguistics).

Prince, Alan, and Paul Smolensky. 1993. "Optimality Theory: Constraint Interaction in Generative Grammar." Technical Report 2, Rutgers University Center for Cognitive Science.

Puškar, Zorica. 2015. "Interactions of Gender and Number Agreement: Evidence from Bosnian/Croatian/Serbian." Unpublished ms., University of Leipzig. (http://home.uni-leipzig.de/zoricapuskar/files/squib_final.pdf; last accessed 3 July 2016)

Ramchand, Gillian, and Peter Svenonius. 2008. "Mapping a Parochial Lexicon onto a Universal Semantics." In *The Limits of Syntactic Variation*, ed. Theresa Biberauer, 219–245. Amsterdam: John Benjamins.

Ramchand, Gillian, and Peter Svenonius. 2014. "Deriving the Functional Hierarchy." *Language Sciences* 46:152–174.

Raz, Shlomo. 1997. "Tigré." In *The Semitic Languages*, ed. Robert Hetzron, 446–456. London: Routledge.

Reesink, Ger. 2002. "Clause-Final Negation: Structure and Interpretation." *Functions of Language* 9:239–268.

Reichard, Ulrich. 2013. "Inference and Grammar: Intersectivity, Subsectivity and Phases." In *Proceedings of the Irish Network in Formal Linguistics 2011*, ed. Catrin S. Rhys, Pavel Iosad, and Alison Henry, 222–244. Newcastle: Cambridge Scholars Publishing.

Reuland, Eric. 2005a. "Agreeing to Bind." In *Organizing Grammar: Linguistic Studies in Honor of Henk van Riemsdijk*, ed. Hans Broekhuis, Norbert Corver, Riny Huybregts, Ursula Kleinhenz, and Jan Koster, 505–513. Berlin: Mouton de Gruyter.

Reuland, Eric. 2005b. "Binding Conditions: How Are They Derived?" In *Proceedings of the HPSG05 Conference*, ed. Stefan Müller, 578–593. Stanford, CA: CSLI Publications.

Reuland, Eric. 2011. *Anaphora and Language Design*. Cambridge, MA: MIT Press.

Rice, Keren. 1989. *A Grammar of Slave*. Berlin: Mouton de Gruyter.

Richards, Marc. 2004. "Object Shift and Scrambling in North and West Germanic: A Case Study in Symmetrical Syntax." PhD diss., University of Cambridge.

Richards, Marc. 2008a. "Defective Agree, Case Alternations, and the Prominence of Person." In *Scales*, ed. Marc Richards and Andrej L. Malchukov, 137–161. Leipzig: Universität Leipzig, Institut für Linguistik.

Richards, Marc. 2008b. "Desymmetrization: Parametric Variation at the PF-Interface." *Canadian Journal of Linguistics* 53:275–300.

Richards, Marc. 2014. "Defective Agree, Case Alternations, and the Prominence of Person." In *Scales and Hierarchies: A Cross-Disciplinary Perspective*, ed. Ina Bornkessel-Schlesewsky, Andrej Malchukov, and Marc Richards, 173–196. Berlin: Mouton de Gruyter.

Richards, Marc, and Theresa Biberauer. 2006. "Explaining Expl." In *The Function of Function Words and Functional Categories*, ed. Marcel den Dikken and Christina Tortora, 115–154. Amsterdam: John Benjamins.

Richards, Norvin. 2010. *Uttering Trees*. Cambridge, MA: MIT Press.

Richards, Norvin. 2016. *Contiguity Theory*. Cambridge, MA: MIT Press.

Riemsdijk, Henk van. 2001. "A Far from Simple Matter: Syntactic Reflexes of Syntax-Pragmatics Misalignments." In *Semantics, Pragmatics and Discourse: Perspectives and Connections. A Festschrift for Ferenc Kiefer*, ed. István Kenesei and Robert M. Harnish, 21–41. Amsterdam: John Benjamins.

Riemsdijk, Henk van. 2002. "The Unbearable Lightness of GOing." *Journal of Comparative Germanic Linguistics* 5:143–196.

Rijkhoff, Jan. 2002. *The Noun Phrase*. Oxford: Oxford University Press.

Rizzi, Luigi. 1982. *Issues in Italian Syntax*. Dordrecht: Foris.

Rizzi, Luigi. 1990. *Relativized Minimality*. Cambridge, MA: MIT Press.

Rizzi, Luigi. 1997. "On the Fine Structure of the Left Periphery." In *Elements of Grammar*, ed. Liliane Haegeman, 281–338. Dordrecht: Kluwer.

Rizzi, Luigi. 2001. "On the Position 'Int(errogative)' in the Left Periphery of the Clause." In *Current Studies in Italian Syntax: Essays Offered to Lorenzo Renzi*, ed. Guglielmo Cinque and Giampaolo Salvi, 287–296. Amsterdam: North Holland.

Rizzi, Luigi. 2008. "On Delimiting Movement." Talk given at the 31st GLOW Colloquium, Newcastle.

Roberge, Paul. 2000. "Etymological Opacity, Hybridization, and the Afrikaans Brace Negation." *American Journal of Germanic Linguistics and Literatures* 12:101–176.

Roberts, Craige. 2002. "Demonstratives as Definites." In *Information Sharing: Reference and Presupposition in Language Generation and Interpretation*, ed. Kees van Deemter and Rodger Kibble, 89–196. Stanford, CA: CSLI Publications.

Roberts, Ian. 2005. *Principles and Parameters in a VSO Language: A Case Study in Welsh*. Oxford: Oxford University Press.

Roberts, Ian, ed. 2007a. *Comparative Grammar: Critical Concepts*. London: Routledge.

Roberts, Ian. 2007b. *Diachronic Syntax*. Oxford: Oxford University Press.

Roberts, Ian. 2010a. *Agreement and Head Movement: Clitics, Incorporation, and Defective Goals*. Cambridge, MA: MIT Press.

Roberts, Ian. 2010b. "A Deletion Analysis of Null Subjects." In *Parametric Variation: Null Subjects in Minimalist Theory*, ed. Theresa Biberauer, Anders Holmberg, Ian Roberts, and Michelle Sheehan, 58–87. Cambridge: Cambridge University Press.

Roberts, Ian. 2012a. "Macroparameters and Minimalism: A Programme for Comparative Research." In *Parameter Theory and Linguistic Change*, ed. Charlotte Galves, Sonia Cyrino, Ruth Lopes, Filomena Sandalo, and Juanito Avelar, 320–335. Oxford: Oxford University Press.

Roberts, Ian. 2012b. "Phases, Head-Movement and Second-Position Effects." In *Phases: Developing the Framework*, ed. Ángel Gallego, 385–440. Berlin: Mouton de Gruyter.

Roberts, Ian, and Anders Holmberg. 2010. "Introduction." In *Parametric Variation: Null Subjects in Minimalist Theory*, ed. Theresa Biberauer, Anders Holmberg, Ian Roberts, and Michelle Sheehan, 1–57. Cambridge: Cambridge University Press.

Roberts, Ian, and Anna Roussou. 2003. *Syntactic Change: A Minimalist Approach to Grammaticalisation*. Cambridge: Cambridge University Press.

Roeper, Tom, and Muffy E. A. Siegel. 1978. "A Lexical Transformation for Verbal Compounds." *Linguistic Inquiry* 9:199–260.

Rooryck, Johan. 2008. "A Compositional Analysis of French Negation." Unpublished ms., Leiden University.

Rosen, Nicole. 2003. "Demonstrative Position in Michif." *Canadian Journal of Linguistics* 48:39–69.

Ross, John R. 1967. "Constraints on Variables in Syntax." PhD diss., MIT.

Ross, Malcolm. 2002a. "Bati-Vitu." In *The Oceanic Languages*, ed. John Lynch, Malcolm Ross, and Terry Crowley, 362–386. Richmond: Curzon Press.

Ross, Malcolm. 2002b. "Kaulong." In *The Oceanic Languages*, ed. John Lynch, Malcolm Ross, and Terry Crowley, 387–409. Richmond: Curzon Press.

Ross, Malcolm. 2002c. "Mussau." In *The Oceanic Languages*, ed. John Lynch, Malcolm Ross, and Terry Crowley, 148–166. Richmond: Curzon Press.

Ross, Malcolm. 2002d. "Sisiqa." In *The Oceanic Languages*, ed. John Lynch, Malcolm Ross, and Terry Crowley, 456–466. Richmond: Curzon Press.

Ross, Malcolm. 2002e. "Taiof." In *The Oceanic Languages*, ed. John Lynch, Malcolm Ross, and Terry Crowley, 426–439. Richmond: Curzon Press.

Rouveret, Alain. 1994. *Syntaxe du gallois: Principes généraux et typologie*. Paris: CNRS Editions.

Rupp, James E. 1989. *Lealao Chinantec Syntax*. Dallas, TX: Summer Institute of Linguistics and the University of Texas at Arlington.

Russell, Bertrand. 1905. "On Denoting." *Mind* 14:479–493.

Russell, Bertrand. 1919. "Descriptions." Excerpt from *An Introduction to Mathematical Philosophy*, 267–288. London: Allen and Unwin. [Reprinted in *Readings in the Philosophy of Language*, ed. Peter Ludlow, 323–333. Cambridge, MA: MIT Press (1997).]

Russell, Bertrand, and Alfred North Whitehead. 1910–13. *Principia Mathematica*. Cambridge: Cambridge University Press.

Rutkowski, Paweł. 2002. "Noun/Pronoun Asymmetries: Evidence in Support of the DP Hypothesis in Polish." *Jezikoslovlje* 3:159–170.

Rutkowski, Paweł. 2007. "The Syntactic Properties and Diachronic Development of Postnominal Adjectives in Polish." Paper presented at Formal Approaches to Slavic Linguistics: The Toronto Meeting 2006.

Rutkowski, Paweł, and Ljiljana Progovac. 2005. "Classification Projection in Polish and Serbian: The Position and Shape of Classifying Adjectives." In *Formal Approaches to Slavic Linguistics 13: The Columbia Meeting 2004*, ed. Steven Franks, Frank Gladney, and Mila Tasseva-Kurktchieva, 289–299. Ann Arbor: Michigan Slavic Publications.

Sabel, Joachim. 2002. "*Wh*-Questions and Extraction Asymmetries in Malagasy." In *Proceedings of the 8th Meeting of the Austronesian Formal Linguistics Association (AFLA 8)*, ed. Andrea Rackowski and Norvin Richards, 309–324. MIT Working Papers in Linguistics 44. Cambridge, MA: MIT, MIT Working Papers in Linguistics.

Sabel, Joachim. 2003. "Malagasy as an Optional Multiple *Wh*-Fronting Language." In *Multiple* Wh-*Fronting*, ed. Cedric Boeckx and Kleanthes Grohmann, 229–254. Amsterdam: John Benjamins.

Sadler, Louisa, and Douglas J. Arnold. 1994. "Prenominal Adjectives and the Phrasal/Lexical Distinction." *Journal of Linguistics* 30:187–226.

Saito, Mamoru, and Naoki Fukui. 1998. "Order in Phrase Structure and Movement." *Linguistic Inquiry* 29:439–474.

Salvi, Giampaolo. 2004. *La formazione di struttura di frase romanza*. Tübingen: Niemeyer.

Samiian, Vida. 1994. "The Ezafe Construction: Some Implications for the Theory of X-Bar Syntax." In *Persian Studies in North America*, ed. Mehdi Marashi, 17–42. Bethesda, MD: Iranbooks.

Sanches, Mary, and Linda Slobin. 1973. "Numeral Classifiers and Plural Marking: An Implicational Universal." In *Working Papers in Language Universals* 11:1–22. Stanford, CA: Stanford University.

Sánchez, Liliana. 2010. *The Morphology and Syntax of Focus and Topic: Minimalist Inquiries in the Quechua Periphery*. Amsterdam: John Benjamins.

Sapir, Edward. 1922. "The Takelma Language of Southwest Oregon." In *Handbook of American Indian Languages: Part 2*, ed. Franz Boas, 1–296. Washington, DC: U.S. Government Printing Office.

Sauerland, Uli, and Fabian Heck. 2003. "LF Intervention Effects in Pied Piping." In *NELS 33*, ed. Makoto Kadowaki and Shigeto Kawahara, 347–366. Amherst: University of Massachusetts, Graduate Linguistic Student Association.

Saul, Janice E., and Nancy Freiburger Wilson. 1980. *Nung Grammar*. Dallas, TX: Summer Institute of Linguistics.

Šaumjan, S. K., and P. A. Soboleva. 1963. *Applikativnaja poroždajuščaja model' i isčislenie transformacij v russkom jazyke*. Moscow: Izdatel'stvo Akademii Nauk, SSSR.

Schafer, Robin. 1994. "Nonfinite Predicate Initial Constructions in Modern Breton." PhD diss., University of California, Santa Cruz.

Schaub, Willi. 1985. *Babungo*. London: Croom Helm.

Schein, Barry. 1992. *Plurals and Events*. Cambridge, MA: MIT Press.

Schifano, Norma. 2015. "Verb Movement: A Pan-Romance Investigation." PhD diss., University of Cambridge.

Schmid, Tanja. 2005. *Infinitival Syntax: Infinitivus pro Participio as a Repair Strategy*. Amsterdam: John Benjamins.

Schütze, Carson. 1995. "PP Attachment and Agreement." In *Papers on Language Processing and Acquisition*, ed. Carson Schütze, Jennifer Ganger, and Kevin Broihier, 95–152. MIT Working Papers in Linguistics 26. Cambridge, MA: MIT, MIT Working Papers in Linguistics.

Schwabe, Kerstin. 2004. "The Particle *li* and the Left Periphery of Slavic *yes/no* Interrogatives." In *The Syntax and Semantics of the Left Periphery*, ed. Horst Lohnstein and Susanne Trissler, 385–430. Berlin: Mouton de Gruyter.

Schwartz, Florian. 2003. "Focus Marking in Kikuyu." In *Questions and Focus: ZAS Publications in Linguistics 30*, ed. Regine Eckhardt, 41–118. Berlin: Zentrum für Allgemeine Sprachwissenschaft.

Seidl, Amanda. 2001. *Minimal Indirect Reference: A Theory of the Syntax-Phonology Interface.* London: Routledge.

Selkirk, Elisabeth O. 1984. *Phonology and Syntax: The Relation between Sound and Structure.* Cambridge, MA: MIT Press.

Sells, Peter. 2001. *Structure, Alignment and Optionality in Swedish.* Stanford, CA: CSLI Publications.

Senft, Gunter. 1986. *Kilivila: The Language of the Trobriand Islanders.* Berlin: Mouton de Gruyter.

Shaul, David Leedom. 1986. *Topics in Nevome syntax.* Berkeley: University of California Press.

Sheehan, Michelle. 2011. "Extraposition and Antisymmetry." In *Linguistic Variation Yearbook 2010*, ed. Jeroen van Craenenbroeck, 201–251. Amsterdam: John Benjamins.

Sheehan, Michelle. 2013a. "Explaining the Final-over-Final Constraint: Formal and Functional Approaches." In *Theoretical Approaches to Disharmonic Word Order*, ed. Theresa Biberauer and Michelle Sheehan, 407–444. Oxford: Oxford University Press.

Sheehan, Michelle. 2013b. "Some Implications of a Copy Theory of Labelling for the Linear Correspondence Axiom." *Syntax* 16:362–396.

Sheehan, Michelle. 2014. "Towards a Parameter Hierarchy for Alignment." In *WCCFL 31: Proceedings of the 31st West Coast Conference on Formal Linguistics*, ed. Robert E. Santana-LaBarge, 399–408. Somerville, MA: Cascadilla Press.

Sheehan, Michelle, and Wolfram Hinzen. 2011. "Moving towards the Edge." *Linguistic Analysis* 34:405–458.

Shimizu, Kiyoshi. 1983. *The Zing Dialect of Mumuye: A Descriptive Grammar.* Hamburg: Helmut Buske Verlag.

Shlonsky, Ur. 1997. *Clause Structure and Word Order in Hebrew and Arabic.* Oxford: Oxford University Press.

Shlonsky, Ur. 2004. "The Form of Semitic Noun Phrases." *Lingua* 114:1465–1526.

Sichel, Ivy. 2007. "Raising in DP Revisited." In *New Horizons in the Analysis of Control and Raising*, ed. William D. Davies and Stanley Dubinsky, 13–34. Berlin: Springer.

Siegel, Muffy E. A. 1976. "Capturing the Adjective." PhD diss., University of Massachusetts, Amherst.

Siewierska, Anna, and Ludmila Uhlířová. 1998. "An Overview of Word Order in Slavic Languages." In *Constituent Order in the Languages of Europe*, ed. Anna Siewierska, 105–149. Berlin: Mouton de Gruyter.

Sigurðsson, Halldór Á. 1988 "From OV to VO." *Working Papers in Scandinavian Syntax* 34:1–42.

Sigurðsson, Halldór Á. 2004. "The Syntax of Person, Tense and Speech Features." *Italian Journal of Linguistics* 16:219–251.

Sigurðsson, Halldór Á. 2010. "On EPP Effects." *Studia Linguistica* 64:159–189.

Sigurðsson, Halldór Á. 2011a. "On UG and Materialization." *Linguistic Analysis* 37:367–388.

Sigurðsson, Halldór Á. 2011b. "Uniformity and Diversity: A Minimalist Perspective." *Linguistic Variation* 11:189–222.

Silverstein, Michael. 1976. "Hierarchy of Features and Ergativity." In *Grammatical Categories in Australian Languages*, ed. R. M.W. Dixon, 112–171. Canberra: Australian Institute of Aboriginal Studies. [Reprinted in *Features and Projections*, ed. Pieter Muysken and Henk van Riemsdijk, 163–232. Dordrecht: Foris (1986).]

Simpson, Andrew, and Zoe Wu. 2002. "Agreement, Shells and Focus." *Language* 78:287–313.

Slade, Benjamin. 2011. "Formal and Philological Inquiries into the Nature of Interrogatives, Indefinites, Disjunction, and Focus in Sinhala and Other Languages." PhD diss., University of Illinois at Urbana/Champaign.

Smith, Kenneth D. 1979. *Sedang Grammar: Phonological and Syntactic Structure*. Canberra: Australian National University, Research School of Pacific Studies, Department of Linguistics.

Soh, Hooi Ling. 2009. "Speaker Presupposition and Mandarin Chinese Sentence-Final *-le*: A Unified Analysis of the 'Change of State' and the 'Contrary to Expectation' Reading." *Natural Language and Linguistic Theory* 27:623–657.

Soh, Hooi Ling, and Meijia Gao. 2006. "Perfective Aspect and Transition in Mandarin Chinese: An Analysis of Double *-le* Sentences." In *Proceedings of the 2004 Texas Linguistics Society Conference*, ed. Pascal Denis, Eric McCready, Alexis Palmer, and Brian Reese, 107–122. Somerville, MA: Cascadilla Press.

Song, Chenchen. 2016. "A Minimalist Study of Complex Verb Formation: Cross-Linguistic Patterns and Variation." Unpublished ms., University of Cambridge.

Sorace, Antonella. 2004. "Gradience at the Lexicon-Syntax Interface: Evidence from Auxiliary Selection." In *The Unaccusativity Puzzle*, ed. Artemis Alexiadou, Martin Everaert, and Elena Anagnostopoulou, 243–268. Oxford: Oxford University Press.

Speas, Margaret. 1990. *Phrase Structure in Natural Languages*. Dordrecht: Kluwer.

Speas, Margaret. 2004. "Evidentiality, Logophoricity and the Syntactic Representation of Pragmatic Features." *Lingua* 114:255–276.

Speas, Margaret, and Carol Tenny. 2003. "Configurational Properties of Point of View Roles." In *Asymmetry in Grammar*, ed. Anna Maria Di Sciullo, 315–344. Amsterdam: John Benjamins.

Spencer, Andrew. 1991. *Morphological Theory*. Oxford: Blackwell.

Sportiche, Dominique. 2005. "Division of Labor between Merge and Move: Strict Locality of Selection and Apparent Reconstruction Paradoxes." Unpublished ms., UCLA. (http://ling.auf.net/lingbuzz/000163; last accessed 2 June 2016)

Sproat, Richard, and Chinlin Shih. 1988. "Prenominal Adjectival Ordering in English and Mandarin." In *NELS 18*, ed. James Blevins and Juli Carter, 465–489. Amherst: University of Massachusetts, Graduate Linguistic Student Association.

Sproat, Richard, and Chinlin Shih. 1990. "The Cross-Linguistic Distribution of Adjectival Ordering Restrictions." In *Interdisciplinary Approaches to Language: Essays in*

Honor of S.-Y. Kuroda, ed. Carol Georgopoulos and Roberta Ishihara, 565–593. Dordrecht: Kluwer.

Starke, Michal. 2009. "Nanosyntax: A Short Primer to a New Approach to Language." Unpublished ms., University of Tromsø. (http://ling.auf.net/lingbuzz/001230; last accessed 2 June 2016)

Starks, Donna, and Diane Massam. 2015. "The Origin of *yes-no* Question Particles in the Niuean Language." *Journal of Linguistics* 51:185–212.

Steriade, Donca. 1982. "Greek Prosodies and the Nature of Syllabification." PhD diss., MIT.

Stevenson, Roland. 1969. *Bagirmi Grammar*. Khartoum: University of Khartoum, Sudan Research Unit.

Stowell, Tim. 1981. "Origins of Phrase Structure." PhD diss., MIT.

Struckmeier, Volker. 2014. "*Ja doch wohl* C? Modal Particles in German as C-Related Elements." *Studia Linguistica* 68:16–48.

Svenonius, Peter. 1994. "On the Structural Location of the Attributive Adjective." In *Proceedings of the Twelfth West Coast Conference on Formal Linguistics (WCCFL 12)*, ed. Eric Duncan, Donka Farkas, and Philip Spaelti, 439–454. Stanford, CA: CSLI Publications.

Svenonius, Peter. 2000. "Introduction." In *The Derivation of VO and OV*, ed. Peter Svenonius, 1–26. Amsterdam: John Benjamins.

Svenonius, Peter. 2006. "The Emergence of Axial Parts." *Nordlyd* 33:49–77.

Svenonius, Peter. 2008. "Review of *Non-projecting Words* by Ida Toivonen." *Language* 84:666–670.

Svenonius, Peter. 2010. "Spatial P in English." In *Mapping Spatial PPs*, ed. Guglielmo Cinque and Luigi Rizzi, 127–160. New York: Oxford University Press.

Svenonius, Peter. 2011. "Spanning." Unpublished ms., University of Tromsø. (http://ling.auf.net/lingbuzz/001501; last accessed 26 December 2015)

Svenonius, Peter. 2016. "Spans and Words." In *Morphological Metatheory*, ed. Daniel Siddiqi and Heidi Harley, 201–222. Amsterdam: John Benjamins.

Swanson, Kirstie. 2011. "Serial Verb Constructions in Bwe Karen." MA thesis, Payap University (Chiang Mai, Thailand).

Sybesma, Rint, and Boya Li. 2007. "The Dissection and Structural Mapping of Cantonese Sentence Final Particles." *Lingua* 117:1739–1783.

Tallerman, Maggie. 1998. *Understanding Syntax*. London: Arnold.

Tallerman, Maggie. 2006. "Challenging the Syllabic Model of 'Syntax-As-It-Is.'" *Lingua* 116:689–709.

Tánczos, Orsolya. 2014. "Cycle by Cycle in the History of *shuisa*." Paper presented at the 16th Diachronic Generative Syntax (DiGS16) conference, Budapest.

Tasseva-Kurktchieva, Mila. 2005. "The Possessor That Came Home." In *Possessives and Beyond: Semantics and Syntax*, ed. Ji-yung Kim, Yury A. Lander, and Barbara Partee, 279–293. University of Massachusetts Occasional Papers in Linguistics 29. Amherst: University of Massachusetts, Graduate Linguistic Student Association.

Tat, Deniz. 2010. "APs as Reduced Relatives: The Case of *bir* in (Some) Varieties of Turkic." In *Proceedings of the 7th Workshop on Altaic Formal Linguistics (WAFL 7)*, ed. Andrew Simpson, 301–315. MIT Working Papers in Linguistics 62. Cambridge, MA: MIT, MIT Working Papers in Linguistics.

Toivonen, Ida. 2003. *Non-projecting Words*. Dordrecht: Kluwer.

Toro, Juan, Luca Bonatti, Marina Nespor, and Jacques Mehler. 2008. "Finding Words and Rules in a Speech Stream: Functional Differences between Vowels and Consonants." *Psychological Science* 19:137–144.

Travis, Lisa. 1984. "Parameters and Effects of Word Order Variation." PhD diss., MIT.

Travis, Lisa. 1994. "Parameters of Phrase Structure and Verb-Second Phenomena." In *Principles and Parameters in Comparative Grammar*, ed. Robert Freidin, 339–364. Cambridge, MA: MIT Press.

Travis, Lisa. 2006. "VP, D^0 Movement Languages." In *Negation, Tense and Clausal Architecture: Cross-Linguistic Investigations*, ed. Raffaella Zanuttini, Héctor Campos, Elena Herburger, and Paul Portner, 127–147. Washington, DC: Georgetown University Press.

Travis, Lisa. 2010. *Inner Aspect: The Articulation of VP*. Dordrecht: Springer.

Trinh, Tue. 2014. "Edges and Linearization." PhD diss., MIT. (http://dspace.mit.edu/handle/1721.1/68523; last accessed 3 July 2016)

Tryon, D. T. 1967. *Nengone Grammar*. Canberra: Australian National University.

Tryon, D. T. 1971. *Iai Grammar*. Canberra: Pacific Linguistics.

Tsimpli, Ianthi. 2013. "(Evidence for) the Language Instinct." In *The Cambridge Handbook of Biolinguistics*, ed. Cedric Boeckx and Kleanthes Grohmann, 49–68. Cambridge: Cambridge University Press.

Tsimpli, Ianthi. 2014. "Early, Late or Very Late? Timing Acquisition and Bilingualism." *Linguistic Approaches to Bilingualism* 4:283–313.

Tucker, Archibald.1994. *A Grammar of Kenya Luo (Dholuo)*. Cologne: Rüdiger Köppe Verlag.

Uriagereka, Juan. 1999. "Multiple Spell-Out." In *Working Minimalism*, ed. Samuel David Epstein and Norbert Hornstein, 251–282. Cambridge, MA: MIT Press.

Vandame, Charles. 1963. *Le ngambay-moundou: Phonologie, grammaire, et textes*. Mémoires de L'Institut Français d'Afrique Noire. Dakar: IFAN.

van den Berg, René. 1989. *A Grammar of the Muna Language*. Dordrecht: Foris.

Vanden Wyngaerd, Guido. 1989. "Verb Projection Raising and the Status of Infinitival Complements." In *Sentential Complementation and the Lexicon: Studies in Honour of Wim de Geest*, ed. Dany Jaspers, Wim Klooster, Yvan Putseys, and Pieter Seuren, 423–438. Dordrecht: Foris.

van der Auwera, Johan, Peter Kehayov, and Alice Vittrant. 2009. "Acquisitive Modals." In *Cross-Linguistic Semantics of Tense, Aspect, and Modality*, ed. Lotte Hogeweg, Helen de Hoop, and Andrej Malchukov, 271–302. Amsterdam: John Benjamins.

Van der Wal, Jenneke. 2016. "Diagnosing Focus." *Studies in Language* 40:259–301.

van Kemenade, Ans. 1987. *Syntactic Case and Morphological Case in the History of English*. Dordrecht: Foris.

Veenstra, Tonjes. 1996. "Serial Verbs in Saramaccan: Predication and Creole Genesis." PhD diss., University of Amsterdam.

Veenstra, Tonjes. 2006. "Head Ordering in Synthetic Compounds: Acquisition Processes and Creole Genesis." In *The Structure of Creole Words: Segmental, Syllabic and Morphological Aspects*, ed. Parth Bhatt and Ingo Plag, 201–222. Tübingen: Niemeyer.

Vennemann, Theo. 1974. "Topics, Subjects, and Word Order: From SXV to SVX via TVX." In *Historical Linguistics: Proceedings of the First International Congress of Historical Linguistics, Edinburgh, September 1973*, ed. John Anderson and Charles Jones, 2:339–376. Amsterdam: North-Holland.

Vikner, Sten. 1995. *Verb Movement and Expletive Subjects in the Germanic Languages*. Oxford: Oxford University Press.

Vilkuna, Maria. 1989. *Free Word Order in Finnish*. Helsinki: SKS.

Vilkuna, Maria. 1995. "Discourse Configurationality in Finnish." In *Discourse-Configurational Languages*, ed. Katalin É. Kiss, 244–268. Oxford: Oxford University Press.

Vincent, Nigel. 1988. "Latin." In *The Romance Languages*, ed. Martin Harris and Nigel Vincent, 26–78. London: Routledge.

Vincent, Nigel. 1997. "The Emergence of the D-System in Romance." In *Parameters of Morphosyntactic Change*, ed. Ans van Kemenade and Nigel Vincent, 149–169. Cambridge: Cambridge University Press.

Waddington, Conrad Hal. 1977. *Tools for Thought*. London: Jonathan Cape.

Walkden, George. 2009. "Deriving the Final-over-Final Constraint from Third Factor Considerations." *Cambridge Occasional Papers in Linguistics* 5:67–72.

Walker, Dale F. 1976. *Grammar of the Lampung Language*. Jakarta: NUSA.

Wang, Yu-Fang, Aya Katz, and Chih-Hua Chen. 2003. "Thinking as Saying: *Shuo* ('say') in Taiwan Mandarin Conversation and BBS Talk." *Language Sciences* 25:457–488.

Watumull, Jeffrey. 2010. "Merge as a Minimax Solution to the Optimization Problem of Generativity." MPhil thesis., University of Cambridge.

Wee, Lionel. 2004. "Reduplication and Discourse Particles." In *Singapore English: A Grammatical Description*, ed. Lisa Lim, 105–126. Amsterdam: John Benjamins.

Werner, Heinrich. 1997. *Die ketische Sprache*. Wiesbaden: Harrassowitz.

Wexler, Kenneth. 1998. "Very Early Parameter Setting and the Unique Checking Constraint: A New Explanation of the Optional Infinitive Stage." *Lingua* 106:23–79.

Whitman, John. 2008. "The Classification of Constituent Order Generalizations and Diachronic Explanation." In *Linguistic Universals and Language Change*, ed. Jeff Good, 233–253. Oxford: Oxford University Press.

Whitman, John. 2013. "Diachronic Interpretations of Word Order Parameter Cohesion." Paper presented at the 15th Diachronic Generative Syntax Conference, Ottawa.

Williams, Edwin. 1980. "Predication." *Linguistic Inquiry* 11:208–238.

Williams, Edwin. 1981a. "Argument Structure and Morphology." *The Linguistic Review* 1:81–114.

Williams, Edwin. 1981b. "On the Notions 'Lexically Related' and 'Head of a Word.'" *Linguistic Inquiry* 12:245–274.

Williams, Edwin. 1982. "Another Argument That Passive Is Transformational." *Linguistic Inquiry* 13:160–163.

Williams, Edwin. 1994. *Thematic Structure in Syntax.* Cambridge, MA: MIT Press.

Williams, Edwin. 2003. *Representation Theory.* Cambridge, MA: MIT Press.

Willis, David. 2006. "Against N-Raising and NP-Raising Analyses of Welsh Noun Phrases." In *Celtic Linguistics,* ed. Robert D. Borsley, Louisa Sadler, Ian Roberts, and David Willis, special issue, *Lingua* 116:1807–1839.

Willis, David, Christopher Lucas, and Anne Breitbarth. 2013. *The Development of Negation in the Languages of Europe.* Vol. 1, *Case Studies.* Oxford: Oxford University Press.

Willson, Heather. 2002. "The Marshallese Complementizer Phrase." MA thesis, Arizona State University.

Willson, Heather. 2005. "Marshallese *yes/no* Questions and Remnant Movement." In *Proceedings of the 12th Annual Conference of AFLA,* ed. Jeffrey Heinz and Dimitris Ntelitheos, 421–435. UCLA Working Papers in Linguistics 12. Los Angeles: UCLA, Department of Linguistics.

Willson, Heather. 2008. "Remnant Movement and the Position of the Marshallese Question Particle." Unpublished ms., UCLA. (http://linguistics.byu.edu/faculty/hwills1/RemnantMvmtMarshallese.pdf; last accessed 21 September 2015)

Wilson, Stephen, and Ayse P. Saygın. 2001. "Adverbs and Functional Heads in Turkish: Linear Order and Scope." In *Proceedings of the Western Conference on Linguistics (WECOL 2001),* ed. Lesley Carmichael, Chia-Hui Huang, and Vida Samiian, 410–420. Fresno: California State University, Department of Linguistics.

Wiltschko, Martina. 2014. *The Universal Structure of Categories: Towards a Formal Typology.* Cambridge: Cambridge University Press.

Wiltschko, Martina. To appear. "Ergative Constructions in the Structure of Speech Acts." In *The Oxford Handbook of Ergativity,* ed. Jessica Coon, Diane Massam, and Lisa Travis. Oxford: Oxford University Press.

Wiltschko, Martina, and Johannes Heim. 2016. "The Syntax of Confirmationals: A Neo-performative Analysis." In *Outside the Clause: Form and Function of Extra-Clausal Constituents,* ed. Günther Kaltenböck, Evelien Keizer, and Arne Lohmann, 303–340. Amsterdam: John Benjamins.

Wunderlich, Dieter. 2001. "Two Comparatives." In *Semantics, Pragmatics and Discourse: Perspectives and Connections. A Festschrift for Ferenc Kiefer,* ed. István Kenesei and Robert M. Harnish, 75–89. Amsterdam: John Benjamins.

Wurmbrand, Susi. 2006. "Verb Clusters, Verb Raising and Restructuring." In *The Blackwell Companion to Syntax,* Vol. 5, ed. Martin Everaert and Henk van Riemsdijk, 229–343. Oxford: Blackwell.

Wurmbrand, Susi. 2014. "The Merge Condition: A Syntactic Approach to Selection." In *Minimalism and Beyond: Radicalizing the Interfaces*, ed. Peter Kosta, Steven L. Franks, Teodora Radeva-Bork, and Lilia Schürcks, 139–177. Amsterdam: John Benjamins.

Yaisomanang, Somphob. 2012. "The Syntax of *yes-no* Questions and Answers in Thai." PhD diss., University of Newcastle.

Yang, Charles. 2016. *The Price of Linguistic Productivity: How Children Learn to Break the Rules of Language*. Cambridge, MA: MIT Press.

Yang, Xiaodong, and Martina Wiltschko. 2016. "The Confirmational Marker *ha* in Northern Mandarin." Unpublished ms., University of British Columbia. (http://syntaxofspeechacts.linguistics.ubc.ca/wp-content/uploads/2014/02/Yang-wiltschko-mandarin-ha.pdf; last accessed 3 July 2016)

Yaohoung, Long, and Guoqiao, Zheng. 1998. *The Dong Language in Guizhou Province, China*, trans. D. Norman Geary. Dallas, TX: Summer Institute of Linguistics and the University of Texas at Arlington.

Yap, Foong Ha, Jiao Wang, and Charles T.-K. Lam. 2010. "Clausal Integration and the Emergence of Mitigative and Adhortative Sentence-Final Particles in Chinese." *Taiwan Journal of Linguistics* 8:63–86.

Zanuttini, Raffaella. 1997. *Negation and Clausal Structure: A Comparative Study of Romance Languages*. New York: Oxford University Press.

Zeijlstra, Hedde. 2004. "Sentential Negation and Negative Concord." PhD diss., University of Amsterdam.

Zeijlstra, Hedde. 2008. "On the Syntactic Flexibility of Formal Features." In *The Limits of Syntactic Variation*, ed. Theresa Biberauer, 143–174. Amsterdam: John Benjamins.

Zeijlstra, Hedde. 2014. "On the Uninterpretability of Interpretable Features." In *Minimalism and Beyond: Radicalizing the Interfaces*, ed. Peter Kosta, Steven L. Franks, Teodora Radeva-Bork, and Lilia Schürcks, 109–129. Amsterdam: John Benjamins.

Zeijlstra, Hedde. 2015. "Left and Right: Explaining FOFC and the Left Position of Specifiers without the LCA." Paper presented at the 4th Cambridge Comparative Syntax conference (CamCoS 4).

Zeller, Jochen. 2013. "In Defence of Head Movement: Evidence from Bantu." In *Diagnosing Syntax*, ed. Lisa Cheng and Norbert Corver, 87–111. Oxford: Oxford University Press.

Zhang, Ling. 2014. "Segmentless Sentence-Final Particles in Cantonese: An Experimental Study." *Studies in Chinese Linguistics* 35:47–60.

Zhang, Niina. 1999. "Chinese *de* and the *de*-Construction." *Syntaxis* 2:27–49.

Zhang, Niina. 2012. "*De* and the Functional Expansion of Classifiers." *Language and Linguistics* 13:569–582.

Zimmermann, Malte. 2015. "Scalar Particles as Alternative-Sensitive Expressions." Paper presented to the Cambridge Linguistic Society.

Zwart, C. Jan-Wouter. 1996a. "On the Status and Position of PPs inside APs in Dutch." Unpublished ms., University of Groningen.

Zwart, C. Jan-Wouter. 1996b. "Verb Clusters in Continental West Germanic Dialects." In *Microparametric Syntax and Dialect Variation*, ed. James Black and Virginia Motapanyane, 229–258. Amsterdam: John Benjamins.

Zwart, C. Jan-Wouter. 1997. *The Morphosyntax of Verb Movement*. Dordrecht: Kluwer.

Zwart, C. Jan-Wouter. 2005. "Some Notes on Coordination in Head-Final Languages." In *Linguistics in the Netherlands*, ed. Jenny Doetjes and Jeroen van de Weijer, 231–242. Amsterdam: John Benjamins.

Zwart, C. Jan-Wouter. 2009a. "The FOFC Asymmetry: A Layered Derivation Perspective." Paper presented at Theoretical Approaches to Disharmonic Word Order, Newcastle.

Zwart, C. Jan-Wouter. 2009b. "Relevance of Typology to Minimalist Inquiry." *Lingua* 119:1589–1606.

Zwart, C. Jan-Wouter. 2011a. "Recursion in Language: A Layered-Derivation Approach." *Biolinguistics* 5:43–56.

Zwart, C. Jan-Wouter. 2011b. "Structure and Order: Asymmetric Merge." In *The Oxford Handbook of Linguistic Minimalism*, ed. Cedric Boeckx, 96–118. Oxford: Oxford University Press.

Zwart, C. Jan-Wouter. 2015. "Top-Down Derivation, Recursion, and the Model of Grammar." In *Syntactic Complexity across Interfaces*, ed. Andreas Trotzke and Josef Bayer, 25–42. Berlin: de Gruyter.

Index

Abels, Klaus, 79, 176–183, 340
Abney, Steven P., 142
Aboh, Enoch, 249
Ackema, Peter, 343
Acquisition, 24–25, 37–38, 42, 46–47,
    94, 189, 249, 268, 270, 290,
    292
    cues to phase boundaries in, 286, 289,
    292
Adjacency, 58–60, 76, 101, 103–104,
    118
Adjective, 125, 127–128
    position in relation to other elements,
    122–123, 125, 128–149, 152
Adposition, 105. *See also* Preposition,
    Postposition
Adverb, 59–60, 97–108, 111–120
Affix, 59, 303, 344. *See also* Prefix,
    Suffix
Afrikaans, 13, 15, 17, 130–134,
    249–250
    nie, 205–209, 280–282, 284
Agglutinating morphology, 85, 92, 98,
    103, 111–112, 329–330
Agree, 48, 51, 168, 171, 184, 259. *See
    also* Agreement; Particle,
    agreement-realizing; PF, PF reflex of
    Agree
Agree-driven incorporation, 72–73
backward Agree, 80, 83–85
long-distance Agree, 263
Agreement, 46, 162, 194, 287, 293–295.
    See also Agree; Particle,
    agreement-realizing

differences between auxiliaries and
    lexical verbs, 188–189, 191–192,
    200, 290
position of agreement morphology,
    334, 337
Akkadian, 254, 256–257
Aldridge, Edith, 247
Alexiadou, Artemis, 182
Anagnostopoulou, Elena, 182
Analytic language, 285, 291
Arabic, 158, 165, 290, 293, 304, 341
Asymmetry, 12, 14, 16, 39–42, 49, 53,
    79–80, 90, 92–95, 101–102. *See also*
    C-command, asymmetric
    in adjunct ordering, 99, 115–116,
    122
    in argument structure, 169
    in Merge, 52
Austronesian, 158–159, 165, 201, 234,
    238, 247
Aux(iliary), 12–14, 41, 57, 61–62,
    67–69, 73
    in Finnish, 297, 299, 301–302
    order in relation to verb and adverb,
    59–60, 98–108, 110–120
    uninflecting, 187–190 (*see also*
    Particle, final auxiliary particle)

Babungo, 219, 220
Bagirmi, 191–193, 201
Baker, Mark, 37
Ban on Improper Movement, 295
Bangla. *See* Bengali
Bantu, 206, 237, 246–247, 339

Basque, 15, 102, 119
Bayer, Josef, 235
Bengali, 17, 256
Berbice Dutch Creole, 159
Bhatt, Rajesh, 107, 111, 124
Biberauer, Theresa, 17, 21–23, 40–41,
    61–66, 76–77, 86, 94, 103, 111, 115,
    117–119, 126, 164, 168, 171,
    207–208, 243, 246, 248–249, 280,
    288, 335
Binding, 45–46, 51, 173, 184, 259
Bislama, 159
Blackings, Mairi, 194–195, 203–204
Bonfim Duarte, Fabio, 198–199
Bongo, 201
Bosnian. See Bosnian/Croatian/Serbian
Bosnian/Croatian/Serbian, 128–131, 134,
    139–140, 143, 230–231, 294
Bottom-pair problem, 52
Bottom-up derivation, 308, 321
Branching Constraint, 53–54
Bulgarian, 138–143, 230–232,
    257–258
Buru, 201
Bwe-Karen, 189–190, 219

Cable, Seth, 105, 194, 259–260, 272
Cantonese, 197–198
Cardinaletti, Anna, 251–252, 260,
    271–272
Case, 18, 47, 91, 162, 168, 249
  position of case affix, 325, 328,
    332–333, 336
Case Resistance Principle, 18
Causative morphology, 35, 334, 336
C-command, 46, 94, 176–177, 332–333.
    See also Linear Correspondence
    Axiom
  asymmetric c-command, 301, 305, 318,
    320
Cecchetto, Carlo, 83–86, 88, 93
Celtic, 38, 155, 158, 160–166
Change, 93, 225. See also Diachrony
Chinese, 198, 209–210, 213, 228–229,
    255, 261. See also Cantonese,
    Mandarin, Jambi-Teochew
    Yixing Chinese, 197

Chomsky, Noam, 33, 36, 44–46, 49,
    51–53, 62, 76, 161, 320, 335,
    337–338
Cinque, Guglielmo, 98–104, 115–117,
    138, 145–146, 148, 152–155,
    158–159, 167–168, 180–184, 266
Clark, Eve V., 25
Clause. See CP
Clitic, 44, 72, 140–141, 170–175, 328,
    336
Coast Tsimshian, 159
Comparative, 123–124, 129, 131,
    133–134, 137–138, 140, 147, 256
C(omplementizer), 15–16, 209–210,
    253–257, 277–279. See also Particle,
    C-particle
Compound, 24–25, 137, 342–345
Condition on Extraction Domain (CED),
    70, 180
Constituent Recognition Domain (CRD),
    80–83, 87
Contact, 22, 204, 225, 279, 290.
Contiguity effect, 287, 292–293, 295
Coordination, 40, 164
CP, 17–19, 65–66, 162
Creole, 158–159, 230
Croatian. See Bosnian/Croatian/Serbian
Cross-Categorial Harmony (CCH),
    31–32, 36, 39
C-selection. See Selection

Defective goal, 171
Deg. See Degree modifier
Degree modifier, 123–124, 133–134
Dem(onstrative), 151–152, 160–163,
    168–173, 176–185, 238–240
  low demonstrative, 158–159, 161, 165
Den Dikken, Marcel, 250
Deutscher, Guy, 256–257
Devos, Maud, 206
Dholuo, 193–194, 217–220
Diachrony, 21–22, 79, 88, 172, 209, 284
Direct modification, 145–147
Directionality, 55, 67, 77, 301. See also
    Licensing direction
Direct object. See Object, direct
Discourse domain, 229, 267

Disharmonic order, 12, 15–16, 20, 25, 28–29, 32, 68–69, 76, 98, 120, 301, 340. *See also* FOFC violation, Inverse-FOFC
and particles, 210, 215, 249
and processing, 82–83, 88, 90, 92
Disjunction marker, 220–221, 247
Distributed Morphology, 323, 341–342
Dominance, 27, 29–36, 33, 35, 39, 67
Dravidian, 22, 38
Drehu, 167
Dryer, Matthew S., 16, 36, 47, 88, 92, 154–155, 158–159, 180–183, 188, 193–194, 201, 222, 291, 325–328. *See also World Atlas of Language Structures*
Duffield, Nigel, 263–264
Dutch, 13–14, 38, 64, 128–134, 245
Được. *See* Vietnamese, *được*
Dwivedi, Veena, 105–108

Early Immediate Constituents, 80, 82–83, 86, 88–92.
Edge. *See* Edge feature; Phase, phase edge
Edge feature, 62, 172. *See also* EPP-feature
EIC. *See* Early Immediate Constituents
Ellipsis, 84
Emonds, Joseph, 54
Emphatic element, 98–99, 104–105, 114, 230, 256
English, 45, 105, 174–176, 266
adverbs, 99, 117–118, 122
compounding, 24–25, 343–344
final discourse particles, 240, 262, 277
and the Head-Final Filter, 121–128, 131–134, 137–138, 147, 149
movement, 74, 99, 117–118
order of demonstrative and noun, 153, 160–161, 166
sentential word order, 14, 16, 68, 304
Epistemicity, 264–268, 270
EPP-feature, 62, 166, 171, 173–174, 181
Erlewine, Michael Yoshitaka, 274
Ernst, Thomas, 19, 98, 115–117
Estonian, 215, 221

Extended projection, 19, 63–66, 289–291
Extension Condition, 49
External argument, 153, 164, 166–169, 173, 180–182, 184–185
Extraposition, 14, 17–19, 71, 90, 164, 233, 284
and the Head-Final Filter, 123–125, 127, 131–135, 139–140, 148

Fabb, Nigel, 194–195, 203–204
Final-over-initial, 12, 14, 231, 233, 240, 243, 279, 284, 286–287
Finiteness, 192–193, 200, 225–226
Finnish, 15, 20–21, 57, 59–62
adverbs, 59, 97–98
and the Head-Final Filter, 128–129
focus particles, 299–300, 230–233, 246, 258, 311, 313–314, 321
sentential word order, 15, 57, 297–300, 302–305, 310–315, 318–319
Flemish, 13
Focus, 104. *See also* Particle, focus particle
FOFC violation, 16–17, 20–22, 25, 30, 32, 58, 65–66, 68–70, 73
and affixation, 329–331, 334–336, 339–344
and auxiliaries, 41, 62, 68–69, 110–111, 119, 299, 301–302, 314–315
in DP, 154–155, 158–159, 161, 163–164, 178–183
and particles, 187, 190–191, 196, 198, 200, 203–204, 206, 208–209, 226–228, 231–233, 235–238, 240, 242–247, 249–254, 257, 263, 265, 270–271, 276–279, 283–284, 287–289, 291, 295
and processing, 83, 85–86, 88–90, 99
Force, 216–217, 230–231, 248, 261, 273
Fox, Danny, 169–170, 320,
French, 99, 118, 128–129, 134, 161
Fyem, 213

Garifuna, 200
Ge'ez, 22

Gender, 293–294, 324
Genitive, 27–28
German, 12–14, 17, 61, 75, 87–88,
    245
disharmony, 32, 38, 75
and the Head–Final Filter, 128–129,
    132–134, 143
particles, 235–236, 246
Germanic, 12–15, 70, 90, 97–98,
    101–102, 133–134, 246, 288
West Germanic, 13, 19, 240, 249–251,
    283
Gilligan, Gary, 323–326, 331–332, 334,
    336
Grammaticalization, 86, 195–197, 207,
    224, 272
Greek, 138, 140, 143, 160, 161, 173,
    188–189, 290
Greenberg, Joseph, 27–31, 39, 40, 122,
    153–155, 324
Grosu, Alexander, 123–124
Guardiano, Cristina, 159–161.

Haddican, William, 119
Haegeman, Liliane, 13, 216
Haider, Hubert, 53–54, 298
Halle, Morris, 36
Harmonic order, 11, 22, 28–29, 33, 36,
    90–92
head-final, 30, 35, 38–39, 58, 64, 71,
    76, 81–82, 85–86, 91, 98, 105–106,
    110, 114, 331
head initial, 30, 37–39, 59, 71, 81–82,
    91, 97, 153, 303
Harmony, 11, 16, 27–32, 35, 39, 292,
    295, 327, 331. *See also* Disharmonic
    order, Harmonic order
and processing, 80, 83, 88, 90–93
Haspelmath, Martin. *See World Atlas of
    Language Structures*
Hausa, 206, 209
Hawkins, John, 15, 31–36, 80–82,
    86–87, 93, 323–326, 331–332, 334,
    336
Head-complement order, 47, 50–51
Head-Final Filter, 121–131,
    134–149

Head-final order, 11–17, 30, 55, 58–65,
    69–71, 74. *See also* Harmonic order,
    head-final; Head-Final Filter; OV
in acquisition, 25
and affixation, 74–75, 325, 329–331,
    337, 343–344
in change, 21–22
in Finnish, 57, 59–60, 63, 298, 302,
    314, 319
and the Head-Final Filter, 136
in order of verb, auxiliary and adverb,
    98, 101–103, 105–110, 114–115
and particles, 190, 199, 235, 241–243,
    251, 260, 272, 286–290
in processing, 81–82, 85–86, 89–92
in relation to the LCA and its
    alternatives, 34–41, 49, 53–55
Head-initial order, 11–17, 19, 30, 55,
    57–65, 71, 74–76. *See also*
    Harmonic order, head-initial; VO
in acquisition, 24–25
and affixation, 325, 329, 343
in change, 21–22
in DP, 153, 164
in Finnish, 57, 59–60, 63, 65, 303, 319
and the Head-Final Filter, 135, 140,
    144–145
in order of verb, auxiliary and adverb,
    97, 100–101, 108, 115, 117–120
in relation to the LCA and its
    alternatives, 36–39, 41, 49
and particles, 190, 200, 208, 211, 225,
    230, 233, 235–238, 240–246, 255,
    257, 273, 279–280, 283, 240,
    242–246, 286–290, 303
in processing, 81–82, 85, 90–91
Head-modifier order, 47
Head-Ordering Principle, 324
Head Movement Constraint, 108, 118,
    179, 341
Head Parameter. *See* Parameter, Head
    Parameter
Hebrew, 158, 160, 165, 167, 341
Hecht, Barbara Frant, 25
HFF. *See* Head-Final Filter
Hindi, 98, 103–114. *See also*
    Hindi-Urdu

Hindi-Urdu, 17, 23, 261
Holmberg, Anders, 40–41, 56–66,
    70–71, 76–77, 86, 97, 103, 111, 115,
    117–119, 126, 164, 243, 246, 258,
    288, 298, 335
Holmberg's Generalization, 304–305
Homophony, 198–200, 203, 205,
    208–209, 211, 213, 223–224, 230,
    257, 263–264, 275, 285
Horvath, Julia, 123–124
Hungarian, 101–102, 124, 128–131,
    160–161, 173

Iai, 159
Immediate constituent (IC), 80–83, 86,
    90
IC-to-non-IC ratio, 80–81
Incorporation, 57–59, 72–75, 170–172,
    240, 250, 295
and affixation, 74–75, 334, 343–344
Indirect modification, 145–147
Indirect object. *See* Object, indirect
Individual-level modification. *See* Stage/
    individual-level modification
Indo-Aryan, 248
Indo-European, 22, 89, 136
Indonesian, 167
Infix, 340
Initial-over-final, 12, 14, 249, 251
Input Generalization, 37, 39, 42, 275,
    285
Inverse-FOFC, 68, 86, 88–92, 246, 301
Iraqw, 89–90
Italian, 84, 99–100, 128, 247, 272
determiners, 160–161, 166, 172, 175
particles, 213, 251–252, 277

Jambi-Teochew, 241, 277–279
Japanese, 15, 34, 38, 64, 75, 136, 260
Jespersen Cycle, 246–247
Julien, Marit, 329

Katu, 167
Kayne, Richard, 12, 33, 40, 49–53, 104,
    144, 148. *See also* Linear
    Correspondence Axiom.
Koopman, Hilda, 47

Lagwan, 213–214
Language change. *See* Change;
    Diachrony
Language contact. *See* Contact
Lardiere, Donna, 24–25
Larson, Richard K., 146
Latin, 15, 21–22, 32, 36, 172
Layered derivation, 278
LCA. *See* Linear Correspondence Axiom
Ledgeway, Adam, 21–22, 25
Left periphery. *See* Periphery, left
    periphery
Lele, 214
Lexical array (LA), 268–270, 272–275,
    278–279, 282, 286–287, 294
Lexicon, 208, 263–264, 281
LF, 46, 48, 50, 76, 176
Li, Yafei, 295
Li's Generalization, 295
Licensing direction, 54, 55, 76
Linear Correspondence Axiom (LCA),
    33–34, 44, 49–56, 59, 61, 67–69, 73,
    79, 103, 152, 270, 301, 323
Linearization, 33, 37, 48, 50, 55–56,
    66–67, 69–72, 74–75, 94, 111, 116,
    147–148. *See also* Linear
    Correspondence Axiom; Linear order
in Finnish, 298, 302–303, 305, 308,
    310, 312, 317–320
and particles, 269–270, 284, 287,
    293–294
Linear order, 30, 33, 43–46, 48–53, 55,
    66, 68, 71, 98, 301–302, 310,
    318–320
and processing, 80, 83, 94
Locality, 41, 45–46, 51, 57, 64
Logical Form. *See* LF
Longobardi, Giuseppe, 171–172,
    175–176

Ma'di, 193–195, 202–205, 282
Macedonian, 130–131, 134, 138–139,
    141–143, 230–232, 257–258
Mahajan, Anoop K., 108
Malagasy, 230, 232–234, 238–240, 275,
    282
Mandarin, 145, 217, 228, 276

Mangarrayi, 89
Marantz, Alec, 323
Marathi, 17, 23, 215, 261
Marshallese, 210–213, 257–258
Merge, 41, 44, 48–49, 52, 74, 268, 275
    external, 41, 72–73, 152, 297, 318–319,
        323
    internal, 51, 53, 73, 153, 297, 323 (see
        also Movement)
Mina, 213
Mixtec, 165, 215–216
Moi, 257
Mood, 191, 193, 253, 267–269, 270,
    290, 334–335
Morphology, 59–60, 85, 323–327, 329,
    331–332
    derivational, 324, 342–343
    inflectional, 103, 323, 331, 334
Movement. See also Ban on Improper
    Movement; Merge, internal;
    Movement trigger; Pied-piping
    A-movement, 62, 117, 168, 181, 296
    Ā-movement, 62, 103, 111, 117, 120,
        233–244, 295–296, 307
    AP-movement, 181–183
    complement movement, 54, 322, 329
    comp(lement)-to-spec(ifier) movement,
        34, 36, 73, 103, 243, 287, 344
    feature movement, 57–58
    FP movement, 172, 182–183, 330, 341
    head movement, 54–55, 77, 85, 92,
        100, 103, 108, 118, 141, 302–303,
        308, 320, 331–334, 338, 341 (see
        also Head Movement Constraint;
        Incorporation)
    NP movement, 153–154, 165, 172,
        181–182
    object movement, 304, 321–322, 338
        (see also Object shift)
    phrasal movement, 58–59, 76, 103,
        117, 119, 141, 147, 338
    remnant VP movement, 111, 167, 337,
        339, 341
    rightward movement, 47, 53, 79, 108
    roll-up movement, 35–36, 40, 103,
        153–154, 182–183, 243, 336–337,
        341

T-to-C movement, 74
verb movement (V-movement), 74,
    287–288, 305, 308, 319, 321–322,
    337–339, 341
V/v-to-T movement, 74, 166, 288, 332,
    341
wh-movement, 51, 53, 98, 153, 209,
    212–213, 307
XP-movement, 75, 172, 252, 331,
    333–334, 340
Movement trigger (^), 40–41, 62–64,
    115, 117, 270. See also EPP-feature
Mulford, Randa C., 25
Mumuye, 193
Mupun, 213–214
Myler, Neil, 324, 334, 342–345

Ndyuka, 159
Neeleman, 79, 176–183, 340, 343
Neg(ation), 105–106, 107–111,
    205–206, 334–335. See also Particle,
    final negation particle
Negative concord, 201, 205–206,
    246–247, 280, 282
Neo-Aramaic, 89–90
Newton, Glenda, 16, 22–23, 248–249
Ngambay, 192–193
Nie. See Afrikaans, nie
-Num(ber), 63, 91, 173–174, 294, 337
    position in DP, 72, 153–155, 159,
        176–181 (see also Universal 20)

Obernauer, Hans-Georg, 235
Object. See also Movement, object
    movement; Object shift; Order of
    object and verb; SOV; SVO; VOS;
    VSO
    direct, 21, 118, 304, 317–320, 324
    indirect, 110, 319–320
Object shift, 305–306, 308–311,
    317–319, 330. See also Movement,
    object movement
Object-verb order. See Order of object
    and verb
Ogbronuagum, 213
Old English, 13
Old Norse, 13

Onset Maximization Principle, 94–96
Optimality Theory, 96
Order of object and verb, 28, 32, 88–89,
  201–202, 230, 270
  "free"/mixed order, 246, 298, 303–305,
    314
  OV derived from VO, 34–35, 51,
    61–62, 304–305 (see also Object
    shift)
  and position of adverb, 100–102, 115
  and position of complementizer, 15–17,
    32
  and position of CP, 17, 19
  and position of determiner, 75, 87–88
  relation to affixation, 74, 323–334,
    336–337, 339, 341–342, 344
Order of subject and verb, 28–29, 32,
  39, 155, 165–167, 184. See also
  SOV, SVO, VOS, VSO
OV. See Order of object and verb

Panagiotidis, Phaevos, 278, 292–294
Pancheva, Roumyana, 124
Parameter, 46–49, 74, 166–167, 305
  Head Parameter, 32, 42, 75–76
  Macro-/microparameter, 37–38
  No-choice parameter, 94, 96
  parameter hierarchy, 38
  parametrisation of the Head-Final
    Filter, 139, 142–143
Päri, 89–90
Parsing, 79–80, 83, 86, 93–96
Participle, 20–21, 302–303, 307
Particle, 187–296
  acategorial (final) particle, 257,
    262–263, 268–272, 275–277, 280,
    286–287
  agreement-realizing, 279–282
  borrowed final particles, 240–242
  in combination with wh-element,
    231–236, 257–259
  C-particle (non-interrogative), 223–230
  defectivity of final particles, 272,
    285
  discourse particle, 193–194, 218, 240,
    245, 334–335
  final auxiliary particle, 191–200

final negation particle, 201–202,
  205–209, 220, 222, 246–247,
  280–282, 284, 286 (see also
  Afrikaans, nie)
focus particle, 113, 236–238, 245, 286
  (see also Finnish, focus particles)
modal particle, 251–252, 263–264 (see
  also Vietnamese, được)
ordering between particles, 271–275
Q(uestion)-particle, 23, 28, 105, 113,
  209–223, 245, 247, 257–263, 282,
  286
sentence-final particle (SFP), 220,
  228–229, 251–252, 273–274, 277
topic(-oriented) particle, 213, 238–240,
  245, 286
verb particle, 309–310
Paul, Ileana, 238
Paul, Waltraud, 261, 273
Performance-Grammar Correspondence
  Hypothesis (PGCH), 80, 83, 86, 91
Periphery, 30, 127, 191, 207, 213, 222,
  229–230, 261, 276, 280, 286
  left periphery, 30, 124, 217, 219, 245,
    259, 266
  of phases, 268, 272, 275, 277–278,
    286, 294
Persian, 89–90, 100–101, 128–129, 221,
  241
Person, 171, 174, 189
Pesetsky, David, 293–294, 320
PF, 147–148, 275, 279, 284, 292
  and linearization, 48–55, 59–60, 67–68,
    70, 76–77, 279, 282
  PF reflex of Agree, 243, 279, 283
Phase, 117, 161, 166–167, 174, 259,
  261, 268, 274, 277–278, 282, 320,
  330–331
  phase edge, 172, 267, 271–272,
    274–275, 286–288, 294
  phase head, 161–162, 172, 267, 285,
    287, 320
Phase Impenetrability Condition (PIC),
  175, 285, 287
Phase-sliding, 272
φ-features, 62, 72, 168–169, 171–174,
  176, 184–185, 339

Philip, Joy, 189, 214, 276
Phonology, 95–96
Phrasal Coherence, 286, 292
Phrase structure rules, 43–47
Pied-piping, 58, 71, 73–75, 77, 154, 249
Plural, 137, 165, 293–294, 325, 333, 339
Polarity. *See* Neg(ation); Particle, final negation particle
Poletto, Cecilia, 247
Polish, 134, 138, 139–140
Pollock, Jean-Yves, 99, 108, 338
Portuguese, 128–129, 134–5, 205, 277, 281
Postposition, 20, 27–28, 62, 240, 249–251, 323–325
PP. *See* Prepositional phrase
Prefix, 16, 74–75, 323–334, 336–343
Preposition, 20, 62, 88–89, 148, 240, 249
  relation to orders of other elements, 27–29, 323–325
Prepositional phrase (PP), 88–89, 162
Processing, 79–83, 87–88, 90–92, 93–94, 127, 148
Pronoun, 40, 305
Proper names, 175
Prosody, 220, 229, 261, 270
Puluwatese, 159

Quantifier, 173–174
Quechua, 212–213

Recessive order, 29–30, 39
Relative clause, 127, 234, 278–279
  covert, 144, 146, 159
  reduced, 125, 144–148, 152
Relativized Minimality, 40–41, 64, 66, 77
Remnant, 75, 77, 141, 165, 173, 182, 276, 272, 315. *See also* Movement, remnant VP movement
Renumeration, 278
Richards, Marc, 75, 168
Richards, Norvin, 209
Riemsdijk, Henk van, 250
Right Roof Constraint, 84, 93

Right-hand Head Rule (RHR), 342
Rizzi, Luigi, 209, 229
Roberts, Ian, 36–37, 40–41, 61–66, 76–77, 86, 94, 103, 111, 115, 117–119, 126, 164, 197, 243, 246, 288, 335
Romance, 19, 21, 24, 38, 343
Romanian, 128–129, 159–160, 165–166, 171–172
Root, 53, 268–269, 341, 344
Roussou, Anna, 36–37, 197
Russian, 124, 138–140, 143, 230–231, 293, 298

Scandinavian, 129, 305–306, 310, 318
Schwartz, Bonnie, 24–25
Scope, 45–46, 51, 163, 213, 274–275, 335
Scottish Gaelic, 163
Scrambling, 51, 87, 106, 111, 115, 304–305, 310
Search, 72–73
Selection, 40–41, 57–60, 63–64, 66–74, 84–86, 147, 307–310
  in Finnish, 301–303, 310–319
  and particles, 232–236, 259–261, 263, 266, 269, 272–275, 286, 288, 335
Semantics, 48–49, 124, 243, 283, 294
Semitic, 22, 158, 341
Sentence-final particle (SFP). *See* Particle, sentence-final particle
Serbian. *See* Bosnian/Croatian/Serbian
Serial verb, 40
Sheehan, Michelle, 17, 22–23, 66–67, 69–71, 87, 94, 147–148, 248–249, 284, 301, 305, 312, 318
Shupamem, 223–225
Simpson, Andrew, 282
Single Engine Hypothesis, 323, 329, 342, 345
Slovene, 128–132, 134, 139–140, 143
Small clause, 50, 84, 318–319
Sorbian, 89, 128–129, 143
SOV, 18, 28, 64, 111, 256, 324, 337, 339
  in Finnish, 297–298, 303–305, 310–312

Spanish, 100–101, 118, 128–129, 160–161, 165–166, 173, 207, 239–240
Speas, Margaret, 267, 337–338
Specifier, 50–51, 70–71
Specifier-Head-Complement Hypothesis (SHCH), 176–177
Sranan, 159
Stage/individual-level modification, 131–134
Stowell, Tim, 18
Strong generative capacity, 27, 30–33, 42
Subject, 49, 155, 161, 165–166, 304–305, 328, 337. *See also* Order of subject and verb; SOV; SVO; VOS; VSO
Small-clause subject, 318–319
Subject-verb order. *See* Order of subject and verb
Subordinator, 16. *See also* Complementizer
Suffix, 16, 24, 30, 58, 112–114, 302
suffixing preference, 323–324, 326–334, 336, 339
Superset Principle, 218
Surface Recursion Restriction, 121
SV. *See* Order of subject and verb
Svenonius, Peter, 57, 143
SVO, 28, 51, 99, 158, 166–167, 297–298, 310
Swedish, 128, 130–134, 143, 244, 307–308
SWITCH-element, 255, 294
Synthetic morphology. *See* Inflectional morphology

Taiwanese, 223–224
Tajik, 89
TAM. *See* Tense/aspect/mood (TAM)
Tenetehára, 198–200, 253
Tenny, Carol, 267
Tense/aspect affix, 325, 330, 332, 336–339, 341. *See also* Tense/aspect/mood (TAM)
Tense/aspect/mood (TAM), 191, 194. *See also* Mood

Teop, 167
Tetun, 213
Thai, 220–221, 223, 247, 298, 304
Thirdfactor, 4, 42
Tidore, 201
Tigré, 22, 89, 90, 341
Tigrinya, 22, 341
Tobelo, 89–90
Topic, 238, 245, 256, 266, 286, 304. *See also* Particle, topic(-oriented) particle
Topicalization, 104, 195, 320. *See also* Topic
Tough-construction, 125, 137–138
Transformation, 44–46
Transitivity (in linear ordering relations), 67–68, 71
Travis, Lisa, 47
Trugman, Helen, 123–124
Turkish, 17–19, 98, 103, 111–114, 136, 241
Typology, 15, 27–30, 36, 42, 165, 275, 304, 323, 326

UCOOL. *See* Universal Constraint on Operational Ordering in Language
Udmurt, 225–227
UG. *See* Universal Grammar
Universal, 20, 42, 151–152, 155, 167, 176, 180
Universal, 21, 121–123, 144
Universal, 25, 39–40
Universal, 26, 340
Universal, 27, 324
Universal Constraint on Operational Ordering in Language (UCOOL), 295–296
Universal Grammar (UG), 25, 31, 33, 37, 42, 46, 60, 64, 79, 86, 90, 93–94, 96, 161, 318
Urdu. *See* Hindi–Urdu

van der Auwera, Johan, 206
van der Wal, Jenneke, 213, 237
Variable, 146, 169–170, 172–176
Variable word order, 101–102, 219
Venetan, 251–252

Verb-object order. *See* Order of object
    and verb
Verb-projection raising, 13, 15, 31
Verb-subject order. *See* Order of subject
    and verb
Vietnamese, 198, 223–224, 255,
    263–266, 268
được, 198, 263–268, 270–271
Vilkuna, Maria, 298–299, 315, 321
Violation. *See* FOFC violation
VO. *See* Order of object and verb
VOS, 165, 167, 275, 288
VS. *See* Order of subject and verb
VSO, 22, 28, 99, 165–167, 199–200,
    275

WALS. *See* World Atlas of Language
    Structures
Welsh, 160, 162–164
West Germanic. *See* Germanic
Wh-in-situ, 51
Williams, Edwin, 123, 169, 295, 342
Wiltschko, Martina, 261, 267
Wolof, 167
World Atlas of Language Structures
    (*WALS*), 16, 28–29, 89–90, 155–158,
    167, 210, 325, 328, 332, 334. *See*
    also Dryer, Matthew S.
Wu, Zoe, 282

Xârâcùù, 159
X-bar theory, 31–32, 34, 43, 46–47,
    49–50, 54

Yapese, 167
Yixing Chinese. *See* Chinese
Yom, 253
Yosondúa Mixtec, 215–216

Zaar, 213
Zhang, Ling, 261
Zhang, Niina, 228, 255
Zwart, C. Jan-Wouter, 17, 52

Linguistic Inquiry Monographs
Samuel Jay Keyser, general editor

1. *Word Formation in Generative Grammar*, Mark Aronoff
2. *X̄ Syntax: A Study of Phrase Structure*, Ray Jackendoff
3. *Recent Transformational Studies in European Languages*, S. Jay Keyser, editor
4. *Studies in Abstract Phonology*, Edmund Gussmann
5. *An Encyclopedia of AUX: A Study of Cross-Linguistic Equivalence*, Susan Steele
6. *Some Concepts and Consequences of the Theory of Government and Binding*, Noam Chomsky
7. *The Syntax of Words*, Elisabeth O. Selkirk
8. *Syllable Structure and Stress in Spanish: A Nonlinear Analysis*, James W. Harris
9. *CV Phonology: A Generative Theory of the Syllable*, George N. Clements and Samuel Jay Keyser
10. *On the Nature of Grammatical Relations*, Alec P. Marantz
11. *A Grammar of Anaphora*, Joseph Aoun
12. *Logical Form: Its Structure and Derivation*, Robert May
13. *Barriers*, Noam Chomsky
14. *On the Definition of Word*, Anna-Maria Di Sciullo and Edwin Williams
15. *Japanese Tone Structure*, Janet Pierrehumbert and Mary E. Beckman
16. *Relativized Minimality*, Luigi Rizzi
17. *Types of Ā-Dependencies*, Guglielmo Cinque
18. *Argument Structure*, Jane Grimshaw
19. *Locality: A Theory and Some of Its Empirical Consequences*, Maria Rita Manzini
20. *Indefinites*, Molly Diesing
21. *Syntax of Scope*, Joseph Aoun and Yen-hui Audrey Li
22. *Morphology by Itself: Stems and Inflectional Classes*, Mark Aronoff
23. *Thematic Structure in Syntax*, Edwin Williams
24. *Indices and Identity*, Robert Fiengo and Robert May
25. *The Antisymmetry of Syntax*, Richard S. Kayne
26. *Unaccusativity: At the Syntax–Lexical Semantics Interface*, Beth Levin and Malka Rappaport Hovav
27. *Lexico-Logical Form: A Radically Minimalist Theory*, Michael Brody
28. *The Architecture of the Language Faculty*, Ray Jackendoff
29. *Local Economy*, Chris Collins
30. *Surface Structure and Interpretation*, Mark Steedman
31. *Elementary Operations and Optimal Derivations*, Hisatsugu Kitahara
32. *The Syntax of Nonfinite Complementation: An Economy Approach*, Željko Bošković

33. *Prosody, Focus, and Word Order*, Maria Luisa Zubizarreta

34. *The Dependencies of Objects*, Esther Torrego

35. *Economy and Semantic Interpretation*, Danny Fox

36. *What Counts: Focus and Quantification*, Elena Herburger

37. *Phrasal Movement and Its Kin*, David Pesetsky

38. *Dynamic Antisymmetry*, Andrea Moro

39. *Prolegomenon to a Theory of Argument Structure*, Ken Hale and Samuel Jay Keyser

40. *Essays on the Representational and Derivational Nature of Grammar: The Diversity of Wh-Constructions*, Joseph Aoun and Yen-hui Audrey Li

41. *Japanese Morphophonemics: Markedness and Word Structure*, Junko Ito and Armin Mester

42. *Restriction and Saturation*, Sandra Chung and William A. Ladusaw

43. *Linearization of Chains and Sideward Movement*, Jairo Nunes

44. *The Syntax of (In)dependence*, Ken Safir

45. *Interface Strategies: Optimal and Costly Computations*, Tanya Reinhart

46. *Asymmetry in Morphology*, Anna Maria Di Sciullo

47. *Relators and Linkers: The Syntax of Predication, Predicate Inversion, and Copulas*, Marcel den Dikken

48. *On the Syntactic Composition of Manner and Motion*, Maria Luisa Zubizarreta and Eunjeong Oh

49. *Introducing Arguments*, Liina Pylkkänen

50. *Where Does Binding Theory Apply?*, David Lebeaux

51. *Locality in Minimalist Syntax*, Thomas S. Stroik

52. *Distributed Reduplication*, John Frampton

53. *The Locative Syntax of Experiencers*, Idan Landau

54. *Why Agree? Why Move?: Unifying Agreement-Based and Discourse-Configurational Languages*, Shigeru Miyagawa

55. *Locality in Vowel Harmony*, Andrew Nevins

56. *Uttering Trees*, Norvin Richards

57. *The Syntax of Adjectives*, Guglielmo Cinque

58. *Arguments as Relations*, John Bowers

59. *Agreement and Head Movement*, Ian Roberts

60. *Localism versus Globalism in Morphology and Phonology*, David Embick

61. *Provocative Syntax*, Phil Branigan

62. *Anaphora and Language Design*, Eric J. Reuland

63. *Indefinite Objects: Scrambling, Choice Functions, and Differential Marking*, Luis López

64. *A Syntax of Substance*, David Adger

65. *Subjunctive Conditionals*, Michela Ippolito

66. *Russian Case Morphology and the Syntactic Categories*, David Pesetsky

67. *Classical NEG Raising: An Essay on the Syntax of Negation*, Chris Collins and Paul M. Postal

68. *Agreement and Its Failures*, Omer Preminger

69. *Voice and v: Lessons from Acehnese*, Julie Anne Legate

70. *(Re)labeling*, Carlo Cecchetto and Caterina Donati

71. *A Two-Tiered Theory of Control*, Idan Landau

72. *Concepts, Syntax, and Their Interface: Tanya Reinhart's Theta System*, Martin Everaert, Marijana Marelj, and Eric Reuland, editors

73. *Contiguity Theory*, Norvin Richards

74. *Impossible Persons*, Daniel Harbour

75. *Agreement Beyond Phi*, Shigeru Miyagawa

76. *The Final-over-Final Condition*, Michelle Sheehan, Theresa Biberauer, Ian Roberts, and Anders Holmberg